International Directory of

COMPANY HISTORIES

International Directory of

COMPANY HISTORIES

VOLUME 66

Editor

Tina Grant

ST. JAMES PRESS

An imprint of Thomson Gale, a part of The Thomson Corporation

Detroit • New York • San Francisco • San Diego • New Haven, Conn. • Waterville, Maine • London • Munich

International Directory of Company Histories, Volume 66

Tina Grant, Editor

Project Editor
Miranda H. Ferrara

Editorial
Virgil Burton, Donna Craft, Louise Gagné, Peggy Geeseman, Julie Gough, Linda Hall, Keith Jones, Lynn Pearce, Maureen Puhl, Holly Selden, Justine Ventimiglia

Imaging and Multimedia
Randy Bassett, Lezlie Light

Manufacturing
Rhonda Williams

Product Manager
Gerald L. Sawchuk

For more information contact
St. James Press
27500 Drake Rd.
Farmington Hills, MI 48331-3535
Or you can visit our Internet site at http://www.gale.com/stjames

LIBRARY OF CONGRESS CATALOG NUMBER 89-190943

ISBN: 1-55862-511-9

BRITISH LIBRARY CATALOGUING IN PUBLICATION DATA

International directory of company histories. Vol. 66
I. Tina Grant
33.87409

Printed in the United States of America
10 9 8 7 6 5 4 3 2 1

CONTENTS

Company Histories

PREFACE

The St. James Press series *The International Directory of Company Histories (IDCH)* is intended for reference use by students, business people, librarians, historians, economists, investors, job candidates, and others who seek to learn more about the historical development of the world's most important companies. To date, *IDCH* has covered over 6,850 companies in 66 volumes.

Inclusion Criteria

Most companies chosen for inclusion in *IDCH* have achieved a minimum of US$25 million in annual sales and are leading influences in their industries or geographical locations. Companies may be publicly held, private, or nonprofit. State-owned companies that are important in their industries and that may operate much like public or private companies also are included. Wholly owned subsidiaries and divisions are profiled if they meet the requirements for inclusion. Entries on companies that have had major changes since they were last profiled may be selected for updating.

The *IDCH* series highlights 10% private and nonprofit companies, and features updated entries on approximately 50 companies per volume.

Entry Format

Each entry begins with the company's legal name, the address of its headquarters, its telephone, toll-free, and fax numbers, and its web site. A statement of public, private, state, or parent ownership follows. A company with a legal name in both English and the language of its headquarters country is listed by the English name, with the native-language name in parentheses.

The company's founding or earliest incorporation date, the number of employees, and the most recent available sales figures follow. Sales figures are given in local currencies with equivalents in U.S. dollars. For some private companies, sales figures are estimates and indicated by the abbreviation *est.* The entry lists the exchanges on which a company's stock is traded and its ticker symbol, as well as the company's NAIC codes.

Entries generally contain a *Company Perspectives* box which provides a short summary of the company's mission, goals, and ideals, a *Key Dates* box highlighting milestones in the company's history, lists of *Principal Subsidiaries, Principal Divisions, Principal Operating Units, Principal Competitors,* and articles for *Further Reading.*

American spelling is used throughout *IDCH*, and the word ''billion'' is used in its U.S. sense of one thousand million.

Sources

Entries have been compiled from publicly accessible sources both in print and on the Internet such as general and academic periodicals, books, annual reports, and material supplied by the companies themselves.

Cumulative Indexes

IDCH contains three indexes: the **Index to Companies**, which provides an alphabetical index to companies discussed in the text as well as to companies profiled, the **Index to Industries**, which allows researchers to locate companies by their principal industry, and the **Geographic Index**, which lists companies alphabetically by the country of their headquarters. The indexes are cumulative and specific instructions for using them are found immediately preceding each index.

Suggestions Welcome

Comments and suggestions from users of *IDCH* on any aspect of the product as well as suggestions for companies to be included or updated are cordially invited. Please write:

The Editor
International Directory of Company Histories
St. James Press
27500 Drake Rd.
Farmington Hills, Michigan 48331-3535

ABBREVIATIONS FOR FORMS OF COMPANY INCORPORATION

AB	Aktiebolag (Finland, Sweden)
AB Oy	Aktiebolag Osakeyhtiot (Finland)
A.E.	Anonimos Eteria (Greece)
AG	Aktiengesellschaft (Austria, Germany, Switzerland, Liechtenstein)
A.O.	Anonim Ortaklari/Ortakligi (Turkey)
ApS	Amparteselskab (Denmark)
A.Š.	Anonim Širketi (Turkey)
A/S	Aksjeselskap (Norway); Aktieselskab (Denmark, Sweden)
Ay	Avoinyhtio (Finland)
B.A.	Buttengewone Aansprakeiijkheid (The Netherlands)
Bhd.	Berhad (Malaysia, Brunei)
B.V.	Besloten Vennootschap (Belgium, The Netherlands)
C.A.	Compania Anonima (Ecuador, Venezuela)
C. de R.L.	Compania de Responsabilidad Limitada (Spain)
Co.	Company
Corp.	Corporation
CRL	Companhia a Responsabilidao Limitida (Portugal, Spain)
C.V.	Commanditaire Vennootschap (The Netherlands, Belgium)
G.I.E.	Groupement d'Interet Economique (France)
GmbH	Gesellschaft mit beschraenkter Haftung (Austria, Germany, Switzerland)
Inc.	Incorporated (United States, Canada)
I/S	Interessentselskab (Denmark); Interesentselskap (Norway)
KG/KGaA	Kommanditgesellschaft/Kommanditgesellschaft auf Aktien (Austria, Germany, Switzerland)
KK	Kabushiki Kaisha (Japan)
K/S	Kommanditselskab (Denmark); Kommandittselskap (Norway)
Lda.	Limitada (Spain)
L.L.C.	Limited Liability Company (United States)
Ltd.	Limited (Various)
Ltda.	Limitada (Brazil, Portugal)
Ltee.	Limitee (Canada, France)
mbH	mit beschraenkter Haftung (Austria, Germany)
N.V.	Naamloze Vennootschap (Belgium, The Netherlands)
OAO	Otkrytoe Aktsionernoe Obshchestve (Russia)
OOO	Obschestvo s Ogranichennoi Otvetstvennostiu (Russia)
Oy	Osakeyhtiö (Finland)
PLC	Public Limited Co. (United Kingdom, Ireland)
Pty.	Proprietary (Australia, South Africa, United Kingdom)
S.A.	Société Anonyme (Belgium, France, Greece, Luxembourg, Switzerland, Arab speaking countries); Sociedad Anónima (Latin America [except Brazil], Spain, Mexico); Sociedades Anônimas (Brazil, Portugal)
SAA	Societe Anonyme Arabienne
S.A.R.L.	Sociedade Anonima de Responsabilidade Limitada (Brazil, Portugal); Société à Responsabilité Limitée (France, Belgium, Luxembourg)
S.A.S.	Societá in Accomandita Semplice (Italy); Societe Anonyme Syrienne (Arab speaking countries)
Sdn. Bhd.	Sendirian Berhad (Malaysia)
S.p.A.	Società per Azioni (Italy)
Sp. z.o.o.	Spólka z ograniczona odpowiedzialnoscia (Poland)
S.R.L.	Società a Responsabilità Limitata (Italy); Sociedad de Responsabilidad Limitada (Spain, Mexico, Latin America [except Brazil])
S.R.O.	Spolecnost s Rucenim Omezenym (Czechoslovakia
Ste.	Societe (France, Belgium, Luxembourg, Switzerland)
VAG	Verein der Arbeitgeber (Austria, Germany)
YK	Yugen Kaisha (Japan)
ZAO	Zakrytoe Aktsionernoe Obshchestve (Russia)

ABBREVIATIONS FOR CURRENCY

$	United States dollar	ISK	Icelandic krona
£	United Kingdom pound	ITL	Italian lira
¥	Japanese yen	JMD	Jamaican dollar
AED	Emirati dirham	KPW	North Korean won
ARS	Argentine peso	KRW	South Korean won
ATS	Austrian shilling	KWD	Kuwaiti dinar
AUD	Australian dollar	LUF	Luxembourg franc
BEF	Belgian franc	MUR	Mauritian rupee
BHD	Bahraini dinar	MXN	Mexican peso
BRL	Brazilian real	MYR	Malaysian ringgit
CAD	Canadian dollar	NGN	Nigerian naira
CHF	Swiss franc	NLG	Netherlands guilder
CNY	Chinese yuan	NOK	Norwegian krone
COP	Colombian peso	NZD	New Zealand dollar
CLP	Chilean peso	OMR	Omani rial
CZK	Czech koruna	PHP	Philippine peso
DEM	German deutsche mark	PKR	Pakistani rupee
DKK	Danish krone	PLN	Polish zloty
DZD	Algerian dinar	PTE	Portuguese escudo
EEK	Estonian Kroon	RMB	Chinese renminbi
EGP	Egyptian pound	RUB	Russian ruble
ESP	Spanish peseta	SAR	Saudi riyal
EUR	euro	SEK	Swedish krona
FIM	Finnish markka	SGD	Singapore dollar
FRF	French franc	THB	Thai baht
GRD	Greek drachma	TND	Tunisian dinar
HKD	Hong Kong dollar	TRL	Turkish lira
HUF	Hungarian forint	TWD	new Taiwan dollar
IDR	Indonesian rupiah	VEB	Venezuelan bolivar
IEP	Irish pound	VND	Vietnamese dong
ILS	new Israeli shekel	ZAR	South African rand
INR	Indian rupee	ZMK	Zambian kwacha

International Directory of

COMPANY HISTORIES

Alternative Tentacles Records

1501 Powell Street, Suite 6
Emeryville, California 94608-2041
U.S.A.
Telephone (510) 596-8981
Fax: (510) 596-8982
Web site: http://www.alternativetentacles.com

Private Company
Founded: 1979
Employees: 6
NAIC: 334612 Prerecorded Compact Disc (Except Software), Tape and Record Reproducing

Alternative Tentacles Records, based in Emeryville, California, is an independent record label owned by Eric Reed Boucher, better known by his stage name, Jello Biafra, former front man for the seminal punk band Dead Kennedys. Although primarily known for releasing albums by the Dead Kennedys and other punk bands—such as Butthole Surfers, D.O.A., 7 Seconds, Winston Smith, NoMeansNo, Neurosis, and Voice Farm—Alternative Tentacles has also released rock and roll, Brazilian hardcore, bent pop, faux-country, and spoken word records from such anti-establishment writers as Noam Chomsky and Howard Zinn. Since the breakup of Dead Kennedys, Biafra has also recorded a number of spoken word records issued by his record company. All told, the label has released about 250 albums, of which more than 150 are still in print. In addition, through its Web site Alternative Tentacles sells books, magazines, videos that reflect the tastes of underground culture, as well as such mundane merchandise as coffee mugs and T-shirts.

A Child of the '60s

Biafra was born in Boulder, Colorado, in 1959. His father was a psychiatric social worker and his mother was a librarian. Biafra was a precocious child, early on displaying a fascination with language. According to his father, when Biafra was only three years old, ''he would startle visitors at the door saying he looked like a Pithecanthroprus erectus.'' He also became interested in music at an early age, delving into his father's large ethnic record collection. However, relations between the two grew contentious, with Biafra enraging his father by comparing him to Stalin and Nixon. The youngster also became an outcast among his peers. Years later, he recalled, ''My heroes in those days were Batman villains. My other friends wanted to be nurses and firemen, but I thought the Riddler and Penguin were much better role models.'' In high school, Biafra rebelled against the country-rock music that ruled the local radio waves, often visiting used record shops where for pocket change he bought records based on interesting covers and liner notes. Many of these records turned out to be seminal influences on the rising punk music scene: the Stooges, MC5, 13th Floor Elevators, Nazz, and Les Baxter. As a teenager, Biafra began using his gift for language to write song lyrics.

In 1978, Biafra enrolled at University of California-Santa Cruz but quit after just two months. He told the *San Francisco Chronicle* in a 1986 profile, ''I was going through the usual teenage anguish stuff. I couldn't see going to college and picking a career out of a hat and hating my own guts, because what I really wanted to do was perform. I've always loved loud, raw music.'' After attending a Ramones concert, Biafra, at the age of 20, decided to form his own band. His band mates shared his taste for unusual names: guitarist East Bay Ray, bass player Klaus Flouride, and drummer D.R. Peligro. Biafra turned in part to the news in the coining of his own stage name. He latched onto ''Biafra,'' the African nation which had become the face of international poverty and starvation, and combined it with Jello, which he believed epitomized U.S. corporate culture. He explained to the *Chronicle*, ''I thought that the two images of Jello and Biafra colliding in the mind were exactly the sort of confrontational question I wanted to raise. Plastic America and its overseas results.'' Moreover, he liked the sound of it. For the name of the band, Biafra turned to a notebook where he jotted down ideas and considered such possibilities as Smegma Pigvomit, Mucus Melanoma, and Calvin Colostomy before settling on Dead Kennedys. Referring to assassinated politicians was offensive to some, but to Biafra the reference was to a self-absorbed, cynical society that resulted from the murder of the Kennedys and Martin Luther King, Jr., the Vietnam war, and the Watergate scandal.

Company Perspectives:

Although it is perceived by many as a ''punk'' label, having released records by Dead Kennedys and others [Alternative Tentacles] is actually best known for its impact on the world of underground culture.

After a week's worth of rehearsal, Dead Kennedys made its first appearance in 1978 at San Francisco's Mabuhay Gardens. The band soon developed a strong following. Biafra proved to be a dynamic performer, often becoming physical with his audience, overturning tables and spilling beer. Despite Biafra's punk antics, the band's songs transcended punk's basic antisocial themes. Rather, Dead Kennedys dealt with politics, poverty, religion, the environment, and later on criticized the punk scene itself, especially the fashion. Dead Kennedys wore jeans and sneakers, eschewing the boots, torn jackets, chains, Mohawk haircuts, and safety pins that would characterize so many bands claiming to be punk. In many ways, Dead Kennedys were the American version of England's Sex Pistols, minus the bondage trappings, and represented an anti-corporate, anti-conservative worldview. The songs were caustic, often humorous, guitar-driven, and manic-paced, forming the foundation of what become known as punk's hardcore sound. Where Biafra and Dead Kennedys differed from many of the punk bands they inspired was in their aversion to the drug scene, which would lead to the downfall, and sometimes death, of many punk musicians.

The Alternative Tentacles Name in the Late 1970s

Dead Kennedys saved their money and in June 1979 produced the band's first single, ''California Uber Alles,'' coining the name ''Alternative Tentacles'' to serve as the label. By self-producing, the band was pursuing an alternative to the ''tentacles'' of mainstream record companies. The single was a success, drawing attention to the band in America and especially Europe, where punk was more popular. Ironically, it also led to a record deal with IRS Records, which released Dead Kennedys' first album, *Fresh Fruit for Rotting Vegetables.* It was intended for distribution by A&M, which thought the group's name was in bad taste. As a result, a small independent label, Fault Products, distributed the album, and upon its release the band launched an uncommonly successful tour of England and Europe for an American punk band. A major part of the interest generated by Dead Kennedys was due to Biafra's engaging persona.

Before the release of *Fresh Fruit,* Biafra accepted the challenge of a friend and ran for mayor of San Francisco in a crowded field of ten candidates, a race won by Dianne Feinstein, who would go on to become a U.S. Senator. The little known 21-year-old conducted the campaign of a talented, seasoned prankster and attracted considerable media coverage. His platform called for the banning of automobiles within city limits, auctioning off important city positions, establishing a board of bribery so that fair prices for liquor licenses and building code exemptions could be established, and forcing all businessmen to wear clown suits from the hours of nine to five. His motto, not surprisingly, was ''There's always room for Jello.'' Nevertheless, some of his ideas were serious, such as the legalization of squatters rights. Although he won less than 3 percent of the vote, receiving 6591 votes, Biafra placed fourth, which by all accounts was a surprisingly strong finish, enough to prompt the Board of Supervisors to ban ''funny names'' from future ballots. More importantly for Biafra and Dead Kennedys, his campaign caught the attention of the British press, which set the stage for the band's European tour in the fall of 1980.

Biafra applied the Alternative Tentacles name to an independent record label he and the members of Dead Kennedys started in 1980 (a year later, the band was made into a partnership known as Decay Music), intending it as a European-based operation that would release and promote the albums of American punk bands, primarily based in the Bay area, unknown to the market. A compilation album called *Let Them Eat Jellybeans* was released, followed by singles from such bands as Black Flagg, D.O.A., Bad Brains, Flipper, TSOL, and Voice Farm. Alternative Tentacles releases made their way back to the United States as import copies, which led to the label becoming a domestic business. Although at first it was essentially a vanity label for Dead Kennedys, in 1982 Alternative Tentacles began to release the work of others, such as Butthole Surfers, the Dicks, the Crucifucks, D.O.A., and TSOL. Early on, distribution and promotion was handled by Faulty Products, but when the company went out of business in 1982, Alternative Tentacles forged a distribution arrangement with another upstart San Francisco label, Mordam Records, an association that would continue into the mid-2000s.

Biafra regarded himself as a poor businessman, but he proved to be dedicated and hardworking, reportedly putting in ten to 14 hours a day. According to the 1986 *Chronicle* article, ''His three employees respect him, but think he's a curiosity. 'He's probably the most unusual boss I've ever had,' says Debbie Dordin, general manager of the company. 'Well . . .' She laughs. 'He's . . .' She laughs again. 'He's on his own timetable. He's meticulous, eccentric and weird. He's conscientious, but he's definitely not a businessman. His input into the company is mostly artistic. As far as a day-to-day influence, that's left up to us.' '' Nevertheless, the Alternative Tentacles had a solid reputation with bands, punk and otherwise. The label was dedicated to treating artists fairly, was known to be scrupulous in paying royalties promptly, and never signed bands to contracts, allowing them to work with outside labels. Despite its unusual way of doing business, Alternative Tentacles was successful enough that other labels sought to buy it, distribute its records, or establish package deals with some artists, but Biafra was never interested in pursuing those avenues. According to guitarist East Bay Ray, however, Biafra was merely the media person and that, in fact, Ray was the one responsible for setting up the label and running it for the first three years.

Alternative Tentacles faced a turning point when it became an object of a criminal pornography charge of distributing harmful matter to a minor pressed by the City of Los Angeles, a case that threatened to drive the label out of business. The charge was related to the Dead Kennedys' third album, *Frankenchrist,* which included a poster by Swedish artist H.R.

Key Dates:

1979: Alternative Tentacles named first used on Dead Kennedys self-produced single.
1982: The label begin producing other groups.
1986: Alternative is cleared on indecency charges.
1997: Former members of Dead Kennedys sue the label over royalties.
2004: The court rules against the label on the royalty suit.

Giger, best known as the Academy Award-winning set designer for the film *Alien.* The poster reproduced a surrealistic landscape by Giger featuring ten sets of male and female genitalia engaged in sexual intercourse.

Giger's work reminded Biafra of the work of Hieronymus Bosch, representing the horrible truth of a contemporary society obsessed with greed. However, to a San Fernando, California mother, whose 14-year-old daughter gave her 11-year-old brother a copy of *Frankenchrist,* as a present, the poster was nothing more than pornography. After failing to get the attention of a television consumer reporter, she turned to the California State Attorney's office, which passed the matter to local authorities. The Los Angeles District Attorney, shortly before he was to run for reelection, agreed with the mother's contention, and on April 15, 1986, Biafra's San Francisco apartment and Alternative Tentacles office and warehouse were raided by vice officers, and a number of copies of the Giger poster were confiscated. Seven weeks later, Biafra and four others were indicted, including the 65-year-old owner of the factory that pressed the album. The defendants faced a $2,000 fine and a year in prison. Although the American Civil Liberties stepped in to help and a legal defense fund was established, the cost of defending the charge placed Alternative Tentacles on the edge of financial ruin. To some observers, the fact that Biafra and Tentacles lacked the financial resources of other music companies made them a convenient target.

The obscenity charges resulted in a lengthy trial, but in the end the jury was deadlocked and the judge dismissed the case. Lead prosecutor Michael Guarino would later admit, "The whole thing was a comedy of errors. . . . About midway through the trial we realized that the lyrics of the album were in many ways socially responsible, very anti-drug and pro-individual." Guarino's involvement with Biafra and Dead Kennedy's would not end there, however. He admitted to the *Washington Post* several years later, "My son adores Jello and plays his music all the time, so my punishment is that I have to listen night after night to everything Biafra has ever performed."

Label Survives 1986 Indecency Charge

Biafra also became the object of attack by the Parents Music Resources Center, co-founded by Tipper Gore. On two occasions, the pair debated contemporary music and the first amendment on the "Oprah Winfrey Show." While Biafra and Alternative Tentacles managed to survive the charges of indecency, the stress of it all contributed greatly to the break up of Dead Kennedys in 1986. According to *San Francisco Weekly,* Biafra's band mates claimed that Alternative Tentacles was owned and controlled by the entire band and that when it broke up they ceded ownership to Biafra alone through an oral agreement. At the time, it did not appear they were giving up much. The label was short on funds as well as new talent to produce. Biafra drifted into what he called spoken word, essentially monologues in the vein of his lyrics, sometimes rants about censorship, grass-roots politics, and other anti-establishment subjects, but he was also capable of well thought out arguments. Over the years, Alternative Tentacles released several of his spoken word albums. The label also released monologues from Noam Chomsky and Howard Zinn, and ventured well beyond punk music to release albums in a variety of styles.

Biafra and Alternative Tentacles would become involved in further legal entanglements in the 1990s. To illustrate the back cover of a 1992 Crucifucks album, the label used a photograph that was originally part of a police public relations campaign to help fend off reductions in the police force. The poster featured a picture of an officer who was pretending to be dead, the text reading, "You wouldn't sacrifice your life for a million bucks." Alternative Tentacles did not contest the charges and a Federal magistrate ordered the record company to pay $2.2 million in damages. The judgment was overturned three months later and the case was ultimately dismissed.

A more difficult legal challenge for Biafra and Alternative Tentacles was a fight between him and the other members of Dead Kennedys, who in September 1998 voted to terminate their relationship with Alternative Tentacles. They claimed that the company had increased the wholesale prices of the group's CDs without telling them and then failed to pay them the higher royalties that resulted. The label manager looked into the matter and agreed that a mistake had occurred but insisted that it was an honest mistake. As a show of his hostility toward his former band mates, Biafra placed the royalty shortage of some $75,000 into a trust account to be released when either he gave his permission or was forced to by a court order. In October 1998, the three Dead Kennedys sued, seeking control of the band's catalog and damages, and the following month Biafra countersued. He contended that the others were upset that he would not agree to allow one of their songs, "Holiday in Cambodia," to be used in a Levi's commercial for its Docker's line. While the three Dead Kennedy's acknowledged that an ad agency had indeed contacted Ray about such a possibility, they had never expressed any interest. Regardless, Biafra claimed he was attempting to preserve the integrity of the band, the record label, and his own reputation. The legal battle between Biafra and the other Dead Kennedy members ended in May 2000 when a judge ruled against Biafra. Alternative Tentacles was ordered to pay nearly $220,000 in damages. Biafra appealed the ruling but eventually let the matter rest.

Alternative Tentacles maintained an office in the United Kingdom until 1997, but closed it down "because employees there were ripping off both AT and our bands—among other things." In 2002, the company moved from San Francisco to offices in Emeryville, California. After 25 years, Alternative Tentacles remained a relatively small business, employing only a handful of people, yet its survival for that length of time was a remarkable accomplishment in itself.

Principal Competitors

Dischord Records; Gearhead Records; Knitting Factory Works.

Further Reading

Athitakis, Mark, "Punks at War," *SF Weekly*, June 23, 1999.

Rubin, Sylvia, "Let's Get Metaphysical," *San Francisco Chronicle*, December 16, 1986, p. 36.

Segal, David, "Jello Biafra: The Surreal Deal," *Washington Post*, May 4, 1997, p. G01.

Sprague, David, "Alternative Tentacles Marks 15 Years of Stretching Limits," *Billboard*, November 26, 1994, p. 11.

Wishnia, Steven, "Rockin' with The First Amendment," *Nation*, October 24, 1987, p. 444.

—Ed Dinger

Arcor S.A.I.C.

Avenida Fulvio Salvador Pagani 487
Arroyito, Cordoba
Argentina
Telephone: (+54) (51) 4303 0281
Toll Free: (800) 57-ARCOR
Fax: (+54) (51) 4310 9501
Web site: http://www.arcor.com.ar

Private Company
Incorporated: 1962
Employees: 13,000
Sales: 2.43 billion pesos ($810 million) (2003)
NAIC: 311320 Chocolate and Confectionery Manufacturing from Cacao Beans; 311340 Non-Chocolate Confectionery Manufacturing; 311821 Cookie and Cracker Manufacturing; 311822 Flour Mixes and Dough Manufacturing; 311919 Other Snack Food Manufacturing; 322211 Corrugated and Solid Fiber Box Manufacturing; 326112 Unsupported Plastics Packaging Film and Sheet Manufacturing

Life is sweet for Arcor S.A.I.C., the privately held firm that has grown to become one of Argentina's two biggest food companies, manufacturing more than 1,500 products. Although Argentina's fertile pampas are noted for their yields of wheat, corn, beef, and, more recently, soybeans, Arcor has achieved its success by making candy, cookies, chocolates, and other sweets, then selling them to customers in more than 110 countries. The company leaves little to chance or outside suppliers, producing its own glucose, flour, dough, cornmeal and corn oil, milk, sugar, marmalade and other preserves, tin cans, corrugated boxes, and plastic film for packaging. A multinational company with factories in several South American countries, Arcor views the whole world as its market.

Candy Factory to Multinational Operation: 1951–90

In 1924, Amos Pagani, a young Italian immigrant, settled in Arroyito, a small town in the province of Cordoba, in order to install a bakery. His five children were put to work making caramel when they reached age ten. Fulvio Salvador Pagani, the second-born, proved the most energetic and daring of the children. In 1951, in partnership with a group of investors that included two of his brothers and members of the Maranzana, Seveso, and Brizio families, Fulvio built a small candy factory in Arroyito. Seven years later, Arcor (its name formed from Arroyito and Cordoba) was producing 60,000 kilos (132,000 pounds) of sweets per day. Its principle was to assure the best quality at the lowest price by supplying itself with its own raw materials. Argentina's closed economy made it difficult to obtain supplies at competitive prices, so Arcor inaugurated its program of vertical integration by constructing its own glucose plant.

Arcor began, in the 1970s, to build its own plants to satisfy its needs—not only for raw materials but also for packaging and energy. In 1970, the company opened a plant in Tucuman; in 1972, one in San Rafael, Mendoza; in 1975, a third in Villa del Totoral, Cordoba; the fourth, in 1978, in San Pedro, Buenos Aires; a fifth, in 1979, once again in Villa del Totoral, for plastic packaging; and in 1980, the sixth, in Parana, Entre Rios. The company also launched operations in neighboring countries: Paraguay in 1976, Uruguay in 1979, Brazil in 1981, and Chile in 1989. Arcor had grown to Argentina's 70th largest company in 1980, with sales of 268.35 billion pesos (about $140 million) and advanced to 46th in 1985. Fulvio's son Luis recalled in a 1998 issue of the business magazine *Mercado* that the key to Arcor's growth in this period "was the reinvestment of profits and the addition of the most modern technology. We invested strongly in technology during the Eighties. When we saw an opening, we were prepared to compete head to head with the multinationals."

Rapid Expansion in the 1990s

At the beginning of the 1990s, Arcor built a plant for chocolates in Colonia Caroya, Cordoba, that was the largest of its type in Latin America and supplied almost half of the Argentine market. The company also constructed a gas pipeline to its Arroyito plant. After Pagani died in an automobile accident at the end of 1990, he was succeeded by his brother-in-law Hugo D'Allesandro, while his eldest son, Luis Alejandro Pagani, was sent to the United States to study business. Luis Pagani assumed

Company Perspectives:

We want to become, in the next few years, the number one candy and chocolate company in Latin America.

the chairmanship of Arcor in 1993. The inauguration of a new corrugated-box factory in Lujan, Buenos Aires, helped consolidate the national leadership in this field of Cartocor S.A., one of the companies that had been integrated into Arcor. Arcor also established a division of foreign commerce with its own marketing department, which encouraged marketing directors in each of the principal markets to create a network coordinating individual strategies according to the country, the consumer, and the brands most sold.

In 1994, Arcor acquired 90 percent of Aguila-Saint S.A. (in full, Cafes, Chocolates Aguila y Productos Saint Hnos. S.A.), a century-old Buenos Aires manufacturer that had been selling confectionery chocolate to Argentine households for generations. The purchase brought with it another chocolate brand, Cabsha. By the end of the year, Arcor was a giant, with sales that year of 718 million pesos and profit an enviable 94 million pesos (with the peso at parity with the dollar). The company competed in 20 categories of candy and chocolates, ranking first in 14 and second in the other six. Exports accounted for about 123 million pesos, or more than 15 percent of sales. Arcor also abandoned its low institutional profile and began a media advertising campaign, including commercials on CNN to reach Hispanics as far north as Mexico.

By now, Arcor's products were being sold in 60 countries. Nechar Alimentos Ltda., the Brazilian caramel, chewing gum, and comfit producer Arcor purchased in 1981, now ranked third in its field, its output having grown more than 30 fold. Nechar was producing chiclets for the entire Western Hemisphere, while in Uruguay Arcor specialized in suckers. In 1995, the company purchased Noel, an Argentine manufacturer of preserves and jams with more than 100 years of name recognition, and opened a state-of-the-art cookie-and-cracker factory in Salto, Buenos Aires. The following year, Arcor established a Peruvian subsidiary, Unidal, which built a candy plant not only to serve the local market but also to export the company's products to neighboring Bolivia, Colombia, Venezuela, as well as to China.

Arcor's sales passed the one-billion-peso mark in 1997. It was the national leader in the production of chocolates, caramels, marmalades, cornmeal, corrugated cardboard, and flexible packing, second in chewing gum and corn oil, and third in cookies. Pagani was aiming for Arcor to be number one in all Latin America in candy and chocolates and saw the company reaching as far north as Alaska by 2005. Some 33 plants were turning out a thousand products. The company was spending 60 million pesos a year on market research, the development of new products, advertising, and promotion. A network of 230 distributors working exclusively for Arcor guaranteed that its products would reach 200,000 points of sale throughout Argentina each week. The company had 35 accounts spread over four advertising agencies.

During 1997, Arcor acquired the Argentine cookie firm LIA and the Brazilian manufacturer of propylene film Koppol. The same year, Cartocor built its fourth plant for corrugated board. In early 1998, the company purchased, for about $200 million, the Chilean candy company Dos en Uno Ltda., including its plant in Argentina and its commercial operations in Brazil, Colombia, and Peru. Dos en Uno ranked second in Chile in chewing gum and chocolates, second in caramels, and third in cookies. Arcor now had 37 plants (30 in Argentina), was employing more than 13,000 people, and was the world leader in caramel production. Also in 1998, the company's revenues reached a record 1.2 billion pesos, and its products were selling in 82 countries.

Other Argentine companies in Arcor's field had been acquired by multinational giants such as Nabisco Holdings Corp., Group Danone S.A., and Cadbury Schweppes PLC. Arcor responded by shifting its focus from low-margin bulk products to ones that could be sold at premium prices for their quality and variety. It also found a relatively cheap way to penetrate the U.S. market by producing private-label candies for Wal-Mart Stores Inc. and Sara Lee Corp. When Brach Confections Inc., the seventh-largest U.S. candy manufacturer, closed its Chicago plant in 2001, it contracted the output to Arcor's Arroyito complex, paying $40 million a year for 30,000 tons of hard candy and chocolates.

Arcor in the New Century

As the 20th century neared its end, Arcor made a major foray into the Brazilian chocolate market—the largest in Latin America—by constructing a $50-million factory, the most advanced chocolate plant in the region, in Braganca Paulista, outside of Sao Paulo. The new factory opened in 1999, but the expense had contributed to Arcor's swelling debt of $310 million as Argentina's economy had fallen into recession, causing company sales to decline. When the Argentine government was unable to pay its own debts in late 2001, the peso was devalued and the national economy suffered a severe blow. Arcor incurred a loss of 122 million pesos (about $37 million) that year but remained current on its interest payments on bank loans and even raised wages for thousands of its employees in the wake of the 40-percent-a-year inflation that resulted from the peso devaluation. Largely because Arcor's net debt of $290 million was all in bank loans—and not in bonds that would have to be redeemed—Pagani was named chief executive officer of the year by *LatinFinance.* Sales rose slightly in 2003, when exports accounted for 24 percent of revenues, and the company was again in the black, earning 85 million pesos (about $29 million). Some of its plants had closed by this time; in 2003, there were 31: 25 in Argentina, three in Chile, two in Brazil, and one in Peru.

Arcor's industrial complex on the outskirts of Arroyito was a virtual city within a city. The company's primary candy factory consisted of hard-candy manufacturing in one building and the production of chewing gum, nougat, and other candies in two other buildings. Sharing the complex was a plant for the production of various corn products, including fructose and glucose, and the company's main distribution center for Argentina. Here, Arcor was also manufacturing paper and cardboard, chemicals, distilled natural oils, essence oils, menthol, and powdered flavors. The entire site was being powered by a gas turbine.

Arcor's plants in San Rafael, Mendoza, and San Pedro, Buenos Aires, were among the foods division's principal plants

Key Dates:

1951: Arcor is founded as a small candy factory.
1958: The company is producing 60,000 kilos (132,000 pounds) of sweets per day.
1980: With six plants in Argentina, Arcor is the nation's 70th largest company.
1989: Arcor now has operations in four neighboring South American countries.
1993: Luis Pagini, the founder's eldest son, becomes chief executive of Arcor.
1994: Arcor ranks first or second nationally in 20 categories of candy and chocolate output.
1998: Arcor's annual sales peak at $1.2 billion; 37 plants are in operation.
1999: Arcor opens a $50-million chocolate factory in Brazil.
2002: Pagani is named chief executive of the year by *LatinFinance* magazine.

for a variety of products. The foods division also included Alicia S.A., which was making powdered products, puddings, desserts, jellies, cakes, juices, cocoa, and ice cream in Recreo, Catamarca; Frutos de Cuyo S.A., processing and packing vegetables in San Juan; Dulciora S.A., producing marmalades and sweets in Villa Mercedes, San Luis; Metalbox S.A., making tin cans in Villa Mercedes; and Alimentos Indal S.A., processing foods and candies in Los Andes, Chile.

The Arcor candy plant in Arroyito—at 78,000 square meters, the largest in the world—and the one in La Reduccion, Tucuman, made up two of the candy division's three facilities. The third belonged to Candy S.A., in Recreo. These units made caramels, chiclets, nougats, cakes, solid and jellied candies, and lollipops. The Arcor plants in Arroyito, Villa del Totoral, and Salto composed three of the four in the cookies division. The fourth was Carlisa S.A.'s plant in Recreo., turning out sweet rolls and nut-and-honey bars. This division also produced crackers, wafers, dried, filled, and coated sweets as well as puddings and salty snacks. The chocolates division had plants in Colonia Caroya and Braganca Paulista. Production included bonbons, dried fruits, icing, chocolate bars, and Easter eggs. Arcor's Bon-O-Bon, a chocolate-covered candy, was the leading chocolate confectionery product in Argentina. The Cofler and Tofi brands were engaged in the highly competitive chocolate-tablet market. Other Arcor brands included Saladix (snacks), Topline (bubble gum), Rocklets (candy), and Whispers (milk chocolate).

All of the basic and raw materials assembled by the agroindustry division—sugarcane, milk, glucose, fructose, and ethyl alcohol— came from Arcor plants in Arroyito, San Pedro, and Rio Seco, Tucuman; a sugar refinery in La Providence, Tucuman; a glucose plant in Tucuman; and some 160,000 hectares (about 400,000 acres) in the states of Salta, Santa Fe, and Santiago del Estero, where some 40,000 heads of cattle grazed. Productos Naturales S.A. was the unit producing flavors, seasonings, and oils. Cartocor S.A. had plants for cardboard and paper boxes and sheets in Arroyito, Parana, and Lujan. Vitopel, S.A., a packaging subsidiary, was the biggest such in Argentina. Founded in 1979, it was located in Villa del Totoral, where it was making bi-oriented polypropylene film for flexible packaging. Both Cartocor and Vitopel were producing for other customers besides the parent company. Vitopel ranked first among Argentine plastic-products manufacturers; Cartocor was third in cellulose and paper.

Principal Subsidiaries

Alicia S.A.; Alimentos Indal S.A. (Chile); Arcor do Brasil Ltda (Brazil); Arcor de Chile (Chile); Arcor de Peru S.A (Peru).; Arcor U.S.A. Inc. (United States); Candy S.A.; Carlisa S.A.; Cartocor S.A.; Dulciora S.A.; Frutos de Cuyo S.A.; Metalbox, S.A.; Productos Naturales S.A.; Vitopel S.A.

Principal Divisions

Agroindustry; Arcor do Brasil; Arcor de Chile; Candy; Chocolates; Cookies; Flavors; Foods; International; Paper and Cardboard.

Principal Competitors

Bagley S.A.; Cadbury Stani S.A.I.C.; Kraft Suchard Argentina S.A.; Nestlé Argentina S.A.

Further Reading

''Arcor Set to Double U.S. Sales,'' *Professional Candy Buyer*, November 1, 2001.

Benechi, Mario, ''Las apuestas de un adelantado,'' *Mercado*, March 1999, pp. 48–50.

''Un dulce sueno continental,'' *Mercado*, January 1998, pp. 40–41.

Forster, Steve, ''Arcor Breaks Through,'' *Candy Business*, November-December 2001, p. 40ff.

Galloway, Jennifer, ''Arcor's Bittersweet Success,'' *LatinFinance*, September 2002, pp. 27–29.

Giglio, Josefina, ''Como hacer de una golosina un mundo,'' *Mercado*, June 1995, pp. 46–48, 50.

Goodman, Joshua, ''The Road to Recovery,'' *Latin Trade*, September 2001, pp. 42–43.

Mandel-Campbell, Andrea, ''Argentinian Candy Company Looks to Sweeten Its Global Pot,'' *Marketing Magazine*, November 24, 1997, p. 6.

——, ''Sweet Success,'' *Latin Trade*, February 1998, p. 26.

''El mundial de Arcor,'' *Mercado*, February 1998, p. 65.

''Quality Rules at Accor,'' *Candy Business*, January-February 2004, p. S40ff.

Ruiz-Velasco, Laura M., and Fatima Cheade, ''Dulce expansion,'' *America economia*, July 1995, pp. 8–9.

Stok, Gustavo, ''Arcor: receta dificil,'' *America economia*, April 23, 1998, pp. 20–21.

''Sweet and Grow,'' *Business Latin America*, February 1, 1999, pp. 6–7.

Tiffany, Susan, ''*ARCOR* Sculpts a Sweet Empire in Latin America,'' *Candy Industry*, February 1996, pp. 16–20, 22–23.

——, ''Investment Is Boon to Market Share,'' *Candy Industry*, February 1997, pp. 29–30.

''Today Candyland, Tomorrow the World,'' *Business Week*, June 4, 2001, p. 31.

Traverso, Lucio, and Juan Quiroga, ''Luis Pagani, Chairman of Grupo Arcor, on the Globalization of Argentine Firms,'' *Academy of the Management Executive*, August 2003, pp. 56–59.

—Robert Halasz

Arnott's Ltd.

11 George Street
Homebush
NSW 2140
Australia
Telephone: (+61) 2 9394 3555
Fax: (+61) 2 9394 3873
Web site: http://www.arnotts.com.au

Wholly Owned Subsidiary of Campbell Soup Company
Founded: 1875 as William Arnott's Steam Biscuit Factory
Employees: 4,900
Sales: AUD 7.4 billion ($5.2 billion) (2002 est.)
NAIC: 311821 Cookie and Cracker Manufacturing; 311911 Roasted Nuts and Peanut Butter Manufacturing; 311919 Other Snack Food Manufacturing

Arnott's Ltd. is the leading Australian manufacturer of biscuits and cookies, which are marketed under the Arnott's brand name. The company commands more than 70 percent of the Australian market and boasts that its products are present in 97 percent of all Australian homes. Arnott's biscuit assortment reads like an honor roll for Australian tea time, with such perennial favorites as Tim Tams, Mint Slice, Full O' Fruit, Iced Vo Vos, and Jatz. The company produces a full range of biscuits, spanning such company-designated categories as plain biscuits, chocolates, creams, and fruit. The company also makes salted snack foods, such as chips, crispbreads, and crackers. The last-named category was boosted by the 2002 acquisition of Snack Foods Ltd., which brought the company two popular brands, Kettle and Rix. Arnott's remains largely focused on the Australian market; nonetheless, the company has also enabled parent Campbell Soup Company to gain a foothold in the Asian region. Arnott's operates factories in Papua New Guinea and in Indonesia, complementing its five factories in Australia. The company's national production presence also enables it to tailor its recipes to meet specific regional tastes. Campbell Soup Company gained full control of Arnott's in the late 1970s. Since the early 2000s, the company's revenues have been estimated at more than AUD 7.4 billion ($5.2 billion).

Building a Biscuit Company: 1850s–1930s

Born in 1827, William Arnott began his career as a baker's apprentice in his native Pathhead, Scotland, before emigrating to Australia in 1847. Arnott settled in Maitland in southern Australia and at first worked for other bakers. In the 1850s, however, he followed the gold rush, setting up a bakery business in the mining fields and catering to the growing population of miners. With money earned from this business, Arnott returned to Maitland and opened his first bakery shop.

After floods destroyed Maitland in the early 1860s, Arnott moved to Newcastle, opening a new shop in rented space on Hunter Street. Arnott began supplying biscuits for the Newcastle shipping industry, and his Ships Biscuits became highly popular as food for long sea voyages. By the end of the decade, Arnott was able to buy the entire Hunter Street building and open a new, larger baker's shop.

Arnott began adding new products, such as sweet biscuits and cakes, and in 1875 set up his first factory, in Newcastle, in order to produce for a larger market. William Arnott's Steam Biscuit Factory soon needed a workforce of 50 in order to turn out some 1.5 tons of biscuits per day. By the early 1880s, Arnott's growing popularity—boosted by the 1882 launch of its Milk Arrowroot—had led the company to Sydney, where it quickly became one of the city's biggest biscuits suppliers. In order to ensure his supply of milk, Arnott bought his own dairy herd during the decade as well.

William Arnott died in 1901, and the company was taken over by his five sons, who were to lead Arnott's on a new era of brand success. The company became one of the earliest Australian producers to advertise its goods under its own brand name, marketed under its trademarked parrot logo first introduced in 1888. The company also began devising new recipes, a number of which became long-standing best-sellers into the 21st century. Two of these in particular, the Iced Vo Vo and the SAO, both launched in 1906, became Australian cultural icons. Other products launched at the time were the digestive cracker Malt 'O' Milk, the Kiel Finger (later renamed the Scotch Finger), Ginger Nuts, and Milk Coffee.

With demand outstripped its production capacity, Arnott's began looking for a site for a new factory and in 1906 broke

Company Perspectives:

Our principles. *Arnott's is the number one grocery umbrella brand in Australia and boasts some of the largest brands in the country. We are committed to providing people with challenging and exciting careers. We are proud of our culture which encourages people to achieve their best in a stimulating team environment. We have six guiding principles: our people create value; we can only achieve working in a team; there is no substitute for quality in everything we do; innovation is essential and rewarded; we must make a difference in our communities; we are committed to winning in retail channels. These principles guide us through every stage of our business from product development, manufacturing, distribution and sales and marketing.*

ground on a six-and-one-half-acre plot in the Homebush section of Sydney. Once considered a remote location, the Homebush area later became one of the central points of the city of Sydney, in part because of Arnott's growing presence there.

After converting its production to supplying troops during World War I, Arnott's resumed its growth in the inter-war period, launching such successful products as the Adora Cream Wafer and the Orange Slice, both launched in 1922, and the Monte Carlo, introduced in 1926. By the end of the 1920s, the company boasted some 150 biscuit varieties which it delivered to an ever-widening circle of customers with the company's own fleet of 19 Albion trucks.

The Depression once again slowed the company's growth, especially since Arnott's scaled back its production to just three days per week at times in order to avoid cutting its workforce. Maintaining its employees placed the company in position to rebound strongly as the economy improved, and by the end of the decade Arnott's production topped 43 million pounds per year.

Strategies for Survival: 1940s to the 1960s

Arnott's once again turned production to support the Australian war effort in the 1940s, while also supplying C-rations to the U.S. forces. During this period, the company dropped most of its biscuit, cake, and cookie varieties, trimming down to just under 20 brands, although these included such company mainstays as the Iced Vo Vo and the SAO. With the end of the war, Arnott's resumed full-scale production for the consumer market, although initial production had by then dropped to just 12,500 tons per year.

The rising economy during the postwar boom years gave Arnott's renewed vigor, and by the end of the 1950s the company's total production had nearly doubled. That decade also marked the appearance of a new generation of important Arnott varieties, including the Jatz crisp, which also became one of the first Arnott products to be featured in television advertising. In the raw materials shortages of the late 1940s, the company devised a new biscuit, the Choc Ripple, using leftover bits of other biscuits. The product proved so popular that the company decided to develop a true recipe for the biscuit, which also inspired the popular Choc Ripple Cake recipe.

The Australian biscuit industry faced a crisis in the 1950s as the popularity of American products turned consumers toward new biscuit and cookie varieties arriving from overseas. Arnott's took steps to head off the American "invaders," launching its own versions of popular American treats, such as the Delta Cream in 1954 and the yeast-based Plaza biscuit, created after the saltine cracker.

This was not enough to keep out the Americans, however. By the mid-1950s, U.S. food powerhouse Nabisco had begun making a serious effort to enter the Australian market, targeting acquisitions of existing companies. In order to fend off any takeovers, Arnott's led the consolidation of a number of prominent regional Australian baked goods companies, including Adelaide's Motteram & Menz, western Australia's Mills & Ware, Queensland's Morrow, and Melbourne's Brockhoff Biscuits, creating the Australian Biscuit Company.

By the 1960s, the combined business had renamed itself Arnott's. The larger company had gained a number of new brands, particularly from the Brockhoff business, which contributed its hugely popular Chocolate Teddy Bear, among others. The early 1960s also saw the launch of a new iconic product for Arnott's: the Tim Tam. Launched in 1963, the Tim Tam was named, according to company legend, for the 1958 Kentucky Derby winner. The chocolate biscuit quickly proved a winner for Arnott's, becoming its best-selling product, selling more than 30 million packs sold each year by the end of the 20th century.

Until then, Arnott's products had typically been sold in tins. The growth of modern self-service supermarkets, however, forced Arnott's to develop new packaging types. By the end of the 1960s, the company had largely abandoned its former tins.

Takeover Pressure: Mid-1960s to the Late 1990s

Into the mid-1960s, the company found itself in the midst of a biscuit "war" after Nabisco launched a new effort to break into the Australian market. In 1964, Nabisco made a takeover offer for Swallow & Ariel, a popular biscuit company based in Melbourne. Arnott's countered Nabisco's bid, and the two sides began a bidding war that eventually set the price at more than double the opening bid, with Arnott's successful in buying a 51 percent stake in Swallow & Ariel. In response, Nabisco set up its Australian operation from scratch. Not to be outdone, however, Arnott's began producing similar products to Nabisco's own, squeezing out its larger U.S. rival by the weight of its own brand name at home.

Buoyed by its success as the dominant biscuit player in Australia, Arnott's began preparing a new era of growth for the 1970s. The company went public in 1970, using the proceeds of the public offering to fuel its increasingly diversified interests. By the end of the decade, the company had moved toward vertical integration with the acquisition of a number of biscuit ingredients supplies, including four mills and preserves and peanut manufacturing facilities. In addition, Arnott's also acquired its own packaging operations during the decade. The company also took advantage of its solid position as Australian biscuit leader to pick up the Australian operations of its chief rival, Peak Freans, in 1975.

Yet Arnott's public listing—and its rapid diversification—exposed it to a fresh attempt at a takeover by Nabisco in the

Key Dates:

1847: Scottish native William Arnott emigrates to Australia and begins working as a baker.
1875: After establishing a successful bakery shop, Arnott opens his first factory in Newcastle.
1906: A new factory is constructed in Sydney.
1956: The company merges with Morrow, Metteram and Menz, Mills & Ware, and Brockhoff to form Australian Biscuit Company.
1963: Tim Tam biscuits are launched.
1970: The company goes public as Arnott's on the Australian Stock Exchange.
1985: Campbell Soup Company gains a minority stake after a takeover attempt by Nabisco.
1992: Campbell Soup acquires a 33 percent stake in the company.
1996: The company acquires Kettles Chip Co. for AUD 20 million.
1997: Campbell Soup acquires full control of Arnott's; Tiny Teddys become the most successful product launch in the company's history.
2001: The company announces a plan to spend AUD 30 million upgrading three manufacturing facilities.
2002: Snack Foods Ltd is acquired for AUD 250 million.
2004: The company introduces Kettle Crunch and Kettle Sensations brands.

1980s. In order to counter the U.S. giant's takeover approach, Arnott's turned to another American company, Campbell Soup Company. Campbell took a 14 percent share of Arnott's, defeating Nabisco's takeover attempt.

The struggle to retain its independence ultimately led to the resignation of the last member of the Arnott family to be involved in the company and the appointment of the first managing director to come from outside of the family. At the same time, Arnott's had been hit hard by an effort, launched in the 1980s, to diversify into snack foods. The company appeared unable to translate its success in biscuits to that of the still-larger snack food market, and in 1990, with losses mounting, Arnott's pulled the plug on its new operations. Soon after, with the Arnott family's announcement of its intention to sell out its control of the company, Arnott's became the subject of a takeover battle. By 1992, Campbell had emerged as the early leader, raising its share of the company to 33 percent, prompting an outright takeover offer.

Arnott's under Campbell: Late 1990s–2000s

Arnott's resisted Campbell's efforts. The slumping Australian economy, however, forced the family's hand. With profits shrinking, Arnott's slowly yielded to the American company, which gained a 70 percent stake by 1994. The company, already hit hard by losses, was dealt a new blow in 1996 when it became the subject of an extortion plot, with a threat to poison its products in an attempt to free a convicted murderer. By 1997, after several years of negotiations, Campbell finally succeeded in gaining full control of the Australian legend.

Campbell's interest in Arnott's came in large part because of the perception of Australia's proximity to the potentially huge Asian Pacific market. Arnott's had already begun exporting its biscuits in the 1970s. With its brand name already established in many of the Asian markets, Arnott's became Campbell's regional spearhead, supported by new production facilities in Papua New Guinea and Indonesia.

Under Campbell, Arnott's also began a renewed attempt to move into snack foods. That effort started in 1996 with the AUD 20 million purchase of the Kettle Chip Company. The move was even seen as heralding a new era of a biscuit-less Arnott's. As managing director Chris Roberts told *The Advertiser* at the time: "The most important step into the future is into the snack food market and out of biscuits."

Fortunately for Australia's biscuit lovers, Arnott's remained committed to its long history as Australia's top biscuit brand. The company continued to develop new biscuit recipes, such as the late 1990s Tiny Teddy biscuits, the most successful new product in the company's history, selling more than five million biscuits in little more than a month.

In the early 2000s, Campbell pumped some AUD 30 million into Arnott's in order to expand the company's production plants in Sydney, Adelaide, and Brisbane. As part of that plan, launched in 2001, the company announced its intention to shut down its Melbourne facility.

The following year, Arnott's took a new step toward developing its revived snack foods division, paying more than AUD 250 million in order to acquire Snack Foods Ltd. That purchase gave the company control of a new range of brands, including the highly successful Rix brand. By the end of that year, Arnott's sales were estimated to have topped AUD 7 billion ($5 billion). In the meantime, the company's Kettle brand had been performing strongly for the company, leading Arnott's to launch new Kettle varieties—Kettle Crunch and Kettle Sensations in 2004.

Principal Competitors

Associated British Foods PLC; Yamazaki Baking Company Ltd.; Morinaga Milk Industry Company Ltd.; Nabisco Biscuit Co.; United Biscuits UK Ltd.; Goodman Fielder Proprietary Ltd.

Further Reading

"Arnott's Competes with Salty Snacks," *B&T Weekly*, April 16, 2004.
"Arnott's Export Sucks up to Ex-pats," *Courier-Mail*, May 14, 2003, p. 11.
"Arnott's Swallows Snack," *Mercury*, July 31, 2002, p. 27.
"Campbell to Snatch Last Slice of Arnott's," *Mercury*, September 10, 1997, p. 27.
Chai, Paul, "Tough Times Bite Arnott's," *Advertiser*, November 15, 1996, p. 19.
Evans, Simon, "Lean Time for Arnott's" *Advertiser*, February 28, 1996, p. 44.
Shoebridge, Neil, "Arnott's Emerges from Its Blackest Hour with a New Will to Win," *Business Review Weekly*, September 22, 1997, p. 84.
Webb, Richard, "Pledge to Keep Arnott's Aussie," *Daily Telegraph*, September 10, 1997, p. 35.

—M. L. Cohen

ASV, Inc.

840 Lily Lane
Grand Rapids, Minnesota 55744
U.S.A.
Telephone: (218) 327-3434
Toll Free: (800) 346-5954
Fax: (218) 327-9122
Web site: http://www.asvi.com

Public Company
Incorporated: 1983
Employees: 151
Sales: $96.38 million (2003)
Stock Exchanges: NASDAQ
Ticker Symbol: ASVI
NAIC: 333120 Construction Machinery Manufacturing

ASV, Inc., is a designer and manufacturer of track-driven vehicles renowned for their ability to traverse a variety of surface conditions while exerting minimal pressure on the ground. All of the company's vehicles use a rubber track suspension system that provides traction on soft, wet, slippery, rough, or hilly terrain. ASV's product lines comprise the R-Series Posi-Track group of vehicles and the Multi-Terrain Loader undercarriage systems it produces through a partnership with Caterpillar Inc. The company conducts its manufacturing activities at a 100,000-square-foot facility in Grand Rapids, Minnesota. The vehicles are sold through Caterpillar's distribution network, which includes dealerships in more than 200 countries. Caterpillar Inc. owns 24.9 percent of ASV.

Origins

Two years of little snowfall forced ASV's founders, Edgar Hetteen and Gary Lemke, to find new occupations. Their livelihoods depended on snowfall: Hetteen, often referred to as the ''grandfather of snowmobiles,'' had founded two companies that pioneered snowmobiles, Arctic Cat and Polaris Industries; Lemke, starting with a small shop in 1968, built one of the largest Arctic Cat dealerships in the country. When high interest rates in the early 1980s exacerbated the financial damage of two winters with only a trace of snow, the pair found themselves insolvent. Lemke's snowmobile dealership in Grand Rapids, Minnesota, foundered, declaring bankruptcy and leaving its owner in debt. Arctic Cat, meanwhile, was in Chapter 11 proceedings. The company would recover, but its collapse in the early 1980s stripped Hetteen of his personal fortune.

Hetteen and Lemke were without money, but they had an idea, one that offered to free them from the caprice of winter weather. Hetteen's feats as a mechanic were legendary to those involved in winter recreation, expressed in the founding of Polaris Industries in 1945 and Arctic Cat in 1961. Lemke, too, was well versed in mechanics, having opened a small shop in 1980 called Marcell Manufacturing that built snow-grooming equipment and an assortment of other small machines used in the construction and snow industries. When his dealership went under at the beginning of the 1980s, Lemke was working on an innovative piece of machinery that both he and Hetteen believed had broad commercial potential. Lemke's sketches of his invention revealed a unique all-season vehicle whose design represented a cross between a snowmobile and a tractor. The vehicle, dubbed the Track Truck, was the size of a small pick-up with rubber tracks that distributed the machine's weight extremely well, enabling the nearly 6,000-pound vehicle to move across a variety of surfaces leaving less of an impression than a human foot. Designed as such, the Track Truck's rubber track system, using rubber wheels and tracks, offered the traction, stability, and low ground pressure needed to operate on soft, wet, muddy, rough, boggy, slippery, snowy, or hilly terrain. Unlike traditional steel tracks, the rubber track system did not cause damage to the surface it operated on, making it particularly useful for groomed, landscaped, and paved surfaces.

Armed with the idea of the Track Truck, but no money to finance its construction, Lemke and Hetteen turned to their friends and neighbors in Marcell, Minnesota, 30 miles north of Grand Rapids. The pair made a presentation to a group of invited guests and, within a short time, succeeded in raising $70,000 from 10 investors. With the start-up capital, Hetteen and Lemke set up shop in a long and narrow tin building in Marcell and began building their first Track Truck. ASV, an acronym for All Season Vehicle, was incorporated in July 1983.

Company Perspectives:

ASV's patented rubber track undercarriage technology is unique and leads a rapidly growing industry of rubber track loaders. Rubber track loaders are widely used within industries such as construction, utility, landscaping, agriculture and the military. ASV's undercarriage technology gives users a unique combination of benefits. It offers mobility superior to traditional rubber tire vehicles, plus flotation and traction surpassing that of steel track machines. The result is a highly versatile work platform that can effectively operate in virtually any environment .

The Track Truck offered several advantages over other track-driven vehicles on the market. ASV's vehicle was smaller and more maneuverable than its competition and it was less expensive, selling for roughly $50,000 rather than the more than $80,000 charged by manufacturers of similar track-driven vehicles. The Track Truck also featured front wheels, which stabilized it on steep grades, and it came equipped with a steering wheel rather than the levers employed by all other track-driven vehicles. Financially, the company was aided greatly by receiving a $100,000 low-interest, economic-development loan from the state of Minnesota, which buoyed manufacturing activity in ASV's tin building, but its principal problem during the 1980s was the Track Truck itself. The vehicle performed admirably, but it suffered from exposure to a limited market. The product only found a receptive audience among those involved in grooming snowmobile and cross-country skiing trails, still leaving Lemke and Hetteen confined to the world of winter recreation. The founders listened to their customers who asked for a more versatile machine and responded with a new product. Although money was scarce, with their research and development coffers empty, Lemke and Hetteen came up with a new product in the late 1980s. The new ASV vehicle, the Posi-Track, was introduced in 1990 and quickly became the driving force of the company, achieving everything the Track Truck had promised to achieve.

The Posi-Track Lends Stability in the 1990s

The Posi-Track Model MD-70 realized Lemke's vision of a multi-use vehicle that would revolutionize the equipment market. Equipped with a rubber track system, the Posi-Track, retailing for $34,000, performed the tasks of small steel-track bulldozers. Unlike the Track Truck, the Posi-Track featured a quick-attach mechanism and three-point hitch. By securing attachments to the hitch, the Posi-Track took on the capabilities of a number of different pieces of equipment, performing the tasks of a mower, a brush cutter, an augur, a backhoe, a snow remover, a plow, and more. The Posi-Track, once outfitted with a remote control unit, was used in the Middle East to disarm bomb-laden tracks. Because its ground pressure was only 1.5 pounds per square inch, the 5,800-pound Posi-Track was virtually weightless, allowing Cargill Inc. to use the machine on its ships to move up and over grain piles. E. & J. Gallo Winery and other California vineyards used the Posi-Track to work between rows of vines, choosing the vehicle because its weight distribution did not compact the soil or create ruts. The applications for the Posi-Track seemed endless, finding customers involved in a variety of markets, including construction, agricultural, landscaping, and wildlife management. "The world is basically our market potential," Hetteen exclaimed in a February 1995 interview with *Corporate Report—Minnesota.*

As the acceptance of the Posi-Track increased, so did the ambitions of ASV's leaders. A dealer network comprising independent construction and farm equipment retailers brought the company in contact with potential customers from California to Maine. By 1994, the company's annual sales reached $5 million, virtually all derived from the sale of Posi-Tracks. At this point, Lemke and Hetteen acted upon the need to expand their company. ASV had outgrown its long and narrow confines in Marcell. In August 1994, they completed the company's initial public offering (IPO) of stock, giving its 10 investors, all of whom would become millionaires, a chance to recoup their investments. The IPO gave ASV $3.3 million in net proceeds, enabling it to reduce its debt, purchase inventory and equipment, and relocate its operations to Grand Rapids. In May 1995, ASV moved into its new offices in Grand Rapids, where it quickly put to use 40,000 square feet of manufacturing space.

Growth came quickly following the move to Grand Rapids, making ASV one of the fastest-growing companies in the United States. After only a year at its new manufacturing facility, the company needed substantially more space. The approval for a financing package for the expansion was received in late 1996, enabling the company to increase the size of its manufacturing facility from 40,000 square feet to 100,000 square feet. The expansion was completed in September 1997. Shortly before occupying its much larger quarters, ASV introduced the Posi-Track HD 4500 series, which was larger and equipped with more features than the MD-70 model. In October 1997, four months after the introduction of the HD 4500, the company introduced the HD 125 (later renamed the DX 4530), the largest of all Posi-Track models produced.

ASV's abilities to offer new models, new technologies, and new features had greatly increased by the late 1990s. Research and development capital, which had been once only a dream, was available to the company in increasing abundance, a product of its success that allowed it to expand and improve its product line. In 1994, ASV spent $30,000 on research and development. By 1997, the company's research and development budget had increased to more than $200,000, enabling it to introduce the HD 4500 and the DX 4530 and, of great significance, to introduce the Maximum Traction and Support System undercarriage in 1997. The new technology, which received a patent in 2001, offered improved traction, power, and reliability and further lessened ground pressure, but most important to ASV's future, the undercarriage system attracted the attention of Caterpillar Inc., the largest manufacturer of construction equipment in the world.

ASV and Caterpillar Form an Alliance in 1998

The interest of officials at Caterpillar in the Maximum Traction and Support System led to an alliance of considerable benefit to ASV. In October 1998, the details of the agreement were revealed. ASV sold 8.7 percent of its stock to Caterpillar for $18 million and gave it the option to purchase a controlling interest in the company within the ensuing decade. Caterpillar,

Key Dates:

1983: ASV is founded and begins development of the Track Truck.
1990: ASV introduces the Posi-Track.
1994: ASV completes its initial public offering of stock.
1995: ASV moves into a 40,000-square-foot manufacturing facility in Grand Rapids, Minnesota.
1998: Caterpillar Inc., intrigued by ASV's Maximum Traction and Support System, forms an alliance with ASV.
2000: ASV introduces its R-Series product line.
2004: Caterpillar increases its stake in ASV to 24.9 percent.

at the time of the announcement, had recently diversified into lighter machinery, making the investment in ASV a good strategic fit for further expansion into the market segment. ASV, for its part, saw its dealer network expand exponentially. In exchange for Caterpillar's stake in the company, ASV gained access to Caterpillar's vast, global dealer network, which comprised 195 dealers in roughly 200 countries. In the United States alone, Caterpillar had 64 dealers, representing 400 separate locations. ''It's just an immediate access to all the things that Caterpillar has,'' Lemke remarked in an October 15, 1998, interview in *Knight Ridder/Tribune Business News.*

ASV and Caterpillar officially began what promised to be a lasting relationship at the end of January 1999, when the alliance was approved by ASV's shareholders. Caterpillar increased its ownership of ASV to approximately 15 percent in October 2000, a transaction that involved the two companies increasing their commitments to each other. Under the terms of the agreement, the companies agreed to jointly develop and manufacture a new product line of Caterpillar rubber track skid steer loaders called Multi-Terrain Loaders, or MTLs. The product offering, which was expected to included five new models, incorporated Caterpillar's patented skid steer loader technology and ASV's soon-to-be patented Maximum Traction and Support System undercarriage. ASV began manufacturing the undercarriage for two MTL models in mid-2001. The beginning of the new decade also saw ASV introduce its own new product line, the R-Series, which debuted with the RC-30 All Surface Loader in the summer of 2000. The RC-30, a compact, ATV-sized vehicle, allowed users to dig, haul, and lift on a scale eclipsing that of larger tractors and skid-steers.

As ASV neared its 20th anniversary, its innovative work was bearing fruit from every branch. Annual sales increased from $43.8 million in 2000 to $96.3 million in 2003. The company's net earnings swelled from $1.4 million in 2000 to $8.7 million. The company's business, which had depended on the Posi-track for 98 percent of its sales in the late 1990s, had diversified, with the introduction of MTLs and the R-Series reducing its reliance on a single product line. The family of R-Series vehicles grew during the early years of the decade, springing from research and development spending that reached $2.6 million in 2003. In early 2003, the company introduced three new models, the RC-30 Turf Edition and the RC-50 Turf Edition, both designed to have minimal impact on grass, and the RC-100, the largest model in the product line. In January 2004, the RC-60 and RC-85 were introduced, adding two new models that ranged in between the 2,935-pound RC-30 and the 9,200-pound RC-100.

As ASV moved passed its 20th anniversary, the company exuded admirable strength. Its commitment to research and development promised to deliver additional innovative vehicles to markets that had come to realize the benefits of rubber track suspension systems. Lemke's pioneering work in the 1980s, coupled with the technological advances achieved by ASV engineers in later years, created what many believed was a superior type of all-season, all-terrain vehicle. The company's electric growth during the late 1990s and early 21st century, which saw annual sales increase from $12 million in 1996 to $96 million in 2003, provided encouragement that ASV's future would bring robust growth. To prepare for the expected surge in demand for its products, the company purchased a vacant manufacturing facility in early 2004. Located in Cohasset, Minnesota, six miles from its existing production facility, the 108,000-square-foot complex was expected to be put use by the end of 2004.

Principal Subsidiaries

ASV Distribution, Inc.

Principal Competitors

Ingersoll-Rand Company Ltd.; Komatsu Ltd.; CNH Global N.V.; Deere & Company.

Further Reading

Brissett, Jane, ''Caterpillar to Buy Grand Rapids, Minn.-Based Maker of Work Vehicles,'' *Knight Ridder/Tribunes Business News,* October 15, 1998.

——, ''Grand Rapids, Minn.-Based Vehicle Maker Stumbles after Caterpillar Deal,'' *Knight Ridder/Tribunes Business News,* June 3, 1999.

Forster, Julie, ''Marcell's Millionaires,'' *Corporate Report-Minnesota,* September 1999, p. 22.

''Grand Rapids, Minn. Tracked Vehicle Maker Gets Patent for Undercarriage System,'' *Knight Ridder/Tribunes Business News,* December 4, 2001.

—Jeffrey L. Covell

Atari Corporation

417 5th Ave.
New York, NY 10016
U.S.A.
Web site: http://www.infogrames.com

Incorporated: 1972
Dissolved: 1998
NAIC: 511210 Software Publishers

Before its merger with disk drive maker JTS Corporation in 1996, the Atari Corporation was a prominent manufacturer of video games and home computers that pioneered the industry of video entertainment. Its history was beset by a series of successes and ultimately defeats: it made money from arcade games, then nearly went bankrupt; it took on new life and astronomical profits in the early 1980s, only to see its industry crash once again, leaving the company to rebuild slowly under different management and then finally succumb to the rise of the PC-based CD-ROM as the preferred medium for computer games. The Atari name, however, was acquired by Infogrames Entertainment in 2001, and that company proceeded to rechristen its U.S. subsidiary Atari Inc.

Nolan Bushnell's Game: The Early 1970s

Atari was founded by Nolan Bushnell in 1972. Bushnell had first become interested in computer games as an engineering student at the University of Utah. After graduation, he worked as a researcher in a Silicon Valley firm, and there he developed his first electronic game, called Computer Space, in 1971. Although this game, like all the other fledgling products before it, was not a commercial success, Bushnell used $500 to start a company with a friend anyway, naming it Atari, a term from the Japanese game of "go" used to politely alert opponents that they are about to be overrun.

Bushnell's second game was a revolutionary development, in that it was far simpler than other games had been. Called "Pong," it was an electronic version of ping pong, played on a screen with a vertical line down the middle and two sliding paddles that batted a blip back and forth. The company first marketed a coin-operated version of this game in 1972 for use in arcades. Since the game could be played by two people in direct competition with each other, Pong was a dramatic departure from the solitary skills of pinball, and it changed the nature of arcade games.

Unfortunately, Atari was unable to reap the rewards of this advance, since dozens of competitors quickly duplicated the game and grabbed a large portion of the market. Within two years of Pong's introduction, its inventors had sold only 10 percent of the machines in existence.

Atari channeled the profits it had made into ventures that turned out to be shortsighted and nonproductive. The company wasted half a million dollars on an abortive attempt to market its products in Japan. In addition, it sunk resources into an attempt to open game arcades in Hawaii. Although Atari introduced a series of new games to follow Pong, formulated in the company's informal, unstructured atmosphere, none caught on as much as its first offering.

Video games for use in the home had first been introduced by Magnavox in 1972, and Atari decided that a logical next step would be to introduce a home version of Pong, to be played on a television screen. Short of funds, the company worked out an arrangement with Sears, Roebuck & Company for the retailer to buy all 100,000 of the devices that Atari manufactured, as well as helping out with funding for Atari's inventories, to guarantee delivery. In the fall of 1975, the home version of Pong was introduced.

Enter Warner Communications: The Late 1970s

Clearly, Atari needed further funds to expand. Rather than sell stock to the public, the company decided to look for a buyer. In 1976, after four months of legal wrangling complicated by a lawsuit filed against Bushnell by his first wife, Atari was sold to Warner Communications Inc. for $28 million. Of this, Pong's inventor collected about $15 million.

By the next year, however, Atari's problems had moved beyond funding. The company's products at the time could be used to play only one game, and consumers were beginning to

Key Dates:

1972: Nolan Bushnell establishes Atari as a computer game developer.
1975: Atari introduces the home version of the Pong game.
1976: Warner Communications acquires Atari.
1982: Pac-Man debuts.
1985: Atari, under new ownership, begins manufacturing home computers.
1996: Financially troubled in the face of competition from Sega and Nintendo, Atari merges with JTS Corporation.
1998: JTS is purchased by Hasbro, which dissolves Atari.
2001: Infogrames Entertainment S.A. acquires Hasbro and the rights to the Atari name; the company's American subsidiary is renamed Atari Inc..

feel that the novelty of playing that one game had worn off. In late 1977 Atari's researchers introduced the Video Computer System, or VCS 2600, which used a semiconductor chip in a programmable device. With this product, the customer gained versatility. Any number of games could be played on cartridges, which were inserted into the set like cassette tapes.

Introduced shortly before the big Christmas selling season, the new games initially failed to conclusively dislodge the old, single-purpose products. In addition, the company had come up against steep competition from several of its competitors, who also had introduced multipurpose video game equipment. Throughout 1978, Atari saw its new product languish on the shelves.

This disappointing news was compounded by administrative confusion at company headquarters. Original Atari employees felt no loyalty toward their new bosses, and top administrators also disagreed with some of Warner's key decisions. After a chaotic budget meeting in New York, Bushnell was ousted from his position as chair of the company.

In his place, executives with backgrounds at large companies were installed, and procedures and practices at Atari became much more businesslike. In an effort to sell off some of the backlogged inventory of slow-moving games that the company had built up, Atari launched a $6 million advertising campaign in the last seven weeks of 1978, designed to clear out inventory and make way for new products.

The strategy worked. At the important, industry-wide Consumer Electronics Show in January 1979, store owners demanded more products to sell. Over the next 12 months, Atari was able to sell all of the game devices it manufactured.

In addition to its game operations, Atari ambitiously branched out into the hotly competitive personal computer field, introducing two models, dubbed the Atari 400 and the Atari 800. These were intended for the home rather than office market. In the company's second year of operation in this field, it lost about $10 million on sales of twice that amount.

With the start of the 1980s, however, Atari's successes in the video game field more than made up for its losses in other areas, as its growth and profits shot up. In January 1980, Atari began an effort to shift the emphasis of the video game industry away from holiday-generated sales, to prove that people were willing to buy video games all year round. To do this, Atari introduced four new video game cartridges late in the first month of the year. The tactic was successful, and demand for the company's product continued to build. By the end of the year, Atari had sold all of the video game machines that it had manufactured. Among its biggest selling cartridges was Space Invaders, an adaptation of a coin-operated arcade game originally designed in Japan.

New Games and New Competition in the Early 1980s

Atari's arcade operations were also going strong. In 1980, the company introduced Asteroids to compete with the Space Invaders arcade game, which was produced by another company. Atari's version proved to be a popular alternative. By the end of the year, 70,000 of the units had been shipped. Overall, revenues from coin-operated games reached $170 million, up from $52 million the year before. In addition to its arcade business, in 1980 Atari also began to explore the market for its products overseas. The company's overall revenues had more than doubled in just one year, topping $415 million, and its operating income had increased by five times.

Because the sale of video cartridges was extremely profitable, Atari introduced new games at a steady pace, releasing titles at the rate of one per month. In 1981, with demand running at feverish pitch, the company decided to ration its product. More than one million cartridges of Space Invaders had been sold. All in all, with its competitors falling by the wayside, Atari was the world's largest producer of video games, holding 80 percent of the American market. At the end of 1981, the company had sold more than $740 million worth of video game equipment and cartridges. In addition, its home computer operations had become profitable, and Atari products dominated the sales of low-priced machines.

To protect its strong market position in the video game field, Atari also began an aggressive effort to shut down video game pirates by taking legal action against them. In November 1981, the company won an important case against a company that was selling a copycat ''Centipede'' game.

Although Atari was aggressive in introducing lucrative new software, it lagged behind in marketing new hardware. Essentially, the company had not followed its introduction of the Video Computer System with a second, more sophisticated generation, except to produce a remote-control model, known as Touch Me, which cost $100 more than the basic set.

The introduction of a Pac-Man cartridge in the spring of 1982, however, helped to stave off these concerns, as the company estimated that it would sell nine million of the games, to reap over $200 million in that year alone. Pac-Man was a breakthrough game, attracting many women and families to the video game market for the first time, and thereby expanding the industry's consumer base. In the fall of that year, Atari also took steps to update its game equipment, introducing a more elaborate version of its game machine, which sold for $350. It also quadrupled its sales of personal computers. In general, Atari poured tens of millions of dollars into research and development, in an effort to stay in front of the competitive industry.

Despite these efforts, however, by the end of 1982, Atari's rise in the industry, which many had believed would continue indefinitely, had been checked. Competition in the video games industry had expanded dramatically as new companies rushed in to the lucrative field. Now, Atari faced more than 30 other game makers, some of which had lured away the company's top game designers, a damaging loss in a field where innovation was suddenly as important as distribution. On December 8, 1982, Atari's corporate parent, Warner Communications, announced that previous sales estimates would not be met because of "unexpected cancellations and disappointing sales during the first week of December," as the New York Times reported at the time. In the wake of this sudden news, the company's stock value dropped precipitously, and several Atari executives were later investigated for insider stock trading, because they had sold off large blocks of stock just before the announcement.

Following this setback, Atari announced in February 1983 that it would fire 1,700 U.S. workers to move manufacturing facilities to Hong Kong and Taiwan. This move set off a wave of protest. In the financial community, it was taken as the sign of a company adrift, since Atari had hired 2,500 new U.S. workers just the year before in a campaign to build up its domestic production capacity, only to undo itself a short time later.

In addition, Atari found itself being challenged by competitors in its home computer business. In May 1983, the company reduced the price of its outmoded 400 computer by two-thirds, from $299 to $100. By the end of its first quarter, losses overall had reached $46 million. In an effort to restore some of the original creative luster to Atari, the company announced an agreement with ousted founder Nolan Bushnell to sell consumer versions of the coin-operated games he was developing in his new business.

By September 1983, quarterly losses had reached $180.3 million, and its nine-month losses reached $536.4 million. The company ended the year with overall losses of $538.6 million on sales of $1.12 billion, half its previous year sales of $2 billion.

Turnaround under Jack Tramiel

To stem Atari's losses, Warner brought in a new head executive who fired more than half the company's 10,000 employees. Nevertheless, costs could not be brought in line with revenues, and the company needed an infusion of further funds to pay for research on new products. Unable to support this continuing drain on its resources, Warner Communications began to look for a buyer for its failing subsidiary. In July 1984, the company announced that it had agreed to sell all Atari operations, with the exception of the small coin-operated arcade video game business and a new telecommunications venture, called Ataritel, to Jack Tramiel, a businessperson who had made his reputation as the head of Commodore International, Ltd., a computer company. The price for Atari was $240 million.

Three days after purchasing the company, Tramiel began his own aggressive effort to cut costs, laying off hundreds more employees and taking steps to collect outstanding funds owed to the company. Unable to sell unwanted video game cartridges, Atari dumped truckloads of them into a landfill in New Mexico. Tramiel installed three of his sons in top management positions, brought in former associates to fill other key spots, and made plans to raise funds through the sale of stock to the public. To Tramiel, Atari was poised to become a computer manufacturer to rival his previous company, despite the fact that its extant computer offering, the 800XL, was outmoded and less powerful than its competitors.

In January 1985, Atari unveiled two new lines of home computers, the XE series-man improved version of the old 800XL made cheaper by a reduction in the number of components and renegotiated contracts with suppliers—and the ST line, a cut-rate imitation of the Apple Macintosh, that used a color screen, fancy graphics, and a mouse, in an effort to move in on the market for Apple computers in the home. By July, the 520-ST had started to make its way into stores. The computer arrived past schedule, with no advertising to announce its presence, and no software to demonstrate its capabilities. Many machines in the first shipment did not work at all because microchips inside had been shaken loose in transit. Nevertheless, with a price of $799, the product initially seemed to have found a receptive public, with a large percentage of sales taking place in Europe.

Despite this good news, Tramiel continued to run Atari in crisis mode. The company's U.S. staff had shrunk to 150, and in May 1985, executives agreed to have one-third of their salaries withheld indefinitely. The company finished out 1985 posting a loss of $26.7 million.

By 1986, the industry in which Atari originally made its mark, video games, was beginning to show signs of life once again. This time, however, product lines were led by sophisticated, expensive Japanese equipment, sold by companies such as Nintendo and Sega. Atari re-entered the field with its old machine, the VCS 2600, which sold for only $40, and also introduced the 7800, a more advanced unit, which sold for twice as much. The company also began a modest advertising campaign for these products for the first time in two years. By the end of the year, these efforts, combined with Atari's home computer sales, had resulted in profits of $45 million, on sales of $258 million. With these strong results, the company was able to offer stock to the public for the first time in November 1986.

With these funds, Atari increased its advertising budget in support of new products it introduced. In 1987, the company began to market a clone of IBM's PC, priced at under $500, as well as a more sophisticated video game console, in addition to introducing products for the desktop publishing field. In October 1987, Atari purchased the Federated Group, a chain of 62 electronics stores based in California and the Southwest, for $67 million. Tramiel hoped that the stores could provide a good distribution outlet for Atari products, and he put his youngest son in charge of the chain. Operating in a depressed area of the country, however, Federated continued to lose money, and the company was forced to shut the stores after just one year.

At the end of 1987, Atari held 20 percent of the U.S. video game market and relied on foreign sales of its home computers, which remained unpopular in the United States, for a significant portion of its income. Overall, the company earned $57 million, on sales that neared $500 million.

Slipping Sales: Late 1980s and Early 1990s

The following year, Atari once again allied itself with its founder, Nolan Bushnell, agreeing to market video games that he had developed. Furthermore, the company announced another big advertising push, in an effort to ensure that the video game crash that had threatened Atari in the early 1980s would not recur. Atari also turned to the courts in December 1988, charging that Nintendo's licensing policies monopolized the market. These moves reflected the continuing lack of demand for Atari's home computer products in the United States, as the company, hampered by its image as a toymaker rather than a high-tech powerhouse, fought for part of this highly competitive market.

In January 1989, Nintendo followed up Atari's suit with a countersuit charging copyright infringement, and by the end of the year, the dispute had reached the U.S. House of Representatives, whose subcommittee on anti-trust echoed Atari's charges. In November 1989, Atari continued its push into the game market by introducing a portable video game player called Lynx, which sold for $200, to compete with Nintendo's popular Game Boy. The company finished out the year with earnings of $4.02 million.

In the spring of 1990, Atari introduced its Portfolio palmtop personal computer. Early the following year, the company came out with a revamped, color Lynx product, and several months later it introduced new notebook computers. Despite these advances, however, Atari was in trouble. Sales of its home computers in Europe began to flag as the company faced increased competition, and in 1991 foreign sales collapsed. In the video games field, Atari's efforts to challenge Nintendo through legal means had been rebuffed, and the company was unable to regain significant market share from its Japanese competitors. By the first quarter of 1992, losses over a three-month period had reached $14 million.

In September 1992, Atari took steps to stem its losses by cutting its research and development expenditures in half and closing branch offices in three states. The company hoped that the introduction of new products, such as the Falcon030 multimedia home entertainment computer would help to revive its fortunes. In addition, the company was working on a more sophisticated video game machine, called the "Jaguar." Nevertheless, 1992 ended with a loss of $73 million.

As Atari began to ship its Falcon030 system to stores in small numbers in early 1993, the company's fate was unclear. Decidedly, it was experiencing another severe downturn, which by the summer had snowballed into what the San Jose Mercury News called a full-fledged financial meltdown: between the second quarters of 1992 and 1993 Atari's sales plummeted 76 percent to only $5.7 million. Sales of its hand-held Lynx games were poor and its Falcon systems were barely visible in the PC marketplace. Atari's hopes now rested on the vaunted 64-bit technology of its soon-to-be-unveiled Jaguar game system, which promised to unseat Sega and Nintendo with the next generation of "high-performance interactive multimedia."

Atari Unravels in the Mid-1990s

In June 1993, IBM signed a $500 million deal with Atari to manufacture Jaguar's hardware, and the first sets hit stores in November. As Jaguar tested the marketplace in 1994, Atari settled a licensing dispute with Nintendo by way of an agreement with former parent Time Warner to raise its stake in Atari to 27 percent. Atari also licensed Jaguar to Sigma Design of California, whose full-motion video technology promised to enable Atari to make the jump from dedicated video game players to the home PC. In September 1994, arch rival Sega also agreed to pay Atari $90 million for the rights to Atari's 70 U.S. game patents. Finally, a partnership with Britain's Virtuality Group seemed to promise a new cutting-edge application for the Jaguar platform: Atari and Virtuality would design a 3-D virtual reality home gaming system to debut in 1995. Within a year of Jaguar's introduction Atari boasted 30 titles for the system, and in mid-1995 Atari announced a CD accessory that would allow CD-ROM games to be played on the Jaguar platform.

All Atari's partnerships and cross-platform efforts, however, could not convince consumers to abandon Sega's Saturn and Nintendo's Playstation for Jaguar, and in October 1995 Atari announced that third quarter revenues had fallen a brutal 40 percent from the previous year. Atari responded by slashing Jaguar's retail price and announcing "Atari Interactive," a new division to make CD-ROM video games for PCs. The writing was on the wall, however, and in January 1996 Jaguar was pulled from the U.S. market.

A month later Atari announced that JTS Corporation, a San Jose-based disk drive maker whose 1994 startup Jack Tramiel had helped fund, would merge with Atari in June. Although Atari publicly maintained that it would continue to market video game consoles and software as a JTS's Atari Division, it soon became clear that Atari's attraction for JTS was not its game technology but its still sizable cash reserves, which JTS would tap to battle disk drive competitors like Seagate and Quantum.

When the JTS merger was finalized in mid-1996 Atari's staff was gutted by 80 percent and its assets liquidated. Some Atari titles lived on through its licensing agreement with Sega, but by the end of 1996 Atari's quarter-century history as an early video entertainment pioneer had come to an end. In February 1998 JTS sold Atari's intellectual property as well as its famous name to Hasbro Interactive, but even this $5 million dollar sale wasn't enough to save JTS, which declared Chapter 7 bankruptcy in February 1999. There was really nothing left of Atari but its name when Hasbro Interactive again sold the company, this time to Infogrames Entertainment S.A., in 2001.

On May 7, 2003, Infogrames announced that it was changing the name of its U.S. operations to Atari. Its NASDAQ symbol was likewise changed to ATAR. Though Atari lived on in name, its future history would be written by Infogrames.

Further Reading

Bernstein, Peter W., "Atari and the Video-Game Explosion," *Fortune,* July 27, 1981.

Biggs, Brooke Shelby, "Success Killed Pac-Man Creator Atari," *Business Journal Serving San Jose and Silicon Valley*, July 22, 1996, p. 1A.

Chronis, George, "The Game's Over for Goldstar, Atari in Next-Gen War," *Video Store Magazine,* January 28, 1996, p. 1.

''Game Maker to Merge: Pong Pioneer to Unite with JTS Corp.,'' *San Jose Mercury News,* February 14, 1996.

Hector, Gary, ''The Big Shrink Is On at Atari,'' *Fortune,* July 9, 1984.

Machan, Dyan, ''Cheap Didn't Sell,'' *Forbes,* August 3, 1992.

Petre, Peter, ''Jack Tramiel Is Back on the Warpath,'' *Fortune,* March 4, 1985.

Shao, Maria, ''Jack Tramiel Has Atari Turned Around—Halfway,'' *Business Week,* June 20, 1988.

——, ''There's a Rumble in the Video Arcade,'' *Business Week,* February 20, 1989.

''U.S. Video Game Firm Gets Back in the Action,'' *Miami Herald,* November 7, 1993.

''Video Games Are Suddenly a $2 Billion Industry,'' *Business Week,* May 24, 1982.

''What Sent Atari Overseas,'' *Business Week,* March 14, 1983.

—Elizabeth Rourke
—updates: Paul S. Bodine; Howard A. Jones

August Storck KG

Waldstrasse 27
Berlin
D-13403
Germany
Telephone: (+49) 30 417 73 03
Fax: (+49) 30 41 77 33 71
Web site: http://www.storck.com/en/index.php

Private Company
Incorporated: 1903
Employees: 4,000
Sales: $967.8 million (2002)
NAIC: 311330 Confectionery Manufacturing from Purchased Chocolate

August Storck KG is the German-speaking region's leading manufacturer of candy and confectionery and is also one of the world's major candy companies. The company's flagship product is Werther's Original, produced by the company since the turn of the 20th century and one of the best-selling and globally recognized candy brands. While August Storck itself accounts for a major proportion of the production of the popular candy, it is also produced or marketed, and sometimes both, under license in a large number of foreign markets—for example, by Alexander Stuart in Australia and by Morinaga in Japan. August Storck has a number of other strong candy brands as well, including the popular Storck Chocolate Riesen, a revival of the company's first branded candy; nimm2, launched in the 1960s as one of the first ''vitamin-enriched'' candies; Campino gummi bears; Mamba fruit chews; merci gift chocolates; and Chocolate Pavot, launched in 2003 to mark the company's 100th anniversary. Headquartered in Berlin, Storck operates production facilities in Halle, Berlin, and Ohrdruf in Germany as well as in Winchester in England and Skanderborg in Denmark. The company has sales subsidiaries in 20 countries, with distribution partnerships in 63 countries. In 2002, the company's total production topped 250,000 tons. August Storck remains privately held and controlled by the founding Oberwelland family. Axel Oberwelland took over as company president—and majority owner—in 2003.

Beginnings and Early Growth: 1903–40s

August Storck was founded in 1903 as the Werther's Sugar Confectionery Factory in the small village of Werther, in Germany's Westfalia region. The company's founder, August Storck (the family's name later became Oberwelland), started the business in a little workshop with just a cooking kettle and panning kettle and three employees in a space not larger than 200 square meters.

The group at first produced a variety of hard candies, which quickly became popular in the local region, and soon reached a respectable production level of 2500 kilos per year. In 1909, company employee Gustav Nebel developed a recipe for a new treat based on a mixture of caramel and cream. Branding of candies had not yet become common practice in Germany at this time. Instead, candies were generally known by the names of their manufacturer or the company's village. The Storck company's new treat became known as Werther's.

The popularity of Werther's helped the business grow strongly in the years leading up to World War I. The company stepped up production, and by the outbreak of the war employed 12 people, with sales throughout most of Westfalia. Yet the devastation of the war put the company's growth on hold. Recovery was slow, hampered by August Storck's ill health. Nonetheless, by the early 1920s the company had once again reached full production, making some 200 different—and unbranded—candy types.

In 1921, Storck-Oberwelland retired and turned over the business to his son, Hugo Oberwelland; nonetheless, the company became known as August Storck KG. Storck continued as a small-scale producer of unbranded candies, although its sales increasingly extended beyond its Westfalia home base. The company's transition to the national level came in the early 1930s with its development of a new, chewy caramel candy.

Storck recognized the potential of the new candy type, and in 1934 the company took the bold move of ending production of all other candy varieties—including the Werther's hard caramel cream—in order to concentrate on its new caramel. The company went a step further, giving one of its candies a name for the first time and becoming the first in Germany to present a wrapped branded candy. Called the ''Storck 1 Pfennig Riesen,''

Company Perspectives:

FOCUS IS ON PEOPLE. This principle is consistently followed by Storck throughout all levels of the company. It is the basis for everything that makes Storck different, special and successful. And its concrete results can be seen in our closeness to the consumer, our responsibility to our employees, our understanding for our trading partners, our trust in our suppliers, and most of all, the high level of credibility of our brands. Storck produces and sells confectionery products that are treasured by people in all corners of the world. Through their quality and uniqueness, our brands give people the good feelings of security, warmth and comfort.

the new candy was individually wrapped and cost just one pfennig. The low price and recognizable wrapping made the candy a national success. By the late 1930s, the company's production had jumped to more than 1,150 kilos and Riesen became Germany's most popular candy. In 1938, in order to keep up with rising demand, the company opened a new production plant in Schotmar, and by the end of that year Storck had produced more than 1,600 tons of Riesen candies.

Yet Storck's good fortune ended with World War II, as shortages of ingredients forced it to shut down production. The company was forced to rebuild at the end of war, and in 1945 inaugurated construction of a new factory, now in the town of Halle. The new plant was designed with an eye on future growth as the company began testing new candy formulas. Nonetheless, the Riesen—produced on the company's 100-meter-long caramel belt—remained the company's core product for some time to come.

Diversifying Brands: 1950s–60s

The booming German economy of the postwar era stimulated pent-up demand for sweets, and by the early 1950s Storck became the country's largest candy manufacturer, producing more than 15,000 tons per year. The company also hired a dedicated sales force, supporting its expansion throughout Germany. In 1953, Storck began exporting its candies for the first time, finding eager markets internationally that included the United States and Hong Kong. The company also began signing on the first of a legion of local licensing partners, enabling it to introduce its brand name into the French, Italian, Austrian, and other markets.

By then, Storck had developed a new branded candy, the Mamba, a fruit chew. Packaging for the Mamba revealed the company's astute sense for marketing—the candy's package featured six pieces, making it easy to share. Introduced in 1953, the Mamba found a ready market and remained a company best-seller into the next century.

Storck continued diversifying its operations in the 1950s. A significant new operation was launched in 1954, when Storck began producing chocolates for the first time. In order to ensure the quality of its milk—and especially cream—supply, Storck entered dairy production as well. The company quickly earned a reputation for the quality of its chocolates. By the end of the 1950s, production had reached 150 tons per day.

Hugo Oberwelland's son Klaus joined the company in the early 1960s, taking charge of its marketing operations. The younger Oberwelland quickly had his first project—that of promoting a new and innovative candy. Launched in 1962, the "nimm2" became one of the world's first vitamin-enriched candies, providing an assortment of essential vitamins and launching a wider trend toward new health food types of products. The nimm2 became the most popular children's candy in Germany and later became a best-seller in more than 40 countries worldwide.

The 1960s proved an era of innovation for the Storck company, as it developed and launched a number of its perennial best-sellers. In 1964, the company released a new specialty "gift" chocolate, the "merci," featuring a selection of individually wrapped chocolates. Merci would later find markets in more than 70 countries. The boost in chocolate sales led the company to open a new chocolate factory in Berlin in 1967.

The company also began developing its own production technologies, and by the mid-1960s had developed a method of molding a smooth, clear, chewable candy, which became known as "gummi" candy. In 1966, the company launched its first gummi brand, Campino, featuring fruit-flavored bear shapes. That product became one of the company's most successful brands, and by the end of the decade Campino alone accounted for some 3,600 tons of the company's total production.

Yet the success of the company's previous brands paled in comparison to its next success. In 1969, Storck relaunched its original caramel cream. Called "Werther's Echte" ("genuine"), the product immediately attracted candy shoppers. Backed by a highly successful marketing campaign featuring a grandfather and his grandson, Werther's Echte quickly imposed itself as one of the world's best-selling candy brands. The candy's success propelled Storck itself into the major leagues among world candy producers. By the turn of the 21st century, production of Werther's alone topped 25,000 tons per year and was sold in some 80 countries.

International Operations: 1970s–90s

Klaus Oberwelland took over as head of the company in 1971, overseeing a company that now manufactured nearly 45,000 tons of confectionery per year. Storck continued developing new brands and candy varieties and in 1973 had a new hit with the launch of Toffifee, which combined caramel, hazelnuts, and chocolate.

By then, the company's operations had begun to expand internationally, with its first sales subsidiary in Austria dating back to 1962. In 1974, the company added a sales subsidiary in the Netherlands, and then opened a subsidiary in the United States, Storck USA LP, established in Chicago in 1977. Other international operations followed—in Belgium in 1979, Switzerland in 1985, and Spain in 1989. The company continued adding new subsidiaries through the 1990s, including Denmark in 1991, Russia in 1996, Poland in 1997, Sweden in 1999, Canada and Hungary in 2000, the Czech Republic in 2001, and Slovenia and Slovakia in 2002.

In the meantime, Storck had also grown by acquisition. The company's first purchase came in 1981 when it bought up

Key Dates:

1903: August Storck-Oberwelland opens a small candy workshop in the town of Werther, Westfalia, Germany, called Werther's Sugar Confectionery Factory.
1909: The company begins producing caramel cream candy, later known as Werther's Original.
1934: The company's launches its first branded candy, Storck 1 Pfennig Riesen, which remains its sole product for nearly 20 years.
1949: The company opens a new factory in Halle, Westfalia, Germany.
1953: Mamba candy brand is launched; the company begins exporting its candies.
1954: The company begins producing chocolate and operating its own dairy production.
1962: Vitamin-enriched nimm2 is introduced; the company opens its first foreign sales subsidiary in Austria.
1967: A Berlin production facility is opened.
1969: Caramel cream, called Werther's Echte, is relaunched.
1977: A sales subsidiary in the United States is established.
1981: The company acquires Germany's Dickmann and its brands.
1988: The company acquires U.K.-based Bendick's of Mayfair and its Winchester, England, factory.
1995: The company opens its first Asian Pacific subsidiary in Singapore.
1998: The company globally rebrands Werther's as Werther's Original.
2003: The company celebrates its 100th anniversary with the launch of Chocolate Pavot brand.

German rival Dickmann. The company then relaunched its popular candy brand as the Super Dickmann. That success was joined by another hit product launch, the Knopper, in 1983.

Storck's next acquisition allowed it to strengthen its foothold in the United Kingdom, where it had begun importing Werther's Echte in 1986. In 1988, the company acquired Bendick's of Mayfair, a popular producer of mint chocolates with a production facility in Winchester, England. Bendick's had been founded in 1930 and held the honor as an official chocolate producer for the British royal family. A later acquisition came in 1999, when Storck bought up a share in Elvirasminde, a Danish candy maker.

Also in 1988, Storck decided the time was right to relaunch the Riesen brand. In order to do so, the company decided to adapt its recipe to meet the taste of modern consumers. Wrapping the original Riesen caramel in dark chocolate, the company created its newest successful brand, Storck Chocolate Riesen.

The fall of the Berlin wall led the company to transfer its headquarters to Berlin in 1989. The company also began looking for a site for a new production facility. In 1993, Storck settled on the town of Ohrdruf, in the former East Germany, which became its largest and most modern factory. The Ohrdruf site particularly emphasized chocolate production and backed up the launch of two new chocolate types, merci Crocant, in 1994, and merci Pur, in 1995.

International Candy Leader in the 21st Century

Storck had increasingly been targeting the overseas market, especially the Middle East and Asian Pacific regions. In order to bring its brands into these areas, the company began licensing its products to local producers and distributors, such as Stuart Alexander in Australia and Morinaga in Japan, among many others. Storck itself added operations in these regions in the 1990s, starting with the opening of Storck Asia Pacific in Singapore in 1995. The company also opened production facilities in the Philippines in the later part of the decade.

Back at home, the company launched a new generation of its vitamin candy in 1996. The nimm2 Lachgummi presented the popular vitamin-boosted candy in chewy form and proved a hit with German children, who propelled the treat to the company's top position among candy brands. The company's winning streak continued into the 2000s with the launch of a new variety of the Campino brand, combining fruit and cream flavors. By 2003, sales of the new Campino had expanded to more than 50 countries. By then, the company's total production had reached more than 250,000 tons per year. Yet the company's Werther's brand had by then become its clear flagship. In 1998, in order to support the candy's international development, Storck decided to rename the candy "Werther's Original."

In 2003, Storck celebrated its 100th anniversary. As part of the celebration, the company launched another new confectionery brand, the Chocolate Pavot, which combined poppy flavors with whipped Marc de Champagne cream. At the same time, Klaus Oberwelland, who had led the company for more than 30 years, turned over the business—as well as majority ownership—to his son Axel Oberwelland. With the fourth generation of the Oberwelland family at the helm, Storck prepared for candy-coated success in the future.

Principal Subsidiaries

Bendick's of Mayfair (U.K.); Elvirasminde A/S (Denmark); OOO Storck (Russia); Storck (Schweiz) GmbH (Switzerland); Storck Asia Pacific Pte Ltd (Singapore); Storck BV (Netherlands); Storck BVBA; Storck Canada ; Storck Ceska Republika sro; Storck Danmark A/S; Storck doo (Slovakia); Storck Hungaria Kft; Storck Iberia Slu (Spain); Storck Mitarbeiter Beteiligungsgeschellschaft; Storck Slovensko; Storck Sverige AB (Sweden); Storck USA LP (United States).

Principal Competitors

Nestlé S.A.; Mars Inc.; Cadbury Schweppes PLC; Wilbur Chocolate Company Inc.; Taiwan Sugar Corporation; Parmalat S.p.A.; Orkla ASA; CSM N.V.

Further Reading

Degen, Rolf, "La manne issu de la planche à dessin," *Tabula*, April 1999.
"Storck Sours UK Sweets," *Marketing*, April 16, 1992, p. 2.
Visto, Cecile S., "US Rejects Storck Candy for Harmful Lead Content," *BusinessWorld*, May 6, 2004.

—M.L. Cohen

Bahamas Air Holdings Ltd.

P.O. Box N 4881
Nassau
Bahamas
Telephone: (242) 377-8451
Toll Free: (800) 222-4262
Fax: (242) 377-7409
Web site: http://www.bahamasair.com

State-Owned Company
Incorporated: 1970
Employees: 680
Sales: $66 million (2004 est.)
NAIC: 481111 Scheduled Passenger Air Transportation; 481211 Nonscheduled Chartered Passenger Air Transportation

Bahamas Air Holdings Ltd., or Bahamasair, is the national airline of the Bahamas. The airline's fleet of eleven aircraft consists of several Dash 8 turboprops and a couple of mid-range Boeing 737 jets. Based at Nassau International Airport (NAS), its scheduled route network connects twenty destinations, including service to Florida. About 1.5 million passengers fly the airline every year. While not known for its profitability, Bahamasair appears vitally important to a country that is heavily dependent on tourism.

Oil Crisis Origins

Bahamasair was formed in the early 1970s to fill a void left by the withdrawal of major airlines from the local market. British Airways stopped serving the Bahamas in 1970 due to the high cost of fuel resulting from the Arab oil embargo. Pan American Airlines would follow suit in 1973 for the same reasons.

Bahamasair was not the islands' first airline. Bahamas Airways Ltd., which had been incorporated in 1936, had also ceased operations in 1973 in spite of a five-year bailout attempt by the British Swire Group. Yet another similarly named airline had been launched in 1968 to provide low-cost service to Europe. Called Air Bahama (International) Ltd., it was sold to Loftleidir in 1969 and renamed Air Bahama in 1976.

Realizing the importance of tourist traffic to its economy, the government of the Bahamas formed Bahamasair in October 1970 as a state-owned enterprise. It was launched with start-up capital of just BSD 9 million.

Bahamasair took over the operations of two small, relatively new airlines, Flamingo Airways (established 1971) and Out Island Airways (formed in the late 1960s). As Jack Ball detailed in an article for *Airliners,* Bahamasair operated a motley fleet of several different types of smaller aircraft, as well as a pair of BAC 1-11 jets.

The airline called on the expertise of Aer Lingus, the Irish state airline that had developed a specialty in providing technical assistance to new airlines in smaller countries. One of the four Aer Lingus consultants, Michael Hayes, was named managing director of Bahamasair in August 1976.

In the mid-1970s, Bahamasair experimented with an amphibious service to Cape Eleuthera while also launching a Nassau-Atlanta route. However, its ambitions were temporarily scaled back in 1976. Bahamasair subsequently focused on developing the Nassau-Miami route, records R.E.G. Davies in *Airlines of Latin America Since 1919.*

The first of the company's mid-range Boeing 737 airliners entered the fleet in the late 1970s. West Palm Beach, Orlando, Newark, and Philadelphia were added to the schedule in 1984 and 1985. In the late 1980s, Bahamasair began flying to Washington Dulles and Miami. On the latter route, the company faced only limited competition from Eastern Airlines. Though important to the local economy, Bahamasair would be unprofitable for decades. It managed an operating profit of less than $1.5 million in 1986.

In November 1988, Bahamasair took over a charter program for Princess Casino Vacation from failed Braniff Inc. Bahamasair soon became the leading carrier to the Bahamas following the bankruptcy of Eastern Airlines in March 1989, leapfrogging Delta Air Lines in the process. Trans World Airlines also cut its service from New York to the Bahamas.

Company Perspectives:

Once formed, the airlines' mission was to serve the Bahamas and its people. There were six objectives set out by Bahamasair that were deemed to have vital roles in the efficiency of its services. The Airline was to serve as the National Flag Carrier and promote the countries' image at home as well as abroad. To provide efficient services throughout the Commonwealth in a cost effective manner. To provide a competitive scheduled passenger, charter and freight service to support commerce and promote the Bahamas Tourist Industry at a profit to the airline. To provide efficient high quality fixed base operations to facilitate and promote general aviation to and within the commonwealth at a profit to the airline. To provide employment opportunities for Bahamians within the framework of government policy. To contribute foreign exchange earnings of the country.

A New Look for the 1990s

In December 1989, Bahamasair introduced a new pastel color scheme reflective of the island's warm beauty. The airline took delivery of two new Boeing 727 airliners, costing $2.6 million, at about the same time. In 1989, the airline also spent $1.9 million to upgrade its Boeing 737s.

Bahamasair entered the 1990s with 600 employees according to one count. It flew to 20 destinations in the Bahamas as well as a handful of cities in the United States. Bahamasair faced enormous competition on the Newark, Philadelphia, and Washington routes and closed them in 1990 as a cost-cutting measure. This freed up planes to bolster service between Nassau and Miami and on domestic routes. The company lost $15 million on revenues of $50 million in 1990.

In the early 1990s, the carrier built its fleet around the 50-seat, de Havilland DHC-8 series 300, a modern turboprop aircraft suited for island hopping. The first few of these models were leased; the airline also placed an order for five Dash 8s worth $56 million. A variety of other aircraft supplemented the fleet, often on a short-term lease basis.

In January 1991, the airline retired its Boeing 737s and Hawker Siddeley 748s. The switch to the Dash 8s left Bahamasair with no jet service to the United States until a Boeing 727 was leased in August 1992. The carrier suffered from a general slowdown in the aviation business due to the Gulf War and a worldwide recession. High fuel costs increased the burden.

The country's tourism ministry launched a promotional campaign for the Out Islands in 1994. Bahamasair participated by improving its service to the Out Islands from Nassau and Freeport.

A proposed merger of several of the Caribbean's airlines, including Bahamasair, Air Jamaica, BWIA, and LIAT, was discussed throughout the 1990s but never finalized. Such a deal would have saved money on marketing and maintenance. The region's carriers were generally unprofitable and Bahamasair was no exception.

Key Dates:

1970: Bahamasair is formed.
1976: The airline focuses on developing a Miami-Freeport route.
1994: Bahamasair features services to Out Islands.
2000: The company's new management is led by Paul Major.
2004: A code-share arrangement with US Airways is announced.

The government of the Bahamas was preparing to privatize several state-owned enterprises, including Bahamasair. The state proposed bringing in a private sector partner while assuming the carrier's existing debts.

New Management in 2000

A new management team led by managing director Paul Major took over in January 2000. By the end of the year, he had announced the ambitious goal of attaining the airline's first ever profit within three years.

Cost-cutting would not be simple, particularly trimming the workforce. Unions staged a two-day sickout in March 2000 that grounded 82 flights and cost the carrier more than $200,000.

In June 2000, Bahamasair entered a ten-year, $15 million contract with Sabre Holdings Corporation for passenger reservation service and other technologies. According to the airline's chairman at the time, Frederik Gottlieb, the carrier was aiming to improve all aspects of its customer service. The company was also exploring code shares with other airlines as a way to boost traffic and revenues.

U.S. airlines curtailed their services to the Bahamas after the September 11, 2001 terrorist attacks. Bahamasair increased its Florida routes to fill the void and to help shore up tourism. However, revenues for 2001 fell $10 million to $61 million.

A restructuring plan was announced in November 2002. It proposed to cut 150 employees from the staff of 716 and to focus on higher volume destinations such as Freeport, West Palm Beach, Orlando, Miami, and Haiti. A twice-weekly Nassau-Havana route was inaugurated the next month using Boeing 737s. These flights were made in conjunction with tour operator Scand American.

Bahamasair had lost a reported BSD 338 million in the 30 years since its founding. Its managers were happy to report one telling statistic—during all that time the airline had not suffered any fatal accidents.

The U.S. invasion of Iraq prompted more Americans to choose the Bahamas as a vacation destination, since it was nearby and perceived as safe. However, major airlines boosted their capacity to the Caribbean at the same time, reported the *Flight International.* Losses in 2003–04 were halved from the previous fiscal year, to BSD 13 million. Revenues were about BSD 65 million.

A long-awaited code share agreement was announced in August 2004. US Airways became Bahamasair's partner in the deal, offering new access to such gateways as Charlotte, Philadelphia, and New York (LaGuardia).

The company sought to increase its revenue base to give it some chance of profitability in light of considerable fixed costs. Bahamasair was planning to expand its service throughout the Caribbean regions with two new Boeing 737 jets. It was also eyeing second-tier destinations such as Raleigh, Cleveland, and Richmond, Virginia. At the same time, the Caribbean was beginning to attract budget airlines from the United States, bringing new competition to Bahamasair from the likes of Airtran Airways and Spirit Airlines.

Principal Competitors

AMR Corporation; Continental Airlines Inc.; Delta Air Lines Inc.

Further Reading

''Bahamas Air Co Meeting Union after Sick-Out, Cancelations,'' *Dow Jones International News*, March 7, 2000.

''Bahamas Airline to Resume Flights to Cuba Following US Embargo Controversy,'' *BBC Monitoring Latin America—Political*, January 8, 2003.

''Bahamasair Has Virtual Monopoly, Majestic Says,'' *Aviation Daily*, April 20, 1989.

''Bahamas Bouncing Back after Rocky Beginning in '89,'' *Tour & Travel News*, August 20, 1990, p. 23.

''Bahamas: Government Announces Proposals to Cut 150 Bahamasair Jobs,'' *BBC Monitoring International Reports*, November 22, 2002.

Ball, Jack, ''Enhancing the Image: An Informal History of Bahamasair,'' *Airliners*, July–August 2004, pp. 56–61.

Blades, Hayden, ''Caribbean Leaders Agree to Set up Regional Airline,'' *Sun Sentinel* (Fort Lauderdale), July 9, 1993, p. 3D.

Culmer, Darrin, ''Roberts Says Bahamasair Seeing Financial Turnaround,'' *Bahama Journal*, July 5, 2004.

Davies, R.E.G., *Airlines of Latin America Since 1919*, Washington: Smithsonian Institution Press, 1984.

Dignam, Dan, ''Bahamasair Cuts Flights from Newark, Washington,'' *Tour & Travel News*, September 17, 1990, p. 35.

——, ''Bahamasair Invests $62 Million to Overhaul Fleet,'' *Tour & Travel News*, December 11, 1989, p. 37.

——, ''PCV Makes Pact with Bahamasair for Charter Flights,'' *Tour & Travel News*, November 20, 1989, p. 43.

Elster, Judy, ''New Nonstop Service to Eleuthera Reduces Transit Time by Half,'' *Travel Weekly*, July 23, 1990, p. 12.

Hall, Hadassah, ''Bahamasair Wants to Expand U.S. Routes,'' *Bahama Journal*, August 16, 2004.

Inniss, Sean, ''Struggling National Flag Carrier to Expand,'' *Nassau Guardian*, National News, June 10, 2003.

James, Canute, ''Bahamas Decides Time Is Ripe for Private Sector Involvement,'' *Financial Times* (London), July 28, 1998, p. 5.

——, ''Caribbean Airlines Urged to Fly One Way,'' *Financial Times* (London), November 28, 2002, p. 33.

Jones, David, ''New for '94: Island Hopping in the Bahamas—Tourism Ministry, Bahamasair Improving Connections to Out Islands,'' *Tour & Travel News*, October 18, 1993, p. 58.

——, ''New Government to Quicken Bahamasair Privatization,'' *Tour & Travel News*, September 7, 1992, p. 38.

Kirby, Mary, ''Bahamasair Aims for First-Ever Profit,'' *Air Transport Intelligence*, October 19, 2000.

——, ''Bahamasair Inaugurates Service to Cuba,'' *Air Transport Intelligence*, December 5, 2002.

Lowman, Ron, ''De Havilland Sells 5 Dash 8s to Bahamasair for $56 Million,'' *Toronto Star*, August 26, 1989, p. C4.

Matthews, Martella, ''Bahamasair Faces Increased Competition,'' *Nassau Guardian*, July 30, 2004.

McKenzie, Tamara, ''30 Years of Bahamasair Losses Led to Cutbacks,'' *Nassau Guardian*, Bus. Sec., July 30, 2003.

''A New Bahamasair,'' *Nassau Guardian*, Editorial Sec., August 4, 2004.

''Prime Minister Describes Finances of Bahamasair and Nassau Airport Project,'' *BBC Monitoring Service: Latin America*, November 24, 1992.

Robertson, Jessica, ''Sickout Cancels Bahamasair Flights, Strands Island Travelers,'' *Associated Press Newswires*, March 3, 2000.

Sidron, Jorge, ''Bahamasair to Lay Off 25% of Staff in Phase Two of Reductions,'' *Travel Weekly*, February 11, 1991, p. 108.

——, ''Islands' Flag Carrier Revamps Fleet, Cuts Service,'' *Travel Weekly*, December 12, 1991, p. 43.

Sobie, Brendan, ''Bahamasair Sees Opportunity for US Expansion,'' *Air Transport Intelligence*, October 18, 2001.

Thompson, Lindsay, ''U.S. Airlines Boost Caribbean Competition,'' *Nassau Guardian*, Bus. Sec., April 16, 2003.

—Frederick C. Ingram

Baltimore Aircoil Company, Inc.

7595 Montevideo Road
Jessup, Maryland 20794
U.S.A.
Telephone: (410) 799-6200
Fax: (410) 799-6416
Web site: http://www.BaltimoreAircoil.com

Wholly Owned Subsidiary of Amsted Industries Inc.
Incorporated: 1938
Employees: 2,000
Sales: $168.6 million (2002)
NAIC: 332313 Plate Work Manufacturing; 333415 Air-Conditioning and Warm Air Heating Equipment and Commercial and Industrial Refrigeration Equipment Manufacturing; 336391 Motor Vehicle Air-Conditioning Manufacturing

Baltimore Aircoil Company, Inc., is a leading producer and exporter of evaporative cooler and heat transfer equipment. BAC supplies products for industry and institutions, including cooling towers, evaporative condensers, aircoil evaporators, and ice thermal storage systems. The company has manufacturing operations in 17 countries around the world. The company's products are sold by a network of 250 independent salespeople.

Origins

The history of the Baltimore Aircoil Company (BAC) dates back to the early days of the refrigeration and air conditioning industries. Established in 1938 by John Engalitcheff, Jr., the company at first manufactured cooling coils.

A native of Moscow, Russia, Engalitcheff had attended Johns Hopkins University on scholarship and graduated with a mechanical engineering degree in 1930. During his lifetime (he died in 1984), he obtained 47 patents on HVAC-related equipment.

According to BAC's official company history, Engalitcheff shut down BAC during World War II in order to enlist in the navy. After the war, the company added evaporative condensers and cooling towers to its product line. Cooling towers removed heat from air conditioning and refrigeration systems by circulating water.

BAC became a significant exporter due to demand for air conditioning technology abroad. An export department was created in 1966. The next year, BAC won a Presidential ''E'' Award for exporting excellence.

In 1956, BAC built a facility in Jessup, Maryland. Three other new plants opened in the 1960s: one in Ontario, Canada (1963), one in Madera, California (1966), and one in Belgium (1968).

New Ownership in the 1970s

Merck & Company, Inc., a manufacturer of pharmaceuticals and specialty chemicals, bought BAC in 1970. Merck expanded BAC's product line and added factories in the Americas, Europe, and the Pacific Rim. The company opened a plant in Paxton, Illinois, in 1973 and one in Milford, Delaware, in 1974. BAC was led then by William E. Kahlert. Named president in 1966 and CEO in 1970, in 1976 Kahlert left to co-found Evapco. Inc.

Mid-1980s Transitions

Before his death in 1984, company founder John Engalitcheff, Jr., was honored by President Ronald Reagan for his contributions to the American Security Council's ''Peace Through Strength'' program.

Amsted Industries, a Chicago-based, diversified industrial manufacturer, bought BAC from Merck in May 1985. The acquisition was done partly to cushion against the cyclical nature of Amsted's railroad products business. At the time, BAC had a dozen manufacturing facilities and 1,900 employees. It earned $8.3 million on 1984 sales of $169.7 million. The Paxton, Illinois, plant was expanded by 20,000 square feet in 1989.

Cooling towers were assembled by BAC in its plants, then erected onsite by either BAC or the client. Another product became popular among institutional clients in the 1980s and 1990s. Thermal storage units, sometimes called ''ice chillers,''

Company Perspectives:

The company's mission is to be the leading provider of products and services for heat transfer and thermal storage in all markets served.

used electricity to freeze water when electricity rates were lowest, then later used water from the melting ice to air condition buildings or cool equipment. Businesses could save thousands of dollars each month by taking advantage of off-peak rates for electricity. BAC continued to work to improve the efficiency of its thermal storage systems.

Keeping Cool in the 1990s

Baltimore Aircoil entered the 1990s with 865 employees, though declining economic conditions led to some layoffs within a couple of years. While the thermal storage business involved some old-fashioned elements—bending steel tubes and cooling buildings with big blocks of ice—in 1997 *PC Week* singled out BAC as a top user of advanced computer technology.

In 1991, BAC began working with Malaysia's Linear Corporation Bhd on the installation of cooling towers in Southeast Asia. BAC and Linear formed a joint venture, BAC Cooling Towers Sdn Bhd, in 1999. The new venture focused on the industrial market for ice thermal storage. By this time, reported Malaysia's *Business Times,* the local cooling towers market was worth MYR 100 a year, while the industrial cooling market was worth one and a half times that. The joint venture was capitalized at $800,000 and expected to see $1.5 million in sales the first year.

A number of industries needed cooling systems, including petroleum, auto, and plastic manufacturing. According to Frost & Sullivan, the total U.S. heat exchanger market was worth $1.5 billion in 1996, when 350,000 units were sold. However, cooling towers relied on chlorofluorocarbon-based refrigerants, which were being phased out due to the Clean Air Act. American manufacturers were also coming under increasing competition for Third World business from European companies, including some backed by large industrial groups.

The ban on CFCs presented new opportunities for BAC, however. In 1995, an ambitious district thermal storage system was installed to cool ten buildings in downtown Chicago. BAC supplied 60 JCE Ice Chiller thermal storage units for the $30 million plant, which was located at the corner of State Street and Adams Street. Other cities such as Denver also turned to district cooling.

In 1999, BAC sold Fort Worth, Texas-based Ceramic Cooling Tower Co. to BDT Engineering, a Tampa, Florida, affiliate of international boiler manufacturer Deutsche Babcock. BAC had acquired Ceramic in 1991 from Fort Worth's Justin Industries. At the time of the sale, Ceramic had 165 employees at two plants.

Freer Trade Abroad after 2001

Relaxed trade restrictions were helping smaller American businesses compete. China's membership in the World Trade Organization further opened a vast new market beginning in December 2001. BAC had formed a joint venture in Daliau, in northern China, in 1998. A BAC official told the *Washington Times,* "We think the Chinese market will eventually be bigger than the United States." A free trade agreement between the United States and Singapore held the prospect of doubling sales in that market after 2003.

Amsted, struggling under a heavy debt, announced it was selling off BAC in February 2001. This decision was canceled, however, by incoming chairman and CEO W. Robert Reum.

In 2004, the company was preparing to move to a new headquarters and 25,000-square-foot research and development facility next to its old site in Jessup, Maryland. Manufacturing operations there, along with 150 jobs, were shifted to plants in Milford, Delaware, and Paxton, Illinois, where there were more blue collar workers. About 200 employees remained at headquarters after the move.

The Paxton and Milford plants were being enlarged. The Paxton plant, which employed about 2,000 people, was increased from 100,000 to 125,000 square feet.

BAC's new HVX Hybrid Wet/Dry Closed-Circuit Cooling Tower, based on the FVX line of closed-circuit cooling towers, was winning industry recognition for its energy and water efficiency. Other new products included aircoil evaporators for food processing and other applications.

Key Dates:

1938: Baltimore Aircoil (BAC) is founded.
1956: Jessup, Maryland, facility is built.
1963: A Canadian factory opens.
1966: A California plant opens.
1968: A Belgium facility opens.
1970: Merck & Company acquires BAC.
1985: BAC is acquired by Amsted Industries.
1991: BAC begins working with Linear Corporation of Malaysia.
2004: BAC moves to new headquarters and shuffles U.S. manufacturing operations.

Principal Subsidiaries

BAC Cooling Towers Sdn Bhd (Malayasia; 30%); Baltimore Aircoil of Canada Inc.; Baltimore Aircoil (Australia) Pty Ltd; Baltimore Aircoil Company (China); Baltimore Aircoil Company (Philippines); Baltimore Aircoil Company SA (Pty) Ltd (South Africa); Baltimore Aircoil International NV (Belgium); Baltimore Aircoil Limited (United Kingdom).

Principal Competitors

Alfa Laval Thermal Inc.; The Burger Cooling Tower Company Inc.; Delta Cooling Towers, Inc.; Evapco, Inc.; Robert Bosch GmbH; SPX Corporation.

Further Reading

"Amsted Aims to Make Presence Felt in Cooling Towers Venture," *New Straits Times* (Kuala Lumpur), Bus. Sec., April 17, 1999, p. 19.

"Amsted Will Buy Merck & Co. Unit for $92 Million," *Wall Street Journal*, April 2, 1985, p. 1.

Anderson, Tom, "New Dimension: Educating Employees on Retirement Spending," *Employee Benefit News*, September 1, 2004.

"BAC to Build New Headquarters, R&D Facility in MD," *Ozone Depletion Network Online Today*, July 10, 2003.

"Baltimore Aircoil: Manufacturing Precision from Mind-Boggling Orders," Pleasanton, Calif.: PeopleSoft, 2002.

"Bank Cuts Cooling Costs with Thermal Storage," *Building Design & Construction*, November 1985, p. 57.

Bernstein, Claire, "Incorporation Shield Springs Leaks," *Toronto Star*, February 7, 1994, p. B3.

"A Big Deal for American SMEs," *Business Times Singapore*, May 3, 2003.

Brainerd, Brian, "Chiller Project under Way," *Denver Post*, November 14, 1997, p. C3.

"Chicago Cooling Plant Uses Ice Storage," *Ozone Depletion Network Online Today*, August 13, 1998.

"Cool Work for Hot Car," *Process Engineering*, April 26, 2002, p. 15.

Dougherty, Carter, "WTO Opens Door to China for Smaller U.S. Firms," *Washington Times*, December 17, 2001, p. D5.

"Eye-Catching," *Daily Record* (Baltimore), March 30, 2000, p. 2A.

"Five Local Companies Make Top 500," *Baltimore Business Journal*, July 3, 1997.

Hinton, David, "Paxton Plant Will Expand, Add Workers," *Pantagraph* (Bloomington, Ill.), July 15, 2003, p. C1.

"Honor Roll of U.S. Exporters," *Business America*, July 2, 1990, pp. 24f.

"Huge Rebates Testify to Efficiency," *Contractor*, October 1998, p. 9.

"Ice Cubes Cool Howard College," *Baltimore Business Journal*, October 8, 1990, p. 15.

Jacobs, Jennifer, "Linear Expect to Return to 'Pre-Crisis' Results This Year," *Business Times*, June 27, 2000, p. 14.

Jones, Sabrina, "Baltimore Aircoil Picks Building Site," *Washington Post*, July 7, 2003, p. E3.

"Linear Signs Deal to Build RM72 Mln Cooling Facility," *Bernama: The Malaysian National News Agency*, January 19, 2001.

MacManamy, Rob, "Putting the Freeze on CFCs," *Engineering News-Record*, April 3, 1995, p. 24.

Marchetti, Michele, "Tapping Top Talent," *Sales & Marketing Management*, August 2004, p. 14.

Morgan, TaNoah, "Baltimore Cooling Equipment Maker to Close Local Plant, Build New Headquarters," *Baltimore Sun*, July 10, 2003.

Siegel, James J., "Amsted Withdraws BAC from Sales Process," *Air Conditioning, Heating & Refrigeration News*, June 4, 2001, p. 5.

Skaer, Mark, "Innovative Cooling Towers," *Air Conditioning Heating & Refrigeration News*, March 3, 2003, p. 16.

Smith, Douglas J., "Power Plant Cooling Systems: The Unsung Heroes," *Power Engineering*, May 2001, p. 55.

Turpin, Joanna R., "Cooling Towers Loom over Expo Crowd," *Air Conditioning, Heating & Refrigeration News*, February 16, 2004, pp. 40f.

Tyler, Kathryn, "The Difference between Life and Death," *HR Magazine*, November 1, 2000, pp. 107–117.

William, Victor, "Linear Corp Teams Up with US Company," *Sun*, April 17, 1999.

—Frederick C. Ingram

Baltimore Orioles L.P.

Oriole Park at Camden Yards
333 West Camden Street
Baltimore, Maryland 21201
United States
Telephone: (410) 685-9800
Toll Free: (888)848-2473
Fax: (410) 547-6277
Web site: http://www.orioles.mlb.com

Private Company
Founded: 1953
Sales: $129 million (2003)
NAIC: 711211 Sports Teams and Clubs

The Baltimore Orioles L.P. is the operating company for the professional baseball team of the same name. As a member of the Eastern Division of Major League Baseball's American League, the Orioles play at Oriole Park at Camden Yards, situated in the heart of Baltimore. The opening of Oriole Park in 1992 ushered in a new era of baseball-only stadiums that paid architectural homage to the ballparks of an earlier era. While the popularity of its home field led to high attendance, success has not transferred onto the diamond in recent years. A team that was a consistent contender for decades has fallen into an extended period of mediocrity. The club is owned by a group of investors headed by attorney Peter Angelos, a gadfly among baseball's generally conservative group of owners. Minority owners of the Orioles include such celebrities as novelist Tom Clancy, political commentator and columnist George Will, filmmaker Barry Levinson, former tennis player Pam Shriver, and legendary sportscaster Jim McKay.

Early 1900s Roots

The Orioles were originally the St. Louis Browns before the franchise was transferred to Baltimore in 1954. Both St. Louis and Baltimore boasted rich traditions in major league baseball during the final decades of the 1800s. The Baltimore Orioles of the 1890s was one of the era's most notorious and celebrated teams, both for its roughhouse ways and adherence to ''scientific baseball,'' which emphasized the use of guile in playing the game. St. Louis originally fielded a team called the Brown Stockings, initially in the National Association, which folded after a single season, then for two seasons in the National League, which was established in 1876. The St. Louis club then joined a rival major league, the American Association, where it won several championships before returning to the National League, along with the Baltimore Orioles, as part of a merger in 1891. The Browns were owned by controversial beer baron Chris Von Der Ahe, who fell out of favor with his fellow owners; St. Louis was stripped of its franchise in 1899. After three years without major league baseball, the city would land an American League franchise three years later. The American League was originally a minor league, the Western League, that changed its name and declared it was the equal to the National League, launching its first major league season in 1901. Baltimore was awarded an American League franchise and the new incarnation of the Orioles played two seasons before the franchise moved to New York City, where the club was renamed the Highlanders and eventually became known as the New York Yankees and emerged as one of the most successful sports franchises in the world. As a result of the Oriole's defection, Baltimore would be without major league baseball for the next half century. St. Louis, on the other hand, would land a National League club, via the 1999 transfer of the Cleveland Spiders, as well as one from the new American League.

Following the 1901 season, the Milwaukee Brewers franchise of the fledgling American League was bought for $35,000 by 33-year-old Robert Lee Hedges, who moved the club to St. Louis, renaming it the Browns. He cleaned up Sportsman's Park where the club played and the Browns over the next dozen years drew well and were profitable. Another rival major league, the Federal League, was formed in 1913, and after completing two seasons it agreed to disband. As part of the settlement with Major League Baseball, Hedges sold the Browns to one of the owners of the St. Louis Terriers, Philip Ball, for $525,000. Hedges made a tidy profit on his investment in the team, becoming the last owner of the Browns to make money on the club. He also held the distinction of giving Branch Rickey his start as a

Company Perspectives:

Oriole Park is state-of-the-art yet unique, traditional and intimate in design. It blends with the urban context of downtown Baltimore while taking its image from baseball parks built in the early 20th century.

baseball executive, naming him the Browns' manager. Rickey would one day revolutionize baseball by refining the minor league farm system of developing big league talent while with the St. Louis Cardinals, and by breaking down baseball's racial barriers when with the Brooklyn Dodgers by signing Jackie Robinson, the first African-America to play major league baseball in the modern era.

The Brown's new owner was a hard-drinking, gruff ex-ballplayer, as well as erstwhile cowhand and construction worker, who made a fortune manufacturing ice machines. Rickey, a teetotaler, campaigned for a national prohibition of alcohol and was promptly shown the door by Ball. It was only the first of many mistakes Ball would make while running the Browns. In 1920 he allowed the National League's Cardinals to share Sportsmen Park, which permitted his local competitor to sell its own park and invest the money in Branch Rickey's farm system. As a result, the Cardinals went on to win several World Series while the Browns became a perennial loser; St. Louis went from being a ''Brown's town,'' to a city that adored the Cardinals. Ball even paid to increase the seating capacity of Sportsman Park, a move that did little to help the Browns, whose attendance declined steadily, but proved a windfall for the immensely popular Cardinals. When Ball died in 1933 the club drew just 88,113 fans for the entire year. One game that season attracted just 34 paying customers. It was no wonder that nobody wanted to buy the team.

The executor of Ball's estate finally turned to Rickey, who recruited Bill DeWitt, Sr., the Cardinals team treasurer, and Donald Barnes, president of American Investment Company, to buy the Browns for $325,000. Barnes put up $50,000, DeWitt $25,000, and the club raised another $200,000 by selling stock at $5 a share. Under new ownership the Browns fared no better on the field or the box office, so that by 1941 Barnes sought permission from the American League to relocate the franchise to Los Angeles. The meeting was held on December 8, 1941, one day after the attack on Pearl Harbor that precipitated the United States' entry into World War II. Because of the sudden uncertainty in the world, Barnes was turned down, but the war did lead to the greatest moment in the Brown's history. In 1944, when the level of major league talent was severely diluted because so many players were serving in the military or alternative service, the Browns were able to win its only American League pennant. Even this moment of glory, however, failed to help the club improve its image in St. Louis. The Browns had the misfortune of meeting the Cardinals in the World Series, losing to their tenants in six games.

Control of the Browns changed hands once again in 1945 when board member Richard Muckerman, along with Bill and Charlie DeWitt, took over the running of the club. The team continued to draw poorly, prompting Muckerman in 1945 to sign and play Pete Gray, a one-armed outfielder, as a gate attraction. The move only succeeded in solidifying the Browns' reputation as baseball's pathetic country cousin. Because the team drew poorly during the postwar years, it had to sell off what little talent it possessed to stay afloat, resulting in teams that even fewer fans wanted to pay to watch. In 1951, Bill Veeck, the former owner of the Cleveland Indians and renowned maverick, bought the Browns with the ambitious goal of driving the Cardinals out of town. The Cardinal's owner was enduring some income tax difficulties, but Veeck's hopes were dashed when millionaire brewer August Busch bought the rival club. Veeck's best known moment while running the Browns came just one month into his tenure, when he had a midget named Eddie Gaedel brought into a game to pinch hit—after jumping out of a cake. With such a compact strike zone, less than two inches after assuming a crouch, Gaedel walked. The next day, the American League banned Gaedel and announced that all future player contracts had to be approved by the league office. Veeck tried others stunts, such as Grandstand Manager's Night, when the fans were able to vote on the starting pitcher and strategic decisions by using placards that said ''Yes'' on one side and ''No'' on the other.

Major Moves in the 1950s

With his genius for marketing Veeck was able to improve annual attendance from 293,790 in 1951 when he took over in mid-season, to 518,796 a year later. Still, the Browns remained last in the league in attendance, and Veeck lacked the money to make the team a true contender. With Busch now in charge of the Cardinals, he looked to move the club, but some of the conservative owners despised his iconoclastic ways and prevented him from returning the Browns to Milwaukee. He was forced to keep the team one more season in St. Louis, and with the fans knowing that the team was slated to leave, attendance collapsed. During a meeting held in September 1953, American League owners voted against Veeck's request to relocate the Browns to Baltimore, which was building a new ballpark and had first made known its interests in procuring the Browns in 1947. The owners knew Veeck was in desperate financial condition: the Browns brought in no money from television or radio; to stay in business during the 1953 season Veeck had been forced to sell his better players; and Veeck could not keep up the mortgage payments on Sportsman Park, so he sold the facility to Busch for $1.1 million. According to some sources, the owners who disapproved of Veeck were determined to keep the Browns in St. Louis until he went bankrupt, at which point the league could dispose of the franchise. Realizing he had no choice, Veeck sold his 70 percent interest in the Browns to a group of some 100 Baltimore investors led by Charles W. Miles for $2,475,000. Once Veeck was out, the American League unanimously approved the transfer of the Browns to Baltimore.

The owners of the new Baltimore Orioles set about the task of building a competitive ball club by hiring a brilliant executive named Paul Richards to serve as general manager. He wrote down in an unpublished manuscript the philosophy and tenets that would guide the club, from operating a farm system to

Key Dates:

1902: American League Milwaukee Brewers move to St. Louis, becoming St. Louis Browns.
1944: Browns win only American League pennant.
1953: Browns move to Baltimore, becoming Baltimore Orioles.
1966: Orioles win first World Series Championship.
1992: Oriole Park and Camden Yards opens.

making a relay throw. It would become known as the Oriole Way, and it would serve as a roadmap for excellence that the Orioles would enjoy for a generation. The farm system developed into the premiere breeding ground for baseball talent for some 20 years, resulting in the Orioles contending for its first pennant in 1960, its first World Series championship in 1966, and having many successful seasons throughout the 1960s, 1970s, and 1980s.

In 1956 James Keelty, Jr., succeeded Miles as president, followed by Leland S. MacPhail in 1960. Ownership changed hands in 1966 when Jerold C. Hoffberger, who headed the National Brewing Company, bought the club. Despite their winning ways, the Orioles failed to draw as well as might be expected, forever placing second in the hearts of Baltimore sports fans, who had developed a passionate following for the Baltimore Colts football team. During Hoffberger's 15-year tenure as Orioles owner, the franchise was essentially a break-even investment, but the Orioles proved to be an excellent promotional vehicle for National Brewing to sell its beer in a very crowded marketplace. When the Hoffberger family sold the company to Carling Brewery in 1976, however, there was little incentive to continue ownership of the Orioles.

In 1979, the Hoffberger family sold the Orioles for $12 million to Edward Bennett Williams, a Washington, D.C., lawyer, prompting some fear that the club might be relocated to a city that would provide better fan support. A former press secretary for Baltimore Mayor William Donald Schaefer, along with two area bankers, at the behest of the mayor, organized a group of volunteers to help sell season tickets. The group became known as the Designated Hitters Club. Following the Orioles' 1983 World Championship, the Club sold 8,200 additional season tickets. The team appeared secure, but in order to take attendance to the next level, to achieve consistent sellouts, it was clear that the Orioles needed to replace antiquated Memorial Stadium with a new ballpark. Both Bennett and Mayor Schaefer were eager to build a new facility, which became especially important to the latter after the beloved Colts moved to Indianapolis in 1984 and the Bullets National Basketball Team move south to Washington D.C. before that. The loss of the Orioles would be a crushing blow to the pride of Baltimore, which would no longer be view as a "big league" city and likely suffer economically. To keep up the pressure, Williams insisted on short-term leases for the use of city-owned Memorial Stadium. Moreover, the team negotiated a no-rent contract. Rather, the Orioles' rent was a percentage of profits, after taxes and expenses were deducted.

While public funding for a new ballpark gained approval, Williams died of cancer in August 1988. In June 1989 New York investor Eli Jacobs and two partners—Orioles president Larry Lucchino and former politician R. Sargent Shriver—bought the franchise for a reported $70 million. Schaefer had become Maryland's governor and was in a much better position to deliver a new ballpark to the Orioles. After much maneuvering in the state legislature, Schaefer was finally able to push through a bill to provide funding for the facility, to begin construction in 1990. The site chosen would be an old railroad depot and warehouse district in Baltimore, an area in desperate need of revitalization.

A New Venue in the Early 1990s

In 1992 the Orioles played it first game in its new 47,000-seat facility, Oriole Park at Camden Yards. It was considered an success even months before the first pitch. The architects chose to ignore the previous generation of American stadiums, multipurpose facilities that were neither well-suited to baseball or football, opting instead to draw inspiration from the baseball-only parks that were built in the early decades of the 20th century, such as Wrigley Field and Fenway Park, perennial fan favorites. They wanted a retro look but with all the modern conveniences. A massive warehouse visible beyond right field provided charm as well as space for executive offices, ticket sale booths, concession kitchens, and a souvenir shop. The critics were first to weigh in with their approval of the new ballpark, and the baseball fans of Baltimore—and the world—concurred, as Oriole Park became a tourist attraction in itself and the club now enjoyed consistent sellouts and attendance topped the 3.5 million mark.

Jacobs began to experience financial difficulties and as early as 1991 began to talk about the possibility of selling the Orioles. In 1993 Jacobs filed for bankruptcy, and the franchise was put on the block. During the course of a spirited, 15-round auction, former Baltimore city councilman and wealthy attorney Peter Angelos, and Cincinnati oil executive William DeWitt, Jr., whose father once owned the Browns, joined forces to bid $173 million and outdistance rival buyers for the club.

Angelos became managing partner of the Orioles, but other than making the playoffs in 1997, the team found it increasingly difficult to compete in the American League's Eastern Division, where the New York Yankees appeared to have an unlimited budget on acquiring players and the Boston Red Sox were desperate in their need to keep up with their fiercest rival. The one bright spot during this period was Orioles player Cal Ripkin's pursuit of Lou Gerhig's seemingly unbreakable record for consecutive games played, which captured the interest of the entire country. The Orioles got away from building the team from within, choosing instead to make costly investments in free agent players, most of whom failed to pan out. Moreover, for several seasons the team had only inexpensive and marginal talent, offering no threat to the division leaders. Some of the charm of Oriole Park also wore off, as many retro-looking ballparks opened up around the country and eclipsed some of its glory. As a result, attendance dipped somewhat, but the franchise was still quite valuable, and in 2004 management again invested in high-priced free-agent players. Should Baltimore

Orioles L.P. be able to once again assemble contending clubs, the team would likely return to the days of regular sellouts.

Principal Competitors

New York Yankees Partnership; The Boston Red Sox; Toronto Blue Jays Baseball Club.

Further Reading

Cohen, Charles, ''Baltimore's Beer and Baseball Baron,'' *Baltimore Business Journal,* November 26, 1999, p. 25.

Goldreich, Samuel, ''Orioles: The Stuff of Legends,'' *Baltimore Business Journal,* August 6, 1993, p. 1.

Golenbock, Peter, *The Spirit of St. Louis,* New York: Avon Books, 2000, 651 p.

Patterson, Ted, *The Baltimore Orioles,* Dallas: Taylor Publishing, 2000, 24 p.

Smith, Fraser, ''If You Build It, They Will Come,'' *Regardie's Magazine,* January-February 1995, p. 73.

Thorn, Jon, et. al., *Total Baseball,* New York: Total Sports, 1999.

Verducci, Tom, ''Losing their Way,'' *Sports Illustrated,* April 26, 1999, p. 42.

—Ed Dinger

Beringer Blass Wine Estates Ltd.

610 Airpark Road
Napa, California 94558
U.S.A.
Telephone: (707) 259-4500
Fax: (707) 259-4542
Web site: http://www.beringerblass.com

Wholly Owned Subsidiary of Foster's Group Ltd.
Incorporated: 1996
Employees: 3,800
Sales: $1.35 billion (2003)
NAIC: 312130 Wineries

Owner of the oldest continuously operating winery in Napa Valley, California, Beringer Blass Wine Estates Ltd. is a leading producer of premium sparkling, table, and fortified wines made from vineyards in Australia, California, Chile, Italy, and New Zealand. Its wines are marketed under a variety of brand names, including Beringer, Wolf Blass, Meridian, Chateau St. Jean, Chateau Souverain, Stags' Leap, Black Opal, Jamieson's Run, Yellow Glen, and Gabbiano. Foster's Brewing Group Ltd.—later known as Foster's Group Ltd.—acquired Beringer Wine Estates in 2000. The company was folded into Foster's wine division and adopted its current moniker in 2001. While its origins date back to the 19th century, Beringer Wine Estates was formed in 1996 to acquire the Chateau Souverain, Meridian Vineyards, Napa Ridge, and Beringer brands from Wine World, Inc., a subsidiary of Nestlé S.A., the global food, beverage, and candy conglomerate. Of these four brands, Beringer by far was the oldest. Generations of the Beringer family retained control over the Beringer brand for nearly a century before selling it to Nestlé in 1971. Under Nestlé's stewardship, the Chateau Souverain and Napa Ridge brands were acquired in 1986 and the Meridian Vineyards brand was introduced in 1990. Beringer Wine Estates subsequently added to its portfolio of brands, acquiring the Chateau St. Jean brand in 1996 and the Stags' Leap brand in 1997. With these wineries under its control during the late 1990s, Beringer Wine Estates ranked as the top seller of premium wines in the United States, controlling more than 14 percent of the domestic market and deriving the bulk of its sales from its Beringer White Zinfandel brand. During the early 2000s, Beringer Blass continued to operate as a leading premium wine group with over 40 brands in its arsenal.

19th-Century Origins

The roots of Beringer Wine Estates stretched back to the mid-19th century, back to the hometown of the company's founders in Mainz, Germany. There, where the Rhine and Main rivers met, Jacob and Frederick Beringer spent their childhood and early adulthood growing up in the fertile, winemaking region known as the Rhine Valley. The two brothers developed an early interest in winemaking, particularly Jacob, but neither would express this passion in any meaningful way in their native Germany. Although the Rhine Valley was renowned for its prized vineyards, the lure of greater opportunities in the burgeoning United States drew each of them away from their homeland. Frederick was the first to go. Frederick left Mainz in 1863 and settled in New York, where the rumors of great promise lived up to their billing. Frederick wrote to Jacob in Mainz, urging his brother to join him in the United States. Intrigued, Jacob packed his bags and set sail for New York in 1868.

For Jacob Beringer, New York was not the mecca of opportunity his brother had described. Frederick's interests were in business, ideally suited to the vibrant and chaotic bustle of New York, but Jacob pined for the more sedate wine business and its rural setting. He had spent his years in Mainz studying winemaking and barrelmaking and had worked as a cellarmaster for a local wine company, becoming more comfortable in a wine cellar than on the streets of New York. Accordingly, Jacob left New York in 1870 and boarded a train for California, where rumor had it that the warm and sunny climate was ideal for growing wine grapes. Jacob took a train to San Francisco—dreaming of grapes while others dreamed of gold—and then traveled north to Napa Valley where he was pleased to find rocky, well-drained soil similar to the soil in his native Rhine Valley.

The conditions in Napa Valley were ideal for winemaking, and Jacob settled in, taking a job as a cellar foreman for another expatriated German winemaker, Charles Krug. By 1875, Jacob

Company Perspectives:

We are unique among the world's major wine producers in operating three separate business channels: Trade, Clubs, and Services. Our Wine Trade strategy is to make and market the world's leading portfolio of international premium wine brands. Our Wine Clubs channel aims to reinforce and further develop its position as the world's leading consumer-direct merchant for premium wine and wine-related products. In Wine Services, our goal is to be the leading supplier of premium packaging and warehousing services to the wine industry, globally.

Beringer was ready to go it alone and, with financial assistance from his brother Frederick, he purchased his first property: the cornerstone of what would develop into the oldest continuously operating winery in Napa Valley. The first project on Jacob's agenda was to build the wine cellars required to store and age wine. To complete the job, Jacob hired Chinese laborers who were returning to the San Francisco area following the completion of the Trans-Continental Railroad and directed them to hand-chisel tunnels into the hillside of rock on his property. The tunnels took years to complete, but once they were finished they served as ideal wine cellars where temperatures remained 58 degrees Fahrenheit regardless of the temperatures in Napa Valley.

Work began on the tunnels in 1876, the year Beringer Winery was formally established. While this time-consuming project was being completed inch by inch, Jacob planted grapes and began building his winery. His first crush took place in 1877, and from there the methodical process of developing a fine wine ensued. It took until the early 1880s before the winery reached full-production capacity, but as soon as there were bottles of wine available Jacob began shipping them to his brother in New York. Frederick, in turn, opened a store and wine cellar in New York in 1880 to make room for the growing number of shipments. Three years after opening the store, Frederick moved to St. Helena to be closer to the family business and began building his home, which was modeled after the Beringer home in Mainz. Dubbed the ''Rhine House,'' the 17-room mansion served as the home for the generations of Beringers. To make room for the sprawling mansion, Jacob's house was put on logs and rolled several hundred feet away.

The Beringer brothers began to distinguish themselves as competent vintners by the end of their first decade of business. In 1887, Beringer wines earned their first domestic awards, followed by international recognition two years later when Beringer's Riesling captured the coveted Silver Medal at the Paris Exhibition. Once given the seal of approval from the European wine community, the Beringer winery began to flourish, as Napa Valley vintners gradually earned the respect of connoisseurs overseas. Beringer's sales and profits swelled accordingly, giving Jacob and Frederick the financial resources to expand their winery and add vineyards. The company's stature increased, and as the century drew to a close, future growth appeared assured. The 1890s proved to be a lucrative decade for the Beringer winery, but as it would turn out, the last decade of the 19th century marked the end of an era at Beringer and the beginning of troubled times.

From the wine company's outset, Frederick Beringer had lent valuable talents to the enterprise. His penchant for business, his wealth, and his financial knowledge had contributed significantly to the company's success during its crucial development from a start-up winery to a recognized producer of premium wines. His death in 1901, however, caused decisive repercussions, stripping the winery of its chief financial wizard. Jacob Beringer's contributions were not to be overlooked—the winery was his inspiration and without his gift for producing wines the Beringer winery could never have existed—but Frederick's death was a loss sorely felt by the Beringer winery. Without the aid of his brother, Jacob Beringer persevered and managed to keep the enterprise running, but another serious blow was delivered five years after Frederick's death. The 1906 San Francisco earthquake reduced the city to rubble and caused widespread damage throughout northern California, devastating the region and severely damaging the Beringer winery. Jacob mended the winery and vineyards, but by the decade's conclusion the combined effect of Frederick's death and the 1906 earthquake had conspired to make the first decade of the 20th century a disaster compared with the prodigious strides achieved during the 1890s.

Prohibition

In 1915, the death of Jacob Beringer, the creator of the award-winning, internationally praised Beringer wines, paved the way for successive generations of Beringers to steward the fortunes of the Napa Valley winery. The first members of the family to take command were Jacob's children, who began their tenure of control just prior to what was perhaps the most anxiety-ridden years vintners could imagine. Prohibition, enacted in 1920, was five years away when Jacob died, but his children ensured the winery would continue to operate by securing a license to produce altar wines. Winery operators without such permission, of course, were forced to exit the business. The dispensation for Beringer went a long way toward giving the company the distinction as the oldest continuously operating winery in Napa Valley during the 1990s.

Permission to keep producing wines during Prohibition also enabled Beringer to increase its production output in anticipation of the repeal of the 18th Amendment. The company produced 15,000 cases in 1932, one year before the production and consumption of alcohol was permitted again, giving Beringer an early lead over its domestic competitors. From 1933 forward, it was business as usual at Beringer, as the company resumed production of its full line of varietal wines. Beringer family members, ensconced in the Rhine House, watched over the operation of the business in the decades following the repeal of Prohibition, adding vineyards occasionally as the company matured into an established veteran of winemaking. Beringer's progress during World War II, the 1950s, and into the 1960s occurred at a leisurely pace, remarkable only for the placid manner in which the company eased its way through the decades. By the 1960s, however, it became clear that the serenity exuded by the company was masking pervasive internal problems. This realization engendered sweeping changes and signaled the end of Beringer family ownership and management after nearly a century of control.

Key Dates:

1875: Jacob Beringer purchases his first property in Napa Valley.
1876: The Beringer Winery is established.
1920: Prohibition is enacted; the company produces altar wines to stay in business.
1971: Beringer is sold to Nestlé U.S.A. Inc.
1986: Chateau Souverain is acquired.
1996: Texas Pacific Group and Silverado Partners acquire the Beringer enterprise; Beringer Wine Estates Holdings Inc. is created to acquire the Chateau Souverain, Meridian Vineyards, Napa Ridge, and Beringer brands from Wine World, Inc.
1997: Beringer goes public; Stags' Leap Winery is acquired.
2000: Foster's Brewing Group Ltd. buys Beringer.
2001: Foster's wine operations adopt the Beringer Blass Wine Estates name.

Early 1970s Nestlé Acquisition

For outsiders, the problems were hard to identify individually, but as a whole industry experts agreed that Beringer's difficulties were caused by decades of ineffective management. Nepotism had led to stagnation. Beringer was not the only wine company suffering from the ills of stagnation during the 1960s. Many of its domestic competitors were family-run businesses that, like Beringer, had failed to maintain their vineyards. Unsatisfactory wines were the result, and the ramification of inferior quality was declining business. By the end of the 1960s, Beringer's difficulties had become grave enough for the family to divest their interests in the company. In 1971, after 95 years of control, the Beringer family sold the Beringer brand name, its wineries, and 700 acres of vineyards.

The new owner was Nestlé USA, Inc., a subsidiary of Nestlé S.A., the global food, beverage, and confection conglomerate based in Switzerland. After acquiring Beringer, Nestlé USA formed a subsidiary company named Wine World, Inc. to superintend the revitalization of the Beringer brand name and the Beringer vineyards. Beringer represented Nestlé's first foray into the wine business, but despite its inexperience the corporation demonstrated shrewd patience in resurrecting the Beringer business. The company took a long-term approach to rebuilding its new acquisition, anticipating it would take between ten and 15 years to orchestrate a complete turnaround. Nestlé, through Wine World, Inc., used this time to bring in new management, new technology, and sophisticated expertise in the art of producing wines. As Nestlé put its revitalization program into effect, the company's efforts were aided by a growing trend among U.S. consumers that would benefit it handsomely for its years of investment. Shortly after Nestlé acquired Beringer, U.S. consumers began to demonstrate a growing interest in high-quality, premium varietal wines. Previously, consumer preferences had favored generic, or "jug" wines, but during the 1970s and 1980s the American palate was becoming more discerning and, consequently, the demand for "European-style" wine was increasing. This general trend worked in Nestlé's favor as the slow process of rekindling the popularity of the Beringer brand in the United States was under way.

Vineyards that had been purchased during the Beringer family era of control received much greater attention under the auspices of Nestlé, such as Beringer's Knight Valley Vineyard located north of Calistoga, California, which was developed into an integral facet of Beringer's operations. Knight Valley and other Beringer vineyards were beneficiaries of sizable cash infusions from the deep coffers of Nestlé, and over time they either recovered their former luster or were substantially improved. The improvements raised the quality of Beringer wines and gradually the brand name was reestablished in the eyes of consumers and wine critics. Although Beringer continued to rank behind such brands as Gallo, Carlo Rossi, Almaden, and Inglenook during the early 1980s, the brand was gaining ground on its competitors by consistently increasing its market share.

At roughly the same time Nestlé management could point to a full recovery of Beringer, the U.S. wine industry was expanding exponentially. Between the late 1970s and the late 1990s, the number of wineries in the country increased from 350 to 950, with much of that growth occurring during the 1980s, a decade when Nestlé was ready to expand as well. By the mid-1980s, Nestlé management felt it had completed its number one priority of reviving the Beringer brand name and was ready to move on to secondary goals. In 1986, the company began expanding, acquiring Sonoma County-based Chateau Souverain, a winery founded in 1943 that specialized in producing red wines, particularly cabernet sauvignon, merlot, and zinfandel. Also in 1986, the company introduced a new brand named Napa Ridge, which used grapes from the coastal regions of California. Expansive vineyards in Santa Barbara were also purchased in 1986 and were used to produce wine for a brand named Meridian Vineyards, which was introduced in 1990.

1990s Bring New Ownership

By the early 1990s, the Beringer enterprise was as healthy as it had been a century earlier when Jacob and Frederick Beringer enjoyed their greatest success. Nestlé management had transformed the venerable company into a leading wine producer that represented a prize for any interested suitor. In the mid-1990s, a potential buyer appeared and set the stage for the second transfer of ownership in Beringer's history.

Eyeing the company with interest was Silverado Partners Acquisition Corp., which was controlled by an investment group that included Napa-based Silverado Partners and a buyout firm named Texas Pacific Group, controller of Continental Airlines. The two investment groups reached an agreement with Nestlé for the acquisition of the Beringer enterprise for $350 million. Once the deal was completed, Silverado Partners and Texas Pacific Group formed Beringer Wine Estates Holdings, Inc. to formally acquire Beringer, which took effect January 1, 1996. Beringer Wine Estates, as the new enterprise in charge of a 120-year-old business, immediately jumped on the acquisition trail to begin expanding its portfolio of properties. Shortly after its formation, Beringer Wine Estates purchased the Sonoma County-based Chateau St. Jean winery, a market leader in the production of premium chardonnay wines. The next acquisition target was the Stags' Leap Winery located in Napa Valley.

Acquired in early 1997, the Stags' Leap Winery was an accomplished producer of red wines, with particular emphasis on cabernet sauvignon, merlot, and petite syrah.

With the additions made in 1996 and 1997 giving the company a total of 9,400 acres of vineyards, Beringer Wine Estates spent the months following the Stags' Leap Winery acquisition planning for an initial public offering (IPO) of stock, hoping the company's stock offering would coincide with a fall harvest expected to be the California wine industry's best ever. Beringer Wine Estates filed with the Securities and Exchange Commission in August 1997 and made its public debut at the end of October 1997, attracting $26 per share. Confident that the years ahead would witness the continued steady rise in annual sales, Beringer Wine Estates' management looked ahead to the remainder of the 1990s and the beginning of the 21st century with considerable optimism. At the time of its IPO, the company ranked as the top seller of premium wines in the United States, and the directors of Beringer Wine Estates were intent on not relinquishing their position.

Changes in the 2000s

Consolidation was forcing many companies in the alcoholic beverage industry to reconsider their strategies at the start of the 21st century, and Beringer Wine Estates was no exception. In August 2000, Texas Pacific Group announced a deal that would not only cement its role as the top premium wine maker in the United States but also position Beringer Wine Estates as a major global player. In one swift move, Texas Pacific Group agreed to sell the company to Foster's Brewing Group for $1.2 billion—a sum that valued the company's stock at nearly 24 percent over its trading price.

The acquisition proved attractive to all involved. For Foster's, the deal marked an important turning point in its growth strategy. As a result of the purchase, Foster's became Australia's first group to gain a strong foothold in the global wine sector. In essence, the deal created the world's first international premium wine company. Foster's, who became known as Foster's Group Ltd. in 2001, had been climbing its way up the wine ranks since its purchase of Mildara Blass Ltd. in 1996. Since that time it had added a variety of different firms to its wine division, including Cellarmaster Wines Pty Ltd., Bourse du Vin International, Maglieri Wines, Windsor Vineyards, Hunter Valley Wine Contractors, and Carter & Associates. The addition of Beringer Wine Estates significantly strengthened its burgeoning wine segment, which officially adopted the name Beringer Blass Wine Estates in 2001. In 2002, wine operations accounted for a greater portion of company sales than beer for the first time in Foster's history.

As a Foster's division, Beringer Blass stood well positioned the wine industry. It was a major player in Australia—the fastest-growing wine exporting country in the world—as well as in the United States, Asia Pacific, and Europe. The company continued its growth in the following years. Full ownership of Castello di Gabbiano was acquired in late 2000, and International Wine Accessories and Etude Wines were purchased the following year. Acquisitions in 2002 included Ponder Wine Estates, the Carmenet brand, and a majority interest in Australia-based Kangaroo Ridge.

Intense competition, an oversupply of grapes, and industry price cuts began to slice into Beringer Blass's profits in 2003 and 2004. Trading in California proved particularly volatile during this time period and proved to be a major challenge since the company relied on the United States for nearly 70 percent of its sales. As such, Foster's took strategic measures to bolster its financial performance. The company cut costs, made changes in management, and launched an aggressive marketing campaign in an attempt to get profits back on track over the next five years. With a longstanding history of success behind it, Beringer Blass would no doubt overcome these obstacles and remain a leader in the wine industry for years to come.

Principal Competitors

E.&J. Gallo Winery; The Robert Mondavi Corporation; Southcorp Ltd.

Further Reading

Evans, Simon, ''Beringer Deal Leaves Rivals an Empty Glass,'' *Australian Financial Review*, August 30, 2000, p. 21.

Ferguson, Tim W., ''Uncorking Beringer,'' *Forbes*, November 3, 1997, p. 42.

''Foster's Acquisition of Beringer Wines Valued at $1.17 Billion,'' *Wall Street Journal*, August 29, 2000, p. B12.

''Foster's Group Ltd.,'' *Wall Street Journal*, June 9, 2004.

Heald, Eleanor, and Ray Heald, ''Beringer's Burgeoning Empire,'' *Quarterly Review of Wines*, Autumn 1997, p. 32.

Palmer, Jay, ''The Coming Glut: Why the Wine Industry's Long String of Price Hikes Is About to End,'' *Barron's*, August 3, 1998, p. 25.

Sinton, Peter, ''Napa's Aussie Link,'' *San Francisco Chronicle*, April 29, 2001, p. E1.

''Texas Pacific Group Gives Farewell to Beringer Wine Estates,'' *Buyouts*, November 6, 2000.

—Jeffrey L. Covell
—update: Christina M. Stansell

Berlex Laboratories, Inc.

340 Changebridge Road
Montville, New Jersey 07045-1000
U.S.A.
Telephone: (973) 487-2000
Fax: (973) 487-2003
Web site: http://www.berlex.com

Wholly Owned Subsidiary of Schering AG
Incorporated: 1979
Employees: 2,400
Sales: $1.2 billion (2003)
NAIC: 325412 Pharmaceutical Preparation Manufacturing

Berlex Laboratories, Inc. is a Montville, New Jersey-based subsidiary of German pharmaceutical Schering AG. Berlex markets some 20 products, such as an oral contraceptive called Yasmin and medicines used to treat multiple sclerosis, dermatological disorders, and cancer. The company also offers diagnostic imaging agents used in performing MRI scans. Berlex's bioscience division is located in Richmond, California. Generating about $1.2 billion in annual sales, Berlex contributes about one-quarter of its parent corporation's total revenues.

Late 1970s Origins

Although Berlex was founded in 1979, the roots of the company date back to the mid-19th century when Ernest Schering open a pharmacy in Berlin, Germany. He would incorporate the business in 1871 as Chemische Fabrik auf Actien and become involved in the production of chemicals, such as mercury compounds, that had uses in both pharmaceuticals and photography. In 1890, a year after Schering died, the company launched its first specialty product, a treatment for gout. Over the next few decades, the company diversified into such areas as electroplating for decorative metals, industrial and laboratory chemicals, and agrochemicals. In the 1930s it merged with a mining and chemical company and the resulting entity was renamed Schering AG. From its earlier days, the company was active in the United States. A subsidiary, Schering & Glatz, was launched in 1876 to distribute medicines produced by the parent company. However, 40 years later during World War I when the United States and Germany became enemies, the German-owned subsidiary was dissolved.

Schering returned to the U.S. market in 1929 by establishing New York City-based Schering Corporation, a subsidiary that focused on hormone research and synthesized steroid drugs. When Germany and the United States were once again pitted against one another in World War II, the company came under scrutiny, largely because its corporate parent was suspected of working closely with the Nazis to produce drugs that might help German pilots to withstand the strains of high altitudes, thus giving them the tactical advantage of being able to fly higher. In 1942 Schering's U.S. subsidiary was seized by the U.S. government, and some ten years later the government elected to sell the business to a private investment group headed by Merrill Lynch. As a result, the U.S.-based Schering Corporation was separated from Schering AG.

Schering AG struggled to rebuild its business during the difficult conditions that prevailed following the war. The company used its expertise in steroids to produce the first birth control pill, simply known as ''the Pill,'' introduced to the European market in 1961. With the profits from this product, Schering was able to diversify and one again try the U.S. market. In 1972 it acquired a half-interest in New Jersey-based Knoll Pharmaceutical, the first of several acquisitions Schering would make in the United States over the next several years.

To complement its five divisions—Drugs, Industrial Chemicals, Fine Chemicals, Agrochemicals, and Electroplating—Schering made some U.S. acquisitions. To become involved in drug development in the United States, in 1979 Schering acquired certain assets of the Internal Medicine division of Cooper Laboratories, Inc., in New Jersey. The interests were folded into a new subsidiary named Berlex Laboratories. From Cooper Laboratories it gained expertise in such areas as cardiovascular disease, birth control, and diagnostic imaging. Berlex also became active in the endocrinology sector. The first product of note introduced by the subsidiary, iodinated contrast agents used in imaging, was shipped in 1982. Later in the 1980s Berlex launched two oral contraceptives, Levlen and Tri-Levlen, as well as Magnevist, the first enhancement agent for use in magnetic resonance imaging.

Company Perspectives:

Berlex's singular approach to developing and making specialized medicines already has yielded innovations in treating multiple sclerosis, dermatological disorders, female health concerns, cancer and in the creation of new diagnostic imaging techniques.

Legal Challenges in the 1980s–90s

After rebuilding its business during the postwar period, Schering AG had bought back all of the subsidiaries it lost because of the war. There was one exception, however: Schering Corporation in the United States, which had grown too large and turned into a major rival. For years the two companies fought over the right to use the Schering trademark in the U.S. market, a matter that reached the boiling point in 1983 when Schering-Plough (the name Schering Corporation took effect after the 1971 merger with Plough Inc.) sued Schering AG, claiming that Berlex had infringed upon its trademark. The resulting litigation dragged on until 1988 when a settlement was reached. Schering AG agreed not to use the Schering name in the United States and Canada in connection with its pharmaceutical products, relying instead on the Berlex trademark so as not to confuse the public.

In 1990 Schering entered the U.S. biotechnology sector by acquiring two San Francisco-area companies: Triton Biosciences and Codon Corporation. A subsidiary of Shell Oil Company, Triton pursued anti-cancer drugs. However, its increasing demands for more funding, without any viable products to show for all of its efforts, had convinced Shell that it would be better off concentrating on its core competency, and it willingly sold the biotech to Schering. Triton had an upside for Schering in that it had two products in clinical trials: Fludara, used in the treatment of refractory chronic lymphocytic leukemia, and Betaseron, a treatment for multiple sclerosis. Established by college professors, Codon raised money by hiring out the expertise of its personnel. Abbott Laboratories helped fund Codon for a period of time, then stepped away, leaving the start-up in a precarious financial position, with just $1 million of operating cash available. Codon eagerly agreed to be acquired by Schering, which was pleased to add the company's expertise in biotechnology manufacturing.

Schering's management was reluctant to impose a German corporate culture on Triton and Codon and elected to allow the biotechs to operate with a great deal of autonomy. As a result, Berlex became bi-coastal and split into two divisions, with the newly formed Berlex Biosciences based in California. While the New Jersey facility operated like a traditional pharmaceutical house, Berlex Biosciences continued to retain the culture of a small high-tech startup. Triton and Codon were consolidated, however, a move that caused some conflict, because the function of some departments overlapped and difficult decisions had to be made over who would be terminated and who would stay. Moreover, the two differed over computers, with Triton committed to mainframe client server architecture and Codon preferring the Macintosh computer. In the end, both mainframe and Macs would be used. For the first few years, consolidation was made difficult because operations were spread throughout the Bay Area. Then, in 1993, Berlex Biosciences was able to bring all the units together in a new facility located in Richmond, California, the Ortho Research Center, which had been built several years earlier by the Ortho Division of Chevron Chemical Company. After Chevron decided to divest Ortho, the center was put up for sale. Berlex paid $53 million for the site and invested another $4 million to retrofit the facility, which was divided into a two-story administration building and a three-story lab building.

New Jersey and California also found themselves in occasional conflict, primarily involving human resources practices such as performance review. To become more efficient in this area, as well as to avoid problems with morale, Berlex revamped its performance review system and rolled it out to both coasts. The California start-up mindset sometimes clashed with the sensibilities of the German corporate parent, the executives of which were more conservative by nature and believed the Americans were moving ahead on projects too quickly. To address this problem and forge better understanding between the two cultures, a work exchange program was established, allowing employees to spend up to one year at an assignment outside their home country. In the end, the East and West Coast arms of Berlex learned to work together, as did the entire American subsidiary with its German corporate parent.

During the first half of the 1990s, Berlex introduced several products into the marketplace. Launched in 1992 was Fludara, a treatment for the most common form of adult leukemia, geared toward patients who did not respond to chemotherapy. A year later, Berlex brought out Betapace, a treatment to help maintain normal sinus rhythm for patients with highly symptomatic atrial fibrillation and atrial flutter (AFIB/AFL). Also in 1993, Berlex introduced Betaseron, a breakthrough in the treatment of multiple sclerosis developed in conjunction with Chiron Corporation. (The product was manufactured by Chiron and sold by Berlex.) A genetically engineered form of interferon, a protein produced by the body to fight viruses, Betaseron was the first medication developed that could reduce the number of spikes in the disease, which could greatly worsen such symptoms as tremors, fatigue, and numbness. The drug Climara, a patch, was another first for Berlex when it was launched in 1995. Climara was the first transdermal estrogen replacement therapy product. The seven-day patch delivered estrogen to women directly into the blood stream, especially useful in the prevention of osteoporosis.

Also in 1995 Berlex introduced Ultravist, an iodinated contrast agent for use in computed tomography. A year later the company offered Feridex I.V., the first liver-specific, as well as the first organ-specific, MRI enhancement agent launched in the United States. To growth its business in imaging agents, in 1996 Berlex forged an alliance with Abbott Laboratories, which maintained a strong hospital product marketing unit. Under terms of the agreement, Abbott would sell Magnevist and Ultravist to hospitals and be responsible for distribution, customer service, and order processing, while Berlex provided technical support. It was a win-win situation for both parties. Berlex was eager to expand sales in its imaging agents, while Abbott was looking to make greater inroads in the diagnostic imaging market.

Key Dates:

1979: Company is formed by Schering AG.
1982: Berlex enters the imaging market.
1988: Trademark suit settled with U.S.-based Schering Corporation.
1990: Biotech Codon and Triton Biosciences acquired.
1997: Headquarters is moved to Montville, New Jersey.

Starting in 1996 Berlex became involved in litigation connected to Betaseron. Biogen Inc. of Cambridge, Massachusetts, developed a drug called Avonex, which relied on a slightly different synthetic interferon. Berlex attempted to block the sale of Avonex because its introduction would violate the company's seven-year period of exclusive marketing. Biogen, on the other hand, contended that it had the right to market Avonex because it gained approval under the federal Orphan Drug Act, which was meant to reward companies for developing drugs used to treat rare diseases. In July 1996 Berlex sued Biogen for patent infringement involving the way Biogen produced the synthetic protein from ovary cells taken from Chinese hamsters. The matter would wend its way through the courts for the next eight years. In the meantime, Avonex dominated the market and became Biogen's flagship product, generating the bulk of the company's annual revenues, which reached $1 billion by 2000.

2000 and Beyond

In September 2000 Biogen won a decision in U.S. District Court, which Berlex appealed to the First U.S. Circuit Court of Appeals. Early in 2002 the two sides appeared to reach a settlement, which called for Biogen to pay Berlex at least $20 million in exchange for a license to the disputed patents. If the appeal sent the case back to the lower court, Biogen also agreed to pay Berlex an additional $55 million. Should the court rule against Biogen entirely, Berlex would be in line for an additional payment of $230 million. In February 2003, the appeals court upheld most of the lower court's ruling but ordered the lower court to re-examine one patent claim. As a result, Biogen was forced to pay Berlex the additional $55 million.

In the final years of the 1990s, Berlex moved to new headquarters in Montville, New Jersey, and introduced several new products. It launched Levlite in 1998, an oral contraceptive with a lower dosage than Levlen. In 1999 Climara became available in a new low-dose form. Another new Berlex drug, also launched in 1999, was Quadramet, used to treat the pain that accompanied metastatic bone cancer. In addition, Berlex acquired two new diagnostic imaging products in 1999: Acutect and Neotect.

The launch of new products accelerated for Berlex in the early years of the new century. In 2000, Levulan Kerstick, used to treat actinic keratoses, was launched, as well as Betapace AF, a replacement for Betapace and generic sotalol taken by patients suffering from atrial fibrillation. In 2001 Berlex launched five products: Campath, used to treat B-cell chronic lymphocytic leukemia; Refludan, a thrombin inhibitor used to treat patients with heparin-induced thrombocytopenia and associated thromboembolic disease; Finevin, an acne medication; Mirena, an implanted contraceptive; and Yasmin, an oral contraceptive. Additionally in 2001 Berlex acquired Refludan, a direct thrombin inhibitor used to treat patients with heparin-induced thrombocytopenia. A year later Berlex acquired Leukine, prescribed for older adults with acute myelogenous leukemia following chemotherapy, after bone marrow transplantation, or peripheral blood stem cell transplantation. In 2003 Berlex introduce Finacea, a topical treatment for rosacea.

After 25 years, Berlex was a clear success for Schering, one of the few European drug makers to crack the U.S. market. The winning strategy was to become a niche company, to focus on specific product lines, such as birth control and multiple sclerosis, rather than to attempt to compete with much larger companies over a broader front.

Principal Subsidiaries

Berlex Biosciences, Inc.

Principal Competitors

Biogen Idec Inc.; Bristol-Myers Squibb Company; Warner Chilcott, Inc.; Wyeth Pharmaceuticals.

Further Reading

Fuhrmans, Vanessa, and Charles Forelle, "Bogen to Pay $55 Million in Deal To Settle Schering Patent Lawsuit," *Wall Street Journal,* February 4, 2003, p. B7.
Sellers, L.J., "Schering AG: Size Doesn't Matter," *Pharmaceutical Executive,* November 1, 2002.
Silverman, Ed, "That Other Schering," *Star-Ledger,* August 8, 2001, p. 47.

—Ed Dinger

Burke Mills, Inc.

191 Sterling Street N.W.
Valdese, North Carolina 28690
U.S.A.
Telephone: (828) 874-6341
Fax: (828) 879-7188
Web site: http://www.burkemills.com

Public Company
Incorporated: 1948 as Burkyarns Inc.
Employees: 167
Sales: $24 million (2004)
Stock Exchanges: Over the Counter
Ticker Symbol: BMLS
NAIC: 313112 Yarn Texturing, Throwing, and Twisting Mills

Burke Mills, Inc., is an American manufacturer, processor, and dyer of yarns primarily for use in the home furnishings and automobile upholstery sectors. Two company facilities produce some 350,000 to 400,000 pounds of yarn a week, which is then marketed throughout the United States, the Caribbean Basin, Mexico, and Canada. Fytek, S.A. de C.V.—a 50 percent owned affiliate headquartered in Monterrey, Mexico—sells Burke Mills products in Central America and South America. The company also makes its product available on a commission basis.

Textile Town Origins

Burke Mills was established in Valdese, a town in North Carolina's Burke County, nestled in the shadows of the Blue Ridge Mountains. That town's origins as a manufacturing hub dated back to the late 1900s, when a group of immigrants left the valleys of Italy's Cottian Alps to settle on land located near the Catawba River, between the towns of Morganton and Hickory, North Carolina.

The Italian immigrants were Waldenses, pre-Reformation Christians whose religious ancestry dated back to at least the 12th century. Persecuted by the official churches and armies of both the Italian and the French governments, the Waldenses first sought refuge in the Alpine valleys of Northern Italy. When the Edict of 1848 granted them religious freedom, they remained secluded on their farms where they increased in number, and prospered so well that there was no longer enough land for farms to sustain the whole community. They migrated to various locations in Europe and the United States, including North Carolina. The area now known as Valdese eventually became the largest Waldensian colony in the world outside of Italy.

The Valdese settlers tried to eke out a living in Burke County, an inland location with poor farm-to-market transportation facilities and terrain broken by streams and mountains. The minimal amount of alluvial soil in the valleys did not allow them to create farms like those they had known in the lush Italian valleys, according to Edward W. Phifer, Jr., in his *Burke: The History of a North Carolina County, 1777–1920.* Unable to develop enough farms to sustain them in their increasing numbers, the Valdenses turned to manufacturing with the same spirit of survival and determination that had characterized their European ancestors—and prospered. It was due to their persevering efforts that the Valdese colony developed a thriving manufacturing economy.

In 1901, the Waldensian Hosiery Mills was established in Valdese. The mill thrived as a family-owned business and was later merged with Alba Hosiery Mills to become Alba-Waldensian, Inc. Valdese resident Leon Guigou was employed at Waldensian Hosiery until 1948 when the 43-year-old decided to strike out on his own. That year, he teamed with Frank Gaddy to perpetuate the entrepreneurial spirit of the area by founding Burkyarns Inc. The fledgling company was situated in a 1,200 square foot building west of Valdese. The weekly goal of the original eight-person work force was to produce 500 pounds of dyed yarn for the hosiery industry.

By 1950 the company had branched out to synthetics, establishing a sound reputation for its dyed rayon, polyester, and acetate wrap yarn. As these materials gained popularity in the 1960s and 1970s, Burkyarns continued to grow and profit.

New Leadership in the 1970s–80s

In 1978, Pakistani entrepreneur Humayun Shaikh—who held several interests in textile and insurance companies in

Company Perspectives:

We at Burke Mills have committed ourselves to the future with major, ongoing capital investments in the latest and most advanced technologies, to satisfy the ever more varied and sophisticated demands of our customers. Our yarns are used in many applications from automotive fabrics, office furnishings and wall coverings, home furnishings, men's and women's clothing, to labels, ribbons and shoestrings.

Lahore, Pakistan—invested in Burkyarns. He joined as a director at the company, and under his leadership, to reflect the widening range of products, the company's name was changed from Burkyarns to Burke Mills. Shaikh became president of the company in 1981 and chairman the following year.

In the early 1980s, Burke Mills management aimed at making the company a world-class manufacturing facility and resolved to upgrade everything to state-of-the-art status. Millions of dollars were spent on machinery, but it soon became obvious that the work force needed additional training in both technical and educational skills. Toward that end, the company formed a partnership with Western Piedmont Community College (WPCC) of Morganton, North Carolina, to train Burke Mills personnel for efficient use of computer-processing equipment and information systems. More than half of the employees volunteered for the training program, where they reportedly developed the skills needed for finding solutions to problems on the job and gained new levels of self-confidence.

During this time, Burke Mills's most important raw materials were unprocessed yarn, dyes, and chemicals. Like all textile plants, the company would dispose of by-products at a landfill. However, environmental concerns over the dumping of yarn, cardboard, plastic tubes, and, perhaps most importantly, cleaning fluid, prompted Burke Mills to find an alternative to the landfill. By recycling its by-products, Burke Mills earned the 1989 North Carolina Small Business Recycling Award.

The healthy economy of the early 1990s favored the purchase of Burke Mills products. Focusing on efficient and cost-effective maintenance of its existing products and markets, Burke Mills enjoyed success. Its business consisted of twisting, texturing, winding, dyeing, processing and selling filament as well as novelty and spun yarn. These yarns were dyed and processed on a commission basis. The company marketed its products throughout the United States, primarily in the East. For fiscal 1993 and 1994, sales to Mexico and Canada amounted to less than one percent of total sales.

Increased demand for package dyed yarns and a continuing strong economy during 1994, coupled with Burke Mills's marketing efforts focused on the home and automotive upholstery markets, brought 1994 sales to $36.2 million and created a backlog of $3.9 million for that fiscal year. Sales to Chatham Manufacturing Company and to Milliken Textile Company exceeded 10 percent of the company's revenue. By 1995, Burke Mills was employing a work force of 356. According to John W. McCurry in the January 1, 1996, issue of *Textile World*, the company boosted its capacity with the introduction of additional automated systems and "found itself in a situation perhaps unique to the United States textiles industry in the 1990s: a dwindling labor supply. Burke County had an unemployment rate which hovered at 2–3 percent, one of the lowest in the United States and a figure labor analysts equated to full employment."

Challenges in the Mid-1990s and Beyond

Challenges in the mid-1990s included significant price increases for the raw materials Burke Mills relied on. To bolster its production capacity, in 1997 the company formed a partnership with Fytek, S.A. de C.V., a yarn company headquartered in Monterrey, Mexico. Fytek provided twisted filament yarns to Burke Mills and to Mexican, Central American, and South American markets; it also distributed Burke Mills yarns to these markets. As a result of the deal, Burke Mills owned 49.8 percent of the stock and 50 percent of the voting control of Fytek.

Burke Mills focused on keeping abreast of technology in 1999, bringing in a new fully integrated system to replace older manufacturing and accounting software.

In the production realm, the company installed newer equipment for dyeing and drying, as well as automated load/unload machines, which reduced labor costs. The manufacture of dyed yarns had undergone dramatic changes over the years. Dyestuffs that had originally been measured by hand became part of a robotics dispensing system that measured and mixed colors to repeatedly and consistently produce any number of shades of the same color. Such automated systems in the dyehouse provided better quality control and more consistent results.

The first step in manufacturing dyed yarn was color matching. Burke Mills labs were equipped with the latest model of color-computer programs. Lab technicians analyzed color samples mailed by clients who wanted colors that matched the exact shade of the samples. The matching process (similar to DNA testing) consisted in breaking down a color into its chemical components. With the help of specialized testing equipment, technicians could produce the exact shade of color that a client wanted. Burke Mills's automated system loaded dyestuff into a mixing container, mixed the solution, and sent it directly into the chosen dye machine. The company's horizontal dyeing system made it the largest fully automated dyehouse in North America; a computerized system controlled the dye mixtures, the times for drying, and for loading and unloading the yarn as a package.

As the 20th century came to an end, despite the improvements made in its mills, Burke Mills found itself in a continually weakening market. Higher costs for labor and raw materials, combined with orders for smaller quantities of yarn per order, pressured the company to increase sales by reducing the prices of its products, thereby lowering gross margins. Because of the special colors specified by its customers, Burke Mills produced on a made-to-order basis. The decline of pounds per order put a strain on the capacity of the older, smaller dye machines while the newer, more efficient larger machines stood idly by, under-utilized and increasing the manufacturing cost per pound of small orders for yarns in a variety of shades and colors. The order mix increased the company's manufacturing cost per pound. Seeking to offset the losses, Burke Mills negotiated with vendors of raw materials for the reduction of prices and adjusted the costs of its overhead structure.

Key Dates:

1948: Burkyarns Inc. is founded.
1979: Burkyarns becomes Burke Mills, Inc.
1989: Burke Mills earns the North Carolina award for recycling of waste items.
1996: Burke Mills automatizes the dying process.
2001: Burke Mills is delisted from NASDAQ and begins trading over the counter.
2003: Burke Mills' net sales drop to an all-time low; the company plans survival.

Yet, during 2000, the price of raw yarn continued to rise, and sales continued to decline. Since Burke Mills operated in a very competitive market, very little of the cost increases could be recovered from sales. Although the company reduced costs, it had to meet expenses of $875,000 for severances, bad debts, recruiting fees, and inventory markdowns that year. Moreover, one of its distributors went out of business, and the entire textile economy continued to falter. In 2001, because Burke Mills failed to meet the NASDAQ minimum bid-price requirements of $1 a share, the exchange delisted the company and moved its stock to the OTC Bulletin Board.

Although Burke Mills had invested heavily in newer and costly, more efficient technology and equipment, it could not stem the flow of lower-priced Asian exports to the United States. It wasn't alone. In 2001, at least 100 U.S. textile mills went out of business and some 60,000 to 75,000 textile workers lost their jobs.

During 2002, the company faced an exceedingly competitive market, a shrinking customer base, erosion in the quality of customer credit, major increases in the cost of natural gas, fuel oil, and insurance, and heavy competition from Asian imports. Sales dropped 20 percent to $29.99 million. While it did not lose any major customers, the weak economy and competition from low-priced imports led Burke Mills customers to downsize their orders. Nevertheless, major improvements were made in efficiencies; labor and overhead costs were reduced, and on-time deliveries improved. There was a major decrease in inventory, costs for labor, and overhead.

Net sales for the first three quarters of 2003 dropped by 21.4 percent to $18,986,000 compared to $24,165,000 in 2002 for the same period. Pounds shipped decreased by 20.5 percent, while the average price of sales decreased by 1.2 percent in a very competitive business environment. The company did not lose any major customers, but textile imports had a negative impact on sales to customers. In other words, in 2003 Burke Mills in particular and the domestic textile industry in general, continued to face very difficult economic times, according to the American Textile Manufacturers Institute (ATMI) Year-End Economic Report of January 12, 2004. ''The crisis that afflicted the industry since the rise in Asian currency manipulation in the late 1990s continued throughout 2003 . . . as the second-worst performance for the industry in the last century,'' according to ATMI.

ATMI noted that ''a huge increase in shipments from China, imports of yarn, fabric, and made-ups jumped 9 percent in 2003, following a huge 26 percent surge [of imports] during 2002. . . . Large Asian exporters, such as India and South Korea, added to the flood of low-cost textiles that entered the United States market.'' However, ''as the dollar weakened against non-Asian currencies, total United States exports of yarn, fabric, and made-ups managed a very modest one percent gain [in 2003]. Although exports to most major destinations—such as Canada, Mexico, and the European Union were down—export growth to the Caribbean Basin countries helped offset the declines to other destinations.''

ATMI President James W. Chesnutt, of the National Spinning Co., expressed guarded optimism. While the U.S. textile industry remained one of the nation's largest manufacturing employers, it was, according to Chesnutt, ''in a fight for its survival. . . . This will be a tough fight, but the industry, for the first time in many years is organized, energized and united.''

Burke Mills continued to operate as well as it could during fiscal 2003; had withstood the strains and pressures brought on by the invasions of foreign products, updated plans for 2004 and still had the creative flexibility and state-of-the art equipment needed to survive the recreation of its industry.

Principal Subsidiaries

Feytek, S.A. de C.C. (50%; Mexico).

Principal Competitors

National Textiles, L.L.C.; Parkdale Mills, Inc; Unifi,Inc.

Further Reading

''Burke Mills,'' *Valdese News*, June 22, 2003.
Herbert, Bob, ''Dark Side of Free Trade,'' *New York Times,* February 20, 2004, p. 25.
McCurry, John W., ''Burke Mills Robotizes Its Dyehouse,'' *Textile World*, January 1, 1996, pp. 78–9.
''Obituaries,'' *Valdese News,* October 3, 2002.
Patterson, Donald W., ''Losses Mount for N.C. Workers; This Could be a Make-or-Break Year for the Textile Industry as a Decades-Old Quota System Is Set to Expire,'' *News and Record* (Greensboro, N.C.), January 16, 2004, p. A1
Phifer, Edward W., Jr., *Burke: The History of a North Carolina County, 1777–1920, With a Glimpse Beyond*, Chapel Hill: N.C.: Bookshop Inc., 510 pp.
''Year-End Economic Report: Textile Industry Crisis Continued in 2003; 2004 to Be a Make or Break Year,'' *American Textile Manufacturers Institute*, January 12, 2004.

—Gloria A. Lemieux

CBS Television Network

51 West 52nd Street
New York, New York 10019
U.S.A.
Telephone: (212) 975-4321
Fax: (212) 975-4516
Web site: http://www.cbs.com

Wholly Owned Subsidiary of Viacom Inc.
Incorporated: 1927 as United Independent Broadcasters, Inc.
Employees: 46,189
Sales: $7.76 billion (2003)
NAIC: 515120 Television Broadcasting

The world's second oldest broadcasting network, CBS Television Network (formerly CBS Corporation) was acquired by Viacom Inc. in 2000. The network provides television programs (including such hits as *Survivor, 60 Minutes,* and *Everybody Loves Raymond*) to more than 200 affiliate stations in the United States, including 20 stations owned by Viacom. During the late 1990s, CBS Television Network reversed a downward slide and rose to become the nation's top network.

Origins

In the late 1920s Arthur Judson, the impresario of the Philadelphia and New York Philharmonic orchestras, approached the Radio Corporation of the National Broadcasting Company (NBC), then the only radio broadcaster in the United States, with an idea to promote classical music by airing orchestra performances; NBC declined. Undaunted, Judson founded his own broadcasting company, which he named United Independent Broadcasters, Inc. (UIB), in 1927.

Lacking the strong capital base NBC was afforded by its parent, RCA, UIB struggled to stay afloat for several months. In the summer of 1927, however, Judson found a rich partner in Columbia Phonograph, a leader in the phonograph record business. Columbia Phonograph bought UIB's operating rights for $163,000; the new company was named the Columbia Phonograph Broadcasting System.

Columbia Phonograph sold UIB's operating rights back to the broadcasting company in 1928, however, apparently because the phonograph company was frustrated by a lack of advertiser loyalty. The broadcasting company's name was then shortened to the Columbia Broadcasting System (CBS), and its finances were greatly enhanced that year when William Paley—the son of a Russian cigar company owner who eventually helped CBS earn its reputation as a classy network—invested $400,000 in the company's stock.

At the time of Paley's CBS stock purchase, the company consisted of only 16 affiliated radio stations and possessed no stations of its own. Paley, who was quickly elected president of the company, tripled earnings in his first year. This success was accomplished by offering to prospective affiliates the network's entire unsponsored schedule at no cost, in contrast to NBC, which charged affiliates for all programs. In return for free programs, affiliates gave CBS airtime for sponsored broadcasts, allowing the network to assure contracted sponsors that airtime would be available. Within a decade, CBS added nearly 100 stations to its network. Since the number of affiliates a network possesses determines the number of people it can reach, which in turn determines what a sponsor is charged, CBS was soon on firm financial ground. By 1930 CBS had 300 employees and total sales of $7.2 million.

Although CBS fared well, NBC continued to dominate the entertainment-oriented broadcasting industry. Paley, viewing news and public affairs as a quick way for CBS to gain respectability, decided to explore the potential for establishing its own network news. In 1930 he hired Ed Klauber to institute a news and public affairs section, and in 1933 the Columbia News Service, the first radio network news operation, was formed. By 1935 CBS had become the largest radio network in the United States.

In 1938 Edward R. Murrow began his career at CBS as head of the network's European division. The first international radio news broadcast was initiated later that year with Murrow in Vienna, Austria, William L. Shirer in London, and others reporting from Paris, Berlin, and Rome. With these newsbreaks, CBS began the practice of preempting regular programming. Interruptions were planned for prime listening time—8:55 to 9:00 p.m.—and were intended to give the network a ''statesmanlike'' image.

Key Dates:

1927: Columbia Broadcasting is founded.
1928: William Paley invests in the radio broadcaster and becomes president of the company.
1938: Edward R. Murrow goes to work for CBS.
1964: Company begins an acquisition spree.
1979: Company begins divesting diverse holdings.
1995: Westinghouse acquires CBS.
2000: Viacom acquires CBS.

CBS entered the recording business in 1938 with the purchase of the American Record Corporation. Later called the Columbia Recording Corporation, it soon became an industry powerhouse.

By the beginning of World War II, CBS employed more than 2,000 people, had annual sales of nearly $36 million, and boasted more than 100 affiliate stations throughout the United States. In 1940 the world's first experimental color television broadcast was made from a CBS transmitter atop the Chrysler Building in New York City and was received in the CBS Building at 485 Madison Avenue. The following year marked the beginning of CBS's weekly broadcasts of black-and-white television programs. Also in 1941, the government ordered NBC to divest itself of one of its two networks, which eventually gave rise to the American Broadcasting Company (ABC).

Post-World War II Activity

Although CBS continued to expand after World War II, NBC was still the industry leader. Under Paley's direction, CBS lured stars away from NBC by devising a plan in which the celebrities could be taxed as companies rather than as individuals, greatly reducing the amount of income they were required to turn over to the government. Jack Benny was the first major star to leave NBC for CBS; soon Edgar Bergen and Charlie McCarthy, Amos 'n' Andy, Red Skelton, and George Burns and Gracie Allen followed. Within a year CBS took the lead from NBC in programming, advertising revenues, and profits—a lead it maintained as the two networks further expanded into television.

In 1946 CBS submitted its color television broadcasting system to the Federal Communications Commission (FCC) for approval. CBS was confident that its color system would be approved, even though existing black-and-white sets could not receive CBS's color broadcasts. The FCC did not approve the system, calling it ''premature.'' In the meantime, RCA had developed a color system that was compatible with existing television sets. The CBS method produced a better picture, however, and in 1950, when both CBS and RCA submitted their systems to the FCC for approval, only the CBS system was approved. But RCA appealed the decision, preventing CBS from marketing its system and gaining time to improve the quality of its own technique. In 1953 the FCC reversed and ruled in favor of RCA.

During the 1950s censorship became an issue in the broadcasting industry. The networks had always been sensitive to censorship pressure: the FCC was given authority to revoke a station's license if it did not serve the ''public interest responsibly.'' In addition, advertisers were given permission to refuse to sponsor a program that they deemed offensive, and network affiliates could pressure the network into discontinuing a controversial program.

Censorship surfaced at all the networks during the early 1950s as U.S. Senator Joseph McCarthy's anticommunist campaign pressured networks and sponsors to blacklist certain actors and writers who were suspected of having left-wing associations. Although CBS was considered the most liberal of the networks, it required 2,500 employees to sign a ''loyalty oath,'' which stated that they ''neither belonged to nor sympathized with'' any communist organization. In 1954 two CBS News commentators began to expose McCarthy's unethical behavior on the television show *See It Now.* The program helped to discredit communist paranoia, but proved so controversial that CBS eventually canceled it.

By this time there were 32 million television sets in the United States, and television had become the biggest advertising medium in the world. The period was marred, however, by a 1956 TV quiz show scandal in which CBS's *$64,000 Question* was shown to be rigged.

In the late 1950s, Paley hired James Aubrey as president of CBS. Aubrey, who purportedly thought that television programming had become too ''highbrow,'' introduced such shows as *The Beverly Hillbillies, Mr. Ed,* and *The Munsters.* These series were extremely popular; in his first two years with CBS, Aubrey doubled the network's profits.

During the early 1960s, CBS embarked on a diverse acquisitions campaign. Before 1964 CBS had made only two acquisitions in its history, but from that year on the company made acquisitions almost every year. In 1964 the network purchased an 80 percent interest in the New York Yankees baseball team, which it sold ten years later. Acquisitions in the fields of musical instruments, book publishing, and children's toys were made throughout the 1960s.

By the end of the decade, CBS had 22,000 employees and net profits of more than $64 million. The network's most notable programming innovation of the decade came in 1968 with the debut of *60 Minutes,* a television news magazine. The 1970s were a period of successful prime-time programming. In 1971 *All in the Family* debuted on CBS, and in 1972 both *M*A*S*H* and *The Waltons* were televised for the first time.

The 1970s, however, were also years of managerial turmoil. In 1971 Charles T. Ireland became the president of CBS but was replaced a year later by Arthur Taylor, who held the position for four years. Taylor was relieved of his duties when the network placed second in the Nielsen ratings for the first time in 21 years. John D. Backe, who had been president of the CBS publishing division since 1973, was chosen as Taylor's replacement.

Meanwhile, in 1976 CBS relieved reporter Daniel Schorr of all duties after he leaked a secret House Intelligence Committee report on the Central Intelligence Agency (CIA) to the Village Voice. He resigned from CBS several months later. And in April 1979, in a case involving CBS and two employees—

correspondent Mike Wallace and producer Barry Lando—the U.S. Supreme Court ruled that journalists accused of libel may be forced to answer questions about their "state of mind" or about conversations with colleagues during the editorial process. The decision was a victory for former Lieutenant Colonel Anthony E. Herbert, who contended that he was libeled in a "60 Minutes" broadcast that aired in 1973.

In 1979 CBS finally began to divest itself of some of its diverse holdings, selling at least one business every year for the next few years. The following year CBS regained dominance in the prime-time TV ratings, a position held by ABC since 1976. One week after CBS took the lead, however, President Backe was forced to resign. He was replaced by Thomas H. Wyman, who had been a vice-president at Pillsbury.

CBS went to court again in 1982 after it aired the documentary The Uncounted Enemy: A Vietnam Deception. The case was the beginning of a long-running battle between CBS and retired U.S. Army General William Westmoreland, who filed a $120 million libel suit against the network. The dispute ended several years later when Westmoreland withdrew his charges on a promise from CBS that the network would publicly attempt to restore his character.

By the early 1980s CBS operations had been divided into six main categories: the broadcast group, which was concerned with programming and production of shows for the network, theaters, home video, and cable TV; the records group; the publishing group; the toys division; the technology center, which was responsible for research and development of new technologies; and various corporate joint ventures, including CBS/FOX Company, a collaboration with Twentieth Century-Fox to manufacture and distribute videocassettes and videodiscs. In 1986 CBS sold its book-publishing business to Harcourt Brace Jovanovich, Inc., for $500 million, and that same year the company sold all of its toy businesses.

In 1983 CBS, Columbia Pictures, and Home Box Office (HBO) joined forces to form Tri-Star Pictures, a motion picture production and distribution company. By 1984 Tri-Star had released 17 full-length films, nine of which it also produced, and in 1985 CBS sold its interest in the company. Another experiment was Trintex, a commercial electronic service that allowed people access to news, weather, and sports information; financial and educational data; and home shopping and banking from a personal computer terminal. Initiated in 1984, Trintex—a project from which CBS withdrew in 1986—was the combined effort of CBS, IBM, and Sears, Roebuck & Co.

In 1985 Ted Turner, owner of Turner Broadcasting System (TBS), announced his intentions to take over CBS. In order to prevent this, CBS swallowed a $954.8 million poison pill by purchasing 21 percent of its own outstanding stock.

In September 1986 Larry Tisch replaced Tom Wyman as chief executive officer of CBS. Tisch had previously served as the chairman of Loew's Corporation, which owned nearly 25 percent of CBS stock at the time. Following a power struggle between Tisch and Wyman, who continued to serve as president of CBS, William S. Paley returned as chairman of the board and Wyman was forced to resign.

Although Tisch was originally to serve only as interim chief executive officer, within four months it was clear that the job was his. He immediately began cutting costs at the network. Trimming $30 million from the news division budget, Tisch tried to reduce programming costs, cut hundreds of jobs, and sold a number of CBS publishing concerns. He also sold CBS Records to the Sony Corporation in 1987 for $2 billion, even though the subsidiary, which boasted such top stars as Michael Jackson and Bruce Springsteen, had been a perennial moneymaker for the company.

Tisch was soundly criticized for selling the number one record company in the industry at a time when the music business appeared to be healthy, and for trying to cut television programming costs when cable TV and other pay services were seducing viewers with a broader and higher quality selection. CBS's prime-time hits were getting old; in 1987 the network came in last in the Nielsen ratings. To make matters worse, CBS viewers tended to be older than the audience advertisers were trying to reach.

In 1988 Tisch, under fire from the CBS board and affiliate stations for lacking any long-term strategy, appointed 38-year-old Kim LeMasters to head the network's entertainment division. LeMasters' task was to find new programming that would appeal to younger audiences.

CBS entered the 1990s absent Paley, who died in 1990. The company soon experienced a pleasant jump in the ratings but was still coping with slumping revenues. In 1990 CBS, like other companies dependent on advertising, saw its income drop precipitously as the country remained stuck in a recession, and prospects for an economic recovery seemed bleak as a war in the Persian Gulf threatened to erupt. Also contributing to the poor fiscal performance that year were the huge hits CBS took on major sports contracts, particularly on professional baseball: the company was forced to swallow $171.2 million in losses.

CBS enjoyed a moral, if not financial, surge in 1991, as the broadcaster's ratings—last among the networks for the previous four years—jumped to number one, the most dramatic recovery in television history. CBS boasted five of the top ten programs, including the number one *60 Minutes,* which became the only show ever to rank first in three separate decades. Although executives from other networks claimed that special events, such as coverage of the World Series and the 1992 Winter Olympics, accounted for the coveted ratings trophy, CBS pointed out that it had beat the competition in regularly scheduled programming and had consistently led NBC and ABC in the weekly ratings races. Industry observers credited this victory to a better stock of shows on CBS as well as an aggressive self-promotional and marketing campaign that outpaced those of the rival networks. Even controversy played to CBS's favor. When U.S. Vice-President Dan Quayle accused the show *Murphy Brown,* the third highest rated show on TV, of irresponsibly celebrating unwed mothers and the breakup of the traditional American family, CBS executives believed the political storm would only lead to greater viewer and advertiser interest.

Financial woes, however, overshadowed these successes. Despite reducing its dividend, cutting $100 million in operating costs, and scaling back personnel by approximately 6 percent—the budgetary ax fell on the company's flagship news division particularly hard—CBS saw revenue fall 8 percent and suffered a loss. Although the networks collectively did their worst business in 20 years, as total ad spending in the country declined for the first time in 30 years, 1991–92 was considered a banner period for television. American viewers were riveted by the Persian Gulf War, the confirmation hearings of Supreme Court Justice Clarence Thomas, and the dissolution of the Soviet Union.

However, CBS was not able to coast on these spectacles. As in 1990, the company racked up huge losses in its sports divisions, proving to some observers what had always been suspected: the network had grossly overpaid for its baseball and football contracts, which were to expire after their respective 1993 seasons. Despite projections of losses for its coverage of the 1992 Winter Olympics, CBS proudly revealed that it had broken even on the Games.

1995 Acquisition by Westinghouse

CBS lost the rights to NFC football games in 1993. This loss, combined with mounting financial losses and the lack of a move into cable, led to a vote of no confidence from one of CBS's top two institutional investors. In response, the beleaguered Tisch sold CBS to Westinghouse Electric Corporation in 1995 for $5.4 billion, marking the beginning of a dramatic era of change for the broadcasting company's new parent company.

Westinghouse, whose massive holdings included defense electronics, power generation, and nuclear engineering businesses, had experienced profound problems during the early 1990s. A lack of strategy, mismanagement, and a costly foray into the financial services business prompted the industrial giant's board of directors to recruit Michael H. Jordan, an executive from Pepsi, to lead the corporation to recovery. Initially, Jordan promised to restore Westinghouse to its former greatness as a technology-driven, industrial heavyweight, but he soon began to look toward other alternatives for the corporation's future. CBS, as it became apparent after Westinghouse acquired the broadcaster in 1995, represented Jordan's vision of Westinghouse's future, perhaps more so than anyone realized.

After abandoning a plan to split Westinghouse's diverse industrial holdings and CBS into two companies, Jordan decided to strip Westinghouse of all its industrial businesses and focus instead on broadcasting. Beginning in 1996, Westinghouse began transforming itself, in essence, into CBS, a process that required the industrial behemoth to peel away all its former strength and move headlong into television and radio broadcasting. In 1996, Westinghouse sold its Knoll Group furniture manufacturing operations, its defense electronics units, and its residential burglar alarm business. The following year, the company sold its Thermo-King business to Ingersoll-Rand for $2.56 billion and its power generation business to Siemens AG for roughly $1.5 billion.

By the end of 1997, Jordan had orchestrated $25 billion in deals to execute his strategy of turning Westinghouse into a broadcaster, a total that not only included the divestitures of the company's industrial holdings but also several important acquisitions. In 1997, Westinghouse paid $4.9 billion for Infinity Broadcasting Corporation, the second largest radio station network in the United States. Also in 1997, Jordan engineered CBS's belated push into cable by acquiring TNN (The Nashville Network) and the U.S. and Canadian operations of CMT (Country Music Television) from Gaylord Entertainment Co. for $1.55 billion. Additionally, CBS launched *Eye on People,* a news and entertainment network expected to bolster the broadcaster's presence in cable.

On December 1, 1997, with much of Jordan's major transformation work completed, Westinghouse changed its name to CBS Corporation and moved its headquarters from Pittsburgh to New York City. Following the sale of its power generation business to Siemens, the only vestiges of the former Westinghouse were the company's nuclear power business and a unit that handled nuclear material for the U.S. government. Both of these businesses were divested in 1998, acquired by Morrison Knudsen and British Nuclear Fuels. What remained was the newly diversified CBS, whose strength during the late 1990s had grown amid the swirl of corporate activity surrounding it. Although the network continued to attract an older audience, CBS's television ratings were encouragingly high during the late 1990s, eclipsing all rival networks. As the broadcaster prepared for the 21st century, ready to begin an eight-year, $4 billion contract with the NFL (having outbid NBC for the rights), the company's new management hoped to engineer a return to the past, back to the years when CBS dominated the industry.

2000 and Beyond

While CBS did return to supremacy, it was achieved under a different corporate structure. In 2000 CBS was acquired by Sumner Redstone's media giant Viacom Inc. for $45 billion. Under Viacom, CBS's cable networks and radio holdings were transferred to other Viacom divisions. CBS gained a new CEO, Leslie Moonves, as former CEO Mel Karmazin went on to take that position at Viacom. Within two years, Viacom had acquired and added to the CBS division the United Paramount Network (UPN), known for such programs as *Buffy the Vampire Slayer* and *America's Next Top Model.*

The ensuing success of CBS was, in part, due to the fact that "reality TV" rocked the television industry. These unscripted shows, featuring ordinary people in sometimes-extraordinary, unrehearsed situations, were a huge hit among viewers, and promised to become a cultural phenomenon with staying power. CBS's reality show *Survivor* was one of the most successful in the genre. *Survivor,* which placed a group of people from all walks of life in a secluded location and charged them with outwitting and outlasting each other in competition, pushed CBS in to first place in the 2002–2003 ratings race. Also instrumental in accelerating CBS's race to the top of the ratings was the show *CSI: Crime Scene Investigation.* The forensics show was a hit, edging the NBC medical drama *ER* away from the top of the Nielsen ratings.

During the 2003–04 television season, CBS introduced some shows that performed well, including *Joan of Arcadia,* and *Cold Case.* The network's most successful show, however, remained *CSI,* primetime's most-watched show (averaging 26.3 million viewers per week). In 2003, the company drew sharp criticism from some as it prepared to air a mini-series on former U.S. President Reagan and First Lady Nancy. When the show's scripts were leaked to the press, conservative and Republican interest groups protested *The Reagans,* which was not a necessarily sympathetic portrayal of its subjects. CBS eventually opted to shuttle the program over to Viacom's cable network Showtime for airing.

Principal Operating Units

Infinity Promotions Group; King World Productions Inc.; Paramount Television Group; Sportsline.com Inc.; United Paramount Network.

Further Reading

Boyer, Peter J., *Who Killed CBS? How America's Number One News Network Went Down the Tubes,* New York: Random House, 1988.

Carter, Bill, "CBS in First Place of Ratings Race for Year," *New York Times,* April 15, 1992.

"CBS Lays Off Hundreds to Cut Budget by at Least $100 Million," *Broadcasting,* April 8, 1991.

"Down to the Core," *Mergers & Acquisitions,* January-February 1998, p. 6.

Goldman, Kevin, "CBS Investors Entertain Disney Rumors, Drive Stock Up," *Wall Street Journal,* April 20, 1992.

——, "CBS Takes $322 Million Pretax Charge on Sports Contracts, Posts Quarterly Loss," *Wall Street Journal,* November 4, 1991.

Greppi, Michele, "Affils Weather Protests," *TelevisionWeek,* November 10, 2003, p. 38.

Kissell, Rick, "Frosh Titles Earn Sked Stripes," *Daily Variety,* January 7, 2004, p. A1.

Halberstam, David, *The Powers That Be,* New York: Knopf, 1979.

McClellan, Steve, "CBS Says Oldies Can Be Goodies, Too," *Broadcasting & Cable,* July 28, 2003, p. 15.

——, "CBS to Break Even on Olympics," *Broadcasting & Cable,* March 2, 1992.

Metz, Robert, *CBS: Reflections in a Bloodshot Eye,* New York: New American Library, 1975.

Paper, Lewis J., *Empire: William S. Paley and the Making of CBS,* New York: St. Martin's, 1987.

Slater, Robert, *This . . . Is CBS: A Chronicle of Sixty Years,* New York: Prentice Hall, 1988.

"Westinghouse RIP," *Economist,* November 29, 1997, p. 63.

—Mark Pestana
—updates: Jeffrey L. Covell; Catherine Holm

Ceské aerolinie, a.s.

Letiste Ruzyne
160 08 Prague 6
Czech Republic
Telephone: (+420) 220 104 310
Fax: (+420) 224 81 04 26
Web site: http://www.csa.cz

Private Company
Incorporated: 1923 as Ceské Statni Aerolinie
Employees: 4,455
Sales: CZK 14.65 billion ($517.50 million) (2002)
NAIC: 481111 Scheduled Passenger Air Transportation; 481112 Scheduled Freight Air Transportation; 481212 Nonscheduled Chartered Freight Air Transportation; 481211 Nonscheduled Chartered Passenger Air Transportation; 488119 Other Airport Operations; 488190 Other Support Activities for Air Transportation

Ceské aerolinie, a.s., also called Czech Airlines or CSA, flies to approximately 70 destinations in more than 40 countries. Its fleet numbers about three dozen Western-made aircraft. Since 2001, CSA has been a member of the Delta Airlines-led Skyteam alliance, which gives its passengers easy access to two dozen international airlines. In addition to scheduled and charter flights, CSA provides an array of aviation support services, including cargo handling, catering, and aircraft maintenance. CSA is controlled by a number of government institutions.

Origins

CSA was founded on October 6, 1923, as Ceskoslovenska Statni Aerolinie, or Czechoslovak State Airlines. The first passenger flight, between Prague and Bratislava, occurred on October 29 with an Aero A-14 Brandenburg biplane piloted by Karel Brabenec.

The airline joined the International Air Transport Association (IATA) in 1929. On July 1, 1930, the carrier used a Ford 5AT to add its first international route, from Prague to Zagreb, in the former Yugoslavia (Croatia). CSA carried about 9,000 passengers during the year, according to *Airlines of the World* by R.E.G. Davies, who also reports that CSA's early fleet included Savoia-Marchetti S.M. 73s, four Airspeed Envoys, and one Saro Cloud, the latter two types made in Britain. Flights to Romania, Austria, and the Soviet Union were added in the early 1930s.

CSA moved to the new airport at Prague-Ruzyni in April 1937. Brussels, Paris, Rome, and Budapest were added to the network within the next two years. However, operations were curtailed on March 15, 1939 due to the Nazi occupation of Czechoslovakia.

Another airline, Ceskoslovenska Latecka Spolecnost (CLS), in which the Skoda Works had a significant interest, had provided domestic and international service after being founded in 1927. It was merged with CSA in 1945.

Cold War Ambassadors

Flight operations resumed on September 14, 1945. After the war, CSA rebuilt its fleet with both the Douglas DC-3 transports of the Allies and their German counterpart, Junkers Ju52s. The route network was restored and the first intercontinental flights—to Cairo and Ankara—added in 1947.

After the Communist coup of 1948, CSA shifted to Russian-made Ilyushin Il-12 airliners. Il-14s made locally under license by Avia were the next upgrade. Seventy-seat, twin-engine Tupolev Tu-104 jets were put into service in December 1957 and used on routes to Moscow, Paris, and Brussels. This aircraft facilitated the expansion of the intercontinental network to Bombay (Mumbai) in 1959.

The international network grew in the 1960s, extending south to Jakarta, Havana, and Africa. Long-range Ilyushin Il-62 aircraft were added in 1969. The next year saw the introduction of service to Montreal and New York. Of the airlines of the Soviet satellites, Czechoslovakia's was perhaps the most visible to the Western world. Another Russian-built airliner, the Tupolev Tu-134, was added in 1971, followed by the Tu-154M in 1988.

Company Perspectives:

In the beginning nature was all. It gave us sustenance, it warmed us and provided us with homes. When it revealed its laws, it bestowed upon humankind a vast gift of knowledge. Its apparent simplicity and innocence were exposed, and humankind peered into the depths of the world's complicated, but perfectly functioning laws. It became enough to stir, to choose one of the many laws of nature and to fulfil one's desires. And so it was that man (not only once) soared heavenward, like a dandelion seed. But nature sent forth greater mysteries and elicited further questions. Why do flocks of birds stay aloft? Why do they always head for their nest? How much patience and work goes into a flowering meadow? What washes up on shore with the ocean's breakers? And why does the intelligent dolphin only guide ships in large pods? Man looked closely at a petal and found that if the perfect network of links is damaged in its structure, the entire flower may wilt. Utter perfection created from myriad superbly functioning, interconnected features, one element complementing the next, patience while awaiting the outcome: add to this the ancient and overwhelming desire of man to overcome time, shorten distances, to fly. From all of this was born an airline. Nature and its fascinating laws attended its birth. To his own benefit, man assessed the speed of the cheetah, the strength of the elephant, the purity of an iceberg, the structural perfection of a leaf and the method and order of the tiny ant, and thus did airplanes take wing with the elegance of a dandelion seed or bird. For the first time—at the threshold of the third millennium—more than three million passengers were borne aloft on the wings of CSA.

New Challenges in the Early 1990s

The ''Velvet Revolution'' that ended communism in Czechoslovakia in the early 1990s meant CSA had to survive on its own. It was a difficult time to go it alone. During a major global recession, even Western European governments were bailing out their flag carriers.

At the same time, CSA was switching its fleet to Western-made equipment. The Airbus 310 was added in 1991, followed by the ATR-72 turboprop and Boeing 737 medium-range airliner the next year. (These were all leased.) The number of destinations continued to proliferate.

As president and board chairman Jiri Fiker told the *Journal of Commerce* in 1992, management was aware of the challenges ahead of surviving in a deregulated environment as the European Union's air market was being liberalized. CSA sought an alliance with a larger airline and found a partner in Air France, which in 1992 led a group acquiring 39.5 percent of the company's stock in a capital and assistance deal worth $60 million. This equity arrangement lasted only a couple of years, however.

At the same time, Czechoslovakia was being partitioned into two separate countries, effective January 1993, necessitating negotiations between the Czech Republic and Slovakia over ownership of the airline. Ceskoslovenske aerolinie, or Czechoslovak Airlines, was renamed Ceske aerolinie, Czech Airlines, on March 26, 1995.

CSA was reborn as a joint stock company on August 1, 1992, with Ceské aerolinie, a.s. being created out of the former state-owned entity Ceské aerolinie, s.p. Air France, one of the original shareholders, sold its interest to state-owned Konsolidacni Banka for $27 million in March 1994.

Mid-1990s Alliances

Prague grew in popularity as an international tourist destination in the mid-1990s. CSA carried nearly 1.5 million passengers in 1995, up 20 percent in one year. Cargo saw a similar increase in business. After several years of losses totaling more than KC $1 billion, the airline was again showing a profit. Turnover was CZK 8.5 billion in 1995. The same year, CSA began a marketing alliance with US carrier Continental Airlines.

Cargo became more important in the mid-1990s. The airline had no dedicated freighters but relied on the belly hold capacity of its passenger airliners. CSA opened a 5,000-square-meter warehouse at Prague's Ruzyne Airport in 1994, which was partly used for third party storage. CSA was one of only two cargo-handling companies there.

ATR-42 turboprops entered the fleet in 1996. The Tupolevs were grounded in 1997, at least as far as scheduled services, though the Tu-154Ms continued to perform some charters for another several more years.

To keep up with capacity demands, CSA placed a $350 million order for ten new Boeing 737s. In 1997, CSA and Boeing created a joint venture (90 percent owned by Boeing) to invest $30 million in Aero Vodochody, the Czech Republic's largest aircraft manufacturer.

Low-Cost Competition after 2000

Under international accounting standards, in 2000 CSA earned $29.5 million, ten times the previous year's figure, on revenues of $436.9 million. The carrier was required to post a loss under Czech accounting standards, which treated leases differently. The company had just under 4,000 employees. International business accounted for more than 80 percent of revenues, reported *Air Transport World.* CSA joined the Skyteam global alliance led by Delta and Air France in 2001.

CSA's transatlantic traffic fell by one-third following the September 11, 2001 terrorist attacks on the United States, prompting the carrier to cut the number of weekly flights from six to four. CSA also canceled orders for three new aircraft as the industry endured a worldwide crisis, and the carrier's planned privatization was delayed. Heavy flooding in August 2002 discouraged international visitors to the Czech Republic.

Turnover rose to $517.5 million (CZK 14.7 billion) in 2002, as pre-tax operating income increased to $26.2 million. CSA carried three million passengers during the year, a figure which rose to a record 3.6 million in 2003. London was its most popular as well as most competitive route. Cargo volume was also up. CSA ended 2003 with 35 aircraft in its fleet.

Dates:

1923: Ceské aerolinie, a.s. (CSA) is founded.
1930: The airlines first international route, to Zagreb, is added.
1962: The company's network stretches south to Havana.
1992: CSA becomes a joint stock company.
1995: CSA is renamed Czech Airlines.
2001: CSA joins Skyteam global alliance.

As low-cost carriers continued to appear in the Czech market, CSA announced plans to build its own low-cost unit. To do this, it attempted to acquire up to 50 percent of Travel Service, a Czech charter operator with subsidiaries in Hungary and Spain. However, acquisition talks fell through in 2003.

CSA management had an optimistic outlook as it grew steadily in the face of a global industry downturn. Airline management aimed to increase the fleet to 50 aircraft by 2006 as CSA expanded operations in both Western and Eastern Europe.

Principal Subsidiaries

Amadeus Marketing CSA S.R.O. (65%); CSA Airtours A.S. (ATO); CSA Services S.R.O. (CSS); CSA Support S.R.O. (SUP); Slovak Air Services S.R.O. (S.A.S.) (Slovakia); Slovenská Konzultacná Firma S.R.O. V Likvidácii (SKF) (Slovakia).

Principal Divisions

Air Crew Training; Charter Transport; CSA Cargo; CSA Catering; CSA Handling; Duty Free; Regular Air Transport.

Principal Competitors

Austrian Airlines; British Airways plc; KLM Royal Dutch Airlines; Lot Polish Airlines; Lufthansa AG; Malév.

Further Reading

''Air France, Investors Agree to Acquire 40% of Czech State Airline,'' *Wall Street Journal*, January 8, 1992, p. A4.

Baker, Colin, ''History: Previous Attempts at Airline Privatisation in Eastern Europe Have Stalled. Will It Be Different This Time Around?,'' *Airline Business*, December 2000, p. 74.

——, ''Living with Change,'' *Airline Business*, January 1, 2003, p. 26.

Boland, Vincent, ''CSA Adopts a New Flight Plan—The Czech Airline Is Seeking a Domestic Partner,'' *Financial Times* (London), November 24, 1994, p. 30.

''CSA—Best Airlines Company in Eastern Europe,'' *English Press Digests*, April 29, 2002.

Davies, R.E.G., *A History of the World's Airlines*, London: Oxford University Press, 1964.

Dokoupil, Martin, ''Czech Airline Plans Expansion Despite Global Gloom,'' *Reuters News*, February 13, 2003.

Dragomir, ''CSA Draws Up Cost-Cutting Program, Says Route Network Will Not Change,'' *Prague Business Journal*, December 3, 2001.

Francis, David R., ''Flying to Freedom Via a Canadian Fuel Stop; Czechoslovak 'Vacationers' Heading to Cuba Defect in Montreal,'' *Christian Science Monitor*, December 2, 1986.

Hastings, Phillip, ''Czechs Tackle Infrastructure,'' *AirCommerce*, August 26, 1996, p. 9.

Henderson, Leslie, ''Prague's Popularity Means Business Is Soaring for Airlines,'' *Prague Post*, Bus. Sec., March 20, 1996.

Hill, Leonard, ''To Prague . . . and Beyond,'' *Air Transport World*, October 2001, p. 55.

Jeziorski, Andrzej, ''Czech Airlines Plans to Launch Charter Division in Early 1998,'' *Flight International*, August 6, 1997, p. 10.

Kayal, Michele, ''Airlines Fight to Survive in Ex-USSR,'' *Journal of Commerce*, Specials Sec., April 24, 1995, p. 8.

——, ''World-Beating Growth Rates,'' *AirCommerce*, April 24, 1995, p. 3.

Mastrini, John, ''Czech CSA Eyes 4-Fold Rise in Air Cargo Capacity,'' *Reuters News*, August 2, 1996.

Novotny, Jiri, ''Czech National Air Carrier CSA's Privatization to Be Delayed until 2004–2005,'' *World News Connection*, November 22, 2002.

Ruzicka, Milan, ''Czechoslovak Airlines Hopes to Survive Recession and Breakup,'' *Journal of Commerce*, November 3, 1992, p. 2B.

''Western Accounting Shows CSA Profitable—Czech Doesn't,'' *CTK Business News*, May 10, 1995.

Woodard, Colin, ''East European Airlines Find Western Partners,'' *Christian Science Monitor*, October 20, 1994, p. 8.

''World Airline Directory Part II—Czech Airlines (CSA),'' *Flight International*, March 27, 1996.

Zivnustkova, Alena, ''Competition in Air-Cargo Market Is Taking Off,'' *Prague Post*, January 31, 1996.

——, ''Czech Air Freshens Up Planes, Even Uniforms,'' *Budapest Business Journal*, April 15, 1996, p. 22.

——, ''High-Flying Professionals,'' *Prague Post,* January 3, 1996.

——, ''Skies Clear Amid Air Battle for Prague,'' *Prague Business Journal*, March 13, 2000.

—Frederick C. Ingram

Chicago National League Ball Club, Inc.

Wrigley Field
1060 West Addison Street
Chicago, Illinois 60613-4397
U.S.A.
Telephone: (773) 404-2827
Toll Free: (800) 347-2827
Fax: (773) 404-4129
Web site: http://www.chicago.cubs.mlb.com

Wholly Owned Subsidiary of Tribune Company
Founded: 1876
Sales: $156 million (2003)
NAIC: 711211 Sports Teams and Clubs

Chicago National League Ball Club, Inc., better known to Major League Baseball fans as the Chicago Cubs, is a subsidiary of the publicly traded media giant Tribune Company. The Cubs have played longer in one city than any other sports franchise. After winning a number of championships in its early history, the Cubs have evolved into sports' most lovable losers, failing to win the World Series since 1908 and not even reaching the Series since 1945. Win or lose, the Cubs have been a perennial favorite on Chicago's WGN television superstation, and draw well at the gate. Often the team's ballpark, Wrigley Field, the second oldest in Major League baseball, is a greater attraction than the team itself. It was the last major league stadium to install lights, and any changes to the facility are met with community opposition, leading to efforts to have Wrigley designated a landmark, which would give the city the power to veto any major renovations.

Late 19th Century Origins

The history of professional baseball dates back to the 1869 Cincinnati Red Stockings, a barnstorming team that took on and defeated all challengers. In 1870 the Chicago White Stockings was formed to challenge the Reds, and in 1871 became one of the founding members of the National Association, baseball's first professional league. At the end of the league's inaugural season, the team's ballpark was destroyed by the great Chicago fire, and the club was forced to withdraw from the National Association for the next two years.

When it resumed play, one of its early boosters, coal baron William A Hulbert, emerged as an officer, and a year later took over as president. Not only would he found the Chicago Cubs, he would have a major influence on the history of professional baseball. The game at the time was poorly run and suffered from the rampant practice of players jumping from one club to another, regardless of contracts. Convinced that he was operating under a disadvantage because of an eastern bias in the game, Hulbert felt no compunction about luring several players away from Boston's perennial championship club. Anticipating retribution from the eastern owners, Hulbert made a preemptive strike; he convinced other club owners to form a new league. Thus, in 1876 the National League was organized, promising to put baseball on a more sound business footing, with contracts honored, no play on Sunday, no drinking, and no gambling. The strongest National Association franchises joined the new league, and the National Association soon disbanded.

Hulbert would become both the president of the National League and the Chicago franchise, which would win the league's first championship. Hulbert died in 1882 at the age of 49, but he had been responsible for a number of important practices in professional baseball, such as having the league determine team schedules (rather than club secretaries), hiring professional umpires, and writing a reserve clause into baseball contracts. This clause bound a player to a club from year to year, and although it prevented contract jumping, it was open to abuse and kept down player salaries. It wasn't until the 1970s that baseball players gained the right to become free agents after fulfilling the terms of their contract.

In 1882 the team's manager, Albert Spaulding, replaced Hulbert as the owner of the Chicago franchise. Spaulding had also been a star pitcher and was already starting to build a sporting goods business that still bears his name. During this early period the Chicago club was known by a variety of nicknames: the White Stockings, Colts, and Orphans. They were also winners, taking the league championship in six of the National League's first 11 seasons. It wasn't until 1902 that the nickname of the Cubs was applied to the team, first appearing in

Key Dates:

1876: The Chicago National League team is founded.
1906: The Cubs moniker is officially adopted.
1908: Cubs win the World Series.
1914: Wrigley Field (originally named Weeghman Park) is constructed.
1921: William Wrigley becomes the Cubs' owner.
1932: Wrigley dies, leaving the team in the hands of his son Philip.
1945: Cubs make another World Series appearance.
1981: The Wrigley family sells the team to Tribune Company.
1988: Lights are installed at Wrigley Field.
2003: Cubs lose final two games of Champion Series, again failing to reach World Series.

a March 27, 1902, article in the *Chicago Daily News.* The name was officially adopted by the club in 1907.

There was also a change in ownership in 1902 when Spalding's agent, James A. Hart, took over. Three years later he was looking to sell. A former newspaperman and press agent for the New York Giants named Charles W. Murphy had been hired to work for the Chicago team, but when he learned of Hart's intentions, he bought the Cubs, using $100,000 he borrowed from his former publisher, Charles Phelps Taft, the older half-brother of William Howard Taft, who would be elected President of the United States in 1908. Because the team was successful, Murphy was soon able to repay Taft, who retained a minority interest.

World Champions in 1908

During Murphy's tenure the club became the first back-to-back winners of the World Series, which pitted the National League Champions against the best team in the upstart American League. The early years of the century were also the golden era for the Chicago Cubs. The 1908 World Championship would be the last in club history through 2003. It was also the period that witnessed the best-known double-play combination in baseball history—Tinkers to Evers to Chance—immortalized in a piece by *New York Times* writer Franklin Pierce. In truth, by modern standards they did not complete a high number of double-plays, and it was ironic that they should be linked together for posterity, given that Tinkers and Evers utterly despised one another.

The Cubs in 1908 were also involved in what was arguably the most controversial moment in baseball history: the "bonehead Merkle" incident. During that season the Cubs were in a tight race with the New York Giants for the National League title when on September 23, 1908, the two teams met in New York's Polo Grounds in a crucial game. The Giants appeared to win the game in their final at bat with a two-out hit, but 19-year-old Giant rookie Fred Merkle, the runner at first, failed to touch second base. Rather, he ran for the clubhouse in center field to avoid the crowd surging onto the field. The Cubs retrieved the ball, or at least claimed they did, and touched second base, thus forcing out Merkle, negating the run, and extending the game. Because a similar circumstance involving the Cubs had occurred earlier in the season, the umpires were alerted to such a possibility and agreed with the Cubs' argument and called out Merkle. The league ruled that the game would be replayed at the end of the season, if necessary. Since the teams were tied in the standings, the game was played, the Cubs won, and went on to defend their World Championship.

Murphy later wore out his welcome with Cubs' fans for trading away popular players and doing little to prevent World Series' tickets getting into the hands of speculators who jacked up the price. He was also becoming unpopular with his fellow owners for unflattering comments he made to the press about Major League Baseball. The National League owners banded together to oust Murphy in 1914, and Taft stepped in to buy Murphy's interest for approximately $500,000. Taft also made it clear, however, that he did not intend to hold the club for very long. Finding no acceptable financial offers, he held onto the team until 1916, finally selling the Cubs to restaurateur Charles Weeghman and a group of partners. Weeghman was the owner of the Chicago Whales of the Federal League, a rival big league that played in 1915, and took Major League Baseball to court. As part of a settlement between the two parties, Weeghman was allowed to buy into the National League. He moved the Cubs to the new Northside ballpark he called Weeghman Park, which he had built the year before for the Whales at a cost of $250,000.

One of Weeghman's minority partners was William K. Wrigley, Jr., a lifelong baseball fan who moved to Chicago from Philadelphia, where he was born in 1861, the son of a soap maker. Wrigley started his own soap business in Chicago, and as an inducement to merchants for carrying his scouring soap he offered baking powder as premium. When baking powder proved more popular than the soap, he began selling the baking powder and offered chewing gum as a premium. Then chewing gum was even more popular, and Wrigley cast his lot with the future of chewing gum. In 1893 he introduced Juicy Fruit and Spearmint gums, and by advertising heavily he was able to make Wrigley's Spearmint the most popular chewing gum in America and make himself a wealthy man. Wrigley loved to spend afternoons at the ballpark with friends, and he quietly began buying up stock in the club so that by 1921 he became sole owner. Single-deck Weeghman Park now became Cubs Park in 1921 and was renamed Wrigley Field in 1926, the same year that plans were announced to add a second deck, which would increase seating to 40,000. Also of note during the 1920s, WGN Radio, on April 14, 1925, broadcast its first regular season Cubs game.

The Wrigley Years

Under William Wrigley's ownership, the Cubs were willing to spend on top players and fielded winning teams, albeit no World Champions. When he died in 1932 he left the chewing gum business and the Cubs to his son, Philip Knight "P.K." Wrigley. Reportedly Wrigley, on his deathbed, elicited a promise from Philip to never sell his beloved Cubs. P.K. Wrigley never did sell the team, but he was also reluctant to spend money on the club. To get fans to come out to Wrigley Field, he decided to sell ambience. He was quoted as saying, "The Fun . . . the sunshine, the relaxation. Our idea is to get the public to go see a ball game, win or lose.'' In 1937 the famous vines were planted on the outfield wall, and bleachers and a new scoreboard would be installed. Wrigley's approach may have angered fans who wanted to root for winners, but his ballpark kept bringing them back. Wrigley Field would remain standing as other cities tore down their vintage ballparks, replacing them with multipurpose stadiums in the 1960s and 1970s. Wrigley Field was the last to install lights, which had begun appearing in the 1930s at major league parks. The Cubs actually purchased lighting equipment in 1941, but on the day after the Pearl Harbor attack that led to America's entry into World War II, Wrigley donated the equipment to the War Department. During his lifetime he never tried installing lights at Wrigley Field. Most owners had turned to lights as an economic necessity, to boost attendance, but Wrigley lacked the need, and since all the other clubs installed lights, not having them made Wrigley Field even more unique.

The Cubs next made it to the World Series in 1945. According to lore, William ''Billy Goat'' Sianis, the Greek-immigrant owner of a local establishment, the Lincoln Tavern, was not allowed to bring his pet goat Murphy into Wrigley Field to watch the fourth game of the series even though the goat had a ticket. Angered that Murphy had been turned away because he smelled, Sianis placed a curse on the team, saying ''Cubs, they not gonna win anymore.'' After the Cubs lost the series to Detroit, Sianis sent a telegram to Wrigley: ''Who smells now?''

After decades of success, the Cubs now became perennial losers, but their fans would at least be able to follow the team's exploits on the newly invented television. On April 16, 1948, WGN-TV broadcast its first game, an exhibition between the Cubs and the crosstown rival White Sox. The fortunes of the Cubs became so bad that in 1960 the team implemented what it called a ''College of Coaches,'' a system in which the team's coaches took turns as manager. The idea was scrapped after five seasons, and Leo Durocher was brought in. He built a strong club that appeared to be on the verge of returning the Cubs to the World Series in 1969. However, the upstart New York Mets began catching up, and although Sianis, who would die a year later, supposedly lifted the curse, the Cubs faltered badly and ended up eight games behind the Mets, who would go on to win the World Series that October.

The Enlightening 1980s

During the 1970s the Cubs would often lead their division only to fall short. In 1977 P.K. Wrigley died, and the family sold the team to the Tribune Company four years later. Tribune was the parent company of WGN, and by buying the Cubs it locked up very valuable programming, which it would then be able to distribute to cable systems via satellite, joining WTBS in Atlanta, which broadcast Braves' games, as a so-called superstation. A new management team was installed with the Cubs, a number of players changed, and the team won a division title in 1984, only to fall short in the playoffs, losing to the San Diego Padres and again failing to reach the World Series.

Because the Cubs came so close to playing in the World Series, Wrigley Field's lack of lights became an issue for Major League Baseball, which wanted all World Series' games played at night in order to attain the highest television ratings. The Cubs began the lengthy process of gaining approval to install lights, a move opposed by baseball purists as well as people who lived in the residential area surrounding the park. Finally, in February 1988 the Chicago City Council passed an ordinance permitting a limited number of night baseball games at Wrigley Field. The first game under the lights at Wrigley was scheduled for August 8, 1988, with the Philadelphia Phillies, but rain caused a cancellation after three-and-a-half innings. The first official night game would have to wait until the next day. Later in 1988, the team reaffirmed its commitment to Wrigley Field by launching a $14 million renovation project that would add 67 mezzanine suites and a new press box.

In 1992 Major League Baseball Commissioner Fay Vincent proposed moving the Cubs from the Eastern to the Western division, an idea that was vehemently opposed by the Tribune Company, which was concerned about having so many West Coast games on WGN that would not only attract fewer viewers but also disrupt the station's highly profitable local news broadcast. In the end, the Cubs stayed, and Commissioner Vincent left. Several years later, baseball would realign further and the Cubs would be placed in the National League's Central division, a change that met with no opposition from the club.

Although the Cubs and their fans were wedded to Wrigley Field, the club was at a disadvantage compared to other teams with larger capacities and revenues from luxury suites, naming rights, and large parking concessions. For years, the Cubs battled with the row houses across the street from the outfield fences where makeshift seating was set up. At first it was just lawn chairs and maybe a kettle grill or two, but the rooftops evolved into revenue-generating enterprises. In 2002 the team constructed large windscreens that blocked some of the view and later in the year sued the rooftop operators. A deal was reached before the start of the 2004 season, with the rooftop owners agreeing to pay the Cubs 17 percent of their revenues. They simply passed that cost onto their patrons, who happily paid the increased ticket price. It was a win-win solution for both sides. The Cubs took in additional revenues, and the rooftop owners were able to book corporate parties in advance, knowing that there would be no disruption.

The Late 1990s and Beyond

In the late 1990s Cubs fans were entertained by the home-run exploits of outfielder Sammy Sosa, but it was the team's development of outstanding pitching that made it a contender. The team made it to the postseason in 2003 and was on the verge of making it to the World Series for the first time in half a century, when once again fate intervened. A Cubs' fan ended up snagging a foul boul that the Cubs fielders might have caught, giving the Florida Marlins new life in game six of the National League Championship Series. The Marlins won that night and closed out the series in seven games, then went on to win the World Series. For the Cubs the cry was once again ''Wait until next year.''

Meanwhile, Tribune Company was interested in expanding Wrigley Field and adding more night games, ideas that once again met stiff opposition from the community. The city threatened to designate Wrigley Field as a landmark, which would prevent the Cubs from doing much without government approval. It was also uncertain how committed Tribune was to its ownership of the Cubs. Because of its investment in the WB Network, WGN was less dependent on the Cubs for programming. Moreover, Tribune appeared ready to launch a major television-station buying spree and could use the $300 million the club would likely fetch. During Tribune's ownership of the Cubs, however, there were periodic rumors that it was about to sell. Whether they would prove to be true this time remained to be seen.

Principal Operating Units

Mesa Cubs; Boise Hawks; Lansing Lugnuts; Dayton Cubs; West Tenn Diamond Jaxx; Iowa Cubs.

Principal Competitors

St. Louis Cardinals, L.P.; Houston Astros Baseball Club; Milwaukee Brewers Baseball Club; The Cincinnati Reds; Pittsburgh Baseball Club.

Further Reading

Gentile, Derek, *The Complete Chicago Cubs,* New York: Black Dog & Leventhal Publishers, 2004, 704 p.

McClellan, Steve, ''Cubs Balks at Vincent Move,'' *Broadcasting,* July 13, 1992, p. 10.

Mullman, Jeremy, ''Fun at the Ol' Ballpark,'' *Crain's Chicago Business,* June 2, 2003, p. A141.

Thorn, John, et. al., *Total Baseball*, Kingston, N.Y.: Total Sports, 1999, 2538 p.

—Ed Dinger

Church's Chicken

980 Hammond Drives N.E., Suite 1100
Atlanta, Georgia 30328
U.S.A.
Telephone: (770) 350-3800
Toll Free: (866) 232-4402
Fax: (770) 512-3920
Web site: http://www/churchs.com

Division of AFC Enterprises, Inc.
Incorporated: 1969 as Church's Fried Chicken, Inc.
Employees: 7,000 (est.)
Sales: $300 million (2003 est.)
NAIC: 722211 Limited-Service Restaurants

A division of AFC Enterprises, Inc., Church's Chicken owns and franchises more than 1,500 fast food chicken restaurants in some 30 states and a dozen countries. About 80 percent of the units are franchised operations. Church's menu centers around Southern-style chicken and features such side dishes as mashed potatoes and gravy, fried okra, cole slaw, Honey Butter Biscuits and Jalapeno Cheese Bombers. In addition to Church's, the parent company owns the Popeyes Chicken & Biscuits chain. Since mid-2004, AFC has been looking to sell off Church's to concentrate on Popeyes.

1950s Origins

Church's founder was George W. Church, Sr. After retiring from a career in the poultry business, working as an incubator salesman, Church was 65 when he decided to launch a business selling fried chicken, pursuing a fast food concept that was ahead of its time. He kept overhead to a minimum and concentrated on offering a high-quality product at a low cost, prepared for carryout to appeal to the increasingly mobile lifestyle of a post-World War II population. In 1952, he opened a walk-up restaurant that was little more than a stand across the street from the Alamo in San Antonio, Texas. It was called ''Church's Fried Chicken to Go,'' an apt name since the restaurant only offered takeout service and sold nothing but fried chicken. As a novelty, the cookers were located next to the window, allowing customers to watch their orders being prepared. It was not until 1955 that he added French fries and jalapenos to the menu. The restaurant was a success, prompting Church to open three more restaurants in San Antonio. However, George Church would not live to see his concept grow further. He died in 1956, and other members of his family took over the operation.

It was George W. (Bill) Church, Jr., who fostered the dream of one day spreading Church's Fried Chicken across the country. When he took over the management of the company in 1962, there were eight locations in San Antonio, and for the time being he was content to concentrate on that limited market. Three years later, Church and his older brother Richard made a key contribution when they developed a marinating formula that could be made virtually anywhere. As a result, Church would be able to spread beyond San Antonio and still maintain a level of quality control on their signature fried chicken. In was also in 1965 that J. David Bamberger joined forces with Church to launch a separate franchise operation.

Bamberger grew up poor in Ohio during the Depression on a four-acre farm that lacked running water and electricity. He worked his way through college by selling Kirby vacuum cleaners on his 40-mile commute to school each day, and after graduating with a business administration degree he stayed on with Kirby. In 1951, he was assigned to work in Tyler, Texas, and later transferred to San Antonio. Bamberger was an exceptional salesman and an even more dynamic motivator of a sales force he managed. One of his salesmen was Bill Church.

As an investor and executive, Bamberger played a key role in the expansion of Church's Fried Chicken, which became the first Texas-based fast-food chain to go national. His idea was to locate units in poor urban neighborhoods, areas that other chains like Kentucky Fried Chicken avoided. About breaking new ground in the hiring and education of employees, Bamberger told *Texas Monthly* in a 2000 profile, ''I sold it to Bill that this was just a step above door-to-door vacuum cleaner sales. We're gonna take the people who are the first to be laid off in a construction job and take them inside, teach them how to clean their fingernails—no one wants to see their chicken handed to them by someone who had to change his car battery that morning—tie a necktie, how to use deodorant, and say, 'Thank

> **Company Perspectives:**
>
> *The Church's concept has always been based on the philosophy of simplicity of operation, starting with a limited menu, equipment designed to do one thing well, people trained to do one thing well and control of operational costs.*

you.' '' In 1967, the first units opened in five other Texas cities, so that by the following year the company was generating sales of $2.7 million from 17 restaurants. The Church family sold its interest in 1968 to the franchise company started by Bamberger and Bill Church. A year later, to fuel the expansion of the chain, the business was incorporated in 1969 as Church's Fried Chicken and taken public. By the end of the year, Church's operated more than 100 restaurants located in seven states.

Leadership Changes in the 1970s

Church's tried to catch up with the segment leader, Kentucky Fried Chicken. By the end of 1974, the chain had grown to 487 units located in 22 states, with total revenues in excess of $100 million. However, CEO Bill Church and Bamberger, his executive vice-president, were no longer in agreement on how to continue growing the business. In 1974, Bamberger quit, citing ''philosophical differences,'' although he remained the company's largest shareholder, owning 1.2 million shares. Picking up the slack was Roger A. Harvin, a childhood friend of Bill Church, who was trained as a plant pathologist but went into the restaurant business in 1967 when he became assistant manager of three Texas Church's restaurants. He then worked his way up through the ranks, became president in 1975, and took on increasing responsibility as Bill Church became less involved in the business. In 1980, Church resigned as chairman of the corporation and Harvin replaced him.

Church's enjoyed a strong run in the 1970s, emerging as the second-largest chain in the chicken segment. The company began to expand internationally in 1979, opening a restaurant in Japan. Also during that decade, Church's became involved in the burger segment, launching a chain called G.W. Jrs. By 1982, the company would operate 62 of these restaurants in Texas. During the early 1980s, however, Church's growth stagnated. There was also disunity at the top levels of management. Early in 1983, James Parker, executive vice-president of operations quit. He was soon followed by chief financial officer William Storm, who resigned according to a company official because of ''philosophical differences with management.'' After leaving the company, Storm criticized Harvin's reluctance to spend money on new concepts or experimentation. Harvin attempted to be more aggressive in the months following Storm's departure. He made a greater commitment to advertising and acquired the Houston-based Ron's Krispy Fried Chicken, a more upscale 74-unit chain that the company hoped would establish it in more upscale, suburban markets, as opposed to Church's traditional inner-city base. In addition, Church's launched a new concept, Charro's, to compete in the charbroiled, Mexican-style area. However, by early November 1983, Harvin resigned and Bamberger returned to replace him. According to press reports, Bamberger engineered Harvin's ouster and stepped in to protect his investment in Church's.

Bamberger served as Church's president on an interim basis until he was able to lure Richard F. Sherman away from the Hardees restaurant chain. The company soon closed more than 100 units and pumped up the advertising budget. Efforts were also made to grow the G.W. Jrs. chain, but management soon gave up on the concept, exiting the burger market in 1985. Because of Bamberger's return, Church's became the subject of constant takeover rumors which maintained that Bamberger was simply dressing up the company in order to sell it. Also during this period, Church's was part of a bizarre rumor that became something of an urban legend in the African-American communities of Memphis, Denver, Detroit, Chicago, and San Diego. According to the stories, Church's was owned by the Klu Klux Klan, which incorporated something into the chicken recipe that would render African-American males either impotent or sterile. The rumors, however bereft of logic, did have a negative impact on Church's sales, according to company memos that came to light during a court case involving a franchisee that sued the company because it had not informed him about the rumors.

In 1985, Church's generated $548 million from 1,500 units, of which fewer than 300 were franchise operations. Sherman and Bamberger tried to strike a 50–50 balance between company-owned and franchised operations as well as taking steps, such as introducing catfish to the menu, to revitalize the chain. Despite management's adoption of a long-range strategy, Church's was still dogged by takeover speculation, for which there was a sound underpinning: most of the company-owned restaurants were located on land owned by Church's, which made the company more valuable than might appear on the surface. In 1987, Sherman resigned and joined forces with Stephen Lynn, the CEO of Sonic Industries and a former Kentucky Fried Chicken executive, to make a bid for Church's. While this $12.25-a-share buyout offer was rejected, another would succeed in early 1989, engineered by Al Copeland, the flamboyant founder of Popeyes Famous Fried Chicken.

Like Bamberger, Copeland grew up poor, a high-school dropout in New Orleans who worked as a soda jerk to help support his mother. After working for his older brother, who ran a chain of donut shops, Copeland became a franchisee when he was just 18. He was running a successful donut operation when he decided to get into the chicken fast food business after a Kentucky Fried Chicken store opened in New Orleans. In 1971, he launched Chicken on the Run, which at first proved to be a disaster. Only when he adopted a spicier Cajun-inspired recipe did the business turn around. He also changed the name to Popeyes Mighty Good Fried Chicken, an allusion to Popeye Doyle, the detective played by Gene Hackman in a hit film at the time, *The French Connection.* Copeland began franchising in 1977, and by the early 1980s Popeyes trailed only Kentucky Fried Chicken and Church's as the largest fast-food chicken chains. Copeland was a one-man management team, but his interests expanded beyond Popeyes to include other restaurant concepts, so that by 1988 he established the positions of president, chief financial officer, and executive vice-president of operations. Two of these slots were filled by executives he hired away from Church's, including CFO Lewis Kilbourne.

Copeland was interested in expanding through acquisitions and soon targeted Church's, which led to speculation that

Key Dates:

1952: George W. Church opens the first store outside the Alamo in San Antonio.
1955: Side dishes are first offered.
1969: The company incorporates and is taken public.
1989: Church's is acquired by Al Copeland and merged with Popeyes restaurant chain.
1992: America's Favorite Chicken Company assumes control of Church's following bankruptcy.
2002: Church's celebrates its 50th anniversary.

Kilbourne, who had signed an agreement not to disclose confidential information when he left Church's, might have revealed company secrets to help Copeland craft an offer. At the very least, Kilbourne was able to persuade Copeland to make a bid despite the two chains' seeming incompatibility. Popeyes, although smaller, was decidedly more upscale than Church's. According to *Restaurant Business,* ''Kilbourne's thinking went this way. Church's was a valid concept that had overexpanded. It was an ideal acquisition target; it had no debt and it was rich in real estate, with some 70 percent of the stores company-owned. Popeyes would buy Church's, slash the losers, and sell off competing stores to Popeyes franchisees for conversion and also to Church's franchises. A much smaller but profitable chain of 600 to 800 stores would be left. Sale proceeds would be used to pare down debt.''

The AFC Purchase: 1980s and Beyond

In October 1988, Copeland offered $8 a share, or $300 million, but by now Church's was headed by Ernie Renaud, the former president of Long John Silver's, and he was showing some success in his turnaround efforts, closing down unprofitable stores and building up the sales volumes in the remaining units. As a result, the price went up, but in February 1989 Copeland finally prevailed, although the final cost was $480 million, funded by junk bonds. The key to making the deal work was the immediate closing of another 100 money-losing units and the sell off of 250 more units. However, after closing the losing stores, Copeland failed to sell off properties because he asked franchisees to pay unrealistic prices. After the first year, only 54 Church's were sold to franchisees instead of 250. Franchisees also became disgruntled because Copeland increased the cost of a reformulated marinade mix as well as the ad fund charges. Efforts to convert Church's stores to the Popeyes' format also proved disappointing.

By 1990, Copeland Enterprises was in default on $391 million in debts, and in April 1991 the company filed for bankruptcy protection. In October 1992, the court approved a plan by a group of Copeland's creditors that resulted in the creation of America's Favorite Chicken Company, Inc. (AFC) to serve as the new parent company for Popeyes and Church's. The former president of Arby's Inc., Frank J. Belatti, became AFC chairman and CEO and promptly moved the company's headquarters from New Orleans to Atlanta. He soon launched efforts to improve relationships with franchisees and upgrade operations and quality. In addition, Popeyes and Church's were placed into separate units, and Church's for the first time in years was able to able to grow without being overshadowed by Popeyes.

In 1993, Hala Moddelmog was named vice-president of marketing. Three years later, she became president, one of the few women to reach the top ranks in the restaurant industry. She grew up in rural Georgia and worked her way through Georgia Southern College before earning a master's in communications at the University of Georgia. She went to work at Arby's as a marketer in 1981, involved in the chain's development of a popular chicken sandwich. After a stint with Bell South, she took a job with Arby's Franchise Association as vice-president of marketing and strategic planning. She then followed Belatti to Church's, where she set about upgrading the chain's image. A new logo was introduced and the restaurant's decor was improved. As president, she introduced honey-buttered biscuits to replace the plain dinner rolls Church's had been serving and invested in ovens to make sure each unit was able to offer them.

Church's pursued a number of ideas during the 1990s to revitalize the business. It opened kiosks and operations in convenience stores and co-branded with the White Castle hamburger chain in several dozen locations. In the mid-1990s, Church's tried a line of Mexican food products, but it proved to be a costly mistake and was quickly discontinued. Nevertheless, the venture taught Moddelmog not to lose sight of what was the core of the Church's franchise. When urged to consider turkey-based additions to the menu, she declined. In 1997, however, she did approve the introduction of spicy chicken wings, which helped to spur a growth in sales. In 1999, Church's added buffalo chicken wings, macaroni and cheese, seasoned beans and rice, and collard greens. Church's ramped up efforts to expand internationally in 2000, with the goal of growing the number of overseas units from 314 in nine countries to 1,000 within four to five years. Central and South American Countries were the immediate target.

When Church's celebrated its 50th anniversary in 2002, the chain was 1,500 units in size, a significant increase over the 1,000 restaurants that remained following Copeland's bankruptcy. Although Church's had experienced some setbacks in the previous decade, Moddelmog generally presided over a successful turnaround. By 2004, however, Church's and Popeyes were no longer compatible operations for AFC, as the two chains were beginning to encroach on each another. AFC had already sold most of its Seattle Coffee Co. brand and was looking to sell off its Cinnabon chain. Belatti decided that AFC needed to concentrate on one of its two chicken brands and elected to divest Church's, hiring Bear, Stearns & Co to evaluate the options. Church's was at its peak value, and it also owned more real estate than Popeyes, giving the chain a better chance to arrange financing. To help in the divestiture, AFC decentralized some functions, a change that made Church's more self-sufficient and therefore more attractive to a potential buyer while enabling the chain to be fully prepared as it embarked once again as an independent business.

Principal Competitors

Chick-fil-A Inc.; KFC Corporation; McDonald's Corporation.

Further Reading

Ely, E.S., "Showdown: How Al Copeland May Yet Skunk Wall Street," *Restaurant Business*, January 1, 1992, p. 60.

Foster, Christine, "Down-Home Girl Makes Good," *Forbes*, November 17, 1997, p. 73.

Fucini, Joseph J., and Suzy Fucini, *Entrepreneurs*, Boston: G.K. Hall & Co., 1985, 297 p.

Lang, Joan, "Church's Is Changing Its Tune," *Restaurant Business*, April 10, 1986, p. 122.

Spielberg, Susan, "AFC Taps Popeyes Prexy, Plans to Pluck Church's," *Nation's Restaurant News*, June 14, 2004, p. 1.

—Ed Dinger

Compuware Corporation

One Campus Martius
Detroit, Michigan 48226
U.S.A.
Telephone: (313) 227-7300
Toll Free: (800) 521-9353
Fax: (313) 227-7555
Web site: http://www.compuware.com

Public Company
Incorporated: 1973
Employees: 8,660
Sales: $1.26 billion (2004)
Stock Exchanges: NASDAQ
Ticker Symbol: CPWR
NAIC: 511210 Software Publishers; 541511 Custom Computer Programming Services; 541512 Computer Systems Design Services

Compuware Corporation is one of the largest software developers in the world, serving some 3,000 corporate clients by developing, marketing, and supporting systems software products that help maximize efficiency and contain costs, among other things. From more than 100 offices in 45 countries, Compuware focuses on information technology (IT) solutions for a wide variety of clients including Ford Motor Co., Blue Cross/Blue Shield, Safeway, and PacifiCorp. Compuware counts among its clients some 90 percent of the *Fortune* 100 companies, and it strives to serve all clients according to its defining principles: the customer, service, excellence, integrity, diversity, diligence, and creativity.

Early Years

Compuware was established in 1973 by three cofounders: Peter Karmanos, Thomas Thewes, and Allen B. Cutting. According to a *Detroit News* report, Karmanos, Thewes, and Cutting pooled $9,000 to establish the company. Their original mission statement was: ''We will help people do things with computers.''

The first office occupied by the fledgling company was located in Southfield, Michigan. Originally, clients came to Compuware for data processing professional services and help with computer installations. In addition, Compuware offered ''programmers for hire'' to provide additional manpower for specific client projects or to create solutions to particular needs. Unlike other companies specializing in software and computer services for a specific industry, Compuware differentiated itself from competing companies by its emphasis on diverse applications of mainframe computer technology. Karmanos, quoted in the company's 20th anniversary publication, stated: ''We were there to help them solve computer problems. . . . We were a resource—a technology resource—to help our customers work smarter and be more productive.''

Compuware continued in its original role as a provider of data processing professional services until 1977 when the company entered the software market with a fault diagnosis tool called Abend-AID. The name Abend-AID was derived from the term abnormal end, which referred to unexpected system errors or failures. These types of problems were often caused by faults in computer programs, changes in system environments, or other errors or failures.

Prior to the availability of Abend-AID, computer programmers confronted with abnormal end situations were required to use manual techniques to test and debug programs. The process involved preparing trial transactions through lengthy procedures such as manually creating experimental entries, writing special test programs, and reviewing program logic. Compuware called this process ''tedious, time consuming, and error-prone.'' The Abend-AID program worked automatically. It intercepted system error messages during actual program execution. This enabled programmers to pinpoint precise error locations and identify the cause of the failure. Abend-AID also offered recommendations for necessary corrections.

Because mainframe computers were critical to business operations, time spent correcting problems often had a significant effect on a company's ability to conduct business. Quick remedies helped reduce the amount of downtime associated with computer problems and helped reduce programmer manpower costs. Abend-AID's success in the marketplace enabled Compuware to become established as a major force in the industry.

Company Perspectives:

Compuware will be the best worldwide provider of quality software products and services designed to increase productivity. We will continue to create practical solutions that meet our customers' needs and surpass their expectations. We will provide an environment for our employees where excellence is encouraged and rewarded and where diversity is promoted at all levels of the company.

A New Focus on Software in the 1980s

Following the introduction of Abend-AID, Compuware organized a products division to sell Abend-AID and other software packages. Although the company continued to provide services, the percentage of total revenue generated by the services division grew smaller as sales from the products division increased. The company's offerings focused on integrated systems software products designed to improve programmer productivity through program testing, data manipulation, interactive debugging, and fault diagnosis.

Interactive analysis and debugging products were tools to help programmers identify and correct errors in software by evaluating the quality of a program's code and logic. They worked by enabling a programmer to use either test or production data and progress through a program one statement or statement group at a time. Whenever an error was detected, the programmer could stop and make an immediate correction. Using this process, programs could be tested one step at a time until they were free from errors. The first software package in the interactive analysis and debugging product line, MBX Xpediter/TSO, was introduced in 1979. In 1983 Xpediter earned Compuware its first International Computer Program (ICP) award, granted in recognition of $1 million in sales.

File and data management software packages were used to automate test data preparation, thereby insuring the integrity of the data manipulated by programs. Compuware launched its line of file and data management products in 1983. The first offering in the line, File-AID, was originally sold under an exclusive marketing arrangement with another company, but rights to the program were purchased by Compuware in 1992. Using File-AID, programmers had immediate and direct access to the data necessary to conduct tests and analyze production work. Although early File-AID products were designed for IBM and IBM-compatible mainframe computers only, subsequent File-AID products were designed for other types of computers.

CICS-dBUG-AID, designed for use with IBM's CICS (Customer Information Control System) was introduced in 1985. The following year, Compuware introduced MVS PLAYBACK, the company's first product in its automated testing line. PLAYBACK simulated an online systems environment that helped computer technicians execute transactions and check data created by manipulation. PLAYBACK streamlined testing procedures by reproducing a real-time environment without requiring that network users staff terminals or even that the communications network be active. Products in the PLAYBACK family offered five phases of testing: the ability to test a single program from a single terminal; the ability to test a single program from more than one terminal; the ability to test the integration of more than one program; the ability to test a program's proficiency at varying production volumes; and the ability to confirm that programming changes made no unexpected consequences in other areas. Subsequent products in the PLAYBACK line permitted the creation of training sessions for network users.

Compuware entered a phase of rapid growth during the second half of the 1980s. In 1987 Inc. magazine ranked Compuware among the fastest growing privately held companies in the United States. Its premier product, Abend-AID, received an ICP $100 million award, and IBM recognized Compuware as a business partner-authorized application specialist. In addition, Compuware expanded its global presence. Following a decision to operate in Europe through wholly owned subsidiaries, Compuware acquired European companies that had been distributing its software products in England, France, Italy, Spain, and West Germany.

To accommodate its expansion, Compuware announced a decision to build new headquarters in 1987. The $20 million facility, located in Farmington Hills, Michigan, provided 165,000 square feet of space in addition to a 4,000-square-foot satellite facility in Southfield, Michigan. When Compuware moved in, it employed 746 people and expected to increase its staff to 995 within a year. The company's annual compound growth rate for the previous five years stood at 34 percent. Software products accounted for 65 percent of revenues; professional data processing services contributed 30 percent; the remaining sales were generated from software developed for specific markets and from educational resources. As the 1980s ended, Compuware broke the $100 million mark in total annual revenue.

Going Public and Further Growth in the Early 1990s

The 1990s brought an increased interest in expansion and growth through acquisition. For example, in 1991 Compuware merged with Centura Software in a move aimed at strengthening its interactive analysis and debugging product offerings. Compuware also increased the attention given to smaller computers. Although the company historically had focused on the sale of mainframe programming software, it released a version of File-AID able to test and edit mainframe data files on personal computers (PCs). File-AID/PC enabled program developers to move blocks of data from mainframes to PCs where they could be scrutinized, copied, edited, modified, or printed. The technology provided a means for discovering programming flaws in a quick manner.

Other new products introduced in 1991 included DBA-XPERT for DB2 (a database management program) and Pathvu/2 (an OS/2 version of a previously released interactive analysis and debugging product). Like its mainframe counterpart, Pathvu/2 provided programmers working with COBOL an automated analysis and documentation tool to evaluate the structure of the programming code. To show what was happening within a program and to document missing elements in the code structure, Pathvu/2 created a graphic display of the program's organization. Compuware reported total revenues of $141.8 million in 1991.

In 1992 Compuware established Compuware Japan Corporation. Compuware Japan's main office was in Tokyo, and

Key Dates:

1973: Three suburban Detroit friends start a company offering computer programming and set-up services.
1977: Company introduces its first software product.
1978: Company expands geographically with an office to serve Baltimore and Washington, D.C.
1987: New headquarters in the Detroit suburb of Farmington Hills are constructed.
1992: Compuware goes public.
1998: Revenues surpass the $1 billion mark.
2003: A new, one million square-foot headquarters facility in downtown Detroit is completed.

company officials hoped to add a branch in Osaka. Compuware Japan planned to focus on adapting existing products for Japanese programmers using Fujitsu and Hitachi hardware in addition to IBM mainframe equipment. The following year, Compuware further expanded its presence abroad with the establishment of Compuware Corporation Do Brasil. Brazil was estimated to be the fifth largest IBM mainframe market in the world. Compuware's move followed a policy change relaxing government-imposed import restrictions on computers and software. Company officials expected the Brazilian subsidiary to be well positioned to serve the emerging Latin American market.

Compuware's initial public offering of common stock occurred in 1992. The stock was offered at $22 per share and 5.5 million shares were sold by the company. Net proceeds (after underwriting discount and other expenses) totaled $111.5 million. In addition, existing shareholders sold 3.9 million shares of common stock.

Despite the successful stock offering, 1992 also marked the first year since Compuware's inception that the company failed to earn a profit, when it reported a net loss totaled at $23.8 million. According to a published statement, the lack of profitability was attributed to special pretax charges of $52.6 million related to expenses surrounding its acquisition of XA Systems Corporation. XA Systems software products were classified primarily as file and data management tools.

In a move designed to augment its fault diagnosis product line, Compuware purchased the Eyewitness product line from Landmark Systems Corporation in 1993. The acquisition increased Compuware's product line to 27 software products. As of March 1993, Compuware had licensed more than 41,000 copies of its products to more than 5,700 customers around the world. Software license fees and maintenance fees produced 74 percent of the company's total revenues. The remaining 26 percent was generated from professional services.

Compuware's Professional Services Division operated branches in seven locations: Baltimore, Maryland; Columbus, Ohio; Colorado Springs, Colorado; Lansing, Michigan; Toronto, Canada; Detroit, Michigan; and Washington, D.C. Most of the revenue generated from the services division was received from business application programming services. Business application programming services were those in which Compuware's programmers wrote original software to perform a particular function. Other services division operations included analyzing business problems and using computer techniques to overcome them; providing conversion services to organizations switching from one type of computer environment to another; systems planning, a service involved in identifying business objectives and information requirements to make recommendations for hardware and software; and consulting. Although revenues earned by the services division typically carried lower profit margins than did revenues earned by the products division, Compuware stated that it remained committed to providing services to its customers.

Despite its growth and expansion, Compuware's executives insisted that the company's basic mission remained unchanged: to help people do things with computers. They acknowledged, however, that the processing power of computers had changed vastly during the company's 20 years in business.

One significant change within the industry was the expanding presence of PCs. Some industry analysts had criticized Compuware's emphasis on mainframe computer technology. In response, Compuware noted that the 36,000 mainframe computers in operation were running "mission-critical systems" applications that were not suited to PC technology. These included credit card authorization services, airline reservations, and online banking. According to Compuware's data, only 13 percent of mainframe computer operators used software to diagnose faults. Even less used software for debugging, file and data management, and automated testing. Compuware's own analysts felt a sufficient base existed for expansion in the mainframe market.

Nevertheless, in 1993 Compuware turned its attention to the PC arena with its acquisition of EcoSystems Software, Inc. The EcoSystems product line included programs designed to be used in PC networks. The PC market differed significantly from the mainframe market because of the wide variety of computer hardware manufacturers and operating systems employed. Two new products were added to the EcoSystem line during the second quarter of 1994 to help network clients schedule batch jobs and better manage database environments.

In early 1994 Compuware acquired Uniface Holding B.V. in a stock trade worth $268 million. Uniface, based in Amsterdam, Netherlands, was a supplier of client-server (network) application and development software. According to Crain's Detroit Business, industry watchers expected the acquisition to provide Compuware with a strong presence in the PC market at a time when its mainframe software licensing was still growing at a rate of about 30 percent. The acquisition also was expected to give Uniface a greater presence in the North American market. Two additional acquisitions in 1994 were Computer People Unlimited, Inc. and Meta Technologies, Inc., both information technology service firms. Compuware also purchased several product lines from other companies, including Advanced Programming Techniques Ltd.'s Oliver and Simon interactive analysis and debugging software. An indication of Compuware founder Peter Karmanos's growing wealth was his 1994 purchase of the Hartford Whalers, a National Hockey League team, which he later moved to North Carolina and renamed the Hurricanes.

In the fall of 1995 Compuware acquired CoroNet Systems of Los Altos, California, a maker of networked applications management software, and renamed the company's product EcoNet. That purchase was followed quickly by several more, including Icons GmbH of Germany, Technalysis Corp. of Minneapolis, Direct Technology Ltd. of England, and Adams & Reynolds, Inc. of Cleveland. Direct Technology made software testing products; the others were computer service firms. Compuware was increasingly offering products and services that addressed the ''Y2K'' computer software problem, and revenues from this business segment were growing rapidly as the magnitude of the problem became known. Annual revenues for fiscal 1996 hit a peak of $614 million. Compuware's overall growth had slowed, however, due in part to the lackluster showing of Uniface, and the company reorganized its structure during the year.

In 1997 Compuware purchased Vine Systems, a London, England-based consulting firm, and NuMega Technologies, Inc., of New Hampshire, which provided debugging services and products to Windows software developers. The following March the company acquired UnderWare, Inc., a Boston software defect tracking tools maker. Additional Y2K products also were being introduced by the company during this period. Sales topped $1 billion for the first time in fiscal 1998, with services accounting for nearly two-fifths of Compuware's revenues.

The company had been growing by leaps and bounds, but was still in the same Farmington Hills, Michigan, headquarters it had occupied for more than a decade. Karmanos was seeking a new home, and the nearby city of Detroit was bending over backward to lure him to its underused downtown. In early 1999 an agreement was reached for the company to move there. Two new buildings were to be constructed at a cost of $1.2 billion. To lure Compuware downtown, the city had agreed to purchase software and services from the company and provide it with huge financial incentives, including cutting the city's business tax. In April Compuware announced record sales of $1.64 billion for the fiscal year with net income of $350 million.

The company's acquisitions continued in the summer of 1999 with the purchase of Data Processing Resources Corp. of Irvine, California. The $450 million deal would give Compuware 3,400 more employees and greatly broaden the company's service business. Compuware's profits had been growing faster than its revenues, leading Business Week magazine to rank it number six on its 1999 list of 50 top-performing companies.

Beginning its second quarter-century in business, Compuware could boast of sales to most of the *Fortune* 100 companies and a 97 percent customer renewal rate. The company was making acquisitions at a rapid clip both to broaden its product line and to boost its presence in the service business. The Y2K problem was providing the company with a temporary surge in income, but it seemed certain that Compuware would be around long after the dust had settled on that particular issue.

2000 and Beyond

The 21st century brought new challenges to Compuware, above and beyond the soon-forgotten Y2K scenario. In 2002, the company embarked on a costly lawsuit against IBM, claiming that IBM had stolen a proprietary software source code. Compuware's external legal fees related to the lawsuit against IBM increased each year, costing the company $12.5 million in 2002, $34.6 million in 2003, and $45 million in 2004.

Such large legal fees, in fact, contributed to Compuserve's restructuring initiative, beginning in late 2002. The company's work force was cut by 1,600. Restructuring efforts also included a focus on acquisition in order to, according to CEO Karmanos, ''fill in product and service gaps.'' Toward that end, Compuware acquired Changepoint Corporation, a project performance management software supplier, for $100 million, and Covisint LLC, an online automotive entity, for $7 million.

Despite burgeoning legal fees and restructuring, Compuware leadership purposefully avoided offshore outsourcing strategies. Instead, the company planned to develop better products and provide better service, according to CEO Karmanos. Said Karmanos, ''I'm not interested in supplemental staffing, I'm not interested in being the cheapest supplier. I'm interested in delivering high-value technology solutions and building a company on that foundation.'' Karmanos suggested that offering more value to customers was key in battling offshore companies.

Meanwhile, Compuware continued to explore ways to offer additional value to customers, to function more efficiently, and to partner with the community. In 2003, the company moved to its new Detroit headquarters, a base for over 4,000 workers which united the company's southeastern Michigan workers and enhanced operations efficiency. Compuware had gained a new client during this time in the Detroit Public Schools, and was recognized for its efforts in saving the school system over $3 million and helping it accomplish technology goals set years prior.

Principal Subsidiaries

Compuware Ltd. (United Kingdom); Covisint LLC.

Principal Competitors

Computer Associates International Inc.; International Business Machines Corporation; Electronic Data Systems Corporation; BMC Software Inc.

Further Reading

Bennett, Jeff, ''Compuware Acquires Covisint for $7 Million,'' *Knight Ridder/Tribune Business News*, June 10, 2004.

Britt, Russ, ''Leaders & Success: Compuware's Peter Karmanos,'' *Investor's Business Daily,* June 19, 1997, p. A1.

Child, Charles, ''Compuware: Riding the Dinosaur,'' *Crain's Detroit Business,* February 15, 1993.

''Compuware Says Microsoft Partnership Paying Off,'' *eWeek,* July 14, 2004.

Compuware: 20 Years of Helping People Do Things with Computers, Farmington Hills, Mich.: Compuware Corporation, 1993.

Cunningham, Cara A., ''Pathvu/2 Taps OS/2 PM Graphics to Analyze COBOL Code,'' *PC Week,* January 6, 1992.

''Detroit Move Like a Return to Home: Compuware Owner Recalls Roots from Childhood in City,'' *Detroit News,* April 11, 1999, p. 1.

Dietderich, Andrew, ''Deciding to Stay Home,'' *Crain's Detroit Business,* June 7, 2004, p. 81.

Doler, Kathleen, ''The New America: Compuware Corp.—Giving Clients More Bang from 'Big Iron,' '' *Investor's Business Daily,* June 17, 1994, p. A4.

Henderson, Tom, ''CompuGrowth: Pete Karmanos Grew Compuware into a Mega-Company—and Defied the Conventional Wisdom in the Process,'' *Corporate Detroit Magazine*, May 1, 1994, p. 10.

Howes, Daniel, "Compuware Pay Cuts Pay Off," *Detroit News*, July 27, 1994, p. 1.
Jones, John A., "Companies in the News: Compuware Expands from Mainframes to Network Jobs," *Investor's Business Daily*, October 25, 1996, p. B14.
Maurer, Michael, "Compuware Merger Wins Raves," *Crain's Detroit Business,* March 28, 1994, p. 1.
Muller, Joann, "No Way to Treat a Crisis," *Business Week*, July 5, 1999, p. 74.
Olson, Lise, "In Software, Compuware's Got the Program," *Detroit News,* June 26, 1988.
Pachuta, Michael J., "Compuware Expands Its Lines, Buys Software Quality Tools," *Investor's Business Daily*, October 2, 1998, p. B8.
Pallatto, John, "Compuware Moves Data Editor to PCs," *PC Week,* September 30, 1991.
Pepper, Jon, "News Special: The Road to Renaissance—Compuware Considering Shifting Suburban Headquarters to Detroit—Move Would Bring 3,000 Jobs to Downtown Area," *Detroit News,* August 24, 1998, p. A1.
Roush, Matt, and Robert Ankeny, "Compuware to Move HQ to Detroit," *Crain's Detroit Business,* April 12, 1999, p. 1.
"SCO, Mett Compuware," *Client Server News*, August 23, 2004.
"Software Growth: Compuware Corp. Keeps Expanding, Here and Abroad," *Detroit News*, January 28, 1987.
Wasswa, Henry, "Compuware Accuses IBM of Ambush Tactics," *America's Intelligence Wire,* August 18, 2004.

—Karen Bellenir
—updates: Frank Uhle; Catherine Holm

Coto Centro Integral de Comercializacion S.A.

Paysandu 1842/62
Buenos Aires, C.F. C1416CDP
Argentina
Telephone: (+54) (11) 4586-7777
Fax: (+54) (11) 4586-7825
Web site: http://www.coto.com.ar

Private Company
Incorporated: 1975 as Carnecerios Integrales S.R.L.
Employees: 17,000
Sales: 2.02 billion pesos ($684.75 million) (2003)
NAIC: 445110 Supermarkets and Other Grocery (Except Convenience) Stores; 445210 Meat Markets

Coto Centro Integral de Comercializacion S.A. (Coto C.I.C.S.A.) runs one of the largest retail chains in Argentina and is the only large retailer that remains wholly under Argentine ownership. Each Coto store is carefully planned and laid out in accordance with the company motto: ''Everything under one roof.'' In order to achieve lower costs and higher quality standards, Coto implements advanced technology to optimize its production, distribution, and storage processes. In addition to food, Coto sells an array of home appliances—some of them under its own label—and household products. The vertically integrated Coto empire includes cattle ranches, slaughterhouses, a manufacturing plant, and shopping centers with food courts, multiplex film theaters, and other entertainment areas.

Beef for Argentina: 1963–87

The son of a Spanish immigrant who became a Buenos Aires butcher, Alfredo Coto started working at his father's market stall at the age of nine. There was no freezer, so the side or two of beef had to be cut and sold by midday. In 1963, when he was 21 years old, Coto became a wholesaler when he purchased the nonkosher rear parts of animals from a Jewish meatpacker. He got out of the wholesale business, however, because he was plagued by non-paying clients and in 1969 returned to retailing by opening a butcher shop with four counters in a neighborhood market. He and his helpers sold, each week, the meat from 100 sides of beef. Because there was so little counter space for cutting the meat, Coto had the sides suspended on three hooks, thereby serving the function of shop windows. For reasons of hygiene, he obliged his workers to wear face masks and place meat remnants in a cold box. This store proved so successful that he began to open more, starting in 1970; soon he was opening four a year. By 1976, he owned a chain of 20 butcher shops. Coto also sold meat to 30 other butcher shops and a dozen restaurants.

As the business grew, Coto and his wife Gloria developed a system that he called ironclad management. This plan consisted, in essence, of cutting costs to the bone. He was vigilant in checking to make sure employees were not shortweighting the customers and pocketing the difference, while his wife organized a group of ''women spies'' who pretended to be shoppers and checked to see if the employees were holding back money. In order to reduce costs further as the business grew, Coto bought a cattle ranch in 1978 and founded, in 1981, a distribution company with its own refrigeration plant. He now had an integrated system of supply and distribution, bringing live cattle to the company's own slaughterhouse and refrigerating the meat. The shops also began selling milk, cooking oil, cheese, and cans of beans. Coto's success attracted the attention of the criminal element, and in 1981 he was kidnapped, beaten, held for 11 days, and released for a ransom payment.

Hypermarkets and Shopping Centers: 1987–2000

However, he had already reached what he considered the saturation point of the meat-selling business, and a visit to the Food Marketing Institute in Chicago in 1981 persuaded him to seek wider horizons. Back in Argentina, Coto opened his first supermarket in Mar de Ajo, a seaside resort where his family vacationed each summer. Soon he was converting some of his butcher shops to supermarkets. In 1991, he bought six stores from a cooperative. By 1992, the recently reorganized Coto Centro Integral de Comercialization consisted of 23 butcher shops and 16 supermarkets.

In the same year, Coto advanced to the next stage: building ''maximarkets'' that averaged some 3,000 square meters (about 30,000 square feet) in size and included takeout bakery, pasta,

Company Perspectives:

We understand the sole way to grow is under a full commitment. Commitment to any product we elaborate, to any supplier we deal with, to any employee we hire, to any product we sell, and, mainly, to any customer we assist.

and rotisserie counters. The chain accepted all credit cards and made a point of speedy home delivery. Sales grew to $450 million in 1992, ranking Coto second only to Carrefour S.A. in its field. Expansion continued, with about half the stores opened in the poorest parts of the Buenos Aires metropolitan area, since Coto maintained that the poor spend more in supermarkets than the rich because they do not eat out often and never go on diets. A profit margin of 17 percent surpassed the typical 15 percent of other chains.

During this period, Coto came to realize that his company needed to achieve greater economies of scale to compete with its rivals. In 1994, he decided to establish ''hypermarkets'': stores of 10,000 square meters (100,000 square feet) that offered a much larger array of nonfood products, including clothing and home electronics. The company also made a $20-million acquisition of the Spinetto shopping mall, which it reopened in 1995 after remodeling. The mall included a food court that seated 900 and the support of some 100 lessees representing top-name stores. Later the same year, Coto opened its first hypermarket, with 6,900 square meters of selling space. Sarandi shopping center, opened in 1996, encompassed 11,000 square meters, had 72 checkout counters, and parking space for 750 cars. The following year, Coto bought the block next to the big Abasto market—once the central market for Buenos Aires—for $9 million, purchased the five Acassuso supermarkets in the northern suburbs of Buenos Aires for $25 million, and acquired the Metro supermarket in the capital's Belgrano neighborhood for $10 million. Coto passed the $1-billion mark in annual revenue in 1996, thereby ranking second only to Carrefour in its field. By 1997, Argentine supermarkets and hypermarkets were accounting for half of all food sales, compared to a quarter in 1989.

Coto and his close associate, Arribal Sanchez, filled Buenos Aires's newspapers with ads trumpeting price cuts on 500 items at a time. Most of them were not true bargains, but 30 or 40 loss leaders lent credibility to the rest of the offers. One 1997 study of the price of a basket of 15 staples found that three chains—Wal-Mart, Carrefour, and Supermercados Norte—offered lower prices than Coto. Moreover, Coto was charged with stocking second-rate brands in place of their ''name'' counterparts, poor service, and lack of hygiene in its older stores. These were not especially serious issues for Coto, since the company did not generally compete with Supermercados Norte, which was usually found in better neighborhoods, or Carrefour, which concentrated on the suburbs.

Controversies shadowed, but did not impair, Coto's growth. In 1994, the company was accused of defrauding the state by paying employees under the table to evade taxes, a practice that allegedly was costing the government $1.5 million a month. Coto was not prosecuted, but it was also accused by rival chains of evading the value-added tax on the difference between sales and expenses. Spokespersons for the firm replied that the refrigeration plant had paid part of what was due and that the heavy costs of building hypermarkets and shopping centers explained the rest. Some of Coto's suppliers said the company solicited them for more and more goods, and when they had become dependent on the chain for survival, it demanded ruinous price cuts. Residents living near Coto branches complained that vehicles took up space for loading and unloading that they were not entitled to use.

By early 1998, Coto had three hypermarkets, the largest and most recent of which consisted of 14,000 square meters covering seven blocks and included an entertainment area with movie theaters, a bowling alley, and a food court for 1,800 people. The company also had a shopping center, 14 maximarkets, 20 supermarkets, 19 butcher shops converted into minimarkets, a refrigeration plant, three cattle ranches, and 11,000 employees. In November 1998, the company opened a huge multistory unit in La Recoleta, one of the best neighborhoods in Buenos Aires.

Coto was up against a formidable international cast of competitors: French, Chileans, Spanish, and Americans (in the form of Wal-Mart stores). ''We are facing savage capitalism,'' Coto told Daniel Weigandt of *America economia.* ''But if Wal-Mart or Carrefour begin selling at below-market prices, we'll tell our suppliers that we have to match them. The strategy is to take 50 leading high-volume products, offer them at 30 percent below cost to attract an enormous clientele for the 100,000 articles of a hypermarket.'' A table at company headquarters stacked with Pepsi Cola, Gatorade, Oreos, and many other goods bore the notice ''Products bastardized by Carrefour'' to remind suppliers that the French retailer, and not Coto, had initiated the price war.

Built at a cost of $30 million in suburban Temperley, a new Coto hypermarket that opened in November 2000 stocked more than 50,000 items, with 60 percent of the space devoted to food. A food court on the second floor served beef dishes, cutlets, chicken risotto, cannelloni pasta, pizza, wine, and desserts. There was a bowling alley with 14 lanes, a 12-screen movie multiplex, an Internet café, a video arcade, bumper cars, and pool tables. By this time, the latest in a series of Argentine recessions had begun to bite deeply, yet Coto had held its operating margins steady the previous year while increasing both sales and operating profit. The company now had seven hypermarkets, two slaughterhouses, and its own distribution center just outside Buenos Aires, built at a cost of $40 million.

Keeping up with the Competition: 2000 and Beyond

By late 2001, Argentina was entering the fourth year of its latest recession, and Coto's reputation for low prices was increasingly working to its advantage. Even residents of La Recoleta, which was better known for stores like Ralph Lauren and Louis Vuitton, were now shopping at Coto, not only for groceries but cosmetics, kitchenware, clothes, and even motor oil and tools for customers doing their own auto repairs to save money. In the previous year, Coto also had introduced its own line of television sets and stereo equipment to compete against better-known but more expensive brands.

Key Dates:

1969: Alfredo Coto opens a butcher shop in a Buenos Aires neighborhood market.
1978: Coto now owns a chain of 20 butcher shops, a cattle ranch, and a slaughterhouse.
1987: Having reached saturation with 50 butcher shops, Coto opens a supermarket.
1992: Coto C.I.C.S.A. has 23 butcher shops and 16 supermarkets.
1995: Coto opens its first hypermarket and its first shopping mall.
1996: The company passes $1 billion in annual revenues.
2000: A new Coto hypermarket is stocking more than 50,000 items.
2003: Some Coto supermarkets are now also functioning as wholesalers.

By that time, Carrefour had been merged with Supermercados Norte and a smaller chain to form Grupo Promodes, a French-owned entity that was now by far the largest retailer in Argentina. Grupo Disco-Ekono—a joint venture of the Dutch firm Koninklijkol Ahold N.V. and Argentina's Velox Retail Holding—also had passed Coto in revenue. To open more stores, Coto took a $175-million credit line from J.P. Morgan Chase & Co. and Rabobank Nederland in 2001. By contrast, some 70 percent of the $755 million that the company invested between 1993 and 2001 had come from its own resources. With the recession deepening in late 2001 and the peso on the verge of collapse, even food sales were falling per square meter of space. Coto began studying the possibility of selling furniture, household goods, and construction materials, plus its own brand-name textiles and toiletries, which came to 10 percent of its annual revenues.

The devaluation of the peso near the end of 2001 was followed by a fall of about 11 percent in national income during 2002. Nevertheless, although the company lost 225 million pesos (about $67.5 million) during the year, Coto raised its revenues by two-thirds, passing Grupo Disco-Ekono. This increase was aided by aggressive promotions based on large discounts for customers who paid with credit or debit cards. It was also attributed to the company's skill in opening stores in good locations at a cost much lower than that of its rivals and to its reputation for low prices. Some 93 percent of its sales were coming from food, the category that falls less in price during times of economic crisis, and Coto was leading the competition in sales per square meter.

The question raised was whether Coto could continue its head-to-head struggle against multinational giants. The devaluation of the peso had almost tripled its debt to Morgan and Rabobank, and this debt had to be restructured in late 2002. This apparently resulted in downsizing, as the company's revenues fell by 28 percent. This placed Coto behind Disco in sales, although it still registered a profit of 172 million pesos (about $58 million).

The future direction of Coto was another source of speculation. According to the Argentine business magazine *Mercado,* Coto had nine hypermarkets, 60 supermarkets, and 26 minimarkets in the fiscal year ended June 30, 2002. There were also three commercial centers, three slaughterhouses, and a warehouse and manufacturing plant. The company ranked first in greater Buenos Aires with one-quarter of the market share in its segment.

The company's private labels were Coto (for products including salad dressings, dairy, ice cream, bakery goods, pasta, and canned and frozen foods), Ciudad del Lago (for groceries, canned products, and dairy), and Top (for home appliances). In addition to its supermarket products, Coto stores offered hot foods for takeout and home delivery. The company's ranches, stocked with Aberdeen Angus and Hereford steers, provided its stores with beef and were considered a future source for leather and beef exports. It was reported in early 2003 that some Coto supermarkets had begun to operate as wholesalers as well as retailers, selling in this form to gastronomical enterprises, small supermarkets, and large kiosks.

Principal Competitors

Carrefour S.A.; Disco S.A.; Supermercados Norte S.A.

Further Reading

Friedman, Michael, and Al Urbanski, ''Argentina Gets Hyper,'' *Progressive Grocer*, November-December, 2001, p. 104.

Krauss, Clifford, ''Upper Classes Stoop to Pinch Every Peso,'' *New York Times*, September 17, 2001, p. B1.

Majul, Luis, *Los nuevos ricos de la Argentina*, Buenos Aires: Editorial Sudamericana S.A., 1997, pp. 173–256.

Torres, Craig, ''Argentine Butcher Cuts Juicy Retail Slice,'' *Wall Street Journal*, June 2, 2000, p. A12.

—Robert Halasz

Dalkia Holding

Quartier Valmy, Espace 21
33, place Ronde
92981 Paris La Défense Cedex
France
Telephone: (+33) 171 00 71 00
Fax: (+33) 1 71 00 71 10
Web site: http://www.dalkia.com

Joint Venture of Veolia Environnement SA and Electrice de France
Incorporated: 2000
Employees: 34,000
Sales: EUR 4.58 billion ($4.77 billion) (2002)
NAIC: 333415 Air Conditioning and Warm Air Heating Equipment and Commercial and Industrial Refrigeration Equipment

Dalkia Holding is Europe's leading provider of energy services. France-based Dalkia's range of services include on-site energy management, including the operation of heating and air-conditioning systems; design and operations of industrial fluid (steam, electricity, compressed air, and so forth) systems; facilities management, including reception and switchboard management services; cogeneration facility operation; and technical services. Dalkia's customers include small and large municipal governments, such as the city of Lyons in France or Kuala Lumpur in Malaysia, as well as industrial and corporate customers. The company serves an impressive number of facilities, including 2,500 industrial sites, 4,000 sports, leisure, and cultural stadiums and centers; more than 9,000 schools and research centers; more than 2,000 hospitals and health care facilities; and more than 4.6 million homes. The 70,000 facilities under the company's management encompass more than 105 million square meters. The company's own power production capacity nears 4,000 megawatts (MW). These operations combined to produce more than EUR 5.1 billion in annual sales ($5.5 billion) in 2003. Some 34 percent of those sales were generated outside of France. Dalkia operates through three primary subsidiaries: Dalkia France; Dalkia International, with operations in 31 countries outside of France; and Dalkia Investissement. Dalkia was created in 2000 through the merger of the energy services operations of Vivendi Environment (now Veolia Environment) and former French electricity monopoly Electricite de France (EdF). Veolia remains the company's largest shareholder with a 66 percent share, while EdF maintains a 34 percent stake.

CGE Diversification in the 1960s

Compagnie Generale des Eaux (CGE), was one of France's first privately owned industrial giants, formed in 1852 under a government then headed by Napoleon III. CGE and its founding shareholders—including members of the Rothschild, Lafitte, and de Morny families—had recognized the emerging market for water supply services as part of the country's early industrialization effort. Lyons became the first city to award its water services contract to CGE in 1853, followed by the city of Paris in 1860.

By the turn of the 20th century, CGE was not only one of France's major water suppliers, it was also one of its largest industrial concerns, with a strong international component as well. By the time of its 100th anniversary, CGE had become a French institution, serving more than eight million customers across a 10,000-kilometer water supply network.

CGE began to diversify in the 1960s. In the end, that diversification process was to result in the company's transformation into the giant globally operating conglomerate Vivendi Universal, one of the world's largest companies entering the 21st century. If Vivendi ultimately became as well known for its media interests, including Time Warner, Universal Music, Havas, and AOL, its initial diversification remained closer to its core as a utilities operator.

One of the CGE's first moves toward diversifying its base came in 1967, when it acquired a stake in Compagnie Générale de Chauffe. That company traced its origins to 1935, when Léon Dewailly created Chauffage Service, one of the earliest specialists in developing and installing heating and air conditioning systems in France. Compagnie Générale de Chauffe (CGC) was itself founded in 1944 to provide heating and air-conditioning

Company Perspectives:

Dalkia offers its customers all services that are not directly linked to their core activity.

Our ambition is to create and maintain an ideal living environment for our customers, so that lasting co-operation is developed as a result. All of this occurs in the ideological context of energy-related efficiency, respect for the environment, attention to quality and a situation where people's health and safety are a priority concern.

systems to the industrial sector. Both companies grew strongly in the aftermath of World War II as France launched a massive reconstruction effort to rebuild its industrial infrastructure. In 1958, CGC extended its business to include facilities management when it was awarded the heating management and facilities maintenance contract for all of the United States' NATO military bases in France.

Chauffage Services and CGC merged in 1960, becoming a French leader in its sector under the CGC name. The company then joined the international market, entering the United Kingdom in 1966 as a founding shareholder of Associated Heat Services (AHS) in partnership with that country's National Coal Board (NCB). CGC later acquired full control of AHS after NCB's exit in 1982.

CGC in the meantime continued its growth, backed by the CGE as its primary shareholder. In 1970, CGC acquired two other heating services specialists, Armand, founded in 1913, and Interchauffage, founded in 1960. The two companies were then merged together under the Armand-Interchauffage name. CGC expanded again in 1976 with the purchase of two new companies, Capelier, a company founded in 1919, and EGCS, which had been founded in 1945. CGC also emerged as an important innovator in the energy services market, especially during the oil crisis of the early 1970s. In response to the soaring price of oil, CGC began developing energy recovery systems and heating systems based on geothermal energy sources in 1973.

Emerging Energy Services in the 1990s

By the early 1980s, CGE increased its stake in CGC to 80 percent before later acquiring full control of the company. This move was made as part of CGE's larger consolidation effort, a process that resulted in the creation of a dedicated environmental services division, later spun off from Vivendi as Veolia Environment. As part of that restructuring, CGC acquired Société Auxiliare de Chauffage in 1982. CGC then restructured its own operations, spinning off its installation operations into a new subsidiary, CGC Entreprise.

CGC acquired another prominent group, Montenay, in 1986. Montenay stemmed from a company founded in 1860. Under Georges Montenay, the company established a coal distribution business in 1929. This business in turn led Montenay to launch a heating services unit in 1947. Montenay went on to develop its own international component, starting in Belgium in 1968. Montenay had been growing through acquisitions in the 1980s. In the years between 1983 and 1986, Montenay had acquired Quintiens, which specialized in industrial and naval electrical systems; Francis & Tytgat, which focused on the electrical and hydraulic systems installation sector; and EIT and UTIBEL. Following its acquisition by CGC, Montenay added several more businesses, including Sanivest and Relaitron.

Montenay and CGC remained separate companies into the 1990s. CGC in the meantime pursued its own growth, with a particular emphasis on France's northern region. In 1990, the company founded CGC Entreprise Nord and acquired several local businesses, including Bouchez, based in Calais since the late 18th century; Bele, based in Dunkirk; and Dehon, based in Saint-Quentin.

By the mid-1990s, CGE had acquired a reputation as a "corporate octopus." Indeed, by then the company had more than 2,200 subsidiaries, with operations ranging from its original water supply services to amusement parks, construction, railroad operations, mobile phones, and cable television. The arrival of Jean-Marie Messier as head of the company in 1996 spelled the dawn of a new era for CGE and its energy services subsidiaries. Messier began refocusing the company toward a dual core of environmental services, on the one hand, and media and communications on the other. As such, CGE began a massive restructuring, spinning off some $25 billion in businesses, such as its construction operations, spun off as Vinci.

As part of its restructuring effort, the company merged CGC and Montenay in 1995, creating the Energy Services division. The following year, that division regrouped its installation operations—including CGC Entrepise, Armand-Interchauffage, and others—under a single entity, Crystal SA. Then, in 1998, after CGE changed its name to Vivendi, the Energy Services division adopted its own name, Dalkia. The following year, the then Vivendi Universal spun off its environmental businesses, including Dalkia, into a new company, Vivendi Environment. In 2002, Vivendi Universal reduced its stake in Vivendi Environment to just over 20 percent. The newly independent Vivendi Environment changed its name to Veolia Environment in 2003.

European Energy Services Leader in the 21st Century

Dalkia continued to build on its international operations in the mid-1990s. In 1995, for example, the company, which had already entered South Korea through a stake in Kukdong Energy, increased its position there with the formation of the joint-venture Hanbul Energy Management Co. The company also added to its position in France with the takeover of rival Bergeon, based in Nice, in 1994. That purchase later led to a degree of controversy, with Dalkia accused of provoking Bergeon's bankruptcy in order to gain control of its contracts.

Vivendi Environment meanwhile had begun looking for a energy supplier partner for Dalkia in the late 1990s. Under pressure by a rapidly climbing debt-load, Vivendi formed an agreement with France's electricity monopoly EdF in 2000 to merge the two companies' energy services operation. Vivendi gained 66 percent of the merged business as well as a much-needed cash injection of some EUR 1 billion. EdF, faced with

Key Dates:

1853: Compagnie Générale des Eaux (CGE) (later Vivendi, then Veolia Environment) is founded.
1935: Chauffage Service is founded.
1944: Compagnie Générale de Chauffe (CGC) is founded.
1960: CGC and Chauffage Service merge as CGC.
1967: CGE acquires a stake in CGC.
1980: CGE acquires control of CGC.
1986: CGC acquires Montenay.
1990: CGC creates an installation division, CGC Entreprise.
1994: CGC acquires Bergeon.
1995: CGC and Montenay merge operations, becoming CGE's Energy Services division.
1998: CGC becomes Dalkia.
2000: Vivendi and EdF merge their Energy Services businesses as Dalkia Holding.
2004: Dalkia acquires 93 percent of Czech Republic's Teplarna Usti.

the loss of its electricity monopoly in France, for its part gained a means of expanding the range of energy services it was able to offer to its own customers.

In exchange for a 34 percent stake in Dalkia, EdF contributed its own energy services businesses. These included Clemessy, founded in 1900, with a specialty in the electrical engineering, industrial maintenance, process automation, and complex systems design, and Citelum, established in 1993 as part of EdF's entry into the market for public lighting and traffic control systems.

Following the merger, Dalkia and EdF established a joint-venture subsidiary, Edenkia, offering comprehensive development and management of energy services systems. Dalkia's international component, named Dalkia International expanded the group's operations in 2001 with the acquisition of Italy's Siram SpA. That purchase gave Dalkia control of the leading energy services operation in Italy. The following year, Dalkia headed north, acquiring DBU Holding, a provider of electro-engineering services in the Netherlands. The addition of DBU enabled Dalkia to take the lead of the energy services sector in that country as well.

Dalkia began targeting the Eastern European market as well, building up a number of contracts in the region in the early 2000s, including operations in such cities as Vilnius, Lithuania, and Poznan, the Czech Republic, in 2003 and 2004. The company also began acquiring a presence in the region as well, buying up a controlling stake in the Czech Republic's Teplarna Usti. In 2004, the company boosted its stake in Teplarna to more than 93 percent. As part of its move into Poznan, the company also agreed to buy a 51 percent share in that city's heat supply operation, Przedsiebiorstwo Energetyki Cieplnej. By then, Dalkia's revenues had topped EUR 5.1, making it the leading energy services company in Europe. With the financial and operational backing of Veolia and EdF, Dalkia appeared certain to remain a major force in the region's energy services sector.

Principal Subsidiaries

Am'Tech Industrie; Citelum; Clemessy; Crystal SA; Dalkia AB (Sweden; 74.79%); Dalkia BV (Netherlands; 74.79%); Dalkia Chile (Chile; 74.79%); Dalkia Energia Y Servicos (Spain; 74.79%); Dalkia Facilities Management AB (Sweden; 74.79%); Dalkia GmbH (Germany; 74.79%); Dalkia Holding SpA (Italy; 75.79%); Dalkia Malaysia (Malaysia; 74.79%); Dalkia Morava (Czech Republic; 74.79%); Dalkia NV (Belgium; 74.79%); Dalkia plc (United Kingdom; 75.79%); Dalkia Pte Ltd (Singapore; 74.79%); Dalkia SGPS SA (Portugal; 74.79%); Dalkia Suisse (Switzerland; 74.79%); Dalkia Technologies; Dalkia Termika (Poland; 74.79%); Edenkia; Ekoterm CR (Czech Republic; 74.79%); Exhor; Finergia (Italy; 75.79%); Prochalor; Prodith; Proxiserve; Serdi; Sicam SpA (Italy; 74.79%); Socup; Sopardel; UAB Vilniaus Energija (Lithuania; 74.79%).

Principal Competitors

United Technologies Corporation; Mitsubishi Heavy Industries Ltd.; ABB Ltd.; Sanyo Electric Company Ltd.; Denso Corp.; Electrolux AB; Al Zamil Group of Cos.; Linde AG; Ingersoll-Rand Company Ltd.; American Standard Companies Inc.

Further Reading

"Dalkia Acquires DBU Holding," *Tribune*, October 24, 2002.
"Dalkia Acquires Teplarna Usti Shares from Severoceske Doly," *Czech News Agency*, April 19, 2004.
"EDF and Vivendi Confirm Energy Service Merger," *Europe Energy*, June 30, 2000.
Toscer, Olivier, "La salade Niçoise de la filiale Dalkia," *Nouvel Observateur*, July 27, 2000.
"Vivendi, EDF Design Energy Services Merger," *Transmission & Distribution World*, December 18, 2000.
"Vivendi Unit Dalkia Inaugurates Biogas Power Station," *Europe Energy*, November 10, 1999.

—M.L. Cohen

Deli Universal NV

Postbus 689
Rotterdam
NL-3000 AR
Netherlands
Telephone: (+31) 10 402 17 00
Fax: (+31) 10 411 76 94
Web site: http://www.deli-universal.nl

Wholly Owned Subsidiary of Universal Corporation
Incorporated: 1869 as Deli Maatschappij
Employees: 3,000
Sales: EUR 1 billion ($1.2 billion) (2003 est.)
NAIC: 511120 Offices of Other Holding Companies; 311423 Dried and Dehydrated Food Manufacturing; 312229 Other Tobacco Product Manufacturing; 423990 Other Miscellaneous Durable Goods Merchant Wholesalers; 424490 Other Grocery and Related Product Merchant Wholesalers; 424910 Farm Supplies Merchant Wholesalers; 424990 Other Miscellaneous Nondurable Goods Merchant Wholesalers

Netherlands-based Deli Universal NV is the wholesaling and distribution arm of Universal Corporation, alongside sister company Universal Leaf Tobacco Company. Deli Universal, which represents the continuation of the former Deli Maatschappij, is itself a federation of independently operating distribution and wholesaling businesses primarily active in the Netherlands. Deli Universal focuses on three core markets: Timber and Building Products, Agri Products, and Tobacco Sheet. The company's Timber and Buildings Products division is subdivided into three primary business units: regional distribution, through the Jongeneel network of 36 lumber centers catering to building contractors in the Netherlands; industrial, primarily through softwood specialist Heuvelman, as well as through its Bouter joinery business based in Bergambacht; and wholesale, through RET, Steffex, and Crailo, which supply wood products such as boards and plywood, as well as doors, ceiling and wall systems, and other materials and products to hardware stores and professional tradesmen and building contractors. Under Agri Products, Deli Universal includes: tea, under the more than 180-year-old Van Rees Group, supplying tea blends to packers worldwide; merchandizing, primarily of rubber, through Corrie, MacColl and Son in Engliand and Imperial Commodities Corporation in the United States; and canned goods, through Imperial Commodities Corporation. Deli Universal's Agri products also include the production and distribution of seeds and specialty grains and beans for confectionery and food processing through subsidiary Red River Commodities. Deli Universal's third division, Tobacco Sheet, is also the link to the company's past as one of the world's primary tobacco importers. This division, operating as Deli HTL in the Netherlands and as DHT in Germany, produces cigar wrappers and binders, as well as filler tobacco for cigars and cigarettes. Deli Universal has been part of the Universal Corporation since 1986.

Indonesian Tobacco Monopoly in the 1890s

The first efforts to cultivate tobacco in the Dutch East Indies in the mid-1850s were largely unsuccessful. These original tobacco crops, planted on the island of Java, yielded only low tobacco grades. Yet Dutch entrepreneurs remained convinced that the region's climate was capable of producing higher quality tobacco. The arrival of Jacobus Nienhuys in the future Indonesia marked the beginning of the colony's growth into a regional center for tobacco.

By the early 1860s, Nienhuys had settled in the region around the Deli River, on the eastern coast of Sumatra, where he began experimenting with tobacco varieties. In 1863, Nienhuys was granted the franchise to a large area along the river in order to establish a tobacco plantation. Nienhuys planted an experimental crop yielding 50 bales of what turned out to be superior quality tobacco. Encouraged, Nienhuys and partner P.W. Janssen began seeking financial backing in order to develop the plantation.

The pair succeeded in raising more than one million guilders by 1867, half of which came from the Nederlandsche Handel-Maatschappij (NHM). Two years later, Nienhuys and Janssen established the Deli Maatschappij with a concession to produce cigar tobacco along the Deli River. By 1870, the company's exports had already topped 207,000 kilos (450,000 pounds). In

Company Perspectives:

Deli Universal seeks to be the leading supplier to professional buyers in each market segment it serves. To accomplish this objective, DU has made extensive investment in companies, staff and value-added customer services. DU is expanding rapidly through internal growth and acquisitions.

The Rotterdam based holding is small, which reflects DU's orientation towards decentralized, capable and leading distribution companies with strong local management.

1871, however, Nienhuys decided to return to the Netherlands. The company sought a replacement, and its choice was Jacob Theodore Cremer.

Then just 24 years old, Cremer had joined the NHM in 1867, arriving in the East Indies in late 1868. Cremer had become interested in the fast-developing tobacco industry in Sumatra and successfully lobbied for the appointment at the head of Deli Maatschappij. Under Cremer—later an important Dutch political figure—Deli Maatschappij grew quickly. By 1883, the year Cremer returned to the Netherlands, Deli Maatschappij's exports had soared to nearly 3.5 million kilos (7.6 million pounds). Cremer had also led the company on a drive to buy up most of the tobacco plantations that had appeared in its wake, and by the mid-1880s Deli Maatschappij already counted more than ten plantations. The company's shareholders had reason to be pleased with their investment. The company's average dividend payments had reached 73 percent, and by 1890 the company itself was valued at 32 million guilders.

Deli Maatschappij succeeded in gaining control of the Sumatran tobacco industry by the turn of the 20th century. In addition to its own plantations, Deli Maatschappij acquired the monopoly on tobacco exports, acting as the broker for other tobacco growers in the region. By then, Sumatra's tobacco had achieved worldwide renown for its quality. The crop became particularly prized as leaf for cigar wrappers. The leaf, with a small central vein—which made more of the leaf usable—was also thinner than other tobacco varieties, making it possible to wrap more cigars at a lower cost.

Tobacco growers in the United States attempted to stem the influx of Sumatra tobacco by demanding high import duties from the government. Even still, the Sumatra leaf, capable of wrapping up to four times as many cigars as U.S.-grown wrapper leaf, remained highly prized and cost-competitive. In the early years of the 20th century, a number of Western tobacco companies set up plantations in Sumatra in order to develop their own supply of the higher-quality leaf. Yet Deli Maatschappij maintained control of its export monopoly as well as control of the world market for wrapper leaf. By the outbreak of World War I, more than 92 percent of all imported wrapper leaf in the United States came from Sumatra.

The enormous profits—in large part as a result of the use of "coolie" slave labor—enabled Deli Maatschappij to invest elsewhere in the world, most notably in the construction of railroads in the United States and elsewhere at the turn of the 20th century. By the 1920s, however, the company's fortunes had begun to decline. Cigar smoking, which had previously dominated the tobacco market, began to wane in the buildup to World War II, and in 1927 sales of cigarettes—wrapped in paper, not in tobacco—surpassed sales of cigars for the first time.

Diversified Trader in the 1960s

The Depression-era dealt the next blow to Deli Maatschappij, as cigar sales plummeted. This period was followed by World War II and the Japanese occupation, which put a virtual standstill to Sumatra's tobacco exports and cut off Deli Maatschappij from its Dutch financial backers. By the end of the war, Deli Maatschappij reentered a dramatically changed market which had seen the emergence of a new class of tobacco giants. In the meantime, the formation of an independent Indonesia and the call to nationalize the industries dominated by the former Dutch colonial power placed Deli Maatschappij under new pressure.

Deli Maatschappij's operations in Sumatra were nationalized in 1958, becoming known as PNP Tobacco. Deli Maatschappij then moved its now greatly reduced operations to the Netherlands. The company maintained an interest in tobacco, however. In 1955, for example, the company had seized control of the United States' American Sumatra Tobacco Corporation, formed in 1910, which had emerged as one of the world's largest sources of wrapper leaf during and after World War II. That company, which had linked New York-based financial partners with farmers in Florida, Georgia, and elsewhere in the South, proved a poor match for its Dutch owners, and the operation was shut down by the early 1960s.

Other activities were more successful for the company, such as its production of tobacco sheets, used for manufacturing cigar wrappers, and other tobacco products. The company also used its long history in the import and export market to develop a diversified trading business. Acquisitions played an important role in the group's diversification. In the mid-1960s, the company acquired the Van Rees Group, a specialist in importing, blending, and merchandizing tea founded in 1819. The company also acquired interests in the rubber market and canned foods markets, which were brought under an umbrella company, Imperial Commodities Corp.

One of the company's most successful diversification efforts came with its purchase of wood products distributor Jongeneel in 1971. That company stemmed from a business founded by Huybertus Jongeneel in 1797 in Utrecht, becoming known as Firma Jongeneel & Zoon in 1800. Jongeneel began expanding beyond the Utrecht market in 1904, although remaining largely focused on its region until the 1970s. As part of the Deli Maatschappij, however, Jongeneel expanded to a national level, and by the beginning of the 21st century had established a network of 34 stores. Deli Maatschappij also acquired interests in the timber and lumber industries and handled trade in such items as sunflower seeds for the confectionery sector, vegetable oils, and coffee.

Deli Maatschappij remained involved in the global tobacco market as well. Following the nationalization of its Indonesian interests, Deli shifted its focus to other markets, becoming a major player in Italy, Greece, and particularly the fast-emerging

Key Dates:

1863: Jacobus Nienhuys begins experimenting with tobacco crops in Sumatra along the Deli River.
1869: Nienhuys founds Deli Maatschappij, which is granted the concession for developing trade in Sumatran tobacco.
1880: After acquiring a number of other tobacco plantations, Deli Maatschappij achieves monopoly control of Sumatran tobacco exports.
1955: American Sumatra Tobacco Corporation is acquired.
1958: Independent Indonesian government nationalizes Deli Maatschappij's tobacco operations in the country.
1960s: Deli Maatschappij enters into a partnership with Universal Leaf Tobacco Company to import and process burley tobacco in Greece and acquires Van Rees Group of tea importers.
1971: The company acquires Jongeneel, a specialist in the wood and wood products market.
1986: Deli Maatschappij merges with Universal, becoming Deli Universal.
1994: Deli Universal acquires Houthandel Heuvelman and Steffex Handelmaatschappij BV.
1998: Astimex is acquired.
2004: Astimex becomes the company's main brand name for wall and ceiling panels.

Brazilian market. Deli Maatschappij's expertise in the import/export market for flue-cured and burley tobaccos brought it into contact with Universal Leaf Tobacco Company for the first time in the mid-1960s, when the two companies entered a partnership to process burley tobacco in Greece. Burley tobacco, the variety used to manufacture so-called ''American'' cigarettes, was then fast becoming the world's most sought-after tobacco type.

That first partnership ultimately led to a full-fledged merger between Universal and Deli Maatschappij. Founded in 1918, Universal had grown into one of the world's largest leaf tobacco distributors, embarking on global expansion in the 1960s. Yet the uncertain future of the tobacco industry, as well as an unsuccessful hostile takeover attempt lobbied against the company, had encouraged Universal to diversify its operations. Universal's early attempts failed to produce the desired results. In 1980, for example, the company entered the fertilizer market, only to see that market collapse soon after. In 1985, the company acquired U.S. title insurance group Lawyers Title Co., but that market too went into a long slump following the crash of the housing market in the late 1980s.

Value-Added Specialist in the 2000s

In 1986, however, Universal found a more successful acquisition—that of Deli Maatschappij. Under the merger, Universal restructured its operations, creating the holding company Universal Corporation. The company's tobacco interests were then combined together into a new, larger Universal Leaf Tobacco, while its trading operations where regrouped under the Deli Universal name.

By the 1990s, Deli Universal's trading operations had emerged as the primary counterpart to Universal's tobacco interests and the main motor for the company's diversified business interests. The company now began to shift its focus toward developing activities in value-added niche markets, moving beyond commodities to more specialized products.

Acquisitions again formed part of this transition, such as the purchase of Houthandel Heuvelman (later Heuvelman Hout) in 1994. That company, founded in 1876, grew into one of the Netherlands' leading suppliers of wood and wood products. Heuvelman also operated its own cash-and-carry store for the building trade, called Megamat, in Rotterdam. In 1995, following its acquisition by Deli Universal, Heuvelman acquired firewood specialist Houthandel van Dooren. In that year, Deli Universal spun off its spice trading operation into a joint venture with Suiker Unie.

Deli added Steffex Handelmaatschappij BV in 1994, a purchase that enabled the company to add the importing and distributing of doors and decorative products in the Netherlands and Belgium. Deli Universal was also active in the lumber market through its control of RET, founded in 1914 as Rubber en Theekistenfabriek in Utrecht. RET, which originally produced crates for Deli's tea and rubber trade, grew into a major Dutch importer of lumber products and developed a particular specialty in the wall and ceiling panel sector.

Deli Universal expanded its lumber products operations again in 1998 with acquisition of Astrimex. Founded in 1946, that company had adopted the Astrimex brand in 1990, which became a top brand of ceiling and wall panels. In 2002, RET and Astrimex's ceiling and wall panel businesses were merged into a single unit. The RET brand for these products was phased out in 2004 in favor of the Astrimex name.

By then, Deli Universal had made a number of other acquisitions. In 2001, the company acquired family-owned Gouderak Holding, based in Eindhoven. Gouderak was then the Dutch and European leader in the recreational wood products sector—that is, garden sheds, screens, decorative borders, and the like. The company strengthened its position in this market in 2002 with the acquisition of Begenco and its well-known Hillhout brand name.

While Deli Universal's operations remained close to its Netherlands base, in 2003 the company began to expand beyond the country's borders when it acquired Germany's JéWé, an internationally operating manufacturer and distributor of products for the do-it-yourself sector. By then, Deli Universal accounted for nearly half of parent company Universal Corporation's annual sales of $2.5 billion.

Principal Subsidiaries

B.V. Deli-HTL Tabak Maatschappij; Bouter & Zn. B.V.; Corrie, MacColl & Son Ltd.; Crailo B.V.; Deli Universal, Inc.; Deutsch-holländische Tabakgesellschaft mbH & Co. KG; Gouderak B.V.; Handelmaatschappij Steffex B.V.; Houthandel H. & P.H. Heuvelman B.V.; Imperial Commodities Corporation; Jongeneel B.V.; Momentum Technologies Inc.; Red River Commodities, Inc.; Red River-Van Eck B.V.; RET; Van Rees B.V.

Principal Divisions

Timber and Building Products; Agri Products; Tobacco Sheet.

Principal Competitors

Imperial Tobacco Group PLC; Gallaher Group PLC; Shanghai Cigarette Factory ; R.J. Reynolds Tobacco Holdings Inc.; Austria Tabak/Gallaher Continental Europe Div.; General Tobacco Co.; Morshansk Tobacco Factory Joint Stock Co.; Cigarrera Biggott Sucesores S.A.

Further Reading

''Ambitions Stirred by New Ugandan Processing Plant,'' *World Tobacco*, March 2004, p. 55.

Bickers, Christopher E., ''Universal Unleashes World's Biggest Processing Plant,'' *World Tobacco*, November 2003, p. 34.

''Feije, Xandra, ''Houthandel RET nu veilig voor buurt,'' *Utrechts Nieuwsblad*, September 12, 2002.

''Gouderak naar Deli Universal,'' *Eindhovens Dagblad*, February 21, 2001.

''Hillhout onder vleugels van Deli Universal,'' *Apeldoornse Courant*, September 12, 2002.

—M.L. Cohen

De'Longhi S.p.A.

Via Ludovico Seitz 47
Treviso
I-31100 TV
Italy
Telephone: (+39) 0422 4131
Fax: (+39) 0422 413652
Web site: http://www.delonghi.it

Public Company
Incorporated: 1903
Employees: 5,870
Sales: EUR 1.28 billion ($1.54 billion)(2003)
Stock Exchanges: Milan
Ticker Symbol: DLG
NAIC: 333415 Air Conditioning and Warm Air Heating Equipment and Commercial and Industrial Refrigeration Equipment Manufacturing; 333414 Heating Equipment (Except Electric and Warm Air Furnaces) Manufacturing; 335221 Household Cooking Appliance Manufacturing; 335224 Household Laundry Equipment Manufacturing

Multi-faceted De'Longhi S.p.A. is a world-leading manufacturer of domestic appliances. Historically a major producer of portable heaters and air-conditioners, the company has expanded to include nearly every category of small domestic appliances in the food preparation and cooking, as well as household cleaning and ironing, segments. The company's products include microwave ovens—De'Longhi is one of Europe's largest manufacturers of microwave ovens under its own brands names and as an OEM (Original Equipment Manufacturer) supplier—as well as table-top and built-in electric and gas ovens, coffee machines, indoor grills, food processors, irons, and vacuum cleaners and other floor care products. In addition to its small domestic appliance production, De'Longhi also designs and manufactures central heating and air conditioning systems for the home, institutional, and industrial sectors. Brands under the company's stable include De'Longhi, Kenwood, Ariete, Elba, Radel, Simac, Supercalor, Superclima, Ariagel, Climaveneta, and Vetrella. Acquisition has played an important part of the group's growth, notably with the purchase of U.K.-based Kenwood in 2001. That acquisition also enabled the company to shift part of its production to Kenwood's manufacturing site in China. In all, De'Longhi operates 13 production facilities and 30 international subsidiaries supporting sales to 75 countries worldwide. International sales account for nearly 75 percent of the group's total revenues, which topped EUR 1.25 billion ($1.5 billion) in 2003. De'Longhi has been listed on the Milan Stock Exchange since 2001. Guiseppe De'Longhi has led the company since the mid-1970s.

Creation of an Appliance Giant: 1970s–80s

De'Longhi SpA celebrated its centenary in 2002—and its transformation from a small parts supplier to one of the world's leading appliance brands. De'Longhi started as a craftsman's workshop in Treviso, in the north of Italy, in what was to become one of the country's most important industrial regions. The De'Longhi family-operated shop began supplying parts to other area manufacturers, developing a specialty in providing components for heating systems. In the 1950s, the shop converted its status, formally incorporating as De'Longhi as it expanded its production. Nonetheless, the company remained a component supplier.

The arrival of a new generation in the form of Guiseppe De'Longhi began the company's transformation in the 1970s. De'Longhi decided to use the company's technical knowledge to develop its own, branded products. As part of this effort, the company stayed close to its historical core of heating systems, and in 1975 De'Longhi debuted its first product, an oil-filled, portable electric radiator.

The success of this product, which carved out a new niche in the home heating sector, set the tone for the company's rapid growth into the next decade. De'Longhi quickly built up a list of products, at first clinging to the heating sector, developing a full range of heating products. As part of this effort, the company made its first acquisition, of Supercalor, in 1979. The success of the company's line quickly took it beyond Italy as well, as sales developed throughout much of Europe in the late 1970s. By 1980, the company had grown sufficiently to attempt to conquer a new and important market—the United States.

Company Perspectives:

The De'Longhi Group operates in two business segments that are linked by the concept of well-being: air treatment products, which bring fresh, pure, and dehumidified air into the home and create optimal well-being conditions for the whole family, and products for food preparation and cooking, house cleaning and clothes ironing that simplify domestic living, providing more quality leisure time.

By the mid-1980s, De'Longhi's revenues had reached the equivalent of EUR 80 million. Its range of products included oil-filled heaters, fan heaters, and gas-fired and kerosene heaters as well. OEM manufacturing, for such well-known brands as Black & Decker, helped the company establish itself as a world leader in portable heaters by the end of the 1980s. In this, the company was aided by its willingness to innovate and to seek out new niche product areas. Such was the case with its launch of the Plus Heat Multi System, the first to combine the advantages of oil-filled, electric and fan heater systems. Yet by then De'Longhi had undergone a dramatic expansion.

The company's true transformation took place in the second half of the 1980s through a series of acquisitions that not only brought it an extended range of brand names but also the technological expertise to make it a leading innovator in a number of new product areas. In 1986, the company acquired Elba, a maker of free-standing ovens and built-in ovens and stove tops. That purchase helped boost the company's own newly introduced oven line, launched with the highly successful ''Sfornatutto'' tabletop oven in 1985.

The success of the Sfornatutto oven in Italy was assured by De'Longhi's quick recognition of the new product's potential. After learning the Italian consumers were reluctant to use their traditional built-in ovens because of the perceived high energy costs of these units, De'Longhi began marketing as a low-cost alternative the Sfornatutto, which, because of its small size, required far less pre-heat time than conventional ovens.

De'Longhi added to its heating technology with the purchase of Radel in 1986. This acquisition gave the company new operations in developing central heating systems based on water-circulating heaters. De'Longhi also sought to extend its operations into another area, that of air conditioners, in the mid-1980s. Confronted by the relatively small market for air conditioners in Europe on the one hand, and by the presence of a number of large players in the more well-developed North American market on the other, De'Longhi decided to call upon its growing tradition for innovation. In 1986, the company introduced the first portable air conditioning system, the Pinguino. That product quickly became one of the most popular air conditioning systems in the world. Following the launch of the Pinguino, De'Longhi acquired Ariagel, adding that company's air conditioning expertise in 1987.

De'Longhi's extended its range of ovens in 1988 with the launch of its first microwave ovens. Despite heavy competition from the growing number of low-cost appliance producers in Asia, De'Longhi managed to carve out a significant place for itself in that sector as well, producing microwave ovens under its own brand name, and as a key OEM supplier as well. This position was reinforced with the creation of a new 60,000-square-foot facility, the largest facility for the production of microwave ovens in Europe.

The company's next acquisition came in 1989, when it purchased Vetrella. That purchase enabled De'Longhi to add production of vacuum cleaners and other floor care systems. In the meantime, the company had another hit product on its hands with the launch of the Friggimeglio, also known as the Roto Fryer, in 1987, the first deep-fat fryer to feature a revolving basket. As one company executive told *Appliance* magazine in 1991: ''We understood we couldn't participate in that category with just another me-too fryer. Instead, we developed a fryer with a rotating basket. It uses 50 percent less oil than any other deep fat fryer. It offers a significant health advantage as well as economy.''

International Leader in the 1990s and Beyond

In the late 1980s and into the 1990s, De'Longhi began solidifying its international presence by opening a number of foreign sales and manufacturing subsidiaries. The company established subsidiaries in Spain and offices in France, Germany, and Belgium. In 1988, the company launched its U.S. subsidiary. The U.K. became another significant market for De'Longhi in the mid-1980s, a trend crowned by the opening of its U.K. subsidiary in 1989. The company moved into head-to-head competition with France's Moulinex in 1990 when it established a full-scale French subsidiary. Three years later, the company opened subsidiaries in the Netherlands, Germany and Japan as well. These were followed by the opening of representative offices in Moscow in 1995, in Shanghai in 1996, in Canada in 1997, and in Belgium in 1999. By the beginning of the 2000s, De'Longhi operated 13 manufacturing plants and subsidiaries in 30 countries, with sales to more than 75 countries around the world.

De'Longhi continued adding to its range of products during the 1990s and into the 2000s. Acquisitions once again provided the motor for part of the company's new product development. In 1995, De'Longhi acquired Simac Micromax, an acquisition that enabled it not only to begin producing irons and ironing systems but also extended its range of food preparation products. Also in that year, De'Longhi launched production of its first coffee maker designs.

The kitchen became a clear company target at the beginning of the 2000s. In 2001, the acquired the U.K.-based Kenwood Appliances Plc, one of the top makers of food preparation equipment and other small appliances both in the United Kingdom and in the global market as well. The Kenwood purchase gave De'Longhi a second strong international brand—next to its own—ensuring it a place among the world's top small appliance companies. Kenwood also brought the company the Ariete brand and line of ironing and floor care systems.

Kenwood, which had been struggling into the 2000s, operated three production plants, including a new facility in China. The addition of this facility gave De'Longhi the opportunity to transfer parts of its own production, which remained heavily concentrated in Italy, to the Chinese plant.

Key Dates:

1902: The De'Longhi family sets up a workshop supplying parts to local industry in Treviso, Italy.
1950s: De'Longhi incorporates, with a specialty in supplying components to the heating appliance industry.
1975: The company's first branded product, an oil-filled portable heater, is launched under Guiseppe De'Longhi.
1979: Supercalor is acquired and the company extends its range of heaters.
1980: Sales begin in the United States.
1986: The company acquires Elba and expands into freestanding, table-top, and built-in ovens.
1987: Ariagel, an air-conditioning specialist, is acquired.
1988: A U.S. subsidiary is created; the company begins production of microwave ovens.
1989: A U.K. subsidiary is created; The company acquires Vetrella floor care appliances.
1990: A company subsidiary opens in France.
1993: Subsidiaries are opened in the Netherlands, Japan, and Germany.
1995: The company launches coffee makers and acquires Simax Micromax, a maker of kitchen appliances and floor care systems.
2001: The company acquires U.K. firm Kenwood Appliance, along with its Ariete brand.
2003: Café Duo coffee maker is introduced.

Following the Kenwood acquisition, De'Longhi launched a public offering, listing its shares on the Milan Stock Exchange. The De'Longhi family nonetheless remained in control of the company. Under the guidance of Guiseppe De'Longhi, the company had expanded strongly since the middle of the 1980s, topping EUR 1.25 billion in revenues in 2003.

Yet the company was far from resting on its laurels and continued to seek out new product niches. This commitment to innovation enabled the company to introduce a new coffee maker, the Café Duo, in 2003. Launched in the United States, the product was part of De'Longhi's plan to focus on U.S. growth, with hopes to quadruple its sales there during the decade. At the same time, De'Longhi remained true to another important part of its history of growth, planning to seek out new acquisitions in the 2000s.

Principal Subsidiaries

Ariete S.P.A.; Climaveneta Deutschland GmbH (Germany); Climaveneta S.P.A.; De'Longhi America Inc.; De'Longhi Australia Pty Ltd.; De'Longhi Canada Inc.; De'Longhi Clima Polska Sp.Zo.O; De'Longhi Deutschland GmbH; De'Longhi Electrodomesticos Espana S.L.; De'Longhi Finance S.A. (Luxembourg); De'Longhi France S.A.R.L.; De'Longhi Japan Corp.; De'Longhi Ltd. (United Kingdom); De'Longhi Nederland B.V.; De'Longhi New Zealand Ltd.; DL Radiators France S.A.R.L.; DL Trading Limited (Hong Kong); Kenwood Appl. (Malaysia) Sdn.Bhd.; Kenwood Appl. (Singapore) Pte Ltd.; Kenwood Appliances plc (United Kingdom); Kenwood International Ltd. (United Kingdom); La Supercalor S.P.A.; On Shiu (Zhongshan) Electrical Appliance Company Ltd. (China; 67%); Promised Success Ltd. (Hong Kong; 67%); Tricom Industrial Co. Ltd (Hong Kong).

Principal Competitors

Siemens AG; Samsung Electronics Co. Ltd.; Sibtyazhmash Joint Stock Co.; Sanyo Electric Company Ltd.; Whirlpool Corp.; Energiya Joint Stock Scientific and Industrial Concern; Aisin Seiki Company Ltd.; Sony Electronics Inc.; BSH Bosch und Siemens Hausgerate GmbH; GE Appliances; Liebherr-International AG; Siemens PLC; Maytag Corporation; LG Electronics Investment Ltd.

Further Reading

Kapner, Fred, ''De Longhi Set to Launch IPO,'' *Financial Times*, June 6, 2001, p. 32.
Liever, Ed, ''Delonghi America Seeks 'Household Name' Status,'' *HFN—The Weekly Newspaper for the Home Furnishing Network*, May 22, 2000, p. 30.
Purpura, Linda, ''Italian Passion,'' *HFD—The Weekly Home Furnishings Newspaper*, November 8, 1993, p. 43.
Quail, Jennifer, ''For Delonghi, Design Focus Isn't Overshadowing Function,'' *HFN—The Weekly Newspaper for the Home Furnishing Network*, May 5, 2003, p. 58.
Stevens, Scot, ''Nurturing the Name,'' *Appliance*, May 1991, p. 54.
Way, Richard, ''Leading Latte,'' *ERT Weekly*, December 5, 2002, p. 20.

—M.L. Cohen

DFS Group Ltd.

First Market Tower
525 Market Street, 33rd Floor
San Francisco, California 94105-2708
U.S.A.
Telephone: (415) 977-2700
Fax: (415) 977-4289
Web site: http://www.dfsgroup.com

Wholly Owned Subsidiary of LVMH Moët Hennessy Louis Vuitton SA
Founded: 1960
Employees: 350
Sales: $127 million (2003 est.)
NAIC: 453220 Gift, Novelty and Souvenir Stores

Hong Kong-based DFS Group Ltd. is the world's largest retailer of duty-free merchandise, specializing in luxury brands and primarily catering to Japanese tourists. DFS operates approximately 150 stores, mostly located in airports, where the company pays a hefty concession fee. The traveling public can purchase merchandise at these shops and avoid the duties—taxes and other charges levied by the local government—as long as the buyer does not use or consume the items while at the location. Historically, tobacco, alcohol, and perfumes have been the mainstays of duty-free retailers. In recent years, DFS has opened ''Galleria'' stores in downtown locations, offering luxury boutique merchandise, contemporary fashion, and local destination products. To purchase items at duty-free prices, customers must show an airline ticket out of the country. Their purchases are then shipped to the airport for pickup at the departure gate on the trip home. DFS is majority owned by the French conglomerate of luxury brands LVMH Moët Hennessy Louis Vuitton SA. Cofounder Robert W. Miller retains a 38 percent interest.

Origins in the 1950s

DFS was founded by Miller and Charles Feeney, both raised in working class communities. Miller grew up in the small town of Quincy, Massachusetts, located in the shadow of Boston. Feeney came from Elizabeth, New Jersey, the son of a nurse and insurance underwriter. During the postwar years following World War II, Feeney joined the army at age 17 and served in Japan and Korea. After being discharged, he used the scholarship the military provided to attend Cornell University, where he studied hotel administration. Because his stipend paid for little more than his tuition, Feeney supplemented his income and honed his entrepreneurial instincts by selling sandwiches door-to-door to fraternities. In Cornell's hotel administration program, Feeney became friends with Miller, a year ahead in school but nearly two years younger. Miller graduated in 1955, and Feeney followed in 1956. Because he still had four months of scholarship money, Feeney attended college in France. He stayed to run a camp for the children of the U.S. Navy fleet stationed in southern France and later met up with Miller in Barcelona. There, in a bar, he told Miller that he thought they could make some money selling merchandise to the fleet. In 1958, they went into business together and began to sell such items as perfume, tape recorders, and transistor radios to navy personnel in Europe. Their emphasis soon switched to selling duty-free liquor and foreign-made cars to U.S. servicemen and tourists on their way home to the United States through a pair of companies: Tourist Internationale Ltd. and Cars International Ltd.

In 1960, Feeney and Miller changed their focus from Europe to Asia, wisely anticipating the potential of selling to the rising class of international businessmen from the region. They launched Duty Free Shoppers, later abbreviated to DFS, and opened duty-free shops at the international airports in Hong Kong and Honolulu. The Duty Free industry actually began aboard international cruise ships in the 1930s. The concept was transferred to international airports in 1947 when Brendan O'Reagan opened a duty-free shop in Shannon, Ireland, which was a major refueling stop for transatlantic flights. The government supported the idea as a way to promote Irish whisky and woolens, and other governments would also soon recognize the potential of promoting tourism and local products by permitting duty-free shopping at their international airports.

DFS continued to concentrate on the military market in the early 1960s. Miller and Feeney passed out literature on navy vessels before they left the United States, outlining DFS car and liquor programs that could be found in Asia. Later they would hire ex-military men to run offices located at U.S. Air Force and Navy bases in Asia. Business was thriving, leading the partners

Company Perspectives:

From its inception DFS has focused on a specific customer—the international traveler.

to expand too aggressively. Soon they found themselves overextended when the U.S. government undercut their business by changing the rules on duty-free liquor and allowing U.S. automakers to sell on military bases. As a result, DFS was forced to shutter its store and was essentially bankrupt by 1965. At this point, the partners turned to outside help. In 1966, they gave 10 percent stakes in the business to British accountant Alan M. Parker and American lawyer Anthony M. Pilaro to help restructure the company. It was Pilaro who brokered a deal with Butlers Bank of Nassau that provided the money DFS needed to exit the car import business. Henceforth, the fortunes of DFS would depend on the tourist trade, in particular Japanese tourists.

Focus on Japanese Travelers in the 1960s

Feeney was the one credited with targeting the Japanese. Twenty years after its defeat in World War II, Japan was emerging as an economic powerhouse. When travel restrictions were lifted in 1966, Feeney correctly surmised that the Japanese possessed a great deal of pent-up desire to travel as well as a demand for western luxury items. He visited the country, learned the language, and became familiar with the Japanese travel customs, which featured lavish gift giving. Travelers would be given a gift of money, Senbetsu, and when they returned they were expected to bear gifts, souvenirs of their trip called omiyage. Japanese couples on their honeymoons would also reciprocate wedding gifts. In addition to the importance of advertising in Japanese travel magazines and tourist guidebooks, Feeney recognized that the vast majority of Japanese tourists, some 80 percent, traveled in package or group tours. Thus, DFS established ties with Japanese travel agencies and began paying tour operators a flat fee for every tourist they brought to a DFS store, as well as commissions as high as 15 percent. Even tour guides and bus drivers were given an incentive to deliver Japanese tourists to DFS stores. Furthermore, DFS took care that it had concessions at the international airports in the countries that the Japanese liked to visit. In addition to Hong Kong and Hawaii, DFS over the next 20 years opened duty-free stores in such locales as Guam, Saipan, Singapore, Anchorage, Los Angeles, and San Francisco. DFS hired Japanese-speaking clerks and made sure that any defective merchandise could be replaced or repaired in Japan.

Retailing in the Asian market proved highly lucrative for DFS, due in large part to Western luxury items commanding a much higher markup than in the United States or Europe. The partners often split 90 percent of the profits the company earned each year, an estimated $3 billion from 1977 to 1995, making Feeney and Miller fabulously wealthy. In the early 1970s, they turned over management of DFS to others. They were both successful in solo business ventures, adding further to their immense wealth, but in many respects they now pursued opposite paths in life. Miller resided with his wife and three daughters in Hong Kong and became famous for a jet-set lifestyle and throwing extravagant parties that rivaled the excesses of America's Gilded Age of the late 1800s. Also reminiscent of that period of ostentatious wealth were the high profile marriages of his daughters, complete with dowries that reportedly ranged from $100 to $200 million. The eldest, Pia, married Christopher Getty, grandson of oil tycoon John Paul Getty; the middle daughter, Marie-Chantal, married Crown Prince Pavlos, the eldest son of the former King Constantine of Greece; and the youngest, Alexandra, married Alexander von Furstenberg, son of Austrian-born Prince Egon von Furstenberg. Equally as wealthy, Feeney, with his wife and five children, lived almost like a recluse—and a pauper. He flew coach, wore a watch worth less than $10, never owned a house or a car, and preferred wearing crumpled old suits. One employee recalled that the first time he met Feeney, his pants were held up by a safety pin. However, Feeney was anything but a miser. In secret, he was giving away most of the millions he had earned from DFS and his other successful ventures. He created a charitable foundation, Atlantic Philanthropies, and in 1984 turned over his share of DFS to it. Then, by the use of off-shore cutout corporations, he gained anonymity to pursue his philanthropic goals. To further protect his identity, he did not even take a tax deduction for his charitable contributions.

DFS faced a challenge early in the 1980s when Host International opened airport and downtown duty-free stores in Honolulu, but DFS's ties to Japanese tour operators proved too formidable an obstacle, and after just nine months Host defaulted on its Honolulu concession. Another rival emerged in 1987 in Hong Kong, when Kiu Fat Investments Corp., backed by the People's Republic of China, won the airport liquor and tobacco concessions. DFS responded by pricing its duty-paid liquor below Kiu Fat's duty-free prices and pressured European design houses not to supply merchandise to Kiu Fat's downtown stores. DFS also launched a service to have the purchased liquor delivered to the airport and checked through to Tokyo or Osaka. In little more than a year, Kiu Fat folded and DFS regained the airport concession. Also during this period, DFS was able to use its contacts with Japanese travel agencies to learn that the honeymoon market was about to shift from Hawaii to Australia and New Zealand. As a result, DFS was able to establish stores in these countries to take advantage of the trade.

The 1980s also saw the interests of the DFS partners begin to significantly diverge. In 1986, the United States overhauled the tax code, which according to the *New York Times,* ''increased [the partners'] isolation by prompting them to restructure the company in a way that put more distance among them. Instead of owners, they became 'shareholder representatives' of tax shelters and charitable foundations they created.'' Isolation turned into conflict later in the decade when Feenery launched retail stores in Hawaii that his partners felt were in competition with DFS. Because he refused to sell the business, the others ousted him from the board of DFS and some subsidiaries. As a way to settle any future conflicts, the four agreed in 1991 to submit differences to a seasoned arbitrator, Ira. M. Millstein, a senior partner in the New York law firm of Weil, Gotshal & Manges. Several years later, Millstein's services would be needed.

In 1994, Feeney decided that the tourist trade was often uncertain and that he preferred a more predictable and conservative investment to fund his charitable foundation. Wanting to sell his stake in DFS, he turned to the most likely buyer, longtime supplier LVMH. His partners vehemently opposed the

Key Dates:

1960: The company is founded by Charles Feeney and Robert Miller.
1966: Alan M. Parker and Anthony M. Pilaro are brought in as partners.
1995: The company's first Galleria store opens in Guam.
1996: Feeney, Parker, and Pilaro sell interests to LVMH.
2004: The company's headquarters are moved to Hong Kong.

idea, but after two years Feeney was able to win over Park. Together they owned 58.75 percent of DFS and could sell majority control to LVMH, which in June 1996 presented a $4 billion bid for the company. Millar and Pilaro insisted that the partners bring the matter to Millstein. According to the *New York Times,* "The central issues quickly boiled down to whether the 1991 agreement required the selling partners to obtain the approval of the nonsellers, and if not, whether a sale would damage the holdings of Mr. Miller and Mr. Pilaro." In the end, Millstein ruled in favor of Fenney and Parker, but he also worked out an agreement with LVMH that would protect the interests of the nonsellers, so that profits would not be inappropriately diverted to the parent company. That same day, Fenney and Parker sold their share in DFS to LCMH for $2.47 billion. (During the course of the sale of DFS to LVMH, Fenney decided it was time to reveal his involvement with Atlantic Philanthropies.)

Miller and Pilaro continued to fight the acquisition, going to court in January 1997, but only days later Pilaro dropped out and agreed to sell his 2.5 percent stake for $105 million. Miller now began to negotiate the sale of his interest, but after several weeks LVMH decided to break off the talks, dissatisfied with his demands, and announced it would run DFS as majority owner with Miller as a shareholder.

Challenges Following 1996 Sale

As had been the case throughout his business career, Feeney displayed an excellent sense of timing, selling his interest in DFS at the peak of its value. Because of an economic crisis in Asia that led to declining tourism, DFS saw its sales drop from $3 billion to $1.5 billion in little more than 18 months from 1995 to 1997, albeit part of that decrease was due to a strategy to close some of the company's airport concessions. In 1995, DFS opened its first Galleria store, in Guam, representing a new direction the company hoped to take. Nevertheless, the Asian crisis precipitated a major restructuring of DFS. It launched a $120 million program to improve its systems and to open more Galleria stores as well as proposed Sephora perfumeries. Nevertheless, matters became so difficult that in March 1998, just a year after LVMH acquired control, DFS had to ask vendors for more time to pay its bills. A few days later, the company announced that it was eliminating 300 jobs and closing five of its 150 stores—two in Hong Kong and the others located in Honolulu; Vancouver, British Columbia; and Queenstown, New Zealand. Management insisted that it was not about to exit the airport business but was eager to lessen its exposure and reposition DFS as an operator of high-quality, specialty stores. The emphasis would no longer be on tobacco, liquor, and perfumes but shift toward fashion.

In September 1998, DFS hired a new president and CEO, Brian E. Kendrick, a turnaround specialist who had been the number two executive at Saks Holdings Inc. Over the course of the next year, DFS rebounded somewhat, due to a revival in the consumption of luxury goods by Japanese tourists. Having guided the company through the Asian economic crisis, Kendrick then left to take a job elsewhere and was replaced by Edward J. Brennan, who had 16 years of experience at R.H. Macy & Co. and Federated Department Stores, and had joined DFS in May 1997. Under Brennan, DFS continued its efforts at diversification, made necessary by the relaxing of trade barriers and other changes affecting the duty-free industry. Sales also improved somewhat, and the company reportedly returned to profitability. Brennan was rewarded in January 2001 by being named chairman in addition to his other titles. However, DFS continued to struggle. A retail flagship store in San Francisco that had opened with much fanfare in late 2000 closed after little more than a year, unable to attract domestic customers. Headcount was reduced, and the company announced that to further cut costs it was reorganizing the business into two major groups: the Asia Group—with divisions in Hong Kong, Taiwan, Korea, and Macau—and the Pacific Group, with operations in Hawaii, Guam, Saipan, and Palau. In addition, a separate North American Division would be located in the company's San Francisco corporate offices.

World events combined to hinder DFS's plans for recovery. The effect of a SARS outbreak as well as the U.S. invasion of Iraq hurt tourism and cut into sales. Matters improved when the company was able to renegotiate airport contracts in Hawaii and Los Angeles. To rebuild the business, DFS returned its focus to the Asian market. In keeping with this initiative, the corporate headquarters was moved from San Francisco to Hong Kong. The company again returned to profitability in the fourth quarter of 2003, but the ongoing viability of the business would likely hinge on a new market, the Chinese traveler and the Chinese mainland.

Principal Competitors

BAA plc; KP Company Ltd.; Compagnie Financière Richemont SA.

Further Reading

"DFS Embraces the Future by Going Back to Its Roots," *Duty-Free News International*, November 15, 2003, p. 1.
Ginsberg, Steve, "DFS Shrinks Globally, Axes Locally," *San Francisco Business Times*, February 8, 2002, p. 1.
Nordheimer, Jon, "Millions of Dollars Couldn't Keep DFS Group Together," *New York Times*, March 12, 1997, p. D1.
"One Life to Give," *Irish America*, December/January 2003, p. 38.
Tanzer, Andrew, and Marc Beauchamp, "Rich, Ruthless and Determined," *Forbes*, October 24, 1988, p. 36.
Weil, Henry, "Soaring Sales at Duty-Free Shops," *Fortune*, April 24, 1989, p. 225.

—Ed Dinger

Donruss Playoff L.P.

2300 East Randol Mill Road
Arlington, Texas 76011
U.S.A.
Telephone: (817) 983-0300
Web site: http://www.donrussplayoff.com

Private Company
Incorporated: 1954 as Donruss Co.
Employees: 115 (est.)
Sales: $25 million (1999 est.)
NAIC: 511199 All Other Publishers

Donruss Playoff L.P. makes trading cards that depict the players of Major League Baseball and the National Football League, as well as some performers from other sports organizations or television programs. The company markets a number of different series each year under the Donruss, Playoff, Leaf, and Score brands, primarily distributing them in the United States through card collectors' hobby shops and mass-marketers like Toys "R" Us. Donruss Playoff's ownership is controlled by Ann Blake, who co-founded Score in the 1980s.

Beginnings

Donruss Playoff traces its roots to 1954, when Donald and Russell Weiner became owners of the Thomas Weiner Company of Memphis, Tennessee, which manufactured hard candy, suckers, and a brand of gum called Super Bubble. They renamed the firm Donruss, using a combination of their first names, and continued to produce a variety of candy and gum products. In the early 1960s, the company began to issue sets of trading cards, one of the first of which was "Idiot Cards" from 1961, which featured cartoons and jokes aimed at the elementary and middle-school market. The 2½ by 3½ inch, thin cardboard cards, which had a full-color front and duotone back, were packaged in waxed paper "wax packs" that included 15 cards and a flat stick of gum and retailed for approximately a quarter. There were 66 different cards, and since each pack contained a random assortment, children would have to buy a number of packages or trade duplicates with their friends to form a complete set.

By the middle of the decade, Donruss had begun licensing entertainment properties for new series of cards. Some of the first such sets were based on the hit 1964 television shows *The Addams Family* and *Voyage to the Bottom of the Sea.* In the latter half of the decade other series based on television's *The Monkees* and *The Flying Nun* were issued as well.

In 1969, Donruss made the national news when a lawsuit over its payment of corporate taxes reached the U.S. Supreme Court. The firm had paid a required $30,000 surtax on accumulated earnings for 1960–61, but then sued the government to get the money back, claiming the earnings did not pass the "purpose test" of being accumulated strictly to avoid taxes. Although a U.S. Circuit Court found in the company's favor, the high court ruled unanimously that Donruss would have to pay the tax, effectively voiding the purpose test for all corporations.

That same year, the Weiners sold the firm to food giant General Mills, under whose ownership operations continued much as they had before, with the company manufacturing a range of candy and bubble gum products and issuing sets of trading cards. In the 1970s, these continued to be based on pop-culture phenomena such as the film *Saturday Night Fever,* television's *Bionic Woman,* and rock and rollers Elvis Presley and Kiss.

Production of Baseball Cards Begins in 1981

Though Donruss was generally doing well with these series, the firm was frustrated by its inability to break into the popular category of baseball cards, which Topps had held exclusive rights to produce since 1956. In 1975, a lawsuit was filed by Topps rival Fleer to try to break the lock on baseball, and five years later a Federal judge ruled that Topps had illegally obtained exclusive rights to use the players' images. Fleer and Donruss immediately worked out agreements with Major League Baseball to issue their own sets of cards, and Donruss's first series hit stores in time for the 1981 season. In August of that year, the judge's ruling was overturned by an appellate court, but Fleer's lawyers discovered a loophole in the Topps contract which allowed cards to be sold if they were not packaged with gum or candy, or if they were sold in combination with some other item. Donruss quickly removed gum and

Company Perspectives:

Now making a name for itself with several innovative autograph and memorabilia insert programs, Donruss maintains it's standing as a company renowned for heritage and innovation.

added three pieces of a Babe Ruth puzzle to its 30 cent, 15-card packs, while Fleer enclosed team logo stickers.

Rather than over-saturating the market for baseball cards, the new competition proved a stimulant. Total sales grew from an estimated 500 million cards a year in the late 1970s to one billion by the mid-1980s as each of the three firms strove to make their card sets distinctive. For its part, Donruss included a 26-card ''Diamond Kings'' subset, which featured paintings of one player from each team by noted sports artist Dick Perez, and other cards that depicted non-player subjects like the San Diego Padres mascot ''The Chicken,'' which thousands of fans mailed to the company to have autographed.

Donruss's initial success with baseball cards was soon followed by problems with distribution and overproduction, however, and in late 1983 General Mills sold the firm to conglomerate Huhtamaki Oy of Finland. Huhtamaki had also recently bought Leaf Confectionery, Inc. of Chicago and Beatrice US Confections, and the three operations were combined under the Leaf, Inc. banner. Together, the companies produced such popular brands as Milk Duds, Heath, Jolly Rancher, Switzer, and Good 'n' Plenty, as well as trading cards and Super Bubble Gum. Huhtamaki, which had been founded in 1920, owned a number of different firms that included makers of beverages, canned and frozen foods, pharmaceuticals, and industrial products. At this time, Donruss had annual sales of approximately $40 million.

The Leaf association proved a boon to the firm, as it provided access to that company's well-established distribution network. In 1985, Donruss began making special cards for Canada, and in 1986 it introduced a new 56-card set called ''The Rookies.'' Sales of cards were continuing to grow and increased approximately 100 percent in both 1986 and 1987 to reach an estimated three billion industry-wide. Topps remained the leader, producing approximately half of the total, with Donruss selling about a quarter and Fleer a shade less. By this time, the concept of baseball cards as collectibles and even investments was gaining wider acceptance, and specialty shops were beginning to spring up around the country to serve customers who now included many adults along with the industry's core audience of teen and pre-teen boys. Prices for the 15-card packs were on the rise, now standing at 45 cents.

The baseball card boom was drawing more competitors into the fray, with Score of Texas and Upper Deck of Anaheim, California, joining the ranks in 1988 and 1989, respectively. Score boosted the cards' quality a notch by using better paper, action photographs, and improved writing on the backs, while Upper Deck went even further, issuing a 700-card set that featured holograms to discourage counterfeiting and opaque foil packaging instead of the traditional waxed paper. Its cards cost 89 cents for 15 and were also sold in complete sets through dealers.

Donruss Introduces Premium Cards in 1990

In the summer of 1990, Donruss took a page from Upper Deck's book and introduced a new, higher-quality card series on top of its standard set. Offered initially only on the West Coast, it was marketed under the Leaf brand name and cost $1.09 for 15 cards and three pieces of a Yogi Berra puzzle. The cards featured a more elegant design, with two-sided color printing on glossy paper, and foil packs, though no full sets were made available to dealers. They would be issued in two batches, one in July and the other in September, so the company could add late player trades and other changes to the second set. Donruss' sister company, Leaf, had itself issued baseball cards in the late 1940s, and the use of the brand name represented a return to that legacy.

In 1991, Topps and Fleer introduced their own deluxe card sets, and, following Upper Deck's lead, all card makers began inserting limited-edition bonus cards into random packs. Struggling to maintain its market share, Topps salted its packages with 300,000 vintage cards, at least one example of each it had produced. Other firms included cards autographed by legends like Mickey Mantle and Nolan Ryan, while Donruss inserted several new limited-edition cards, as well as 5,000 signed by Cubs All-Star Ryne Sandberg. The year 1991 also saw the launch of the Donruss Learning Series, a program for elementary and middle school children that used baseball cards to help teach history, geography, and math with workbooks and a set of 55 cards designed specifically for the program.

Baseball card mania was now at a high point, with sets of premium cards whose suggested price per pack was just over $1 commonly selling for $2–$3 or more at hobby shops, and still more new competitors preparing to enter the market. The companies' focus on limited edition inserts was not greeted enthusiastically in all quarters, however, and Donruss was criticized for including four random ''preview cards'' of forthcoming Leaf series, such as the stylish black-and-white Studio line, only in full sets of its standard cards, which necessitated the purchase of a complete set to obtain a handful of rare cards. The company would ultimately add two separate sets of Leaf previews in different batches of the 1991 full sets.

In the summer of 1991, Donruss began expanding its Memphis plant from 256,000 square feet to nearly 400,000. It would continue to make trading cards and bubble gum at the facility, where employment grew from 550 to 720.

In 1992, with sales of standard card lines plunging in the face of more attractive higher-end versions, Donruss announced that it was severely curtailing its production and doubling the basic cards' retail price to 99 cents a pack. At the same time, their quality was upgraded, and they were packed in foil, while certain limited-edition and autographed cards would be included at random. One subset would be the popular Diamond Kings cards, which would henceforth be produced only in limited quantities. The year 1992 also saw the firm create card series for use as giveaways by McDonald's, Coca-Cola, and Cracker Jack, and introduce a new, cheaper line of cards called ''Triple Play.'' The latter set contained 264 cards and was sold in 12-packs that also contained a rub-off game card. Priced at 59 cents, they were geared toward the youngest collectors, who

Key Dates:

1954: Candy maker Thomas Weiner Co. is renamed Donruss.
1960s: The company begins producing trading cards based on television programs.
1969: Donruss is acquired by General Mills.
1981: After Fleer wins a lawsuit against Topps, Donruss produces its first baseball cards.
1983: General Mills sells Donruss to Huhtamaki Oy of Finland.
1990: The company introduces a line of premium cards.
1993: Hockey cards are added.
1996: Huhtamaki sells Donruss sports card lines to Pinnacle Brands, Inc.
1999: Bankrupt Pinnacle sells Donruss to Playoff Corp.
2001: Playoff takes the name Donruss Playoff L.P.; baseball card production resumes.
2003: The company slices a rare Babe Ruth jersey into pieces for insertion into card packs.

were increasingly being ignored in a market that was more and more aimed at teenagers and adult investors.

A study by Salomon Brothers of market share for card makers at this time highlighted the dramatic changes that had occurred since the 1980s. First place was now held by newcomer Upper Deck with 24 percent, followed by Topps with 22, Fleer with 20, Score with ten, Donruss with eight, and the remainder of the pie divided up by smaller companies like SkyBox and Classic.

In 1993, Donruss branched out into hockey cards, which were launched in the fall with a suggested price of $1.79 a pack. The company also introduced the Leaf Limited line, which featured cards that utilized both holograms and metal foil. Inspired by the previous year's Topp's Finest series, Leaf Limited would be restricted to 5,000 cases. At more than $5 per pack of six cards, it was Donruss's most expensive offering to date.

Sports Strikes Wreak Havoc for Card Industry in 1994

The year 1994 proved disastrous for many sports card manufacturers. A major baseball strike forced cancellation of the latter half of the season and soured many on the game, while a lockout of National Hockey League players threw that sport into disarray for a time as well. Simultaneously, the proliferation of card makers and their increasing emphasis on limited-edition series, along with a sizable drop in the resale value of recent cards, was causing large numbers of collectors to rethink their devotion to the hobby. Further aggravating factors included the actions of the players' associations, which signed deals with unlimited numbers of companies for high licensing fees that drove up card prices, and the chicanery of certain unscrupulous dealers, who found ways to remove valuable insert cards before packs were put out for public sale or even stooped to counterfeiting desirable cards. By the end of 1994, sales of baseball and hockey cards had fallen an estimated 40 percent, and Donruss's revenues were down by nearly half to approximately $50 million.

The company took several measures to regroup under new head John Williams, who had previously run Huhtamaki's Polarcup packaging unit. In 1995, the firm, which had recently become known as Donruss Trading Cards, Inc., began developing a line of entertainment cards, along with what it called interactive cards. It was soon marketing a set of nearly 100 Ace Ventura cards, based on the hit Jim Carrey movies.

The company's sales slump was dragging down Huhtamaki's profits, however, and in May of 1996 the Finnish company sold Donruss's baseball and hockey card lines to Pinnacle Brands, Inc. for approximately $41 million, and then sold the entertainment card and game businesses to U.S. Playing Card Co. Coming in the aftermath of Fleer's merger with smaller rival SkyBox International, the Donruss sale reduced the number of major card companies to four.

New owner Pinnacle Brands was a Texas company that had evolved out of baseball card maker Score, which now primarily made football and NASCAR cards. It had started in 1970 as Optigraphics, which made special "moving-image" cards, and became Score when it entered the baseball card market in 1988. Its founders and owners, Ann Blake and John Flavin, had divorced in 1992, with Flavin continuing at Score and Blake leaving to found a company called Cardz Distribution. After Score became Pinnacle, Flavin sold his own stake in the firm.

Under the aegis of Pinnacle, Donruss continued to release various lines of baseball and hockey cards, including such items as Leaf insert cards printed on actual pieces of metal and others printed on leather and wood. Such strategies did not succeed in reversing the company's fortunes, however, and in July of 1998 Pinnacle Brands, Inc. and subsidiaries filed for bankruptcy. A year later, the Donruss, Score, and Leaf brands, excluding their baseball and hockey licenses, were acquired by Playoff Corp. of Grand Prairie, Texas, after a heated bidding war with representatives of Fleer and Upper Deck. Playoff, which was owned by Ann Blake, had grown out of her Cardz operation and now produced several lines of high-end football cards. It generated some $25 million in annual revenues. In the months following the sale, new series of Leaf, Score, and Donruss Elite cards were issued, and in 2000 the firm added a new 36,000-square-foot distribution facility and launched a line of cards based on the Japanese animated television series *Dragonball Z.*

Baseball Cards Return in 2001

In early 2001, the company became known as Donruss Playoff L.P. and won a license from Major League Baseball Properties and the Major League Baseball Players Association to produce cards for the forthcoming season. The firm would make sets for the two "lost" years of 1999 and 2000 as well. During the year, Donruss Playoff also moved its headquarters from Grand Prairie to Arlington, Texas, where it planned to eventually open a visitors center and memorabilia museum.

In 2002, the company issued a set of 150 Diamond Kings cards and sold most of the original paintings on Internet auction site eBay. Other new card series contained insert cards that held pieces of bats and uniforms used in actual games by 100 current and past players, a practice copied from Upper Deck. Another of Donruss's insert sets, inspired by one from Topps, turned to the designs of the earliest baseball cards, using ornate gold borders and canvas-like paper. The year 2002 also saw the firm produce entertainment cards for programs such as *Buffy, The Vampire Slayer* through its new Score Entertainment division and introduce the first U.S.-produced Spanish-only baseball card set, the 225-card Super Estrellas. A six-card pack, which included a mini-poster, retailed for $1.99.

Donruss stirred up controversy in 2003 when it announced plans to slice up a rare game-worn Babe Ruth jersey, for which it had paid $264,210 at auction. It would randomly insert 2,100 cards bearing pieces of the shirt into packs over the next several years. The company responded to critics of the jersey's shredding by stating that it gave average fans a chance to own a piece of history and brought out the legendary Yankee's 86-year old daughter to give the cutting her stamp of approval. Also in 2003, Donruss created a first-ever set of cards for players of the 17-year old Arena Football League, which would be sold at games and via the teams' Web sites. The following year, the company launched a baseball card insert series called Fans of the Game, which depicted baseball-loving performers like Regis Philbin, Charlie Sheen, Joe Mantegna, and *Sopranos* star James Gandolfini.

With a half-century of history behind it, Donruss Playoff L.P. continued to focus on the production of collector-oriented sports and entertainment trading cards. The firm had been chastened by the card market shakeout of the 1990s and was now focusing on high quality or limited production items which offered such bonus features as player autographs and slices of game-worn uniforms and equipment.

Principal Subsidiaries

Score Entertainment.

Principal Competitors

The Upper Deck Company, LLC; The Topps Company, Inc.; Fleer/Skybox International LP.

Further Reading

Alm, Richard, ''Pinnacle Brands Purchases Donruss Trading Card Rights,'' *Dallas Morning News*, April 19, 1996, p. 1D.

Bailey, Arnold, ''Collectors' Corner: Diamond Kings Sets Offer Ornate Gems from Antiquity,'' *Providence Journal*, June 8, 2002, p. D23.

——, ''Collectors' Corner: Ruth's Jersey Tears Some Up,'' *Providence Journal*, September 6, 2003, p. C2.

——, ''Collectors' Corner: Gandolfini Among Heavy Hitters Included in 'Fans of the Game' Set,'' *Providence Journal*, March 28, 2004, p. D8.

Bayee, Chris, ''Baseball Card Companies Now Focusing on Incentives,'' *Tulsa World*, May 10, 1991, p. B1.

Fatsis, Stefan, ''Candy Firms Gobbling up Competitors, Brand Names,'' *Washington Post*, August 7, 1988, p. 204.

''General Mills in Pact to Sell Bubble Gum Unit,'' *Dow Jones News Service*, November 22, 1983.

Grimes, Chuck, ''Card Companies Getting Bullish,'' *News & Observer* (Raleigh, North Carolina), August 10, 1991, p. C3.

——, ''These Rookies a Winning Set,'' *The News & Observer, Raleigh, NC*, September 28, 1991, p. C3.

Guyon, Janet, ''Two Gum Producers in Sticky Situation over Baseball Cards,'' *Wall Street Journal*, August 27, 1981, p. 13.

Hammonds, Keith, ''In Baseball Cards, Topps Still Leads the League,'' *New York Times*, April 25, 1982.

Jennings, Dana Andrew, ''Forget That '52 Mantle Baseball Card: 'New Stuff' Has the Industry Booming,'' *Wall Street Journal*, April 21, 1989.

——, ''Trading Cards Contend in a Whole New Ball Game,'' *New York Times*, August 6, 1995, p. H33.

Johnson, Harold, ''Baseball Card Boom—5 Firms Now Share $500 Million a Year,'' *San Francisco Chronicle*, July 19, 1989, p. A3.

McLinden, Steve, ''Arlington, Texas, Sports-Card Maker Donruss-Playoff Makes Name for Itself,'' *Fort Worth Star-Telegram*, September 3, 2002.

——, ''Grand Prairie, Texas, Company Acquires Sports-Card Brands from Rival,'' *Fort Worth Star-Telegram*, July 21, 1999.

Monahan, Chris, ''Reaching a New Pinnacle,'' *Orange County Register*, April 23, 1996, p. D2.

Simmons, Bill, ''Sports Trading-Card Shuffle Boom! Collectors, Dealers Feel Effect—Too Much of Good Thing,'' *Boston Herald*, December 9, 1994, p. 3.

Simon, Rand, ''Companies Forgetting the Kids in Race to Profits,'' *Toronto Star*, November 2, 1991, p. B6.

''The Supreme Court Ends Tax Defense for a Corporation,'' *New York Times*, January 14, 1969.

Trejo, Frank, ''Arlington, Texas, Company Scores with Spanish Baseball Cards,'' *Dallas Morning News*, October 11, 2002.

Wesley, John C., ''Cutting the Babe to Pieces Misses the Point,'' *Patriot-News*, November 2, 2003, p. D1.

Wisby, Gary, ''Card Firm Cashes in on Diamond Gems,'' *Chicago Sun-Times*, May 4, 1987, p. 1.

Woods, George, ''Donruss Develops Glossy Line,'' *Dallas Morning News*, June 23, 1990, p. 8B.

—Frank Uhle

THE E. W. SCRIPPS COMPANY

The E.W. Scripps Company

312 Walnut Street, 28th Floor
2800 Scripps Center
Cincinnati, Ohio 45202
U.S.A.
Telephone: (513) 977-3000
Fax: (513) 977-3721
Web site: http://www.scripps.com

Public Company
Incorporated: 1890 as Scripps-McRae League
Employees: 7,800
Sales: $1.87 billion (2003)
Stock Exchanges: New York
Ticker Symbol: SSP
NAIC: 511110 Newspaper Publishers; 511140 Database & Directory Publishers; 515120 Television Broadcasters; 515210 Cable and Other Subscription Programming; 551112 Offices of Other Holding Companies

The E.W. Scripps Company is a diverse U.S. media company with interests in newspaper publishing, broadcast television, national television networks, and interactive media. Scripps operates 21 daily newspapers, 15 broadcast TV stations, four cable and satellite television programming networks, and a television retailing network. Scripps's media businesses provide Internet content and advertising services. Network television brands of Scripps include: Home and Garden Television (HGTV), Food Network, Do It Yourself Network (DIY), and Fine Living. Eighty-five million U.S. households are reached by HGTV; and Food Network reaches 84 million households. Scripps network web sites include FoodNetwork.com, HGTV.com, DIYnetwork.com, and fineliving.com. Network programming from Scripps is available in 86 countries across the globe. Scripps's Shop at Home Network (a television retailing subsidiary) reaches almost 48 million full-time equivalent U.S. households. Five million of these households are reached via Shop At Home affiliated broadcast stations, which are owned by Scripps. The Shop At Home Network markets an expanding range of consumer items to television viewers and to customers on the Internet at shopathometv.com. Scripps operates Scripps Howard News Service and United Media. United Media is a worldwide licensing home and syndicator of newspaper features and comics, including ''Peanuts,'' ''Dilbert,'' and more than 150 other comics and features.

''Penny Press'' Origins

The E.W. Scripps Company began life in 1878 as Scripps and Sweeney Co. when 24-year-old Edward Willis Scripps, with his cousin John Sweeney and other family members, founded his first newspaper, the *Cleveland Penny Press.* Scripps had $10,000 in capital and owned 20 percent of the paper. The rest was owned by his half-brothers George Henry and James Edmund Scripps—each of whom received 30 percent stakes in the company—and other partners.

E.W. Scripps was a populist who thought that most newspapers were geared towards the rich. He wanted his newspaper to keep the poor informed through short, simple stories that could be understood by those without extensive education. He got many of these ideas from James E. Scripps, an English immigrant who started the *Detroit Evening News* in 1873. E.W. also added his interest in personal stories to the mix, later giving a raise to an editor who published the fact that he had been fined $10 for riding a horse while intoxicated.

At the time the *Cleveland Penny Press* was founded, most newspapers had a party affiliation. They also sold for more than a penny, and many contemporaries were skeptical that the Press would succeed. E.W. Scripps' formula proved successful, however, and within weeks the *Cleveland Penny Press* had a circulation of approximately 10,000. It was not a profitable operation, however, until James E. Scripps ordered E.W. to run the paper for $400 a week.

As soon as the *Penny Press* was making money, E.W. persuaded his brothers to buy the *St. Louis Chronicle.* He then spent a year in St. Louis managing the paper. E.W. bought a 55 percent interest in the *Penny Post*—part of which was already owned by James E.—went to Cincinnati to manage it, and changed the paper's name to the *Cincinnati Post.* He subsequently began taking on political corruption and winning circulation.

Company Perspectives:

Scripps aims at excellence in the products and services we produce and responsible service to the communities in which we operate. Our purpose is to continue to engage in successful, growing enterprises in the fields of information and entertainment. The company intends to expand, to develop and acquire new products and services, and to pursue new market opportunities. Our focus shall be long-term growth for the benefit of shareholders and employees. Scripps Company is guided by the motto, "Give light and the people will find their own way."

From 1887 to 1889 James E. Scripps was in Europe receiving medical treatment while E.W. managed the *Detroit News*. Although E.W. expanded advertising and circulation, James E. was angry with the changes his brother made; upon his return, James E. removed E.W. from every position he could. In 1890 E.W. started his own paper, the *Kentucky Post*, in Covington, across the Ohio River from Cincinnati.

Also in 1890 E.W. Scripps entered into a partnership with his business manager, Milton McRae; the two called their newspaper company the Scripps-McRae League. McRae handled day-to-day management of the papers and received one-third of the profits, while Scripps set editorial guidelines and long-term policy. In 1890, with his business running smoothly, Scripps began building a ranch outside of San Diego, California.

In 1894 George Scripps joined Scripps-McRae. This gave the group a controlling interest in the *Cleveland Press*. Later in the 1890s the group started the *Akron Press* and *Kansas City World*. As his chain expanded, E.W. Scripps chose young, growing towns to start new newspapers. He invested as little in machinery or plants as possible, usually buying old presses and renting run-down buildings. He would then hire young ambitious editors who were given a minority stake in their paper; many of them became rich if their newspapers succeeded. With E.W. Scripps spending most of his time in California, McRae often exceeded his authority and put editorial pressure on newspaper editors. Scripps would periodically venture out of California, discover what McRae was doing, and reverse it.

Scripps next began a series of West Coast newspapers unassociated with the Scripps-McRae League group. They included papers in Los Angeles, San Francisco, Fresno, Berkeley, and Oakland, California, as well as Seattle, Tacoma, and Spokane, Washington. In 1900 George Scripps died, leaving his stock to E.W. James E. Scripps contested the will, however, and James E. and E.W. settled out of court. E.W. was forced to give all of his stock in the Detroit newspapers to James E., who in return gave E.W. all of his stock in newspapers outside Detroit.

In 1902 Scripps started the Newspaper Enterprise Association (NEA), a service for exchanging and distributing illustrations, cartoons, editorials, and articles on such specialized subjects as sports and fashion. Newspapers in the Scripps chain paid a monthly fee and received information and illustrations none of them could have afforded individually. Although the NEA was originally only for Scripps papers, demand for its services was so great that it soon became available to any newspaper.

In 1906 Scripps entered another period of expansion, buying or starting papers in Denver and Pueblo, Colorado; Evansville and Terre Haute, Indiana; Memphis and Nashville, Tennessee; Dallas, Texas; and Oklahoma.

Wire Service in the Early 1900s

In 1907 Scripps combined the NEA, the Scripps McRae Press Association, and Publishers Press into the United Press Association wire service in order to provide 12,000 words of copy a day by telegraph to 369 subscribers in the United States. A similar service, the Associated Press (AP), already existed and was far larger and better financed. Scripps viewed AP as monopolistic and too close to the establishment and deliberately set out to oppose it. AP was also geared toward morning newspapers, while most of Scripps's were evening newspapers. Scripps therefore had each of his papers send out stories from their area during the day and combined them with information gathered at offices set up in important news producing cities such as Washington, D.C., and other world capitals.

In 1908 E.W. Scripps retired from active management, appointing his son James G. Scripps chairman of the board. During World War I, E.W. was a passionate advocate of U.S. intervention on the side of the Allies and moved to Washington, D.C., to push his cause. Shortly thereafter, a family crisis erupted, during which Scripps's son James detached the five West Coast newspapers and the Dallas Dispatch from the chain. In 1918 United Press caused a storm of controversy when it reported the end of World War I four days before it actually ended. E.W. Scripps's health started declining during the war, and by its end he was largely living on his yacht. In 1920 he gave direct control of the chain to his son Robert and Roy W. Howard and in 1922 incorporated all of his stock, news services, and newspapers into the E.W. Scripps Company, based in Cincinnati. The profits went to the Scripps Trust, set up for his heirs.

Despite his semiretirement, Scripps had the energy to direct a last burst of expansion in the 1920s. He made Roy Howard chairman and business director in 1921. Howard had played an important role in building the United Press. By 1924, he was placed in full charge of both business and editorial by E.W.'s son Robert. The newspaper chain was renamed the Scripps Howard League. Beginning in 1921, newspapers were bought or started in Birmingham, Alabama; Indianapolis, Indiana; Baltimore, Maryland; and Pittsburgh. Sales for 1925 came to about $28 million. In 1926 the Denver-based Rocky Mountain News and Times were bought.

At the time of E.W. Scripps's death in 1926, the Scripps Howard League was the second largest newspaper chain in the United States, after William Randolph Hearst's. E.W. Scripps was one the most successful newspaper owners of the era of the so-called Press Barons. Because of his reclusive personality, though, he was one of the least known. He stood up for the working class but in many ways despised them. In addition, he encouraged his newspapers to crusade for female suffrage but considered women inferior to men.

Key Dates:

1878: Edwin Willis Scripps establishes the *Cleveland Penny Press.*
1890: Scripps-McRae is created to oversee Scripps's newspaper holdings.
1907: United Press wire service established.
1922: Company changes name to E.W. Scripps Co.; the E.W. Scripps Trust is created.
1935: Scripps enters the radio broadcast industry.
1940: Scripps takes over the National Spelling Bee from a Louisville, Kentucky, newspaper.
1962: The Scripps Foundation is incorporated.
1982: Company sells UPI wire service to Media News Corporation.
1988: Company goes public.
1994: Home and Garden (HGTV) cable network launched.
2002: Fine Living cable network launched.

In all, Scripps started 32 newspapers. Some of them did not stay in business long; some were unsophisticated but remained fiercely independent. Their emphasis on human interest stories was welcomed by new immigrants who had lost their former communities.

Roy Howard's stock holding in the company was small, but with his strong personality he influenced the Scripps heirs and took working control of the company, managing it as if it were his own and bringing his own family into the company hierarchy. In 1927, Scripps Howard bought the *New York Telegram.* Four years later, it purchased the *New York World* and merged the two newspapers into the World-Telegram. In 1936 Howard gave up his position as chairman of the chain and became president.

In the 1930s United Press built a network of bureaus in South and Central America and in the Far East, though its coverage was weaker in Europe, and it remained smaller than AP. Also that decade the newspaper chain began to shrink as less-profitable papers were sold or consolidated and six-day evening papers began to lose their appeal. During World War II Ernie Pyle came to fame as a Scripps Howard columnist reporting from the European battle theater, before losing his life on a Pacific battlefield.

Postwar Growth

After World War II Scripps Howard's sales grew dramatically, from nearly $50 million in 1940 to more than $100 million in 1948 and $140 million in 1952. Profits, however, were not increasing. Due to the rising cost of labor, newsprint, and printing machinery, profits were hovering around $10 million, according to Forbes magazine. In 1953 E.W. Scripps's grandson Charles E. Scripps became company chairman at the age of 33, and Roy Howard's son Jack R. became company president at the age of 42. By this time Scripps Howard had 19 newspapers with a total circulation of four million. The company was also expanding into broadcasting and owned radio and television stations in Cleveland and Cincinnati as well as in Knoxville and Memphis, Tennessee. The Scripps family trust still owned nearly 75 percent of the company. Management was decentralized with general operations conducted in New York, editorial policy in Washington, and finances in Cincinnati.

In 1958 United Press merged with the Hearst Corporation's troubled International News Service to become United Press International (UPI). Hearst gained five percent ownership of UPI, but most former International News Service employees were laid off. Also that year Scripps bought the *Cincinnati Times-Star* and merged it into the Post, giving the company control of all of Cincinnati's daily newspapers. The *Cincinnati Enquirer*—which had been acquired in 1956—was carefully kept separate from the other papers to diminish possible charges of a monopoly. In 1964, however, the U.S. Department of Justice accused Scripps Howard of owning a monopoly and ordered it to sell the *Enquirer.* The *Enquirer* was far stronger financially, but the trust's lawyers advised the firm that it would be better off selling it, rather than trying to sell the *Post.*

In the meantime, Scripps continued building its broadcast division, buying WPTV in West Palm Beach, Florida, for $2 million in 1961. In 1963 the broadcast properties were taken public under the name Scripps Howard Broadcasting Company. The initial offering quickly sold out, leaving the E.W. Scripps Company with two-thirds ownership.

Roy Howard died in 1964. One of the problems Jack Howard—who had succeed Roy Howard as president in 1953—faced was that the company was still run for the beneficiaries of the E.W. Scripps trust, and the trustees' lawyers sometimes had a large role in significant corporate decisions. More importantly, with the rise of television after World War II, evening newspapers across the United States found their circulations declining: people read the newspaper in the morning and watched the news on television in the evening. In addition, management of Scripps had become so conservative that critics charged it had no long-range plans and did little beyond preserve its assets. More and more Scripps newspapers took advantage of a law that allowed newspapers in danger of failing to partially merge with stronger rivals, keeping only editorial departments separate. By 1980, 8 of the 16 remaining Scripps dailies were in such arrangements, a higher percentage than any other major chain.

In 1976 Jack Howard retired as president of E.W. Scripps but remained a director of E.W. Scripps and chairman of Scripps Howard Broadcasting. Edward Estlow became E.W. Scripps's first CEO who was not from the Scripps or Howard families; he had been the chain's general business manager.

Scripps slowly began to change in the 1970s. In 1977 the company bought for $29 million the 90 percent of Media Investment Co. that it did not already own. Media Investment had holdings in some of Scripps's newspapers and radio and television stations. The purpose of acquiring the investment company was to permit employees to own shares in the diversified E.W. Scripps Company.

Refocusing and Going Public in the 1980s

UPI losses were continuing to increase—$24 million between 1975 and 1980. In addition some of Scripps's newspapers were operating in the red, including the flagship *Cleveland*

Press. In 1980 Scripps sold the *Press* for an undisclosed amount to Cleveland retailer Joseph E. Cole. The chain then had 16 daily newspapers, making it the seventh largest in the United States. Scripps continued a policy of not reporting financial data, but the *Wall Street Journal* cited its sales at approximately $550 million.

In 1981 the E.W. Scripps Company began looking for a buyer for UPI. Estlow said that part of the reason was the possibility that the beneficiaries of the Scripps trust fund might bring legal action forcing the closing or selling of the wire service. In 1982 the firm found a buyer for UPI: Media News Corporation, a private firm started for the purpose of buying UPI, which had 224 bureaus and 2,000 employees. The purchase price was not disclosed, but industry analysts felt it could not have been much more than the value of UPI's assets, which the New York Times estimated were worth about $20 million.

In the early 1980s Scripps began funneling money into its chain of weekly business journals. The publications were losing readership and advertising revenue, and some criticized them as lacking hard news. In 1985 Lawrence A. Leser became president of Scripps and quickly began making changes. He sold many of the weeklies, as well as a videotape publishing business, and concentrated on building the cable, broadcast, and daily newspaper operations, particularly in the rapidly growing South and West.

In 1986 the company bought two television stations from Capital Cities Communications and the American Broadcasting Co. Scripps paid an estimated $246 million for WXYZ in Detroit and WFTS in Tampa. The company was also building a string of cable television systems. In 1986 Scripps merged with the John P. Scripps newspaper chain, which was comprised of six California newspapers and one Washington newspaper.

These purchases, along with a cable system being built in Sacramento, left the company with millions of dollars in debt. Partly in an effort to pay off this debt, the Scripps family members who controlled the Scripps trust fund decided to take the company public. In 1987, as a prelude to its stock offering, the firm officially released financial data for the first time, reporting operating income of $150 million on sales of $1.15 billion. It owned 20 daily newspapers and nine television stations and cable systems in ten states. The 1988 stock offering left the Scripps trust with approximately 75 percent ownership of the company.

In December 1988 the E.W. Scripps Company formed Scripps Howard Productions to produce and market television programs. In February 1989 it sold the six-day Florida Sun-Tattler for an undisclosed amount and bought Cable USA's system in Carroll County, Georgia. Profits for 1989 were $89.3 million on sales of $1.27 billion.

In 1990 Scripps began the SportSouth Network to provide regional sports programming on cable television in six southern states. Most of the firm's revenue continued to come from newspapers, but it believed that future growth would come from cable television. As of the early 1990s, the firm had 672,000 cable subscribers, making it one of the 20 largest cable system operators in the United States.

The E.W. Scripps Company also negotiated to buy WMAR-TV in Baltimore from Gillett Holdings for $154.7 million. Scripps backed out of the deal at the last minute and was sued by Gillett. The firms settled out of court, and Scripps bought the station for $125 million in cash. In late 1991 the company announced a modernization of the *Pittsburgh Press* delivery systems. The modernization, which would cause hundreds of layoffs, resulted in a crippling strike that lasted well into 1992; the newspaper was sold on December 31, 1992.

Increased Emphasis on Television in the 1990s

In 1993 the E.W. Scripps Company sold its Pharos Books and World Almanac Education units to K-III Communications and also sold its four radio stations, its television station in Memphis, Tennessee, and newspapers in Tulare, California, and San Juan, Puerto Rico. These moves occurred at the same time that the company was shifting to an increased emphasis on television and specifically on television content—as opposed to simply broadcasting. In March 1994 the E.W. Scripps Company purchased Cinetel Productions, a leading independent producer of cable-television programming. Ownership of Cinetel helped the company launch a new cable network, Home & Garden Television (HGTV), in late 1994. HGTV, which was available in 48.4 million cable homes by early 1999, marked the beginning of the company's cable narrowcasting strategy—what it called "category television." The aim was to become the predominant player in particular cable television categories. HGTV's category was that of home decorating, improvement, and maintenance; landscaping; and gardening.

In 1994 Charles E. Scripps retired as company chairman, having served in that position since 1953, and was succeeded by Lawrence A. Leser. Two years later, William R. Burleigh was named president and CEO. Meantime, the E.W. Scripps Company continued to deemphasize its broadcasting side when it sold its cable systems to Comcast Corporation in November 1995 for $1.58 billion. On the newspaper side, the company divested its Watsonville, California, daily in 1995 and spent $120 million in 1996 to acquire the *Vero Beach Press Journal*, a daily. In August 1997 the E.W. Scripps Company traded its daily newspapers in Monterey and San Luis Obispo, California, to Knight-Ridder, Inc. for the Daily Camera, a newspaper in Boulder, Colorado. In October of that same year the company paid $775 million in cash—the firm's largest acquisition in history—for the media assets of Harte-Hanks Communications Inc., which included five daily newspapers in Texas and one in South Carolina, a group of community newspapers in Texas, and a television and radio station in San Antonio.

This purchase immediately led to the company's acquisition of a second cable category network as the television and radio station were traded for a 56 percent controlling interest in the Food Network, a cable network featuring programming on food and nutrition. In early 1999 the E.W. Scripps Company sold the community newspapers it gained via Harte-Hanks to Lionheart Holdings LLC, a community newspaper group based in Fort Worth, Texas.

In May 1998 the company sold Scripps Howard Productions, and later that year Cinetel Productions changed its name to Scripps Productions. E.W. Scripps Company launched its third cable category network, Do-It-Yourself, in 1999. The company's category television unit was its fastest-growing operation, with revenues reaching $148.6 million in 1998, an increase of 76.5 percent over the previous year.

2000 and Beyond

As it entered the 21st century, the company's ten broadcast television stations (six ABC, three NBC, and one independent) reached an estimated 10 percent of all American homes. Scripps was one of the largest U.S. independent operators of ABC affiliates, and the company's cable television networks experienced fast and continuous growth as well. HGTV climbed to more than 78 million subscribers in the early 2000s, while the Food Network had more than 75 million subscribers.

During this time, E.W. Scripps named a new leader. Ken Lowe first became president and then CEO of the company. Lowe had joined E.W. Scripps in the 1980s, working in the radio broadcast department. He moved on to the cable operations in the 1990s and there conceived and implemented his idea for the Home and Garden network HGTV. Scripps revenues in 2001 reached $1.4 billion, with the majority (51 percent) generated from the newspaper business. Nineteen percent of 2001 revenues came from broadcast television, 24 percent from category television, and the remaining six percent from licensing and other media. Scripps' subsidiary, Shop At Home Network, LLC (acquired in whole in 2002), launched a web site during this time, allowing program viewers and Internet surfers to shop electronically. Shop at Home Network programming also continued to be transmitted via satellite to cable television systems, direct broadcast satellite systems, and television stations. Sales for Shop At Home Network in 2002 were $195.8 million.

By 2002 Scripps newspapers were serving 20 markets in the United States, spanning Washington State to Florida. Readership totaled 1.4 million daily and 1.7 million on Sunday, making Scripps the ninth largest publisher of newspapers in the United States. Two hundred fifty of Scripps newspapers sponsored the annual Scripps Howard National Spelling Bee, a tradition since the 1940s, in which by the early 2000s some ten million children participated annually.

Also during this time, the company launched the Fine Living Network, dedicated, in the words of a company spokesperson, ''to the pursuit of personal passions and the art of getting the most from every moment in life.'' Programs ranged in subject matter from travel and financial planning to yoga instruction and party planning. In 2004, due largely to its cable programming operations, and the advertising dollars it generated, Scripps announced higher than predicted profits, prompting a two-for-one stock split for its shareholders.

Principal Operating Units

Newspapers; Broadcast; Scripps Networks; Retail Television; Licensing and Other Media.

Principal Competitors

Gannett Company Inc.; The Hearst Corporation.

Further Reading

Abrams, Bill, ''Capital Cities, ABC to Sell 2 TV Outlets to Scripps Howard,'' *Wall Street Journal,* July 29, 1985.

Astor, David, ''Scripps Decides to Keep United Media,'' *Editor and Publisher,* August 21, 1993, pp. 34–35.

Baldasty, Gerald J., *E.W. Scripps and the Business of Newspapers,* Urbana: University of Illinois Press, 1999, 217 p.

Brendon, Piers, *The Life and Death of the Press Barons,* New York: Atheneum, 1983, 288 p.

Casserly, Jack, *Scripps: The Divided Dynasty,* New York: Donald I. Fine, 1993, 236 p.

Cauley, Leslie, ''Scripps Quickly Proves an Outsider Can Start a Cable-TV Network,'' *Wall Street Journal,* November 13, 1998, pp. A1+.

Cochran, Negley D., *E.W. Scripps,* New York: Harcourt, Brace and Company, 1933.

Downey, Kevin, ''Pursuing a Passion for Media,'' *Broadcasting & Cable,* January 19, 2004.

''E.W. Scripps Co.,'' *Mediaweek,* May 17, 2004, p. 17.

Garneua, George, ''Scripps Buys Six Dailies,'' *Editor and Publisher,* May 24, 1997, pp. 6–7, 29.

Fass, Allison, ''Extra, Extra,'' *Forbes,* September 6, 2004, p. 200.

Gilbert, Nick, ''E.W. Scripps: Purring Without Garfield,'' *Financial World,* May 24, 1994, pp. 14+.

Jessell, Harry A., ''E.W. Scripps: Building, Growing with HGTV,'' *Broadcasting and Cable,* March 2, 1998, pp. 18–22.

Katz, Richard, ''Scripps Tills Lush Niche Cable Garden,'' *Variety,* August 24, 1998, p. 18.

King, Michael J., ''Weakened Chain,'' *Wall Street Journal,* November 28, 1980.

Lillo, Andrea, ''Merger Gives Scripps 100 Percent of TV Shopping Network,'' *Home Textiles Today,* January 5, 2004, p. 17.

Lipin, Steven, ''Scripps to Acquire Harte-Hanks's Media Assets,'' *Wall Street Journal,* May 19, 1997, pp. A3, A4.

Pace, Eric, ''U.P.I. Sold to New Company,'' *New York Times,* June 3, 1982.

Phillips, Stephen, and David Lieberman, ''Extra! Extra! Get Yer Share of Scripps,'' *Business Week,* July 11, 1988.

Robichaux, Mark, ''Comcast to Buy E.W. Scripps's Cable Systems,'' *Wall Street Journal,* October 30, 1995, p. A3.

''Roy W. Howard, Publisher, Dead,'' *New York Times,* November 21, 1964.

''Scripps Acquires all of Shop At Home,'' *Mediaweek,* January 5, 2004, p. 21.

''Scripps and Howard,'' *Forbes,* October 1953.

Sherman, Jay, ''Campaign Ads Brighten Profits,'' *TelevisionWeek,* July 19, 2004, p. 18.

Trimble, Vance H., *The Astonishing Mr. Scripps: The Turbulent Life of America's Penny Press Lord,* Ames: Iowa State University Press, 1992, 547 p.

——, ed., *Scripps-Howard Handbook,* 3rd ed., Cincinnati: E.W. Scripps, 1981, 400 p.

—Scott M. Lewis
—updates: David E. Salamie; Catherine Holm

East Japan Railway Company

2-2, Yoyogi 2-chrome
Shibuya-ku, Tokyo 151-8578
Japan
Telephone: (81) 3 5334-1151
Fax: (81) 3 5334-1110
Web site: http://www.jreast.co.jp

Public Company
Incorporated: 1987
Employees: 77,009
Sales: $24 billion (2004)
Stock Exchanges: Tokyo Osaka Nagoya
Ticker Symbol: 9020
NAIC: 485112 Commuter Rail Systems

East Japan Railway Company (JR East) is the largest passenger railway company in the world. Approximately 16 million passengers travel on its 4,665-mile network each day. The company operates a five-route shinkansen, or bullet train, that travels between Tokyo and the eastern mainland of Japan. While transportation accounts for the majority of JR East's sales, the company is also involved in real estate, advertising, publicity, hotel operations, information services, housing development, construction, car rentals, and credit card services. JR East was once a government-owned entity; it became fully privatized in 2002.

Early History

East Japan Railway Company was the largest of the six regional passenger companies into which Japan's state-owned railroad company, Japan National Railway, was divided in April 1987. Japan's railroad first began as a national railroad, since at the beginning of the Meiji Restoration no other organization could finance such a large project. The first railroad, opened in September 1872, ran from Shimbashi, west of Tokyo, to Yokohama in Kanagawa Prefecture, the main port near Tokyo. It was 23.8 kilometers long, with a gauge of 1,067 millimeters. To finance its construction, the Japanese government raised £1 million in London by issuing bonds through the Oriental Bank.

British engineers such as Edmund Morel, John Diack, and John England supervised the line's construction, giving advice to the Japanese government on railroad management and technology. Most of the materials and machines were brought from Britain as well. The British engineers were paid high salaries; for instance, the foreign general manager in the railroad office earned ¥2,000 per month, whereas the highest-ranking minister in the Japanese government earned only ¥800 per month. Most of the foreign railroad engineers left Japan by the end of the 1880s. The Japanese had learned enough about railroad construction and management from the British, and Japanese government-sponsored students of modern railroad technology had returned home from Britain to apply their expertise to domestic railroad construction.

One of these students was Masaru Inoue, who had studied civil engineering and mining at University College in London. He was invited to participate in the construction of the first Japanese railroad, and as head of the ministry of transport took the lead in railroad construction and in forming Japanese railroad policy. He was responsible for the government's decision to build all the railroads itself, but soon realized the difficulty of funding the project. Economic problems and a shortage of government funds meant that the construction of private railroads had to be permitted, though the government provided subsidies and other assistance.

The first and largest private railroad was the Nippon Railroad, operating between Ueno, Tokyo, and Aomori, the largest city in the north of Japan's main island. The Nippon Railroad was financed mainly by the daimyo, or nobles, who had received compensation from the government for losing their former status at the time of the Meiji Restoration. The first stretch of the railroad opened in 1883, and its success induced the railroad boom from the end of the 1880s. As a result of the boom in railroad construction, the total length of the private railroad soon came to exceed that of the national railroad by a considerable margin: in 1905, the mileage of the private railroads attained 5,282 kilometers, compared with the national railroad's 2,414 kilometers.

Private Railroads Are Nationalized: 1906

There was a lobby in the Japanese government for the nationalization of the private railroads. After the Russo-Japanese War,

Company Perspectives:

The JR East Group will aim to function as a corporate group providing high quality and advanced services with railway businesses at its core while achieving sound management. For this purpose, every individual employee of the group will endeavor to support safe and punctual transportation and supply convenient and high-quality products. Every employee will take on the challenge of improving the standard of services and raising the level of technology in order to further gain the confidence and trust of customers. As a "trusted life-style service creating group," we will go forward with our customers to contribute to the achievement of a better living, the cultural development of local communities, and the protection of the global environment.

the military powers were especially anxious to nationalize major private railroad companies to facilitate through-traffic on all trunk lines, particularly in the event of an emergency such as war. Much discussion took place in the Diet, and there was strong opposition from the private railroad shareholders.

In 1906, 17 private railroad companies were nationalized as Kokuyo Tetsudo or Japan National Railway (JNR). The financial compensation paid to the private shareholders was equal to approximately double the paid capital. From the national economic viewpoint, the nationalization of the railroads made it possible to mobilize assets into other heavy industries. About ¥450 million—equal to about two-thirds of Japan's industrial, mining, and transport assets in 1907—were paid in the form of national debt to shareholders, who converted it into cash and invested it in other key industries. As the result of the nationalization, the government controlled 4,833 kilometers including unopened lines, 1,118 locomotives, 3,067 passenger carriages, 20,884 freight carriages, and 8,409 employees. The national railroad's share of transport increased drastically from the pre-nationalization level of 32 percent to 90.9 percent, in terms of lines in operation. In terms of passengers per kilometer and tons per kilometer, the national railroads had 83.8 percent and 91.4 percent of the total respectively, compared with 37.7 percent and 29.4 percent before nationalization. The national railroad had gained a monopoly in land transportation.

Accordingly, the management structure had to be changed. In 1907 Tetsudosagyo-kyoku (the Railroad Bureau) was reorganized to become Teikoku Tetsudo-cho (the Imperial Railroad Department), and in 1908 the latter was placed under the direct control of the Cabinet, changing its name to Tetsudo-in (the Railroad Ministry). Tetsudo-in was composed of five Control Divisions: Hokkaido, Tobu, Chubu, Seibu, and Kyushu. These divisions had a certain degree of autonomy.

The first president of Tetsudo-in was Shimpei Goto, who had been president of the South Manchuria Railroad for about three years. He established Kokutetsu Dai Kazokushugi (JNR familism), an ideology designed to unify a staff of about 90,000 into a kind of family, bringing together numerous employees who had belonged to various private railroad companies.

Goto also made efforts to change from narrow gauge—10.67 centimeters—to standard gauge—14.35 centimeters, though almost all the private and national railroads had adopted the former. It is not clear why the Meiji government had originally adopted narrow gauge, but Shigenobu Okuma, who had negotiated with the British over the introduction of the railroad system into Japan, remarked that the government had not foreseen the kind of problems that would be incurred as a result of its choice of gauge. The British engineers' recommendation of narrow gauge had been based on Japan's economic climate at that time. Goto wished to increase traffic capacity by widening the gauge. However, there was strong opposition to the change from the military powers. In the end, the government chose to extend the railroads rather than widen the gauge. Japan National Railway had to wait until the introduction of the Shinkansen (Bullet Train) in 1964 for its conversion to standard gauge.

In 1910 Japan had 7,838 kilometers of railroad; by 1930 it had increased to 14,574 kilometers. The national railroad was, however, easily affected by the politicians who promoted the construction of lines in certain regions in order to win local support, regardless of profitability.

Japan National Railway increased the amount of passenger and freight traffic from the mid-1910s to the 1920s. Forty-five million tons of freight were transported in 1916, as opposed to eighty-one million tons in 1926. In 1916 the number of freight carriages was about 43,000, increasing to about 60,000 in 1926. However, from the latter part of the 1920s, especially during the Great Depression from 1929, JNR's freight transport growth was slow, with a 17 percent increase from 12.5 billion tons per kilometer in 1926 to 14.5 billion tons per kilometer in 1935, a sharp contrast to the freight traffic growth rate of 79 percent in the 11 years from 1916 to 1926. Passenger traffic was similarly affected. In the 1910s and 1920s, passenger numbers had increased rapidly, especially season ticket holders, as workers tended to commute by train from the expanding suburbs. In the latter part of the 1920s JNR faced increasing competition from motor vehicles. In 1930 JNR's freight traffic revenue in the 50-kilometer range fell by 41 percent owing to competition from trucks. As for passenger transport, JNR faced competition from bus services for short-distance journeys of between five and 20 kilometers. Urban transport was gradually taken over by private and municipal electric trams and private electric railroads, and by the subway system, which first opened in 1927. However, JNR still held a strong position and its business flourished, especially long-distance transportation. It also launched bus services, connecting with railroad stations, in 1930. Bus services acted as feeders for the railroads as well as replacing railroads in areas where the demand for transport was not strong, but some form of transport was essential.

The development of civil and mechanical engineering was an important part of JNR's history, culminating in high-technology systems such as the Shinkansen. The construction of early railroad lines was undertaken by Japanese civil engineers, though initially under the guidance of British engineers. By 1880, however, the time of the Kyoto-Otsu project, Japanese engineers were able to carry out all types of construction, including a tunnel of 18 kilometers.

JNR was also able to manufacture rolling stock at an early stage, first by importing the main parts and later obtaining them from Japanese suppliers. Passenger and freight carriages were relatively easy to manufacture, compared to locomotives. At the

Key Dates:

1872: Japan's first railroad is opened.
1906: Seventeen private railroad companies are nationalized as the Japan National Railway (JNR).
1949: JNR is organized as a public company.
1964: The Shinkansen (bullet train) is introduced.
1987: JNR is privatized and divided into six regional passenger companies; East Japan Railway Company (JR East) is formed as a result.
1993: Shares of JR East are listed on the Tokyo, Osaka, and Nagoya stock exchanges.
2002: The Japan Railway Construction Public Corporation sells its remaining shares of JR East; the company becomes fully privatized.

beginning of the 1880s, almost 100 percent of passenger carriages and freight cars were manufactured in Japan. By contrast, most of the locomotives were initially imported from Britain, but from the 1890s American locomotives were introduced, mainly in Hokkaido, in the north of Japan's main island, and German locomotives in Kyushu, south of the main island. The dominance of British locomotives was gradually eroded by these newcomers.

It took some time for Japanese engineers to master locomotive manufacturing. The first domestic-built locomotive was made in 1893 under the guidance of Richard Trevithic, a grandson of Richard Trevithic, one of the pioneers of British railroad engineering. As the length of lines and volume of transport increased, the number of Japanese-produced locomotives grew as Japanese familiarity with Western technology increased, especially through maintenance and repair. The nationalization of the railroads promoted the growth of the indigenous locomotive industry, because at the time of nationalization 147 types of locomotives from different countries and different manufacturers came under government control. It proved difficult for the government to combine these in one system. By 1912, Japanese factories had produced 162 locomotives and JNR ceased to import locomotives. At that time, 6.7 percent of the total locomotives available at that time were Japanese-made. Between the wars, Japanese factories gradually increased the locomotive manufacturing capacity. Japanese locomotives performed well, even in comparison with western locomotives.

The early introduction of electricity to the railroads indicated the formation of a technocratic element in JNR. Electrification was urgently needed to increase speed and capacity. Around the end of the 1910s, high coal prices became another reason for accelerating electrification. The electrification of the lines was largely restricted to urban areas and some hilly areas such as Yokokawa. By 1935 JNR had electrified 579 kilometers of its lines, but this was only about 4 percent of its total track length. The private railroad companies were more active in converting from steam to electricity because they were more innovative, operating in urban areas over relatively short distances. Generally speaking, JNR's profitability increased along with freight volume.

In World War II, JNR buildings and lines sustained heavy damage and JNR was under strong pressure from the government to cooperate in military transportation. During the war JNR lost 10 percent of its rolling stock, including 891 locomotives, about 14 percent of JNR's total. About 20 percent of JNR's buildings, including stations and warehouses, were destroyed, and 1,600 kilometers of track were damaged, about 5 percent of the total. 65 percent of the tonnage of ships owned by JNR was lost. About ¥1.8 billion was estimated lost as the result of war damage.

Postwar Changes

Following the war, JNR had to rebuild its transport facilities and begin to reform its management structure, including its relations with the government. During the occupation period, JNR was under the control of the Railway Transportation Office of the 3rd Transportation Military Railway Service of the U.S. army, but was left to operate by itself. In 1949 JNR was reorganized as a public corporation, as were the Nippon Telegraph and Telephone Public Corporation and the Japan Tobacco Monopoly Corporation, though they were still owned and heavily supervised by the government. JNR was to be run as an independent profit-making unit outside the government budget, though considerable subsidization was needed, especially for investment in new lines. JNR's management was regulated and supervised by the Ministry of Transport. Increases in fares, freight rates, and employees' wages had to be approved by the Diet.

Freight and passenger volumes increased particularly rapidly during the period of strong economic growth which began in the 1960s. Freight volume in 1955 was 81.8 trillion tons/km, rising to 341.9 billion tons/km in 1970, an increase of 4.2 times. Over the same period, passenger traffic rose 3.5 times from 165.8 billion persons/km to 587.2 persons/km. Modernization of JNR could be measured by the rate of electrification of the lines and the growth in the percentage of double tracks among JNR lines. Only 9.8 percent of the lines were electrified in 1955, but by 1984 it had risen to 43.4 percent. Only 12.7 percent of JNR lines were double tracks in 1960, against 27.1 percent in 1984. The number of steam locomotives decreased from 3,974 in 1960 to 1,601 in 1970, in contrast to the dramatic increase in electric locomotives from 4,534 in 1960 to 12,582 in 1970. In provincial areas single track was laid, as it was cheaper and adequate for low levels of traffic. The conversion from steam to electricity and the introduction of diesel engines were the preferred ways of increasing capacity rather than the conversion of lines from single to double track.

Development of the Shinkansen (Bullet Train): 1964

The most significant event in the postwar development of JNR was the introduction of the Shinkansen (bullet train) in 1964, for a distance of 515 kilometers between Tokyo and Osaka. The maximum speed attained was 200 kilometers per hour, which made it possible to shorten the time of the journey from six and a half hours by the earlier trains to four hours by Shinkansen. The Shinkansen reached peak performance in time for the increase in passenger demand for the Tokyo Olympic Games, which opened in 1964. The sum of $80 million, estimated to cover total construction costs for the Shinkansen, was borrowed from the World Bank. The total cost when it was completed in 1961 was nearly double the original estimate. The Shinkansen line was extended westward to Okayama in 1972 and then to Hakata, the largest city in Kyushu, in 1975. In 1982 the Shinkansen line was extended further, northward from Ueno, Tokyo to Morioka in Iwate prefecture, and to Niigata.

As a result of heavy investment in the Shinkansen and modernization of old lines, JNR's accounts were in the red from the latter part of the 1960s. The deficit was exacerbated by the comparative decline of freight transportation by rail as against other forms of land transport, and the costs of maintaining a work force of 400,000 employees. JNR's performance was particularly poor in provincial areas which were responsible for 94 percent of the total deficit in 1970, although they represented only 8 percent of JNR's total traffic. The railroads' share of freight and passenger transport was decreasing dramatically. In 1950 the railroads had a 51 percent share of all freight traffic compared with 9 percent for road transport and 39 percent for coastal shipping, but in 1980 the railroads' share was only 8 percent, compared with 41 percent for road transport and 51 percent for coastal shipping.

Privatization in the Late 1980s

JNR's deficit grew rapidly in spite of huge subsidies from the government, and was a major political problem. JNR's total accumulated debt in 1987 was ¥37.5 trillion (US$357 billion), the result of employees' pension financing, retirement payments, and the construction of new Shinkansen lines. The Diet, the government, and JNR made several attempts to resolve the problem. However, none of these plans were successful. Eventually, in 1982, the government's Second Special Committee for the Rationalization of Administration (Daini Rincho) proposed the privatization of JNR as a solution to its deficit. This occurred during the course of discussions on the simplification of public sector administration in general. Following the recommendation of the committee, a new committee, Kokutetsu Kanri Jinkai, was established to carry out the privatization of JNR.

At this time JNR was operating more than 20,000 kilometers of railroads nationwide, with about 200 railroad lines, 500 stations, and 600 kiosks. JNR's assets also included 45,500 railroad cars and ¥41.5 billion of capital investment in 155 related businesses with 58,500 hectares of land. The biggest problem was to reduce the number of personnel, which totaled 276,000.

In April 1987, ending its 115-year-old history as the state railroad firm, the Japanese National Railway was divided into six regional passenger companies—Hokkaido Railway Company, East Japan Railway Company, Tokai Japan Railway Company, West Japan Railway Company, Shikoku Railway Company, and Kyushu Railway Company—and one freight company, Japan Railway Cargo, with four other companies, including JNR Settlement Corporation (JNRSC), charged with custody of JNR's assets and the clearing of debt through real estate sales and public share offerings. The total work force was reduced by 61,000 to 215,000.

In April 1988, the company's first anniversary, the six regional passenger companies and one freight company reported total pretax profits of ¥151.6 billion, four times greater than the initial target. In 1989 the seven Japan Railway group companies posted total current profits of ¥211.8 billion, which represented a 39.8 percent jump from the previous year, over 70 percent greater than projected in their business plan. The following fiscal year, the seven companies announced a 26.7 percent increase in total profits from the previous year, and in the fourth year the total profits of the seven companies reached ¥387.6 billion, a 44.4 percent increase from 1989.

JR East in the 1990s and Beyond

Success for JR East continued into the early 1990s. At this time, many of Japan's nationalized companies continued their privatization process by offering shares on the stock market. JR East was the first regional passenger company to go public in October 1993 when 62.5 percent of its shares were listed on the first section of the Tokyo stock exchange.

JNRSC, JR East's majority shareholder, was restructured and then dissolved in October 1998. The company had failed to liquidate certain assets and debt continued to linger. In fact, by 1998 debt was hovering at 28 trillion yen. As such, the Japanese government passed new legislation that required the seven regional companies to pay off 180 billion yen in debt. The government, in turn, was responsible for 23.5 trillion yen in debt that would be paid from the national treasury. The Japan Railway Construction Public Corporation (JRCC) was created to oversee the debt reduction process and handle the remaining assets of the regional railway companies.

In August 1999, JRCC made a second public offering of JR East shares, bringing the company one step closer to full privatization. Meanwhile, JR East worked to control costs and shore up profits as passenger volume declined during an economic downturn. The company continued to focus on upgrading and maintaining its railway system while branching out into new areas. As part of its strategy, JR East developed shopping centers and hotels near its stations in the Tokyo area.

The company entered the new millennium on solid ground. It adopted a new business plan, New Frontier 21, in 2000. According to the company, the plan's five key points included: creating customer value and customer satisfaction; business innovation utilizing advanced technologies; harmony with society and coexistence with the environment; creating motivation and vitality; and raising shareholder value.

JR East became fully privatized in 2002 when JRCC sold its remaining shares. Free from government involvement for the first time in its history, JR East forged ahead with its New Frontier 21 strategy. The company enjoyed success from its new Suica transport cards. Over nine million passengers were using the card just two years after its introduction. It also extended its Tohoku Shinkansen line to Hachinohe in late 2002. JR East remained active in other business ventures as well. The JR Shinagawa East Building was opened in 2004 along with the Hotel Dream Gate Maihama, which was built under railway tracks at Maihama station at the entrance to Tokyo Disney Resort.

With its eye on the future, JR East planned to expand its Shonan-Shinjuku line, complete upgrades and developments at its Omiya and Shinagawa stations, refurbish its Tokyo-area stations, and construct a route that would join the Ueno-Tokyo portion of the Tohoku line, the Takasaka line, and Joban line with the Tokaido line. This would create an additional travel route connecting the northern and southern portions of the

Tokyo metropolitan area. As the largest fully-privatized passenger rail company in the world, JR East appeared to be on track for success in the upcoming years.

Principal Subsidiaries

Tokyo Monorail Co. Ltd. (70%); JR Bus Kanto Co. Ltd.; JR Bus Tohoku Co. Ltd.; East Japan Transport Technology Co. Ltd. (58.6%); Tohoku Kotsu Kikai Co. Ltd. (50.7%); Niigata Rolling Stock Machinery Co. Ltd. (40.5%); JR East Mechatronics Co. Ltd.

Principal Divisions

Transportation; Station Space Utilization; Shopping Centers & Office Buildings; Other Services.

Principal Competitors

Keihin Electric Express Railway Co. Ltd.; Keio Electric Railway Co. Ltd.; Keisei Electric Railway Co. Ltd.

Further Reading

Friedland, Jonathan, ''Tokyo: Off the Rails,'' *Far Eastern Economic Review*, June 30, 1994, p. 60.

Haddock, Fiona, ''JR East Goes West,'' *Asiamoney*, July 2002, p. 6.

Hara, Nobuko, ''JR East Puts Privatization Back on Track,'' *Euromoney*, November 1993, p. 67.

Harada, K., Nippon no Kokutetsu, Tokyo: Iwanamishoten, 1984.

''Japan - Task of JNR Settlement Corp. Still Unfinished,'' *Asahi Shimbun*, November 2, 1998.

''JNR Settlement Corp. Ends Operations,'' *Japan Transportation Scan*, October 26, 1998.

Minami, R., *Railroads and Electric Utilities,* Tokyo: Toyo Keizai Shimposha, 1965.

Nippon Kokuyu Tetsudo Hyakunenshi, 17 vols., Tokyo: JNR, 1969–1972.

Nippon Tetsudoshi, 3 vols., Tokyo: JNR, 1919–1921.

Noda, M. et al., *Nippon no Tetsudo,* Tokyo: Nippon Keizai Hyoronsha, 1986.

Smith, Charles, ''Markets: Riding on Success,'' *Far Eastern Economic Review*, September 9, 1993, p. 63.

Umemura, Shinji, ''JNR Division and Privatization a Success,'' *Japan 21st*, July 1992, p. 38.

—Takeshi Yuzawa
—update: Christina M. Stansell

Easton Sports, Inc.

7855 Haskell Avenue, Suite 200
Van Nuys, California 91406-1902
U.S.A.
Telephone: (818) 782-6445
Toll Free: (800) 347-3901
Fax: (818) 782-0930
Web site: http://www.eastonsports.com

Private Company
Incorporated: 1985
Employees: 500
Sales: $187.6 million (2003)
NAIC: 339920 Sporting and Athletic Good Manufacturing

Easton Sports, Inc., is a privately owned Van Nuys, California-based manufacturer of sports equipment. The company has been a consistent innovator, primarily in its use of aluminum in its products. Easton designs and manufactures archery equipment, baseball and softball bats, hockey stick shafts and blades, and hockey skate blades. It also makes tent tubes and bicycle components. The company is headed by Jim Easton, the son of the company's founder.

Doug Easton Begins Making Arrows in the 1920s

Although Easton Sports, Inc. was not formed until 1985, the company traces it heritage to the youth of James Douglas (Doug) Easton. When he was just 15 years old, Easton became an archery enthusiast under fortuitous circumstances. In the fall of 1921, he was hunting near his home in Watsonville, California, when a shotgun propped up against a car fell, discharged, and seriously wounded him in both legs. For much of the next year, he was confined to the hospital and his home while recuperating. To help him pass the time, a friend gave Easton a copy of a new book written by Dr. Saxton T. Pope, *Hunting with the Bow & Arrow.* Easton became fascinated with archery and as soon as he was able he began to craft bows from yew wood and wooden arrows from straight grained woods like cedar and pine. His excellent work was quickly recognized, especially his arrows, which were soon regarded as the best tournament arrows in the country. At 17, while shooting a round of archery at San Francisco's Golden Gate Park, he met an older man who complimented him on his craftsmanship. Easton credited his work to a book written by Saxton Pope, only to learn moments later, when the man extended his hand, that he had been conversing with his mentor.

Easton made bows and arrows on a part-time basis for the next ten years, supporting himself primarily by driving a delivery truck. He then decided to devote himself entirely to his craft and in 1932 moved to Los Angeles, opening Easton's Archery Shop. Here he made friends with some of Hollywood's elite who shared his enthusiasm for archery. Easton began producing broadheads and in 1938 toyed with a broadhead design that used an aluminum ferule. Having outgrown his shop, Easton moved to a larger facility in Los Angeles, and it was here that be began to experiment with aluminum as an arrow shaft, the result of his frustration with the inconsistencies of wood. He presented his first set of aluminum arrows to Larry Hughes, a local archery champion. Over the next two years, Hughes enjoyed strong results with his experimental arrows, culminating in his winning the 1941 National Championship. However, Easton would not be able to take advantage of Hughes' success because World War II soon intervened, and for the next several years the military commandeered all supplies of aluminum.

A year after the war ended, when aluminum finally became available again, Easton continued his work on metal arrows, which soon led to his first trademarked aluminum arrow shaft, the 24SRT-X. By 1949, Easton stopped making finished aluminum arrows, electing instead to manufacture the shafts and avoid competing with his customers. In 1953, he incorporated the business as Jas. D. Easton Archery, but it was still very much a one-man shop, supplemented with help from his wife, young son James, and occasional part-timers. The 24SRT-X was so successful, however, that in 1956 he hired his first two full-time employees. A year later, he needed more room and moved the business to Van Nuys, where he took over a new 10,000-square-foot building. Over the next decade he introduced the XX75, which would become the best selling arrow shaft in history.

James Easton Joins His Father in 1960

Before hiring outside help, Easton attempted to convince his son, who was by now studying engineering, to quit college and

Company Perspectives:

80-plus years of sporting goods manufacturing success doesn't happen by accident. It's the result of constant innovation and unwavering commitment to being the best. Look inside to find out more.

come work for him. Jim Easton refused, took a job with an aircraft manufacturer, and completed his studies at night. Upon graduation, he kept his job, but after five years he soured on the idea of working for a large company, and in 1960 went to work for his father. The two soon came into conflict over the direction of the business, and it was only due to the prodding of the younger Easton that the company began to expand beyond archery. In 1964, Easton introduced aluminum ski-pole shafts. The company even moved beyond sports in 1967 when it used its expertise in precision tubing to make the thermal shroud for the seismometer used on the Apollo moon landing. In 1969, Easton first became involved in team sports through the production of aluminum baseball bats. Although it did not invent the aluminum bat, Easton developed the technology that made them a viable product. The only advantage of early aluminum bats over wooden bats was that they did not break. Otherwise, they were too heavy, poorly balanced, and hit the ball no further than their wooden counterparts. Easton's engineers worked on the problem and eventually developed equipment to make the walls of the bat thinner while maintaining their curved shape.

As Easton was working out the technical problems of producing a superior aluminum bat, the company's founder died from cancer on December 31, 1972, leaving his son Jim in charge. At the time, Easton was making aluminum baseball bats under a private-label arrangement with another company. Easton insisted on having its name printed somewhere on the bat to ensure that its work was recognized and prevent the customer from building a reputation due to Easton's quality then later dropping Easton in favor of a cheaper source. When the other company refused, Easton launched its own bat brand in the mid-1970s and sold it through an independent distributor, Curley-Bates Company. By the end of the decade, Easton had developed a superior product that was able to command a premium price.

For a time, Jim Easton attempted to take advantage of the company's expertise developed in drawing aluminum tubes to precision tolerances for arrow shafts. Easton positioned itself as a custom house for companies in need of work that a standard mill could not provide. In the end, Jim Easton felt the company was simply becoming a job shop, one that was vulnerable to the vagaries of economic cycles, and he concluded that the business was better off devoting its energies to product development. In 1976, Easton began to make tent tubing and two years later was contracted by PRINCE to manufacture aluminum tennis racket frames. In the late 1970s, an Easton engineer who was an amateur hockey player began working on an aluminum hockey stick. In 1981, the company gained approval for its stick from the National Hockey League, and a marketable model was introduced a year later.

During the 1980s, Easton completed a pair of acquisitions. In 1983 it bought Hoyt Archery Company, maker of high-end bows and accessories. Two years later, Easton acquired Curley-Bates, its aluminum bat distributor. The company was renamed Easton Sports, Inc., and Jim Easton made plans to expand it beyond bats, setting the lofty goal of transforming Easton Sports into the world's top team sports manufacturer of hardgoods. To further that ambition, the Easton brand name would have to gain greater recognition, product lines would have to be expanded to all seasons of the year, and the company would have to gain an international presence. In late 1987, Easton Sports opened an automated warehouse in Salt Lake City to better distribute the company's products and support its long-term goals.

In 1986, Easton Sports Canada was launched and the company began to produce mast and boom tubing for sailboards and bike frame tubing. Easton then tried to bring out its own line of bicycles but soon found that the economics did not work: the company's frames were too expensive to factor in the other costly components of the bike. In 1990, the money-losing venture was brought to a halt. The company was more successful in adding to its line of baseball and softball bats and expanding its hockey business. It introduced composite-based golf shafts in 1990 and ventured as far afield as developing aluminum drum sticks. Also in 1990, the company opened the Easton Sports Lab to further its research and development efforts.

Easton saw its revenues grow from $13 million in 1977 to $90 million ten years later, topping the $100 million mark in 1991. It was succeeding in a competitive marketplace, taking on much larger rivals like Wilson, Spalding, and Mizuno, as well as Nike, which was aggressively moving beyond the athletic shoe niche. In 1991, Jim Easton explained to *California Business* the company's three-pronged approach to doing business in such a climate: "Our strategy is to have a performance product first, to break in the sport and get a reputation. And once you've got that, then you can bring out other good quality products. Otherwise, you're in a commodity business, and you're just trying to sell by price."

Easton continued to dominate the market for aluminum arrows, enjoying an 80 percent market share and producing some 16 million aluminum arrows a year. In 1992, nine out of ten Olympic archers used Easton arrows. From 1972, when archery was reintroduced as an Olympic sport, until 1992, every gold medal winner used Easton arrows. All told, archery products accounted for 30 percent of Easton's total revenues. The company introduced the XX78 arrow shaft in 1992, and in 1995 it expanded externally with the acquisition of French arrow manufacturer Beman.

New Opportunities in the 1990s

Easton was also developing a formidable line of hockey products, but they took time to catch on. A major step towards acceptance came in the late 1980s when top goal scoring forward Brett Hull began to use Easton aluminum sticks on the ice, but the turning point took place in 1990 when superstar Wayne Gretzky, who had been traded two years earlier to the Los Angeles Kings, visited Easton to try its sticks. He liked the product so much that he agreed to a seven-year, $2 million endorsement deal, providing Easton with instant credibility in the hockey world. By 1994, more than 150 NHL players would be using Easton hockey products. The company introduced its

Key Dates:

1922: Doug Easton begins making arrows and bows.
1939: Easton first uses aluminum to make arrow shafts.
1953: The business is incorporated.
1964: Aluminum ski-pole shafts become the company's first non-archery product.
1972: Doug Easton dies and is replaced by his son James.
1985: Easton Sports is formed through acquisition.
1990: Wayne Gretzky signs an endorsement deal for an aluminum hockey stick.
1995: Easton introduces a composite hockey blade.
1999: The world's first two-piece baseball bat is introduced.

Ultra Lite composite plastic hockey stick and X-Treme Graphite blade, developed with significant input from Paul Kariya of the Anaheim Mighty Ducks and other NHL players. Although Easton was capable of producing hockey sticks and blades much lighter than traditional wood versions, it was the players who advised the developers about the need for weight in certain situations, such as winding up for a slap shot. As a result, Easton added weight to the composite material to produce a stick that was lighter than wood and stronger, yet provided the feel that a player required. The sticks proved so popular with professional players, that Easton signed very few to stick deals, because most of them simply preferred to use Easton sticks whether they were compensated or not. By 2000, nearly 40 percent of NHL players used Easton sticks, far more than any of the older, traditional brands like Bauer, Titan, CCM, and Koho.

Easton also became involved in other ice hockey and roller hockey products. In the late 1990s, the company introduce its parabolic blade technology for ice skates, the patented Razor Blade skating system, which used a flex zone between the holder and the runner to transfer energy from the foot to blade, resulting in 25 percent tighter turns and better glide while allowing the skater to conserve energy. The stainless steel blades could also be removed from the graphite holder and replaced. In 2001, Easton introduced the Z-Air Skate, which created a comfortable, high-performance hockey skate combining a thermally activated composite construction, air-foamed latex ankle pads, and side cut tongue to fill in empty space around the foot. These were also the first skates to provide a drainage system to release moisture and keep them lighter, stiffer, and dryer after a game. In addition, they were heat moldable for a tighter fit or to make them ready to wear right out of the box. Along with sticks and skates, Easton developed protective hockey gear: gloves using a special foam to pad the back of the hand where players were often stick checked, shoulder pads and caps using Easton's proprietary Bio-Dri liner treatment to help keep players cool, a spinal pad called Spine Tec, and a three piece system that combines all the upper-body pads into a single unit capable of moving in unison. For the lower body, Easton developed pants that also used the Bio-Dri and Spine Tec technology as well as other high-tech padding.

Although Easton enjoyed tremendous growth with its hockey products, it also remained in the forefront of aluminum softball and baseball bats technology. In the early 1990s, however, the company became a victim of its own success when it introduced a titanium softball bat that performed so well that softball associations banned it, maintaining that the bat was dangerous and would add too much of an offensive component to the game. Despite this setback, Easton continued its innovations in bat design. In 1997, it launched the Redline series, introducing the first Scandium bat to the marketplace. Two years later, Easton offered the ConneXion series of bats, the first two-piece system that significantly reduced vibration and offered a more forgiving sweet spot. To round out its bat product lines, Easton began producing wooden bats, which remained the only material allowed in Major League Baseball. The company's use of wood came by way of expansion. In 1999, Easton acquired Stix Baseball Inc., an Orlando, Florida-based wooden bat manufacturer. Easton also became involved in a related sport, developing bats for the game of cricket.

During the late 1990s and early 2000s, Easton expanded in a number of directions. In 1998, the company entered the aftermarket bicycle component business. To supplement its tent pole business, it added tent stakes and other accessories, as well as snow shoes that used an aluminum alloy. In the hockey segment, Easton added apparel and equipment bags. Although Easton remained a relatively small player in the sporting equipment industry, it was well respected for its technology and marketing skills and was well positioned to enjoy long-term success. Over the years, Jim Easton was approached by suitors wanting to buy the company and investment bankers looking to take it public, but he remained content to keep the business private and family owned. Jim Easton's son Greg had already held top management positions in the company and appeared poised to carry on the tradition started by his grandfather, who as a teenager almost died from a gunshot wound and survived to found a sports empire.

Principal Subsidiaries

Easton Development, Inc.

Principal Competitors

Amer Group plc; The Hockey Company; Mizuno Corporation.

Further Reading

Barrier, Michael, "Hitting the Bull's-Eye," *Nation's Business*, January 1992, p. 67.
Brinsley, John, "Sticking to It," *Los Angeles Business Journal*, February 14, 2000, p. 14.
Svetich, Kim, "Jas. D. Easton Inc.: The Product Is Performance," *California Business*, October 1992, p. 12.
Taylor, John H., "Make Mine Aluminum," *Forbes*, December 7, 1992, p. 150.

—Ed Dinger

Edgars Consolidated Stores Ltd.

PO Box 100
Crown Mines
2025
South Africa
Telephone: +27 11 495 6000
Fax: +27 11 837 5019
Web site: http://www.edcon.co.za

Public Company
Incorporated: 1929
Employees: 10,766
Sales: ZAR 10.53 billion ($1.87 billion) (2004)
Stock Exchanges: Johannesburg
Ticker Symbol: EDCON
NAIC: 452111 Department Stores (Except Discount Department Stores); 452990 All Other General Merchandise Stores

Edgars Consolidated Stores Ltd. (Edcon) is South Africa's leading retail group. The Johannesburg-based company operates more than 650 stores under a variety of fascia throughout southern Africa, including South Africa, Botswana, Swaziland, Lesotho, and Namibia. Clothing retail is the company's main focus, accounting for some 85 percent of its total revenues of ZAR 10.53 billion (US $1.87 billion) in 2004. The company's Edgars department store chain offers a full range of men's, women's and children's clothing, footwear, and accessories, as well as cosmetics and related department store items at 151 locations. Generally located in shopping malls, the Edgars chain also includes the operation of Red Square cosmetics boutiques and Accessoreyes sunglasses boutiques as stand-alone shops and in-store corner shops. Edcon's other major operation is its United Retail fashion clothing division, which serves as the logistics and administrative arm for the company's Jet Stores, Cuthberts, Sales House, and Legit store formats. Originally operated as independent entities, the United Retail formats also have been bundled into a growing chain of multi-brand shops since the early 2000s. The company also operates the 12-store ABC footwear chain. Together, United Retail and Edgars give Edcon control of nearly one-third of southern Africa's retail clothing market. With future growth in this area limited—in large part because of anti-competition concerns—Edcon has begun exploring new retail formats to take it forward into the new century. In 2002, the company acquired general merchandise discount store format Super Mart, which operates at nearly 25 locations. Edcon plans to rebrand the stores as Jet Mart and rapidly expand the chain on a national and regional level. Also in 2002, Edcon acquired CNA, South Africa's leading newsstand and bookstore retailer, with 186 stores, featuring books, magazines, newspapers, stationery, audio visual products, greeting cards, and the like. In 2004, Edcon moved into housewares and home furnishings with the acquisition of the Boardmans homestore chain, which operates 25 stores in South Africa. American-born Steve Ross holds the company's CEO spot. Edcon trades on the Johannesburg Stock Exchange.

Founding a South Africa Retail Leader in the 1920s

Edgars was founded as a small retail shop on Johannesburg's Joubert Street in 1929—just as the world's economy slumped into the Depression era. The Edgars store held on, however, and in 1935 began its long climb to the top of South Africa's retail market. In that year the store moved its premises to Cape Town. The year 1935 also marked the entry of Sydney Press into the company. Press initially joined the store as a part-time worker in order to meet the busy Christmas season. Yet Press, and other members of his family, quickly became the driving force behind the Edgars chain.

Sydney Press took charge of opening a second Edgars store, returning the brand to Johannesburg with a store on Eloff Street in 1937. That year, the company also opened branches in Springs, Benoni, and Germistown. The Edgars extension continued into the end of the decade, with new stores in Durban and on Johannesburg's Field Street, among other locations. Sydney Press's brother Hubert joined the company in the early 1940s, taking charge of various administrative and accounting functions. Another brother, Basil, joined in 1944, taking charge of the group's mail-order business.

Edgars went public in 1946, listing on the Johannesburg stock exchange. The company launched an expansion of its

Company Perspectives:

The Group's business mission is to create value: by providing our customers with the right products and outstanding personal service; and by providing customers with payment options and financial services to meet their individual lifestyles and financial needs.

goods offerings, adding men's and boy's clothing to its original women's wear fashions. Through the end of the decade, the company's stores grew to include footwear, fabrics and other household textiles, and jewelry. Edgars also extended its reach to neighboring Zimbabwe, opening its first store there in 1949.

The 1950s marked an era of strong growth for the Edgars chain, and by 1960, the company already boasted nearly 140 stores. The company stepped up its expansion in the new decade, more than doubling its stores by 1965. The mid-1960s marked the launch of an acquisition phase, starting with the purchase of the Sales House brand in 1965. In that year, also, the company picked up U.K.-based Werff Fashion Stores, which operated 26 stores. Edgars' U.K. expansion was short-lived, however, and in 1971 the Werff chain was sold off again.

Diversifying in the 1970s

In the meantime, the company had acquired another strong South Africa store format, Jet Stores, which featured seven supermarkets in 1965. The company later transformed the Jet brand into one of the country's leading fashion retailers, a process begun in the early 1970s with a massive expansion—between 1971 and 1972 the company opened nearly 80 Jet stores. Part of this stock came from another aborted expansion effort, the acquisition of five Dan Hands furniture stores in 1970. After a rapid expansion, with 35 new stores opened before the end of 1971, the company sold off the brand in 1972.

Instead, Edgars returned its focus to its Edgars chain. In the mid-1970s, the company opened a new generation of ''flagship'' stores, the first of which opened in Parow in 1975. A second flagship opened in Durban the following year. The flagship format continued to grow, and included a 10,000-square-meter store opened on Market Street in Johannesburg in 1976. Serving the company's logistics needs was its new distribution center, opening in Johannesburg that same year. That building was joined by a new corporate headquarters in 1978, in time for the company's 50th anniversary.

By the early 1980s, under Sydney Press, Edgars had grown to a nationally operating business posting sales of more than ZAR 200 million per year. The company attempted a new expansion, acquiring the Ackermans Chain Stores group from Greatermans in 1981. The Ackermans format featured discount clothing and textiles. The extension failed, however, and Ackermans was sold off again in 1984.

In the meantime, Sydney Press, who had guided the company for more than 45 years, lost control of Edgars in 1982. In that year, and reportedly while Press lay in a hospital bed following open-heart surgery, control of the company was taken by South African Breweries (SAB). The event sparked the beginning of a longstanding family feud among the Press family.

Under SAB, however, Edgars flourished. New CEO and managing director Vic Hammond steered the company on its greatest expansion, and by 1990, when Hammond stepped down, the group had established itself as a South African retail empire with sales of nearly ZAR 2 billion. Part of that expansion came from the 1983 launch of a third-generation Edgars flagship format.

Restructuring for the New Century

Edgars continued to grow strongly into the first half of the 1990s, more than doubling sales to top ZAR 4.2 billion by 1995. By then, the company's retail network of more than 520 stores covered a total selling space of 643,000 square meters. In addition to the Jet and Edgars formats, the company operated a number of other store brands, including Cuthberts shoe brand, which had pioneered self-service shoe sales in South Africa; the more traditional ABC shoe stores; Sales House; and Smiley's Wearhouse.

Into the second half of the 1990s, the Edgars chain began expanding its store formats. The Edgars chain in particular expanded through the addition of a number of new in-store concept boutiques, including the Red Square cosmetics corner and a sunglasses department, Accessoreyes. Other boutiques tested by the company during the period included a denim corner, The Issue; a sportswear boutique, Starting Block; and Studio Quattro, which sold watches and jewelry. In addition to being developed as in-store corners, the company also launched a number of self-standing boutiques.

Yet Edgars' growth came to a sudden halt in the late 1990s. Despite steadily growing sales totals, the company had become less and less profitable. By 1998, the group's profits dipped by more than 60 percent—sparking the group's share price to crash as well. With shares dipping as low as ZAR 14 per share—down from a peak of ZAR 170 at mid-decade—the company found itself in dire straits. Employee morale was low, sparking a six-week strike by store workers in 1998. Even longtime majority shareholder SAB jumped ship, unbundling its shares in the company.

In desperation, the company went on a worldwide headhunting effort, bringing in the United States' Steve Ross, formerly with Sears Roebuck, as group CEO. Under Ross, Edgars was renamed Edgars Consolidated Stores Ltd. and listed on the Johannesburg Stock Exchange, becoming known as Edcon. Ross then led the company on a drastic restructuring, reducing store sizes—by as much as half—and consolidating the company's retail operations into two major components. Edgars remained the company's department store focus, while United Retail, created in 2000, took over as a single logistics and administrative umbrella operation for the company's other retail formats. The company then hired Accenture and Comparex to take over its internal IT operations, putting into place a more flexible and efficient infrastructure. Also as part of its IT effort, the company launched two e-commerce sites, edcon.co.za and edgars.co.za.

The changes made in the company began to take hold in the early 2000s. By 2001, the company's profits were once again

Key Dates:

1929: The first Edgars department store opens in Johannesburg.
1935: Edgars moves to Cape Town; Sydney Press joins the company as a temporary employee.
1937: Press opens the second Edgars, returning to Cape Town.
1946: Now led by Sydney Press, Edgars goes public with a listing on the Johannesburg Stock Exchange, and begins a period of strong growth.
1960: Edgars tops 135 stores.
1965: Edgars tops 300 stores; Sales House and Jet Supermarkets are acquired.
1975: The company launches the first of the second-generation flagship Edgars stores.
1982: South African Breweries acquires control of Edgars and the company begins major expansion.
1990: Sales near ZAR 2 billion.
1996: The company launches new small-format boutique concepts, including Accessoreyes and Red Square cosmetics.
1998: Steve Ross becomes CEO and leads a restructuring; the company is re-listed on the Johannesburg exchange and changes its name to Edgars Consolidated Stores (Edcon).
2002: Edcon's operations extend beyond clothing and textiles with the acquisitions of Super Mart and CAN.
2004: Edcon acquires Boardmans housewares retail chain.

gaining strongly. The company's retail operations now spanned almost 430 locations, which, given the group's concept boutique shops, gave the company nearly 725 retail store fascia. By the end of its 2002 year Edcon's sales had topped ZAR 7.4 billion, and the company had consolidated its dominance of the South African retail scene with a market share of some 29 percent.

Yet Edcon recognized that its command of the South African retail clothing market gave it little room to grow in the near and mid-future. Acquisitions of other clothing retailers were likely to raise anti-competition concerns. Instead, the company became determined to expand beyond the clothing sector.

Edcon made its first move in this new direction in 2002, with the acquisition of Super Mart, a general merchandiser. The Super Mart purchase also enabled the company to move into the lower- to middle-income retail brackets. Edcon immediately began plans to expand the chain, reaching 17 stores by 2003, with plans to open four new stores in 2004. The company also planned to rebrand its new general merchandise operations under the new name Jet Mart.

Edcon's new expansion move involved the purchase of most of the CNA newsstand retail chain. Founded in 1896, CNA had grown into a major South African retailer of books, magazines, and newspapers, stationery, and related items, with nearly 200 stores across the country. Yet CNA fell on hard times in the late 1990s, and by 2002 had entered liquidation procedures. Edcon won the bid to take most of the company in November 2002. After integrating CNA into its retail network, including consolidating its logistics and other operations, Edcon acquired a further chunk of the CNA chain, adding 32 more stores from ThisDay Media Stores in November 2003. Under Edcon's control, CNA quickly regained its profitability.

By the end of its 2004 fiscal year, Edcon appeared firmly revitalized, with earnings expanding by as much as 75 percent and sales soaring past ZAR 10 billion. The company continued to seek out new growth opportunities, and in early 2004 the company announced its entry into the housewares and furniture sector with the purchase of Boardmans, a 25-store chain founded in 1982. The company also acknowledged its interest in acquiring new store formats and retail sectors in the near future. Edcon had shaken off its difficulties of the previous decade and now prepared for further growth in the 21st century.

Principal Subsidiaries

Bookwise Pty Ltd.; Cannon Clothing Pty Ltd.; Celrose Clothing Pty Ltd.; Central News Agency (Swaziland) Pty Ltd.; CNA Properties Pty Ltd.; Edcon Sourcing Pty Ltd.; Edgars Stores (Lesotho) Pty Ltd.; Edgars Stores (Namibia) Ltd.; Edgars Stores Ltd. (Zimbabwe); Elixer Marketing Pty Ltd.; Ellesse SA Pty Ltd.; Jet Supermarkets Botswana Pty Ltd.; Laure Fashions Pty Ltd.; Reactor Clothing Pty Ltd.; Shoecorp Shoe Stores Pty Ltd.; Supermart Pty Ltd.; United Retail Ltd.

Principal Competitors

Woolworths Holdings Ltd.; Mr. Price Group Ltd.; Foschini Ltd.; Brandcorp Holdings Ltd.; Galvanising Techniques; Wooltru Ltd.

Further Reading

Claasen, Larry, ''Edcon Goes on Buying Spree to Become the Wal-Mart of SA,'' *Business Day,* December 24 2003.

''Edcon Goes from Strength to Strength,'' *Sunday Times Business Times,* April 5, 2004.

''Edgars Stores Benefits from Extensive Branch Network,'' *Zimbabwe Independent,* September 29, 2000.

Silove, Heidi, ''Edcon Strategy Has Goal of Sustaining Turnaround,'' *Business Day Management Review,* March 23, 2004.

—M.L. Cohen

Edward**Jones**

Serving Individual Investors Since 1871

Edward D. Jones & Company L.P.

P.O. Box 66906
St. Louis, Missouri 63166-6906
U.S.A.
Telephone: (314) 515-2000
Toll Free: (800) 343-8000
Fax: (314) 515-3269
Web site: http://www.edwardjones.com

Wholly Owned Subsidiary of The Jones Financial Companies
Incorporated: 1922
Employees: 8,500 (est.)
Total Assets: $3.47 billion (2003)
NAIC: 523120 Securities Brokerage; 523920 Portfolio Management; 524210 Insurance Agencies and Brokerages

Edward D. Jones & Company L.P. is one of the world's largest brokerage networks, with more than 8,000 offices across the United States, Canada, and England. Almost all Jones offices are one-person affairs, and the firm aims primarily at individual investors who have relatively small accounts. Until the 1980s, Edward Jones offices were found exclusively in rural areas, but the firm expanded into suburbs as well as into big cities, including Chicago and Detroit. Jones brokers specialize in low-risk investments, and its customers are usually in the market for the long haul. While the average mutual fund customer buys and sells a fund every three years, Jones customers on average hold on for 20 years. On several lists maintained by *Forbes* and other business publications, Edward Jones consistently ranks among the top companies to work for in the United States and Canada.

Early Years

Edward D. Jones of Edward D. Jones & Co. was not the same Edward D. Jones remembered on Wall Street as the Jones of Dow Jones. This Edward D. Jones was a broker in St. Louis, Missouri, who opened his own firm in 1922. In 1943 Jones's firm merged with an older investment firm, Whitaker & Co., founded in 1871. The brokerage was nothing out of the ordinary until Edward D. Jones's son Edward Jones, Jr., joined the company in 1948. Jones, Jr., known as Ted, studied agriculture at the University of Missouri, then worked for a while on Wall Street. He had always liked small towns, and was comfortable with farmers and rural people. Up to that point, Jones brokers worked rural territories only as so-called TNT brokers, looking for clients from Tuesday til Thursday, before heading back to the St. Louis office. Ted Jones decided that the brokerage would do well to branch into small towns directly, to offer investment services to people that big city firms usually overlooked. Jones, Sr., disagreed with his son, but Ted went ahead anyway, and opened the first Jones branch in 1955 in the tiny town of Mexico, Missouri. When Ted Jones took over as managing partner of the brokerage in 1968, he pressed ahead with his plans to infiltrate rural America. Most offices were in the Midwest, and from the start they followed the Jones pattern still used today: a one-man office, pushing conservative investments.

Even before Ted Jones took over as managing partner, he instituted a broker training program unique in the industry. Jones trained college graduates who had no specific background in the securities industry. While learning the ins and outs of the financial markets, Jones trainees also polished their people skills and learned to hone in on potential investors. Then they were sent to a town where they knew no one. The new broker was required to make 1,000 cold calls, knocking on doors like the storied Fuller brush man or encyclopedia salesman. To reach the quota often took many months of eight- to ten-hour days pounding the pavement. Only after this grueling initiation was completed was the new broker allowed to open an office. It took a particular kind of person, and not your typical broker, to go for the Jones approach. But the scheme apparently built intense company loyalty among Edward D. Jones's scattered crew. Ted Jones commented on his brokers' training in a June 12, 1986 article in the Wall Street Journal, ''If it's beneath your dignity, then go work somewhere else.'' But for the brokers who could stand the isolation from co-workers, the small town atmosphere, and the exhausting cold calls, there was money to be made. Jones offices prospered, and the company grew.

The number of Jones brokerages expanded gradually through the 1970s, filling the Midwest. The Jones formula seemed to work

Company Perspectives:

At Edward Jones our way of doing business is face-to-face. That means you'll not only find us online, you'll often find us right around the corner as well. Our investment representatives live and work alongside the investors they serve. Doing so has taught us a valuable lesson: Investing is not a one-size-fits-all proposition. Individual investors are real people, each with his or her own personal long-term financial needs and goals. At Edward Jones, we offer real solutions—solutions tailored specifically to your individual needs and goals.

in town after town, from Spearfish, South Dakota, to Paris, Illinois. One area Jones tried and failed to penetrate was Florida. The firm made a big push there in the mid-1970s, attempting to recruit brokers from other firms. This did not work, and Jones bowed out of the state. By 1978, Jones operated just over 200 brokerage offices. At that time, the offices were linked by a teletype system, which let them communicate with each other and also keep up with moving stock quotes. However, the network had grown too big for the teletype technology, and brokers had trouble getting their quotes because of tied-up lines. The company therefore switched to using Merrill Lynch's toll-free number for stock quotes for a time, and eventually upgraded to a sophisticated computer and satellite network.

Under New Leadership in the 1980s

Ted Jones stepped down from managing the firm in 1980, and he was succeeded by John W. Bachmann. Bachmann had begun working for the firm one summer when he was in college, and his first position in the head office is variously described as janitor or messenger. When he took over, Edward D. Jones & Co. had approximately 300 offices, still almost entirely in the Midwest. Bachmann launched the company into a rapid expansion. By the mid-1980s, the firm had close to a thousand offices spread across 36 states. The new managing partner did not deviate from the traditional Jones-style training, but was if anything more avid about it than his predecessor. Bachmann was a disciple of the management expert Peter Drucker, who is credited with turning management into an academic discipline. Bachmann engaged Drucker as a consultant in the early 1980s. Drucker apparently liked Jones's structure, which he saw as a strong center surrounded by the relatively autonomous satellites of the one-person offices. Bachmann's vision of the company, fueled by his work with Drucker, went beyond the small-town markets the company had already extensively cultivated. The new managing director realized that there were many Jones-type customers outside small towns—people with low amounts to invest, worried about retirement income, who would enjoy Jones's conservative investment advice and friendly, personal service. These investors were overlooked by the big investment houses like Merrill Lynch and Charles Schwab, who tended to go after wealthy clients first. Thus Bachmann began training new brokers and opening new offices at a furious pace. Beginning in 1981, Jones grew in terms of number of brokers at 15 percent a year all the way into the mid-1990s.

The company made money as it expanded, with a return on equity of typically close to 30 percent, considered quite high in the securities industry. Even as Jones moved into new geographic areas, penetrating big cities such as Atlanta and Chicago, the company clung to its basic strategy, pushing low-risk investments for individual investors. Jones brokers did well. Figures for the late 1980s asserted that many were making over $100,000 a year.

But there was some evidence that not all Jones's approved transactions were as low-risk as they should have been. The company was involved in a number of lawsuits and complaints in the mid-1980s, brought by customers who were angry at investments that went sour. In the early 1980s, Jones sold its customers debenture issues for Baldwin-United, an insurance carrier, and these bonds were in default within a year. Other troublesome transactions that Jones pushed were energy partnerships offered by a firm called Petro-Lewis and real estate partnerships offered by one Southmark Corporation. These and other ill-fated ventures aggressively pushed by Jones brokers led Matthew Schifrin of Forbes magazine to claim in an August 22, 1988 article that Jones made its money by "peddling a good proportion of overpriced junk." Schifrin's article also reported on a class-action suit brought against Jones by 24,600 investors who had lost money in 1983 on limited partnership shares in something called Natural Resource Management Corp. Customers claimed they had been led to expect a 15 percent minimum return. Instead, every $1,000 invested ended up worth only about $50. Jones management, including managing partner John Bachmann, had a big stake in Natural Resource Management, leading to allegations of conflict of interest. Jones settled these complaints out of court.

Another stumble in the mid-1980s was Jones's expansion into the home mortgage market. The firm started to offer its customers home mortgages in 1986, but over two years, the company lost money on these transactions because the one-person offices were overwhelmed with the required paperwork. The mortgage program was discontinued in 1988. In 1987 the firm organized itself as a limited partnership. This made it officially the Jones Financial Companies, L.P., which acted as a holding company for Edward D. Jones & Co. At the time of the reorganization, Jones posted its sales as $268 million.

Expansion Through the 1990s

By the early 1990s, Jones had over 1,500 offices in 45 states across the United States. While the company still had its biggest presence in the Midwest, Jones planned to push into territory where it was under-represented, including southern California, New England, and Florida. By 1991 Jones offices could be found in every state except Hawaii, Alaska, Delaware, and Massachusetts, and 40 percent of those offices were not in small towns but in suburbs. Managing principal John Bachmann reiterated for the Wall Street Journal on February 12, 1991 that "geography doesn't really matter, anyway." Jones was after a particular kind of customer, and that customer could be found just as well in suburban Connecticut as in Sandwich, Illinois. By this time, Jones was an interesting combination of high technology and old-fashioned style. Every Jones office was fitted with a satellite dish, and the isolated brokers tuned in frequently to videos broadcast from headquarters. Some of these leaked to the press in an embarrassing way, giving a glimpse of the seemingly low-key Jones behind the scenes. Just after the Persian

Key Dates:

1955: The first Edward Jones office opens in Missouri.
1960: The company employs 60 brokers in nine offices.
1979: Edward Jones installs computers and printers in its 200 branch offices.
1986: The firm's 1,000th office opens in Stoughton, Wisconsin.
1994: Offices in Canada are opened.
1997: The firm begins operations in London.
2001: Edward Jones branch offices number 8,000.

Gulf War a Jones principal dressed as "Stormin' Norman" Schwarzkopf, the successful general of that conflict, urged Jones brokers on the satellite broadcast to boost the firms sales with "Operation Bonus Bracket." The presentation stressed that brokers could make more money for themselves and the firm by pushing specific investments, which had added fees.

The satellite dishes were also sometimes controversial in small towns, where they represented an architectural anomaly. The Edward D. Jones office in Beaufort, South Carolina, was picketed in 1991 by demonstrators who thought the obtrusive satellite dish did not belong in the town's historic business district. Otherwise, the satellite dishes kept Jones brokers in constant touch with headquarters and enabled them to make transactions for their customers in mere seconds. Although the firm still presented an image of down-home conservative advice and one-on-one consultations, it was nevertheless completely modern in the way it did business, and increasingly branching out from its small-town customer base.

By 1994 Jones had penetrated every state except Alaska and Hawaii, with more than 2,600 offices. These offices were in small towns, in suburbs, and to a large extent in big cities, too. The company had over 80 brokerage offices in Chicago, for example. That year Jones also made its first move internationally, opening several offices in suburban Toronto, Ontario, Canada. The move across the border happened after five years of research showed that Canadians matched the Jones investor profile almost perfectly. Jones's typical customer in the mid-1990s was an individual in his or her mid- to late 50s, with grown children and a low or nonexistent mortgage. These people were concerned primarily with investing for retirement. They were baby-boomers—people born just after World War II, and now nearing the end of their working lives. The United States was not the only country that had experienced a postwar baby boom. Canada and Europe had them, too, and so Jones began aiming for customers there. In the mid-1990s Jones discussed extravagant plans, saying it would open 300 to 350 Canadian offices over the next five years, investigate Europe, and think about Mexico. Jones's leader Bachmann told the St. Louis Business Journal on July 25, 1994 that he had been approached by Japanese firms interested in a joint venture, but that he was not ready to go to Asia yet.

Jones paused its expansion a bit in 1995 and 1996 to make some internal changes. The firm invested $150 million to upgrade its computer and satellite technology. It had the largest satellite network in the securities industry. It also delved into the Internet, so that by 1997 it had one of the largest client/server systems on the web, and each Jones office had its own home page. Another improvement the company made was to shorten its name from Edward D. Jones & Co. to simply Edward Jones: this was easier to fit on storefront signs. In the mid-1990s Jones also took a second look at some urban markets that had not done as well as expected. Jones had wanted to build a strong presence in Detroit in the early 1990s, but had less than 30 offices in the Detroit metropolitan area by 1996. At the end of that year, Jones started over, announcing it would open over 200 brokerages there over the next several years. By 1997 Jones was back on its expansion tear, hoping to open 100 new offices a month. A large percentage of these new offices were in urban areas. John Bachmann told Fortune magazine on October 13, 1997 that his job now was "to see how large and how important we can become" without selling the limited partnership. As Jones became more and more a mass-marketer, it would make it easier to afford national advertising. Other brokerages were competing for Jones customers, so opening more offices made sense. Merrill Lynch planned in the late 1990s to move into the kinds of rural areas that had long been Jones's mainstay, and banks, too, were increasingly offering some of the investment services that only brokers had handled in the past. Bachmann's plan for Jones was to bring the number of brokerages up to 10,000 by the year 2004.

Edward Jones came to England in 1998, opening its first office in Norwich. A year later the firm had over 80 offices in England, mostly in small towns south of London and in the Midlands. Jones sent some of its most successful U.S. brokers over to England. Here, too, Jones brokers carried on as they did in the United States, beginning with cold calls, knocking on doors, leaving leaflets and business cards, inviting people to investment seminars. The following year, the firm established a foothold in Scotland.

Jones's rapid expansion seemed to pay off. Revenues grew 25 percent in 1998, up to $1.3 billion, and Jones's return on equity remained the envy of the securities industry.

2000 and Beyond

By this time, Edward Jones was well-known for the attention it paid to the professional development and satisfaction of its work force. In 2000, Edward Jones dedicated the A.F. McKenzie Training Center in Ontario; some 400 Edward Jones investment representatives comprised the company's sales force in that country. The company was named the number one firm to work for in Canada by the magazine *Investment Executive* in a 2001 survey. Also that year, as the 8,000th Edward Jones branch worldwide opened for business, *Fortune* ranked the company first in its 2002 listing of "100 Best Companies to Work for in America" while *Kiplinger's Personal Finance* ranked the company first among full-service brokers. By 2003, when 600 Edward Jones offices were operating in Canada, *Business Magazine* had ranked Edward Jones high among the top 50 places to work in Canada. Canadian operations remained an important focus for the firm, and expansion was rapid. By 2004, Edward Jones served more than 150,000 Canadian clients. The company planned to have 3,000 offices in Canada, with 500 of these located in the Province of Quebec. The first five Quebec offices had opened in 2002, representing Edward Jones's first penetration of an English and French-speaking market.

The firm was also recognized for its customer service. A 2002 survey, by J.D. Powers and Associates, of customer satisfaction among full-service investors saw Edward Jones tie for first place. In a national research study in 2003 and 2004 by Forrester Research, Edward Jones was the highest-ranking brokerage named on this list, and placed second in the customer advocacy ranking.

Edward Jones was not immune to increased scrutiny from the U.S. Securities and Exchange Commission (SEC) in 2003 and 2004, as they investigated charges that many mutual fund companies were forming revenue sharing agreements, a practice dubbed ''pay to play'' in which brokerage houses took large payments from funds that they recommended highly to customers while the customers were not informed of such payments. In 2004 the SEC considered taking action against Edward Jones, based on such an inquiry. Edward Jones's 2003 revenue-sharing payments totaled almost $90 million in 2003.

Nevertheless, Edward Jones's reputation for customer and employee satisfaction remained strong. The firm's long-term investment track record was lauded by *Barron's* in 2004, a notable feat given the tough investment climate of the early 2000s. In addition to its investment offerings, Edward Jones offered credit card and life insurance products, continuing to focus on a clientele of individuals and small businesses.

Principal Competitors

Merrill Lynch & Co. Inc.; The Charles Schwab Corporation; Raymond James Financial Inc.

Further Reading

Berman, Phyllis, ''Door-to-Door in Harpenden,'' *Forbes,* June 14, 1999, pp. 86–88.

Burns, Greg, ''Can It Play Out of Peoria?,'' *Business Week,* August 7, 1995, pp. 58–59.

Cocheo, Steve, ''Is Main Street a State of Mind?,'' *ABA Banking Journal,* April 1994, p. 52.

Cowell, Alan, ''U.S. Concern Solicits British Investment Funds,'' *New York Times,* June 1, 1999, p. C3.

Desloge, Rick, ''Edward D. Jones to Stock New Offices,'' *St. Louis Business Journal,* August 5, 1991, p. 1A.

Feder, Barnaby J., ''The Last-Stand Partnership on Wall Street,'' *New York Times,* June 21, 1998, p. BU7.

Hansen, Bruce, ''Pounding the Pavement,'' *Memphis Business Journal,* July 8, 1991, p. 1.

Jacobs, Sanford L., ''To This Broker, Paris Is in Illinois, New York in Limbo,'' *Wall Street Journal,* June 12, 1986, p. 1.

Johannes, Laura, ''SEC Weighs Action Against Edward Jones,'' *Wall Street Journal,* March 31, 2004, p. C1.

McReynolds, Rebecca, ''Ed Jones, America's Community Banker,'' *US Banker,* September 1997, p. 58.

Power, William, and Michael Siconolfi, ''Edward D. Jones Takes 'Rallying the Troops' to Literal Heights,'' *Wall Street Journal,* July 12, 1991, pp. C1, C8.

Power, William, ''Keeping Up with Down-Home Joneses,'' *Wall Street Journal,* February 12, 1991, pp. C1, C13.

Roush, Matt, ''Edward Jones Makes New Expansion Effort,'' *Crain's Detroit Business,* November 4, 1996, p. 18.

Schifrin, Matthew, ''Jonestown,'' *Forbes,* August 22, 1988, pp. 61–64.

Siconolfi, Michael, ''An Alien Saucer Tries to Plop Down in Historic Beaufort,'' *Wall Street Journal,* June 17, 1991, p. A1.

Teitelbaum, Richard, ''The Wal-Mart of Wall Street,'' *Fortune,* October 13, 1997, pp. 128–30.

Van Allen, Peter, ''The One-Horse Broker Is Going Suburban, Too,'' *American Banker,* April 10, 1997, p. 12.

—A. Woodward
—update: Catherine Holm

El Paso Corporation

1001 Louisiana Street
Houston, Texas 77001
U.S.A.
Telephone: (713) 420-2600
Fax: (713) 420-6030
Web site: http://www.elpaso.com

Public Company
Incorporated: 1928
Employees: 11,855
Sales: $12.1 billion (2002)
Stock Exchanges: New York
Ticker Symbol: EP
NAIC: 486210 Pipeline Transportation of Natural Gas

With over 55,000 miles of pipeline in its arsenal, El Paso Corporation—formerly known as El Paso Energy and the El Paso Natural Gas Company—owns and operates one of the largest natural gas transmission systems in North America and is one of the region's largest independent natural gas producers. The company expanded rapidly in the mid- to late 1990s, acquiring Tenneco Energy, Sonat Inc., and Coastal Corporation in multibillion dollar deals. El Paso faced controversy in the early 2000s related to its involvement in California's energy crisis. In addition, accounting errors forced it to restate its financial performance from 1999 to 2003. The revisions slashed the value of its oil and gas assets by $2.7 billion. El Paso has been divesting non-core assets and restructuring in attempt to revamp its image.

Early History

Paul Kayser, a young Houston attorney, founded El Paso Natural Gas in 1928. In 1929, Kayser obtained a franchise from the El Paso City Council to sell natural gas to the city. He proposed construction of a 200-mile pipeline that linked El Paso with natural gas wells located near the city of Jal, New Mexico. After obtaining financing for the ambitious project, he immediately began hiring work crews and securing equipment and supplies.

Pipeline construction methods at the time were crude in comparison to techniques developed during the mid-1900s. The lines were built by hand and the men who worked on the lines had to be extremely tough. Difficulties related to building Kayser's pipeline were amplified by the fact that his pipes would cross some of the most difficult terrain in the southwestern United States. The pipeline had to cross 200 miles of rivers, mountains, and deserts, and it had to be built to withstand all types of natural disasters. Although the work was tedious and time-consuming, Kayser's crews pioneered new methods of welding, ditching, and crossing unique terrain. The line was finished and put into service in 1930.

Unfortunately for Kayser and his fledgling start-up, the Great Depression began shortly after the building of the pipeline. El Paso generated profits of $283,000 during the pipeline's first year of operation, but the Depression-era economy threatened to quash the venture. Fortunately, the city of El Paso continued to buy Kayser's gas. The company was able to pay its debts and to expand its pipeline system during the early 1930s. The company built new lines extending to the copper mining areas of southern Arizona and northern Mexico and in 1934 extended service to Tucson and Phoenix, Arizona.

During the late 1930s, El Paso enjoyed steady growth. It built new pipeline systems extending throughout the oil- and gas-rich Permian Basin in south Texas and extended lines north and west to accommodate growing regional demand. By the late 1930s, the company was generating revenue of about $5 million annually and was beginning to post strong profit gains. Expansion slowed during World War II as the nation's labor and resources were steered toward the war effort. Following the war, El Paso benefited from strong demand for natural gas in the growing southwestern United States. As the postwar economy and population boomed, cities throughout the region demanded energy sources to fuel growth and development.

El Paso experienced explosive growth in the late 1940s. Gains during that period were due in part to the completion of a 700-mile pipeline reaching from El Paso's Permian Basin operations to California. El Paso began supplying gas through a 26-inch pipeline and also began construction of new, larger pipelines aimed at the burgeoning California market. As a result of those efforts, El Paso's assets rose from about $23.5 million in 1945 to $285 million in 1950. Meanwhile, sales increased from

Company Perspectives:

The root word of stewardship, steward, means custodian or keeper. The key idea behind this value is service. As active stewards of El Paso, we serve our fellow employees, our customers, and our shareholders by consistently building long-term value. Of all our five values, this value has the most intrinsic worth. By embracing the idea of stewardship and striving to get it right, El Paso is continuously working toward excellence as a company.

$9 million to $41 million and net income climbed to a record $9 million in 1950.

Growth and Diversification: 1950s–70s

During the early 1950s, El Paso continued to post steady gains as demand for its natural gas increased. It built or purchased pipes reaching as far north as Ignacio, a small town in southern Colorado, and continued its westward expansion, bolstering its feeder pipes going to California and increasing sales throughout Arizona and New Mexico. By 1955, El Paso captured nearly $30 million in profits annually from about $180 million in sales. By the early 1960s, those figures had risen to more than $40 million and $400 million, respectively.

El Paso's big gains during the late 1950s were partially attributed to its 1957 acquisition of part of the operations of Pacific Northwest Pipeline Corporation. The acquisition gave El Paso a presence in several western and northwestern states, with pipelines reaching as far as Washington and connecting to other companies' networks in Canada. In addition to geographic expansion, El Paso began to diversify during the 1950s into related oil and chemical businesses. It created El Paso Products Company as a subsidiary to manufacture chemicals from natural gas derivatives. Despite forays into other industries El Paso remained focused on buying, transporting, and selling natural gas.

After 35 years of leadership, El Paso's founder left his chief executive duties during the early 1960s. The company's president, Howard Boyd, replaced Kayser. Kayser had transformed his company from a tiny start-up supplier with 200 miles of pipeline to a $500 million corporation with 20,000 miles of pipe delivering gas throughout the western United States. Throughout his reign, he remained committed to the pragmatic development of natural resources and sound business practices. ''There is nothing more vital to our economy than the orderly, wise, and free use of our precious natural resources developed under practical, intelligent conservation policies,'' Kayser stated in 1954.

El Paso continued to grow at a rapid pace during the late 1960s and early 1970s. Although natural gas industry profits were generally cyclical, El Paso's overall sales and earnings grew during the period. By the early 1970s, El Paso operated one of the nation's largest pipeline systems. It stretched from northern Mexico to the northeast tip of Washington, with extensions throughout the Southwest and reaching into Wyoming, Idaho, and Oregon. Although federal regulators kept El Paso from operating its own pipes in specified regions, its lines connected with those of other operators to give El Paso access to markets in California, Kansas, Oklahoma, and Nevada.

Partly in an effort to minimize its exposure to cyclical gas markets, El Paso diversified during the late 1960s and 1970s. By 1974, non-gas operations contributed about one-third of El Paso's annual $1.3 billion in revenues. The company's largest non-gas division was its petrochemical business, which manufactured a variety of chemicals used in the growing synthetics industry. El Paso also became heavily involved in the fiber and textile industries, particularly nylon, rayon, and other synthetics. Other El Paso's subsidiaries were involved with mining, gas and oil exploration, insurance, copper wire, and real estate development.

One of El Paso's most intriguing and promising ventures during the 1970s was a venture into liquefied natural gas. In 1969, El Paso reached what it termed a ''historic agreement'' with Sonatrach, an Algerian national oil and gas company. Under the arrangement, the Algerian company would deliver a billion cubic feet of natural gas in liquid form daily to El Paso Natural Gas. El Paso would then distribute the low-cost gas through its pipeline network. The ambitious project required the construction of a nine-ship fleet of special tankers to be owned and operated by El Paso, as well as the construction of storage terminals on the East Coast and in Algeria. El Paso moved 230 employees to Algeria for the project. Liquefied gas deliveries commenced in 1978 and made a significant contribution to El Paso's bottom line.

Although El Paso's liquefied gas venture represented an important success during the 1970s, its non-gas-related operations were generally less fruitful. El Paso jettisoned some of those operations and posted losses from major activities like chemical and fiber manufacturing. To make matters worse, El Paso was harmed by a Supreme Court decision in 1974. For several years, federal regulators had been trying to renege on their decision in the late 1950s to allow El Paso to acquire its northern operations. El Paso fought their efforts but was defeated. In 1974, El Paso was forced to divest the holdings, effectively terminating its natural gas operations north of New Mexico and Arizona.

Despite some setbacks, El Paso managed to sustain long-term growth during the 1970s. Sales dipped following the 1974 divestiture but surged back up to $1.15 billion in 1975, rising to more than $2 billion in 1978. Earnings, however, fluctuated around $50 million to $60 million annually. El Paso's huge revenue gains during the late 1970s reflected turbulence in energy markets.

El Paso benefited from the Natural Gas Policy Act which was passed in 1978. That act basically allowed El Paso to begin competing with other Texas companies for the purchase of natural gas reserves. El Paso greatly increased its reserves after the act was passed, building up a sizable reserve base near its Permian Basin pipeline operations as well as in other regions of the country. It simultaneously boosted its output capacity to meet the expected surge in demand during the 1980s.

As a result of strong natural gas markets and El Paso's increased output capacity, sales topped $2 billion in 1978, rose past $3 billion in 1980, and then increased to nearly $4 billion in

Key Dates:

1928: Paul Kayser establishes El Paso Natural Gas.
1930: The company's pipeline is finished and put into service.
1957: Part of the operations of Pacific Northwest Pipeline Corporation are acquired.
1969: El Paso reaches a liquefied natural gas agreement with Sonatrach, an Algerian national oil and gas company.
1983: Burlington Northern Inc. buys El Paso.
1992: Burlington completes the spin-off of El Paso Natural Gas Co.
1996: El Paso acquires Tenneco Energy.
1999: Sonat Inc. is purchased.
2001: The company buys Coastal Corporation in a $24 billion deal.
2002: FERC rules that El Paso is guilty of manipulating the California natural gas market.

1981. In 1981, El Paso reported record earnings of $147 million. Unfortunately, El Paso's profit gains were short-lived. During the late 1970s and early 1980s, industry competitors had hustled to boost natural gas output capacity with expectations of strong demand. However, a weak economy and a newfound emphasis on energy conservation slowed market growth. Supply outstripped demand in 1982, and natural gas prices dropped. Furthermore, El Paso's chemical businesses suffered major setbacks in 1982. Although El Paso's sales rose to $4.3 billion in 1982, its net income dropped to $53 million.

The Burlington Purchase: 1983

The El Paso Company, as it became known in the 1970s, ceased to exist as an independent corporation in 1983. The company was purchased by Burlington Northern Inc. and became a wholly owned subsidiary. Burlington was a $9 billion conglomerate active in mineral development, timber and forest products, and rail carrier systems. Although El Paso was experiencing some problems at the time, Burlington viewed the company as an excellent complement to its existing mineral development operations.

The acquisition seemed like a good move, particularly in light of new federal legislation scheduled to take effect during the mid-1980s. The legislation had effectively deregulated certain aspects of the natural gas industry. Prior to the mid-1980s, El Paso, in accordance with the Natural Gas Act of 1938 and the Natural Gas Policy Act of 1978, was in the business of purchasing gas from other producers, transporting the gas, and then selling it to local distribution companies. Its business began to change in 1984. Federal legislation passed in 1984 had a tumultuous effect on prices, transportation, and contractual relationships between customers and suppliers. The net effect was that natural gas industries and markets became more competitive. As a result, El Paso shifted from merchant to distributor during the late 1980s and early 1990s. Rather than owning the natural gas it transported, it simply provided transportation services for a fee charged to the owners and/or buyers.

El Paso prospered under Burlington's management. Over the next few years, Burlington spun off or sold several of El Paso's nonperforming divisions and streamlined the company's natural gas operations. El Paso's conversion to transportation services, moreover, was well timed. During the late 1980s, gas prices remained suppressed. While many of Burlington's competitors went deep into debt buying up reserves, Burlington emphasized the service end of the industry through El Paso. Going into the early 1990s, El Paso was recognized as the low-cost provider of natural gas transportation services in its market.

In the early 1990s, Burlington changed its business strategy. After shunning the natural gas exploration and production business for several years, it decided to shift its focus to take advantage of a projected upturn in natural gas prices. During the early 1990s, Burlington sold most of its subsidiaries and reinvested the proceeds into natural gas reserves.

The El Paso Spin-off: 1992

Burlington completed the spin-off of El Paso Natural Gas Company on June 30, 1992. William A. Wise was selected to act as president and chief executive of the once again independent El Paso. The 45-year-old Wise had been with El Paso since 1970, working as an attorney and then serving in various management positions. Wise was credited with helping the company make a transition to transport services during the late 1980s and with helping to make El Paso a low-cost industry leader. When El Paso regained its independence, its pipeline consisted of a 20,000 mile network connecting three oil producing regions in Texas, Oklahoma, and New Mexico to buyers primarily in California, Arizona, New Mexico, and Texas. Sales during 1993, its first full year of operation, topped $900 million, about $90 million of which was net income.

El Paso was in a relatively strong position in its industry going into the mid-1990s. It was the largest supplier of natural gas to the state of California and had successfully changed from merchant to transporter in compliance with new (1992) federal regulations. However, it was also facing obstacles. Most notably, the California gas market was becoming glutted, dampening profits in El Paso's most important region. Nevertheless, investors were enthusiastic about El Paso's chances, as evidenced by a doubling of the company's stock price between 1992 and early 1994. El Paso was pinning its long-term hopes on the rapidly expanding Mexican market, to which it had unsurpassed access. It was also engaged in an ambitious effort to vastly increase its access to the northern California natural gas market.

Problems in the Mid-1990s and Beyond

As part of its growth strategy, El Paso embarked on an impressive acquisition journey during the mid- to late 1990s. Three of the company's largest acquisitions significantly added to its holdings. El Paso acquired Tenneco Energy in 1996 in a $4 billion deal. Wise commented on the purchase in a December *Inside F.E.R.C.* article. "This watershed event unites the strengths of two seasoned organizations and caps 18 months of growth and change in our business." Wise went on to claim that the acquisition solidified the company's "place as a major player in domestic and international natural-gas transmission, gathering, processing and marketing, as well as electric power development.'' Indeed, as a result of the purchase El Paso gained control of the only coast-to-coast natural gas pipeline in the United States. Shortly after the purchase, the company adopted the El Paso Energy corporate moniker.

El Paso's next big move came in 1999 when it made a $6 billion play for Sonat Inc., a natural gas transporting and marketing firm. In order to clear regulatory hurdles, El Paso was forced to sell off its East Tennessee natural gas pipeline, 17 compressor stations, a liquefied natural gas facility, and Sonat's Sea Robin pipeline and its one-third interest in the Destin pipeline. The joining of El Paso and Sonat created the largest natural gas transmission system in North America. The company rounded out its spending spree with the $24 billion purchase of Coastal Corporation in 2001. Coastal had become an attractive target, mainly because of its natural gas reserves, and El Paso was eager to add it to its growing arsenal.

Over the past six years, El Paso had transformed itself into a leader in natural gas pipelines, gas processing, exploration and production, field services, and merchant energy, and the company planned to expand further into liquefied natural gas and telecommunications. Its revenues had also grown dramatically from $2.9 billion in 1995 to $21.9 billion in 2000. The company changed its name to El Paso Corporation in 2001.

El Paso began to face significant challenges during 2001. The Enron Corporation bankruptcy and the ensuing loss of investor confidence in energy companies forced the company to clean up its balance sheets. At the same time, El Paso came under fire for its alleged involvement in California's energy crisis. An August 2001 *BusinessWeek* article summed up the situation, reporting, ''State and federal regulators are investigating charges that El Paso used its control of a key pipeline to sharply boost the price of natural gas flowing into the state. El Paso says it certainly didn't manipulate the market and blames higher prices on California's unique energy problems.'' In the end, however, the Federal Energy Regulatory Commission ruled that El Paso had manipulated the supply of natural gas in California in 2001 and early 2002. The company eventually reached a $1.6 billion settlement but continued to assert its innocence in the matter.

By 2002, El Paso was struggling under a mountain debt. As such, the company began a major sell off of its non-core assets. Over $3 billion in assets were jettisoned in 2003. Additional holdings were sold the following year, including part of its interest in GulfTerra Energy Partners, its refinery in Aruba, domestic power plants, various production properties, and chemical operations. At the same time, the company became entangled in a proxy fight with displeased shareholders that had watched the company's stock fall by 90 percent in recent years. Wise was ousted during the turmoil and Doug Foshee was tapped to oversee El Paso's turnaround.

During 2004, Foshee worked to reposition El Paso. According to the company, it planned to focus on pipeline operations in the United States and Mexico, production in the United States and Brazil, and marketing and trading. It also continued to clean up its accounting records. In 2004, the company revised its 1999–2003 figures, which resulted in a $2.7 billion drop in the value of its oil and gas assets. The move left it subject to an investigation by the Securities and Exchange Commission. While the past several years were indeed tumultuous for El Paso, the company appeared to be slowly emerging from the problems it had encountered in the early 2000s.

Principal Divisions

Southern Pipelines; Western Pipelines; Eastern Pipelines; Non-regulated Business.

Principal Competitors

AEP Inc.; Duke Energy Corporation; The Williams Companies Inc.

Further Reading

''El Paso Restatement to Cut Value of Oil, Gas Assets by $2.7 Billion,'' *Wall Street Journal*, August 24, 2004, p. A6.

''FERC Approves Merger between El Paso, Sonat,'' *Pipe Line & Gas Industry*, November 1, 1999, p. 102.

Fisher, Daniel, ''Hot Seat; Things Get Worse for El Paso Chairman Bill Wise,'' *Forbes*, October 28, 2002, p. 62.

Graebner, Lynn, ''Mojave Pipeline Fate Is Near: Gas Project Hinges on Who Would Regulate It,'' *Business Journal-Sacramento*, December 20, 1993, p. 1.

Grunbaum, Rami, ''Gas Ignites Burlington Resources' Growth,'' *Puget Sound Business Journal*, July 17, 1992, p. 1.

''It's Official. Tenneco Energy Now Part of El Paso Energy Corp.,'' *Inside F.E.R.C.*, December 16,1996, p. 4.

''New Aspirations,'' *International Petroleum Finance*, March 31, 2001.

Palmeri, Christopher, ''Pipeline Glut,'' *Forbes*, March 28, 1994, p. 71.

Pulley, Mike, ''Mojave Makes Move; PG&E Cuts Its Staff,'' *Business Journal-Sacramento*, March 1, 1993, p. 1.

Smith, Whit, ''It Was a Long Time Coming but El Paso and Coastal Have Finally Tied the Knot,'' *Upstream*, March 30, 2001.

''Thriving under Suspicion,'' *BusinessWeek*, August 6, 2001.

Wetuski, Jodi, ''About El Paso,'' *Oil & Gas Investor*, February 2004, p. 45.

—Dave Mote
—update: Christina M. Stansell

European Investment Bank

100, boulevard Konrad Adenauer
L-2950 Luxembourg
Telephone: (+352) 43 79 1
Fax: (+352) 43 77 04
Web site: http://www.eib.org

Government-Owned Company
Incorporated: 1958
Employees: 1,213
Total Assets: $289.14 (2003)
NAIC: 522293 International Trade Financing; 522110 Commercial Banking

As the primary financial arm of the European Union, the European Investment Bank (EIB) is also the world's largest bank and the world's largest lender, topping even such better-known institutions as the World Bank and the International Monetary Fund. The bulk of the non-profit bank's lending remains focused on the member states of the European Union. Of the more than EUR 42 billion in loans signed in 2003, nearly 80 percent went to support infrastructure, industrial, high tech and other investments within the European Union. Germany remains the single-largest contributor to the EIB's capital base and is also its top recipient—largely in order to support development in the former East Germany regions—accounting for more than 19 percent of all loans in 2003. Spain is the next-largest recipient, with loans of about 19 percent as well. EIB has also played an important role in supporting the ''accession'' of the EU's newest member states from Eastern Europe, which joined in 2004 and expanding the EU to 25 states. The EIB has been providing infrastructure and other development loans to these regions on a massive scale since the late 1980s. Nonetheless, since the early 2000s, the EIB has been shifting away from its traditional role as a financing institution and instead has been redeveloping itself as a motor for European economic growth and competitiveness. In this capacity, the EIB has shifted a significant percentage of its lending portfolio towards high-technology investments and to the SME (small and mid-sized enterprise) segment, including medium and long-term loans, venture capital, and other financial backing. The bank also supports the so-called TENs (Trans-European Networks) projects linking all of the EU or at least several of its member states, such as the preparation of a European-wide broadband network. The EIB is based in Luxembourg and operates independently of the European Union government, while deriving its capital base of more than EUR 250 billion from contributions from each EU member. The EU states also provide the EIB with its strong Triple AAA rating by providing financial guarantees. Since 2000, EIB has been a member of the EIB Group, which also includes the European Investment Fund (held at 60.5 percent by EIB itself). Philippe Maystadt, former Belgian finance minister, has been president of EIB since 2000.

Financing the European Community in the 1960s

The European Investment Bank was created by the Treaty of Rome—which established the basis for the European Community—in 1958. Codified under Articles 129 and 130 of the treaty, the EIB's role was to provide financing in the form of loans for Europe's major infrastructure projects. Special emphasis was placed on infrastructure projects benefiting all five of the EC's initial members, particularly those that contributed to the smooth and balanced creation of a common market. Another initial function of the EIB was to serve as a means of compensating the presumed ''losers'' of an inter-European union, that is, ensuring that resources were to be directed toward the weaker economies among the EC's partners.

As the strongest and largest of the five initial EC countries, Germany played a prominent role in defining the nature of the new bank. At that country's insistence, for example, the EIB's capital base was developed through funds raised on the international capital markets, rather than through direct subsidies from member countries. Instead, member countries provided the financial guarantees for the EIB's bonds, which in turn enabled the EIB to achieve a Triple AAA rating among market analysts. This rating made the EIB's bonds all the more attractive among the international investment community.

Another feature of the EIB was that it was established as an independent entity within the EC, with its headquarters in Luxembourg, rather than in Brussels. Directorships were created for

Company Perspectives:

Our mission is to further the objectives of the European Union by making long-term finance available for sound investment.

each member state, as well as for the EC as a whole. While the EIB was expected to cooperate with the other institutions of the EC, its independence meant that it was able to establish its own lending objectives, rather than serve as a financial tool for the EC's political agenda. (Other EC structures, such as the European Social Fund, were established for these objectives.) In this way, the EC's investment and social "adjustment" priorities remained independent from each other. This meant, too, that the EIB was established purely as a lending agent and not as a grant-making authority.

The EIB came into being under the presidency of Italy's Pietro Campilli, who was succeeded after just one year by Paride Formentini, also from Italy. The bank's initial capital base stood at one billion "units of account" (ua)—the currency measurement put in place before the creation of a virtual European currency, the ECU, itself supplanted by the euro in 1999. Italy, the poorest of the original five EC members, became the primary recipient for the EIB's infrastructure and development lending. The EIB also quickly extended its lending activities beyond the EC itself, making its first loans on extra-community projects in 1962. The EC remained, however, the EIB's primary focus.

For the most part of its first decade or so of existence, the EIB played a largely secondary and supporting role. This was in large part because the booming economies among the member nations during the late 1950s and through the 1960s meant that the states themselves were better able to shoulder the burden of their infrastructure development. At the same time, the establishment of a common customs union proceeded strongly. This success meant that there was less of a need to call upon the EIB for assistance in financing the putting in place of the common market among members.

Growing up in the 1970s

The shock of the economic crisis that struck Europe in the early 1970s brought about a refocus in the EIB's role and objectives. The dwindling economies of the original EC member countries made it more difficult for the individual nations to pursue their separate and often disparate national policy objectives. At the same time, the enlargement of the EC, with the addition of the United Kingdom, Denmark, Ireland, and others in the 1970s, followed by the joining of Greece, Spain, and Portugal into the mid-1980s, had brought the EC a still more diversified landscape of economic and infrastructure development.

These factors led the EC to begin taking steps toward developing a European-wide economic policy. The EIB in turn began adopting lending patterns more closely associated with EC economic strategies and objectives. Another important factor in this shift was the fact that the EIB achieved the best rates on its own borrowing from the international market when the projects it proposed to support were directly in line with the EC's own sanctioned policies. In turn, such projects, which received additional guarantees from the EC states, were also viewed as low risk, which also helped the EIB borrow on better terms.

The addition of new countries to the EC brought the EIB's first capital enlargement in 1973, when the banks lending base was expanded to 2.025 billion ua. The larger financial base, coupled with the development of European-wide policies at the European Parliament, led the EIB to draft its own regional lending policy starting in 1974. Under its new policy, the EIB now expanded its lending focus to include industrial development loans in the depressed industrial regions of the growing EC membership. At the same time, the EIB benefited from the creation of a new structural fund, the European Regional Development Fund (ERDF). The EIB began co-financing many of the ERDF's own projects, providing the EIB with a low-risk means of diversifying its portfolio and expanding its range of operations.

The EIB also began lending specifically to the growing number of European Community "associates," particularly countries seeking admission to the EC. The Mediterranean region became a favored target for EIB lending projects. The EIB became responsible in the 1980s for assisting associate countries such as Greece, Spain, and Portugal in achieving requirements for EC admission. In order to fulfill its new mandate, the bank enlarged its capital base twice in the 1980s, to ECU 14.4 billion in 1981 and to ECU 28.8 billion in 1986. Spain in particular became one of the largest beneficiaries of the EIB's new Mediterranean focus and remained the second-largest recipient of EIB loans into the 2000s.

European Growth Motor in the New Century

Another important focus for the EIB, stemming from the oil crises of the 1970s, was the promotion of alternative energy developments in Europe, especially the development of nuclear energy capacity in the member states. Yet the EIB also found itself exposed to a degree of criticism for its environmental policies—or, rather, its perceived lack of environmental concern. In 1984, the EIB countered this criticism with the adoption of a first environmental policy statement. This was, however, considered too weak in its language by many observers and was unable to prevent the EIB's lending to such environmental disasters as the bridge between Sweden and Denmark, the Lihir Gold Mine in Papua New Guinea, and the Lesotho hydroelectric dam, which forced the displacement of more than 20,000 people as well as flooding a large portion of a highly fertile agricultural region.

In the late 1980s and early 1990s, the EIB began developing a number of new markets. On the one hand, the bank began focusing more of its loan portfolio on financing the SME market, as well as telecommunications and urban transport initiatives among EC member countries. In 1989, the EIB also began providing financing to countries in the former Eastern Bloc as these emerged from Soviet rule, lending to Poland, Romania, Hungary, Bulgaria, the Czech Republic, and Slovakia. The EIB stepped up its operations in the region toward the late 1990s as these countries prepared their applications to join the 15 members of what by then had become known as the European Union (EU).

Key Dates:

1958: European Investment Bank (EIB) is established following the Treaty of Rome, which created the European Community (EC).
1962: EIB makes its first loans outside the EC.
1975: The adoption of a new regional policy more closely aligns EIB with EC policy objectives.
1978: EIB begins lending to "Club Med" states (Spain, Portugal, Greece).
1988: EIB begins providing loans to small and mid-sized enterprise (SME) and industrial markets.
1989: The bank begins lending to eastern European countries.
1992: EIB tops the World Bank in lending for the first time.
2000: Libson European Council establishes new long-term objectives, including development of Europe into the world's largest knowledge-based economy.
2003: EIB drafts a new policy, Innovation 2010 Initiative, in support of the Lisbon council objectives.
2004: The bank's capital is increased to EUR 162 billion after ten new countries join the European Union.

In keeping with its growing portfolio, the EIB increased its capital again, doubling its base to ECU 58 billion in 1991. By 1995, after Finland, Sweden, and Austria had joined the EU, the bank's capital base had climbed to ECU 62 billion. By 2004, with the expansion of the EU to 25 states, the bank's capital base had swelled past EUR 163.7 billion. Meanwhile, the EIB had long become the world's largest lending bank, having surpassed even the World Bank in 1992.

Following the Lisbon European Council in 2000 and the appointment of a new president, former Belgian finance minister Philippe Maystadt, the EIB announced a shift in its objectives. While the EIB intended to continue providing infrastructure and policy support to the European Union as it had for more than 40 years, in the new century the bank was determined to play a significant part in achieving the Lisbon summit's stated objective of making Europe the world's most competitive high-technology and knowledge-based economy by 2010.

As part of this shift, EIB quickly refocused its lending portfolio, shifting an increasing percentage of its loans toward supporting high-technology and venture capital programs, as well as the SME market. In support of this effort, the EIB drafted a new policy, called "Innovation 2010 Initiative," in June 2003, providing for increasing emphasis on projects corresponding to the Lisbon Council objectives. At the same time, EIB braced itself for a new boom in its lending portfolio as the EU embraced ten new members in 2004. As the world's largest bank, and as the lending institution backing one of the world's major markets, EIB remained a powerful force in the global economy in the new century.

Principal Subsidiaries

European Investment Fund (60.5%)

Principal Competitors

World Bank; International Monetary Fund; European Bank for Reconstruction and Development.

Further Reading

Brown, Paul, "EIB Governors Are Urged to End Secrecy," *Guardian*, June 1, 2004, p. 14.

Colomer, Nora, "Uncharted Financial Territory Lies Ahead for New EU members," *Asset Securitization Report*, April 19, 2004.

"EIB: Enlargement-related Changes Explained," *European Report*, May 8, 2004, p. 103.

Fleming, Stewart, "Low Profile, High Aims," *Business Week*, October 20, 2003, p. 70.

"Investment Bank Takes New Role in EU Growth Plan," *Irish Times*, October 31, 2003, p. 59.

Lankowski, Carl, "Financing Integration: The European Investment Bank in Transition," *Law and Policy in International Business*, Summer 1996, p. 999.

Milner, Mark, "European Investment Bank Seeks to Spread Its Wings outside the Union," *Guardian*, October 25, 1999, p. 20.

Norman, Peter, "The Catalyst of Europe," *Financial Times*, February 7, 2001, p. 16.

Robinson, Karina, "Laying Europe's Building Blocks," *Banker*, May 1, 2004.

Tremlett, Giles, "EIB: Brussels Is Trying to Spike a Damaging Report on the World's Biggest Bank," *Observer*, March 7, 2004, p. 4.

—M.L. Cohen

Food Lion LLC

2110 Executive Drive
Post Office Box 1330
Salisbury, North Carolina 28145-1330
U.S.A.
Telephone: (704) 633-8250
Fax: (704) 636-5024
Web site: http://www.foodlion.com/

Wholly Owned Subsidiary of Delhaize America Inc.
Incorporated: 1957 as Food Town Inc.
Employees: 73,000
Sales: $8 billion (2003 est.)
NAIC: 445110 Supermarkets and Other Grocery (Except Convenience) Stores

Food Lion LLC is one of the largest supermarket chains in the United States. The company operates more than 1,200 stores in 11 states, primarily in the southeast and mid-Atlantic regions. By cutting its overhead dramatically, Food Lion has been able to offer ''everyday low prices'' to consumers and still manage to reap some of the highest profits in the supermarket industry. Faced with a struggling economy and increased competition in the form of supercenter outlets, Food Lion has responded with some store closures and work force reductions, but has also sought to revitalize the grocery shopping experience through the introduction of a store concept called Bloom, intended to provide a uniquely convenient layout and competitive prices.

Before the Lion: The 1950s–60s

In December 1957 Ralph W. Ketner, Brown Ketner, and Wilson Smith opened a Food Town supermarket in Salisbury, North Carolina. The three men had worked together in the grocery business for some time at a small chain that was owned by the Ketners' father but had recently been sold to Winn-Dixie. Dissatisfied with their new employer, the Ketners and Smith set out to open their own chain of supermarkets. By calling on everyone they knew in Salisbury for a small investment, the trio slowly raised enough capital to begin operations. Although growth was sluggish for the first ten years or so, those early investors made out very well in the long run. After numerous stock splits, an initial investment of 100 shares, originally valued at $1,000, was worth more than $16 million by the end of 1987.

During Food Town's first decade, the company tried every kind of gimmick available to entice customers into its stores. Contests, free pancake breakfasts, trading stamps, beauty pageants, and other promotions captured shoppers' attention, but not their sustained business. By 1967, after a full decade of operations, Food Town had only seven stores, and earned less than $6 million that year.

In 1967 Ralph Ketner formulated the strategy that would launch Food Town's dramatic rise in the retail food industry. Ketner, the story goes, locked himself in a Charlotte, North Carolina, motel room with six months worth of invoices and an adding machine. When he emerged three days later, he had determined that prices could be slashed on 3,000 items, and, if sales volume increased by 50 percent, the company would still show a profit. Gambling that the reduced-price strategy would adequately expand its repeat-customer base, Food Town implemented his plan. Ketner later remarked, ''One thing about taking a gamble: when you're already broke you can't do much damage.'' Soon the company adopted an unusual new slogan: LFPINC, which stood for ''Lowest Food Prices In North Carolina,'' and shifted its advertising emphasis from print to television. Ketner's gamble was a winner; increased volume soon more than made up for the price reductions.

The Lion Acquisition: 1970s

The 1970s were a period of tremendous growth for the company. By 1971, sales were nearly $37 million. Although it occasionally snapped up a particularly appealing acquisition, Food Town preferred to build its chain from within. The company tended to construct more smaller stores rather than fewer larger ones to provide greater convenience. In 1974 the second-largest Belgian supermarket chain, Delhaize Freres & Cie, ''Le Lion,'' purchased a majority of Food Town's shares. Delhaize ''Le Lion'' signed an agreement to vote with Chairman Ralph Ketner for ten years on all policy issues. The company's growth accelerated dramatically in the late 1970s and the 1980s. Food

Company Perspectives:

Food Lion associates know we: are a diverse, proud and enthusiastic team; are knowledgeable, friendly and efficient; are passionate about selling food; are trusted, respected, and rewarded; realize our full potential here; respond to local product needs; and ferociously eliminate unnecessary cost.

Town opened stores in Virginia in 1978 and in Georgia in 1981. In 1977 the chain operated 55 stores; by 1987, it ran 475.

In 1982, Food Town was sued by the owner of several supermarkets in Virginia which operated under the name Foodtown. The court restricted the use of Food Town's name in certain markets due to the similarity. As a result of this action and in anticipation of similar problems with another group of stores in Tennessee, the chain decided to change its name. The new name, Food Lion, was selected partly because the Belgian chain Delhaize had a lion logo, but also because the chain could save money in changing the signs on its stores: only two new letters, an "L" and an "I," needed to be purchased since the "O" and the "N" could be shifted over. This type of frugality was characteristic of the chain. In 1983, Food Lion carried its new banner into Tennessee as sales surpassed the $1 billion mark.

In the summer of 1984, the National Association for the Advancement of Colored People (NAACP) organized a boycott of Food Lion stores because the chain had declined to sign a "fair share" agreement. The agreement called for raising the number of African Americans in management, increasing minority employment, and pledging to do business with minority-owned vendors and construction firms. The NAACP moved its annual board meeting from New York to Charlotte, North Carolina, to attract attention to its protest. The boycott ended in September when Food Lion signed an agreement with the NAACP to increase minority opportunities with the company.

Growth and Prosperity in the 1980s

Food Lion branched into Maryland in 1984. Early the following year, the company acquired Giant Food Markets Inc. of Kingport, Tennessee. It soon sold the 22 Jiffy Convenience Stores that came with the Giant deal, sticking to what it did best—the conventional supermarket trade.

In January 1986, Tom Smith became CEO of Food Lion, replacing Ralph Ketner, who remained chairman. Smith, who had once worked as a bagger for a Food Town store, returned to the company in 1971 as a buyer and became president and chief operating officer in 1980. Smith steered Food Lion on the same course as Ketner had, stressing low prices and efficient service. The company topped the $2 billion sales mark at the end of Smith's first year as CEO.

By the late 1980s, Food Lion had become the dominant force in the regions in which it did business. Stunning earnings and market share encouraged the chain's further expansion. In 1987 Food Lion prepared to extend its territory into Florida. Food Lion saw Florida's increasing population and the relatively high prices of chains already in the area, such as Winn-Dixie and Publix, as an excellent opportunity for expansion. The chain planned to double its number of outlets by first tapping Florida's shoppers, then possibly moving westward through Alabama, Mississippi, and Louisiana. After nine months of market-softening advertising proclaiming "when we save, you save," three Food Lion stores opened in Jacksonville, Florida. The response was phenomenal; security guards had to be hired to help people form orderly lines at cash registers. By the end of the year, Food Lion had plans for 20 more stores and a distribution center of 1,000,000 square-feet to be built in nearby Green Cove Springs. That facility positioned Food Lion for eventual entry into other Florida markets such as Tallahassee, Tampa, and Melbourne.

Since Ralph Ketner formulated Food Lion's everyday low-price strategy in 1967, the company stressed doing "1,000 things 1% better," an attitude that was responsible for Food Lion's operating expenses of only 13 percent of sales, compared to a 19 percent average in the industry. Food Lion cut costs in a variety of inventive ways: recycling banana boxes to ship cosmetics and health products and using exhaust from freezer motors to help heat the store in the winter, for example. Food Lion also used aggressive inventory strategies, ordering enormous quantities of products to save through volume buying.

New Challenges in the 1990s

By the end of the 1980s, Food Lion was the fastest-growing and one of the most profitable supermarket chains in the country. In 1990 alone, Food Lion opened 20 more stores, while sales hit $5.6 billion (beating Smith's goal of $5 billion set five years earlier). Earnings of $172.6 million for the year equated to a 3.1 percent margin, besting the industry average of one percent. Smith set a new goal of reaching $14 billion in sales by 1995. He also became chairman of Food Lion in 1990, replacing Ketner, who remained on the board of directors.

To keep the company growing, Smith broke with tradition by targeting a state noncontiguous to the ones Food Lion already operated in: Texas. That market appeared vulnerable to a low-price operator because food prices there averaged 15 percent higher than Food Lion's. By the fall of 1991, Food Lion had opened 41 stores in the Dallas-Fort Worth area. Sales for 1991 increased 14.3 percent to $6.4 billion, and the firm's margin remained steady and healthy at 3.2 percent.

The following year, however, Food Lion faced several challenges. In November, toward the end of a year in which Food Lion opened 131 new stores and expanded to Oklahoma and Louisiana, ABC's PrimeTime Live news magazine television show aired a story claiming that Food Lion stores had knowingly sold spoiled meat, fish, and poultry to its customers. The report included hidden-camera videotape appearing to show Food Lion employees masking the spoiled states of the products by rewrapping products whose sell-by dates had passed. Through the power of television, the effect of this negative publicity was immediate and significant. Chainwide same-store sales plunged 9.5 percent in November.

Particularly hard hit were stores in the states into which Food Lion had only recently expanded: Florida, Texas, Oklahoma, and

Key Dates:

1957: Food Town is established in Salisbury, North Carolina.
1974: Belgian grocer Delhaize acquires Food Town.
1982: Company changes its name to Food Lion.
1986: Tom Smith, who started at the company in the 1950s as a grocery bagger, becomes CEO of Food Lion.
1999: A new management team seeks to revitalize Food Lion.
2001: Food Lion becomes part of Delhaize's umbrella company for its American holdings.

Louisiana. Compounding Food Lion's difficulties were its less-than-robust sales in these new markets, especially Texas. Some analysts contended that Food Lion had misread the Texas grocery market. In any case, 1992 ended with a disappointing sales increase of 12.5 percent and a decreased margin of 2.5 percent. The full brunt of the PrimeTime story was felt in 1993 when sales increased only 5.7 percent and the firm barely broke even, posting net income of only $3.9 million due in large part to a $170.5 million charge incurred in order to close 88 stores, about 50 of them in the poorly performing Texas and Oklahoma markets. Ketner announced early in 1993 that he would not seek reelection to the Food Lion board, citing his frustration with constantly being outvoted on key board matters. Ketner had reportedly opposed some of Smith's expansion plans.

Food Lion sued ABC for fraud and racketeering, claiming that ABC had concocted the story. Smith also fought back on several other fronts. He moved to quickly boost customer confidence in the quality of Food Lion products by offering money-back guarantees. Moreover, the number of planned new stores was scaled back in favor of the expansion and remodeling of existing stores. This was seen as particularly important in markets such as Dallas-Fort Worth, where customers who might be attracted by low prices were turned off by the smaller size, smaller selection, and no frills of most Food Lion stores. Many of the remodeled stores featured the addition of a deli/bakery. In 1994, 65 stores were remodeled, with the number of renovations increasing to 121 in 1995. By contrast, Food Lion opened only 47 new stores in 1995.

Finally, Smith moved to address an ongoing conflict with the United Food and Commercial Workers Union (UFCW), which had been attempting to organize Food Lion for years. The UFCW had brought to the attention of the U.S. Department of Labor claims that Food Lion had violated child-labor laws and had forced some of its workers to work extra hours without receiving overtime pay. Rather than continuing to fight, Food Lion agreed to a $16.2 million settlement in 1993. Two years later, however, the matter had not been completely resolved since as many as a thousand Food Lion employees opted out of the 1993 settlement to pursue independent claims. Food Lion began to settle these suits in 1995 (without any admission of wrongdoing), adding hundreds of thousands if not millions of dollars to the amount it agreed to pay in 1993.

During 1995—a year in which sales growth continued to slow (a 3.5 percent increase to $8.21 billion, well below Smith's $14 billion goal of five years earlier) and the company's margin fell further to 2.1 percent—Food Lion's lawyers and public relations staff remained busy. New reports from the consumer watchdog group Consumers United with Employees (CUE) claimed that Food Lion had a "chronic problem" with selling out-of-date infant formula and over-the-counter drugs. Food Lion maintained that CUE was biased because of its connections to labor unions and cited an inspection by the U.S. Food and Drug Administration of 63 Food Lion stores which resulted in an overall "excellent" rating. Food Lion even conducted its own investigation of some of its competitors' stores to show that they too were selling a certain percentage of out-of-date items, thus implying that Food Lion was being unfairly singled out for an industry-wide problem. The firm did, however, agree to refund CUE for 1,088 cans of outdated infant formula CUE had purchased from Food Lion stores. In mid-1995 it also filed a $100 million lawsuit against the UFCW, former employees, and others alleging a conspiracy to destroy the company through the continuing attacks.

The company also remained embroiled in a lawsuit against ABC, alleging fraud, trespassing, and breach of fiduciary duty in the way that ABC had conducted its investigation and in its use of hidden cameras. The company was seeking $100 million from ABC in damages, profits made by ABC from the PrimeTime broadcast, and attorneys' fees.

The 2000s and Beyond

The lawsuit dragged on until 1997, when $5.5 million dollars in punitive damages was awarded Food Lion. The presiding judge reduced the settlement to $315,000, but after another appeal, the Fourth U.S. Circuit Court of Appeals reduced the settlement to a payment of only $2 because the court decided that as the public had not actually been harmed by ABC's broadcast, the North Carolina fraud and unfair trade practices statute had not been violated. Food Lion spokespeople expressed disappointment, but were pleased that "the court recognized that ABC's manipulative and illegal tactics caused unwarranted damage to our company."

Food Lion continued its expansion, acquiring 11 stores from its North Carolina competitor Food Fair in May 1996. At the same time they began testing two new store concepts. The first was the store within a store, at four new locations, two of them in North Carolina and two in Virginia. The typical Food Lion market at this time averaged 33,000 square feet, but these expanded stores, featuring health and beauty care areas, expanded pet supply sections, and larger beverage areas, ranged from 40,000 to 50,000 square feet. The other new store concept was Stock N Save, a no frills version of Food Lion carrying only a fourth of what was typically carried in one of their markets.

Food Lion grew steadily, acquiring nearly all of west central Florida's 100 Kash 'n Karry supermarkets in late 1996. The company's efforts in Texas did not prove as successful, and after five years of effort Food Lion pulled out of the Lone Star state, as well as from Oklahoma and Louisiana, for a total casualty of 61 stores. Food Lion had begun the store expansions just as several other grocery chains were advancing into the same regions, and just as ABC aired its Prime Time news report about the company.

Revitalization and Expansion in the 2000s

After the failed expansion into the southwest Food Lion focused on its core base by renovating existing stores and upgrading their technology. Tom Smith, the 30-year Food Lion CEO, abruptly stepped down in April 1999 and was replaced by Bill McCanless, who led Food Lion into another acquisition, this time of food chain Hannaford and helmed the company toward other new experiments, the addition of international food sections, and self-scanning checkout machines. In August 2000 McCanless added the duties of company president as a 25-year Food Lion veteran stepped down from the post.

During this time, parent company Delhaize reorganized its U.S. holdings, establishing Delhaize America Inc. to oversee the Food Lion, Hannaford, and Kash n' Karry chains, among others. Food Lion's stock was converted to that of Delhaize America, which would by 2001 become wholly owned by the European Delhaize conglomerate. The presidency and eventually the CEO position at Food Lion passed to Rick Anicetti, formerly of the Hannaford chain.

Throughout the first half of the first decade of the 21st century Food Lion continued to experiment with new formats, opening in-store pharmacies, creating its own brand of low-fat ice cream, and remodeling large numbers of stores. They aided the reconstruction efforts in Florida in the wake of Hurricane Charley in August 2004 by contributing truckloads of food and raising money for the Hurricane Charley Disaster Relief Fund.

Despite some store closings in January 2003 Food Lion continued to prosper overall. The company debuted a new store concept in North Carolina during this time. Named Bloom, the pilot store was designed to offer consumers the most convenient shopping experience available, and toward that end reorganized the traditional store format to bring convenience items to the front of the store. Moreover, Food Lion won a steady stream of awards from the Environmental Protection Agency for its successful efforts in reducing energy consumption of heating and refrigeration systems as well as a reduction of energy used by light bulbs. They were the only grocery store to be so honored.

Principal Competitors

Wal-Mart Stores, Inc.; Winn-Dixie Stores Inc.; Publix Supermarkets Inc.

Further Reading

Elder, Laura, "Mauled by Competition, Grocer Food Lion Retreats From Texas," *Houston Business Journal,* October 10, 1997, p. 8A.

"Food Lion," *Supermarket News,* March 18, 1996, p. 2.

Gilligan, Gregory J., "North Carolina-Based Grocery Chain Purchases Competitor Supermarkets," *Knight Ridder/Tribune Business News,* August 18, 1999.

Johnson, Lori, "Food Lion Opens First 'International World'," *Business Journal Serving Charlotte and the Metropolitan Area,* October 8, 1999, p. 3.

Ketner, Ralph W., *Five Fast Pennies,* Salisbury, N.C.: R.W. Ketner, 1994, 227 p.

Konrad, Walecia, "Food Lion: Still Stalking in Tough Times," *Business Week,* June 22, 1992, p. 70.

"The Lion in Winter: Tom Smith Tells How He Plans for Food Lion to Come Roaring Back," *Business North Carolina,* June 1994, p. 28.

Mathews, Ryan, "Can Five Wrongs Make One Right?," *Progressive Grocer,* June 1995, pp. 53–61.

Napoli, Lisa, "In the Media Jungle, the Lion Weeps Tonight," *Business North Carolina,* March 1993, p. 16.

Nhan, Tawn, "Food Lion Struggles to Recapture Cost-Conscious Supermarket Business," *Knight Ridder/Tribune Business News,* May 19, 1996, p.5.

Parks, Liz, "Food Lion Sinks its Teeth into Self Scanning," *Drug Store News,* March 6, 2000, p. 23.

Poole, Claire, "Stalking Bigger Game," *Forbes,* April 1, 1991, pp. 73–74.

Tosh, Mark, "Can Food Lion Recover?," *Supermarket News,* December 21, 1992, p. 1.

Weinstein, Steve, "Food Lion on the Prowl," *Progressive Grocer,* October 1990, p. 78.

Wineka, Mark, and Jason Lesley, *Lion's Share: How Three Small-Town Grocers Created America's Fastest-Growing Supermarket Chain,* Asheboro, N.C.: Down Home Press, 1991, 265 p.

Zwiebach, Elliot, and David Ghiteman, "Delhaize Names New President for Food Lion," *Supermarket News,* August 28, 2000, p. 1.

Zwiebach, Elliot, "Food Lion Focuses on Its Core Markets," *Supermarket News,* June 1, 1998, p. 16.

——, "Food Lion Struggles Back," *Supermarket News,* November 8, 1993, p. 1.

——, "Remodels Set as Food Lion's First Step for Kash n' Karry," *Supermarket News,* November 11, 1996, p. 2.

—Tom Tucker
—updates: David E. Salamie; Howard A. Jones

FOOTE CONE & BELDING

Foote, Cone & Belding Worldwide

100 West 33rd Street
New York, New York 10001
U.S.A.
Telephone: (212) 885-3000
Fax: (212) 885-2803
Web site: http://www.fcb.com

Wholly Owned Subsidiary of The Interpublic Group of Companies Inc.
Incorporated: 1942
Employees: 6,000
Sales: $452 million (2003)
NAIC: 54181 Advertising Agencies

With a history dating back to 1873, Foote, Cone & Belding Worldwide is one of the oldest providers of advertising and marketing services. It is part of the Interpublic Group of Companies, Inc., and has a network of 197 offices in 109 countries around the globe. Through the years Foote, Cone & Belding has created successful advertising campaigns for GlaxoSmithKline, Kraft Foods, J.P. Morgan Chase & Co. and Hilton.

Early History

The history of Foote, Cone & Belding begins in 1873 with the founding of the Lord & Thomas advertising agency and the career of Albert D. Lasker. It was Lasker who, along with John E. Kennedy and Claude Hopkins, revolutionized the advertising industry and brought it into the 20th century. Lasker built his agency until it became one of the largest and most successful in the world and is said to have ruled over it in an almost dictatorial manner. Furthermore, he did not take his own success lightly, nor did he wish to conceal it. In the words of the noted advertising man David Ogilvy, Albert Lasker ''made more money and spent more money than anyone in the history of the business.''

In the 1930s and 1940s the most important accounts at Lord & Thomas were the American Tobacco Company and the Pepsodent division of Palmolive. The former was owned and operated by the controversial George Washington Hill; its principal product, Lucky Strike cigarettes, provided nearly one-fourth of Lord & Thomas' business. Pepsodent was at the time the largest-selling toothpaste on the market, and was particularly important to Lasker who was a large shareholder in the company.

During the Depression consumer product companies and advertising agencies alike were often faced with the possibility of failure. Most corporations that survived did so because they were large enough to weather years of economic difficulty and were run by powerful, energetic men with large personal stakes in their respective companies. Albert Lasker was used to doing business with such men; he liked the challenge of bargaining with strong personalities. When the business world began to change in the early 1940s, his interest in advertising began to diminish. Fairfax Cone wrote of Lasker's relationships with his clients, that they ''had been cemented at the top. When their structure began to change, when he became a supplier instead of a valued consultant, Mr. Lasker lost interest in the business. He saw that the day of the individual owner or the lasting partnership of two or three men in any large undertaking was gone. Business had become too big for that.''

Lasker called together his three regional heads—Foote of New York, Cone of Chicago, and Belding of Los Angeles—to tell them that he was retiring from advertising in order to pursue other interests and that, as of December 31, 1942, Lord & Thomas would close its offices permanently. To say the least, the three men were surprised by the news. Originally, Lasker thought he could divide Lord & Thomas' business by apportioning accounts to each of the three according to geographical location. This plan meant, in effect, that the agency would be divided into three separate firms. Then Lasker changed his mind and decided it best to keep the company intact with each man directing a regional headquarters: Foote, Cone & Belding Company was born. Lasker made Foote president, Belding chairman of the board, and Cone chairman of the executive committee.

Foote, Cone and Belding did not purchase Lord & Thomas. It was willed to them by Albert Lasker. The sole financial condition was that each man raise $32,000 as security for a $100,000 loan Lasker obtained for them through a Chicago investment bank. The only other stipulation was that the name of Lord & Thomas be retired along with Mr. Lasker.

Company Perspectives:

Every person at Foote Cone & Belding—at every level, across every discipline and in every office—is in the business of creating ideas that will benefit our clients. Ideas that both sell today and build brand value. This is our point of difference. It is at the heart of everything we do, and, frankly, we believe we do this better than any other agency. It is why clients hire us. It is the standard we set for ourselves. It is how we measure our results.

A New Beginning

Since the change of ownership was sudden and unexpected, many people inside and outside the advertising industry were shocked. Many industry analysts did not believe that the new firm was viable. Its harshest critics expected FCB to lose most or all of its clients and fall from the ranks of the major agencies. Foote, Cone & Belding was not taken seriously, particularly by the media. A January 4, 1943, *Time* magazine article commented that, "To the advertising world it was almost as if Tiffany had announced that from now on it would be known as Jones, Smith & Johnson."

The critics, however, focused primarily on the name change and not the more salient facts. The new agency was able to retain nearly all of the old Lord & Thomas customers, the most important of which was George W. Hill's American Tobacco account. Moreover, it won a number of new lucrative accounts, including Toni home hair permanent products, Hiram Walker Whiskey, and Marshall Field and Company, not to mention ad contracts for a few Samuel Goldwyn movies.

Yet the question still remained—who were Foote, Cone and Belding? They were barely known to each other, much less to those outside the company itself.

Emerson Foote was born in Alabama and raised in California. His college career consisted of one semester at the University of California, after which he sought work in the advertising business. He tried on various occasions to obtain a job with the research department of Lord & Thomas' San Francisco office in the early 1930's, but without success. The Depression was under way and virtually no one was hiring. So in 1934 Foote opened up his own firm, Yeomans & Foote, only to find the competition within the industry too intense for the small company to survive. A short time later, Foote's work came to the attention of the J. Stirling Getchell agency which offered him a job developing an ad campaign for a new automobile manufacturer called Chrysler. Foote accepted the job, but when Getchell died in 1938 the firm was dissolved and Foote was once again seeking employment. He applied to Lord & Thomas, and this time he was hired—as an assistant account executive for Lucky Strike cigarettes. In this capacity he met George W. Hill. Foote impressed Hill and was subsequently put in charge of the entire American Tobacco Company account. Simultaneously he was promoted to the position of general manager of Lord & Thomas in New York, a position he still held at the time of Lasker's retirement.

Don Belding, the oldest of the three men and director of the Los Angeles office, was unique for an advertising man in that he avoided being transferred from city to city doing agency business. He spent all of his career in the western United States. A native of Oregon, Belding had been an artillery man in World War I, a Western Union telegraph operator, and the publisher of a small newspaper before he entered advertising. After spending a year in the hospital for a war related illness, he enrolled in a veterans' training program. Part of his training included a government paid internship at Lord & Thomas of San Francisco. Years later Lasker opened an office in Los Angeles which Belding took charge of in 1938. There he used his experience in copywriting and accounts management to provide services for clients such as Lockheed, Sunkist, Purex, and Union Oil.

Fairfax Cone, like his two partners, spent his early life in California. He attended the University of California at Berkeley and worked for the San Francisco Examiner in the ad department. He had taken up drawing as a child and had become quite accomplished. He was colorblind, however, and later realized that because of this difficulty any advancement as an artist was impossible. He turned to copywriting and obtained work at a number of small San Francisco advertising agencies. When he went to work for Lord & Thomas, Cone began writing campaigns for the Southern Pacific Railroad and Dollar Lines ocean travel, and also became proficient at selling vacations as consumer products.

In 1934 Cone temporarily left Lord & Thomas to work for J. Stirling Getchell on the Plymouth and De Soto automobile accounts. During this period, Cone became afflicted with a seriously debilitating illness. What was at first thought to be a severe case of jaundice, turned out to be hypoglycemia. The correct diagnosis and proper treatment were seven years in coming, and during the interim Cone was forced to live half his life in bed.

Cone left Getchell and returned to Lord & Thomas in 1936 as manager of the agency's San Francisco office. He remained on the West Coast until 1941 when Albert Lasker asked him to move to New York to help out with a new campaign for Lucky Strikes. His stay in New York was brief. He no sooner became acquainted with George Hill than he was transferred to Chicago to work on the troubled Pepsodent account. A year and a half later, Cone found himself one-third owner of one of the largest advertising agencies in the world.

By 1946 the new firm of Foote, Cone & Belding had answered its critics and had proven itself the suitable heir of Lord & Thomas. Then publication of a book that became a best-seller threw the agency into turmoil and a three year period of readjustment. *The Hucksters,* by a former FCB copywriter named Frederic Wakeman, was supposedly a fictional account of the less reputable side of the advertising business. The two main characters of the book included an overbearing, unscrupulous owner of a large corporation and an advertising account executive who wasn't reluctant to lie in order to sell his client's merchandise. It was generally believed within the industry that the first character was patterned after George W. Hill and the second after Emerson Foote. The book caused a stir of controversy and was soon made into a major motion picture.

Because of the unflattering portrayal of the George Hill character, many people in the industry felt Hill would take the

Key Dates:

1873: The Lord & Thomas agency is founded.
1942: Foote, Cone & Belding Company is formed after Albert Lasker's retirement.
1948: Foote leaves the firm.
1957: Belding retires from the agency.
1962: Foote, Cone & Belding goes public.
1994: Foote, Cone & Belding becomes True North Communications.
2001: The Interpublic Group of Companies buys True North Communications and restores the Foote, Cone & Belding name.

American Tobacco account away from Foote, Cone & Belding. That did not happen. Instead, he awarded the company with a new five million dollar account for Pall Mall, American Tobacco's second best-selling cigarette.

In 1948 George Hill died. Leadership of his company passed to Vincent Riggio, a man with whom Emerson Foote felt he could not do business. On Foote's recommendation the American Tobacco account, fully one-fourth of the agency's business, was terminated by the agency. Emerson Foote, suffering from manic depression and thinking that he may have given up too much in relinquishing the account, had a nervous breakdown. He subsequently sold his stock at below market value and left the firm.

Triumphs and Disappointments in the 1950s–60s

The year 1948 marked something of a watershed for Foote, Cone & Belding. The agency was successful in obtaining a number of what were to become long-standing accounts. Foote, Cone & Belding began handling the advertising for, among others, Latex elastic products and Dial deodorant soap. It was also instrumental in putting the Hallmark Playhouse, precursor to the Hallmark Hall of Fame, on television.

Throughout the 1950s Foote, Cone & Belding continued to gain new clients and expand the services rendered to those already on its roster, particularly in the areas of radio and television. The firm had long employed Bob Hope as spokesman for Pepsodent and Arthur Godfrey for Toni and Frigidaire; now it had Red Skelton and George Gobel selling Johnson's Wax and Dial Soap respectively. At this time, Foote, Cone & Belding also created ad campaigns for Paper-Mate pens, Clairol hair coloring, and Kool-Aid.

The news was not all good, however. In 1951 the company lost the Pepsodent account to McCann-Erickson, leaving FCB without the two accounts (Pepsodent and American Tobacco) that had been the bedrock of Lord & Thomas' business. Pepsodent later returned to the firm, but with a much weaker market share. Then, in 1955, General Motors withdrew the Frigidaire account from Foote, Cone & Belding and took its business elsewhere.

The withdrawal of the Frigidaire account coincided with what at first promised to be the brightest chapter in the Foote, Cone & Belding story, but which turned out to be the darkest. In August of 1955, J.C. Doyle of the Ford Motor Company asked Fairfax Cone if he would be interested in doing the advertising for a new Ford automobile. Cone accepted the invitation and FCB, along with 10 other agencies, entered into the most extensive bidding competition ever seen in the ad industry. After 22 weeks and countless campaign presentations, Foote, Cone & Belding was finally awarded the account. The firm was instructed to find a suitable name for the new ''E'' (Experimental) car; after a month of brainstorming the agency had created the ''Edsel.''

The failure of the Edsel as an automobile is well-known; it cost the Ford Company close to $350 million. What is not recognized very often is that the Edsel was an advertising failure as well. The fiasco proved a cardinal rule of advertising—an advertisement, by itself, can aid or inhibit the sales of a good product, but it cannot, no matter how excellent the art and copy, save an inferior product. The Edsel was a product so out of step with prevailing market conditions that it was a losing venture from the beginning. In the words of Fairfax Cone, ''The trouble with the Edsel was almost everything.'' Cone and company worked diligently through the years of 1956, 1957, and 1958 to make the Edsel appealing to the American consumer, but without success. In the winter of 1959 the last Edsel crossed the assembly line.

The agency's resilience was soon apparent; the Edsel did not destroy Foote, Cone & Belding, nor even hinder its growth. The company acquired new accounts for Zenith, Dole pineapple, Contac, Fritos, True cigarettes, Sunbeam, People's Gas, International Harvester, Sara Lee, Monsanto, Ralston-Purina, Merrill Lynch, and Falstaff beer.

In 1957 Don Belding retired from the firm at the age of 60, and the agency came increasingly under the direction of Fairfax Cone and company chairman Robert Carney. Carney, a shrewd lawyer and businessman, urged the agency to go public, which it did in 1962. By 1965 the company's shares were being traded on the New York Stock Exchange.

During the 1960s the agency made strides in cementing its relationships with the major clients on its roster and in enhancing their images. Its work for Kimberly-Clark, a client of Lord & Thomas since 1923, is particularly notable. Two Kimberly-Clark products, Kleenex and Kotex, have become so well known that the names themselves are now household words used to define an entire line of products. With FCB's research and marketing help, Kimberly-Clark emerged as one of the leaders in the manufacture of paper towels, napkins, paper uniforms and paper dresses. Similar work by the company was done for Armour/Dial and S.C. Johnson & Son.

Nowhere, though, was Foote, Cone & Belding advertising more visible and prolific than on television. Fairfax Cone, who had long considered advertising and television mismatched, nonetheless brought the firm to the forefront of this area of the industry. By 1969 the company was responsible for $110 million worth of advertising time on television. Products advertised by Foote, Cone & Belding were the sponsors of such shows as *Rowan and Martin's Laugh-In, The Dean Martin Show, The Jackie Gleason Show, The Ed Sullivan Show, The Smothers Brothers Comedy Hour,* and *Ironside.*

The Business of Advertising in the 1970s

The 1970s marked a shift in emphasis for Foote, Cone & Belding. The agency began to focus less on advertising as an art and more on advertising as a business. Following the trend started by the other large agencies, Foote, Cone & Belding actively sought to acquire subsidiaries and build a more comprehensive international network of company offices. In January of 1972 it purchased the predominantly female-operated Hall & Levine agency (which it later sold in 1978), in 1973 it bought Whalstrom & Company, in 1975 Honig-Copper & Harrington, and in 1978 merged with Carl Byoir & Associates. In the international arena, Impact/FCB was established in Belgium and France, Jessurun/Bauduin-FCB in Amersterdam, Lindsay Smithers-FCB in Johannesburg and Capetown, and FCB/SPASM in Sydney and Melbourne.

Expansion on this scale, however, was costly, and fiscal 1974 was marred by a $1,410,000 loss the agency suffered as a result of the failure of its FCB Cablevision venture. Any agency operating in the international market is prone to the trials and tribulations of currency fluctuations; Foote, Cone & Belding was no exception.

In June 1977 Fairfax Cone died. With his passing, the firm and the advertising industry as a whole lost one of its most distinguished men. He had been one of advertising's staunchest defenders and most articulate critics. Foote, Cone & Belding had grown large and profitable under his tutelage. At the time of his death, it was an international agency with resources and services rivaling those of the biggest worldwide firms. Furthermore, Foote, Cone & Belding was able to achieve this eminence without resorting to what Cone called dishonest, tasteless, and gimmick-ridden advertising.

The advertising industry during the 1970s was marked by more than just business expansion. Most of the major agencies, FCB included, went through a period of creative malaise. The difficulties involved in the management of what was now a sprawling bureaucracy, and maintaining a balance between the creative and financial operations of the business, contributed to this problem.

Growth in the 1980s

In 1981 Foote, Cone & Belding emerged from its slump; 10 of its entries were ranked in Advertising Age's 100 Best Commercials, more than that of any other agency. This accomplishment revealed a renewed commitment to creativity. The approach did not always work (FCB lost Hallmark in 1981), but it revitalized Foote, Cone & Belding's image, and between 1982 and 1984 the agency won a record number of new accounts. The year 1984 was especially lucrative because Levi Strauss and a number of other major clients substantially increased their advertising budgets to meet the demand created by the Los Angeles Olympics.

However, FCB encountered financial difficulties. The firm went on a subsidiary buying spree between 1981 and 1984, amounting to over $23 million in purchases. The fiscal strain of this expansion was felt in 1985 and made even worse by the fact that many clients, preparing for a more sluggish economy and a drop in sales following the Olympics, reduced expenditures for advertisements. The result of these developments was that despite the 1985 increase in total revenues (including subsidiaries), the agency's net income dropped 14 percent, driving its share price down.

Present chairman and chief executive officer of Foote, Cone & Belding, Norman W. Brown, fought to keep the firm from becoming a takeover target. With the aid of outside consultants, the company implemented a new budgetary system that included profit-planning models for each office. The strategy was that the decision-making process within management would be less time consuming and more efficient and that financial planning would be more farsighted.

The 1990s Brings Change

Nevertheless, Foote, Cone & Belding's financial difficulties were not over. The economy in the 1990s was marked by a recession that took its toll on the advertising industry. Along with staffing and expenditure cuts, the company and its peers faced strained relationships with clients. During this era of budget reductions, there was a greater push to secure as many clients as possible and Foote, Cone & Belding desperately needed an edge over other firms. As part of its strategy, the company adopted a holding company structure under the name of True North Communications in 1994. This change placed True North in a position to own more than one advertising agency. In an attempt to diversify, the company restructured itself with the creation of three subsidiaries, TN Media, TN Technologies and TN Services.

Unfortunately, True North Communications proved to need much more than a name change. Although it had 190 offices across the globe and billings of more than $7 billion, it continued to lack a competitive edge over its peers. To further complicate the situation, its endeavor to merge with Publicis Communications of France failed in 1996. Its joint venture in Europe also fell apart one year later as Publicis commenced an ill-fated hostile takeover of True North. At the same time, Foote Cone's relationship with clients began to deteriorate further. The company lost its accounts with Citicorp and Mazda Motor—the latter terminated its contract due to the True North acquisition of Bozell, Jacobs, Kenyon & Eckhardt, which provided advertising for Chrysler. In an attempt to shore up revenues, Foote Cone and Bozell considered joining efforts in order to attract global corporate clients.

Despite heartened efforts to succeed in the global market, True North Communications put itself up for sale in 2001. The company had lost the $1.5 billion DaimlerChrysler account the previous year, and believed a sale was its best option. The Interpublic Group of Companies came to its rescue and completed its $2.1 billion acquisition in 2001. Interpublic immediately restored the Foote, Cone & Belding name, hoping that the historical moniker would attract new customers.

Indeed, under the charismatic leadership of CEO Brendan Ryan the company won many new clients such as Samsung, Boeing and Taco Bell. Interpublic and Foote, Cone & Belding however, continued to encounter many difficulties. Although Interpublic had become quite large, it did not have as many global accounts as other agencies of its size. The reorganization had also brought layoffs in the New York office. FCB lost the AT&T Wireless business worth $400 million. In addition, some of Foote, Cone & Belding's clients conflicted with those brought by Interpublic, and there were clients that complained of account problems. To make matters worse, Interpublic's stock was faltering, dropping by fifty-five percent between 2001 and 2004. Nevertheless, Foote, Cone & Belding Worldwide remained poised in the midst of these difficulties. Its history, dynamic leadership, and list of impressive clients would no doubt allow it to prevail for years to come.

Principal Competitors

Arnold Worldwide Partners; Saatchi & Saatchi; TBWA Worldwide Inc.

Further Reading

Beatty, Sally Goll, ''Foote Cone Gets 3Com Account Following a String of Setbacks,'' *Wall Street Journal,* October 27, 1997, p. 1.

——, ''True North, in Shift of Direction, Says Pact With Publicis is Over,'' *Wall Street Journal,* March 1, 1996, p. B5.

''Business Brief—Interpublic Group of Cos.: Foote Cone & Belding Cuts Include up to 80 Layoffs,'' *Wall Street Journal,* September 10, 2001, p. A4.

Cone, Fairfax M., *With All Its Faults: A Candid Account of 40 Years in Advertising,* Boston: Little Brown, 1969.

Goldman, Kevin, ''Foote Cone & Belding is Aiming to Make a New Name for Itself,'' *Wall Street Journal,* December 12, 1994, p. B7.

Gunther, John, *Taken at the Flood: The Story of Albert D. Lasker,* New York: Harper, 1960.

Johnson, Bradley, ''Did True North Pick Best Partner in IPG?,'' *Advertising Age,* April 5, 2004, p. 6.

Khermouch, Gerry, ''The Shock Waves Rocking Interpublic Scandal has Scared Off Clients and Endangered its Grand Strategy,'' *Business Week,* December 2, 2002, p. 54.

Kranhold, Kathryn, ''True North to Discuss Scenarios for Merger of Foote Cone, Bozell,'' *Wall Street Journal,* September 7, 1999, p. B10.

Lublin, Joann S., ''Agencies Foresee Unkinder, Rougher 1991,'' *Wall Street Journal,* December 27, 1990, p. B2.

MacArthur, Kate, and Tobi Elkin, ''So, What's in a Name? History,'' *Advertising Age,* July 9, 2001, p. 1.

Melcher, Richard A., and Gail Edmunson, ''A Marriage Made in Hell; How the Foote Cone-Publicis Alliance Hit the Rocks,'' *Business Week,* December 22, 1997, p. 40.

O'Connell, Vanessa, and Nikhil Deogun, ''True North is in Talks to Sell Itself to Expand,'' *Wall Street Journal,* January 29, 2001, p. B9.

Sampey, Kathleen, ''Ryan's Hope: The Worst is Over,'' *Adweek,* August 12, 2002, p. 5.

Vranica, Suzanne, ''FCB Chief Sets Creativity Improvement as Top Priority,'' *Wall Street Journal,* April 6, 2001, p. B6.

—update: Christina M. Stansell

Frankfurter Allgemeine

ZEITUNG FÜR DEUTSCHLAND

Frankfurter Allgemeine Zeitung GmbH

Hellerhofstrasse 2-4
D-60327 Frankfurt am Main
Germany
Telephone: (+49) (69) 7591-0
Fax: (+49) (69) 7591-1743
Web site: http://www.faz-verlag.de

Private Company
Incorporated: 1949 as Frankfurter Allgemeine Zeitung GmbH
Employees: 1,137 (est.)
Sales: EUR 458 million ($575 million) (2003)
NAIC: 511110 Newspaper Publishers; 511130 Book Publishers; 511140 Database and Directory Publishers; 323110 Commercial Lithographic Printing

Frankfurter Allgemeine Zeitung GmbH publishes the German daily newspaper *Frankfurter Allgemeine Zeitung—FAZ* for short. Created by about 300 editors and a tightly knit network of correspondents worldwide, *Frankfurter Allgemeine* is published Mondays through Saturdays, read by roughly one million readers daily, and distributed to 148 countries. In addition to putting out *Frankfurter Allgemeine,* Frankfurter Allgemeine Zeitung GmbH publishes the weekly newspaper *Frankfurter Allgemeine Sonntagszeitung* and the regional daily newspaper *Rhein-Main-Zeitung* in the Frankfurt region. The company also owns the regional daily newspaper *Märkische Allgemeine,* which is distributed in the Potsdam region, as well as a number of commercial printing businesses and book publishers. Other activities include information broker services, electronic databases, and logistics services to other newspaper publishers. Frankfurter Allgemeine Zeitung GmbH is majority-owned by the FAZIT-Stiftung Gemeinnützige Verlagsgesellschaft mbH, a non-profit foundation.

Postwar Origins

Frankfurter Allgemeine Zeitung (FAZ) was the brainchild of a group of dedicated democratic minds whose goal it was to establish a politically independent daily newspaper with national reach in Germany after World War II. Its initiation and early days were mainly determined by the newspaper's first business manager, Otto Klepper. Klepper, a lawyer and social democrat, became Prussia's minister of finance during the Great Depression. After Hitler's National Socialists came into power in 1933, Klepper left the country to escape from their terror campaign against social democrats. During his exile, he connected with other German emigrants and developed a political vision for a post-Hitler Germany. Determined to help establish a democratic society after the war, Klepper returned to Germany and helped found Wirtschaftspolitische Gesellschaft (Wipog), a nonprofit organization to promote democracy based on a social market economy, in 1947. Convinced that the success of a democratic postwar order heavily depended on politically independent media, he came up with the idea to publish an independent daily newspaper. With a meager DEM 100,000 in funding from Wipog, Frankfurter Allgemeine Zeitung GmbH (FAZ-Verlag) was founded in 1949, and Klepper became the first business manager of the publishing venture.

The company's corporate charter stipulated that the editorial direction of the newspaper be collectively determined by an editorial management team consisting of the five founding editors. One of them, Erich Welter, a journalist, editor, and lecturer with a background in politics and economics was a consultant to the Mainz-based regional daily newspaper *Allgemeine Zeitung* after World War II. Before the war, he had worked for the *Frankfurter Zeitung,* another daily newspaper in the Frankfurt am Main region, which was banned by the Nazis in 1943. Many of the newspaper's former editorial staff ended up working for *Allgemeine Zeitung* after the war. From this group of former colleagues, Welter recruited the first editorial team of the *Frankfurter Allgemeine Zeitung.*

On November 1, 1949, the first issue of *FAZ* was published. As stated by the leading editorial team on page one, *Frankfurter Allgemeine* was to be "a voice of Germany in the world." However, in its 16 pages there was no mention of the country's past under Hitler. In 1950, after less than a year, Otto Klepper, disgruntled with *FAZ'* editorial direction, resigned as FAZ-Verlag's business manager and later as Wipog's chairman. While it was his vision to create a politically independent newspaper with a critical view of postwar Germany, *FAZ* soon drifted into the mainstream of the dominant public opinion, which was strongly

Company Perspectives:

Editorial Peak Performance. Frankfurter Allgemeine Zeitung *has time and time again been regarded as one of the world's best newspapers.* Frankfurter Allgemeine Zeitung *owes this reputation to its detailed, exclusive background reporting and solid analysis. The clear distinction between news and commentary is one of its basic editorial principles. The results are competence and trustworthiness, from which its advertisement business benefits.*

influenced by the new political powers and by the veil of silence that covered the country's shameful Nazi past. However, the second part of Klepper's vision—to create a newspaper for the whole German nation—was soon to become true.

Modest Existence in the 1950s

While *Frankfurter Allgemeine* quickly gained a considerable distribution during the second half of the 1950s, the early years were difficult and quite modest. The paper's editorial staff worked out of two apartments in Frankfurt am Main, together with the administrative and advertising department. The offices of the latter turned into bedrooms every night for the tenants who lived there. Another group of editors was located in Mainz, where the paper was printed. Manuscripts and correspondence were transported back and forth by messengers, first by train and later by motorcycle. Frequently, editorial staff and publishers switched offices back and forth between Frankfurt and Mainz. In October 1950, *FAZ* moved to new offices in Frankfurt's Börsenstrasse, where the whole staff worked under one roof for the first time. Printing of the newspaper was also moved to Frankfurt, a few blocks down from its new offices, where *Frankfurter Rundschau,* another Frankfurt-based daily newspaper, was printed. On the floor that FAZ-Verlag had initially rented, editors and secretaries sat at their desks on garden chairs from local apple wine bars. When it was raining, many of them had to bring an umbrella into the office to stay dry. If an editor wanted to go on a business trip, it was expected that he traveled after his daily work at the office was done and showed up on time the very next morning. However, the staff was highly motivated to make the "newspaper for all of Germany."

The subscribers of *Allgemeine Zeitung's* national edition became *FAZ*'s initial reader base. Until the mid-1950s, *FAZ* sold fewer than 100,000 copies daily on average. Parts of Germany's population struggled to make ends meet, unemployment was high, and money was tight. However, when the German economy began to pick up speed again in the mid-1950s, *Frankfurter Allgemeine*'s revenues rose steadily. In 1959, an average of more than 200,000 copies daily were sold for the first time. In the same year, the newly founded nonprofit foundation FAZIT-Stiftung Gemeinnützige Verlagsgesellschaft mbH became the majority shareholder of *Frankfurter Allgemeine* to ensure its independence.

Growth and Diversification until 1989

FAZ's evolution into a national German newspaper was closely connected with the postwar economic boom under the political leadership of Christian Democrat Konrad Adenauer. His chief economist Ludwig Erhard, who had studied with the same liberal socialist—Franz Oppenheimer—as Welter and promoted the idea of a socially "softened" model of capitalism called *Soziale Marktwirtschaft*—social market economy. A cofounder of Wipog after the war, Erhard used *FAZ* as a medium to propagate this idea. Soon *FAZ* became the voice of Germany's politically conservative entrepreneurial elite and remained so for many decades to come.

In 1961, FAZ-Verlag moved its headquarters to Frankfurt's Hellerhofstrasse. Around the same, time FAZ-Verlag's management decided to change printers. From then on, *FAZ* was printed by Frankfurter Societäts-Druckerei. During the "economic miracle" years and in the decades after, the company greatly expanded its readership and distribution—nationally as well as internationally. Nationally, the number of *FAZ* readers grew by roughly 50,000 each decade. Internationally, the *Frankfurter Allgemeine* became a highly respected publication which was soon distributed in most countries around the world. In 1988, a brand-new office building was added to the newspaper's headquarters to contain the growing editorial and administrative staff. FAZ-Verlag had succeeded in creating a highly regarded national print medium that was very attractive to advertisers. Roughly 70 percent of the newspaper's revenue was generated from advertising, in particular from national and international classified ads for jobs and business advertising. As *FAZ* grew considerably in size through advertising, its content expanded accordingly. For example, a full-color supplement, the *Frankfurter Allgemeine Magazin,* was added to the paper's weekend edition. In addition to the *Frankfurter Allgemeine,* FAZ-Verlag launched the business newspaper *Blick durch die Wirtschaft,* the daily newspaper *Rhein-Main-Zeitung,* and a Sunday edition of the *FAZ* in the Frankfurt/Main region. Over the years, FAZ-Verlag also established a tightly knit logistics arm that distributed its newspapers.

Although the newspaper business was thriving, FAZ-Verlag's management realized that it was economically unsound to depend on one main source of income that was extremely vulnerable to economic downturns. Consequently, the company began to branch out into new business activities in the 1980s and 1990s. FAZ-Verlag offered information broker services from its electronic databases, published business books, and even launched its own business radio program. The company acquired minority or majority shares in a number of book publishers, commercial printers, a book retail chain, and in the business news wire service Vereinigte Wirtschaftsdienste as well as in the radio and TV channels Radio/Tele FFH and RTL plus.

After the Berlin Wall fell in 1989, FAZ-Verlag acquired Märkische Verlags- und Druck-GmbH, the publisher of the eastern German regional daily newspaper *Märkische Allgemeine Zeitung* in Potsdam, including its large printing department. Beginning in 1994, a part of the daily *FAZ* edition was printed in Potsdam. Another acquisition in eastern Germany was Berlin-based Deutsche Zeitungsverlag GmbH, the publisher of the East German daily newspaper *Neue Zeit.* While *Märkische Allgemeine* successfully established itself as the leading subscriber-based newspaper in the state of Brandenburg surrounding Berlin, *Neue Zeit* ceased publication in 1994.

Key Dates:

1949: National daily newspaper *Frankfurter Allgemeine Zeitung* is launched in Germany.
1959: Newly founded FAZIT-Stiftung becomes majority shareholder.
1961: FAZ-Verlag moves to new headquarters on Frankfurt's Hellerhofstrasse.
1979: *FAZ* circulation passes the 300,000 mark.
1990: FAZ-Verlag acquires Märkische Verlags- und Druck-GmbH.
2001: The national weekly newspaper *Frankfurter Allgemeine Sonntagszeitung* is introduced.

New Highs and New Lows after 1995

After the reunification of Germany in 1990, the growth of *FAZ* circulation slowed while the newspaper's advertising business declined significantly. With job classifieds down almost 30 percent and paper prices up more than 20 percent, FAZ-Verlag slipped deeply into the red. At the same time, competition intensified among both newspaper publishers and print and electronic media for pieces of the shrinking advertising pie. To make up for its losses, FAZ-Verlag streamlined its various shareholdings and sold off its lucrative stake in private TV-station RTL plus. In 1995, the company launched a highly acclaimed image campaign in major news and business magazines with the heads of well-known individuals from Germany's intellectual, political, and cultural scene buried in the *FAZ,* accompanied by the newspaper's traditional slogan: ''There's always a smart head hidden behind it.'' Beginning in 1996, the number of *FAZ* copies sold on average started climbing again, by about 4,000 copies a year. In the business year 1996, FAZ-Verlag passed the DEM 1 billion mark in total sales for the first time. Two years later, the number of *FAZ* copies sold daily on average exceeded 400,000—another first.

By 1999, FAZ-Verlag's 50th anniversary year, the company seemed to be back in good financial standing. Over 1.1 million people read the *Frankfurter Allgemeine*. The average number of *FAZ* copies sold daily peaked at 408,411. Advertising revenues had jumped a healthy 28 percent within two years. There were 500 editors working for the newspaper—a record number—supported by a worldwide network of 40 correspondents. The goal of the founders had been reached: *Frankfurter Allgemeine* had become a newspaper for the whole of Germany—roughly four-fifths of the daily copies were sold outside of the Frankfurt am Main region—and a voice of Germany in the world. In the summer of 1999, a thousand opinion makers on the international scene were asked which newspaper was the best in the world, and *Frankfurter Allgemeine Zeitung* ranked third after the British *Financial Times* and the American *New York Times*. The newspaper's design had not changed much in 50 years: Its title as well as feature article headlines were printed in an old-fashioned German typeface; there was no picture on the front page; and, although technically possible and used by other competitors, the whole paper was still printed in black and white. *Frankfurter Allgemeine* even decided to disregard the new spelling rules introduced in Germany because the paper's managing editors thought they were not clear enough.

However, while *Frankfurter Allgemeine* tried to preserve the paper's traditions, formidable challenges were looming. On one hand, the late 1990s brought a new generation to the paper's editorial management team after the managing editors who had shaped *FAZ* through the years of the Cold War retired. The younger journalists did not have the black-and-white worldview held by their predecessors. The world had grown more complex and so had the ideological battles. In addition, the loyal readers of *Frankfurter Allgemeine* had come of age along with the paper: Three-fourths of its readers were at least forty years old. On top of that, a major market force had emerged in the mid-1990s that threatened FAZ-Verlag's core business—the Internet. Not only was more and more high-quality content available online, often for free, but the new medium almost instantly developed into a thriving job marketplace, eroding *Frankfurter Allgemeine*'s main source of advertising revenues.

To counteract this threat, the company initiated a number of new ventures. In 1999, FAZ-Verlag launched the ''Berlin Pages,'' a daily supplement for the German capital, while the unprofitable *FAZ-Magazin* ceased publication. Another publishing venture took the form of the free advertising weeklies *Sunday* and *Sunny*. One year later, the company introduced an English edition of *FAZ* in cooperation with the *International Herald Tribune*. Another major step followed in 2000 when *FAZ* put out an online version of the paper and strengthened its Internet arm to include an information broker and other online services. Finally, in September 2001, the company tackled the German market for Sunday newspapers with the national launch of *Frankfurter Allgemeine Sonntagszeitung (FAS)*. Also among FAZ-Verlag's new ventures was the creation of a logistics firm that offered distribution services to other publishers, an idea that proved immediately successful.

After three record years, the company's expansion came to a sudden halt in 2001. In the aftermath of the bursting of the so-called ''Internet Bubble,'' FAZ-Verlag's advertising business plunged, and the company slipped deeply into the red again. By 2002, FAZ-Verlag had lost more than half of its advertising revenues. With financial resources dwindling, the company abandoned most of its new ventures and launched a comprehensive cost-cutting program. For the first time in its history, *FAZ* fired a number of editors for economic reasons. In mid-2004, FAZ-Verlag announced that the company had made the turnaround and was expecting to become profitable again. Two of the company's main goals were to reach the break-even point with *FAS* and to streamline and strengthen the Internet edition of *FAZ* and other online services. While the company was not in immediate danger of going under, signs abounded that FAZ-Verlag would not have an easy ride. In 2004, for example, Axel Springer Verlag, which had dominated the German market for Sunday papers for decades before the launch of *FAS,* launched *WELT KOMPAKT,* a new national daily newspaper.

Principal Subsidiaries

Verlagsgruppe Märkische Verlags- und Druckgesellschaft mbH; Union Verwaltungsgesellschaft mbH; Deutsche Verlags-Anstalt GmbH; Prestel Verlag; F.A.Z. Institut für Management-, Markt-

und Medieninformationen GmbH; Medienservice GmbH & Co. KG; Maincom Telemarketing Services GmbH; Verlagsgruppe Leadermedia.

Principal Competitors

Verlagsgruppe Handelsblatt GmbH; Financial Times Deutschland GmbH & Co. KG; Axel Springer AG.

Further Reading

Hofmann, Gunter, ''Die Grammatik der FAZ,'' *Zeit*, August 17, 2000, p. 30.

Mussey, Dagmar, ''German Newspapers in Sunday Battle,'' *AdAgeGlobal*, November 2001, p. 16.

—Evelyn Hauser

Fresh Enterprises, Inc.

100 Moody Court
Thousand Oaks, California 91360
U.S.A.
Telephone: (805) 495-4704
Toll Free: (877) 225-2373
Fax: (805) 374-1144
Web site: http://www.bajafresh.com

Wholly Owned Subsidiary of Wendy's International, Inc.
Founded: 1990
Employees: 2,213 (est.)
Sales: $250.5 million (2002 est.)
NAIC: 722211 Limited-Service Restaurants

A subsidiary of Wendy's International, Inc., Fresh Enterprises, Inc. is a Thousand Oaks, California-based company that operates the Baja Fresh Mexican Grill chain of more than 300 fast-casual restaurants located in some 26 states and Washington, D.C. Baja Fresh trades on a reputation for serving Mexican food using the freshest ingredients and avoiding the use of microwaves, freezers, or MSG. A sign that has graced the design of the main counter over the years reads, "No can-openers, no freezers, no lard." Steak is hand-trimmed, USDA Choice; chicken breasts are served boneless and skinless, marinated, and charbroiled; and salsa is prepared daily. Made-to-order items include burritos, tacos, salads, quesadillas, nachos, and such specialties as chicken picado, steak picado, taquitos, fajitas, and enchiladas. Side orders include guacamole and chips, cebollitas, salsa, black or pinto beans, rice, and rice and beans. Because preparation time at Baja Fresh is much longer than rival fast-casual Mexican restaurants, such as McDonald's owned Chipotle Mexican Grill, management is taking steps to simplify the menu.

First Restaurant Opens in 1990

Baja Fresh was founded in 1990 by James Magglos and his wife Linda, who had no experience in the restaurant business. In 1978, when he was in his early 20s, Magglos began operating an automobile detail and window tinting shop in Westlake Village, California, but he always harbored a dream of one day running a restaurant. He also loved Mexican food. As Magglos told the *Ventura County Star* in a 1997 profile, "I just wanted to have a great place and serve food the way I like it." To launch their restaurant, Magglos and his wife took out a third mortgage on their home. In Newbury Park, where the couple lived, they found an affordable location, one that over the years had housed a number of eateries: Uncle Stink's Hot Dogs, Porky's Ribs, and Casey's Hamburgers. In August 1990, the first Baja Fresh Mexican Grill opened on this site. The quick-service restaurant was an immediate success, tapping into several trends. A number of Mexican food concepts were emerging from California, but the emphasis on fresh ingredients helped to differentiate Baja Fresh from many of its competitors and proved popular with customers who were becoming more health conscious about their eating habits. "We make everything in our stores fresh daily. It's not processed somewhere else and sent to us," Magglos explained to the *County Star.* "A tomato is a real tomato and we make it into salsa. Another thing is our chicken. We use only chicken finger, which is that small piece of meat under the chicken breast. It's like the filet mignon of the chicken, the tenderest, most flavorable part. And there are only two on each chicken." Baja Fresh also benefited from the rising popularity of the fast-casual restaurant concept, which was not quite fast food and not quite full service. The price points were higher than fast food, but the ingredients were fresher. Although they lacked the ambience and service of a full-service restaurant, fast-casual restaurants were quicker and more convenient, a combination that appealed to the fast-paced lifestyle of many customers. Baja Fresh also distinguished itself because of "intangibles," as described by Magglos to the *County Star:* "For example, our stores are immaculate from the front to the bathroom. We're the type of establishment where the health inspector will have lunch after he does his job. All of our people make more than minimum wage. Even our dishwashers get vacations, so we have an attitude in our stores that is different."

The Maggloses added two more Baja Fresh restaurants in 1991 and another three while launching a franchising effort in 1993. Because Baja Fresh proved so popular, enjoying something of a cult following, Magglos received many inquiries about franchises, but he was selective about the partners he

Company Perspectives:

Baja Fresh is all about choices that fit the way you eat.

would accept. The first franchise unit, and the seventh overall in the Baja Fresh chain, opened in Oxnard, California, in November 1994. The first franchise owners were Darren Utley and his father-in-law John Dobbert. Utley had owned eight Domino's Pizza franchises but had been a regular customer at the Baja Fresh restaurant located in Simi Valley and loved the food so much that he decided to drop Domino's in favor of Baja Fresh. Dobbert, a former school teacher, also had strong experience as an entrepreneur and had been involved in running a restaurant as well as owning three Penquin Frozen Yogurt franchises.

Because Magglos was selective about franchisees, the Baja Fresh chain grew at a slow pace during the first half-dozen years. It eventually expanded beyond southern California and outside the state itself, with unit openings in Phoenix, Las Vegas, and Denver. By the end of 1997, there were 34 restaurants generating $33.7 million. Another 13 units would open in 1998 as the chain gained a toehold on the East Coast with openings in Fairfax, Virginia, and Rockville, Maryland. Sales in 1998 improved to $54.9 million. About a quarter of the 47 units were company owned.

Turning Point in 1998

Baja Fresh also reached a major turning point in late 1998: the Maggloses sold a controlling interest in Fresh Enterprises to Greg Dollarhyde and Pete Siracusa, both of whom were involved with another fast-casual chain, Rusty Pelican, which Siracusa founded. Magglos retreated from day-to-day operations, retaining a minority interest with his wife and a seat on the board of directors, while Siracusa assumed the chairmanship and Magglos became president and chief executive officer. Dollarhyde, a graduate of Cornell University's prestigious School of Hotel Administration, had experience working at Pizza Hut, served as vice-chairman of Kenny Rogers Roasters, and had been president and chief executive of Country Harvest Buffet. Supplying the financial backing for the deal was Catterton Partners, a Greenwich, Connecticut-based private equity firm that made a specialty of restaurant investments. The firm owned a controlling interest in Wolfgang Puck Food Co. and also invested in P.F. Chang's China Bistro, La Madeline French Bakery & Café, and Caribou Coffee. Also taking minority positions in Fresh Enterprises was Minneapolis-based Oak Investment Partners and New York-based Grumman Hill Group.

Some of Baja Fresh's loyal customers expressed concern that the sale of the chain would lead to a drop off in quality, but Dollarhyde remained committed to the concept of relying on fresh ingredients, and he became even more of a stickler for quality control than the chain's founders. During most of the first year he was in charge, expansion took a backseat to the design and implementation of systems to protect the integrity of the supply chain and ensure consistency among restaurants, whether they were company owned or franchise operations. Dollarhyde supplemented Baja Fresh inspectors with independent secret shoppers. Rather than have employees measure and bag spice for beans, with the danger that quality might vary between stores, he had the suppliers provide prepacked spice packages and precisely measured sacks of beans. Restaurant refrigerators were organized with dated containers to make sure no ingredients were kept for an extended length of time. Grated cheese, for example, had to be used within 24 hours, whereas other restaurants would add corn starch and continue to use the cheese, despite the detrimental effect on taste and texture. Customers were not only reassured by the changes Dollarhyde made after taking over, they patronized Baja Fresh in even greater numbers.

While Dollarhyde laid the foundation for maintaining quality control that would allow Baja Fresh to expand more rapidly without compromising its principles, the chain added just ten new restaurants in 1999, bringing the total to 57. Revenues for the year increased to $74.8 million. In 2000, Baja Fresh added 39 units and sales reached $106.8 million. The chain expanded even more rapidly in 2001, opening 55 restaurants and growing sales to $176.7 million, to go with operating income of $6.5 million. Moreover, same-store sales grew by 7.8 percent over the previous year.

In 2002, Baja Fresh awarded a franchise agreement for Greater Boston, Massachusetts, to Northern Foods Services Inc., an experienced Rockville, Maryland-based restaurant company that agreed to develop at least 14 Baja Fresh restaurants in five years and as many as 30. Also in 2002, Baja Fresh signed a franchise agreement with Lettuce Entertain You Enterprises, headed by well-respected restaurateur Richard Melmann, to develop 16 Chicago-area restaurants. Lettuce Entertain You operated three dozen restaurants, including such successful Chicago establishments as Ambria, Everest, Shaw's Crab House, Tru, Wildfire, Foodlife, and Nacional 27. In addition, the company operated restaurants at the Paris Las Vegas resort. Like other Baja Fresh franchisees, Melmann started out as a customer. His son first took him to a Baja Fresh restaurant, and later, at a baseball game, he met a Baja Fresh investor, ex-basketball star Rick Barry, who encouraged him to become involved in the business. Later in 2002, Allen Bernstein, the CEO of the Morton steakhouse chain, also came on board, securing the rights to develop at least 16 Baja Fresh restaurants in his native Long Island.

Baja Fresh under Wendy's: 2002 and Beyond

To finance continued expansion, in May 2002 Fresh Enterprises registered with the Securities and Exchange Commission its intention to make an initial public offering of stock (IPO). At this stage, the Baja Fresh chain totaled 157 units, of which 72 were owned by the company and 85 were franchise operations. The goal of the offering was to raise $57.5 million, with $30 million earmarked for expansion and an unspecified amount to be used to pay down debt. Banc of America Securities was slated to serve as the lead underwriter, but the offering never took place. Instead, Wendy's stepped in and offered $275 million for 100 percent of Fresh Enterprises, a deal that Banc of America would now broker. Dollarhyde and the officers of Catterton Partners weighed the potential of an IPO against the $275 million in cash that Wendy's put on the table and quickly decided that going with Wendy's was the wiser choice. Catterton and the other investors made a tidy profit, while

Key Dates:

1990: The first restaurant opens.
1994: The first franchised restaurant opens.
1998: Greg Dollarhyde is named CEO after the sale of the company to Catterton Partners.
2002: Wendy's acquires the Baja Fresh chain.
2004: Dollarhyde is replaced by William Moreton.

Dollarhyde was able to stay on to run Fresh Enterprises as a Wendy's subsidiary and now had the resources and the financial backing of a corporate parent with deep pockets. For Wendy's, acquiring Baja Fresh at a premium price made sense because it was playing catch-up with the likes of McDonald's Corp., which had entered the fast-casual segment by acquiring Boston Market and Chipotle Mexican Grill. Wendy's hope was that the Baja Fresh chain could grow to between 600 and 700 units within five years. To accommodate that growth, Fresh Enterprises leased additional office space. Earlier in the year, it agreed to lease half of an office building under construction in Thousand Oaks, some 12,000 square feet, but now added the remaining 10,000 square feet.

By the end of 2002, the Baja Fresh chain numbered 210 units and revenues topped the $250 million mark. Dollarhyde expressed his delight with the company's new ownership, telling *Chain Leader,* ''A good 25 percent of my job was finding money, recruiting money, developing money and communicating with people who gave me money.'' In addition, by forgoing the IPO, he did not have to deal with the pressures that came with the public markets. However, he would soon find out about the pressures that came with heading a subsidiary of a large public company like Wendy's. Baja Fresh began to post disappointing results, with same-store sales declining by 4.6 percent in 2003. A sluggish economy and the chain's rapid expansion were blamed, as well as the effects of over saturation in the southern California market where Baja Fresh restaurants took customers from one another. Cooking so many items to order, in many ways a strength of the chain, also led to lengthy service times, which were almost twice as long as Chipotle. To make matters worse, while Baja Fresh was blaming the economy for poor results, Chipotle enjoyed a 24.5 percent increase in comparable-restaurant sales for 2003. As a result of its poor performance in 2003, Baja Fresh cost Wendy's nine cents in share earnings for the year.

Although it was unclear whether he quit or was fired, Dollarhyde was replaced as chief executive in April 2004 by William Moreton, former chief financial officer of Panera Bread Co. Moreton also had executive experience at Quality Dining Inc., where he was CFO, and Houlihan's Restaurant Group, which he helped to put into bankruptcy during his days as a banker with Credit Agricole and then joined to restructure. This task began his direct involvement with the food service industry.

Moreton conducted a market-by-market review of operations, and in August 2004 the company slowed down its plans for expansion, as well as deciding to close five underperforming restaurants, thereby exiting Atlanta, Georgia; Charlotte, North Carolina; and Tucson, Arizona. Baja Fresh also began looking at ways to improve service time. One solution was to reduce the size of the menu, which featured many made-to-order items that extended service times. Nevertheless, the chain wanted to introduce new products in all of its major categories in order to prevent the menu from becoming stale to regular customers. The obvious solution was to rotate some items on and off the menu, a practice that Moreton used at Panera to good effect. Baja Fresh also looked to improve its advertising, taking advantage of the input available from Wendy's marketing personnel. Although the chain had suffered the first major setbacks in its 15-year history, Baja Fresh remained a strong concept and continued to enjoy the backing of its corporate parent.

Principal Divisions

Baja Fresh Mexican Grill.

Principal Competitors

Chipotle Mexican Grill, Inc.; Moe's Southwest Grill, LLC; Rubio's Restaurants, Inc.; Santa Barbara Restaurant Group.

Further Reading

Bertagnoli, Lisa, ''Bringing up Baja,'' *Chain Leader*, September 2002, p. 52.

Hamstra, Mark, ''Dollarhyde, Investors Buy Baja Fresh Burrito Concept,'' *Nation's Restaurant News*, December 14, 1998, p. 6.

Hamstra, Mark, ''Go East Young Burrito: Taqueria Chains Migrate Out of California,'' *Nation's Restaurant News*, July 13, 1998, p. 39.

Liddle, Alan J., ''Freshening up the Baja Brand,'' *Nation's Restaurant News*, August 23, 2004, p. 76.

Mitchell, John, ''Fresh Approach Paying Dividends,'' *Ventura County Star*, October 18, 1997, p. D1.

Papiernik, Richard, ''Wendy's Fast-Casual Foray Adds Baja Fresh Buy,'' *Nation's Restaurant News*, June 10, 2002, p. 1.

—Ed Dinger

Fruth Pharmacy, Inc.

RR1 Box 332
Point Pleasant, West Virginia 25550
U.S.A.
Telephone: (304) 675-1612
Fax: (304) 675-7338
Web site: http://www.fruthpharmacy.com

Private Company
Founded: 1952
Employees: 500 (est.)
Sales: $113 million (2003)
NAIC: 446110 Pharmacies and Drug Stores

Based in Point Pleasant, West Virginia, Fruth Pharmacy, Inc., operates 22 drugstores, generally 10,000 square feet in size, of which 13 are located in western West Virginia and nine in southern Ohio. In addition, the family-run company operates a stand-alone gift store, the Honey Bear Tree, in Cross Lanes, West Virginia. This venture grew out of the chain's strong giftware program, which sets it apart from the competition. Fruth also emphasizes customer service, since it is unable to compete on price with larger competitors. However, many Fruth drugstores are also located in small towns that fly under the radar of large discount stores. As a result, they have often served as one of the few retailers in a community and have traditionally offered a little bit of everything, including such services as utility bill collection, money orders, lottery tickets, and package mailing. As a result, Furth has also become a place where small town residents look to purchase gifts, especially during the Christmas season. Each year the chain mails a 16-page circular promoting its seasonal gifts, many of which are the result of buying trips to the Far East conducted by Fruth's management. The chain also enjoys excellent gift sales at other times of the year, especially during Halloween and Valentine's Day. Nevertheless, the bulk of Fruth's sales still come from prescriptions. Several of the company's executives, including its founder, are licensed pharmacists.

Founding and Growth: 1952–90s

Fruth Pharmacy was founded by Jack E. Furth in 1952. His parents owned a drug store in Mason County, West Virginia, and Fruth grew up around the pharmacy business. In truth, however, the store centered on the soda fountain. After enrolling at Duke University to major in chemistry, Fruth realized that although he enjoyed working in the laboratory, he did not care for the solitude and preferred the experience of retailing. To combine his interests in chemistry and retailing he made the practical decision of becoming a pharmacist. After two years at Duke, Fruth transferred to Ohio State University to enter pharmacy school. Upon graduation in 1951 he spent the next year and half working as a pharmacist in Springfield and Xenia, Ohio, for the Gallagher Drug Co. He then returned home to West Virginia to launch his own business, opening a pharmacy—complete with soda fountain—in the town of Point Pleasant. He operated out of this location for the next eight years before building a new store.

Jack Fruth did not add a second store until 1963, when he bought the Corrick Drug Company. Unfortunately, six years later the store burned down, leaving him with just the Point Pleasant operation. In 1970, Corrick's longtime president, Don Pullin, came to work for Fruth as a pharmacist and would become instrumental in the growth of the company. In 1975, Fruth again added a second location, buying the White Cross Pharmacy in Huntington, West Virginia, a community that would be the eventual home of three Fruth drugstores. Over the next seven years, with Pullin serving as president, Fruth added four more stores. By the end of 1982, the chain for the first time was posting $1 million in revenues each month. To further its growth, the small chain joined Associated Chain Drug Stores, a group founded in 1926 to help drug stores combine their buying power as well as offering other services. By the end of the 1980s, Fruth doubled in size, with 12 stores in West Virginia and Ohio.

In 1989, Associated Drug merged with Affiliated Drug Stores, a rival buying group that was founded several years after Associated. Jack Fruth was named the first chairman of the new organization, which he said represented a new spirit among

Company Perspectives:

We cater to the needs of our customers by providing the best customer service in town. Fruth's pharmacists are on duty 7 days a week and are dedicated to serving your every prescription need. That's why we're known as . . . Your Hometown Pharmacy.

drug store chains. He told *Drug Store News* in April 1989, "It used to be that two chains in the same market wouldn't speak to each other; now we're anxious to work together, so we all have a chance at the business. The feeling is no longer that as drug chains, we're competitors. Our competitors are the deep discounters, the combos, the hyper-markets, the HMOs, and mail order. If mail order or a Kmart takes away business, we all suffer."

Over the next five years, Fruth added another five stores and upgraded its pharmacy operation with a new computer system, Synercom Pharmacy System, which helped to process third-party insurance claims. For Jack Furth, it was part of the changes the pharmacy business had undergone since he entered the field 30 years earlier, when most transactions for prescriptions were done on a cash basis. Synercom was chosen because it combined technical sophistication with ease of use, allowing the chain's pharmacists to begin using it as quickly as possible. All Furth pharmacies were connected to a central system, which pooled the information and helped management to determine what to carry and to set price changes. Each night, files were updated so that the next day the stores had new information on supply and pricing. In addition, customers' prescriptions could be included in the system and they could be filled at any Fruth location.

Branching Out in the 1990s

Fruth added two new stores in 1993, bringing the total to 18, and the business was generating $35 million in annual sales systemwide. The chain continued to thrive despite the poor economic conditions that prevailed in its area of operation. With the closing of many of the steel mills and coal mines in the region, whose workers provided a base of income for local retailers, Fruth had found itself operating in a market with one of the lowest per capita incomes in the nation. The company also faced a new challenge on the big box front in the form of Wal-Mart. By serving markets too small for Wal-Mart, Fruth was protected somewhat, while in larger markets where Wal-Mart entered, Fruth would see an immediate drop in sales. Generally, however, within six months the store would have won back its market share, despite not being able to compete on the basis of price. The key was the chain's commitment to customer service.

Although Fruth's stores were relatively small, they often had five or six associates available on the sales floor to help customers. Moreover, the practice of offering a wide variety of merchandise, started by Jack Fruth at his first store, continued to pay dividends. The stores were especially known for their giftware sections, which offered items ranging in price from $2.99 to more than $400. High-end items included collectible figurines, decorative lamps, dolls, and glassware. Because it was a high-margin business, giftware was especially attractive to management, which made buying trips several times a year. Thus, new merchandise regularly appeared on the sales floor, prompting many customers to stop by to see what had come in.

The stores were also quick to stock seasonal merchandise and to hold decorating contests in order to give customers a different look. Aside from giftware, buyers for the other departments were given a great deal of latitude in replacing merchandise, so that on average departments were refreshed every other month. In addition, the stores made a point of being responsive to customer requests and would place special orders for merchandise if necessary. As a result, the Fruth stores averaged about $2 million each in revenues in fiscal 1994, a notable achievement.

In the mid-1990s, Fruth had to contend with shrinking margins on its pharmacy business, which placed greater emphasis on controlling costs and maximizing the giftware business. A 20,000-square-foot addition was made to its warehouse to speed up the shipment of merchandise. Starting in 1995, Fruth began installing a new point-of-sale (POS) scanning system in all of its stores. This system, combined with an expanded warehouse, helped the chain to better control inventory and avoid having items run out of stock. The chain also strengthened its gift business by making buying trips to Hong Kong to stock up on seasonal products, artificial flowers, toys, and general merchandise. To maximize its buying power, Fruth began to travel with buyers from other drug store chains. During fiscal 1994, Fruth stores enjoyed a strong increase in average sales per store, to $2.8 million, as total revenues topped $50 million.

Struggles and Recovery: Mid-1990s and Beyond

In the fall of 1996, Fruth added stores in Eleanor and Ripley, West Virginia, and in February 1997 a store was opened in Gallipolis, Ohio, bringing the total number of Fruth drugstores to 21. There was some talk about entering the Kentucky market but mostly the chain was looking to fill in the areas in which it had already established a presence. The Ohio opening was remarkable given that the company was recovering from a December 1986 fire that completely destroyed its Point Pleasant 30,000-square-foot distribution center and some adjacent office space. All told, Fruth lost more than $2 million worth of inventory, of which $1.2 million was covered by insurance. Nevertheless, the company lost all of its Valentine's Day merchandise. Fruth quickly rented two floors in Gallipolis, some 30 minutes away, to house replacement inventory and cobbled together office space in Point Pleasant banks and churches for buyers and administrators. The accounting operation was moved to temporary quarters in Gallipolis.

The chain had essentially recovered from the shock of the fire when in March 1998, a levy broke in Waverly, Ohio, flooding its makeshift storage facility and depositing 18 inches of water in area Fruth stores. Although the stores had to be closed for a day, the pharmacy departments continued to serve customers. Despite fire and flood, the chain continued to show strong growth, with sales for fiscal 1997 up 9 percent to $60

Key Dates:

1952: Jack Fruth opens his first drugstore.
1963: Fruth's second store opens but later burns down.
1975: The company adds a second location.
1994: Average sales per store reaches $2 million per year.
1996: Fire destroys a distribution center.
2002: The chain tops $100 million in total sales.

million. The fire also resulted in the building of a more modern warehouse in September 1997, as well as a separate 10,000-square-foot corporate office complex, adding a multimedia meeting room that could also be used as a training center to help bolster Fruth's reputation for superior customer service.

Around this time, Fruth began a program to remodel two or three stores a year. Management also looked to grow the chain by acquisition and was regularly approached by independent drug stores interested in being acquired. The goal was to reach the 25-unit mark by 2002, but it would not be met. Instead, the company focused on internal growth. The chain's POS system was providing information that management was now able to use to adjust its mix of merchandise. For example, cosmetic products were deemphasized while more bath and body items were added, as were sugar-free and snack foods. Sales for fiscal 1998 grew to $65 million, an 8.3 percent increase over the previous year.

In early 2000, Fruth opened its first non-pharmacy operation, a gift, card, and floral shop it named the Honey Bear Tree, which took over a 9,500-square-foot store in Cross Lanes, West Virginia, that had previously housed a Rite Aid drugstore. The upscale decor, featuring dark wood cabinetry and diffused lighting, was divided into separate ''rooms'' where different product lines and brands were featured, such as Yankee Candles and Precious Moments. While Honey Bear Tree was up-market in many respects, it also attracted customers by offering half-price greeting cards. Fruth also opened its 22nd drugstore in fiscal 2000, taking over a former Kroger supermarket in Nelsonville, Ohio. In addition, the chain invested in adding drive-through window pharmacy operations to nine of its stores. At the same time, Fruth continued to use POS data to prune its shelves of unnecessary and redundant merchandise. As a result of these efforts, sales approached $80 million in fiscal 2000.

Traditionally, Furth's advertising budget was devoted almost entirely to circulars, but in 2000 the chain tried advertising on television after a vendor asked if Fruth would be interested in spending some co-op money on a commercial for a Christmas tree stand. A large number of customers reported seeing the commercials, which led management to eliminate one circular each quarter to use for television advertising the following year. The reallocation of funds proved highly successful. The chain advertised during morning talk shows and evening news programs shortly before seasonal promotions. As a result, Valentine's Day sales were up 18 percent and Christmas sales improved 20 percent, while overall sales for fiscal 2001 increased by 13.2 percent to $90 million. The chain also took advantage of television advertising by becoming involved in a segment with a local station called ''Ask the Pharmacist,'' which allowed viewers to have their pharmacy questions answered by a Fruth pharmacist.

Fruth celebrated in 50th anniversary in 2002, and for fiscal 2001 (which ended June 30, 2002) the chain saw annual sales top the $100 million mark for the first tine, reaching $105 million, a 10.5 percent increase over the previous year. Although the chain was not adding stores, it continued to modify its merchandise mix and broaden the range of its giftware. One of the greatest challenges Fruth faced at this stage was recruiting new pharmacists willing to move to western West Virginia and southern Ohio. The latest store to open, for example, was able to hire only one pharmacist, who had to handle the entire load for the first six months in operation. To help alleviate this problem, in 2003 Fruth started an extern program with West Virginia University to attract young pharmacists to the area.

Although Jack Fruth was well into his 70s, he remained chairman and had no intention of selling the chain of drugstores he founded, although he would likely find a number of willing suitors. For years he had emphasized treating employees like family and customers like friends. In keeping with this approach, his succession plan called for the company to one day be owned by its employees.

Principal Subsidiaries

Honey Bear Tree.

Principal Competitors

Drug Emporium, Inc.; Kmart Corporation; Rite Aid Corporation; Wal-Mart Stores, Inc.

Further Reading

Ball, Susan, ''Fruth Adds Right Chemistry to Recently-Merged Group,'' *Drug Store News*, April 17, 1989, p. 3.

Forinash, Danny, ''After Defying the Odds, Fruth Pharmacy Celebrates 50th Anniversary,'' *State Journal*, November 8, 2002, p. 22.

''Fruth Goes to Great Lengths to Ensure Success,'' *Chain Drug Review*, February 17, 1997, p. 24.

Johnsen, Michael, ''Focusing on Competitive Niche,'' *Drug Store News*, April 29, 2002, p. 126.

Prior, Molly, ''Fruth Pharmacy: Remodeled Stores Drive Sales Gains,'' *Drug Store News*, April 28, 2003, p. 125.

—Ed Dinger

Galey&Lord

Galey & Lord, Inc.

980 Avenue of the Americas
New York, New York 10018
U.S.A.
Telephone: (212) 465-3000
Fax: (212) 465-3025

Private Company
Incorporated: 1988
Employees: 4,790
Sales: $436.8 million (2003)
NAIC: 313210 Broad Woven Fabric Mills, Cotton; 313210 Broad Woven Fabric Mills, Manmade Fiber and Silk; 313311 Broad Woven Fabric Finishing Mills

Galey & Lord, Inc., develops, manufactures, and markets fabrics for the apparel and home furnishings industries, particularly high-quality woven cotton and cotton-blended apparel fabrics and printed fabrics. Galey & Lord sells its products to uniform and sportswear manufacturers of men's, women's, and children's wrinkle-free slacks, pants, and shorts. Known for innovative fabric dyeing and finishing techniques, this long-established company also produces khaki, corduroy, and wrinkle-free fabrics. Galey & Lord's acquisition of Dominion Textile's Swift Denim division in 1998 made it one of the largest producers of denim in the United States. Nevertheless, the company filed for bankruptcy protection in 2002 and again in 2004.

Origins in the 19th Century

Partners William Galey and Charles Lord founded Galey & Lord in 1886 to market fabrics to the apparel industry. The pair established the company as a selling agent for their other business, Aberfoyle, a mill in Pennsylvania. The firm grew steadily, and by 1922 it also functioned as sales agent for Camerton Mills. During the Great Depression, Galey & Lord manufactured a fabric common for civilian work wear—khaki. Though expensive, khaki earned its place as a conventional apparel fabric at this time.

World War II marked a turning point for the company's khaki fabric. During the war, Galey & Lord began selling khaki to the U.S. military. The trademark Camerton Army Cloth became the standard issue for uniforms. Thus, the company gained a reputation as the ''King of Khaki,'' and Galey & Lord maintained its position as a leader in the khaki market into the 1990s. The company sold 75 million yards of the fabric in 1996. Manufacturers used 70 percent of that khaki for men's wear. In the past, only consumers 45 years old and older wore khaki. By 1996, though, 15- through 20-year-olds sported khaki, too.

Khaki itself changed a lot through the decades, especially with the advent of business casual wear. Modern khaki fabrics came in a variety of colors such as tan, putty, olive, black, navy, sage, and chocolate, and Galey & Lord manufactured about 70 percent of its khaki with special sueded or napped finishes during the 1990s. One thing about khaki that remained constant, however, was the fabric's competitive pricing. ''Khaki is a category,'' explained Galey & Lord vice president Cheryl Blanchette in the *Daily News Record.* ''It has staying power, and the fashion influence is driving it. It is really being driven by consumers looking for an alternative to denim. The overall popularity of khaki is in the casualization of America. The young generation has always liked denim and now is looking for an alternative. The fashion influence of khaki is big. There are a lot of new players in khaki apparel.'' Some of Galey & Lord's more well-known customers for khaki included Calvin Klein, Ralph Lauren, Tommy Hilfiger, Guess, Polo Jeans, Liz Claiborne, the Gap, Banana Republic, L.L. Bean, and Land's End.

Part of Burlington in the Postwar Era

Shortly after the end of World War II, J. Spencer Love, creator of Burlington Industries, purchased Camerton Mills—and Galey & Lord as part of the acquisition. Burlington manufactured fine cotton and cotton-blended fabrics under the Galey & Lord name, so blended fabrics became synonymous with Galey & Lord. The company remained a division of Burlington Industries until 1987, when Asher Edelman threatened a takeover of the company. Burlington management engineered a leveraged buyout of Galey & Lord to fend off the attempt. The division was spun off to a Burlington executive—Arthur Wiener—for $150 million. Citicorp Venture Capital financed the spinoff and retained 39 percent of the new company's shares. Wiener became chief executive

Company Perspectives:

The Company is committed to being an industry leader in providing superior customer service. The key elements of this tactic include providing timely and complete order delivery, building partnerships with customers, providing electronic data information services, and providing inventory management support.

officer of the now independent Galey & Lord, headquartered in New York City and Greensboro, North Carolina. The company's strategy for the future involved manufacturing fabrics that were made differently than those of competitors by experimenting with dyeing and finishing. Wiener eventually made Galey & Lord a public company in 1992.

That year the company also created a new synthetic fabrics division. A converting operation under the direction of Edward Delfoe, the division supplied dyed and printed synthetic fabrics to Galey & Lord customers. The company established a batch dyeing facility at its Society Hill, South Carolina, plant to print and dye polyester/rayon, acrylic, and wool blends, mainly for two-piece dressing.

Corduroy Makes a Comeback: 1990s

In 1993, Galey & Lord once again saw a trend emerging in corduroy. The fabric, popular in the 1970s, began to regain acceptance after falling from favor with consumers in the 1980s. Corduroy sales for the company rose 7 percent in 1993 and remained strong in 1994 when clothing manufacturers began offering five-pocket jeans in corduroy. By 1996, more and more consumers considered the fabric another alternative to denim, causing a resurgence in its prominence.

At this time, Galey & Lord was the only vertically integrated corduroy manufacturer in the United States, and the company produced a very different corduroy than in the past. For example, the fabric became available in a wider range of colors and textures. Softness became a priority for corduroy. Consumer tastes dictated that eight-wale corduroy replace 14-wale corduroy (unless the 14-wale fabric was very soft), and four- or six-wale corduroy became the fabric of choice for fashion items. Alternate ribbing also varied the look of the fabric now, and the wearing season of corduroy lengthened as well. Although corduroy pants remained a staple throughout the fall and winter seasons, corduroy shorts became popular as an item for spring wardrobes.

Galey & Lord received substantial business in the United States and Europe from the sale of its corduroy. In 1996, the company saw a 30 percent increase in its corduroy business. As Bob McCormack, president of apparel fabric marketing for Galey & Lord told the *Daily News Record* in early 1997: "We see a very optimistic future for corduroy.... The biggest growth is in the men's area." Buyers of Galey & Lord corduroy included Levi, Lee, Wrangler, Guess, Mossimo, Penney, and the Gap.

In 1994, Galey & Lord purchased the decorative prints division of Burlington Industries. This acquisition marked the company's entry into the non-apparel fabric market. Renamed Galey & Lord Home Fashion Fabrics, the new subsidiary supplied home decorator fabrics for bedspreads, comforters, and curtains. The company also launched Group II, a second printed apparel fabrics division. Galey & Lord Prints, the company's first such unit, printed on polyester and rayon blends or on 100-percent rayon. This new division printed on 100-percent cotton—and limited rayon challis—for the women's, men's, and children's wear markets. Galey & Lord executives appointed Leon Hecht and Joe Richards, both from Cranston Apparel Fabrics Company (a division of Galey & Lord's competitor Cranston Print Works) as heads of Group II. Galey & Lord located both the first division and Group II at its specialty plant in Society Hill, South Carolina. Late in 1994, Wiener explained to *WWD* that "we feel the print market is beginning to turn around, and the new division gives us additional products with which to address the market and pick up some additional."

Despite Wiener's optimism, printed fabrics did poorly for the year. In the middle of 1995, industry analysts predicted a "violent shakeout" in the printed fabrics industry, but they also anticipated an upswing the following year. Nevertheless, by the fourth quarter of 1995, Galey & Lord announced the closing of its printed apparel fabrics business. Conditions in this segment of the industry had been deteriorating since 1992. Raw material costs rose consistently during this time; the market remained soft, and low-price imports heightened existing competition.

Ironically, sales volumes for printed fabrics increased during this time; however, weak operating results ate away Galey & Lord's profit margins. Sales in 1994, for example, totaled $30.1 million for printed fabrics—6.7 percent of net sales. Yet the company sustained $9.4 million in operating losses that year. Likewise in 1995, sales in this area again amounted to 6.7 percent of sales—$33.8 million—but operating losses reached $13.4 million. In fact, losses for printed apparel in the first nine months ending in June 1995 were $9.7 million compared to an operating profit of $37.3 million for the apparel, woven apparel, and home furnishings divisions. As Wiener explained in the *Daily News Record,* "The losses had become too large to justify continuing the businesses without a firm belief that a turnaround could be completed near-term."

In addition to the operating losses, Galey & Lord expended $14 or $15 million more to close the divisions. The company also laid off 450 workers, most from the Society Hill plant in South Carolina and some from the sales office in Greensboro, North Carolina. Executives from the printed apparel divisions—Hecht, Richards, and Maria Damiano—left the company.

Ron Loeser, a partner with the converter Omega Textiles, summed up the situation in *WWD:* "It's really scary what's happening. When a company with the resources like Galey & Lord decides it can't make it in the print business, there are some serious problems with it, the overall business." David Caplan, chief executive officer of another converter Metro Fabrics, agreed: "I hate to see any of the competition go out of business. Good healthy competition is important. Arthur Wiener is a tremendously bright man who runs a fantastic company. This is a step backward for the industry."

At the heart of these concerns was the need for better margins among manufacturers. Demand for prints remained

Key Dates:

1886: William Galey and Charles Lord establish Galey & Lord.
1922: By now, Galey & Lord is the sales agent for Camerton Mills.
1987: Burlington Industries spins off Galey & Lord; Arthur Wiener is named CEO.
1992: Arthur Wiener takes Galey & Lord public.
1994: The decorative prints business of Burlington Industries is acquired.
1996: Galey & Lord purchases six facilities in Mexico.
1998: The Polymer Group sells Swift Denim to Galey & Lord.
2002: Galey & Lord declares bankruptcy.
2004: The company emerges from bankruptcy and then files a second time later in the year.

strong during this time, as was evidenced by Galey & Lord's sales figures, but the business itself shifted. Operating costs grew as the prices of raw materials rose domestically, which encouraged the purchase of imported goods. The implementation of the General Agreement on Tariffs and Trade (GATT) further cultivated import use since access to U.S. markets expanded with the elimination of textile and apparel import quotas for several countries by the year 2005.

However disappointing the performance of printed apparel, the showing by Galey & Lord's wrinkle-free fabrics compensated at least to a small degree. In 1995, Galey & Lord dominated this market with 100-percent cotton fabrics. Wrinkle-free fabrics accounted for 75 percent of Galey & Lord's men's wear sales and 14 percent of women's wear sales. One of Wiener's goals became expanding this area. As he revealed to *WWD:* ''Developing more wrinkle-free products to fit into women's wear manufacturing and women's wear garments is one of the key challenges we've given to our merchants and product development people.'' Customers for wrinkle-free fabrics included Hagar, Levi Strauss, and Farah.

Acquisitions in the Mid- to Late 1990s

In 1995, Galey & Lord signed a letter of agreement to purchase the South Carolina textile firm Graniteville Company, a subsidiary of Triarc Companies, Inc. Though this would have doubled the size of Galey & Lord, the company canceled the merger due to undesirable conditions within the retail, textile, and apparel sectors. Fees and expenses associated with the aborted venture totaled $1.6 million.

Nevertheless, Galey & Lord successfully acquired Dimmit Industries the following year. Dimmit Industries sewed and finished pants and shorts for the casual wear market. Galey & Lord purchased the company from Farah for $22.8 million and acquired six manufacturing facilities in Piedras Negras, Mexico, in the process. These plants were to produce men's slacks and shorts from Galey & Lord fabrics, launching the company into the business of apparel manufacturing. Galey & Lord, in effect, became a full-service supplier to its established customer base after the acquisition. The company used its fabrics to make garments—apparel made in North American Free Trade Alliance (NAFTA) countries as opposed to the Far East—for its established customer base, thereby increasing business at its six manufacturing plants in North Carolina, South Carolina, and Georgia. Bob McCormack, a Galey & Lord executive vice-president, explained the company's rationale in *WWD:* ''We are trying to protect the business we have in the United States by better servicing our customer base. As competition from overseas intensifies, we will be able to offer them a complete package.''

The company established a new subsidiary—G & L Service Company, North America, Inc.—to run operations in Mexico. In 1996, the six Mexican plants operated at full capacity. Galey & Lord planned expansions to the facilities in 1996 and 1997.

Throughout its history, Galey & Lord had been associated with innovations in fabric. The company historically dyed and finished fabrics to differentiate items that it produced from its competitors' goods. In 1996, Galey & Lord purchase special wet and face finishing equipment to further its reputation in quality yarn-dyed fabrics despite the expense. ''It's not a question of whether we can afford this development work,'' said Wiener in the *Daily News Record.* ''We can't afford not to do it.''

During the late 1990s, the company's strategy was to continue to develop its practice of unique dyeing and finishing. It also planned to produce better and different fabrics of world-class quality and to change fabrics as dictated by market demands. Above all, Galey & Lord intended to grow. ''We have four internal goals to execute,'' Wiener told the *Daily News Record.* ''We will continue to grow our core fabric business in the Carolinas and Georgia, with product development, to supply apparel yard goods to domestic, NAFTA, and international customers. We will expand our garment business to use those fabrics. We are constantly looking at acquisitions. If we see the right one, we will do it. We will be in the Pacific Rim in a joint venture. There are 4.5 billion people in Asia, and 700 million can buy our products. We must find a way to participate in this market. We will be larger through acquisition and growth. G&L's good growth pattern won't be reversed. How big we will be depends on what comes along that is right.''

The CEO's words foreshadowed the largest deal in Galey & Lord's history. In 1998, the company doubled its sales after completing a $480 million acquisition of Dominion Textile's Swift Denim division. The denim division was first transferred to the Polymer Group and then to Galey & Lord. The deal secured Galey & Lord's position as the second largest denim manufacturer in the world. The company also gained Klopman International and Polymer's foreign operations in Tunisia in this transaction. While Galey & Lord management applauded the deal, many analysts were concerned about the high level of borrowing the company undertook, mainly because the denim market had seen a marked decline during the 1990s.

Changes in the 21st Century

Sure enough, as early as 1999, there were distinct signs that Galey & Lord's financial performance was deteriorating. Indeed, losses began to mount as the company entered the new millennium. After struggling in a lackluster retail environment,

Galey & Lord filed for bankruptcy protection in 2002. By that time, its losses had reached $850 million. The company pledged not to cut operations and continued to manufacture fabrics during the proceedings.

In March of 2004, Galey & Lord exited bankruptcy protection after more than two years. The company emerged as a private company with John J. Heldrich at the helm. (Arthur Wiener announced his retirement at this time.) As part of the company's reorganization plan, General Electic Capital Corp. provided a financing package worth $70 million.

Events happened quickly during the next few months in 2004. Galey & Lord announced in June that it would close a weaving plant in Georgia in August. Approximately 450 employees would be laid off by the decision to consolidate the plant. Overall, the company had cut about 2,200 jobs since 2002. In July, Galey & Lord revealed that Patriarch Partners LLC, an investment firm with major holdings in the textile industry, was interested in acquiring the company. The transaction, however, needed to be approved by the company's lenders.

Less than one month later, Galey & Lord filed for bankruptcy for a second time. The company had not been able to fulfill its post-bankruptcy obligations. Patriarch Partners made a $188 million offer to buy Galey & Lord out of bankruptcy court. As part of the deal, Patriarch Partners would assume $130 million of Galey & Lord's debt. Patriarch Partners seemed optimistic that if the acquisition were successful, Galey & Lord would eventually regain its financial footing and continue to be a leading producer of denim, corduroy, and khaki in the textile industry.

Principal Subsidiaries

Swift Denim Group.

Principal Competitors

Avondale Inc.; Milliken & Company Inc.; Mount Vernon Mills, Inc.

Further Reading

Adams, Tony, ''Big Changes Loom on Horizon for Textile Manufacturer Galey & Lord,'' *Columbus Ledger-Enquirer* (Georgia), August 20, 2004.

''Business Brief—Galey & Lord Inc.: Stake of 40% Now is Held by Citibank, Certain Units,'' *Wall Street Journal*, April 5, 1999, p. 1.

Eliot, Edward, ''Galey & Lord Raises Effluent Treatment to a Higher Level,'' *Textile World*, May 1995, p. 73.

''G & L to Buy Six Factories from Farah,'' *WWD*, May 21, 1996, p. 15.

''Galey & Lord Agrees to Be Acquired by Patriarch Partners; Investment Firm Commits to Working with Management to Execute Long-Term Strategic Vision for Global Textile Maker,'' *Dow Jones News Service*, July 21, 2004.

''Galey & Lord Forms Division,'' *Daily News Record*, July 14, 1992, p. 10.

''Galey & Lord Inc. Forecasts Loss,'' *Wall Street Journal*, July 25, 2001, p. A.4.

''Galey & Lord Launches Its Second Unit for Prints,'' *WWD*, September 13, 1994, p. 18.

''Galey & Lord to Close Two Apparel Print Units in the Fourth Quarter; Will Take $14–$15 Million Charge in September Quarter,'' *Daily News Record*, July 21, 1995, p. 3.

''Guilford Mills to Sell Unit, as Galey & Lord Files for Chapter 11,'' *The Wall Street Journal*, February 20, 2002, p. 1.

Krouse, Peter, ''Getting into Jeans,'' *Greensboro News & Record*, February 8, 1998, p. E1.

McNamara, Michael, ''Converters: Girding for a Fallout,'' *WWD*, July 25, 1995, p. 10.

——, ''Galey & Lord's Strategy: More Wrinkle-Free,'' *WWD*, February 9, 1994, p. 22.

Maycumber, S. Gray, ''King of Khaki and Court of Corduroy,'' *Daily News Record*, February 17, 1997, p. 58.

Patterson, Donald W., ''Galey Free from Bankruptcy; Galey & Lord Is Now a Private Company With a New President and CEO, John J. Heldrich,'' *Greensboro News & Record,* March 9, 2004, p. B8.

——, ''Galey & Lord Files 2nd Time; the Struggling Textile Company Says the New Bankruptcy Filing Is Tied to a $188 Million Buyout,'' *Greensboro News & Record,* August 20, 2004, p. B6.

''Textile Maker Will Shut Georgia Plant,'' *St. Louis Post-Dispatch*, June 9, 2004, p. B03.

—Charity Anne Dorgan
—update: Christina M. Stansell

Gannett Company, Inc.

1100 Wilson Boulevard
Arlington, Virginia 22234
U.S.A.
Telephone: (703) 854-6000
Fax: (703) 558-4638
Web site: http://www.gannett.com

Public Company
Incorporated: 1923
Employees: 53,000
Sales: $6.71 billion (2003)
Stock Exchanges: New York
Ticker Symbol: GCI
NAIC: 511110 Newspaper Publishers; 513120 Television Broadcasting

Referring to itself as a diversified news and information company, Gannett Company, Inc. owns 101 daily newspapers, including the best-selling daily newspaper in the United States, *USA Today,* which is also available in 60 countries worldwide. Gannett also owns more than 20 television stations covering roughly 17 percent of the United States. Although the company's focus is primarily in its newspaper and broadcasting properties, it operates a news service and is also involved in commercial printing, telemarketing, data services, and news programming. The company also owns and operates over 130 web sites in the United States and another 80 in the United Kingdom. Headquartered in Arlington, Virginia, Gannett maintains offices in 43 states, the District of Columbia, Guam, the United Kingdom, Belgium, Germany, Italy, and Hong Kong.

Origins

Gannett was the brainchild of Frank Gannett, who paid his way through Cornell University by running a news correspondence syndicate; when he graduated he had $1,000 in savings. Gannett got into the media business in 1906 when he and several associates bought the *Elmira Gazette* in Elmira, New York, with $3,000 in savings, $7,000 in loans, and $10,000 in notes. They bought another local paper and merged them to form the *Star-Gazette,* beginning a pattern of mergers to increase advertising power that the company would follow throughout its history. Six years later, in 1912, Gannett bought the *Ithaca Journal,* beginning his toehold in upper New York state. The company gradually built up a portfolio of 19 New York dailies by 1989.

In 1918 Gannett and his team moved to Rochester, New York, a city whose papers would turn out to be among the company's strongest. Many of Gannett's rising executives were groomed at the Rochester papers. The group purchased two newspapers upon their arrival and merged them into the *Times-Union.* The papers' holdings were consolidated under the name Empire State Group. In 1921 the *Observer-Dispatch* of Utica, New York, was acquired. In 1923 Gannett bought out his partners' interests in the Empire State Group and the six newspapers the group then owned, and formed Gannett Co., Inc. Gannett appointed Frank Tripp general manager. Tripp helped run the everyday business of the papers, and the two were close allies for years. The Northeast was Gannett's focus for the next 25 years, and the company expanded aggressively with acquisitions there. Another key executive, Paul Miller, joined the company in 1947, becoming Gannett's executive assistant. By then, the company operated 21 newspapers and radio stations.

The company's role as a leader in technology began in 1929, when Frank Gannett co-invented the teletypesetter. Gannett newsrooms were among the first to use shortwave radios to gather reports from distant sources. In 1938, before color was used much in newspapers, many Gannett presses were adapted for color; much later, with its *USA Today,* the company would continue to be a leader in color use. Other advantages included a corporate plane that helped reporters get to the site of news quickly. Frank Gannett died in 1957, but not before he saw Miller named president and chief executive officer. Miller oversaw the company's expansion from a regional to a national chain in the next decade.

Gannett News Service, as the company became known, was founded in 1942 as Gannett National Service. The wire service subsidiary provided the company's local papers with national stories from Washington, D.C., and 13 bureaus. The stories often

Company Perspectives:

The information company. Newspapers. Television. Internet.

featured a local angle or local sources. A television news bureau was added in 1982. Through all these years, Gannett grew by buying existing newspaper and radio and TV stations. In 1966 it founded its first newspaper, *Florida Today*. It was the work of Allen Neuharth, who later was to become the founder of *USA Today*. Neuharth brought the new paper to profitability in 33 months, an incredible feat in the newspaper business, according to analysts. Because the paper was near the National Aeronautics and Space Administration (NASA), it was dubbed ''Florida's Space Age Newspaper.'' The paper was ultimately redesigned to emphasize state and local news and was promoted and sold with *USA Today*, which provided national and international coverage.

Gannett went public in 1967. In 1970 Miller assumed the title of chairman, and Neuharth was promoted to president and chief operating officer from executive vice-president, making him the heir-apparent to the top position in the company. Neuharth went on an acquisition spree, leading the company to its current size and status in the media world. He became chief executive officer in 1973 and chairman in 1979.

1970s: Growth Through Acquisitions

Two notable mergers were those with Federated Publications in 1971 and with Speidel Newspaper Group in 1977. Two years later, Gannett merged with Combined Communications, the biggest such merger in the industry at that time, for $400 million. The Evening News Association joined the Gannett family later when Gannett bought it for $700 million. One near merger was with Ridder Publications. That company's president, Bernard H. Ridder, Jr., was a golfing mate of Miller. Ridder had concluded that the only way his small, family-held company's stock would ever reach its full potential was for Ridder Publications to merge with a big media company. The two talked, but Ridder proved to be more interested in Knight Newspapers because it had less geographic overlap with Ridder than did Gannett. However, in 1989 Gannett and Knight-Ridder implemented a joint operating agency to combat the decline in newspaper advertising revenues in Detroit, Michigan. The cooperative venture was the largest ever merging of two competing newspapers' business operations. The arrangement called for the Knight-Ridder's *Free Press* and Gannett's *Detroit News* to divide revenues equally. Since Gannett held more of Detroit's market share before the merger, it took a loss during the venture's first year, 1990.

In 1986 Neuharth retired as chief executive officer, passing the baton to John Curley. Curley had been president and chief operating officer since 1984; he joined Gannett in 1970. Curley took on the title of chairman in 1989. A newsman like most of Gannett's heads, Curley was editor and publisher of several Gannett papers and was founding editor of *USA Today*.

Neuharth continued as chairman of the Gannett Foundation, which was established in 1935 by Frank Gannett to promote free press, freedom of information and better journalism, adult literacy, community problem-solving, and volunteerism. Neuharth spent as freely at the foundation as he had at the company, giving $28 million to various programs in 1989 alone. Despite criticism from some Gannett newspaper executives, Neuharth also oversaw the Foundation's move from Rochester, New York, to Arlington, Virginia, where *USA Today's* offices were located. Interior design of the charity's new headquarters ran to $15 million.

With expenses rising faster than assets, Neuharth sold the Foundation's ten percent share of Gannett Co. back to the company for $670 million. On July 4, 1991, the philanthropy's name was changed to the Freedom Forum, and its mission was changed to focus on First Amendment and other strictly journalistic issues. Gannett Co. created a $5 million fund to replace money withdrawn from the Gannett Foundation's more community-oriented charities. Other accomplishments of the company in the early 1990s included: increasing the company's use of recycled newsprint to 20 percent of total usage, over 180,000 tons; being named one of the United States' top 20 places for African Americans to work; and becoming the first news service to syndicate a weekly newspaper column dedicated exclusively to gay and lesbian issues.

Neuharth had said in 1982 when he started *USA Today* that it would begin making annual profits in three to five years. By 1990 the paper had had quarterly profits but never a full year of profitability. Between 1982 and 1990, *USA Today* sapped the company of an estimated $500 million. September 1992 marked ten unprofitable years for *USA Today*. But with 6.6 million readers daily, the United States' most widely read newspaper also celebrated record advertising and circulation revenues. *USA Today* executives claimed that had the U.S. economy not been in recession, the paper would have been in the black by 1990. Fortunately, the rest of Gannett's business was strong enough to offset *USA Today's* annual losses. Curley, the paper's president and publisher, hoped that cost-containment measures, lower newsprint prices, and other savings in the production-distribution process would bring *USA Today* into profitability.

The year 1991 was Gannett's most difficult since the company went public in 1967. The company slipped from second to third in rankings of the top U.S. media concerns as a result of Time Warner's leapfrog to first place. Annual revenues dropped two percent and net income was down 20 percent from the year before. Fifty-five of Gannett's 86 local dailies raised circulation prices, and circulation barely rose.

Yet the national daily newspaper was another demonstration of Gannett's leadership role in the use of technology, as well as journalism. The paper also was an innovator in graphics, especially in the use of color. Media observers credited *USA Today's* use of color as the spur for industry-wide interest in color graphics. The copy for the paper was composed and edited at *USA Today's* Arlington, Virginia, headquarters, then transmitted via satellite to 36 printing plants in the United States, Europe, and Asia.

$5 Billion in Revenues: 1990s

Gannett's most significant activity during the 1990s took place in the divestiture and acquisition arena, an area that some

Key Dates:

1923: Frank Gannett buys out his partners in the newspaper business and forms Gannett Company Inc.
1929: Frank Gannett invents the teletypesetter.
1942: The Gannett wire service is established.
1967: Company goes public on the New York Stock Exchange.
1982: *USA Today* begins publication.
1999: Gannett acquires Newsquest plc.

observers believed the company needed to explore more fully. Critics contended that Gannett, renowned for its financially conservative approach, should loosen its purse strings and adopt a more aggressive acquisition strategy. Confronted with suggestions that the company should purchase a movie studio or a television network, Gannett management demurred, preferring to keep its focus set on its core businesses. ''We aren't complicated people,'' Curley informed the *Wall Street Journal* in late 1995. ''We like newspapers and TV stations. If you run them very well, they can do very well. . . .'' Despite the company's penchant for financial discipline and its steadfast adherence to its existing businesses, the 1990s saw Gannett explore new business opportunities and express more than a modicum of acquisitive might.

Gannett began the process of adding and paring away businesses in 1995. That year, the company shouldered past rival bidders such as Ellis Broadcasting and NBC in its $1.7 billion acquisition of Greensville, South Carolina-based Multimedia, Inc. The acquisition gave Gannett 11 daily newspapers, 50 other newspaper publications, five network-affiliated television stations, two radio stations, and production and syndication control for television shows hosted by Phil Donahue, Sally Jesse Raphael, Rush Limbaugh, and Jerry Springer. The acquisition of Multimedia also ushered Gannett into the cable business, giving the company 450,000 cable television subscribers. As the company delved into the previously foreign territory of operating cable television systems and controlling television programming, it withdrew from two other businesses. In 1996 the company sold its outdoor advertising division to Outdoor Systems of Phoenix, divesting the business to free its resources for the development of its newspaper and broadcast properties and to facilitate the incorporation of the Multimedia properties into its fold. Louis Harris & Associates, Gannett's polling subsidiary, also was sold in 1996, a year that saw the company enter into a joint venture with Knight-Ridder and Landmark Communications to form an Internet service provider called InfiNet, created to help publish newspapers online.

Deal-making continued to predominate at Gannett headquarters as the company entered the late 1990s. The company had exchanged six of its radio stations for a television station in Tampa, Florida, in 1996; in 1998, it exited the business entirely by selling its remaining five radio stations to Evergreen Media. As the company's radio properties disappeared, the number of its television stations increased with the acquisition of three stations in Maine and South Carolina. Before the end of the decade, the company completed two more significant deals, which, in keeping with the trend established in the 1990s, included a divestiture and an acquisition. In 1999, the company sold the cable assets obtained in the Multimedia acquisition. According to company officials, the decision to divest the cable properties was not based on a strategic decision, but represented an opportunity to realize a significant profit. Gannett sold the cable business to Cox Communications for $2.7 billion, a move that the company's treasurer described as ''a grand-slam deal'' in the July 31, 1999, issue of *Editor & Publisher*. In a separate announcement, Gannett revealed that it was acquiring 95 percent of Newsquest plc, the largest regional newspaper publisher in England.

The cumulative effect of the acquisitions and divestitures completed during the latter half of the 1990s lifted Gannett's revenues above $5 billion by the end of the decade. Although the company shied away from headlong leaps into other areas of the media industry—unlike many of its competitors—Gannett's consistent record of financial growth suggested that there was no pressing need to develop into a comprehensive, broadly diversified media conglomerate.

The Early 2000s

As the 1990s rolled to a close Gannett became embroiled in a $10 million dollar lawsuit with banana giant Chiquita Foods International. In May 1998 the *Cincinnati Enquirer*, a Gannett-owned newspaper, ran an 18-page exposé on the banana titan, alleging numerous questionable business practices, but it was soon alleged that *Enquirer* reporter Mike Gallagher had illegally obtained Chiquita voice-mail messages. By June 28, 1998, the *Enquirer* had retracted the story upon the front page of its Sunday edition. Repercussions from the suit would extend into the next century as the reporter and his managing editor filed suits of their own.

Gannet acquired Sacramento's KXTV Channel 10 in February 1999, although it sold its Multimedia Cablevision Inc., a 515,000-subscriber operation it had picked up in 1995 through its acquisition of Multimedia. By October 1999, Gannett was back in purchasing mode, picking up eight papers in the new York area from the Tucker Communications group; additionally, the company expanded in to Great Britain, picking up 11 British dailies. The trend continued in to 2000, when Thomson Co. agreed to sell Gannett 21 daily papers for $1.13 billion in June.

Long time Chief Executive Officer John J. Curley stepped down from Gannett in June 2000, passing the mantle to his right-hand man, President and Vice-Chairman Douglas H. McCorkindale. Curley remained chairman until early 2001, when he retired, leaving McCorkindale chairman, president, and CEO. The orderly changeover caused nary a ripple in Gannett's stock; McCorkindale had been Curley's associate for so long that investors seemed assured that the firm would continue on familiar patterns. Certainly the company strategies remained the same. In that same month Gannett bid on yet another British company, Newscom, publisher of four daily newspapers, for $702 million, then cut a check for $2.6 billion for *Arizona Republic* and *Indianapolis Star* publisher Central Newspapers. The acquisitions mounted through the rest of the early 2000s, and by 2004 Gannett controlled three Scottish papers and 11 related magazines, as well as 34 publications from Brown County Publishing Company, including *The Green*

Bay News-Chronicle. Profits for the company remained on the upswing into the middle of 2004, and CEO Corkindale was voted in by directors to remain chairman until 2006, two years longer than originally scheduled.

Such success did not come without some controversy. As late as 2003 the lawsuits related to the Chiquita Banana stories in the *Enquirer* were still in the courts. Ultimately the courts decided in favor of former editor Larry Beupre and awarded him a $550,000 settlement for his claim that he had been the company's scapegoat. There was likewise trouble in Hawaii, with *Honolulu Star-Bulletin* owner David Black accusing Gannett of various unsavory business practices, including various legal manipulations that rendered it cost-prohibitive for his paper, a rival to the Gannett-owned *Honolulu Advertiser*, to purchase newsprint.

In late 2004, however, even with occasional assaults, Gannett was clearly secure financially and in its role as an industry leader. The company remained a steady draw for talented minority workers, thanks in no small part to Gannett's aggressive recruitment drives aimed at promising college graduates. In 2004, a titanic merger looked to be in the works between the television operations of Gannett and Hearst-Argyle, following the relaxation of duopoly rules by the Federal Communications Commission (FCC). A merger of the two companies would come close to dominating 35 percent of the market place, near the allowable cut-off ministered by the FCC. Critics suggested that a merger would further shrink both jobs and diversity of viewpoints in areas controlled by both companies, but that remained to be seen.

Principal Subsidiaries

USA Today; USA Weekend; Newsquest plc; Gannett News Service; Gannett Offset; Gannett Retail Advertising Group; Gannett Media Technologies International; Nursing Spectrum; Texas-New Mexico Newspapers Partnership; Captivate; Clipper Magazine Inc.; 101 Inc.; Army Times Publishing Company; Gannett UK Ltd.

Principal Competitors

The News Corporation Ltd.; Knight-Ridder Inc.; The Associated Press; The E.W. Scripps Company; The Hearst Corporation.

Further Reading

Calabro, Lori, "Douglas McCorkindale: Confessions of a Dealmaker," *CFO: The Magazine for Senior Financial Executives,* March 1991.

Case, Tony, "Two Old Marketplace Enemies End Up the Best of Partners," *MEDIAWEEK,* March 15, 1999, p. 18.

Cosco, Joseph, "Loyal to the Core," *Journal of Business Strategy,* March-April 1996, p. 42.

Cose, Ellis, *The Press,* New York: Morrow, 1989.

Crain, Rance, "Readers Find Newspapers 'Boring . . . Dull'," *Advertising Age,* September 14, 1992.

Donaton, Scott, "Media Reassess As Boomers Age," *Advertising Age,* July 15, 1991.

Endicott, R. Craig, "100 Leading Media Companies," *Advertising Age,* August 10, 1992.

Ferraro, Cathleen, "Dallas-Based Media Firm Trades Television Stations with Gannett Co.," *Knight Ridder/Tribune Business News,* February 26, 1999.

Fisher, Christy, "A Decade of 'USA Today': Color It Red," *Advertising Age,* August 31, 1992.

Fitzgerald, Mark, "Stockholder Proposal Seeks Closing of USA Today," *Editor & Publisher,* April 4, 1992, p. 12.

Foust, Dean, "Patching the Cracks in the House That Al Built," *Business Week,* December 16, 1991.

"Gannett: USA's Tomorrow," *Economist,* November 25, 1989.

Garneau, George, "A Flat Year Expected for 1992," *Editor & Publisher,* January 4, 1992.

——, "Gannett Foundation's Revised Mission," *Editor & Publisher,* June 8, 1991.

——, "Newspaper Financial Reports," *Editor & Publisher,* August 8, 1992.

Henderson, Barry, "Gannett to Sell Off Recently Acquired Cable Systems," *Kansas City Business Journal,* September 1, 1995, p. 3.

Kerwin, Ann Marie, "Advice for the Next Century: Future Role of Newspapers Discussed by Panel," *Editor & Publisher,* August 8, 1992.

McClellan, Steve, "Multimedia Buy Boosts Gannett into Top 10," *Broadcasting & Cable,* July 31, 1995, p. 36.

Moses, Lucia, "Exit Strategy for No. 1 Man at No. 1 Chain," *Editor & Publisher,* May 8, 2000 p. 12.

Moses, Lucia, "Thomson Sale Reshapes Gannett, CNHI Groups," *Editor & Publisher,* June 12, 2000 p. 5.

Mott, Frank Luther, *American Journalism: A History, 1690–1960,* New York: Macmillan, 1962.

Noak, David, "Top Gannett VP Vetted Chiquita Story Package," *Editor & Publisher,* July 25, 1998, p. 16.

Powell, Dave, "Technology and Imagination Are the Stuff from Which Businesses Can Be Built," *Networking Management,* March 1991.

Rengers, Carrie, "Where Gannett Went Wrong," *Arkansas Business,* October 19, 1992, p. 22.

Sacharow, Anya, "The Merger," *MEDIAWEEK,* November 27, 1995, p. 12.

—Lisa Collins
—updates: April Dougal; Jeffrey L. Covell; Howard A. Jones

General Cigar Holdings, Inc.

387 Park Avenue South
New York, New York 10016-8899
United States
Telephone: (212) 448-3800
Toll Free: (800) 273-8044
Fax: (212) 561-8979
Web site: http://www.cigarworld.com

Private Company
Incorporated: 1906 as United Cigar Manufacturers Company
Employees: 35
Sales: $182.2 million
NAIC: 312229 Other Tobacco Product Manufacturing

General Cigar Holdings, Inc., makes and markets imported handmade and hand-rolled premium cigars made with long filler and all natural tobacco leaf. The company's most popular brands include Macanudo, Punch (MPP), Hoyo de Monterrey, Cohiba, and Partagas. Through its subsidiary, Culbro Tobacco, it grows, cures, ages, and processes the majority of Connecticut Shade tobacco in the world. The company also owns Club Macanudo cigar bars in New York and Chicago. Once known as Culbro Corporation General Cigar Holdings is 65 percent owned by Swedish Match AB. The remaining shares are held by the Cullman family, which founded the company.

1840s–1940s: Origin and Development of Family Cigar Business

Tobacco and the Cullman family have been intertwined since the mid-19th century. In 1848, during the time of revolution in Europe, Ferdinand Kullman, a wine merchant from Germany, immigrated to the U.S. In America, he continued to sell wines and, according to family history, began selling cigars as well. He changed the family name to Cullman.

Ferdinand's son, Joseph, began working at age 14 for a tobacco merchant in New York City. He was involved in buying and selling leaf tobacco. His work became prosperous enough for him to send his son, also called Joseph, to college. In 1904, Joseph Jr. graduated from school and entered the tobacco business. Called ''Mister Junior,'' the young Cullman began buying a variety of tobacco, including Havana seed, Connecticut broadleaf, some Cuban tobacco, and also tobacco grown in Ohio and Wisconsin. He followed his father by importing Sumatra tobacco from the Dutch East Indies, and traveled to tobacco auctions in Amsterdam for Indonesian wrapper tobacco.

In 1906, the Cullman family formed its cigar-making operations into the United Cigar Manufacturers Company. It was listed on the New York Stock Exchange that same year. Soon, Joseph Cullman Jr. became interested in another aspect of the tobacco business, namely tobacco-growing in Connecticut. Although tobacco for cigars was already being grown there, the type was Connecticut broadleaf, a dark, maduro-style wrapper. Joseph began growing Havana seed (or Cuban seed, as it was also known) in the fertile Connecticut River Valley fields, and the wrapper that grew was lighter. Before long, it became very popular with cigar consumers, and the Cullmans became one of the largest growers of wrapper leaf in the entire state.

United Cigar Manufacturers grew quickly in its first decade; it paid its first dividends in 1909, aided by a series of acquisitions of other cigar makers. This all took place at a time when the cigar industry itself was undergoing a rapid consolidation, especially among the largest tobacco companies, including American Tobacco and Consolidated Cigar Corp. In 1917, United Cigar Manufacturers changed its name to General Cigar Co., Inc., to reflect its growing holdings.

The following year, General Cigar moved to change the face—and structure—of the U.S. cigar industry. Before the early 1920s, cigars had been primarily sold as local brands or under private labels. Across the United States, there were hundreds of small-volume cigar names. General Cigar alone represented about 150 different brands. In 1918, the company moved to establish the first national cigar brands. It dropped nearly all of its brands, and instead concentrated on the manufacturing, sales, and advertising for five core brand names. Each of General Cigar's brands—which included White Owl, Van Dyck, Wm. Penn, and Robt. Burns—hit a different price point. Advertising became important; General Cigar was among the first

Company Perspectives:

General Cigar Company is the largest manufacturer and marketer of premium, imported, hand-made or hand-rolled cigars—those made with long filler and all natural tobacco leaf. Through another subsidiary, Culbro Tobacco, it grows, cures, ages and processes the majority of the Connecticut Shade tobacco in the world.

companies to recognize the potential of the new radio networks that were developing. General Cigar was soon sponsoring radio programs and announcing its products on a national scale. The company's net profits rose from $1.5 million in 1914 to $2.7 million by 1919. Cigar sales were on the rise throughout the country, reaching a high of 8.5 billion cigars sold in 1920.

During the 1920s, the cigar industry began to suffer from image problems. The rise of organized crime during Prohibition, and the image of the stogie-chomping gangster—developed in part by Hollywood, and personified by such actors as Edward G. Robinson—gave the cigar an aura of disrespect among the public. Later that decade, the cigar industry faced a second crisis, when American Tobacco began promoting new, machine-rolled cigars. Its advertising asked: "Why run the risk of cigars made by dirty yellowed fingers and tipped in spit?" The image proved disastrous for the cigar industry as a whole. Cigar makers rushed to convert their manufacturing from hand-rolled to machine-rolled products, but cigar sales plunged through the 1930s. During this same time period, the cigar industry was hit hard by the rise in cigarette use across the United States. Cigar consumption never recovered to its early 1920s peak. General Cigar saw its sales fall steadily. While in 1924, General Cigar had posted sales of $23.7 million and a profit of $2.3 million, by 1939, its fortunes had dropped to less than $19 million in sales, with a slight $880,000 profit.

The cigar industry fought to improve its image, organizing the Cigar Institute of America in 1940. As the United States prepared to enter World War II, the cigar's image was helped by Winston Churchill's ever-present cigar. Also, Hollywood was coaxed to take cigars away from its movie villains, and give them instead to heroes. More and more, cigars became props for the film industry's romantic leads, softening the public's—and especially women's—resistance to cigars. General Cigar's sales climbed again, to $22 million in 1941, and $27 million in 1943. The following year, General Cigar again jolted the industry with the rollout of its Robt. Burns Cigarillo. The Cigarillo was a scaled-down panatela cigar, resembling more closely a cigarette than the old-style stogie. Wrapped in a lighter-shade wrapper tobacco, it had a milder taste than the traditional cigar. The Cigarillo helped pull General Cigar's revenues up to $35.6 million by 1947.

In the 1940s, another generation of the Cullman family followed the cigar making tradition. Edgar Cullman, who had been employed in the U.S. Treasury in Washington, made a decision to return home and begin working in his father's tobacco business. Because he was new to the craft, his father advised him to learn how to roll a cigar and how to grow tobacco. Edgar soon joined a small cigar company in New York City called Anton Bock. During that time, cigar makers used two-, three-, and four-year old tobacco, and blended them and aged them together. For three days each week, Edgar learned how to sort and shake Cuban tobacco, how to open bales, how to moisten tobacco, and how to count the leaves. He also learned how to roll cigars. The other two days, especially during the summer growing season, he spent his time in the tobacco fields or in the sheds, learning how to grow and cure the leaves that hung from rafters for initial curing. During the winter, he inspected warehouses where the tobacco was processed and bulked before it was sorted into grades.

1950s–90s: Expansion and Diversification

While Edgar continued to learn the craft of cigar-making and tobacco, General Cigar was turning its efforts toward research, developing new tobacco products and manufacturing techniques. In the 1950s, General Cigar introduced Homogenized Tobacco Leaf (HTL), a blended, continuous band of binder tobacco that not only allowed for a more uniform product and a milder taste, but also enabled the high-speed manufacture of the smaller-shaped cigars at significant cost-savings. General Cigar soon formed a separate department for its research and development efforts, and automated machinery and equipment, selling its machines to other manufacturers. General Cigar had neglected the marketing of its own cigars, however, and sales remained flat, hovering around $35 million into the mid-1950s.

General Cigar's R&D efforts began to pay off in the late 1950s, and its sales began a steady climb, to $45.2 million in 1956 and to $62 million in 1960. Licensing of its HTL systems and other equipment brought in growing income from royalty and licensing fees, from $680,000 in 1958 to $1.1 million in 1960. With about 37 percent of its common stock controlled by Bush Terminal Company, General Cigar gained a reputation as the industry's technological leader. Analysts noted the company's unbroken record of paying dividends each year since 1909. Per capita consumption of cigars had risen steadily through the 1950s, to 134 cigars per adult male per year, up from 116. By 1961, General Cigar was firmly entrenched in its second-place industry position, behind leader Consolidated Cigar Corp. Most of General Cigar's sales were in the low and medium price segments, with the Cigarillo dominating the five-cent segment, and its White Owl brand competing for leadership of the ten-cent segment. By then, General Cigar operated eight manufacturing facilities, four processing plants, and about 50 warehouses.

While the Cuban revolution placed a burden across the cigar industry, General Cigar controlled some 800 acres of tobacco-growing land in Connecticut, supplying more than half of its wrapper leaf needs. Nevertheless, the company was forced to write off its Cuban operations, and sales sagged. Late in 1961, Edgar Cullman led an investment group in the purchase of 37 percent of General Cigar's stock, raising that stake to 45 percent by the following year. Cullman soon assumed the presidency of General Cigar and began to revitalize its operations.

Among General Cigar's innovations was the introduction of a new Robt. Burns cigar, a Cigarillo with a plastic tip called a Tiparillo. The Tiparillo was launched with a heavy promotional campaign—estimated at around $5.5 million in 1962—

Key Dates:

1906: The Cullman family establishes a cigar-making business called United Cigar Manufacturers Company.
1917: United Cigar changes its name to General Cigar Company Inc. 1944: The company introduces Cigarillo, a scaled-down panatela cigar resembling a cigarette in size and shape.
1962: General Cigar begins promoting new Cigarillo cigar with plastic tip, called Tiparillo.
1971: General Cigar introduces Macanudo cigars, which become the company's most popular premium brand.
1976: General Cigar changes its name to Culbro Corporation to reflect diversified acquisitions.
1980s: Culbro sells several of its diverse companies to regain profitability.
1996: Company begins operating the Club Macanudo cigar bar in New York.
1997: Culbro Corporation is split into two public companies: General Cigar Holdings, Inc., and Griffin Land & Nurseries.
2000: Swedish Match buys 64 percent of General Cigar Holdings, Inc.

featuring the slogans "Cigars, Cigarettes, Tiparillos?" and the soon-to-be famous "Should a gentleman offer a Tiparillo to a lady?" Sales began slowly, but by 1963, they had taken off, raising General Cigar's revenues to $69 million, and giving the company the dominant position in the small cigar market.

The Surgeon General's report on smoking in January 1964 proved a new—if short-lived—boon to the cigar industry. Throughout the following year, millions of cigarette smokers switched to cigars, and especially smaller cigars. General Cigar reaped the benefits of this movement, particularly with its Tiparillo brand. The company also introduced its Ultra homogenized wrapper tobacco, which, like HTL, produced substantial cost savings in cigar production, adding more royalties and licensing fees to the company's income. In order to meet the surge in demand, General Cigar expanded its production capacity.

The company also began a series of acquisitions in the 1960s, including Gradiaz, Annis & Co. and its premium cigar labels, and the Cullman Bros. Farms. In 1964, General Cigar expanded beyond cigars, with the acquisition of Metropolitan Tobacco Co. and New Jersey Tobacco Co., and into wholesale distribution, with activities focused on cigars, cigarettes, candy, tobacco, drugs, and other items. Year-end revenues for 1964 jumped to $193 million.

The 1967 acquisition of the Connecticut wrapper tobacco and nursery operation of American Sumatra Tobacco Corporation, followed by the 1969 purchase of Ex-Lax Inc for $33 million, helped revenues climb to $246 million. The mid-1960s boom in cigar sales lasted less than a year, however, which left General Cigar with production capacity far outreaching demand. The Ex-Lax acquisition had given the company a relatively stagnant product. To worsen matters, General Cigar almost immediately sold off that company's Feminine Hygiene division, which was the only one with growth potential. General Cigar next moved into the salted snack foods market. For $26 million, it purchased Bachman Foods subsidiaries, and Helme Products, Inc. and its smokeless tobacco.

The 1971 introduction of a new line of cigars, Tijuana Smalls, designed for the growing baby-boomer youth market, brought General Cigar's revenues to $265 million, at a time when cigar sales overall continued their long decline. During this period, General Cigar also initiated real estate development operations, converting portions of its 6,300-acre holdings into industrial and warehouse sites.

In 1971, General Cigar began making Macanudo cigars, having purchased a cigar producing facility in Jamaica, Temple Hall, and its Macanudo brand in 1968. The brand was made with a unique blend of tobacco grown by the company. Edgar Cullman brought his 30-plus years of tobacco experience to bear, and the wrapper was made from a specially developed, pickled, and processed seed of tobacco. In the 1970s, the company also purchased the U.S. rights for Partagas cigars from the Cifuentes family, who had been the maker in Cuba until Castro took over.

In 1976, in order to underscore its diversified operations, General Cigar changed its name to Culbro Corporation. By the end of the 1970s, the company's fortunes had dwindled. The Bachman brands of pretzels and potatoes were largely regional—marketed in Pennsylvania and in some northeastern states. Culbro attempted to take the Bachman label national, to the extent that the Bachman brand name was given to all of the company's snack products—which included the products of newly acquired Cains Marcelle Potato Chips Inc. and the potato/corn snack division of Fairmont Foods Co.—most of which had been local, yet successful brands. But the Bachman brand failed to inspire consumer interest and ran into distribution difficulties, so that, despite steady rises in the salted snack food market, Bachman began losing money, including $9 million on 1978 sales of $80 million.

At the beginning of 1980, Culbro sold off its Bachman division and took a substantial loss. Meanwhile, cigar sales slumped as new and stiffer tobacco taxes, and growing levels of smoking restrictions, were added across the country. Despite revenues of $430 million in 1979, Culbro followed its $4.5 million loss in 1978 with a loss of $21 million in 1979. The following year, Culbro left the proprietary drug market as well, selling that division, including Ex-Lax, to Sandoz Ltd. of Switzerland for $94 million, and returning Culbro to profitability. By 1987, Culbro had sold off its Helme Tobacco smokeless tobacco operations, and its Metropolitan Distribution Services, as well as the remains of its snack food business.

Despite these difficulties, Culbro still retained more than 6,000 acres of land, worth about $6 million at purchase price value, but many more times that if converted to industrial or residential use. Then, in 1983, Culbro acquired all of the outstanding shares of Eli Witt Company. Culbro's revenues began a steady climb through the rest of the decade, from $626 million in 1983 to $1.1 billion in 1991. Through Eli Witt, Culbro began a new string of acquisitions, including Certified Grocers of Florida, Inc., and Trinity Distributors in 1993, and the southern divisions of NCC L.P.s wholesale distribution business. As part of that last transaction, Culbro sold part of its Eli Witt common stock to MD Distribution Inc., reducing Culbro's share—and unilateral control—of Eli Witt to 50.1 percent. In April 1994, Culbro deconsolidated Eli Witt from its financial statement.

Nearly half of Culbro's 1994 sales of $185 million came from its General Cigar consumer products division, which by then included the distribution of the strong-selling Djeep lighters, sold primarily through Wal-Mart. Still the company struggled as its stock prices remained stagnant. Soon, however, the cigar industry would see a reversal in the long-time decline of cigar sales, primarily from a renewed interest in high-end and hand-rolled cigars.

In 1995, Tabacalera, a Spanish tobacco monopoly, offered $100 million for a 50-percent interest in the General Cigar division of Culbro. CEO Edgar Cullman, Jr., declined the offer, deciding instead to reinvigorate the company's original business, in particular its premium, high margin cigars, including the Macanudo and Partagas labels. The following year, Cullman opened a cigar lounge in Manhattan called Club Macanudo, which became extremely popular and profitable. He then began to consider a major acquisition in the cigar business, a transaction that might necessitate a public offering of Culbro stock. In order to receive the highest net dollars from an offering, it was felt that Culbro would be better preserved as a "pure play" cigar company. As a result, Cullman decided to split Culbro into two public companies that would operate independently. The tobacco business would belong to General Cigar Holdings and all nontobacco business would become a new company called Griffin Land & Nurseries. The split went into effect on February 27, 1997.

Also during this time General Cigar Holdings acquired the privately-held Villazon & Company, Inc., adding the brand to its growing list of premium cigars. Cigar consumption continued to increase in the closing years of the 1990s, stimulated by a number of factors that included the improving image of cigar smokers, an expanding base of educated, affluent adults in their 30s and 40s who enjoyed smoking cigars, and a high increase in restaurants and clubs where cigar smoking was encouraged. Although 1998 saw another slump, which the company attributed to a mismatch between buying patterns by retail outlets and consumption patterns, Cullman remained optimistic about the company's ability to regain success in the marketplace.

Through all the fluctuations in business, General Cigar Holdings remained a leading manufacturer and marketer of premium cigar brands, which now included the premium brands of Macanudo, Punch (MPP), Hoyo de Monterrey, Cohiba, and Partagas. General Cigar's mass market cigar sales included Garcia y Vega, White Owl, and Tiparillo. Still, the company's stock price began to dip, and investor worries were not eased when a lawsuit was brought against the company during this time by Cubatabaca, which alleged that General Cigar Holdings was guilty of trademark infringement.

1999 and Beyond: Major Deals with Swedish Match

Financial aid came in the form of an international conglomerate with deep pockets. In 1999, General Cigar Holdings entered into an agreement with Swedish Match AB to sell its mass-market cigar business, including its number one natural leaf wrapper brand, Garcia y Vega, along with White Owl, Tijuana Smalls, and Tiparillo, for $200 million in cash. General Cigar made the deal to focus more attention on its branded premium cigar business, which was the largest portion of the company's sales profits. The agreement would allow General Cigar to supply Swedish Match's tobacco needs. In addition, Swedish Match's sales force in the United States would sell a select number of General Cigar's premium brands then sold through mass-market distribution channels. Swedish Match would take ownership of two manufacturing plants in Alabama and the Dominican Republic, including machinery and equipment, inventories, and trademarks.

In January 2000 General Cigar Holdings was again taken private in a deal that saw Swedish Match acquire a 64 percent interest in the cigar maker. The remaining 36 percent would remain in the Cullman family. The move was made to help the cigar company improve shareholder value, and help both companies develop, expand, and consolidate the cigar business globally. The deal was closed in New York in May, positioning Swedish Match as a leading global cigar company, and allowing for General Cigar to tap into the former company's European market share.

By 2004, General Cigar Holdings had become the largest manufacturer and marketer of premium, imported, hand-made or hand-rolled cigars made with long filler and all natural tobacco leaf in the United States. Through its Culbro Tobacco subsidiary, it continued to grow, cure, age, and process most of the Connecticut Shade tobacco in the world. It was the owner of 1,100 acres of prime land in the Connecticut River Valley, and leased an additional 500 acres in Connecticut and 80 acres in the Dominican Republic to grow leaves and, recently, also Candela wrapper leaves. The company continued to demonstrate the Cullman family commitment to cigar tobacco leaf quality as well as its pledge to market and manage one of the most successful premium cigar making companies in the world.

Principal Subsidiaries

General Cigar Co., Inc.; Culbro Tobacco; Club Macanudo.

Principal Competitors

Altadis USA Inc.; Swisher International Group, Inc.; Altria.

Further Reading

"Swedish Match Buys General Cigar Unit," *U.S. Distribution Journal,* July 1999, p. 64.

"General Cigar Sells Mass Market Business," *United Press International,* March 26, 1999.

"General Cigar Smells Like Success in Midst of Smoke-Filled Rooms; Analysts Hot for Macanudo Maker's Stock," *Crain's New York Business,* September 29, 1997, p. 4.

"General Cigar Smokes a Sleeker Stogie," *Business Week,* December 14, 1968, p. 72.

Ginsburg, Stanley, "Everything Went Wrong for Edgar Cullman," *Forbes,* March 3, 1980, p. 90.

—M.L. Cohen
—update: Nancy K. Capace

Everyone deserves a good meal.™

Golden Corral Corporation

5151 Glenwood Avenue, Suite 300
Raleigh, North Carolina 27612
U.S.A.
Telephone: (919) 781-9310
Fax: (919) 881-4686
Web site: http://www.goldencorral.net

Wholly Owned Subsidiary of Investors Management Corporation
Incorporated: 1972 as Golden Corral Corporation
Employees: 3,700
Sales: $1.247 billion (2003)
NAIC: 72211 Full-Service Restaurants

Having started with one small steakhouse, Golden Corral Corporation has grown into one of the nation's strongest family restaurant chains. The ability to adapt to changing tastes allowed Golden Corral to continue growing during the 1980s and 1990s as changes in eating habits and increased competition brought drastic change to the family steakhouse business. Success continued in the 2000s as well—by 2003 the company operated and franchised 467 restaurants throughout the United States, serving 167.5 million guests that year.

1970s Origins

Golden Corral was born in 1973, when James H. Maynard and William Carl were unable to convince Ponderosa, Bonanza, Western Sizzlin', or any of the other major chains that they were financially worthy of a franchise. Undaunted, they mapped out the plans for their first steakhouse in a North Carolina library and raised money by selling shares to friends from high school and college. The first Golden Corral opened in 1973 in Fayetteville, 40 miles from the company's Raleigh headquarters. The motif was western and the emphasis was on meat and potatoes. Patrons raised their hands for their orders when the waitresses, or ''steerettes,'' called out their numbers. During the 1970s, about 90 percent of Golden Corral customers raised their hands for red meat.

The new company counted on freshness to separate itself from other budget steak houses. From the beginning, each Golden Corral restaurant cut its own steaks from fresh, USDA Choice beef. ''Nobody in America at the time was doing that,'' Maynard told *Restaurant Hospitality*. ''We started with a seven-ounce sirloin and ran up to a 12-ounce. We cut top butts, tenderloins, filets, and ribeyes.'' Golden Corral charged only slightly more for its fresh steaks than the other budget chains did for their frozen, imported steaks. The company also set itself apart by focusing on small-town America, opening most of its units in markets with almost no direct competition. In addition, Golden Corral distinguished itself by avoiding franchising agreements; many Golden Corral managers became partners, owning 20–30 percent of the units they ran.

They may have started on a shoestring, but Golden Corral's cofounders had big plans. ''We set out from day one to do multiple units,'' said Maynard. Using money from sales and lease-backs, bank loans, and internally generated cash, the young company grew rapidly. By 1979, Golden Corral owned more than 100 restaurants. By the end of 1980, the total was 151. The 1982 purchase of 193 restaurants from Sirloin Stockade, a Kansas-based competitor, further swelled the ranks. Approximately 100 Sirloin Stockades became Golden Corrals, either owned outright by the privately held company or managed under the Golden Corral banner through a leasing agreement with parent company Investors Management Corporation (IMC). By the mid-1980s, there were 430 Golden Corral restaurants. Each unit averaged about 5,000 square feet in size and about $1 million in annual sales.

The company continued to add restaurants and make a profit throughout the 1980s, but increased competition, the recession, and changes in American eating habits threatened to make the steakhouse a dinosaur. As consumption of red meat dropped and demand for fresh green foodstuffs grew, Golden Corral and its competition first added salad bars and then expanded them. Some Golden Corral units gave up more than 30 seats to make room for salad bars up to 27 feet long. Expanding the dining room added 75 seats but reduced parking. Waste and spoilage shrank profit margins because employees were not trained to handle fresh fruits and vegetables. On top of that, market researchers reported that family steakhouse chains were losing market share to fast-food restaurants and to more upscale chains like TGI Friday's and Chili's.

Company Perspectives:

At Golden Corral restaurants, our goal of pleasing each and every guest is made possible through the dedicated efforts of our caring and knowledgeable co-workers. Since the beginning, they have been preparing and serving the highest quality food at reasonable prices in a clean, friendly atmosphere thereby fulfilling the Golden Corral mission of making pleasurable dining affordable.

By 1987, Golden Corral had more than 500 restaurants in 38 states; revenues reached $457 million in 1988. The company never lost money, but as its market share and profit margins grew leaner, Golden Corral—like competitors Bonanza, Western Sizzlin', Quincy's, and Western Steer—began trimming money-losing units. It eventually cut 87 restaurants (although several would reopen as Ragazzi's, an Italian chain also owned by Investors Management). The company also began taking a long, hard look at what it would take to begin growing again.

New Directions in the Late 1980s

Leading the company in its new direction were Maynard, now chairman and treasurer, and Theodore M. Fowler, president and soon-to-be CEO. Fowler, who started as an area supervisor in 1977, succeeded Maynard as president in 1982 and as CEO in 1989. (Cofounder Carl left Golden Corral in 1984 but remained a director.) Following a series of strategy sessions in 1988, Golden Corral decided to ask its customers which way it should go. The company hired market researchers to poll current and potential customers on their attitudes about every aspect of "the experience of eating in a restaurant," Fowler told *Business/North Carolina.* "We wanted to design a concept better than anything else in the market."

Golden Corral's late 1980s soul-searching resulted in a number of changes of direction for the company. Most readily apparent to customers was the Metro Market concept. The company hired architect Jerry Cook to design a prototype based on its market research. The first Metro Market, in Lawton, Oklahoma, was a far cry from the dark, wagon-wheeled decor of the earlier Golden Corral. It was light, airy, and large, although at 7,800 square feet it fell about halfway between the older units and the model the company eventually would adopt. Most importantly, it replaced the old salad bar with a U-shaped buffet court that took up about a third of the floor space.

The first seven Metro Market, or GC-10, restaurants opened in 1991. At approximately 10,000 square feet and able to seat 400 to 440 customers, the new units dwarfed the old, which averaged 5,000 square feet and 175 seats. The centerpiece of the new units was, of course, the food bar, dubbed the Golden Choice Buffet. Entering a cafeteria-style line, customers could still order a fresh-cut USDA choice-grade steak; now, however, they could also opt for any of up to 170 all-you-can-eat items. A typical Golden Choice Buffet might include Salisbury steak, chicken pot pie, fried chicken, shrimp, and meatballs and gravy among the entrees and corn, green beans, carrots, turnip greens, creamed potatoes, and baked potatoes with six different toppings among the vegetables. A health-conscious diner could balance the many fried items with fresh fruit and salad fixings. At the Brass Bell Bakery, the ringing of a brass bell every 15 minutes signaled that more fresh bread, rolls, and pastries were coming out of the oven. For those who saved room, there were plenty of choices for dessert, too.

To many, the new Golden Corral hardly seemed to be a steakhouse anymore. About 80 percent of the customers ordered the food bar, either alone or with an entree. Only about 20 percent still ordered steak. "That's why we call it a steak, buffet, bakery concept," Fowler told *Business/North Carolina.* Whatever they called it, it worked. The average customer spent $5.45 at the first Metro Markets, down from the $6 average at the older units. The combination of menu management and sheer volume, however, boosted annual earnings at the best performing of the newer restaurants to nearly $3 million, close to triple the $1 million average of the old restaurants. In *Restaurant Hospitality,* Fowler explained why the food bar worked. "The genius is to have a lot of great tastes at four cents an ounce, which then allows you to offer more expensive items like chicken wings or shrimp at ten cents an ounce." A large, well-trained staff that kept large numbers of people moving through the lines also helped.

The location of the new restaurants marked another departure for Golden Corral. Moving away from its almost exclusive commitment to small communities, the company designed its GC-10 units for markets of 50,000 or more, although it planned a limited number of smaller and medium-sized restaurants for areas of 18,000 to 35,000 and 35,000 to 50,000 people. In 1993 and 1994, the company estimated that 60 percent to 70 percent of its new units would be Metro Markets. Most of the first wave of new units were located in the southern states of Texas, Oklahoma, North Carolina, and New Mexico.

Focusing on Franchising in the 1990s

Another major change was Golden Corral's decision to hitch its growth plans to an aggressive franchising effort. The company took its first tentative steps in this direction between 1988 and 1991, when it franchised some 55 troubled outlets to its most talented general managers. In 1991, it awarded seven new franchises. The franchising effort began in earnest in 1992. Larry Tate, vice-president of franchising, told *Southeast Food Service News* that Golden Corral intended to award 40 franchises that year. "But the concept took off so well," Tate said, "that we closed the year with 102 new franchises." The company planned to open two new franchises and one company store per month in 1993, boosting the total to three franchises and one company store per month in 1994.

To insure that a commitment to franchising did not compromise Golden Corral's reputation for quality and value, the company said it would award franchises only to qualified applicants, train them well, offer them support, and continue to adapt to shifts in customer tastes. The company set its franchising fee at a modest $40,000 but estimated the total commitment involved in opening a new Golden Corral at about $2 million per location. Golden Corral required potential franchisees to have $300,000 in liquid assets and a net worth of $1.5 million. Previous restaurant experience was necessary, as was the com-

Key Dates:

1973: James H. Maynard and William Carl open the first Golden Corral.
1979: By now, Golden Corral owns more than 100 restaurants.
1982: The company acquires 193 restaurants from Sirloin Stockade.
1991: The first seven Metro Market concept restaurants open.
1992: Aggressive franchising efforts begin.
1993: The first international Golden Corral opens in Juarez, Mexico.
1997: The firm signs a $45 million franchise agreement with Frisch's Restaurants Inc.
2003: Golden Corral celebrates its 30th anniversary; 24 new restaurants are opened.

pletion of a 12-week training program that taught a franchise operator every task performed at a Golden Corral restaurant.

As Golden Corral remodeled and expanded, it also reorganized. In 1991, Fowler's management team completed three years of examining the company's corporate structure by giving more decision-making authority to restaurant managers and their regional supervisors. The company added two geographic divisions, for a total of six, and moved the positions of marketing manager, human resources and training director, division administrator, and district manager from its Raleigh, North Carolina, headquarters to the six divisional offices. The changes resulted in Golden Corral division headquarters in Raleigh; Washington, D.C.; Tampa, Florida; Kansas City, Kansas; Dallas; and Houston. Golden Corral's divisional offices also offered support to franchises.

Golden Corral opened a Center for Training and Development in 1991 to train restaurant managers, prospective managers, and training professionals. The center marked the company's effort to standardize training, which in the past had varied from restaurant to restaurant. It also indicated a growing trend in the restaurant industry. In an economy with a shrinking number of young job-seekers and increased competition, the possibility of training and advancement helped companies attract people with the potential to move into management.

The early returns on Golden Corral's reinvention of itself were promising. Following several years of near-zero growth, Golden Corral's system-wide sales were $449 million in 1991, up 27 percent from 1990. Total sales increased to $481 million in 1992 and to $514 million in 1993. In July 1992, *Restaurants and Institutions* cited the company's emphasis on value when it named Golden Corral one of "10 Great Growth Chains." Earlier that year, the same magazine's "Choice in Chains" survey of 2,500 U.S. households named Golden Corral the best steak chain. According to *Southeast Food Service News,* Golden Corral had also become the largest privately owned company in North Carolina.

In February 1993, Golden Corral celebrated its 20th anniversary in Fayetteville, the site of the company's first restaurant. During the celebration, company executives emphasized their lofty plans to open 500 new restaurants and triple revenues to $1.7 billion within five years. By the end of the decade, the company planned to celebrate the opening of the 1,000th Golden Corral restaurant. "We want to make Golden Corral the largest family restaurant chain in the world," Larry Tate said.

Later in 1993, IMC announced a five-year development deal that would bring Golden Corral 47 units closer to its goal of 1,000 restaurants. Under the terms of the agreement, Corral Midwest, Inc., agreed to purchase 26 existing Golden Corral units and open up 47 new Metro Market units. Corral Midwest, the largest Golden Corral franchisee, planned to open the new units in Indiana, Illinois, Iowa, Kentucky, Missouri, Kansas, Oklahoma, Nebraska, and Tennessee. IMC, Citicorp Venture Capital, and several members of the Corral Midwest management have ownership stakes in the franchise concern. Golden Corral also announced a 14-restaurant deal with the Winston Group of Atlanta and an 18-unit agreement with Golden Partners of Fort Smith, Arkansas.

The first international Golden Corral opened in Juarez, Mexico, in July 1993. A Juarez investor planned to open five restaurants, and a franchisee in Monterrey, Mexico, planned eight more. The south-of-the-border Golden Corrals differed from their northern siblings in one important respect—they planned to serve alcohol.

The many challenges Golden Corral faced as it entered the mid-1990s included maintaining uniform quality as it took on new franchises and planning how to break into the nation's largest markets with a restaurant concept that required 2.5 acres of space. Just above its niche loomed the more upscale steak chains; the cheaper fast-food joints lurked below. The obstacles were many and its goals ambitious, but Golden Corral's ability to recreate itself to meet its customers' desires boded well for its chances of growing into one of the largest family restaurant chains in the world.

Success Continues in the Late 1990s and Beyond

While Golden Corral fell short of its goal of 1,000 units by 2000, the company continued to experience success in the late 1990s. During 1997, the company moved into the Miami, Fort Lauderdale, and New York City markets. Fifty-five restaurants were opened that year, and the company secured a $45 million franchise agreement with Frisch's Restaurants Inc., a Big Boy restaurant operator in the Midwest. By 1998, there were over 450 restaurants in operation. With plans to open an additional 70 stores that year, Golden Corral stood as one of the fastest-growing family restaurant chains in the United States.

As sales inched toward the $1 billion mark at the start of the 21st century, Golden Corral moved into the Northeast—a region known for its high real estate prices. In 2000, the company announced that it planned to open 17 franchises over a five-year period in the Boston area. It also set plans in motion to enter Detroit, St. Louis, and Cleveland, as well as Idaho and Oregon.

A new restaurant design called the "strata" was launched in 2000. This style—known as display cooking in the restaurant industry—positioned the kitchen in the front of the restaurant and allowed guests to watch the preparation of salads and other buffet items. Sales surpassed $1 billion in 2001, a sure sign that customers liked the new restaurant setup.

Franchising continued to play a key role the Golden Corral's success. By this time, franchise locations outnumbered company-owned stores three to one. An October 2001 *Business North Carolina* article summed up the advantages of franchising, observing that ''franchising gives Golden Corral a way to leverage outside capital without giving up equity. Franchisees absorb the risk and cost of building and operating restaurants, and the company doesn't pile up debt and interest costs.'' The article also gave insight to potential problems related to franchising, reporting that ''the down side is that Golden Corral shares profits with franchises and can see its image charred if one stumbles.''

That had yet to happen, however, and Fowler and Maynard forged ahead with their expansion plans. The company chalked up its 12th consecutive year of sales increases in 2003 as it celebrated its 30th anniversary. By now, 54 out of 467 restaurants were reaching over $4 million in annual sales. In 2004, Frisch's—the company's largest franchisee—announced that had signed a contract to open 21 new restaurants in Columbus, western Pennsylvania, and southern Michigan. Frisch's planned to operate 62 Golden Corral units by 2011.

With over 30 years of success under its belt, Golden Corral had secured an envious position in the restaurant industry. *Nation's Restaurant News* had ranked it as the leader in the grill-buffet category for the eighth straight year in 2003, and *Entrepreneur* magazine had listed it as the top franchiser in the family steakhouse segment for nine consecutive years. While intense competition and dollar-conscious consumers would no doubt remain obstacles for Golden Corral in the years to come, the company appeared to be on track for continued success.

Principal Competitors

Metromedia Restaurant Group; Ryan's Restaurant Group Inc.; Western Sizzlin Corporation.

Further Reading

Carlino, Bill, ''Golden Corral Parent Agrees to Franchise Acquisition Plan,'' *Nation's Restaurant News*, August 30, 1993, p.3.

Carlson, Eugene, ''Golden Corral Bucks Slowdown with Shift in Direction,'' *Raleigh News and Observer,* May 2, 1993, p. F1.

Chaudhry, Rajan, ''10 Great Growth Chains,'' *Restaurants and Institutions*, July 22, 1992.

Coolidge, Alexander, ''Frisch's to Open 21 More Golden Corrals,'' *Cincinnati Post*, July 26, 2004, p. B7.

Degross, Renee, ''Turning Buns into Dough,'' *Raleigh News & Observer,* February 14, 1998, p. D1.

Douglas, Linda Brown, ''Restaurant Chain to Get 47-Store Franchise,'' *Raleigh News and Observer,* August 20, 1993, p. C7.

''Downscaling Concepts to Upscale Profits,'' *Nation's Restaurant News*, August 30, 1993.

Farkas, David, ''The Reincarnation of Golden Corral,'' *Restaurant Hospitality*, February 1992.

''Golden Corral Revamps Operations; Restaurants to Get More Authority,'' *Raleigh News and Observer,* March 7, 1991, p. C6.

''Healthy Vittles at the Corral,'' Raleigh, North Carolina, *Raleigh News and Observer,* February 9, 1992, p. 1F.

Koteff, Ellen, ''Ted M. Fowler Jr.,'' *Nation's Restaurant News*, October 9, 1995.

Marshall, Kyle, ''Breaking ''Em in at Golden Corral,'' *Raleigh News and Observer,* September 25, 1991, p. C8.

''North Carolina Restaurant Chain on Aggressive Growth Track,'' *Southeast Food Service News*, March 1993, p. 1.

Olson, Chris, ''Golden Corral Rounds up Second Location in Omaha,'' *Omaha World-Herald*, October 17, 1998.

Piecoro, Nick, ''Golden Corral Moving into Region,'' *Patriot Ledger*, June 8, 2000.

''Round Them Up,'' *Business-North Carolina*, October 1, 2001, p. 36.

Thompson, Samantha, ''Gold in Them Thar Corrals,'' *Raleigh News & Observer,* October 28, 2000.

Williams, Bob, ''Revved up for Fast Move into Mexico,'' *Raleigh News and Observer,* November 14, 1993, p. F1.

Wittebort, Suzanne, ''Golden Corral Relishes Lean Times,'' *Business/ North Carolina*, May 1992, p. 47.

—David B. Rice
—update: Christina M. Stansell

Goodwill Industries International, Inc.

15810 Indianola Avenue
Rockville, Maryland 20855
U.S.A.
Telephone: (301) 530-6500
Toll Free: (800) 664-6577
Fax: (301) 530-1516
Web site: http://www.goodwill.org

Nonprofit Company
Founded: 1902
Employees: 82,370
Sales: $2.21 billion (2003)
NAIC: 45331 Used Merchandise Stores; 56132 Temporary Help Services; 62431 Vocational Rehabilitation Services

Goodwill Industries International, Inc. is the umbrella organization for independently operated, nonprofit, community-based affiliates that provide job-based and employment services for people with disabilities. It includes 207 member organizations in the United States, Canada and 23 other countries. Goodwill Industries has 1,900 retail stores that are stocked with donated clothing and household goods. Almost 85 percent of the revenues are directed into training and placement programs. The company has long been North America's leading nonprofit provider of vocational services for people with disabilities and other special needs, and one of the world's largest private-sector employers of people with disabilities. Goodwill Industries International served over 600,000 people in 2003.

Early History

Goodwill Industries was founded in 1902 by the Rev. Edgar James Helms, a Methodist minister who came to head the Unitarian Church's multidenominational Henry Morgan Memorial Chapel in Boston's South End slums. At the time, the chapel's attendees were largely alcoholics and indigents lured inside by the smell of hot coffee and stew. When the chapel was full, the doors were locked and the visitors treated to a fire-and-brimstone sermon. However, Helms disapproved of this tactic for reform. Instead, he began using the baptistery tank to pipe in water to showers installed in the basement, in order to clean up his charges. Next, he made space for a nursery where working mothers could leave their children. Helms then issued an appeal for used clothing to give to the poor and hired poverty-stricken seamstresses to repair the clothing before selling it cheaply to the needy.

This self-help system expanded with the donation of 1,000 burlap bags from a coffee-importing firm and also grew to include the donation, repair, and resale of used furniture and other items. The effort became institutionalized under the name of the Morgan Memorial Industries and Stores. However, Helms drew criticism from some professional social workers of the day, who objected that Helms did nothing to check that his charity employees were the most worthy of help. Moreover, the Unitarian church eventually withdrew its support of the project. Helms subsequently found sponsorship from the Methodist Church and his next self-help effort manifested itself in Brooklyn, where the Goodwill Industries name was born.

By 1919 Goodwill Industries training shops and stores had opened in Cleveland, Denver, Los Angeles, and Brookline, Massachusetts, and the Methodists were planning to invest $305,000 for plants in New York, Buffalo, Philadelphia, Pittsburgh, St. Paul, and other cities. The plan called for 30 of these centers, training 120,000 people a year and spending $2 to $3 million annually for wages. An important new manpower supply was tapped in the numbers of disabled servicemen returning from World War I. Skilled workers taught the newcomers the best and quickest ways to repair donated materials and, when they became skilled themselves, the pupils were recommended to commercial shops and factories. The store for the sale of remade articles served a double purpose, offering training as salespersons, stenographers, and bookkeepers.

Helms took his message overseas in 1926, when he began a world tour, laying the ground for what was to become Goodwill Industries International. He traveled to Europe, the Middle East, Japan, Korea, Ceylon, and the Philippines. Organizations based on the Goodwill idea sprang up in Mexico, the Caribbean, and South America, and eventually in Asia, Africa, and Great Britain. An international department within Goodwill's corporate office was not formed until 1969, however. The Goodwill

Company Perspectives:

Goodwill Industries will enhance the quality and dignity of life for individuals, families, and communities on a global basis, through the power of work, by eliminating barriers to opportunity for people with special needs, and by facilitating empowerment, self-help, and service through dedicated, autonomous local organizations.

Industries International Foundation was later established in the mid-1980s to help fund special programs for Goodwill's network outside North America.

More than 60 cities in the United States and various communities in foreign countries had Goodwill Industries institutions by 1932. The Buffalo chapter, for example, paid more than $60,000 in 1930 to 100 persons for what it called ''Jobs from Junk—Wages from Waste.'' These wage-earners were described in an article as including ''men and women with nervous diseases; mental quirks, social complexes and maladjustments; paralysis victims, capable of training, maybe, in the use of feeble limbs, but who in regular business channels has time to try?''

The Great Depression changed Goodwill's direction. People with disabilities did not become the major focus of its work until the mid-1930s, when mass unemployment convinced the organization it needed to restrict its services to a smaller segment of the population. Their efforts yielded a payoff to others in need, for a woman's entire restyled outfit, including a silk dress and warm winter coat, could be purchased for $6.80, while a man's similar clothing, including suit and overcoat, cost only $8.50. A bed with springs and mattress sold for $6.50, and a reconditioned stove for $10.

Goodwill at Mid-Century

When Goodwill Industries celebrated its 50th anniversary in 1952, there were 101 plants in the United States. In 1951 the company took in $13.6 million in revenue and paid $8.2 million in wages. Of the 17,545 handicapped men and women employed by Goodwill that year, about 30 percent had found full- or part-time jobs in private industry by May 1952. Many others had established their own shops. The Goodwill agencies were 90 percent self-supporting and completely nondenominational, although some still were receiving financial aid from the Methodists. There were another seven Goodwill agencies in Canada and seven more scattered from Shanghai to Lima, Peru.

A 1953 *Saturday Evening Post* article listed the main donations to Goodwill as consisting of clothing, shoes, furniture, repairable household appliances, toys, and books. Interesting stories began to crop up concerning Goodwill donations. In one incident, a painting donated to the Boston chapter was found to have been painted by the Venetian Renaissance master Gentile Bellini and was sold to the Museum of Fine Arts for a handsome sum. One woman who donated a gas range forgot to remove the roast she had cooked for dinner and called in to reclaim it. Farmers contributed such items as two bales of hay, a brace of rabbits, a horse, and a nanny goat, who devoured most of the fiberboard lining of the truck while in transit.

The *Post* article went on to report that the Norfolk Goodwill specialized in the acquisition and restoration of Early American antiques, the Denver agency specialized in silverware, and the Michigan affiliates excelled in furniture making. Fort Worth was outstanding for returning ranching gear to working condition. The Los Angeles chapter was the biggest operation, employing some 1,500 persons and doing more than $1 million worth of business annually. It was followed by Detroit, Boston, Chicago, and San Francisco. Milwaukee, Denver, St. Louis, and Cincinnati had the best-equipped physical rehabilitation centers. Chicago led all affiliates in securing contract work from manufacturers. The Dallas chapter, cited as representative, employed about 400 persons a year and always paid slightly more than the minimum wage. More than 98 percent self-supporting, it owned its own building, machinery, and fleet of trucks and employed a staff medical director, psychologist, and chaplain.

An accounting of the Goodwill personnel employed in 1952 found that 6 percent were blind, 47 percent physically handicapped in other ways, 15 percent emotionally handicapped, 19 percent aged, and the remaining 13 percent, who were not handicapped, largely consisting of supervisory and transportation workers. Some 60 Goodwill ladies' auxiliaries and service clubs like the Lions and Rotarians helped raise money through such devices as annual bazaars.

By 1968 the Goodwill Industries workshop network had reached 135, employing over a year's time a total of some 50,000 handicapped persons. A survey found that the percentage of employees with some neurological, mental, or social affliction had risen to 42 percent in 1966, compared to 32 percent in 1960. The percentage of physically handicapped persons fell from 20 to 15 percent over this period. The executive director of the Philadelphia chapter said the mentally retarded and emotionally distressed were more difficult to rehabilitate and often less productive than the physically handicapped, leading to increased costs. Some workshops said they were laying off handicapped workers because of the scheduled increase in the federal minimum wage to $1.80 an hour in 1969. Although ''sheltered'' workshops employing the handicapped could pay as little as half of the regular minimum wage, the U.S. Department of Labor was requiring that they match the percentage increase on all their wages.

Aiding the Needy in the 1990s

By the 1990s Goodwill Industries was again concentrating on a wider segment of the needy population: not only the disabled but those socially and economically disadvantaged. It was, by the middle of the decade, serving people with a range of barriers to employment, including lack of education, welfare dependency, a criminal record, and advanced age. The largest single group of people served by the organization in the mid 1990s were those with vocational disadvantages such as welfare dependency, illiteracy, a history of criminal behavior, or past substance abuse. People with mental retardation made up the second-largest group of those served.

The federal-state vocational-rehabilitation system, the public welfare system, and the U.S. Department of Labor together accounted for more than half of yearly referrals to Goodwill. Other individuals were referred privately and through state mental

Key Dates:

1902: Rev. Edgar James Helms establishes Goodwill Industries.
1926: Helms brings his message overseas.
1953: The *Saturday Evening Post* features Goodwill in an article.
1969: The company forms an international department.
1994: Goodwill changes its name to Goodwill Industries International Inc.
1999: Goodwill launches the first and only nonprofit Internet auction site in the United States.

health/mental retardation offices. Goodwill organizations in many communities established basic-skills programs offering tutoring in reading and basic math. Partnerships were formed with community organizations such as Literacy Volunteers of America.

High-tech training such as computer operation and word processing was increasingly popular in Goodwill's rehabilitation programs. The Honolulu affiliate was training individuals for work in the thriving local hospitality industry. The Iowa City, Iowa, chapter offered training for retail occupations. The New York City Goodwill was working with major banks to train people in financial-services areas. The most common types of training programs also included food service, janitorial and building maintenance, and horticulture. Training courses ranged in length from six weeks to several months. When Goodwill graduates were hired by a business in the community, Goodwill job coaches were available to provide long-term, one-on-one training and adjustment support.

Industrial and service contract work had become an increasingly important source of revenue for Goodwill Industries by 1995, when it accounted for $214 million, or more than 20 percent of combined revenues. Goodwill Industries was providing contractual services support to the following major industries: automotive, airline, aircraft, aerospace, lumber, pharmaceutical, paper manufacturing, electronics, recycling, printing, hospital, and corrugated products. Labor-intensive work included mechanical and electronic assembly, packaging, inspection, custodial services, groundskeeping, stockkeeping, data entry, and mailing. In addition, Goodwill Industries was providing custodial, groundskeeping, and food-service support to federal-, state-, and local-government agencies.

Goodwill's retail revenues continued to grow steadily. It was a full-line discount retailer with a special emphasis on clothing, but donations being sold also included linens, furniture, shoes, small appliances, hardware, housewares, collectibles, books, and recordings. In 1981 the Chicago chapter came out with its own line of designer jeans, called "Goodies." Although used, they came with a designer label and sold for $4.99, compared to $1.50 for Goodwill's other used jeans. A Denver outlet began selling used ski equipment in 1993, most of it in good shape but coming with a disclaimer for liability. Goodwill's combined retail revenues reached $513.5 million in 1995, up from $359.3 million in 1991.

Unsalable donated items were being sold as scrap material or in wholesale markets. In 1993 Goodwill Industries processed close to 700 million pounds of donated textiles, and more than 99 percent of it was sold either in Goodwill retail stores or on the salvage market for other uses. Some member organizations had become involved in materials recycling: sorting and sometimes processing materials like paper, aluminum, and glass.

Goodwill Industries of America Inc. changed its name to Goodwill Industries International, Inc. in 1994. In 1995 Goodwill employed nearly 52,500 people in its own facilities, retail stores, and industrial contract programs. Its member organizations in North America collectively served more than 130,000 people in vocational and rehabilitation programs. Of these, nearly 25,000 found competitive jobs in the community as a result of Goodwill training. There were 1,427 retail outlets in 1995. A 1994 survey found that five of every six dollars in Goodwill Industries income went for program spending, which ranked the organization in the top ten social-service charities in the United States in that category. Goodwill affiliates contributed to the parent organization on a purely voluntary basis.

Moving Goodwill Industries into the Next Millennium

Throughout its history, Goodwill had always changed with the times. As a way to attract a new kind of shopper, Goodwill Industries launched its e-commerce website in 1999. This site was the first and only nonprofit Internet auction site in the United States. Five years later, the website was still successful. It averaged 13,000 visitors per day. In a press release, George W. Kessenger, the President and CEO of Goodwill International said that, "The site has brought a whole new world of shoppers and donors in contact with Goodwill." The site had more than 100,000 registered buyers and since its inception had raised more than $15 million.

A change had occurred on the retail side of Goodwill Industries as well. A new store format increased retail sales 10 percent between 2001 and 2002. In 2000, Portland, Oregon, stores started an advertising campaign that was compared to trendy ads ran by Target Corporation and the Gap Inc. The Portland stores were a part of the Columbia Williamette chain of Goodwill. Columbia Williamette operated 24 retail stores in the United States and was the most successful chain in North America. Indeed, over 84 million pounds of foods were donated to these area stores in 1999. Across the country, a new 23,000 square-foot store opened in Fort Worth, Texas. This was double the size of a regular Goodwill retail store and included a coffee shop and a used bookstore.

In efforts to encourage people to become financially responsible, Goodwill Industries began a partnership with the Federal Deposit Insurance Corporation (FDIC) in 2003 to educate its recipients on the banking system. The training program employed the FDIC's Money Smart curriculum and showed people how to budget, save, and use a checking account. Later that year, Goodwill also made its voice heard in Washington, D.C., urging Congress to reauthorize the 1998 Workforce Investment Act (WIA). The implementation of the WIA, as it had been written, had greatly affected people with disabilities. Goodwill recommended that steps be included so all workers would have access to training that would allow them to be placed in more skilled positions.

By 2004, Goodwill Industries International had grown into a network of 207 member organizations with locations in the United States, Canada, and 23 other countries. There were 1,900 retail stores. The revenues from these, as well as those from shopgoodwill.com, funded programs for people with disabilities and welfare recipients. Almost 85 percent of the revenues were directed into training and placement programs. Goodwill thrived and was dedicated to fulfill the goals of its vision statement: "We at Goodwill Industries will be satisfied only when every person in the global community has the opportunity to achieve his/her fullest potential as an individual and to participate and contribute fully in all aspects of a productive life."

Further Reading

Calame, Byron E., "Institute Lays Off Handicapped Workers Due to Pay-Floor Hike," *Wall Street Journal*, January 23, 1968, p. 23.

"Enterprise of the Heart," *Time*, May 5, 1953, p. 96.

"Going Once, Going Twice, Going Strong; shopgoodwill.com Celebrates Five Years," *Business Wire*, August 25, 2004.

"Goodwill Industries and FDIC Team Up for Strong Financial Futures," *Ascribe News*, March 13, 2003.

Goodwill Stores Aim to be Hip While Helping—Ad Campaigns, Site Décor Use Color, Creativity to Fight Firm's Stigma," *Wall Street Journal*, July 3, 2000, p. 1.

Howell, Debbie, "New-look Thrift Shop Begs Question, How Good Will Goodwill Get?" *DSN Retailing Today*, August 6, 2001, p. 2.

Keeler, Ralph Welles, "Men and Goods Repaired," *World Outlook*, May 1919, pp. 18–19.

"Low-Income American Workers Need Congressional Investment; Goodwill Calls For Stronger Workforce Legislation," *Ascribe News*, August 29, 2003.

Perry, George Sessions, "They Give Them a Second Chance," *Saturday Evening Post*, October 3, 1953, pp. 40+.

Troy, Mike, "Unconventional Retailer Maintains Superstore Growth," *DSN Retailing Today*, October 7, 2002, p. 6.

Wattles, Janet B., "Jobs from Junk—Wages from Waste," *Scientific American*, February 1932, pp. 84–85.

—Robert Halasz
—update: Christina M. Stansell

Granaria Holdings B.V.

Postbus 233
Den Haag
NL-2501 CE
The Netherlands
Telephone: (+31) 70 312 11 00
Fax: (+31) 70 312 11 50
Web site: http://www.granaria.nl

Private Company
Incorporated: 1912
Employees: 7,500
Sales: EUR 8.4 billion ($8.4 billion) (2002 est.)
NAIC: 424410 General Line Grocery Merchant Wholesalers; 237210 Land Subdivision; 531210 Offices of Real Estate Agents and Brokers; 551112 Offices of Other Holding Companies; 336399 All Other Motor Vehicle Parts Manufacturing; 335912 Dry and Wet Primary Battery Manufacturing

Publicity-shy Granaria Holdings B.V. is a Dutch-owned holding company with substantial real estate investments in the Netherlands, as well as controlling stakes in EaglePicher Holdings in the United States, and in The Nut Company, Europe's leading producer, marketer, and distributor of nuts and related snack foods. Granaria is controlled by the Netherlands' Wyler family, which includes brothers Joel and Daniel Wyler. Founded as a grain trader in the early part of the 20th century, Granaria changed its tack in the early 1990s, redeveloping itself as a hands-on industrial investor. Granaria's interests in the food processing industry led it to form The Nut Company, merging its own Klijn brand of nuts and snacks with those of Ultje and Felix, both controlled by Germany's May-Gruppe, in 1999. The Nut Company now controls much of the European nuts and snack market, with top brands including Klijn in the Netherlands, Jack Benoit in France and Italy, Ultje in Germany and Austria, and Felix, made in Poland for the broader European market. In all, The Nut Company operates production facilities in the Netherlands, Germany, Poland, and France and is directly managed by Daniel Wyler. EaglePicher Holders is the new name for the diversified industrial group Eagle Picher Industries, based in the United States. EaglePicher, part of the Granaria fold since 1998, has been transitioning as a technologies company since the early 2000s, providing a range of products, such as batteries, micro fluid filtration systems, precision machined components, and a variety of other products for the automotive, space, aerospace, nuclear, defense, and other industries. The company also operates in the zinc distribution, pharmaceutical, and semi-conductor markets. Granaria itself owns more than 60 percent of EaglePicher, sharing ownership with the company's management and with financial partner ABN Amro bank. Granaria remains a privately held, family controlled company, with total annual revenues estimated at nearly EUR 8.4 billion ($8 billion) in the early 2000s.

Grain Trader to Investment Vehicle in the 1990s

Louis Wyler started as a grain trader in the early 1900s, exporting grain produced by Dutch farmers to food cooperatives in Germany. By 1912, Wyler had gained control of the trading operation. Wyler transferred the company's headquarters to Rotterdam. Granaria, as the company was called, soon grew into a leading Dutch specialist in grain trading and also developed a significant share of the country's feed import market.

Granaria's growth took off following World War II and the arrival of Wyler's son, Martin. By the late 1970s, The younger Wyler had built Granaria into the clear leader in the Netherlands grain trading market, while also building up a globally operating commodities trading wing as well. In 1980, Wyler stepped back from direction of the company, and sons Joel and Daniel Wyler took over as the company's heads. Martin Wyler retired in 1983.

Joel Wyler, then 31 years old, had worked at a Swiss trading firm and a hotel investment company before joining the company in 1976. He was followed soon after by younger brother Danny. The Wyler brothers began refocusing Granaria from the start, selling off much of its global commodities business in 1980 and turning the company's attention toward investment in the Dutch agricultural sector. Danny Wyler himself left the company during the 1980s in order to continue to head up its former commodities business under its new owners. Mean-

Company Perspectives:

Granaria Holdings today holds interests in several industrial companies, venture capital, corporate recovery and real estate. Granaria is actively pursuing further growth in its investment portfolio.

while, through the 1980s, Granaria added a number of operations, such as Spellman's Oliefabrieken BV, which processed oilseeds in its plant in Rotterdam; Silo Gerritsen BV, which operated a network of grain and seed silos in the Netherlands; and Imko Gelria, which emerged as the largest peanut processing operation in Europe.

Danny Wyler rejoined Granaria in 1988. The Wylers then attempted another diversification in the late 1980s that made their name somewhat notorious in the Netherlands. Transport along the Dutch canal system remained a tightly controlled, highly unionized, and restricted market in the 1980s. Yet in 1988, the newly named Dutch minister Nellie Smit-Kroes—a close friend of the Wyler family—gave the Wylers permission to begin transporting their own goods along the country's canal system. Granaria went ahead and purchased a fleet of German tugboats. Yet the company immediately found itself under attack as the canal unions blockaded the canal system in a violent confrontation that required the intervention of the country's military police. Ultimately, Smit-Kroes was forced to rescind the decision to allow competition on the country's canal routes. Granaria then claimed some NLG 63 million in compensation and damages. The company ultimately agreed to a claims settlement worth more than NLG 9 million (approximately $4.5 billion) in 1989.

The canal crisis led Granaria to exit the trading sector altogether in 1990, when it sold its remaining operations in that area to fellow Dutch company Schouten Giessen NV. The Wylers nonetheless retained ownership of the Granaria name, with the company now known as Granaria Beheer, or Holdings.

Two Pronged Industrialist in the 21st Century

Granaria began acquiring a number of industrial operations in the 1990s. At first, the company remained close to the food processing industry and achieved strong growth in its peanuts processing operation. The company attempted to expand beyond nuts into other food categories as well. In 1992, for example, the company took over struggling Belgian pâte producer Sanpareil. Yet Granaria proved unable to turn around that company and in 1993 sold it off again. The Wylers also became involved in another, more controversial investment, when Joel Wyler became a shareholder and director of World Online, headed by another family friend, Nina Brink.

In the meantime, Danny Wyler continued to lead the company's efforts to develop its food processing businesses under the Granaria Food Group umbrella. A more successful investment for Granaria came through its 1997 acquisition of Klijn Noten, the leading brand of nuts, dried fruits, chips and crackers, and related snack products in the Netherlands. That purchase gave Granaria control of Klijn's NLG 90 million ($45 million) in annual sales, boosting the total revenues estimated under Granaria's control to NLG 400 million ($200 million). Combined with Granaria's existing nut processing operations, the company now controlled the number two spot in the European peanuts and nuts market.

Granaria quickly parlayed its Klijn investment into a world-class operation. In October 1999, the company agreed to merge Granaria Food Group with the nut processing business of Germany's May-Gruppe, then the leading nut and peanut processor in Europe, with control of top German and Austrian brand Ultje; French and Italian leader Jack Benoit; as well as the Felix Snack food brand, with sales throughout Europe. The merger created the clear European leader in the sector, with a turnover estimated at more than EUR 400 million ($350 million).

By 2000, the merger had cleared scrutiny from competition authorities, which judged that the competition from globally operating snack foods companies would make it difficult for the merged business to fix prices in Europe. Another factor contributing to the favorable decision was that despite the strength of its brand names, these represented just 20 percent of the merged company's operations, with the bulk of its revenues coming from sales to private label distributors. With the merged process completed, the company took on a new name, becoming The Nut Company. Danny Wyler became directly involved in the company's direction, taking up the position of chairman.

During this period, Joel Wyler had found his own direction within Granaria. In 1998, the company agreed to acquire the U.S.-based Eagle Picher Industries, paying $700 million for the diversified producer of gallium and germanium as well as a variety of products and components for the automotive, aerospace, nuclear, defense, and other industries. As Joel Wyler told *The Financial Times* in a rare interview: "Granaria wanted to have another core business, another engine for growth, in the US. Eagle-Picher is a leading player in every niche market in which it operates. That's a good basis for growth, and that's what we like so much about the company—in addition to which, it's so diversified, it's a solid base against cyclical influences."

Yet Eagle Picher, which began as a Cincinnati paint company in 1842, had fallen on hard times in the 1990s owing to its exposure to some $2 billion in claims stemming from its earlier involvement in the asbestos industry. Eagle Picher had gone into Chapter 11 reorganization in the early 1990s, emerging from bankruptcy only in 1996. The company's ownership had been transferred to a trust, which handled the investments needed in order to pay off its claims.

Granaria agreed to acquire the company's industrial operations in a three-way deal backed by ABN Amro, which brought in Eagle Picher's management as part owners of the company as well. Nonetheless, Granaria placed itself in control of the company, with Joel Wyler serving as company chairman. The addition of Granaria's nearly $900 million in annual sales, together with the rising sales from The Nut Company, enabled the company's revenues to swell past an estimated EUR 1.5 billion at the beginning of the 2000s.

Eagle Picher began a series of its own acquisitions into the 2000s with the goal of diversifying its operations. Toward this

Key Dates:

1912: Louis Wyler takes control of a grain trading firm, which moves to Rotterdam and becomes known as Granaria.
1980: After years of expansion, new leaders begin divesting the company's global trading operations and investing in food processing businesses.
1988: Granaria buys a fleet of tugboats in Germany and attempts to begin transporting its own grains in the Netherlands' canal system.
1990: Granaria sells the rest of its trading arm and refocuses itself as a holding company.
1992: Granaria acquires Sanpareil, a Belgian maker of pâte, but sells this company again the following year.
1997: Granaria acquires the Klijn nut and snack food brand, which becomes part of Granaria Food Group.
1998: Granaria acquires the U.S.-based Eagle Picher Industries.
1999: Granaria merges Granaria Food Group into nuts operations of May-Gruppe, which becomes known as The Nut Company.
2000: Eagle Picher launches a restructuring in order to become a more diversified technology group.

end, the company acquired Carpenter Enterprises Ltd. in 1999. That purchase boosted Eagle Picher's trade with the automotive industry, with a range of precision machined components. In 2000, the company made a new purchase, buying BlueStar Battery Systems Corporation for $4.9 million. That company, which changed its name to Eagle Picher Energy Products Corp., or EPEP, produced lithium-based batteries for the U.S. military.

Granaria then led Eagle Picher on refocusing efforts, selling off a number of operations. In 2000, for example, the company sold off Ross Aluminum Foundries and Michigan Automotive Research Corporation, as well as its Cincinnati Industrial Machinery, Fluid Systems, and Rubber Molding division. In 2001, the company exited its Construction Equipment Division, which was followed in 2002 with the sale of parts of the group's Precision Products division. The company's refocusing continued through 2003, with the sales of parts of the Hillsdale UK Automotive division and parts of the companies germanium-based operations. After transferring its headquarters to Arizona, the company changed its name to EaglePicher Holdings in 2004.

Despite the high-profile nature of its two core holdings, Granaria remained a reclusive and highly private family-owned organization. The Wyler-controlled investment vehicle had successfully transformed itself from a trading house to a diversified industrial group, with extensive real estate and other holdings as well. The company's total assets were estimated at more than EUR 8.4 billion in the early 2000s, while its industrial operations alone approached the EUR 2 billion mark. Under the hands-on leadership of Joel and Daniel Wyler, Granaria readied itself for the future.

Principal Subsidiaries

EaglePicher Holdings Inc.; The Nut Company NV.

Principal Competitors

Johnson Controls Inc.; Compaignie Financiere Alcatel; Hitachi Chemical Company Ltd.; Exide Technologies; Azimut Brabork; Yuasa Corporation; Rayovac Corporation; Beech-Nut Nutrition Corporation; Columbia Empire Farms Inc.; Guy's Snack Foods Inc.; Los Angeles Nut House; Georgia Nut Company.

Further Reading

''Commission Clears Granaria, LTJE and Felix Nut Snack Venture,'' *European Report*, March 4, 2000.
''Granaria and May-Gruppe Merge,'' *Eurofood*, October 7, 1999
''Granaria Left Hand Op Amerikaanse Eagle-Picher,'' *Telegraaf*, January 6, 1998.
''Granaria Pays $700M, Lands Eagle-Picher,'' *American Metal Market*, February 27, 1998.
Kunnen-Jones, Marianne, ''Wyler Honored as International Studies Fellow,'' *University of Cincinatti News*, August. 30, 2001.
Miller, Joe, ''Dutch Firm to Buy Eagle Picher,'' *European Rubber Journal*, February 1998, p. 10.
Tomkins, Richard, ''Eagle Picher Sold for Dollars 743m cash,'' *Financial Times*, February 26, 1998, p. 19.
Van der Velde, Leo, ''Harde noten,'' *Haagsche Courant*, November 14, 2000.
''Wylers Sell Trading Business to Focus on Europe Operations,'' *Milling & Baking News*, March 6, 1990, p. 50.

—M.L. Cohen

Greif Inc.

425 Winter Road
Delaware, Ohio 43015
U.S.A.
Telephone: (740) 549-6000
Fax: (740) 549-6100
Web site: http://www.greif.com

Public Company
Incorporated: 1926 as Greif Bros. Cooperage Corporation
Employees: 9,800
Sales: $1.9 billion (2003)
Stock Exchanges: New York
Ticker Symbol: GEF
NAIC: 322213 Setup Paperboard Box Manufacturing; 322211 Corrugated and Solid Fiber Box Manufacturing; 322214 Fiber Can, Tube, Drum, and Similar Products Manufacturing; 322215 Nonfolding Sanitary Food Container Manufacturing; 322212 Folding Paperboard Box Manufacturing

Greif Inc., formerly Greif Bros. Cooperage Corporation, is a leading producer of industrial packaging products such as steel, fibre and plastic drums, and drum closure systems. Grief also makes corrugated shipping containers and manages timberlands in the United States and Canada. It has been involved in the bulk packaging industry since its foundation in 1877. Michael J. Gasser became CEO in 1994 after succeeding John Dempsey, who had led the company for nearly half a century. With Gasser at the helm, Greif has focused on international expansion. Van Leer proved to be its most successful acquisition as it doubled the company's size and provided opportunities in the markets of Europe, Asia, and Latin America. With more than 9,800 employees in more than 40 countries, Greif aims to be a global leader in industrial packaging products and services.

Origins

The company, founded in Cleveland in 1877 by four brothers from the Greif family, was initially a manufacturer of wooden staves, headings, barrels, and kegs. By 1926, Greif owned 216 manufacturing plants and eight divisional offices, as well as timberlands, logging equipment, sawmills, and cooperages.

John Raible (later characterized by William Baldwin of *Forbes* as ''a wealthy investor with enough other interests to make cooperage only a sideline'') took over from the founding Greif brothers in 1913. It was perhaps the worst time in the history of the cooperage industry for less than interested management. Wooden packaging, although buoyed during the first two decades of the 20th century by the rise of the petroleum industry, was devastated by the one-two punch of prohibition and the development and introduction of 55-gallon steel drums. Although Greif Bros. sales more than tripled from $11.4 million in 1940 to $36.1 million in 1946, its profitability decreased; net income increased by only 67 percent from $720,000 to $1.2 million during the same period. It was increasingly clear to some observers that traditional cooperage companies would have to diversify or die.

New Vision in the Postwar Era

In 1946, John Dempsey, a 33-year-old accountant, mounted a challenge to Raible's corporate control. Dempsey's wife and mother-in-law had held stakes in the company, and he accumulated enough other shares to garner a controlling interest in 1946. While the new leader continued to buttress the cooperage business with the acquisition of timber acreage in the postwar era, he also tried to develop a proprietary machine to make the lightweight, disposable kraft-paper drums that were replacing old-fashioned wooden barrels in shipping.

Dempsey assigned a team of Greif mechanics the task of designing a proprietary fibre drum machine, but their attempts were unsuccessful. Faced with the imminent demise of his company, Dempsey acquired the rights to a drum winder from an outside inventor. Throughout the postwar era, he purchased the equipment necessary to manufacture steel, plastic, and paper packaging and containers. The company also boosted its container capabilities with the acquisition of an interest in Brooklyn's Carpenter Container Corp. in 1948. By the mid-1950s, revenues from the new operations had drawn about even with the original cooperage business.

Company Perspectives:

We will achieve superior return on assets while consistently increasing revenue. We will strive to be one of the most desirable companies to work for in our industries, focusing on establishing a work atmosphere in which our employees can excel. We will continually add value to our customer relationships, with an emphasis on providing packaging solutions on a global scale. We will capitalize on our leadership position and pursue profitable growth in the Industrial Packaging & Services business. We will pursue internal growth in addition to strategic acquisitions to profitably expand the Paper, Packaging & Services business. We will grow our Timber business both in terms of land holdings and revenue generation.

Dempsey's reorganization was costly. Sales declined by 15 percent from $31.7 million in 1946 to $26.9 million in 1949, and profits dropped by 40 percent, from $2 million to $1.2 million. In fact, it took the company more than a decade to regain the annual revenue and net income records established in the late 1940s; it was not until 1959 that Greif Bros. recovered its record fiscal levels of $40 million sales and $2 million profit.

Although Dempsey eliminated half of the company's 240 factories by 1963, he parlayed Greif Bros.' relatively small, but widespread, plants into a competitive advantage. Having production facilities near its clients' plants helped the company forge close ties with those customers, as well as to save on Greif's own shipping costs. By the early 1960s, Greif's product line had expanded to include steel drums, plywood drums, fibre drums, corrugated cartons, wire products, and multiwall bags. In 1964, the company's headquarters was moved south from Cleveland to Delaware, a suburb of Columbus, Ohio.

Greif's sales more than doubled over the course of the decade, from $45 million in 1961 to $103 million in 1971. Net income followed suit, growing from $2.1 million to $5.5 million as the company grew accustomed to its new emphasis. The company formally recognized its exit from the barrel-making business by dropping "cooperage" from its name in 1969.

Expansion in the 1970s

Unlike some of its larger, more diversified rivals such as Continental Group, International Paper, and Mobil's Container Corp. of America, Greif Bros. did not buy or build any paper mills, even though the company had hundreds of thousands of acres of timberland. Instead, the company acquired 50 percent of Macauley & Co. and its Virginia Fibre Corp. when they were created in 1974. Company namesake Robert Macauley was a "longtime Dempsey associate" and Greif Bros. board member. Dempsey believed that by limiting the parent company's investment in this capital-intensive business he would limit its exposure to risk and debt. By the early 1990s, however, Greif had increased its stake in Virginia Fibre to 100 percent.

Greif expanded via acquisition during the 1970s, acquiring Chipboard, Inc. and Narad, Inc. Although the disposition of these purchases is unclear, it appears that they developed into Greif's Michigan Packaging Company and Down River International, Inc. subsidiaries. Michigan Packaging was founded in 1967 and grew into a corrugated sheet board company with three plants in the eastern United States. Established in 1963, Down River started out manufacturing corrugated boxes and evolved into a specialty producer of corrugated honeycomb filler for packaging and other applications. Acquisitions helped fuel a dramatic decade of growth. Sales nearly tripled from $103 million in 1971 to $307 million in 1981, and net income more than quadrupled, from $5.5 million to $25.2 million. This high level of profitability, combined with the stable majority ownership of the Dempsey family, allowed Greif to fund plant expansions and modernizations internally without incurring debt.

According to William Baldwin of *Forbes,* Greif ranked second only to Continental in the American fibre drum industry into the early 1980s. At 5 percent, Greif's average annual sales increases slowed significantly from the double-digit rate of the 1970s, but outpaced the fibre can industry's overall annual growth rate of 3.5 percent from 1982 to 1988. Annual profits increased at an average of three percent each year to a peak of $30.3 million in 1988.

But while sales continued to increase fairly steadily in the waning years of the decade and into the early 1990s, Greif's net income declined by more than one-fourth to $22.1 million in 1990. The reduced profitability was attributed to high capital investments ($66 million in 1989 alone), raw materials price increases, customers' price sensitivity, and increased global competition in Greif's primary markets. The company combated these trends by concentrating more intensely than ever on customer service. In the early 1990s, for example, Greif designed an ingeniously simple new shipping drum for Kraft General Foods. The custom-made containers revised the traditional cylindrical drum shape into a cube with rounded corners, allowing vastly more efficient transportation and storage. Whereas Kraft's trucks could hold 500 of the traditional cans, they could pack in 640 of the new drums.

Greif's 1990s-era environmental efforts included production of recycled and reusable packaging. The company's Greif Board subsidiary had been producing recycled-content corrugated board and kraft paper for nearly 30 years, and was working to incorporate more post-consumer corrugated board into its products. In 1993, Greif's Canadian container subsidiary worked with Ingersoll-Dresser Pump Co. to develop an award-winning reusable container for chemicals and hazardous materials. Progressive efforts such as these reflected Greif's heritage of meeting market challenges and helped ensure its place in the packaging industry.

By the mid-1980s, John C. Dempsey's more than $300 million personal fortune ranked him as one of America's richest individuals, according to *Forbes* magazine. Dempsey was known among his colleagues and friends as "a deeply righteous person who gave of himself." His strongly-held religious beliefs were reflected in an illustration that graced the back cover of Greif Bros.' annual report virtually every year he was CEO. It was a photo of the corporate board room featuring Warner Sallman's famous "Head of Christ" painting. Dempsey served as Greif's chairman and CEO for 47 years, until 1994, when the 80-year-old's failing health forced his retirement from day-to-day leadership to the honorary post of chairman emeritus. Dempsey was succeeded by Greif Bros.' vice-president and controller, Michael J. Gasser. The new leader noted that the

Key Dates:

1877: Greif Bros. is founded in Cleveland, Ohio.
1946: Jack Dempsey becomes chairman of Greif.
1964: Company headquarters are moved to Delaware, Ohio.
1967: Michigan Packaging is established.
1994: Michael J. Gasser succeeds Dempsey as CEO.
2001: Greif purchases the Van Leer industrial packaging division of Huhtamaki Van Leer Oyj of Finland.
2003: Company shortens its name to Greif Inc.

moral principles embraced by his predecessor would "continue to play an integral part in the Company's operating policy."

A Change in Leadership in the Mid-1990s

The advent of new leadership for the first time in nearly half a century ushered in what the new CEO called "an era of great anticipation and virtually unlimited potential" in his first annual letter to shareholders. Gasser vowed to evaluate and reorganize Greif Bros.' operations, and even suggested the possibility of diversification and acquisition in pursuit of "aggressive growth." In 1995 the company applied to have both its classes of stock listed on the National Association of Securities Dealers Automated Quotes, suggesting the possibility of an equity flotation to fund expansion.

As the new CEO had promised, Greif expanded almost immediately. In September of 1996, the company acquired Kyowya Corrugated Container Co., a packaging supply maker from Huntington, West Virginia. Less than six months later, Greif made plans to purchase the steel drum operations of North American Packaging Corp. The next year, Greif completed its acquisition of Sonoco Product Co.'s industrial-container business. The company also decided to pursue Sonoco's intermediate bulk-container business. The corrugated box maker, Great Lakes Corrugated Corp. in Toledo, Ohio, was next in a long list of acquisitions in the late 1990s. In order to manage all of the new business, Greif consolidated 18 plants in 1998 as part of a restructuring plan. It was decided that three plants would close in the United States.

Growth in the New Millennium

Up until this point, Greif's operations had been successful, but relatively small. Some of its business was exclusive to North America, like the management of 280,000 acres of timberlands in the United States. The acquisition of the Van Leer industrial packaging division from Huhtamaki Van Leer Oyj of Finland in 2001 changed its position. Royal Packaging Industries Van Leer NV of Amsterdam was already a global producer of steel, fiber, and plastic drums and bulk containers. Greif's size doubled in the $540 million deal, and it gained a foothold in the markets of Europe, Asia, and Latin America.

Success for Greif continued in 2003. The company increased its ownership of CorrChoice, a producer of corrugated sheets, to 100 percent. CorrChoice began as a joint venture in 1998, and operated seven corrugated sheet feeder plants in the United States. The business increased and performed well outside of North America with the opening of a steel drum facility at a port near Shanghai in China. This operation supported the petroleum, chemical, agrochemical, pharmaceutical, and food and fragrance industries. In the same year, Greif removed "Bros." from its title and became Greif Inc. The company hoped that this modification would promote a unified and global image.

Greif showed no signs of slowing down going into 2004. The company opened a plant in Perm, Russia to produce large steel drums. Greif had additional plans to expand business globally and Gasser set goals for Greif to become an organization that was "more market-focused and performance-driven." In order to support employees, plans were made to open the "Greif Center of Excellence," which would educate its people in "The Greif Way." Michael J. Gasser remained extremely optimistic about the role of Greif for years to come with his statement, "Positive change is occurring in every Greif plant, office and distribution center around the world. We are, indeed, making Greif a better partner with our customers, a stronger and more competitive force in the marketplace, and a more valuable long-term investment for our shareholders."

Principal Subsidiaries

CorrChoice, Inc.; Great Lakes Corrugated Corporation; Heritage Packaging Corporation; Michigan Packaging Company; MultiCorr Corporation; OPC Leasing Corporation; Ohio Packaging Corporation; Van Leer.

Principal Divisions

Industrial Packaging & Services; Paper, Packaging & Services; Timber.

Principal Competitors

Longview Fibre Company; Smurfit-Stone Container Corporation; Temple-Inland Inc.

Further Reading

Allen, Michael Patrick, *The Founding Fortunes: A New Anatomy of the Super-Rich in America,* Truman Talley Books, 1987.
Baldwin, William, "Homely Virtues," *Forbes,* July 19, 1982, p. 54.
"Business Brief—Greif Bros. Corp.: A Charge of $27.5 Million Planned for 3rd Quarter," *Wall Street Journal,* June 15, 1998, p. 1.
Eckhouse, Kimberly, "Shaped-Up Shippers More Space- and Cost-Efficient," *Food Processing,* May 1993, p. 134.
"18-Year Veteran Named Greif Bros. President," *Columbus (Ohio) Dispatch,* November 2, 1995, p. 2B.
"Greif Bros. Buys Sonoco Business," *Wall Street Journal,* April 1, 1998, p. 1.
"Greif Bros. Plans Acquisition," *Wall Street Journal,* September 11, 1996, p. B7.
"Greif Bros. Plans Purchase," *Wall Street Journal,* February 13, 1997.
"Greif Bros. Will Buy Packaging Division in $500 Million Deal," *Wall Street Journal,* October 30, 2000, p. 1.
Matthews, Tom, "Greif Adds to Operation with Plant in Russia," *Columbus Dispatch,* July 16, 2004, p. 1B.
Niquette, Mark, " 'Bros.' History at Greif," *Columbus Dispatch,* February 25, 2003, p. 1C.
"They're in the Money," *Cleveland Plain Dealer,* October 14, 1986, p. 1A.

—April Dougal Gasbarre
—update: Christina M. Stansell

GREY

Grey Global Group Inc.

777 Third Avenue
New York, New York 10017
U.S.A.
Telephone: (212) 546-2000
Fax: (212) 546-1495
Web site: http://www.greyglobalgroup.com

Public Company
Incorporated: 1917 as Grey Studios
Employees: 10,500
Sales: $1.3 billion (2003)
Stock Exchanges: NASDAQ
Ticker Symbol: GREY
NAIC: 541810 Advertising Agencies

Grey Global Group Inc., formerly Grey Advertising Inc., is one of the world's largest advertising agencies with offices in 83 countries around the globe. The company provides integrated communications services to a wide variety of clients whose products include some of the most well-known American brand names, and Grey prides itself on its longstanding relationships with these clients. From its base in New York's fashion industry, Grey has grown to become an advertiser of foods, cars, electronics, drugs, and other products. The WPP Group PLC made a $1.4 billion play for Grey in 2004.

Early History

Grey Advertising got its start on August 1, 1917, when 18-year-old Larry Valenstein founded Grey Studios. Too young to be sent overseas to fight in World War I, and having left college, Valenstein borrowed $100 from his mother and leased an office at 309 Fifth Avenue in New York. The fledgling entrepreneur set up shop as a direct mailer. Valenstein had worked previously as an errand boy at another direct mail firm, and he felt that he had learned enough at that job to strike out on his own. Valenstein's new business got its name from the color of his office's walls: slate gray.

Every six months, Grey Studios produced direct mail folders in which New York's furriers advertised their wares. As the business grew, Valenstein added new employees, taking on an art director and an assistant. Four years after its founding, Grey Studios moved to its second set of offices. Located at 41 East 29th Street, the company's two tenement rooms also served as a home for its art director. Needing extra help, Valenstein hired 17-year-old Arthur Fatt as an office boy in 1921.

It was Fatt, with a flair for salesmanship, who suggested several years later that the company replace its biannual mailers with a magazine published nine times a year and designed to showcase the products of the company's clients. After Fatt presented his boss with the title *Furs & Fashions* and a dummy issue, Valenstein was persuaded, and Grey Studios launched the publication.

Furs & Fashions soon became a success, and with the capital generated from this publication, Grey Studios was able to move from direct mailing to advertising, a logical outgrowth of the direct mail business, and a long-sought goal of the company. In 1925, Valenstein and Fatt renamed the company Grey Advertising.

Grey placed its first national advertisement in the August 1926 issue of the *Ladies Home Journal.* Drawing on the company's longstanding relationship with the fur industry, it featured a spot for Mendoza Fur Dyeing Works, Inc., of New York, for which the agency was, incidentally, never paid.

In 1930, Grey Advertising moved to its third New York location, on East 30th Street, just off of Fifth Avenue. In the 1930s, the company built on its historical affiliation with the New York garment industry, of which the fur industry was a part, to develop a reputation as an advertiser for retail stores and their merchandise. As a Seventh Avenue-area firm, based in the world of fashion, Grey Advertising became known as a soft goods specialist, dedicated to promoting manufacturers who retailed their wares in department stores. By 1938, the company was earning $250,000 a year in billings.

Grey's leaders concentrated on attracting high-quality creative talent throughout the 1940s, despite the fact that the entry of the United States into World War II made recruiting workers in a wartime economy difficult. Grey Advertising continued to turn a profit during the war years. As the American economy

Company Perspectives:

In these uncertain times, we have stayed true to the singular purpose that has always guided us; to build the value of our clients' brands. We focus relentlessly on our clients, judging our performance by their growth and our prospects by the faith they show in us. This enduring strength is rooted in our souls and permeates our vision and our work. It's what makes our client relationships long and strong and sets us apart from other companies in our industry.

boomed in the aftermath of the war, the agency's sales reached $1 million a year.

Despite this success, Grey's leaders realized that their competitors in the New York advertising industry were growing at a faster rate than they were, mainly as a result of their work for companies that manufactured packaged goods. These products, sold in grocery stores or drug stores, as opposed to department stores, had low prices, were sold in large quantities, and brought unparalleled prestige and professionalism to an advertising agency. In 1946, Grey acquired its first packaged goods client, the Mennen Company.

By the end of the 1940s, Grey's size and profits had grown so large that its two leaders instituted an employee stock-ownership plan, so that their coworkers could also participate in the company's good fortune. In 1955, Grey notched another important packaged goods client, Block Drug.

In the following year, Valenstein moved up to chairman of the agency, and Fatt became president of Grey. Shortly thereafter, the company scored its biggest coup in the packaged goods field. In 1956 Grey added manufacturing giant Procter & Gamble to its client list, after the company's previous ad agency had gone out of business and many of its employees had moved over to Grey.

Part of the importance of packaged goods clients lay in their heavy use of television advertising, and as the medium grew in importance throughout the 1950s, Grey increased its involvement with television advertising. As the manufacturers who advertised on television saw their businesses grow, so did the advertising agencies who worked for them. In addition, Grey began to hone its prowess at market research during this time by focusing on the broader picture of market strategy, as opposed to narrow campaigns for a single product.

International Expansion in the Late 1950s

In 1959 Grey opened its first international office, in Montreal. In that year, the agency's billings reached 44.61 million. Two years later, Valenstein and Fatt gave up their day-to-day duties at the agency they had created and became chairmen of Grey's executive committee. Herbert Strauss, an agency employee since 1939, took over as president.

With Strauss at the helm, Grey began a dramatic geographical expansion. In 1962, the company opened an office in Los Angeles called Grey-Western Division. In addition, the agency looked east, purchasing part of an English agency called Charles Hobson.

This was followed, in 1963, by expansion to Japan. Also in that year, Grey became one of the first advertising agencies to branch out into public relations by establishing Grey Public Relations, the company's first subsidiary. By the next year, Grey's billings had topped $100 million, more than doubling in just five years. In addition, the company had moved into Belgium, France, Germany, and Italy. Toronto, the company's second Canadian office, would be added in the next year. Overseas offices were responsible primarily for handling the international needs of Grey's American clients.

By 1965 Grey employed nearly 900 people, who were newly installed in seven floors of a new office building on Third Avenue in Manhattan. Despite its large size, the agency stressed teamwork and balance among its different departments, thereby engendering creative problem solving. In August 1965 Grey became the fourth national advertising agency to offer stock to the public, selling 290,000 shares in the company at $19.50 a piece. Selecting its clients carefully to assure high-quality management and strong growth potential in the products it advertised, Grey included Bristol-Meyers, Revlon, and Greyhound, along with Procter & Gamble, on its roster of accounts. To help service these accounts, the agency opened offices in Australia, Spain, and Venezuela.

By 1967, its 50th year in business, Grey Advertising boasted $221 million in billings. In the following year, the company opened offices in San Francisco and Austria. Two years later, Edward H. Meyer took over the post of chairman of the board, and the company began to supplement its global growth with expansion through the acquisition of subsidiaries. Meyer sought "to expand the geographic range of the business and the communications range of the business," as he told an interviewer from *Advertising Age.* In keeping with this policy, the company entered the business of healthcare communications in 1970, inaugurating Grey Medical, in addition to adding a unit called Crescendo Productions.

This was followed by the acquisition of Statter, Inc., in 1971. Also in that year, the company opened offices in The Netherlands and Argentina. After its purchase of North Advertising, Inc., the eighth largest advertising agency in Chicago, the company inaugurated Grey-North. A second midwestern office also was founded that year, when the company opened Grey-Twin Cities in Minneapolis-St. Paul.

Gains and Losses in the 1970s

In 1972, Grey won the Goodrich Tire Company's $6 million a year passenger car tire account with a creative proposal focusing on the new technology involved in radial tires. This capped a year-long stint in which the company had won approximately $63 million in new business. Grey had landed a $16 million small car account from the Ford Motor Company in August 1971, and followed this up by acquiring business from the Singer Company, Calgon Corporation, Carter-Wallace, and General Electric. At the same time, however, the company lost $13 million of billings, from clients including Ballantine beer, the Howard Johnson Company, and a Procter & Gamble deter-

Key Dates:

1917: Grey Studios is founded by Larry Valenstein.
1925: The company is renamed Grey Advertising Inc.
1956: Grey begins its relationship with Procter & Gamble.
1959: An international office is opened in Montreal.
1965: Grey becomes the fourth national advertising agency to go public.
1976: Grey forms a joint venture with a Swiss advertising firm creating Steinman and Grey.
1980: Conahay & Lyon is purchased by Grey-2, forming a joint agency.
1983: The company forms Grey Strategic Marketing.
2000: Grey Advertising creates Grey Global Group as a holding company; Grey Worldwide becomes its advertising unit.
2004: The WPP Group offers nearly $1.4 billion for Grey.

gent. Building on this stint of new business, Grey opened foreign offices in South Africa and Brazil in 1973, and also established its Grey Entertainment & Media subsidiary to handle communications and entertainment advertising.

In 1974, Grey won a $16.5 million Navy recruiting account from the U.S. government, which it subsequently lost in the next year. The company filed a formal protest over the loss of the business with the General Accounting Office and threatened to sue, claiming it had been unfairly stripped of the account. Grey's attempt to press a legal claim to the Navy work came to an end in September 1977, when a court dismissed its claim. Also during this time, Grey lost its Ford Motor account.

In the mid-1970s, Grey added offices in Sweden, Norway, and New Zealand. The company also invested in a consumer research firm, Market Horizons, and Lexington Broadcast Services, a television syndication service. Grey's overseas business flourished, and in 1976, the agency formed a joint venture with a Swiss advertising firm, creating Steinman & Grey. This fell apart, however, just one year later. A further setback occurred in 1977, when the company lost a client of 20 years, Greyhound.

In the following year, however, the company rallied back, winning a prestigious automotive account, the American Motors Corporation. In the late 1970s, Grey's international expansion continued as the company added foreign affiliates in Chile, Hong Kong, and Uruguay. Moreover, the company branched out to the Hispanic market in the United States, acquiring Font & Vaamonde, an agency that specialized in this work.

The 1980s saw Grey's expansion through acquisition continue apace. In 1980 the company's subsidiary Grey/2 bought another New York firm, Conahay & Lyon, for $1.4 million, thus forming a joint agency. In addition, the company returned to its roots when it opened Grey Direct, a direct marketing concern. This holding was augmented in the following two years by the purchase of the Beaumont-Bennett Group, a sales promotion and co-op advertiser, and Rada Recruitment Communications, which prepared job recruitment materials. In 1983, the company formed Grey Strategic Marketing, a subsidiary that offered long-term planning services. Foreign offices added in the early 1980s included Denmark, a second stab at the Swiss market, Singapore, Peru, and Mexico. In addition, the company formed Grey Reynolds Smith, a wholly owned subsidiary in Canada.

A New Business Plan in 1983

In late 1983, Grey inaugurated a new five-year business plan and set out to remake its corporate image. The company took steps to elevate the importance of creative work within its corporate culture, hiring new people in this area, and promoting creative executives from within the company. In an effort to increase the respect and prestige afforded creative talent at the agency, Grey installed its employees in expensive new offices and inaugurated a worldwide prize for the best creative work. With these measures, the agency hoped to shake its image as a traditional, hidebound shop, lacking in new ideas.

These efforts started to show fruit as the agency notched a number of big new clients in the mid-1980s, including Mitsubishi Motors of America, Red Lobster Restaurants, and Miss Clairol. In early 1986, the agency took steps to insure that this success would not make Grey the object of a hostile takeover, despite the fact that the company's longstanding employee stock ownership plan meant that 55 percent of the company was held by Grey employees. To further strengthen its defenses, the agency rearranged the structure of its stock offerings. During this time, the agency purchased Gross Townsend Frank Hoffman, a medical advertising firm, just one month before it sold off Grey Medical, its old unit. By the end of the year, Grey billings had topped $2 billion.

Grey's steady acquisition of properties that complemented its central advertising unit helped to make the company one of the world's few fully integrated marketers by the mid-1980s. In this way, the company was able to lessen the impact of clients' gradual shift away from traditional advertising to more creative forms of promotion. With its various units, Grey had the capability to handle all aspects of a client's marketing needs, including advertising, promotions, direct mail, and public relations. For accounts like the hospital chain Humana, Grey was able to coordinate a unified, interrelated campaign, which used mailings to follow up on television advertising, reinforcing one message through many media. For its client Kool-Aid, the agency adopted a similar approach, tying television commercials to ads in Sunday newspaper comic sections, which in turn keyed in to in-store displays with coupons for stuffed animals, sunglasses, and skateboards. In addition, the company arranged promotional events, with appearances by Kool-Aid's mascot, a smiling pitcher.

In the late 1980s, Grey shed some of the holdings it had acquired during its period of rapid expansion throughout the late 1970s and 1980s. The company transferred its Chicago shop to a Swiss firm, and in November 1988, Grey sold for $38 million its LBS Communications (formerly Lexington Broadcast Service), a television syndicate whose high cash flow had made Grey ripe for takeover.

Despite these divestments, the company continued to grow. The agency got into the audiovisual corporate communications business in 1988, with its purchase of Gindick Productions. Although Grey refrained from merging with another ad agency of its size during the period of industry consolidation in the late 1980s, Grey made "an average of 20 to 25 acquisitions a year," Chairman Meyer told *Advertising Age.* "Grey's attitude is to keep its culture and character consistent and make small mergers one at a time, with specific companies for specific reasons in specific countries in specific communications skills," he elaborated.

Responding to Global Changes in the Late 1980s–90s

In 1989 Grey turned its attention to coming changes in the world market and took steps to prepare for European economic union in 1992. The company formed a European management board in April to coordinate its agency network, as the continent became more and more a single market. In addition to this regional strength, Grey also had built up a strong network in Asia, with agencies in Japan, Taiwan, the Philippines, Hong Kong, Australia, New Zealand, Malaysia, Thailand, Singapore, and India.

As its business became more international, Grey looked to strengthen its other communications enterprises such as public relations, direct-response mailings, and promotional services—and expanded their scope to an international level, in keeping with its advertising activities. By 1991, the company had 188 offices in 40 countries.

Despite the recession that hampered the American economy in the early 1990s, Grey continued to turn a profit. In 1991, the company reported earnings of $528 million. These were lower than expected as a result of the expensive shuttering of Levine, Huntley, Vick & Beaver, an agency subsidiary based in New York that had fallen apart after the loss of its primary account, Subaru cars, and the departure of its management.

Although the company was known for solid strategic planning, Grey's reputation on Madison Avenue suffered for lack of innovation during the mid-1990s. A new creative director brought change to the company, and they began to win midsize accounts. Grey won $160 million in new business in 1994.

Grey grew in cyberspace as well. In 1999, the company formed MediaCom Digital, a strategic developer that connected all advertising services. Later that year, Grey Advertising purchased media buying agency Beyond Interactive in order to increase its online media business. The purchase was meant to act as a counterpart to other Grey businesses such as Grey Direct and media.com. Beyond Interactive opened up offices in China and Mexico the following year.

Changes in the New Millennium

In order to manage the company's subsidiaries effectively, Grey Advertising Inc. set up a holding company in 2000 under the Grey Global Group name. Its advertising division adopted the Grey Worldwide corporate moniker. The company had not been through a reorganization since 1970—the year Edward Meyer was elected CEO. Grey was not alone in its restructuring. The creation of Grey Global came at a time when advertising agencies across the globe were becoming increasingly diversified.

In the early years of the new millennium, Grey continued to grow on many levels. In an effort to increase Grey's email services worldwide, Grey Direct added Englishtown.com to the clientele of Grey eMMetrics, its email marketing division, in 2001. With 60 million email messages sent each month, Englishtown.com became its highest volume client. This new client had the ability to track the success of each email initiative and to analyze returns to determine the most efficient advertising strategies.

Procter & Gamble, which accounted for 10 percent of Grey's business, kept Grey Global Group as one of two agencies responsible for the majority of its global advertising accounts in 2002. With this decision, Grey gained additional international business for Zest soap and Torengos snack products. At the same time, however, Grey suffered blows to its reputation when three former executives were indicted by the Justice Department for conspiracy to control bids and allocate contracts.

Despite global advertising growth as a result of the Summer Olympics, Grey's future as the last independent agency of its kind came into question in 2004. The company hired Goldman Sachs Group Inc. and J.P. Morgan Chase & Co. to discuss the possibility of a sale. Grey's revenue was $1.3 billion in 2003, but labor costs and real estate expenditures took their toll on profit margins. Grey had become an attractive takeover target, especially with clients such as Procter & Gamble, GlaxoSmithKline PLC, Nokia Corp., and BellSouth Corp., and industry analysts began to speculate that Edward Meyer, Grey's longtime chairman and CEO, might relinquish control after 34 years. Sure enough, the United Kingdom's WPP Group PLC—the second largest advertising firm in the world—offered $1.4 billion for Grey in September 2004. With a sale on its horizon, Grey Global looked to be on track for changes in the future.

Principal Operating Units

Grey Healthcare; GCI; G2; Grey Interactive; Grey Direct; Market Data Solutions; Grey Worldwide; APCO; MediaCom; Alliance; J. Brown Agency; Gwhiz; Wing Latino.

Principal Competitors

The Interpublic Group of Companies Inc.; Publicis Groupe S.A.; WPP Group PLC.

Further Reading

Alter, Stewart, "Grey Locks Up to Block Buyouts," *Advertising Age,* March 24, 1986.

——, "Grey Out to Shed Gray Image," *Advertising Age,* January 21, 1985.

Beardi, Cara, "Grey Goes Global with E-mail Marketing," *Advertising Age,* September 24, 2001, p. 67.

"Big Creative Idea Won Goodrich Tires for Grey," *Advertising Age,* September 25, 1972.

Bold, Ben, "P&G Pools Global Ads into Publicis and Grey," *Marketing,* November 21, 2002, p.5.

Goldman, Kevin, "Grey Livens Up Its Image, Using Creative Touch to Win Accounts," *Wall Street Journal,* April 4, 1994, p. B6.

Gray, Ralph, "AMC Cites 'Discipline' in Naming Grey for Cars," *Advertising Age,* March 6, 1978.

"Grey Advertising Inc.'s Beyond Interactive Has Its First Client in Asia," *Wall Street Journal,* April 19, 2000, p. 1.

Honomichl, Jack J., ''Strategic Research Role Makes Grey Unique,'' *Advertising Age,* June 14, 1976.

''How an Ad Agency Hits the $100-Million Mark,'' *Business Week,* January 23, 1965.

Johnson, Bradley, ''Grey's Allure Hidden Behind Fat Costs and Weak Margins,'' *Advertising Age,* July 5, 2004, p. 6.

Kalish, David, ''Space Invaders,'' *Marketing & Media Decisions,* November 1988.

Lafayette, Jon, ''Meyer Readies Grey for Europe in 1992,'' *Advertising Age,* April 24, 1989.

Mand, Adrienne, ''Behind Beyond; Grey Explains Acquisition,'' *Adweek,* August 23, 1999, p. 44.

Menzies, Hugh D., ''Grey Agency Plans Offering,'' *New York Times,* August 21, 1965.

Petrecca, Laura, ''Grey Revamps Agency, Names New Managers,'' *Advertising Age,* April 24, 2000, p. 13.

Ramirez, Anthony, ''Do Your Ads Need a Superagency?,'' *Fortune,* April 27, 1987.

Revett, John, ''Grey Threatens Lawsuit As Navy Shifts Ad Account to Ted Bates,'' *Advertising Age,* September 8, 1975.

Sanders, Lisa, ''Third Former Grey Exec Indicted in Print Probe,'' *Advertising Age,* December 16, 2002, p. 4.

''Stardust Memories,'' *Greyline: Grey Advertising Inc. News,* August/September 1982.

Steinberg, Brian, and Dennis K. Berman, ''Grey Global Hires Advisers, Explores a Possible Sale,'' *Wall Street Journal,* June 28, 2004, p. B3.

White, Erin, and Ben Winkley, ''WPP Scrutinizes Grey Global, Weighing a Possible Acquisition,'' *Wall Street Journal,* August 23, 2004, p. B4.

—Elizabeth Rourke
—update: Christina M. Stansell

H.J. Russell & Company

504 Fair Street
Atlanta, Georgia 30313
United States
Telephone: (404) 330-1000
Fax: (404) 330-0922
Web site: http://www.hjrussell.com

Private Company
Incorporated: 1957
Employees: 1,833
Sales: $303 million (2003)
NAIC: 233320 Commercial and Institutional Building Construction; 233220 Multifamily Housing Construction; 531110 Lessors of Residential Buildings and Dwellings; 531190 Lessors of Other Real Estate Property

H.J. Russell & Company is the largest African American owned real estate and construction company in the United States. Through four main divisions—Construction, Program Management, Property Management, and Real Estate—the firm provides a broad range of services including construction contracting and management, the development and construction of urban residential structures, the management of residential and commercial properties, and environmental management. The property management division manages some 12,000 apartment units, condominiums, and public housing units. H.J. Russell & Company is based in Atlanta, with project offices in Chicago, Dallas, Miami, Phoenix, St. Louis, and New York. Apart from its main businesses, a subsidiary, Russell's Concessions International Corporation, operates food and beverage concessions in major airports throughout the country, while The Russell Foundation manages founder H.J. Russell's philanthropic activities.

Great Depression Background

The history of H.J. Russell & Company is largely a history of the perseverance and vision of one man, Herman J. Russell. Russell was born in 1930 in Summerhill, an impoverished neighborhood in Atlanta. The youngest of eight children, Russell grew up during the hardships of the Great Depression, a time that exerted an early and decisive influence on his dream to have his own business. ''As much as I wanted to work . . . there were no jobs,'' Russell recalled on the occasion of his company's 50th anniversary, explaining ''That's one of the reasons my desire was so great to be my own boss.'' He became his own boss at a young age. When he was eight years old, he began doing chores for neighbors. At ten, he got a paper route. All the while as a child, he also worked for his father's small plastering company, Rodgers Russell Sr. Plastering Company, mastering the plaster trade by the time he turned 12.

Another key moment occurred when Russell was a teenager and planned to open a shoeshine parlor on a vacant lot on his street. He first needed to get city approval to use the residentially zoned land for a commercial purpose. In a 1996 interview in *Nation's Business,* Russell recalled, ''I went before this totally white City Council, and I'll never forget, one councilman said to me, 'Nigger, why can't you just shine shoes on your front porch?' That did something to me that day. It was just like lightening striking me. I said to myself, 'I'm going to make a difference. I'm going to do something to turn that kind of attitude around'.''

Though poor and with little formal education, Russell's father, in addition to the plaster trade, taught Russell to save money. By the time he was 16, Russell had saved enough money to buy a vacant lot from the city of Atlanta, where, with the help of friends, he built a duplex. The rental income from those two units was enough to pay for his college education at Tuskegee Institute where in 1952 he was granted a degree in building construction.

Launching a Company in the 1950s

That same year, Russell returned to Atlanta and founded his own company, H.J. Russell Plastering Company. With little more than an old pick-up truck and a single employee, the new company began doing small plastering and repair jobs in Atlanta. Despite the racial segregation in Atlanta's construction trades, segregation that made it nearly impossible for African Americans to bid successfully on large jobs, Russell through unrelenting determination moved on to bigger projects, purchasing and improving other pieces of land—at first in his own Summerhill neighborhood and later in other parts of the city—

Company Perspectives:

Our Mission: To continue as a profitable enterprise that: is known for delivering superior services and products; enhances the quality of life of our community; earns the loyalty of its employees through demonstrated commitment to their development and reward of exemplary performance; is recognized as a national leader in the construction and real estate industries.

and building homes. By the mid-1950s the company had grown to employ a work force of 25. In 1957 Russell also inherited his father's company, valued at approximately $15,000, and renamed it H.J. Russell & Company.

The company continued to grow, concentrating on the construction of duplexes, small apartment buildings, and other rental properties for low and middle income families. Most were projects that remained in the firm's hands after completion and provided the company with an additional source of regular income. As a result of this focus, Russell established the Paradise Management Company in 1959 to manage its residential and commercial properties.

New Inroads in the 1960s

In 1962 Russell solidified its building activity with the establishment of the H.J. Russell Construction Company. By that time, Russell was doing well enough to attract the interest of the Atlanta Chamber of Commerce, and in November a letter was sent inviting Russell to join the organization. When it issued the invitation, the all-white Chamber of Commerce was unaware that Russell was African American. He accepted and became a member before the group discovered its "mistake." The story of H.J. Russell becoming the first black member of the Chamber of Commerce made front-page news in Atlanta. Almost 20 years later, in 1980, the organization had changed significantly; Russell was then voted the second black president of the Chamber of Commerce.

The company grew rapidly in the 1960s, thanks in part to the introduction of government programs intended to spur residential construction, particularly in the South. The company's construction division was one of the largest builders of HUD affordable housing during President Richard Nixon's administration. That experience led to Russell performing on lucrative contracts for large construction projects. In 1963 he was selected to do the plastering on Atlanta-Fulton County Stadium, then being built for the Atlanta Braves baseball team. Later in the decade, the company came into its own with other high profile projects in downtown Atlanta such as the construction of Citizens Trust Building in 1969 and the fireproofing and plastering for the Equitable Building in 1968, the latter being the largest contract of its kind ever awarded to a black-owned firm.

Consolidation in the 1970s

Two developments helped solidify H.J. Russell & Company's position as one of the Southeast's pre-eminent construction contractors. First, the building programs of Department of Housing and Urban Development (HUD) of the 1970s required participation of minority-owned companies in contracts. Second, the election of Atlanta's first black mayor, Maynard Jackson, provided Russell's firms with new business in the city. Jackson inaugurated affirmative action programs that required white-owned companies with city contracts to subcontract with minority-owned companies. The solid reputation for good work and dependability that H.J. Russell & Company had by then established made it a natural partner in such projects. Still, despite participation in such programs, some 75 percent of the company's work remained through private contracts in the 1970s and 1980s.

H.J. Russell & Company continued to work regularly on prestigious construction projects in and around Atlanta, including the Ashby Street MARTA station in 1972 and the Delta Air Lines headquarters. The company also began diversifying its business interests in the 1970s through purchases made by H.J. Russell. He founded the City Beverage Company, a nationwide distributor of beer and other beverages; he obtained a 50-percent interest in DDR International, Inc., which managed construction projects; he obtained a majority share in Russell-Rowe Communications, the owner of a television station in Macon, Georgia; and he established Concessions International, the operator of restaurant units at several U.S. airports. In 1972 he joined the Omni Group, which purchased two major professional sports franchises: the Atlanta Flames of the National Hockey League and the Atlanta Hawks of the National Basketball League. The investment made Russell the first African American to share ownership in a major sports franchise. In 1973 when *Black Enterprise* magazine published its first ranking of the top 100 companies, H.J. Russell & Company was 22 on the list, with annual sales of $6 million and about 500 employees. As of 2004, the company has appeared on the list every year since.

"Rocketing Growth" in the 1980s

By 1981 Russell was well-recognized for his success. His personal wealth was estimated at over $10 million, and he was a regular recipient of honors from various business, civic, and educational organizations. The Atlanta University School of Business inducted him into their Entrepreneurs Hall of Fame in 1982. The Georgia State University's College of Business Administration inducted him into the Business Hall of Fame in 1985. In 1986 he was the Atlanta Business League's Chief Executive Office of the Year.

H.J. Russell described the decade of the 1980s as "a time of rocketing growth" for his company. At the beginning of the decade, the company's annual sales totaled more than $50 million and its work force numbered approximately 500. During this time, the firm was selected to work on the Georgia Pacific Headquarters, slated to be the second tallest structure in Atlanta. H.J. Russell was also named one of the contractors on the Hartsfield Atlanta International Airport's main terminal complex, a job that significantly expanded the firm's reputation as one of the country's most reliable builders of transportation facilities.

The company expanded geographically mid-decade when its project management division set up offices in Birmingham, Alabama. New clients there included the City of Birmingham, the Birmingham Turf Club, the Birmingham Airport Authority, and the Birmingham/Jefferson County Civic Center Authority. The H.J. Russell division responsible for residential property

Key Dates:

1946: Herman Jerome Russell buys his first parcel of land and builds a rental duplex.
1957: Russell inherits a family business and renames it H.J. Russell & Company.
1960: The company takes on its first major project, developing 12 residential units.
1963: Russell becomes first African American member of Atlanta Chamber of Commerce.
1973: H.J. Russell & Company makes the first *Black Enterprise* top 100 list.
1980: Russell is elected president of the Atlanta Chamber of Commerce.
1986: Company opens a branch in Birmingham, Alabama.
1994: Four subsidiaries are united as divisions of H.J. Russell & Company.
2003: Russell is succeeded as CEO by son Michael Russell.

development saw impressive growth as well, and in 1987 H.J. Russell & Company renovated and enlarged its own corporate offices to more than 42,000 square feet.

Preparing for Russell's Retirement in the 1990s

It was a golden business opportunity for H.J. Russell & Company when in 1990 Atlanta was chosen to host the Summer 1996 Centennial Olympic Games. Moreover, the decision to locate the Olympic stadium in Summerhill provided an occasion for Russell (H. J., as he was usually called) to return to the neighborhood in which he had grown up. H.J. Russell & Company was selected to help build the stadium and other Olympic facilities which were part of an urban renewal effort in the badly deteriorated section of Atlanta. Groundbreaking for the stadium took place in May 1993.

That year H.J. Russell & Company had total sales of $152 million and was ranked fourth on the *Black Enterprise* list of top minority-held companies. The firm underwent a major reorganization at the beginning of its 1995 fiscal year. Its four construction and real estate companies were united within H.J. Russell & Company. Presidents of the former subsidiaries were named vice-presidents of the newly-combined firm. The consolidation was undertaken to streamline company operations—and hence maximize profits—by creating a single strategic plan for all divisions with a single financial officer. Russell's son, H. Jerome Russell, was named president and chief operating officer of H.J. Russell & Company, while youngest son Michael was named vice-president of joint venture construction. Russell's daughter and oldest child, Donata Russell Major, became vice-president of Concessions International Corporation. The reorganization was perceived as the first step in Russell's easing his way into retirement and passing control of the company into the hands of his children.

The second chapter of the changing of the guard at H.J. Russell & Company was a surprise to observers. In 1996 Russell announced that he would step aside as company CEO, and that the position would be taken over by R.K. Sehgal, who would also be named vice-chairman of the firm. The Sehgal news was startling not only because the man's flamboyant, jet-setting image was so at odds with the conservative, reserved face of H.J. Russell & Company. What was most unexpected was that an outsider—even one who had taken the Law Companies Group from $50 million to 350 million in annual revenues in a ten-year period—would be granted such an unprecedented degree of control in the Russell family business. Russell explained to the press that an important reason for the Sehgal move, in addition to bringing his experience to the company, was that Sehgal might mentor the Russell children and prepare them for the inevitable day when they would take over the reins at the firm. Sehgal had turned down offers from larger companies to accept the Russell offer. Part of the deal, reportedly, was that he was given a large ownership stake in the company, although majority ownership remained with the Russell family. Sehgal officially took over his new positions in April 1997. The Sehgal era was short-lived. He and Russell reportedly failed to agree on a vision for the firm, and by the end of 1998 Russell had returned to the CEO's office.

Annual revenues topped $172 million in 1997, and the firm employed more than 1,500 workers (including concessions personnel). H.J. Russell & Company continued to work on high-profile projects, in Atlanta and elsewhere in the United States, through the decade of the 1990s. These included the Birmingham Civil Rights Institute and the Georgia Dome in 1992, Coca Cola Company corporate headquarters in 1993, the BMW-Zentrum manufacturing plant in Greenville, South Carolina in 1994, Wachovia Headquarters in Winston-Salem, North Carolina in 1995, The McCormick Place expansion in Chicago in 1996, the Roswell Park Cancer Research Institute in Buffalo New York in 1998, and the St. Louis Missouri City Justice Center and Atlanta's Phillips Arena in 1999. During this time, the company sold the Macon, Georgia, television station it had owned since the 1970s.

New Leadership in the 2000s

In 2003 H.J. Russell retired as CEO a second time. This time he was succeeded by Michael, the younger of his two sons. The choice was a surprise—many had expected Jerome to get the job. The decision was reached at a family meeting at which all of the Russell children expressed what they most wanted to do for the company. Jerome wanted to concentrate on the real estate development side of the firm. Naming Michael CEO would enable Jerome to give his undivided attention to that division. Donata was interested in the nonprofit arena, including entrepreneurship, youth development and mentorship. She was named president of the Russell Foundation. The CEO position was ideal for Michael, who was most interested in growing H.J. Russell & Company and pushing it to the next level. Russell himself, who remained chairman, went into what he called semi-retirement. This, he explained, meant that he would work only nine to ten hours a day instead of the 14 to 15 hours he formerly logged.

Philanthropy was also part of the company's legacy as it moved further into the 21st century. Throughout his business life Russell has been as dedicated to improving the community in which his companies operated as in expanding his own business opportunities. He developed his companies with an eye toward the ongoing improvement of the black community in Atlanta. This is evident in the numerous residential properties he developed and built in the city. In addition he gave his time and office to fundraising for programs for disadvantaged youth, and he donated land to black churches in Atlanta. In the 1960s he contributed money that made possible the establishment of the *Atlanta Inquirer*, an important organ of the civil rights movement in Georgia. He elected to locate the headquarters of his firm in a run-down area of Atlanta to encourage its rehabilitation. In 1999 he contributed a total of $4 million to the entrepreneurship programs of Clark Atlanta University, Georgia State University, Morehouse College, and his alma mater Tuskegee Institute. The Russell Foundation continued to oversee Russell's philanthropic efforts throughout the United States.

As the 2000s progressed CEO Michael Russell was expected to expand the company's work in revitalizing urban areas in and beyond its Atlanta base. It had already begun work on building apartments, condos, and a retail mall on an eleven-acre area in Newark, New Jersey.

Principal Subsidiaries

Concessions International Corporation.

Principal Divisions

Construction; Program Management; Property Management; Real Estate.

Principal Competitors

Brasfield & Gorrie, LLC; CBL & Associates Properties, Inc. (CBL); Choate Construction Company.

Further Reading

Barrier, Michael, ''Entrepreneurs Who Excel,'' *Nation's Business,* August 1, 1996, p. 18.

Booker, Lorri Denise, ''Tax Breaks for Developer are Opposed,'' *Atlanta Journal,* December 2, 1987, p. B1.

Copeland, Larry, ''He Altered Atlanta in More Ways Than One,'' *USA Today,* December 3, 2003, p. 8B.

''Georgia Builder Finding Road to Growth,'' *New York Times,* March 5, 1981, p. D1.

Harte, Susan, ''Jerome Russell: COO of Family Empire Not Angling for Top Spot,'' *Atlanta Journal-Constitution,* November 18, 2001, p. 2P.

Holmes, Tamara E., ''Herman J. Russell Passes Torch,'' *Black Enterprise,* January 2004, p. 19.

Holsendolph, Ernest, ''Creative Move Bolsters Future of H.J. Russell,'' *Atlanta Journal and Constitution,* November 23, 1996, p. G3.

——, ''Russell Learned to Save, to Give,'' *Atlanta Journal and Constitution,* November 7, 1999, p. 2H.

Mitchell, Cynthia, ''Focus on R.K. Sehgal,'' *Atlanta Journal and Constitution,* December 1, 1996, p. R4.

Poole, Sheila M., ''H. J. Russell: Atlanta Patriarch,'' *Atlanta Journal-Constitution,* January 21, 2002, p. 1B.

——, ''H. J. Russell President Resigning to Start Firm,'' *Atlanta Journal and Constitution,* November 12, 1992, p. 3.

Saporta, Maria, ''Builder H.J. Russell Puts Outsider at Helm,'' *Atlanta Journal and Constitution,* November 21, 1996, p. D1.

——, ''Construction Icon Gives Up CEO Job,'' *Atlanta Journal-Constitution,* October 7, 2003 p. 1D.

——, ''Reorganization Sets Stage for Succession at H.J. Russell & Co.,'' *Atlanta Journal and Constitution,* June 21, 1994, p. C1.

White, Paula M., ''Changing the Guard: Herman Russell Steps Down as Company CEO,'' *Black Enterprise,* April 1, 1997, p. 16.

—Gerald E. Brennan

The H.W. Wilson Company

950 University Avenue
Bronx. New York 10452
U.S.A.
Telephone: (718) 588-8400
Toll Free: (800) 367-6770
Fax: (800) 590-1617
Web site: http://www.hwwilson.com

Private Company
Incorporated: 1903
Employees: 500
Sales: $39 million (2002 est.)
NAIC: 511140 Database and Directory Publishers

The H.W. Wilson Company is a leading reference publisher specializing in indexes and abstracts, primarily selling to libraries. The headquarters of the privately-owned company is located on the Harlem River in the Bronx borough of New York City, and another facility is maintained in Dublin, Ireland, where 120 professional abstracters are employed. Wilson is best known for its *Readers' Guide to Periodical Literature.* Other major titles include *Famous First Facts, Current Biography,* and *Book Review Digest.* All told, the company publishes 15 full-text periodicals databases, seven biography databases, 18 index and eight abstracts databases, five collection development catalogs, an art image database, and a large number of reference monographs. In recent years, Wilson has placed increasing emphasis on electronic distribution of its databases, eventually switching from tape formats to the Internet through the introduction of WilsonWeb.

Origins in an 1800s Bookstore

Wilson's founder, Halsey William Wilson, was born in Wilmington, Vermont, in 1868. Orphaned at the age of two, he was raised by his maternal grandparents in Massachusetts and later, at the age of 12, went to live with relatives in Iowa. After studying at the Beloit Academy in Wisconsin, Wilson began attending college at the University of Minnesota in 1885. Money was a concern for the young man, who was only able to take classes intermittently while holding down a series of part-time jobs, including janitor, job printer, newspaper delivery, and bookseller. In December 1889 Wilson and his roommate, Henry S. Morris, pooled $400 to establish a bookstore, Morris & Wilson, that initially operated out of their dormitory room and served the university community. The business proved so successful that it was able to soon relocate to a room in the school's "Old Main" building.

Wilson became more devoted to growing the bookstore than pursuing his studies. When his partner graduated two years later and moved away, Wilson continued to run the bookstore alone. Wilson never completed his degree at Minnesota and likely ceased taking classes in 1892. He married Justina Leavitt, a teacher and school administrator, in 1895, and she helped Wilson run the business before becoming highly active in the women's suffrage movement. In 1898 Wilson bought out Morris, becoming the sole proprietor.

As a bookseller, Wilson had to constantly search through publishers' catalogs in order to keep track of currently published books that his customers might want. It was tedious and time-consuming work that prompted him to long for a comprehensive, up-to-date index of published works. He eventually decided to create such an index himself. What made the concept work economically was Wilson's idea to keep the publication current by placing each entry on a printer's "slug," which could then be later sorted with slugs from new entries. It may have been an obvious solution to someone who had experience as a job printer, but it was a revolutionary concept in bibliographical publishing. In February 1898 Wilson first published *Cumulative Book Index,* a comprehensive alphabetic list of currently published books in English, featuring the key elements of future Wilson indexes: the listing of author, title, and subject. The work sold for $1 to 300 subscribers, who would then receive periodically updated versions.

Introducing the Reader's Guide *in 1901*

Wilson continued to run his bookstore even as he expanded his bibliographical publishing. He soon hired his first editor, Marion E. Potter, who would work for the company for the next

Company Perspectives:

The company's mission is to give guidance to those seeking their way through the maze of books and periodicals, without which they would be lost.

55 years. In 1899 Wilson brought out a list of books in print, called *United States Catalog.* Two years later he turned his attention to the indexing of magazine articles, hoping to apply the techniques he developed with books. While *Cumulative Book Index* and *United States Catalog* attracted both booksellers and libraries as customers, a magazine index would be dependent almost entirely on the library trade. After studying existing services and consulting with librarians, Wilson developed his second revolutionary contribution to reference publishing, one that made a magazine article index economically viable: a sliding scale for charging subscribers, based on the amount of usage. Thus, larger libraries, based on holdings, paid a higher rate than smaller ones. In 1901 he published the first issue of the *Reader's Guide to Periodical Literature,* which proved an instant success and helped to firmly establish Wilson as the worldwide leader in his field.

In 1903 Wilson incorporated his business as The H.W. Wilson Company, which still included the original bookstore, the profits of which were used to subsidize his increasing focus on index publishing. Wilson continued his practice of consulting with library personnel in the development of new products, as he expanded his efforts into specialized fields. In 1905 he brought out *Book Review Digest,* edited by his wife, followed in 1907 with the launch of the *Debater's Handbook* series (which later became the Wilson Reference Shelf series), *Index to Legal Periodicals* in 1908, and a year later *Children's Catalog,* the first of many lists of books recommended to public and school libraries. Wilson recognized that his *Reader's Guide to Periodical Literature* had stimulated an interest in older magazines, and so in 1910 he started the Periodicals Clearing House to sell back issues.

Because the publishing industry was centered in New York City, Wilson found that operating out of Minnesota was not in the best interest of his publishing operation, which mostly served customers in the eastern part of the country. In 1913 he finally sold his bookstore and relocated his company, taking with him several key employees to White Plains, New York, located 25 miles north of New York City. The demand for his indexes was so great that Wilson soon outgrew this space, and in 1917 he bought a five-story building in The Bronx, which became the foundation of the company's current headquarters. This new facility was large enough to handle the full range of the company's activities, including editing, printing, and distribution. In 1929 even this plant proved too small for Wilson's expanding business and an adjoining eight-story building was added. A 30-foot lighthouse was constructed on top, which became a landmark along the Harlem River and also served as the company's logo.

From the time Wilson moved his operation to The Bronx until he stepped down as chief executive in 1952, the company introduced a number of significant bibliographical works. In 1929 it first published *Education Index* and *Art Index.* The *Vertical File Service Catalog,* a list of pamphlets and similar material indexed by subject and including descriptive notes and prices, was launched in 1932. To serve libraries with smaller holdings, Wilson published *The Abridged Readers' Guide* in 1935. A year later the company brought out an index of books, periodicals, and pamphlets concerning the library profession called *Library Literature.* In 1938 Wilson published *Bibliographic Index* and in 1940 introduced *Current Biography,* a monthly publication that provided biographical sketches of people in the news. *Biography Index* was then introduced in 1946.

Wilson was able to take full advantage of several trends: the proliferation of published works, resulting both from mainstream publishers and scientific and scholarly research, and the increase in the establishment of public and school libraries. Recognizing the importance of librarians to his business, Wilson joined library associations, named librarians to his board of directors, and sponsored library awards. He also continued to work closely with librarians on the products his company turned out, including some that were useful although unprofitable. The business, in general, was never highly profitable but it always paid a dividend, due in large part to the company's unique niche. Because it was in essence a monopoly—Wilson himself considered his bibliographical products a public utility—the company was saved the expense of a sales force. Moreover, because Wilson had such a head start in the field, it was cost prohibitive for another company to enter the market.

Wilson was well into his 80s when his health began to fail. He turned over the responsibility of day-to-day affairs in 1952 and became chairman of the board. In many ways he was a paradox. On the one hand, he proved to be an innovative entrepreneur, a supporter of women's rights, and one of the first employers to offer stock sharing and pensions. He had no children and gave most of the company's stock to employees. After his death, most of the profits were paid to the employee-owners. (When they died, shareholders were required to sell back their stock to the company.) On the other hand, Wilson paid low salaries, was often petty in his frugality, and very much paternalistic and puritanical. Behind his back, he was called Pop or Papa. He fought against the unionization of his employees, ultimately failing, and was known to rail against federal income tax and the New Deal social legislation of the 1930s. He did not drink or smoke, and banned alcohol at all company picnics and parties. Nevertheless, he promoted women to key positions in the company and was one of the first employers to hire physically handicapped workers. He was also unassuming, working at a rolltop desk in a corner of the editorial offices without a private secretary. After he died in 1954, his will established a charitable foundation that benefited the library profession and former employees in need.

Replacing Wilson as CEO and president in 1953 was Howard Haycraft, who went to work for the company after graduating from the University of Minnesota in 1929. He is best remembered today for his scholarly book about mystery fiction, *Murder for Pleasure,* published in 1941 and still in print a half-century later. He also edited a number of anthologies of detective fiction. As an editor at Wilson he worked on such titles as *The Junior Book of Authors, British Authors of the 19th Century,*

Key Dates:

1889: Halsey Wilson and Henry Morris start a Minnesota bookstore.
1898: Wilson buys out Morris and begins publishing the *Cumulative Book Index.*
1901: *Reader's Guide to Periodical Literature* is first published.
1903: H.W. Wilson is incorporated.
1913: Wilson sells the bookstore and moves to White Plains, New York.
1917: The company is relocated to The Bronx.
1954: Halsey Wilson dies.
1985: The company's first electronic product, a version of the *Reader's Guide,* debuts.
1997: The WilsonWeb web site is launched.

America Authors, and *20th-Century Authors.* He headed Wilson until 1967, then served as chairman until retiring in 1970.

Challenges in the 1970s–90s

Haycraft was succeeded by Leo M. Weins, who came to Wilson in 1957 from the American Library Association, where he served as Comptroller. He was responsible for a number of advancements at Wilson, including the expansion to Dublin, Ireland, and leading the company into the electronic age. It was also during his tenure that the company became complacent and lost its competitive edge. In the early 1970s, an ex-librarian named Anthony DeStephen recognized a chink in Wilson's armor; the company had failed to copyright its books. He took 70 years worth of *Reader's Guides,* had the material set overseas, and then reorganized the material alphabetically. He then sold the material to Information Access Co. (IAC) to produce competing products. Wilson could have easily done the same thing as DeStephen, and it even passed up the chance to acquire IAC at an early stage, but failed on both counts. IAC was acquired by Ziff-Davis, which grew the enterprise, and sold it to Thomson Corporation in 1994 for $465 million. Wilson was also slow to embrace the computer age, clinging to print technology.

In 1985 the company offered its first electronic product, *Reader's Guide to Periodical Literature,* but its WILSEARCH proprietary set of search commands proved cumbersome. Not only did Wilson fall behind the competition in delivering data electronically, it also lost some of its edge with librarians.

In 1992 the company became involved in a censorship flap. A regular columnist for *Wilson Library Bulletin* wrote a satirical questionnaire that inquired about the sexual habits of its librarian readers. Although the magazine was mailed to its subscribers, 80-year-old CEO Weins was so incensed about the piece that he insisted the editor fire the columnist. The editor refused, and even resigned in protest, as did several other columnists for the magazine. Weins had overrun copies of the magazine destroyed and refused to make copies available at the upcoming annual conference of the American Library Association. Normally the sample copies of the latest issue of *Wilson Library Bulletin* would be prominently displayed at the Wilson booth and given out to visitors. This time, however, conference goers were offered a memo written by Weins explaining why he took the actions he had. At a membership meeting at ALA a resolution was passed condemning the company for its "flagrant act of censorship." Other journals were also quick to condemn Weins' actions.

The Future of Wilson

Wilson saw its revenues steadily decline during the early 1990s. In January 1995 Wein announced his retirement. He was replaced as president and CEO by Harold Regan. After graduating from St. John's University and completing his military duty in Vietnam, Regan earned an M.B.A. in Labor Relations Law from Long Island University. He then became director of personnel and labor relations at Rheingold Breweries, Inc. He joined Wilson in 1974, in charge of human resources and corporate administration. He became a vice-president of the company in 1984 and two years later was elected to the company's board of directors.

Regan faced a difficult challenge in turning Wilson around and almost did not receive a chance to try. Thomson offered a bid of approximately $80 million to acquire the company in 1995, but the board turned it down. Regan began to bring in new people to help revitalize the company, established joint ventures with technology partners, and joined the competition in becoming more involved in full-text licensing. The company also launched a Web site, WilsonWeb, to make many of its products available through the Internet. As the company moved into the new century, it steadily improved its Web capabilities, adding PDF page images to its full text articles and refining its Web search capabilities and offering other enhancements. The days of operating as a virtual monopoly were long past. Whether Wilson would be able to successfully reinvent itself and find a way to compete against much larger and better financed rivals and still remain privately owned, was very much an open question.

Principal Divisions

WilsonWeb.

Principal Competitors

The Thomson Corporation; Reed Elsevier Group plc; ProQuest Company.

Further Reading

Barrett, William P., "Mousetrapped," *Forbes,* December 29, 1997, p. 58.

Lawler, John, *The H.W. Wilson Company: Half a Century of Bibliographic Publishing,* Minneapolis, Minnesota: University of Minnesota Press, 1950.

Nelson, Milo, "QE2 and WLB Run Aground," *Information Today,* September 1992, p. 30.

—Ed Dinger

Hanmi Financial Corporation

3660 Wilshire Boulevard, Penthouse S
Los Angeles, California 90010
U.S.A.
Telephone: (213) 382-2200
Fax: (213) 384-0990
Web site: http://www.hanmi.com

Public Company
Incorporated: 1982 as Hanmi Bank
Employees: 372
Total Assets: $1.78 billion (2003)
Stock Exchanges: NASDAQ
Ticker Symbol: HAFC
NAIC: 551111 Offices of Bank Holding Companies; 522110 Commercial Banking

Hanmi Financial Corporation is the largest Korean-American bank in the Los Angeles area, boasting assets of nearly $3 billion and 30 branch offices. The company operates as the holding company for Hanmi Bank, a community bank that conducts general business banking, offering commercial loans, U.S. Small Business Administration loans, commercial mortgage loans, real estate construction loans, and consumer lending and banking services. Hanmi Financial concentrates on serving the multi-ethnic population of Los Angeles, Orange, and San Diego counties, particularly those of Korean descent.

Origins

Hanmi Financial's operating entity, Hanmi Bank, was incorporated in August 1981, beginning what would be an impressive rise within Los Angeles's Korean-American business community. The bank officially began business more than a year later, receiving its license by the California Department of Financial Institutions in December 1982. Hanmi Bank opened on Olympic Boulevard, to the southeast of Koreatown, a Los Angeles community that served as the base for area's Korean-American community. By the end of the 20th century, Los Angeles's Korean-American community represented a substantial portion of the region's population, numbering 800,000 persons. Hanmi Bank was established to assist and to benefit from the growth of the large, yet closely-knit Korean enclave. Hanmi developed a reputation in commercial and small-business lending, but it would take years before its lending abilities were sufficient to attract widespread recognition.

Hanmi Bank began lending to and taking deposits from consumers at its original location on Olympic Boulevard, gradually gaining the clientele and financial resources to broaden its scope. The company grew by adding branches and by expanding the financial services it offered. Hanmi Bank opened its second branch on Olympic Boulevard, referred to as its Vermont branch, in the fall of 1985 and opened its third branch in the downtown section of Los Angeles the following spring. The company, like other Korean-American banks in the area, sought to cater to all of the financial needs of its community. The community, in turn, typically demonstrated a preference in dealing with banks run by those of Korean heritage, which provided a stable business base for a bank able to meet the various financial needs of its largely Korean clientele. Hanmi Bank took an important step toward developing a portfolio of services in the fall of 1988, when the company established a Small Business Administration department and began providing loans qualified by the U.S. Small Business Administration, an independent agency of the federal government. Before the end of the decade, the company added a fourth banking facility, opening a branch on Garden Grove Boulevard in the summer of 1989.

Hanmi Bank entered the 1990s set to experience a decade of profound growth. During this definitive era of development, the company was led by Benjamin Hong, a highly influential leader in southern California's Korean-American banking community. Before joining Hanmi as the bank's president and chief executive officer in 1988, Hong served as senior vice-president of First Interstate Bank and as the director of international finance at Northrup Corp., among various other executive banking positions. Hong, in his mid-50s when he arrived at Hanmi, spent six years at the bank, departing in 1994 to lead Nara Bancorp, one of Hanmi's chief rivals at the end of the decade. Although he only spent part of the 1990s at Hanmi, his influence over the company extended into the 21st century, as it did over much of Koreatown's banking community. Hong not only groomed

Company Perspectives:

The name "Hanmi" was formed by the combination of two Korean words meaning "Korean-American." From our inception, and to our very core, we are connected with the Korean-American community. We have grown with our community's support, and our community has grown with our help.

Hanmi's future executives during his tenure at the bank but also trained the principal executives of the community's other leading banks, presiding as the patriarch of the cast of chief executive officers competing for the hotly contested business of Korean-Americans at the beginning of the 21st century.

Hanmi rose to prominence during the 1990s, becoming the bank of choice for many Korean-Americans living in the greater Los Angeles area. The company's growth was underpinned by favorable conditions, as the immigrant population increased 35 percent in the 1990s, triple the rate for the population as a whole. Further, according to a Small Business Administration report, Korean-Americans were the most entrepreneurial of U.S. ethnic groups, averaging one business for every eight people. Hanmi, intent on participating in the growth of its mainstay community, grew by strengthening its reputation and by evolving into a more comprehensive financial institution through the expansion of the services it offered. Physically, expansion was minimal during the 1990s—only one new branch was established, a unit opened in 1992 on Western Avenue—but the company's services were broadened, enabling it to assist in and to profit from its community. In 1995, the company opened an automobile loan center, the same year its downtown branch, which set the benchmark for all Hanmi branches, exceeded $100 million in deposits. In 1997, the bank reached a financial milestone when its assets reached $500 million. The following year, Hanmi achieved the ultimate distinction. In April 1998, the company edged ahead of its closest rival, Pacific Union Bank, which was founded by a South Korean company in 1974, to become the largest Korean-American bank in terms of assets. After 16 years of well-executed development, the bank reigned as the region's biggest contender, but in the years ahead the company would feel pressure from a handful of competitors, each vying to capture Hanmi's leadership position.

Consolidation Begins in the Late 1990s

By the time Hanmi reached preeminence, the competition among the pack of Korean-American banks in southern California was beginning to intensify. Within several years, the banks would begin to consolidate, with the largest of the banks assuming a predatory posture, each poised to acquire its rivals. Hanmi joined the fray in September 1998 when it acquired First Global Bank. Based in Los Angeles, First Global owned three branches, controlled $44.9 million in loans, and held nearly $78 million in deposits.

At the time Hanmi turned to acquisitions as a means to achieve growth, the bank's former leader was guiding his company on an identical front. Benjamin Hong, in charge of Nara Bancorp Inc. for four years when Hanmi purchased First Global, was beginning his bid to surpass his former company. In 1998, Hong ordered the purchase of Korea First Bank in Flushing, New York, owned by Seoul-based Korea First Bank, the majority owner of Pacific Union Bank. The race to supremacy was just beginning in Los Angeles's Korean banking market as an era of coexistence among the banking firms gave way to a period of predation.

Hanmi pressed ahead with internal expansion before making its next move on the acquisition front. In 1999, the bank began offering mortgage loans after establishing a mortgage department in July. The following spring, Hanmi made the greatest geographic leap in its history by opening a branch in San Diego. Next, the bank's executives reorganized the company, giving it a corporate structure tailored for the period of consolidation that awaited. In March 2000, Hanmi Financial Corporation was incorporated as a holding company for Hanmi Bank. In June 2000, the reorganization was completed when Hanmi Financial Corporation became the holding company for Hanmi Bank.

Hanmi triggered a more aggressive acquisitive posture in the Korean-American banking community with an announcement in May 2001. The company announced it had agreed to purchase California Center Bank for $103 million, a deal that would give Hanmi $480 million in assets and make the company, with roughly $1.5 billion in assets, nearly twice as large as its closest competitor, Pacific Union Bank. In a June 11, 2001 article in the *Los Angeles Business Journal,* an unidentified industry source described the events leading up to the announcement, describing a bidding process that included Hong's Nara Bancorp. "Nara made several overtures to CCB (California Central Bank) for the purpose of acquiring it," said the industry source. "CCB contacted Hanmi, and Hanmi put in a bid that was driven by Nara's bid. In a lot of ways, that was a defensive move from Hanmi's standpoint. Both had courted CCB for quite a while, but Nara's overture forced CCB's hand."

The race to acquire was kindled by Hanmi's bid for California Central. Chung Hoon Youk, Hanmi's president and chief executive officer, realized the need to expand through acquisitions. In a June 11, 2001 interview with the *Los Angeles Business Journal,* Youk remarked, "Mainstream banks are coming into our market. To efficiently compete, we need to be bigger." Hong echoed the thought in a May 22, 2001 interview with *American Banker,* "Consolidation is the natural evolution to increase the competitiveness of larger banks. If there are any banks for sale, we would pursue them very aggressively." The leaders of several other Korean-American banks voiced similar strategies, creating a stir among industry observers who waited expectantly for the next big deal. The agreement to purchase California Central ended up falling through—a Hanmi spokesperson said California Central "got cold feet and abruptly got out of the negotiation process," according to the July 30, 2001 issue of the *Los Angeles Business Journal*—but the collapse of the deal only fueled bankers' interest in consolidation.

In the wake of the abandoned California Central acquisition, Youk and his management team expanded internally while they weighed their options on the acquisition front. In 2001, the year the company registered on the NASDAQ, Hanmi opened a

Key Dates:

1981: Hanmi Bank is incorporated.
1982: Hanmi Bank opens for business in December.
1988: Hanmi Bank begins providing Small Business Administration loans.
1995: Hanmi Bank establishes an automobile loan center.
1998: Hanmi Bank acquires First Global Bank.
2000: Hanmi Financial Corp. is formed as the holding company for Hanmi Bank.
2004: Hanmi Financial acquires Pacific Union Bank, its closest competitor.

branch on West Olympic Boulevard in Koreatown and an office in Irvine. Another branch, the company's Fashion District branch, was established in December 2003, but before the opening there were sweeping changes in the leadership of Los Angeles's Korean-American banking community. In little more than a week, three chief executive officers, all of whom had offices within three blocks of each other, resigned, vacating their posts in the midst of the market's consolidation. On April 21, 2003, the president and chief executive officer of Pacific Union Bank, Woon Seok Hyun, announced his resignation, effective May 22, 2003. Later that week, Hong announced he would resign from Nara Bancorp by the end of the year. On April 30, 2003, Chung Hoon Youk announced he was leaving Hanmi at the end of the week, resigning to fulfill his dream of becoming a professor.

While the other leading banks turned to the task of replacing their chief executive officers, Hanmi searched to fill its own leadership void. The company, in July 2003, selected Jae Whan Yoo, whose banking career encompassed nearly three decades of service, beginning in 1976 when Yoo began working for Bank of America in Seoul. During the 1990s, Yoo served in several senior management positions at the $22-billion KorAm Bank. Immediately before joining Hanmi, Yoo served as a director and board member of the $57-billion Industrial Bank of Korea.

New Directions in 2003

Not long after Yoo's appointment, Hanmi made an announcement that significantly altered the dynamics of Los Angeles's Korean-American banking community. On December 23, 2003, the company announced it had struck a deal to buy Pacific Union Bank, the second-largest Korean bank in the Los Angeles area. Pacific Union was put up for sale by its majority owner, Seoul-based Korea Exchange Bank, the previous month, whetting the acquisitive appetites of the Korean banks in the Los Angeles area. Hanmi entered into a bidding war with three other banks and emerged victorious, sealing an agreement to acquire Pacific Union's $1.1 billion in assets for $295 million in cash and stock. The effect of the Pacific Union acquisition outstripped the deal to acquire California Central by more than a factor of two, giving Hanmi assets of nearly $3 billion and significantly widening the gulf separating it from its competitors. The largest and second-largest banks had agreed to merge, promising a dominance that had to dishearten the other banks jockeying as consolidators. Hanmi stood to be the largest Korean bank in the Los Angeles area by far.

A little more than 20 years after first beginning business on Olympic Boulevard, Hanmi held sway as the premier Korean bank in the Los Angeles area. The acquisition of Pacific Union was completed in April 2004, giving Hanmi a tremendous boost to its stature and presenting its executives with the difficult challenge of integrating Pacific Union into its operation. The company announced it intended to close as many as seven branches that geographically overlapped with existing Hanmi branches. Hanmi, in a bid to further achieve efficiencies from the integration of Pacific Union, announced it would lay off between 100 and 150 employees and consolidate certain functions such as data processing. As the company addressed itself to embracing Pacific Union, its executives could look forward to steering the area's preeminent financial institution toward a promising future.

Principal Subsidiaries

Hanmi Bank.

Principal Competitors

Nara Bancorp Inc.; Saehan Bank; Wilshire State Bank; Center Financial Corporation.

Further Reading

Berry, Kate, "Korean Bank Bucks Tradition," *San Diego Business Journal*, March 22, 2004, p. 22.

Dougherty, Conor, "In Close-Knit Koreatown, Aborted Deal Creates Stir," *Los Angeles Business Journal*, July 30, 2001, p. 3.

——, "Korean Banks Seeks Strength with Mergers," *Los Angeles Business Journal*, June 11, 2001, p. 3.

"Hanmi Bank Acquisition," *Los Angeles Business Journal*, May 14, 2001, p. 38.

"Hanmi Financial Corporation Announces Selection of Jae Whan Yoo as CEO & President," *Internet Wire*, June 27, 2003.

Kuehner-Hebert, Katie, "L.A.'s Biggest Korean Bank Extends Lead," *American Banker*, December 24, 2003, p. 1.

——, "L.A.'s Korean Banks Facing Consolidation," *American Banker*, May 22, 2001, p. 1.

——, "Spare Change: L.A.'s Koreatown Is Splitsville for CEOs," *American Banker*, May 12, 2003, p. 5.

—Jeffrey L. Covell

Harpo Inc.

110 North Carpenter Street
Chicago, Illinois 60607
U.S.A.
Telephone: (312) 633-0808
Fax: (312) 633-1976
Web site: http://www.oprah.com

Private Company
Incorporated: 1986 as Harpo Productions, Inc.
Employees: 70
Sales: $314.5 million (2002 est.)
NAIC: 512110 Motion Picture and Video Distribution

Based in Chicago, and with additional offices in Los Angeles, Harpo Inc. is one of the most successful production companies in the history of entertainment, one of the largest black-owned companies in the world, and the brainchild of one of the television industry's highest-paid performers ever, Oprah Winfrey (Harpo is Oprah spelled backwards). With productions ranging from made-for-TV movies and miniseries, to feature films and books, a magazine, videotapes, and CDs, Winfrey's reign as the Queen of Entertainment has extended almost from the inception of the company, winning both her and her company and show numerous awards.

Background

Oprah Winfrey, the woman who would realize enormous success as the founder of entertainment giant Harpo Inc., had the most inauspicious of beginnings. The story of her success includes overcoming incredible odds with a singular determination that inspires her audience. Born in 1954 to teenage parents in Mississippi, Winfrey lived in terrible poverty on her grandmother's farm before moving to Milwaukee at age six to live with her mother. There, she was sexually abused by male relatives, and at the age of 14, Winfrey gave birth to a premature baby, who died shortly afterwards. After running away and being kicked out of a juvenile detention home because all the beds were filled, she was finally sent to Nashville to live with her father, Vernon Winfrey. A barber and businessman, Vernon provided the discipline that was lacking in his daughter's life, instituting a strict curfew and stressing the value of education. Under his guidance, Oprah quickly changed her life's direction.

Broadcasting in the Early 1970s

In 1973, at the age of 19, Winfrey was hired as a reporter by WVOL, a radio station in Nashville, and her broadcasting career was off and running. During this time, she went to Tennessee State University, where she majored in Speech Communications and Performing Arts. In her sophomore year (1975), she moved to WTVF-TV in Nashville, becoming the first and youngest African American woman anchor at the station.

In 1976 Winfrey moved to Baltimore, where she joined the staff of WJZ-TV news as a news co-anchor. Two years later, she became, in addition to her duties as reporter and anchor, the host of that station's program ''People Are Talking.'' In January 1984, Winfrey moved again, to Chicago, to host WLS-TV's program ''AM Chicago,'' a local half-hour talk show with sagging ratings, scheduled opposite Phil Donahue's top-rated show. One month after Winfrey became the host, the program had become the number one show in the city, and the producers gave Winfrey an extra half-hour for the show. In September 1985, they renamed it ''The Oprah Winfrey Show.'' Also that year, Winfrey would costar, along with Whoopie Goldberg, Danny Glover, and Rae Dawn Chong, in Steven Spielberg's movie *The Color Purple,* based on the novel of the same name by Alice Walker. Her poignant performance (and her first-ever acting experience) as Sofia would win her a nomination for an Academy Award and a Golden Globe Award for Best Supporting Actress. The following year, she would costar with Matt Dillon in *Native Son,* the second movie adaptation of Richard Wright's 1940 classic novel.

Incorporating in the Mid-1980s

Winfrey's love for the screen and her desire to bring quality entertainment projects into production were what prompted her to form her own production company, Harpo Productions, Inc., in 1986, with Winfrey as the chairman and Winfrey's agent, Jeffrey Jacobs, as the president and chief operating officer (COO). Early that year, Jacobs managed to buy the syndication

Company Perspectives:

Oprah Winfrey is most interested in concentrating on those topics that can actually help people improve their lives—shows on battered women and alcoholism, for example, or on building relationships with family members. This will both increase the power of the show and make people feel better about their lives.

rights to the show and began distributing it through King World Productions. On September 8, 1986, ''The Oprah Winfrey Show'' was televised nationwide. Less than a year later, the program was ranked the top syndicated talk show in the United States, pushing out longtime leader ''Donahue.'' In June 1987 the show received three Daytime Emmy Awards for Outstanding Host, Outstanding Talk/Service Program, and Outstanding Direction. In June 1988 ''The Oprah Winfrey Show'' was awarded its second consecutive Daytime Emmy Award as Outstanding Talk/Service Program. The show would remain the number one talk show for 12 consecutive seasons, receiving a total of 32 Emmys, seven of which went to the host. Also in 1988 Winfrey received the International Radio and Television Society's ''Broadcaster of the Year'' Award, making her the youngest person and only the fifth woman ever to receive the honor.

Harpo's first co-produced project was *The Women of Brewster Place,* a film released in 1989, in which Winfrey costarred with Paul Winfield, Robin Givens, and Moses Gunn, which recounted the lives of the female denizens of an inner-city brownstone, adapted from the Gloria Naylor novel. The film would later inspire a television miniseries of the same name. Other productions, such as *Kaffir Boy,* Mark Mathabane's autobiography of growing up under apartheid in South Africa, followed, as well as the 1998 feature film *Beloved,* based on the Pulitzer Prize-winning novel by Toni Morrison. Winfrey would spend ten years producing and would star in the film, directed by Jonathan Demme.

In October 1988, Harpo Productions made television history when it announced that it had assumed ownership and all production responsibilities for ''The Oprah Winfrey Show'' from Capitol Cities/ABC, making Oprah Winfrey the first woman in history to own and produce her own talk show. That year, the company spent $20 million to buy and renovate a huge, 100,000-square-foot television and film production facility located in downtown Chicago to house its headquarters, where ''The Oprah Winfrey Show,'' as well as other Harpo Entertainment productions, would be produced. When originally purchased, the old complex featured three stages, screening rooms, production offices, a darkroom, kitchen facilities, and indoor parking. The renovation added office space, a gym, a larger stage for Winfrey's daily show, and an updated look for the exterior of the old building.

In addition to her roles as television host and CEO of a production company, Winfrey found time for social causes and philanthropy. Committed to helping children of abuse, Winfrey initiated The National Child Protection Act and testified before the U.S. Senate Judiciary Committee to establish a national database of all convicted child abusers. On December 20, 1993, President Clinton signed into law the Oprah Bill.

During this time, Winfrey had formed a new division called Harpo Films. In 1995 ABC and Harpo Films announced a three-year agreement under which Harpo would produce six made-for-television movies for the network under the ''Oprah Winfrey Presents'' banner, extending the relationship between ABC and Harpo, which had already produced several miniseries, movies, and primetime specials for the network. The first title in the ''Oprah Winfrey Presents'' program was *Before Women Had Wings,* followed by the four-hour miniseries *The Wedding,* based on the Doubleday novel by Dorothy West, the last surviving member of the Harlem Renaissance. The company also optioned the rights to *The Keepers of the House,* a Pulitzer Prize-winning novel written by Shirley Ann Grau, chronicling the lives of a wealthy white Southern landowner, his black housekeeper, and their three children from the 1930s to the 1960s. Other projects in the pipeline for the company included adaptations of *Their Eyes Were Watching God,* based on a novel of the same name by Zora Neale Hurston, which was slated for airing in 2005.

In 1991, after eight years in syndication, Winfrey was at a crossroads both personally and professionally and began to think about retirement from the talk show industry, which had become characterized by scandal and theatrics. Instead, however, she opted to alter the focus of her show, moving from popular controversies to featuring poetry, music, literature, authors, and actors, as well as human issues such as dealing with the loss of a child, weight loss topics, and the like. The following year, Winfrey signed an unprecedented contract with distributor King World, extending her show through the end of the 20th century. Winfrey also became one of King World's largest shareholders, with more than a million shares to her name. At the conclusion of the 1995–96 television season, Winfrey was honored with the most prestigious award in broadcasting, The George Foster Peabody Individual Achievement Award. Winfrey also was recognized by *Time* magazine as one of America's 25 Most Influential People of 1996.

By that time, Winfrey was only the third woman in history (along with Mary Pickford and Lucille Ball) to own a major studio, and was personally worth an estimated $98 million. She also topped the *Forbes* list of the highest paid entertainers in the United States, bumping Bill Cosby out of the spot. In September 1996, Winfrey announced the formation of Oprah's Book Club, an on-air reading club, created with the idea of inspiring more Americans to read. All of the books Winfrey selected for the program became instant bestsellers, averaging over a million copies sold each.

At the start of the 1997–98 television season, Winfrey announced the creation of Oprah's Angel Network, a national effort encouraging her audience to do charitable work and make charitable financial contributions. One of the hallmarks of the Angel Network was The World's Largest Piggy Bank, a campaign that encouraged viewers to save their small change for a national fund to provide scholarships for college students; another was the volunteer work with Habitat for Humanity to build homes for the poor.

Total revenues at Harpo for 1997 reached $150 million, a 7.1 percent increase over the previous year. Also in 1997,

Key Dates:

1973: Oprah Winfrey begins her broadcast career as a reporter in Nashville.
1984: Winfrey hosts a morning talk show in Chicago, which will become ''The Oprah Winfrey Show.''
1986: ''The Oprah Winfrey Show'' earns three Emmy Awards.
1988: Harpo Productions assumes ownership and all production responsibilities for ''The Oprah Winfrey Show,'' making Oprah the first woman in history to own and produce her own talk show.
1996: Oprah's Book Club is formed.
2000: *O* magazine premieres.
2004: Harpo signs an agreement to extend The Oprah Winfrey Show through the year 2011.

Winfrey was named *Newsweek*'s ''Most Important Person'' in books and media, and TV Guide's ''Television Performer of the Year.'' She was also awarded a People's Choice Award for ''Favorite Television Performer.''

The Late 1990s and Beyond

The late 1990s brought some challenges to Winfrey and her company. A group of Texas cattle owners filed a lawsuit against her in 1998 alleging libel due to comments she made on her show about Mad Cow Disease. The trial was watched closely by First Amendment rights advocates worldwide, and the jury eventually found Winfrey innocent. While the lawsuit was ongoing, Winfrey took over a local theater in Amarillo, Texas, turning it into an impromptu set for her show.

In October 1998 oprah.com, an online web site co-developed by ABC Internet Group and Harpo Productions, was launched, allowing more input from Winfrey's huge following of fans. Two months later, Winfrey announced the creation of Oxygen Media, a new cable channel targeted at women. Joining the venture were big hitters in the entertainment world, including Geraldine Laybourne, Marcy Carsey, Tom Werner, and Caryn Mandabach. Other backers included America Online and ABC. By the end of the 20th century, ''The Oprah Winfrey Show'' claimed a viewership of some 20 million throughout the world.

In April 2000, Harpo joined forces with the Hearst Corporation to create the premiere issue of *O, The Oprah Magazine*—Oprah's lifestyle magazine for women. A 500,000-circulation rate base was planned for the bimonthly magazine, which went to a monthly issue later that year. Harpo and Hearst promoted the magazine as a personal growth guide for women ages 18 to 49. Oprah planned to appear on the cover of each issue, and begin and end each issue with a first and last word, exhorting readers to use their lives to ''make a difference in somebody else's.'' The magazine also included departments and columns on finance, personal growth, ''Phenomenal Women,'' dreaming big, and dream jobs. After the first issue debuted, editor in chief Ellen Kune resigned but cited family demands and denied any tension between herself and Oprah. Advertisers lined up quickly to secure ad space in the new magazine, proving the influence of the Oprah brand, characterized as intelligent, empathic, spiritual, and courageous.

By 2004, Oprah's talk show, boasting 23 million viewers, had been the top-rated daytime show nationwide for 17 years. As the show's contract with King World came to an end, Oprah suggested that she might leave the show. However, she eventually renewed the contract through the 2010–11 television season, planning to tape 140 episodes per year, with a final year consisting of 130 shows and celebrating the program's 25th anniversary. Oprah said that the renewed contract would give her company a chance to create and develop more projects and shows, as it had the very successful ''Dr. Phil'' show, starring psychologist and advice guru Dr. Phil McGraw.

Oprah, and Harpo Inc., continued to accumulate accolades from the business world. Harpo was ranked among *Black Enterprise's* ''Industrial Service 100,'' garnering notice as the largest business with majority African-American ownership. Oprah was also the first to receive the Bob Hope Humanitarian Award, presented at the 2002 Emmy Award show. In 2004, Oprah was awarded ''Favorite Talk Show Host'' at the 30th Annual People's Choice Awards, reflecting the enduring popularity of her show.

Principal Subsidiaries

Harpo Films, Inc.; Harpo Productions, Inc.; Harpo Video, Inc.

Principal Competitors

Martha Stewart Living Omnimedia Inc.; Lifetime Entertainment Services.

Further Reading

Albiniak, Paige, ''Oprah Wears Its Age Well,'' *Broadcast & Cable,* January 20, 2003, p. 47.

Borden, Jeff, ''A Secret Not Even Oprah Will Air: Declining Ratings,'' *Crain's Chicago Business,* August 14, 1995, p. 1.

——, ''A West Side Story: Oprah As Producer,'' *Crain's Chicago Business,* March 26, 1990, p. 19.

——, ''When Money Can't Cut It: Next on 'Oprah'!,'' *Crain's Chicago Business,* January 11, 1993, p. 9.

Coe, Steve, ''Winfrey Signs Film Deal with Disney,'' *Broadcasting & Cable,* November 6, 1995, p. 58.

Curry, Sheree R., ''Advertisers Line Up for Oprah Book,'' *Advertising Age,* October 25, 1999, p. S6.

Freeman, Michael, ''Oprah Winfrey's,'' *MEDIAWEEK,* March 21, 1994, p. 16.

''Harpo Scores First Non-Oprah TV Deal,'' *Crain's Chicago Business,* July 2, 1990, p. 1.

''King World Agrees to Pay $150 Million in 'Oprah' Deal,'' *Wall Street Journal,* September 25, 1998, p. B7.

Lloyd, Fonda Marie, ''Footprints in Time: 25 People Who've Blazed an Indelible Trail of Black Business Progress Since 1970,'' *Black Enterprise,* August 1995, p. 108.

McClellan, Steve, ''Upheaval at Harpo?,'' *Broadcasting & Cable,* October 31, 1994, p. 14.

Melcher, Richard, ''Next on Oprah: Burned-Out Talk-Show Hosts?'' *Business Week,* October 2, 1995, p. 64.

Melcher, Richard, and Kelley Holland, ''What Women Really Want?'' *Business Week,* December 7, 1998, p. 50.

Mullman, Jeremy, ''Oprah Winfrey, 50, Chairman, Harpo Inc.,'' *Crain's Chicago Business,* June 7, 2004, p. W84.

Nathan, Paul, "The Right Backup," *Publishers Weekly,* September 25, 1995, p. 16.

Noglows, Paul, "Oprah: The Year of Living Dangerously," *Working Woman,* May 1994, p. 52.

"Oprah, ABC Extend Pact," *Broadcasting & Cable,* October 23, 1995, p. 24.

"Oprah Magazine Editor Resigns," *Mediaweek,* June 5, 2000, p. 5.

"Oprah Reups with King World," *Broadcasting,* August 8, 1988, p. 37.

"Oprah: The Winner Who's Taking It All," *Broadcasting,* March 27, 1989, p. 35.

" 'Oprah' Staying at King World," *New York Times,* September 25, 1998, p. C17.

"Oprah Winfrey Renews Contract," *TelevisionWeek,* August 9, 2004, p. 4.

"Oxygen Media," *Wall Street Journal*, November 25, 1998, p. B12.

Schlosser, Joe, "King World Locks in Oprah," *Broadcasting & Cable,* September 28, 1998, p. 6.

Sellers, Patricia, "The Business of Being Oprah," *Fortune,* April 2002.

Shahoda, Susan, "Oprah Winfrey Buys Historic Chicago Film & Television Complex," *Back Stage,* September 30, 1988, p. 4.

"Spiritual Awakening," *Mediaweek,* April 3, 2000, p. 74.

Winters, Rebecca, "A Daytime Diva in the Jury Box," *Time,* August 30, 2004, p. 71.

—Daryl F. Mallett
—Update: Catherine Holm

Heijmans N.V.

Graafsebaan 13
's-Hertogenbosch NL-5248 JR
The Netherlands
Telephone: (+31) 73 528 91 11
Fax: (+31) 73 528 93 00
Web site: http://www.heijmans.nl

Public Company
Founded: 1923
Employees: 10,018
Sales: EUR 2.6 billion ($3 billion) (2003)
Stock Exchanges: Euronext Amsterdam
NAIC: 237310 Highway, Street, and Bridge Construction; 237110 Water and Sewer Line and Related Structures Construction; 237990 Other Heavy and Civil Engineering Construction; 531210 Offices of Real Estate Agents and Brokers

Heijmans N.V. has built a road to the number three position in the Netherland's construction industry, trailing only Koninklijke Volker Wessels Stevin and BAM. Headquartered in 's-Hertogenbosch, in the Netherlands, Heijmans owes its growth to a steady stream of acquisitions throughout the 1990s and into the 2000s, including Koninklijke IBC, completed in 2001, and the United Kingdom's Leadbitter, in 2003. Heijmans operates through four primary divisions. Homes & Offices encompasses the group's property development and home and office construction business, chiefly through subsidiaries Heijmans IBC Vastgoedontwikkeling and Heijmans IBC Bouw. Traffic & Transport, the company's historical activity, is chiefly operated under the Heijmans Infrastructure division, and specializes in the design, development, construction, and maintenance of roads and other transport infrastructure projects. Industry & Production includes Heijmans construction services for the industrial sector, and also manufacturers and distributes building materials, including prefab hulls, concrete, brickwork, roofing, and insulating plates. The company's fourth division is Heijmans International, which is leading the group's development beyond the Netherlands into Belgium, Germany, and the United Kingdom. The Netherlands nonetheless remains by far the group's strongest market, at 84 percent of its EUR 2.6 billion sales in 2003. Heijmans, along with others in the Dutch construction industry, has run afoul of the Netherlands' competition authorities, facing charges of price fixing, market sharing agreements, and other anti-competitive practices. In response, the company has developed a new charter for good conduct. Heijmans is listed on the Euronext Amsterdam Stock Exchange. Guus Hoefsloot was named chairman of the company in 2004.

Street Builder in the 1920s

Rosmalen native Jan Heijmans was just 20 years old when he went into business for himself as a street builder. Heijmans' first project was a contract for paving the road in front of the Den Bosch train station. Hampered by the difficult economic climate of the late 1920s and 1930s, and by the Nazi occupation of the country during World War II, Heijmans remained a small company. Yet Heijmans was also well-positioned to take advantage of the vast reconstruction needed in the Netherlands following the war. During this period, the company also extended its business beyond street-building into the general construction sector.

During the 1950s, Heijmans began participating in a number of international infrastructure projects, notably in Turkey and the Middle East. The company also grew through acquisition, buying up restoration and renovation specialist Koninklijke Van Drunen. Joining the company during this time were Heijmans sons Theo, Lambert, and Gerard—later joined by youngest brother Jan in 1966. Each was expected to start at the bottom levels of the company and work their way up to a position on the company's board of directors. Founder Jan Heijmans died at the age of 63. By then, he had decided to concentrate the company's activities in the Netherlands, where it began competing for national contracts. The company also extended its operations to cover a wider range of construction markets during this time. As part of that effort, in 1975 Heijmans acquired HBS Den Bosch, a move which brought the company into the distribution of building materials. HBS Den Bosch later grew into one of that sector's largest companies in the Netherlands.

Heijmans remained a modest-sized business, among many others in the highly fragmented Dutch construction industry

Company Perspectives:

As a company Heijmans wishes to make a significant contribution to construction in the countries in which it operates. Aspiring to operate as a full-service construction and property development company, Heijmans focuses on all of the activities in the value chain, from consultancy services and design to maintenance and management. The wealth of knowledge and experience that exists within the organization combined with the entrepreneurial skills that Heijmans is renowned for make Heijmans the obvious choice: innovative in its approach to the market and in its development of products and concepts, transparent to the parties that have an interest in the company, highly versatile in its range of products and services and concerned about its social environment. Heijmans is aware of its social responsibility and carries out its activities safely, with due concern for the environment and in accordance with the relevant legislation and regulations.

through the 1980s. Toward the end of that decade, however, the sector began making its first movement to consolidation, particularly in view of the coming single European market slated for 1992. Heijmans began positioning itself as a central player in the emerging market in the late 1980s with the naming of Joop Janssen as company chairman.

Under Janssen, Heijmans set itself a goal of topping NLG 1 billion in sales before the mid-1990s, a level that would place the company among the Netherlands' top construction groups. Janssen first set to work improving the company's margins, shifting the group's property development operations toward the middle and higher-end ranges. By the mid-1990s, the company had successfully improved its margins in its home building activities from less than 1 percent to as high as 6 percent. Janssen also led the company on an early wave of acquisitions.

Becoming a Dutch Leader in the 2000s

By the early 1990s, Heijmans had already outgrown its corporate structure as a family-owned company. In order to achieve further growth, the company required capital. Faced with the option of allowing itself to be bought up by a larger company, Heijmans instead chose to go public. In 1993, the company listed on the Euronext Amsterdam Stock Exchange.

The listing provided Heijmans with the capital to begin a steady series of acquisitions that lifted the company to the number three spot in the Netherlands by the turn of the 21st century. By 1994, the company had already achieved its objective, topping NLG 1 billion in sales that year. The company launched its buying spree in earnest in 1995, acquiring Noorlander Beheer and NV Algemene Ondernemingen VAG, adding more than EUR 90 million to its total annual sales. The company continued in 1996, adding such companies as Exters Beheer, Van Helvoirt Beheermij, Holding De Enk, and Vos en Teeuwissen. That year also marked a new extension outside of the Netherlands with the purchase of Belgium's BAB, or Belgische Asfalt- en- Betonmaatschappij.

These acquisitions on the whole shared similar traits in that nearly all were small, locally operating companies. Heijmans, which had adopted a decentralized, divisional structure in the 1970s, generally maintained that policy for its new acquisitions, leaving existing management in place. In this way, the company was able to complete its national network while remaining close to its local markets.

Larger acquisitions leading up to 2000 included Vebo Holding and Walcherse Bouw Unie in 1997; Verenigde Bedrijven Van Lee, a company with sales of EUR 63 million; Van Zwol Groep, with sales of EUR 45 million, in 1999; Van den Berg, a EUR 59 million company; and Verengide Hijbeek Bedrijven, with sales of EUR 33 million, in 2000. Also in 2000, the company continued its Belgian expansion, picking up that country's Van den Berg BV, which added its expertise in fiber optic cable construction and some EUR 45 million in sales.

By the end of 2000, Heijmans' annual sales had already topped EUR 1.5 billion, representing a 25 percent increase in just one year. Yet, while acquisitions provided some 10 percent of the rise in the group's revenues in 2000, organic growth remained the primary growth generator.

That situation changed dramatically in 2001, when the company announced its acquisition of family-controlled Koninklijke IBC. Like Heijmans, IBC was a major player in the Dutch housing market, with sales of some EUR 750 million per year. IBC also complemented Heijmans' Belgium expansion with its own operations in that country. The combined group now represented more than EUR 2.3 billion in revenues per year, placing it as number three in the Dutch construction market behind Koninklijke Volker Wessels Stevin and BAM. Following the merger with IBC, Jan Heijmans, the last of the founding family still serving on the company's board of directors, announced his decision to retire.

Heijmans made a new attempt to gain scale in the Netherlands, making a bid for the construction operations of rival Hollandsche Beton Groep (HBG), which was then in the process of negotiating a sale of its dredging business. The deal would have created one of the top five European construction groups. However, HBG ultimately rebuffed Heijmans' offer.

International Targets for the New Century

With little room for dramatic growth in the Netherlands, Heijmans began developing plans for further international expansion. Germany became the group's new objective in a so-called ''oil slick'' expansion strategy that limited the company's acquisition targets to nearby markets. Heijmans was also careful to choose only profitable companies for its expansion, preferring to leave purchases of struggling businesses to turnaround specialists. Consequently, in November 2001, the company first looked to pick up Martin Wurzel Baugesellschaft, based in Jullich, in Germany's North Rhine Westphalia region, but called off that acquisition early in 2002.

Instead, the company began discussion with the creditor banks of another German group, Phillip Holzmann, which had gone into bankruptcy proceedings. By May 2002, the company had reached an agreement to acquire the first of three companies from the Holzmann group—Dubbers-Malden, based in the Netherlands' Gelderland region along the German border—afterward purchasing Franki Grundbau in Hannover and Holz-

Key Dates:

1923: Jan Heijmans starts up a road building business in Rosmalen, the Netherlands.
1966: After completing several projects in Turkey and the Middle East, Heijmans decides to focus on its domestic market.
1975: Heijmans diversifies, with operations in all construction sectors, and acquires HBS Den Bosch.
1988: Joop Janssen is named company chairman and begins transforming Heijmans from regional company to one of the Netherlands largest construction companies.
1993: Heijmans goes public on the Amsterdam Stock Exchange.
1996: The company begins a new surge of international expansion, acquiring Belgische Asfalt-en-Betonmaatschappij (BAB) in Belgium.
2001: The company caps its acquisition drive with the purchase of Koninklijke IBC, making Heijmans the third-largest construction company in the Netherlands.

mann's Grafenwohr operation, near Nuremberg. These acquisitions placed Heijmans in a position to compete for high-rise construction contracts and engineered construction and public works projects in Germany's southern and western regions.

From Germany, Heijmans' eye turned to the United Kingdom. The company made a first entry into that market via a joint venture with CA Blackwell, forming Heijmans Blackwell Remediation Ltd., which focused on soil-cleaning operations in the United Kingdom and Ireland.

By then, Heijmans, along with other groups in the Netherlands' construction industry, faced scrutiny from the country's monopolies and competition authority, the Nma, which accused the company of, among other things, having paid off a French company in order to secure a construction bid. The company was also accused of price fixing and a number of other fraudulent practices and was ultimately fined some EUR 14 million. In response, Heijmans became one of the first in the industry to adopt a new standard code of practice.

In the meantime, Heijmans continued seeking out new acquisitions, the most significant of which was the Proper-Stok Groep, which added its revenues of EUR 150 million to the group in 2002.

At the beginning of 2003, Heijmans completed its entry into the U.K. market when it announced that it had agreed to acquire Leadbitter Ltd. That company, with operations largely in public sector projects—including schools, hospitals, leisure facilities and housing—had seen its revenues increase from just £300,000 pounds in 1993 to more than £110 million in 2002 under owner Bob Rendell. The addition of Leadbitter gave Heijmans a firm foothold for future expansion into the United Kingdom.

Joop Janssen retired from the company in September 2003, having built Heijmans from a small regional construction company to one of the Netherlands' top three leaders. Janssen had personally brought in his replacement, former HBG executive Guus Hoefsloot, whom he had met during the takeover discussions for that company. Under Hoefsloot, the company turned its attention toward achieving its next strategic objectives—stepping up the share of its international operations to at least 20 percent of revenues by 2008.

Principal Divisions

Heijmans International; Heijmans Nederland; Heijmans IBC; Heijmans Industry and Production; Heijmans Belgium; Heijmans U.K.; Heijmans Germany.

Principal Competitors

RWE AG; Consolidated Contractors Company; Nippon Oil Corporation; Bouygues S.A.; JFE Holdings Inc.; VINCI S.A.; China Civil Engineering Construction Corporation; United Engineers Malaysia Bhd.; Skanska AB; Hochtief AG; Royal BAM Group N.V.; Colas S.A.; Construtora OAS Ltda.; ENCOL S.A.

Further Reading

Bechtold, Kees, "Bouwconcern Hiejmans is na nieuwe fraude terug bij af," *Brabants Dagblad*, February 16, 2004.
——, "De laatste Heijmans neemt afscheid," *Brabants Dagblad*, May 4, 2001.
Board, Laura, "Heijmans Prepares to Bid for Rival," *Daily Deal*, June 27, 2001.
"Enhanced Focus in a Difficult Market," *Europe Intelligence Wire*, September 4, 2003.
"German Coup for Heijmans the Builder," *Algemeen Dagblad*, May 30, 2002.
"Heijman Walks away from Holzmann Deal," *Daily Deal*, June 26, 2002.
Leitch, John, "Heijmans Makes Move into UK with Leadbitter Purchase," *Contract Journal*, February 12, 003, p. 2.
Major, Tony, and Ian Bickerton, "Heijmans Chases Holzmann Units," *Financial Times*, April 23, 2002, p. 29.
Mees, Henk, "Groei Heijmans kent geen grenzen," *Brabants Dagblad*, March 15, 2002.
——, "The Netherlands Has Got Heijmans Measles," *Brabants Dagblad*, May 10, 2002.

—M.L. Cohen

Ideas today for the cars of tomorrow

Hella KGaA Hueck & Co.

Rixbecker Strasse 75
D-59552 Lippstadt
Germany
Telephone: (+49) (2941)38-0
Fax: (+49) (2941) 38-7133
Web site: http://www.hella.com

Private Company
Incorporated: 1899 as Westfälische Metall-Industrie Aktien-Gesellschaft
Employees: 22,811
Sales: EUR 3 billion ($3.5 billion) (2003)
NAIC: 336321 Vehicular Lighting Equipment Manufacturing; 333512 Machine Tool (Metal Cutting Types) Manufacturing; 335314 Relay and Industrial Control Manufacturing; 335122 Commercial, Industrial, and Institutional Electric Lighting Fixture Manufacturing; 335129 Other Lighting Equipment Manufacturing (pt); 336211 Motor Vehicle Body Manufacturing (pt)

Hella KG Hueck & Co. is one of the leading European suppliers of lighting accessories to the worldwide automotive industry with a global market share of roughly 10 percent. Key customers include car manufacturers Audi, BMW, Volkswagen, Ford, Opel, Volvo, Renault, Daimler-Chrysler, and Scania-DAF. Based in Lippstadt, Germany, the company operates more than 60 production facilities in 18 countries around the world. In addition to lighting for passenger cars, commercial vehicles, motorcycles, boats, and bicycles, Hella also makes automotive plug-in relays, sensors, and remote controls as well as whole front-end modules. Hella also supplies replacement headlights, rear lights, fog lights, and other lighting equipment to car dealers and garages, with this aftermarket business accounting for roughly 45 percent of total sales. Together with a number of strategic partners, Hella develops innovative electronic, lighting, and wiring systems for motor vehicles. The company is owned by the German Hueck family.

Growth in the Early 20th Century

While the Hueck family, a Westphalian family of industrialists, played a major role in Hella's history beginning in the early 1920s, it was the Jewish Windmüller family—one of the oldest non-aristocratic families in Westphalia with predecessors reaching back to the late 13th century—that determined the company's initial success. Company founder Sally Windmüller took over his father's feed store in Lippstadt, Westphalia, after his death in 1877 and expanded it slowly but steadily. By 1888, the business employed four people and sold its products to a growing number of customers outside the region. After marrying in 1891, Windmüller started making specialty metal products such as fittings and harnesses for horse carriages. In 1895, Windmüller acquired the machinery of Cöppius-Schulte-Röttger, a nearby manufacturer of lamps that had gone bankrupt. In the same year, a new factory building was erected in Lippstadt and 30 employees began to make lamps for horse carriages and bicycles.

Windmüller's new venture took off. By the late 1890s, the company had grown to a medium-sized business, employing 122 workers. To finance the company's further growth, Windmüller invited a handful of business partners to become investors in his enterprise. In 1899, the company was transformed into Westfälische Metall-Industrie Aktien-Gesellschaft—Westphalian Metals Industry Ltd. (WMI), a public limited company.

While fittings, harnesses and lamps for carriages, bicycle lamps, and lanterns remained a significant part of WMI's production in the early years, it was the rise of the automobile as a means of mass transportation that spurred the company's continuous growth throughout the 20th century. The first cars that cruised Germany's unpaved roads in the early 1900s had lamps similar to horse coaches: paraffin, candle, or gas lamps. However, lighting was not standard equipment in the already extremely expensive vehicles and was therefore considered a luxury. To drum up business, Windmüller, who was the first to own an automobile in his hometown, used his vehicle as a sales tool. He equipped his car with the lighting fixtures his company made and drove around town. He also visited trade shows in Germany and abroad, showing off WMI's products. Soon the

Company Perspectives:

Quality—from the rough design draft to the finished headlamp. Customer satisfaction based on quality in every aspect of a product is a decisive factor for success, now more than ever before. The corporate strategy of the international Hella Group has set its sights on three goals: First, offering customers first-class products and services at competitive prices. Second, providing employees with opportunities for dedicated, successful and personally satisfying work. Third, gaining and maintaining a position as a first-class automotive supplier.

company's product range also included bulb horns, which were crafted by some 40 instrument makers from Saxony that joined the workforce in Lippstadt. The company's newly established advertising department and traveling salesmen marketed WMI's products throughout Germany and Europe. By 1905, WMI was a thriving mid-sized business with almost 200 employees that exported its products to many Western European countries as well as to Hungary and Russia.

The year 1906 saw the first light bulb suitable for use in automobiles invented by German light bulb manufacturer Osram. Two years later, WMI began to make battery-powered electric lamps for cars, including sidelights, rear lights with a red glass cover, and license plate lights. In 1908, the company also launched an innovation of its own—the ''Hella'' headlight system. ''Hella'' doubled the range of illumination compared to the headlights used up until then and surpassed them by far in terms of the intensity of the light beam it put out. It became a bestseller. To keep up with the growing demand, a brand-new factory was built in 1911. WMI took on the production of additional accessories for carriages and cars, including whip holders, locks, ashtrays, and a variety of handles. By 1912, subsidiaries had been established in London, Paris, Vienna, Barcelona, Milan, and New York. During World War I, the company was required to manufacture war goods, including handguns, grenades, and other weapons components. While exports came to a sudden halt, WMI's revenues increased rapidly during the war but stood at roughly half of the prewar turnover in the following business year, 1918–19.

Although the company founder lost his majority stake in WMI soon after it became a stock corporation, Windmüller had never been challenged as the company's executive director by the other shareholders before 1920. His visionary leadership and skillful management was the driving force behind WMI's success. However, after Germany's defeat in World War I, Windmüller, determined to keep the business alive during a time of extreme shortages in raw materials and other supplies, approved the purchase of scrap metals, tools, and recyclable products from German army stocks, which was illegal. A regional law suit was brought against him in 1921 in which he was charged with causing damage to the state. Consequently, he was put on probation and was required to pay a heavy fine. Almost overnight, the company founder lost all of his business property, including his residence, as well as his post as executive director of the enterprise he had led to become one of Germany's leading manufacturers of lighting fixtures. Windmüller and his family moved to Berlin, where he ran WMI's sales agency for eastern Germany and Eastern Europe. However, the company founder retired soon after and died in 1930 at age 72, while his wife fled Nazi Germany and moved to Portugal shortly before the World War II broke out.

Battle for Economic Survival: 1920s–30s

After Windmüller's departure, WMI was left without a leader. Due to a number of share capital increases, the company's shares were widespread among various investors. This happened at a time when Germany slipped into serious political and economic turmoil. The government had financed the Great War by printing money and issuing bonds. After Germany's defeat, the national debt load became almost unbearable with the high reparations the country was obliged to pay. While the money printing presses kept putting out ever more bank notes, their value began to drop, then plunge, and finally vanish. Only a currency reform in the fall of 1923 was able to stop this economic nightmare which left a deep mark in WMI's balance sheets. With exports down to almost zero, the domestic market shrunk due to bankruptcies and the lack of purchasing power.

Meanwhile, there were two major groups of shareholders fighting over the company's management. One group consisted of bankers who tried to gain a majority share in WMI by raising the company's share capital in 1920. The other group was the Hueck family, whose company was a major supplier of semi-finished brass products to WMI. The CEO of the Eduard Hueck company, Oskar Eduard Hueck, had begun to buy WMI shares after World War I in order to gain more influence over a major customer. Hueck's brother Alfred, a lawyer, challenged the legality of the 1920 share capital raise and finally won the lengthy legal battle. By the time the case was settled, Oskar Eduard Hueck had acquired a 60-percent majority stake in WMI. In 1923, Hueck became chairman of the company's supervisory board. Three years later, he brought into the company Dr. Wilhelm Röpke, a cousin of his wife, who soon after became WMI's director of commerce.

While WMI's leadership conflict was resolved, the German economy went on a roller coaster ride. A short recovery after the introduction of the new *Goldmark* was followed by a severe plummet in sales in late 1925. To cut their losses, WMI's management decided to close the factory completely for the first two months of 1926. However, by the middle of the year demand picked up again and at times became so strong that the company was unable to fill all orders. Up until October 1929, when the stocks at the New York Exchange took a severe plunge, WMI's revenues and profits went up. The stock market crash turned the economic situation around once again. In the early 1930s, Germany, along with the rest of the world, slipped into a deep depression, resulting in a downturn on WMI's balance sheets. The German economy picked up speed again after Adolf Hitler and his National Socialist Party took over the political leadership. The Nazis pushed the country's motorization forward by abolishing the motor vehicle tax, which significantly boosted WMI's lamp sales for cars. In 1936, the company equipped the forerunner of the Volkswagen ''Beetle'' with lighting fixtures and horns. In the same year, the company secured an exclusive contract with the Ford Motor Company as their sole supplier for

Key Dates:

1899: Merchant Sally Windmüller founds Westfälische Metall-Industrie Aktien-Gesellschaft (WMI).
1908: The company starts manufacturing battery-powered lamps for automobiles.
1921: Windmüller leaves the company.
1926: The "Hella" brand logo is registered.
1936: WMI becomes an exclusive supplier to the Ford Motor Company.
1951: WMI is transformed into a private company.
1959: The company becomes a limited partnership.
1961: A first production facility abroad opens in Australia.
1986: The company is renamed Hella KGaA Hueck & Co.
1987: Dr. Jürgen Behrend becomes a personally liable partner.
1991: Hella introduces the xenon headlamp.
1992: The company takes on front-end module manufacturing for Volkswagen.
1999: A joint venture with the German Behr GmbH is formed.
2000: The company's first factory for lighting equipment in the United States begins operations.

headlamps, horns, and other accessories. By 1939, Ford had become WMI's single most important customer. However, the outbreak of World War II in the same year suddenly cut the company off from its export markets once again.

As the size of WMI's workforce fluctuated heavily during these chaotic times, so did the company's product range. In the second half of the 1920s, WMI supplied headlamps and break lights to major German automobile manufacturers. In 1926, the "Hella" brand logo was introduced and used for all of the company's products. WMI's range of accessories for cars was expanded to include rear reflectors, rear-view mirrors, cigar lighters, and windscreen washers. However, when the demand for these items dropped during the Depression years, the company started making household goods such as kettles, saucepans, cans, and spoons. During the early 1930s, more than one-third of WMI's sales were generated by products for bicycles, motorcycles, and motor boats. However, in the second half of the decade, the company manufactured an increasing amount of military goods. With the onset of World War II, WMI produced specially designed lamps for military motor vehicles as well as tools, measuring instruments, and ammunitions. After an increase from roughly 350 in 1925 to 830 three years later, the company's payroll dropped to 300 by 1930. However, by 1939 the number of workers had grown more than fivefold, reaching 1,700 in that year. As most men left the company to serve in the military, WMI replaced them with female workers and later with forced laborers, prisoners of war, and concentration camp prisoners.

Headstart after World War II

Fortunately, WMI's facilities survived the World War II in good shape. Only a few weeks after the war had ended in Germany, the military administration of the victorious Allied Forces allowed the company to resume operations. Besides a few measuring instruments that were confiscated, the company's machinery and other equipment were intact. While Germany's car manufacturers and other industries rebuilt their plants during the postwar years, WMI began to make whatever was in demand: coffee pots, crankshafts, bicycle lamps, alarm clocks, headlamps for the British Rhine army, a vegetable drying installation, a sugar beet processing plant, and crop spraying equipment. Starting out with the remaining 45 employees after the war, the company's payroll soon grew back to a considerable size, reaching 1,500 by 1948.

By that time, the German auto industry began to pick up speed again. The number of motor vehicles in the country grew tenfold in the decade following the currency reform, reaching roughly 1.7 million by 1959. During the 1950s, a considerable amount of WMI's sales to automakers came from Volkswagen, which equipped its VW Beetle with lighting fixtures from Lippstadt. However, WMI was also able to revive its prewar business relationship with Ford and delivered the first blinking turn signals for the Taunus and Goliath models in 1951. Between 1950 and 1955, exports roughly doubled. Besides the United States, the company also shipped their products to Austria and Switzerland, Benelux, and Scandinavia. In 1957, a Brazilian manufacturer acquired a license for a number of Hella products.

In 1950, Oskar Eduard Hueck's second son, Arnold, a physicist, joined the company. One year later, the Hueck family was able to acquire the remaining shares in WMI, which was then transformed into a limited liability company. In 1959, WMI's legal form was changed again. The company became a private limited partnership and Hueck's son became an executive general partner besides Wilhelm Röpcke. Röpcke's son Reinhard joined the company in 1957 and became an executive general partner nine years later.

The new management team led the company through the explosive growth years of the "German economic miracle." In the 1950s, the company's product range was expanded by windshield wiper and washer control systems and rotating beacons for police cars and special vehicles. To keep up with demand, production capacity was continually expanded during the 1950s. When the company ran out of space at its site in Lippstadt, new facilities were acquired in other German cities, including Todtnau, Paderborn, Hamm-Bockum-Hövel, and Bremen. A second building in Lippstadt was acquired in 1958. As a result, WMI's sales tripled during the 1950s, passing the DEM 100 million-mark in 1959 for the first time. In that year, the company's workforce had grown to more than 5,500.

International Expansion: 1960s–80s

The extraordinary growth of the "economic miracle" years in Germany, along with mass motorization in the 1960s, provided a solid basis for WMI's growth in the coming decades. However, it was the company's early international expansion that later enabled WMI to quickly follow its customers from the auto industry to wherever on the globe they set up shop. The first step into that direction was the establishment of WMI's first production plant outside of Germany, set up in 1961 in Australia. During the 1960s, 1970s, and 1980s, the company expanded its network of foreign subsidiaries into South America, Asia, and Western Europe. In 1986, WMI was renamed Hella KGaA Hueck & Co. After the Berlin Wall fell in 1989 and the Soviet Union dissolved in 1991, the company also expanded into the eastern part of Germany, the Czech Republic, Slovakia, and Slovenia.

By the mid-1990s, Hella had become a global supplier to some of the world's biggest automakers with roughly DEM 3 billion in sales and a workforce of 17,000. A worldwide network of production plants—often right next to the customer's assembly lines—made ''just in time'' delivery possible. However, competition among automakers was rising, resulting in constant pressure on their suppliers to lower cost. In order to compete as an original equipment manufacturer (OEM), Hella had to integrate not only its production regimen, but also its research and development efforts ever more closely with the new product development cycles of the company's customers. While these development cycles became shorter, the variety of designs increased. As a result, Hella's engineers had to do more development work while profit margins were shrinking.

The company responded by introducing new, innovative lighting solutions, by venturing into new markets, and by initiating a number of joint ventures with other suppliers to the auto industry. In 1991, Hella introduced the xenon headlamp at the International Auto Exhibition in Frankfurt. The innovative lamp, based on xenon gas, doubled the light output compared with conventional halogen headlights and cut the energy consumed by the lamp by one-third. Mass production of the xenon headlights for BMW began in 1992. Five years later, Hella launched the bi-xenon headlamp system with both a high and a low beam. Although more expensive than halogen lamps, xenon lamps significantly increased a driver's field of vision at night. To lower development and production cost for the growing variety of car models—each with a distinctly different headlight design—Hella's engineers came up with a modular system based on tiny light emitting diodes. This LED-technology allowed the combination of pre-produced light modules in an unlimited number of variations. First introduced in 1992 for break lights in a BMW convertible, the modular system was soon also used in other rear lights. In addition to use in passenger cars, Hella lighting fixtures were also employed in commercial vehicles and trailers, motorcycles, bicycles, boats, and trains. In 1996, the company spun off Hella Aerospace GmbH as an independent subsidiary for aviation lighting, which was later sold to Goodrich Corporation in the United States. Along with lighting fixtures, the company took on the production of other components, such as switches and relays, remote controls, electronic controls, and sensors.

Company Transformation in the 1990s and Beyond

To counteract dwindling profit margins in the auto lighting business, Hella's management decided to broaden its strategic focus and to transform the company from a component supplier to a systems partner. Because of its limited size and financial resources, Hella aimed to achieve this goal by forming strategic partnerships with other independent component suppliers. Beginning in 1992, a new Hella plant in eastern Germany put out whole front-end modules for a number of Volkswagen models. In the late 1990s, Hella launched two joint ventures for front-end modules—one in Argentina and one in Brazil—with its first licensee, Brazilian lighting component manufacturer Industrias Arteb. In 1999, Hella established a joint venture with the German Behr group, a supplier of air conditioning and motor cooling units and a long-standing business partner. The new venture developed a front-end module for the Czech car maker Skoda. In 2001, Hella entered two strategic partnerships that resulted in new joint ventures: one with Japanese lighting components manufacturer Stanley Electric and one with German automotive wiring specialist Leoni Bordnetz-Systeme. Two years later, Hella announced a strategic alliance with Japanese manufacturer Taiko Device Techno & Co. to jointly market automotive relays. Another joint venture was established with German automotive electronics manufacturer Micron Electronic Devices in 2004.

At the beginning of the 21st century, the company's OEM-business for automotive lighting components slipped into the red. However, Hella's aftermarket business remained a strong and profitable revenue source. To further strengthen this area, Hella introduced the ''Hella Service Partner'' system aimed at building strong loyalty to the company among German car repair shops. Dr. Jürgen Behrend, a personally liable partner since 1987 and Hella's CEO since 1993, saw the company's future in intelligent automotive systems that are developed, manufactured, and marketed by a network of independent suppliers such as Hella. While it remained to be seen if this strategy would secure the company's future as a family-owned enterprise in an increasingly consolidating market, it was clear that Hella's future heavily depended on the continued success of Europe's automakers.

Principal Subsidiaries

Hella Handel Austria GmbH; Hella NV/SA (Belgium); Hella Australia Pty Ltd.; Hella Arteb S.A. (Brazil); Hella North America, Inc. (United States); Hellamex, S.A. de C.V. (Mexico); Hella, Inc. (Canada); Hella Trading (Shanghai) Co.; Hella CZ, s.r.o. (Czech Republic); Hella Polska Sp. z o.o. (Poland); Hella A/S (Denmark); Hella A/S (France); Hella Limited (United Kingdom); Hella Ireland Ltd.; Hellanor A/S (Norway); Hella B.V. (Netherlands); Hella s.p.a. (Italy); Hella S.A. (Spain) Electra Hella's S.A. (Greece); Hella Hungária Gépjármüalkatrész-Kereskedelmi Kft. (Hungary); Hella Korea Inc. (HKI) (South Korea); Hella-New Zealand Limited (New Zealand); Hella-Phil, Inc. (Philippines).

Principal Competitors

Valeo SA; Visteon Corporation; Magneti Marelli Holding SpA; Robert Bosch GmbH; Delphi Corporation; Catalina Lighting, Inc.; Johnson Controls, Inc.; Koito Manufacturing Co. Ltd.; Ichikoh Industries Ltd.

Further Reading

Chew, Edmund, ''Hella Hopes Stanley Alliance Bolsters Business,'' *Automotive News*, October 22, 2001, p. 18H.

——, ''Hella: Modular Lighting System,'' *Automotive News Europe*, July 30, 2001, p. 19.

——, ''Hella Says Its Size Is Just Right,'' *Automotive News*, October 11, 1999, p. 32X.

——, ''Hella Sees Recovery in Lighting,'' *Automotive News*, October 7, 2002, p. 18.

——, ''Hella Works to Remain Family Owned Company,'' *Automotive News*, October 9, 2000, p. 24F.

Costa, Mara, ''Germany's Hella Forming Brazilian Venture,'' *Plastics News*, May 10, 1999, p. 13.

''Das Familienunternehmen ist für Hella eine zeitgemässe Form,'' *Frankfurter Allgemeine Zeitung*, June 18, 1999, p. 41.

''Germany's Hella Launches Production in 2nd Plant In Slovakia,'' *Europe Intelligence Wire*, September 29, 2003.

Graham, Alex, ''Suppliers Race to Dominate Adaptive Headlamps,'' *Automotive News*, December 16, 2002, p. 28A.

''Hella Forms Alliance with Japanese Auto Supplier,'' *Automotive Industries*, March 2003, p. 61.

''Hella kooperiert mit japanischer Stanley,'' *Frankfurter Allgemeine Zeitung*, September 12, 2001, p. 29.

100 Years of Hella: From a Lamp Workshop to Global Supplier to the Automobile Industry, Lippstadt, Germany: Hella KG Hueck & Co., 1999, 176 p.

Pryweller, Joseph, ''Partner Buys Hella's Share in N. American Lighting,'' *Automotive News*, October 12, 1998, p. 32E.

''UK: Hella Forms New Electronics Joint Venture,'' *just-auto.com*, June 14, 2004.

—Evelyn Hauser

HERCULES

Hercules Inc.

Hercules Plaza
1313 North Market Street
Wilmington, Delaware 19894-0001
U.S.A.
Telephone: (302) 594-5000
Fax: (302) 594-5400
Web site: http://www.herc.com

Public Company
Incorporated: 1912 as Hercules Powder Company
Employees: 5,116
Sales: $1.85 billion (2003)
Stock Exchanges: New York
Ticker Symbol: HPC
NAIC: 325520 Adhesive Manufacturing; 325510 Paint and Coating Manufacturing; 325998 All Other Miscellaneous Chemical Product and Preparation Manufacturing

Hercules Inc. manufactures specialty chemicals and materials used in the pulp and paper, food, pharmaceuticals, personal care, paints and adhesives, and construction materials industries. The company has four main divisions. Aqualon is a leading provider of products that are used to change the physical properties of water-based systems. FiberVisions holds a leading industry position as a producer of thermal bond polypropylene staple fiber and various textile fibers. Hercules' Pinova division is the only pale wood rosin derivatives producer in the world. Its Pulp and Paper unit supplies the industry with performance, process, and water treatment solutions. Challenges in the late 1990s and early 2000s forced Hercules to restructure and sell off various assets. The company successfully fought off a proxy fight waged by International Specialty Products Inc. in 2003.

Early History

The Hercules Powder Company was one of the several small explosives companies acquired by the Du Pont Company in the 1880s. By the beginning of the 20th century, Du Pont had absorbed so many of its competitors that it was producing two-thirds of the dynamite and gunpowder sold in the United States. In 1912, a federal court, citing the Sherman Anti-Trust Act, ordered Du Pont broken up. It was through this court-ordered action that the Hercules Powder Company was reborn, a manufacturer of explosives ostensibly separate from Du Pont.

The division of the Du Pont Company into Du Pont, Atlas Powder Company, and Hercules Powder Company was intended to foster competition in the explosives industry, but in reality the antitrust agreement allowed the connection between Hercules and the parent company to remain intact. The new company was staffed by executives who had been transplanted from the Du Pont headquarters across the street into the main offices of Hercules in Wilmington, Delaware. As *Fortune* magazine remarked in 1935, "The Hercules headquarters is in Wilmington and breathes heavily Dupontizied air." Not only did the Du Pont family retain a substantial financial interest in Hercules, but as late as 1970 the president of Hercules was related to the Du Pont family.

The Hercules Powder Company was set up as a fully developed business entity, complete with several explosives factories, a healthy segment of the explosives market, and a $5 million "loan" in its treasury. It operated successfully and made a profit from its very first year. Given its early advantage, it is not surprising that Hercules developed into one of the larger chemical companies in the United States.

Hercules began as an explosives company serving the mining industry, gun owners, and the military. In the first month of operation, its facility in Hazardville, New Jersey, exploded. Hercules had plants up and down the East Coast, however, and the loss of the Hazardville plant was not financially disastrous. Like other manufacturers of explosives, Hercules preferred many small plants to a few large ones. Due to the company's risks involved in product transportation, these plants were located in proximity to customers, rather than near the source of raw materials.

The company's first big break came in 1916 when Hercules signed a lucrative contract to supply Britain with acetone, a contract that stipulated, however, that no known sources of

Company Perspectives:

At Hercules, we strive to increase our competitive advantage through work process redesign; understand and meet our customer requirements; create more efficient and cost effective business processes throughout the Company; utilize and develop the skills and energy of all employees to achieve continuous improvement; reinforce our Company-wide applications knowledge and strength to add value through innovation to our customer's products and operations; focus on our business, manufacturing, application, and technology strengths in several key markets including pulp and paper, coatings and adhesives, food, pharmaceuticals and personal care, construction and hygiene; and strengthen the growth and profitability of our businesses through product and service extensions combined with small bolt-on acquisitions that fit closely with our product and market positions and make excellent short and long term financial sense.

acetone be used. Hercules sent ships out to the Pacific to harvest giant kelp, which was used to produce the solvent Britain needed. That same year, Hercules paid large dividends on its stock shares. The company also benefited from its sale of gunpowder to the army.

In 1920, Hercules began to manufacture cotton cellulose from the lint left over from cotton seeds once the high-quality cotton has been extracted. Cotton cellulose is a fiber that has hundreds of industrial uses. When treated with nitroglycerine it becomes nitrocellulose, important in the production of lacquers and plastics. Hercules quickly became the world's leading maker of cotton cellulose. This early effort at diversification in no way threatened Du Pont, which also manufactured nitrocellulose but only for its own uses.

Expansion into Naval Stores in the 1920s–30s

Throughout its history, Hercules proved successful at transforming a previously worthless substance into something useful. However, for every time Hercules succeeded in this kind of endeavor, there were prior failures. The company's foray into naval stores is an example of this. Naval stores is a term that refers to products derived from tree sap and recalls the early use of pitch to caulk boats. Gums, turpentine, and various adhesives are all referred to as naval stores. In 1920, a Senate committee predicted that the virgin pine forests from which high-quality naval stores were derived would soon be exhausted and that there would be no naval stores industry left in the United States. The management at Hercules saw, or thought it saw, a chance to corner the naval stores market.

Hercules joined forces with Yaryan, one of the few companies that distilled rosin from tree stumps rather than pitch. After buying rights to pull stumps and building a new rosin distilling plant, Hercules quickly became the world's largest producer of naval stores. However, a problem soon arose: the expected shortage of naval stores never materialized. Hercules, the Senate Committee, and the naval stores industry overlooked the fact that pine trees grow back rather quickly and that with proper management there would be plenty of pitch. Hercules was stuck with fields full of stumps, facilities to process the stumps, and a large amount of inferior turpentine. Turpentine derived from stumps is dark in color and hence unsuitable for some uses in finishing and painting furniture.

Endowed with sufficient capital (a legacy from Du Pont), Hercules was able to salvage its naval stores division by developing a paler turpentine and convincing its customers that wood (as opposed to pitch) naval stores were a bargain. In 1935, naval stores, the second largest of the company's investments, provided the smallest percentage of company sales. Naval stores and products derived from them eventually became a mainstay of the company, albeit one with slow growth. Not until the mid-1970s did the naval stores division emerge as a profitable endeavor. It was its explosives division which ensured the company's financial stability throughout the Depression.

By 1935, Hercules had five divisions: explosives, naval stores, nitrocellulose, chemical cotton, and paper products. Chemical cotton is made from the short fibers of cotton unsuitable for weaving which are then pressed into sheets and sold to industries as a source of cellulose. The paper products division began in 1931 with the purchase of Paper Makers Chemical Corporation, which provided 70 percent of U.S. demand for the rosin ''sizing'' used to stiffen paper.

At the time of America's entrance into World War II, Hercules was the country's largest producer of naval stores and the third-largest producer of explosives. Business was good during the war, and company coffers were stuffed with both legitimate and illicit gains. Hercules, Atlas, and Du Pont were convicted of a joint price-fixing scheme, and Du Pont was assessed a $40,000 dollar fine. Hercules' annual reports during this period concentrated on plans for reducing the company's staff once the war ended because the demands of the war had swelled the company's workforce to twice its previous size.

Postwar Diversification

Three years after the war ended, Hercules emerged from what a later industry analyst called ''a big sleep.'' The demand for nitrocellulose, paper chemicals, and naval stores, products Hercules was depending on in peacetime, was growing at a snail's pace. Sales were averaging an unremarkable $200 million a year. However, in the 1950s the company entered two markets it would later dominate: DMT and polypropylene.

Consistent with its ''waste not, want not'' approach to new chemicals, Hercules began to use waste gases from refineries to manufacture polypropylene, an increasingly important type of plastic. Polypropylene was used for food packaging, among other things. DMT is the chemical base for polyester fiber and was sold as a commodity to both chemical and polyester makers, including Du Pont. Besides these new products Hercules continued to look for new uses for naval stores from which it already derived chemicals used in insecticides, textiles, paints, and rubber.

Between 1955 and 1963, Hercules saw its sales double, due in large part to government contracts. In 1959, Hercules diversified into rocket fuels and propulsion systems for the Polaris, Minuteman, and Honest John missiles. Sales of aerospace equipment and fuels accounted for almost 10 percent of sales in 1961, 15 percent in 1962, and 25 percent in 1963. Throughout

Key Dates:

1912: Hercules Power Company is formed as a result of a court-ordered breakup of Du Pont.
1916: The company signs a contract to supply the Britain with acetone.
1920: The manufacture of cotton cellulose begins.
1959: Hercules diversifies into rocket fuels and propulsion systems.
1968: The company changes its name to Hercules Inc.
1989: Hercules acquires full ownership of the Aqualon Group.
1998: BetzDearborn Inc. is acquired.
2000: CP Kelco is formed.
2003: International Specialty Products Inc. wages an unsuccessful proxy fight.
2004: Hercules' stake in CP Kelco is sold.

the Vietnam War, Hercules continued to derive approximately 25 percent of its profits from rocket fuels, anti-personnel weapons, and specialty chemicals such as Agent Orange and napalm.

The man who presided over Hercules in the 1960s was George Thouron, a relative of the Du Ponts. He described Hercules' policy towards expansion as ''sticking close to profit-producing fields.'' A profile in *Fortune* magazine described Thouron as a quiet man. As the article noted, ''his main interest is in his prize Guernsey cattle.''

Thouron knew that the war in Vietnam would not last forever and undertook an ambitious reorientation of the company toward the production of plastics, polyester, and other petrochemicals. A contemporary observer remarked that ''few companies have expanded further or faster than Hercules Inc.'' Herculon, the company's synthetic fabric, had garnered almost 11 percent of the market for upholstery material. A water soluble gum called CMC also made money for the company. CMC was as versatile as Herculon was stain-resistant: it made its way into products as diverse as ice cream, embalming fluid, diet products, and vaginal jelly. ''From womb to tomb,'' one company pundit quipped. In 1968, the company changed its name from Hercules Powder Company to Hercules Inc.

The 1960s and early 1970s were an auspicious time for Hercules. Although the foray into plastics had required large capital and research expenditures that depressed earnings, Hercules remained a profitable and steadily growing company. High inflation actually helped the synthetics industry since the prices of natural fibers outpaced the cost of synthetics.

Overcoming Challenges in the 1970s

In 1973, however, Hercules learned that oil can be economically as volatile as nitroglycerin. The Arab oil embargo was a disaster for the petrochemical industry, and if the embargo were not enough, two years later the demand for naval stores crashed just months after a rosin shortage had been predicted. Hercules, anticipating a shortage, had ordered millions of pounds of rosin at twice the usual price. Around the time that the first rosin-laden ships arrived it became clear that Hercules' customers, also fearful of a shortage, were overstocked with the material. The rosin problem, combined with a drop in the fibers market, caused sales to drop 90 percent. Hercules stock went down 17 percent. The year 1975 was not a good one for most chemical companies, but the difficulties that Hercules experienced were more than its share.

Werner Brown was the company's president during these years. In 1977, he was promoted and chose Alexander Giacco to be the next president. Hercules had become an inordinately large company; its overheads and the size of its workforce were both excessive. In his first year as president, Giacco fired or forced into retirement 700 middle managers and three executive vice-presidents. Giacco had a managerial style that differed from that of the mild-mannered Brown, and his restructuring of the company reflected that. Giacco streamlined Hercules to make it more of a monarchy. ''He runs the company like an extension of himself,'' said one analyst. In order to stay in touch with the various divisions, Giacco invested in advanced communications equipment and computers. He also reduced the managerial levels between himself and the foremen from 12 to six. His position in the company is suggested by his description of a new product. ''I heard Gene Shalit say that candy wrapping paper made too much crinkling noise in movie houses. So we developed a candy wrapper that has no crinkle.''

In many ways, Giacco's plan for Hercules resembled the strategy his mentor, Werner Brown, mapped out in the early 1970s: shift from commodity to value-added (specialty) chemicals, get rid of unprofitable divisions, and derive more profits from existing product lines. Giacco also led the company away from its long-standing tradition of basic chemical research into more immediately profitable, application-based inquiry. After the fiasco in 1975, when two unrelated markets crashed at the same time, Hercules has experimented with the proper combination of products taking to heart the teachings of economist Charles Reeder: ''There's a simple two word answer to why chemical company earnings vary all over the lot. The words are 'product mix.' ''

This product mix had eluded Hercules. One thing was certain, however: Hercules' mix would not include petrochemicals. In 1975, 43 percent of its fixable assets were in petrochemicals, but within a decade these assets were liquidated. Naval stores, responsible in 1985 for a decline in operating profits, also fell out of favor. Demand for CMC, the binding agent, declined because the oil industry was not using it for drilling. Propylene fibers and film, food flavors and fragrances (relatively new ventures), paper chemicals, aerospace, and graphite fibers were included in the future recipe for success. The company's plants for manufacturing DMT and explosives were among two dozen sold between 1975 and 1985.

One shining success during this period was the growth of the stagnant polypropylene market. Hercules entered into a joint venture with the Italian firm Montedison, with whom it had previously teamed up in the pharmaceutical company Adria Labs, in order to take advantage of Montedison's newly developed, extremely efficient process for manufacturing polypropylene. Because the material cost so little, Giacco promoted the use of it to replace other materials in all types of products, including cigarette filters. It was mixed with polyethylene to produce a synthetic wood pulp replacement.

The company's herbicide business, maintained during the 1960s, was not profitable and its liabilities continued to haunt Hercules well after it closed the Reasor-Hill plant in Jacksonville, Arkansas. After five years of class action litigation on behalf of U.S. veterans exposed to Agent Orange, the company paid $18 million in 1983 to settle claims in the case. Its product's extremely low levels of the impurity dioxin, which was perceived to be the primary pathogen in Agent Orange, mitigated the portion Hercules paid of the total $180 million settlement with several other manufacturers.

The overall success in its aerospace business segued nicely with its line of graphite composites, which had steadily gained acceptance during the 1970s to become a mainstay in high performance aircraft. In 1986, Dick Rutan and Jeana Yeager flew the company's Magnamite carbon composites into the history book when their experimental craft the Voyager circled the globe.

Management Changes in the Late 1980s–90s

David Hollingsworth succeeded Giacco as chairman and CEO in 1987. After Hollingsworth sold the company's share of the HIMONT polypropylene venture to Montedison, Giacco resigned from the board, offended at the loss of a sure growth center. As in the last period after the top office changed hands, several poorly performing, mature businesses were sold off. Advanced materials and flavors and food ingredients—particularly natural additives based on pectin and carrageenan—were the focus of intended growth. In 1989, the company bought out Henkel KgaA's share of the Aqualon Group, formed in 1986 to make cellulose derivatives and water-soluble polymers.

The 1990s were another period of readjustment. Hercules impressed investors with its 1991 introduction of Slendid, a fat substitute made from citrus pectin (it would first be used in a commercial product five years later, in J.R. Simplot frozen French fries). However, its aerospace unit, which surged forward in the late 1970s, suffered serious setbacks in its program to develop engines for the Titan IV program. Overall, the year was a disappointing start for a new CEO, Tom Gossage. He would devote the next five years to enhancing the company's value to shareholders and succeeded in building Hercules' market value to nearly three times what it was when his tenure began (from $1.6 billion to $4.4 billion).

In 1996, another CEO, R. Keith Elliott, took the reins at Hercules. The company's successful composites business was sold to Hexcel Corporation that year. A new, lower cost carrageenan plant was being built in the Philippines. Hercules entered a joint venture of its polypropylene fiber business with Jacob Holm & Sons A/S (Denmark) in 1997. Earlier it had signed agreements to co-produce hydrogenated hydrocarbon resins in China with the Beijing Yanshan Petrochemical Company. One of the smaller CMC subsidiaries, Aqualon do Brasil, was sold to Grupo Gusmao dos Santos. In 1997, Hercules and its partner Mallinckrodt Inc. sold their Tastemaker venture to Roche for $1.1 billion.

Obstacles in the Late 1990s and Beyond

The late 1990s and early 2000s were tumultuous times for Hercules. The company made several moves that proved to be problematic. In 1998, the company acquired BetzDearborn Inc. for $2.4 billion and the assumption of $700 million in debt. The deal was designed to bolster Hercules' paper chemicals business and give it a foothold in the water and industrial process treatment industry. Benefits of the merger failed to reach fruition and company debt continued to grow. As such, Hercules decided to sell the water treatment portion of BetzDearborn to GE Specialty Materials for $1.8 billion in 2001. It also sold the majority of its resin assets that year.

In another move to reduce debt, the company joined with Monsanto Company to create CP Kelco, a venture that combined both Hercules' and Monsanto's food gums business. Problems arose, however, when CP Kelco filed $430 million suit against Pharmacia, the former parent company of Monsanto, claiming its food gum business was undervalued at the time of its formation in 2000. Hercules decided to sell its 28.6 percent stake in CP Kelco in 2004.

Management changes also continued during this time period. Elliott was replaced by COO Vincent Corbo in 1999. Corbo resigned in 2000, and the company tapped former CEO Gossage to lead the company. William Joyce was named CEO the following year. Joyce's short career with Hercules was marred by a vicious proxy fight waged by International Specialty Products Inc. (ISP) and its chairman Samuel J. Heyman. ISP held a 10 percent stake in Hercules and fought to gain control of the company's board of directors in 2003. Heyman was publicly critical of Joyce and the company's decision to sell BetzDearborn, claiming Joyce had not acted in the company's best interest. Despite ISP's efforts, Hercules managed to maintain control of its board and remained intact. Heyman resigned from the board and ISP eventually sold most of its shares.

In late 2003, Joyce left Hercules to head up Nalco Company. John K. Wulff was named chairman while Craig A. Rogerson assumed the role as president and CEO. The past several years had been challenging, but Hercules now operated as a slimmer, more efficient company and earned a profit in 2003—a good sign that business was back on track. Nevertheless, the company and its peers in the chemical industry faced several obstacles. Wavering demand and high energy and raw material costs would no doubt keep Hercules on its toes in the years to come.

Principal Divisions

Pulp & Paper; Aqualon; FiberVisions; Pinova.

Principal Competitors

Akzo Nobel N.V.; The Dow Chemical Company; Rhodia.

Further Reading

Brown, Werner C., and Alexander F. Goacco, *Hercules Incorporated: A Study in Creative Chemistry*, New York: Newcomen Society in North America, 1977.

''Building Successful Global Partnerships,'' *Journal of Business Strategy*, September–October 1988, pp. 12–15.

''Career Journal: Who's News,'' *Wall Street Journal*, October 7, 2003, p. B10.

Chang, Joseph, ''Battle for Hercules Heats up as Critical Annual Meeting Looms,'' *Chemical Market Reporter*, July 14, 2003, p. 1.

——, ''Hercules Victorious in Proxy Fight,'' *Chemical Market Reporter*, August 4, 2003, p. 2.

Corbo, Vincent J., ''Five Great Myths about Hercules,'' Merrill Lynch Chemical Conference, March 12, 1997.

Dyer, Davis, and David B. Sicilia, *Labors of a Modern Hercules: The Evolution of a Chemical Company*, Boston: Harvard Business School Press, 1990.

''Hercules Inc. Signals Proxy Fight May Lead to End of Sale of Itself,'' *Wall Street Journal*, April 13, 2001, p. B2.

Plishner, Emily S., and William Freedman, ''The Labors of Hercules,'' *Chemical Week*, August 23, 1995, pp. 29–31.

Rotman, David, ''Hercules Looks to Regain R&D Strength,'' *Chemical Week*, May 1, 1996, pp. 56–57.

Walsh, Kerri, ''Hercules to Sell BetzDearborn,'' *Chemical Week*, May 23, 2001, p. 17.

——, ''J. M. Huber Buys CP Kelco Stake From Hercules,'' *Chemical Week*, February 4, 2004, p. 25.

Wood, Andrew, and Jarret Adams, ''Hercules Buys BetzDearborn for $3.1 Billion,'' *Chemical Week*, August 5, 1998, p. 7.

—updates: Frederick C. Ingram; Christina M. Stansell

Holt and Bugbee Company

1600 Shawsheen Street
Tewksbury, Massachusetts 01876
U.S.A.
Telephone: (978) 851-7201
Fax: (978) 851-3941
Web site: http://www.holtandbugbee.com

Private Company
Incorporated: 1906
Employees: 40
Sales: $42 million (2003)
NAIC: 321912 Cut Stock, Resawing Lumber, and Planing

Holt and Bugbee Company is located some 30 miles north of Boston in Tewksbury, Massachusetts. It is a fifth generation, family-owned company that acts as a wholesale distribution yard with a 500,000-board-feet inventory of the finest hardwood and softwood lumbers. One of the largest suppliers of hardwoods in the Northeast, it also maintains branches in Mt. Braddock and Boyertown, Pennsylvania. Holt and Bugbee imports lumber from around the world to its facilities, where the wood is cut, shaped, seasoned, and distributed for specialized uses by architectural millwork shops, boat builders, cabinet makers, furniture makers, and lumber yards.

Holt and Bugbee deals in a variety of woods that serve a wise range of uses. Ash White, a shock resistant hard wood with bending qualities, is sold for use in making furniture, paneling, flooring, molding, sporting goods like baseball bats, and tool handles. Basswood is a soft, lightweight wood suitable for carvings, luggage, drawing boards, blinds, and picture frames. Another soft wood is Butternut, generally known as White Walnut. It is an attractive rich tan color and used to make paneling, kitchen cabinets, interior trim, molding, and millwork. Cherry is a hardwood that comes in wide range of color from a dark reddish brown to a creamy white, and finds a variety of uses in furniture, paneling, flooring, clock cases, and kitchen cabinets. Drawn from the same family as Lauan, Meranti Dark Red is a favorite wood for use in ship building and is also suitable for paneling, molding, interior trim, and millwork. Mahogany South American is a stable wood that ages to a rich golden brown on exposure and is popular for woodenware, furniture, cabinetry, and paneling. Holt and Bugbee also offers Maple Hard Sugar, a relatively hard and heavy wood that is suitable for a number of uses, including furniture, woodenware, paneling, flooring, and interior trim. Soft Maple lacks the hardness and strength of Hard Maple but is suitable for many of the same uses, if strength and hardness are not as essential, as in the manufacture of some types of furniture, paneling, and molding. One of the most popular hardwoods in recent years is Red Oak, which is both attractive and strong and is readily available in the United States. It is used widely in furniture, flooring, cabinets, paneling, and interior trim. White Oak has some of the same traits as Red Oak, but its close grains makes it water resistant, offering greater protection from fungi and insects. It is used in marine applications and is also popular in furniture, paneling, flooring, molding, millwork, and interior trim. Yellow Poplar is a versatile soft wood that is suitable for paint-grade work and is used to make interior trim, store fixtures, drawer sides, molding, and millwork. American Black Walnut offers a warm, rich appearance and comes in a range of colors and grain ranges, making it ideal for fine furniture, jewel boxes, and cabinetry as well as paneling, flooring, molding, and interior trim. Holt and Bugbee also offers Teak, ideal for marine applications such as boat decking and trim. It is also used in the construction of fine furniture, paneling, and flooring.

The company's main 24.5-acre facility includes nine dry kilns with a capacity of 1,000,000 board feet, a 20,000-square-foot automated grading station able to accommodate 30 width and length selections, and a 70,000-square-foot automated machining facility. Holt and Bugbee employs a computerized laser system that is able to increase yield and minimize wood waste, a high-speed molder production facility, an on-site tooling shop, and a computerized milling optimizer that can detect wood defects and automatically determine and execute the proper number of cuts to maximize yield. Holt and Bugbee maintain a ten-person sales team that covers the United States from Maine to as far south as Virginia and as far east as Ohio.

19th Century Origins

Holt and Bugbee was established in Winchester, Massachusetts, in 1825 by John Cutter when he opened a sawmill to rough-cut Mahogany logs. At the time, New England saw mills

Company Perspectives:

Like many longstanding New England firms, the company started business with a simple trade and over the past 176 years has adapted its function to survive in an increasingly complex and demanding world.

relied on the supply of local timber, which was quickly being stripped, either by clearing for agricultural uses or by cutting for lumber and fuel. Area mills grew to rely on coastal schooners delivering native lumber from other parts of the United States, supplemented by the occasional shipment of exotic hardwoods from the Caribbean islands, Africa, and South America. These supplies were acquired in trade for the products produced by New England's growing industries, such as textiles and shoes. Cutter relied on a more mundane product that he used to arrange trade with a sea captain: block ice wrapped in seaweed, which would be transported to South America and traded for rough Mahogany logs. Over the next 25 years, Cutter's yard prospered, expanding beyond Mahogany to include other hard and soft woods. He was joined in business by his son-in-law, Stephen Holt, in 1850, and together they ran the company, known as Cutter & Holt, until Cutter's death in 1860. Holt took on a new partner, John Bugbee, and the company was renamed Holt and Bugbee. A family member of Bugbee, a nephew named George Tousey, became involved in the business in 1895. The company moved to Boston and was incorporated in the state of Massachusetts in 1906. Then, in 1911, it moved the operations to Charlestown, Massachusetts, the company's home for the next six decades.

John Bugbee assumed the presidency of the firm, a position he held for decades and did not relinquish until his death in 1928. All told, he worked at Holt and Bugbee for nearly 70 years. He was succeeded as president by George Tousey, who headed the company for the next 21 years. When Tousey died in 1949, Osmund O. Keiver took over as president, but after just four years he was replaced by Tousey's widow. She ran Holt and Bugbee for five years before retiring in 1958 and turning over the reins to her son-in-law, Roger Curtis Pierce. Born in Boston, he graduated from Boston Technical High School and Hebron Academy before attending Boston University. With the advent of World War II he joined the Army Corps of Engineers, serving in India and Burma. He married Mary Tousey and in 1950 went to work for her family's business.

Relocation in the 1960s

In the mid-1960s, Charlestown began to undergo redevelopment, and Holt and Bugbee elected to moved out of Boston to Tewksbury, Massachusetts, 30 miles north. In 1967, the company relocated to a five-acre site in Tewksbury that offered a larger warehouse and yard storage capabilities. The company also installed a state-of-the art warehousing and lumber handling system. More importantly, however, Tewksbury was well situated, close to Interstate 93 and 495 and Route 128, making Holt and Bugbee more accessible to the entire New England market. Delivery trucks would now be able to quickly reach metropolitan Boston and the suburbs west of the city as well as Salem in forty minutes and the entire Worcester area in less than hour.

By the time Holt and Bugbee celebrated its 150th anniversary in 1975, it added greatly to its new home. The company's operation now covered ten acres and included complete planning and milling facilities, housed in a new 15,000-square-foot steel building, which included planers, moulders, gang rips saws, band resaw jointers, and cut-off saws. Shed space was increased from the initial 25,000 square feet to nearly 50,000 square feet. Holt and Bugbee was well known as one of the best equipped wholesale lumber yards on the entire East Coast. It handled more than 30 species of hardwood and softwood, serving such markets as boats, musical instruments, architectural millwork, and furniture. The company also enjoyed a strong business supplying lumber to New England schools for use in woodworking in industrial arts and vocational educational training programs.

Holt and Bugbee enjoyed one of its strongest periods of growth during the 1980s. The growing demand for its products led to further need for kiln capacity. As a result, the company increased its number of kilns to nine, possessing a capacity of one million board feet, which provided an additional benefit. Holt and Bugbee had always offered hardwoods in certain thicknesses—8/4, 10/4, 12/4 and 16/4—as specialty items, but now these thicker sizes became part of the standard product line. During the 1980s, the company placed greater emphasis on service. Because many customers needed to sort to width and length in hardwoods, the company built a 20,000-square-foot automated grading system, capable of 30 width and length selections. The call for machined products also grew. Twenty years earlier Holt and Bugbee began to offer the machining of Hardwood lumber as a customer service, the demand of which steadily grew. To meet the need, the company added a 70,000-square-foot machining expansion that included the most sophisticated woodworking machinery available. Other improvements to the yard included the 1983 installation of an industrial boiler and Pneumafil dust collection system, which were fueled by wood waste of the milling operation. An increase in business also meant an increase in personnel. In 1987 the company added a second floor to its office accommodations.

The 1990s and Beyond

In May 1990, Roger Pierce died in his sleep at the age of 68, and his wife, Mary, succeeded him as president of the firm. During her tenure Holt and Bugbee expanded beyond Massachusetts for the first time. In 1993, the company bought ten acres of land in Mount Braddock, Pennsylvania, located south of Pittsburgh. A year later, a lumber yard operation opened on the site. Mount Braddock was well situated for Holt and Bugbee's business, located close to important sources of North Appalachian hardwoods, including some of the world's best Cherry. The facility would include an automated sticking facility, three air dying sheds (with a 300,000 board-feet capacity), six dry kilns (with a 350,000 board-feet capacity), an automated grading and sorting facility, planer, rip saw, rail siding and container loading services, and an inventory of two million board feet of lumber.

Mary Pierce stepped down as president in 1995, replaced by her son, Phillip T. Pierce. In 1999, the company established

Key Dates:

1825: The company is founded by John Cutter.
1850: Stephen Holt, Cutter's son-in-law, joins the company.
1860: Cutter dies, John Bugbee joins company, which is renamed Holt and Bugbee.
1906: The company is incorporated.
1967: The company moves to Tewksbury, Massachusetts.
1994: Hold and Bugbee begin operations in Mt. Braddock, Pennsylvania.
1999: Operations are established in Boyertown, Pennsylvania.

Holt and Bugbee Hardwoods in Boyertown, Pennsylvania, located some 40 miles northwest of Philadelphia. It was a smaller facility than the ones in Tewksbury and Mount Braddock, offering just milling services, but it included a 38,000-square-foot warehouse and an inventory of 500,000 board-feet inventory of lumber. The operation was strategically located, allowing Holt & Bugbee to better serve customers in the mid-Atlantic region.

As Holt and Bugbee entered a new century, just 25 years short of its bicentennial, it remained very much a family business, with a number of relations holding key positions. As it had done when John Cutter traded ice for Mahogany, the company continued to import hardwoods from around the world, as well as stocking wood native to the United States. At the same time, the company stayed current with the latest technologies while maintaining a tradition of craftsmanship, kept abreast of customer's changing needs, and positioned itself to enjoy continued prosperity.

Principal Subsidiaries

Holt & Bugbee Hardwoods; Holt and Bugbee Export Co., Inc.

Principal Competitors

Higgins Lumber Company; Mac Beath Hardwood Company; Luthier's Mercantile International, Inc.

Further Reading

"Holt & Bugbee—Definitely Not Run of the Mill," *National Hardwood Magazine*, October 1988.

—Ed Dinger

Hong Kong Dragon Airlines Ltd.

Dragonair House
11 Tung Fai Road
Hong Kong International Airport
Lantau
Hong Kong
Telephone: (852) 3193-3193
Fax: (852) 3193-3194
Web site: http://www.dragonair.com

Private Company
Incorporated: 1985
Employees: 2,544
Sales: HKD 10 billion ($1.28 billion) (2003 est.)
NAIC: 481111 Scheduled Passenger Air Transportation; 481112 Scheduled Freight Air Transportation; 481211 Nonscheduled Chartered Passenger Air Transportation; 481212 Nonscheduled Chartered Freight Air Transportation; 488119 Other Airport Operations; 561520 Tour Operators

Hong Kong Dragon Airlines Ltd., better known as Dragonair, is Hong Kong's second largest airline. Founded in the mid-1980s as a charter operator, the airline has evolved from an independent startup to a well-connected regional force. Dragonair flies a young fleet of Airbus jets to about 30 destinations in Asia. More than three million people fly the airline every year. Its cargo operations extend as far as Europe and the Middle East. China National Aviation Company Ltd. (CNAC) is the company's largest shareholder (43.29 percent). CITIC Pacific Ltd. (28.50 percent), Cathay Pacific Airways Ltd. (17.79 percent), and Swire Pacific Ltd. (7.71 percent) also have significant holdings.

Company Takes Wing in 1985

Hong Kong Macau International Investment Company was formed by Hong Hong investors in 1984. Backers included the family of textile tycoon Chao Kuang-piu. According to the *Christian Science Monitor,* the purpose of the group was to demonstrate confidence in Hong Kong's future after the scheduled turnover of the colony from Great Britain to the government of the People's Republic of China. Mainland China investment vehicles controlled 40 percent of Dragonair's shares.

The group established Hong Kong Dragon Airlines Limited, or Dragonair, in 1985. Hong Kong shipping executive Sir Yuekong Pao was named Dragonair's chairman. Pao invested $7.7 million of his own money in the venture. Stephen H. Miller was the company's general manager.

Flight operations began in July 1985 with a Boeing 737 flight between Hong Kong and Kota Kinabalu, Malaysia. The first flights were charters to China and tourist destinations in other Asian countries.

Dragonair was the first local competition for Cathay Pacific Airways Ltd. in forty years. (Another new player, Air Hong Kong, focused exclusively on freight. It was later acquired by Cathay.) Dragonair announced the scope of its ambitions in January 1987 with the order of two long-range MD-11 aircraft. However, it was not able to gain the scheduled routes it needed to compete effectively. Y.K. Pao sold his holdings to the Chao family in 1989.

Changing Hands in 1990

CITIC Pacific Ltd. (part of PRC-owned China International Trust & Investment Corp.), Swire Pacific Ltd., and Cathay Pacific (itself backed by Swire) acquired an 89 percent stake in Dragonair in 1990. The family of Dragonair chairman K.P. Chao reduced their holding in the company from 22 percent to 6 percent. *Airline Business* reported that Cathay and its parent company Swire Pacific paid HKD 343 million ($44 million) for their combined 35 percent stake.

The change in ownership was followed by a period of cooperation between British-backed Cathay, Mainland China authorities, and Dragonair. Cathay transferred its routes to Beijing and Shanghai to Dragonair in March 1990. Dragonair continued to fly to secondary destinations in the region, including Dhaka, Bangladesh; Kagoshima, Japan; and Pattaya and Phuket, Thailand.

Cathay also gained the right to manage the smaller airline for fifteen years. Dragonair leased a Lockheed L-1011 Tristar from

Company Perspectives:

With its international flight crew and traditional Asian hospitality on the ground and in the air, Dragonair is aiming higher to provide a pleasurable and comfortable flying experience.

Cathay Pacific for service to the mainland, which became the focus of its route development. Dragonair was provided access to Cathay Pacific's reservation systems. Within a few months, Dragonair's monthly passenger count doubled to 60,000.

In 1992, Dragonair bought a 30 percent holding in Hong Kong ground handling company International Aviation Services (IAS), later Hong Kong International Airport Services, Ltd. (HIAS). The remaining shares were acquired in 1994.

Dragonair began shifting to an Airbus fleet in 1993 with the arrival of a half-dozen mid-sized A320s. Widebody A330s were added to the fleet in 1995.

By the mid-1990s, Dragonair was flying to 20 destinations, including 14 in China. It carried more than one million passengers a year and operated a fleet of nine planes. The airline was believed to have been profitable by 1991 and reported earnings of HKD 722 million ($93 million) in 1995. A planned flotation was shelved, however.

China National Aviation Corporation (Group) Ltd. (CNAC Group), the civil aviation unit of the Chinese government, acquired a controlling interest in Dragonair in 1996. (Before this, CNAC had begun to set up its own competing carrier, to be called China Hongkong Airlines.) The 35.86 percent stake cost HKD 1.97 billion. (CNAC later raised its holding to 43 percent). CNAC chairman Wang Guixiang was subsequently named chairman of Dragonair, replacing one of the founders, Chao Kuang-piu. Also in 1996, Dragonair formed a maintenance and repair joint venture with Dah Chong Hong.

A period of expansion followed the CNAC investment. Dragonair opened new routes and acquired new equipment. In the spring of 1997, both Dragonair and Cathay Pacific temporarily grounded their new Airbus 330 jets due to problems with the Rolls-Royce Trent 700 engines.

With CNAC backing, Dragonair was poised to capitalize on increased traffic to Mainland China after the time of the July 1997 transfer of sovereignty. The opening of Hong Kong's new Chek Lap Kok in April 1998 was another factor in favor of expansion. Asia was seen as one of the world's leading growth areas in aviation demand—at least until the Asian financial crisis hit later in the year. This setback was only temporary, and the region was soon leading forecasts for both passenger and cargo growth. Cathay Pacific veteran Stanley Hui was named Dragonair CEO in 1997 after seven years with the airline.

Cargo Operations Grow after 2000

Dragonair moved into a brand-new headquarters at Chek Lap Kok airport in the end of June, 2000. It also unveiled new

Key Dates:

1985: Dragonair is established.
1990: CITIC Pacific, the Swire Group, and Cathay Pacific acquire an 89 percent stake.
1996: CNAC acquires a 36 percent interest, which is later upped to 43 percent.
2000: A new company headquarters opens; cargo service to Europe is launched.
2005: The company plans to enter the U.S. cargo market.

uniforms and a new advertising campaign, as well as its own frequent flyer program, dubbed ''The Elite.'' Dragonair joined the regional frequent flyer program Asia Miles in September 1999 and the JAL Mileage Bank in June 2001.

In the summer of 2000, Dragonair began flying dedicated freighters on routes to Shanghai, China, and Europe and the Middle East (Hong Kong-Dubai-Amsterdam-Manchester), using leased Boeing 747s. Cargo service to Osaka was added in May 2001. Dragonair also bought two 747s, which were delivered in 2001. A cargo route to Xiamen, China, opened in 2002. Dragonair also began freight and passenger service to Taipei, Taiwan, in July of that year. This brought Dragonair into competition with Cathay Pacific again for the first time in a dozen years. At the same time, Cathay Pacific filed for permission to once more fly directly to the Chinese mainland.

Dragonair's net profits rose 60 percent to HKD 540 million in 2002. By this time, reported *Aviation Daily,* cargo operations accounted for 30 percent of revenues. Freight volume increased nearly fifty percent in 2002, to 20,095 tons.

The airline's fleet expansion continued in 2003 despite the war in Iraq. This was due to an apparently insatiable market for travel to and from Mainland China and Taiwan. However, the SARS threat forced the airline to temporarily reduce its flight schedule by 63 percent in the spring of 2003. The bird flu crisis caused a similar disruption a year later.

In November 2003, Dragonair began a scheduled service to Bangkok and the next month joined China Southern Airlines in a codeshare arrangement for Hong Kong-Guangzhou traffic. The airline began flying to Tokyo's Narita Airport in April 2004. Codeshare flights for several destinations were operated in partnership with Air China beginning in February 2004.

The passenger market rebounded in 2004, driven by newly affluent Chinese tourists. Dragonair increased frequencies and scrambled to hire additional flight attendants to meet demand.

Cargo continued to see consistent growth. Dragonair began operating a Hong Kong-Shanghai freight route on behalf of DHL in June 2003. Dragonair used a leased Airbus A300 freighter to start a cargo service to Nanjing in June 2004. A second daily European loop, to Frankfurt and London, followed a month later. In mid-2004, the carrier had five Boeing 747 freighters and 26 Airbus passenger airliners.

A route to Sydney was scheduled to open in the second half of 2005. Manila, Philippines, and Seoul, Korea, were other anticipated destinations. Dragonair also planned to begin service to the United States in 2005, at first with cargo flights. The airline was planning to more than double its freighter fleet to nine Boeing 747s by 2008.

Principal Subsidiaries

Dragonair Holidays; Hong Kong International Airport Services Ltd. (HIAS); LSG Lufthansa Service Skychefs (31.94%); Hong Kong Airport Services Ltd. (HAS) (30%); Dah Chong Hong-Dragonair Airport GSE Service Ltd. (DAS) (30%); Das Aviation Support Ltd. (DSL) (30%); Wise Counsel Ltd. (WCL) (30%).

Principal Competitors

Cathay Pacific Airways Ltd.; China Airlines Ltd.; CR Airways Ltd.; EVA Airways Corporation.

Further Reading

Bailey, John, "The Dragonmaster," *Flight International*, May 12, 1993, p. 29.

Barling, Russell, "Dragonair Freighter Spree Targets US," *South China Morning Post* (Hong Kong), May 7, 2004, p. 3.

——, "Dragonair Plots New Europe Loop," *South China Morning Post* (Hong Kong), February 20, 2004, p. 2.

Bangsberg, P.T., "Dragonair Boosts Airbus Fleet; Two A320s Ordered, Five More Optioned," *Journal of Commerce*, October 30, 1996, p. 3B.

Berfield, Susan, "A Plane Tale of Caution," *Asiaweek*, May 29, 1997, p. 1.

Dennis, William, "Dragonair Launches Narita Service with Tourism Campaign," *Aviation Daily*, February 2, 2004, p. 5.

Done, Kevin, "SARS Wreaks Havoc on Asian Airlines," *Financial Times* (London), April 12, 2003, p. 19.

"Dragonair Fleet Expansion Goes According to Schedule," *Aviation Daily*, April 9, 2003, p. 5.

Evans, David, "Dragonair Lifts Fleet as Freight Demand Soars," *South China Morning Post* (Hong Kong), Bus. Sec., October 6, 2000, p. 2.

Ionides, Nicholas, "Dragonair Snubbed as CNAC Continues Its Dogfight with Cathay," *South China Morning Post* (Hong Kong), Bus. Sec., March 25, 1996, p. 8.

Lee, Isabel, "China Tourists Lift Dragonair," *South China Morning Post* (Hong Kong), June 19, 2004, p. 5.

Lewis, Paul, "All Change," *Flight International,* May 28, 1997, p. 31f.

Lo, Joseph, "Carriers Hit Turbulence," *South China Morning Post* (Hong Kong), September 17, 2002, p. 1.

Kristof, Nicholas D., "Dragonair: A Gnat That Roars," *New York Times,* March 9, 1987, p. D10.

Mackey, Michael, "Growing Up," *Air Transport World*, November 2000, p. 112.

Ng, Eric, "Dragonair to Fly to Sydney Next Year," *South China Morning Post* (Hong Kong), June 1, 2004, p. 2.

Page, Paul, "Flying Dragon: Hong Kong's Younger Airline Isn't Afraid of Competition, and Dragonair Has an Expansion Plan to Prove It," *Air Cargo World*, November 2002, pp. 26f.

Putzger, Ian, "Bigger Dragon: While Passenger Trade Has Been Falling, Hong Kong's Dragonair Has Been Planning a Big Freight Expansion," *Air Cargo World*, July 2003, pp. 18f.

Rosenberg, Barry, "Dragonair Aims to Breathe Its Own Fire," *Overhaul & Maintenance*, December 2001, p. 31.

Smith, Patrick, "Hong Kong Airlines Vie for the China Trade," *Christian Science Monitor*, Bus. Sec., August 27, 1985, p. 20.

Tabakoff, Nick, "Airlines' Expansion Reaches for the Skies," *South China Morning Post* (Hong Kong), New Era Life Sec., July 1, 1997, p. 47.

Thomas, Geoffrey, "Lucky Dragon: Hong Kong's Second Airline Finds Opportunity, Success in the China Market," *Air Transport World*, June 2002, pp. 32+.

"Under Their Wings," *Economist*, May 21, 1994, p. 75.

Whitaker, Richard, "Second Strings," *Airline Business*, April 1992, pp. 38+.

——, "Taming the Dragon; Freight Fortunes," *Airline Business*, August 1990, p. 44.

Willoughby, Jack, "A Free Market?," *Forbes*, March 23, 1987, p. 158.

—Frederick C. Ingram

In-Sink-Erator

4700 21st Street
Racine, Wisconsin 53406
United States
Telephone: (262) 554-5432
Toll Free: (800) 558-5712
Fax: (262) 554-5712
Web Site: http://www.insinkerator.com

Wholly Owned Subsidiary of Emerson Electric Company
Incorporated: 1938 as In-Sink-Erator Manufacturing Company
Employees: 1,000 (est.)
Sales: $341 million (2003 est.)
NAIC: 335228 Other Household Appliance Manufacturing; 333120 Construction Machinery Manufacturing

Racine, Wisconsin-based In-Sink-Erator is the world's largest manufacturer of food waste disposal units and hot water dispensers. The company has a sales and service presence in more than 80 countries, and produces millions of disposal units every year. In-Sink-Erator produces eight models of food disposal units, which range from ⅓ horsepower to 1 horsepower and are priced from $50 to $250. In-Sink-Erator products are available through wholesalers as well as such retail outlets as Ace, Tru Serv, The Home Depot, Lowe's, and Menard's.

1930s Origins

In-Sink-Erator originated from an innovative approach to a classic inconvenience. In 1927, John W. Hammes invented the first food waste disposer in his basement workshop. As the story goes, Hammes was inspired to create a more convenient way to dispose of food waste after he saw his wife wrapping food scraps in newspaper before throwing them into the waste can. Standing over the sink, he envisioned a means of shredding food scraps into tiny pieces, so that they could be carried away through the drain.

Born in Iowa in 1895, Hammes worked as a farmer and then a carpenter before becoming a building contractor in Racine, Wisconsin. He oversaw new construction as well as projects to transform old churches, factories, and other buildings into modern retail stores and apartment buildings. At one point, some 85 percent of Racine's apartment construction was attributed to Hammes. Hammes applied for his architect's license from the state of Wisconsin in 1931 and served as Racine's consulting architect from 1933 to 1935. Thus, before his emergence as an appliance industry pioneer, Hammes had already made a significant impact on the city of Racine.

After producing an initial food disposal unit in his basement, Hammes made arrangements with the owner of a local machine shop to use the facilities for 25 cents an hour, so that he could produce decent prototypes. According to an article in the August 7, 1955, *Racine Sunday Bulletin:* "The owner asked if he knew how to run metal working machines, and without a moment's hesitation, Hammes replied yes. As soon as the owner left the room, John began trying different levers and dials. In just a few minutes, he knew how to run a lathe."

Eleven years of testing and development followed the creation of Hammes' initial disposal unit. According to the same *Racine Sunday Bulletin* article: "As the years went on, he made different models and tried them out in his own kitchen sink. The house in which they were living at this time had a cesspool in the back yard, and John would put on his hip boots and wade in the ground waste to check the size of the particles after grinding in the hand-made disposer." On August 27, 1935, Hammes obtained U.S. Patent No. 2,012,686 for his Garbage Disposal Device.

Eventually, Hammes was ready to introduce his food disposer to the general public. Along with his two sons, Quinten and Ever, Hammes established the In-Sink-Erator Manufacturing Company in 1938. The company set up shop in a small facility on Clark Street and produced 52 disposal units during its first year. From the very start, the new company was challenged to convince cities and towns that its product would not cause problems for municipal sewer systems. In fact, many communities banned the device until its impact on sewage systems could be determined.

In-Sink-Erator's growth was gradual during the 1940s due to the initial slow rate of disposal adoption, the fact that the

Company Perspectives:

Our sales force has always been aimed at the customer and our management team has always been focused on the industry because we think it's the right thing to do. We don't want to just look at ways of making more disposers—we want to help make the industry a better place. That commitment has been evident during our entire history.

company could not advertise because a significant share of its resources were devoted to capital expenditures, and the eruption of World War II. Aside from manufacturing disposal units for hospital ships, In-Sink-Erator's attention was focused on making defense parts during the war years.

Following the war, In-Sink-Erator was able to resume consumer sales of food disposal units. As the economy boomed, so did the company's success. As an early write-up explained, "progress was made almost immediately. Many cities modified their codes. In addition, others passed ordinances requiring disposers, since in their research, these communities found the disposer to be of great help in getting rid of garbage at lower cost and with improved sanitation."

Postwar Development

When electric motors were difficult to find during the mid-1940s, due to the war effort, In-Sink-Erator decided to manufacture its own. Previously, the company had purchased and modified motors from another manufacturer. Eugene Wieczorek, who joined the company as a teenager in 1941 and later became vice-president of advanced planning, bet John Hammes $1 that he could design a better motor in-house. He won the bet, and the company soon gained the ability to make close-coupled motors for its own use and for other companies. In fact, In-Sink-Erator once supplied fractional horsepower motors used in some of the earliest garage door openers. However, the company later decided to concentrate its efforts within the plumbing field. In-Sink-Erator soon added an automatic reverse feature to its disposals, which served to make them last longer.

By the late 1940s, Hammes' idea had caught the attention of other manufacturers. By this time, 18 other firms were producing food disposal units. These competitors sought to capture a share of a convenience appliance market that was burgeoning along with the growing number of women in the work force. In-Sink-Erator responded with its own marketing efforts, including a fleet of pink station wagons that were piloted by the company's salespeople. The wagons made it possible for reps to tote 45-pound disposal units with them as they made calls on plumbers and plumbing inspectors in various cities.

An important differentiating factor for In-Sink-Erator was the company's distribution channel. Unlike competitors, which sold disposal units to appliance dealers, In-Sink-Erator sold its products exclusively through plumbing contractors—a point that was emphasized on the exterior of its pink wagons. "Casting our lot with the plumbers was a turning point," explained long-time Sales and Marketing Vice-President Robert M. Cox in *In-Sink-Erator: The First 50 Years*. He noted, "Our consistent relationship with the plumber over the years has been, in my mind, the single key to our being able to outdistance our competitors."

In-Sink-Erator started the 1950s by moving into a new, larger facility. The additional capacity was needed as the company created a commercial division to serve restaurants, as well as such institutions as hospitals. As In-Sink-Erator expanded during the 1950s, it faced growing national competition from the likes of Whirlpool, General Electric, Waste King, and KitchenAid. In order to compete, the company added a direct sales force in 1952 and formed a network of authorized independent service representatives in 1954.

Just as his company was poised for explosive growth, John Hammes died in 1953, at the age of 57. It was around this time that In-Sink-Erator began to struggle with several quality problems as well as the growing costs of production. Rather than risk everything John Hammes had built, measures were quickly taken to turn things around. Ev Hammes challenged the company to produce a new disposer of high quality that would cost less to make. The result was In-Sink-Erator's Model 77 disposer, the first in the industry to include a five-year parts warranty.

Along with the development of new products, the company continued to advance on the marketing front through national advertisements. The first In-Sink-Erator print ad campaign aimed at the consumer marketplace began in 1956. Ads included the tag line, "Darling, you're much too nice to be a garbage collector," and appeared in such national magazines as *Vogue*. On the television front, In-Sink-Erator reached out to the nation with commercials featuring George Burns and Doris Day.

Explosive Growth and Expansion in the 1960s

The 1960s were a time of remarkable growth for the food disposal industry in general, and In-Sink-Erator in particular. By 1960 the industry was selling approximately 750,000 units annually. That year, some 75 communities required disposers nationwide, including Beverly Hills, California; Columbus, Ohio; Denver, Colorado; Detroit; and St. Paul, Minnesota. Amidst this growing rate of adoption, In-Sink-Erator made it more convenient to install or replace its disposers. The company's Quick Lock mounting system was introduced in 1960 and quickly became a standard feature in future models, giving the company a design edge over its competitors.

The industry's rapid growth led to physical expansion at In-Sink-Erator, which again moved to larger facilities in Racine. In 1963, In-Sink-Erator experienced its second unexpected leadership loss in ten years when President Quinten A. Hammes died. Hammes and his father were remembered for their pioneering roles within the industry. Interestingly, in 1963 In-Sink-Erator discovered that one of the original 52 disposal units produced by John Hammes in 1938 was still in working condition.

During the second half of the 1960s, the company was led by Chairman Ever J. Hammes and President George E. Shoup. In 1966, the company secured a major client when it began producing Kenmore disposal units for Sears Roebuck and Company. The deal made In-Sink-Erator the world's top food disposal manufacturer, accounting for one of every three units produced. Moreover, as In-Sink-Erator grew, the company gained greater control over the quality and availability of parts

Key Dates:

1927: John W. Hammes invents the first food waste disposer in his basement workshop.
1935: Hammes obtains a U.S. patent for his Garbage Disposal Device.
1938: Hammes establishes the In-Sink-Erator Manufacturing Company.
1945: Company focuses on making defense parts for the war effort.
1952: Facing national competition, the company adds a direct sales force.
1966: In-Sink-Erator secures Sears Roebuck as a client and becomes the world's top food disposal manufacturer.
1968: Emerson Electric acquires In-Sink-Erator.
1973: In-Sink-Erator acquires H&H Precision Products and enters the hot water dispenser market.
1978: In-Sink-Erator accounts for half of all food disposer units sold in the United States.
1980s: In-Sink-Erator begins marketing dishwashers.
1993: The company produces its 50 millionth food waste disposer.
2001: Annual sales reach an estimated $341 million and the company produces about 75 percent of all food disposers worldwide.

needed to manufacture its disposers. Following the decision to manufacture its own motors during the 1940s, In-Sink-Erator introduced a stamping operation in 1966, and added aluminum die casting capabilities in 1969.

A defining moment in In-Sink-Erator history took place in 1968, when Emerson Electric acquired the company. A *Fortune* 500 company, St. Louis-based Emerson was a world leader in the areas of appliances and tools; electronics and communications; heating, ventilation, and air conditioning; industrial automation; and process control.

Amidst continued growth in the industry, In-Sink-Erator developed its Badger line of disposal units in 1969. This inexpensive, reliable product line was targeted at the new residential construction market and was made possible by capital investment in new tooling and manufacturing equipment.

Market Leader: 1970–90s

As part of Emerson Electric, In-Sink-Erator saw its sales double from 1968 to 1973. That year, the company acquired H&H Precision Products and entered the hot water dispenser market. In addition, it also began manufacturing trash compactors. By the early 1970s, In-Sink-Erator enjoyed a strong market for food disposers. In 1972 alone, 2.7 million units were sold by the industry, with an estimated 30 million units in place throughout the United States.

In 1972, an important leadership change took place when John A. Rishel was named president of In-Sink-Erator. A long-time appliance industry executive, Rishel remarked on the reason for In-Sink-Erator's success in a profile of Racine's companies: "This company has been uncommonly successful because of its people," he explained, adding, "Nowhere else have I ever seen such teamwork, craftsmanship, care, sales expertise, service and follow-through. It has built an industry as well as a company."

In 1974, In-Sink-Erator captured one-third of the market and strengthened its leading position among disposer manufacturers. The following year, company sales doubled from 1973 levels, and within three years In-Sink-Erator models accounted for half of all food disposer units sold in the United States. As of 1978, the company employed approximately 800 workers and had expanded its manufacturing plant to cover 388,000 square feet.

By the 1980s, the food disposal appliance industry had evolved considerably over previous decades. Advancements in technology enabled manufacturers to produce units that were more reliable and efficient, quieter, and more affordable. In addition, food disposers were achieving international adoption at an increasing rate. At In-Sink-Erator, product evolution was evident in the 1980 introduction of the company's Classic model, which it dubbed "a super premium food waste disposer." By 1986, In-Sink-Erator achieved an enviably low product failure rate. Among the company's disposals that were under warranty, failures occurred at a rate of only 0.8 per 1,000. Following its success with food disposers and trash compactors, In-Sink-Erator also began marketing dishwashers during the 1980s.

During this time, In-Sink-Erator formed a relationship with home improvement retailer Lowe's and thereby increased its retail presence. As the decade unfolded, the company also began forging relationships with wholesale distributors and was able to achieve strong increases in both sales and market share. By In-Sink-Erator's 50th anniversary in 1988, an estimated 75 percent of all contractors included garbage disposals in new residential homes. By this time, D.L. Seals had been named president of In-Sink-Erator.

Although the company did not release sales figures, industry observers in the early 1990s estimated that the company's revenues totaled about $200 million. A major development occurred in 1993, when the company produced its 50-millionth food waste disposer. In honor of the milestone, a ceremony was held and the unit was put on permanent display in the company's lobby.

It also was in 1993 that In-Sink-Erator was preparing to release a computer-controlled home water purification system called Aquabest, marking its first new product introduction in about 15 years. Development of the new system, which carried a retail price tag of $700, involved the acquisition of 12 patents, and cost millions of research dollars, had begun in 1989.

In-Sink-Erator scored a major win on the retail front when it secured The Home Depot as a client. During the 1990s, some 80 communities throughout the United States made food waste disposers mandatory. In addition, more than 80 countries had adopted the appliances, as foreign markets discovered the environmental advantages of food waste disposal.

2000 and Beyond

In late 2000, In-Sink-Erator began test piloting an Internet procurement system with some of its distributors, with a goal of launching it in early 2001. The e-commerce system was in addition to electronic data interchange (EDI), which In-Sink-Erator had used for some time. The new Web-based system gave distributors the ability to place and check on the status of orders, review product specifications, and more.

As of the early 2000s, In-Sink-Erator continued to place a premium on its workers. In addition to cross-training them to keep their work as interesting as possible, the company also offered tuition reimbursement for those wishing to pursue college or vocational courses. In addition, In-Sink-Erator developed its Skills Center, which offered courses that sought to expand employees' knowledge and increase their ability to gain promotions. Among the courses offered at the center were blueprint reading and computer systems and software, as well as such fundamentals as mathematics.

The company also carried on the tradition of quality established by John Hammes many years before. In the November/December 2000 issue of *ASA News*, In-Sink-Erator Marketing Communications Manager Jim Magruder said: ''We subject our disposers to conditions they'll never see in a lifetime of use. We run diluted acid through them for days at a time to measure corrosion, and we constantly turn them on and off to make sure the motors work properly and don't burn out. We also challenge their grinding capability with large quantities of frozen steak bones and wood cubes. If a unit doesn't pass the test, we investigate to determine the problem and then immediately make necessary design or production adjustments.''

According to independent reports, by 2001 In-Sink-Erator had estimated annual sales of $341 million and produced about 75 percent of all food disposers worldwide. In addition to its own branded line of appliances, the firm produced disposers that were marketed under other manufacturers' names. Heading into the mid-2000s, Jerry Ryder was In-Sink-Erator's president. The company was well-positioned for growth, with a market presence in 80 countries and subsidiaries in Australia, Canada, and the United Kingdom.

Principal Competitors

Anaheim Manufacturing Company; General Electric Company.

Further Reading

Fauber, John, ''Tapping a Market: Firm Here Develops Water Purifier,'' *Milwaukee Journal Sentinel*, November 7, 1993.

In-Sink-Erator: 50 Years of Quality, Racine, Wisc.: In-Sink-Erator, 1988.

''In-Sink-Erator Manufacturing Co.,'' *Racine Sunday Bulletin*, August 7, 1955, p. 20.

''In-Sink-Erator Milestone. 50 Million,'' *Racine Journal Times*, July 28, 1993.

In-Sink-Erator: The First 50 Years, Racine, Wisc.: In-Sink-Erator, 1988.

''John W. Hammes,'' *Southeastern Wisconsin: Old Milwaukee County*, Chicago: S.J. Clarke, 1932.

Martin, Mary Jo, ''In-Sink-Erator,'' *ASA News*, November/December 2000.

Pfankuchen, David, ''Traced By Head of Firm,'' *Racine Journal Times*, August 30, 1973, p. D2.

The In-Sink-Erator Story, Racine, Wisc.: In-Sink-Erator, 1978.

Wicklund, Pete, ''Clean Living,'' *Racine Journal Times*, October 22, 2001, p. B2.

—Paul R. Greenland

Kiabi Europe

100 rue du Calvaire
Hem F-59510
France
Telephone: (+33) 3 20 81 45 00
Fax: (+33) 3 20 81 49 49
Web site: http://www.kiabi.fr

Private Company
Incorporated: 1978
Employees: 4,500
Sales: EUR 2.2 billion ($2.5 billion) (2003 est.)
NAIC: 448110 Men's Clothing Stores; 448120 Women's Clothing Stores; 448130 Children's and Infants' Clothing Stores; 448140 Family Clothing Stores; 448150 Clothing Accessories Stores

Kiabi Europe is a leading French clothing retailer, operating 110 stores in France as well as 12 stores in Spain and three stores in Italy. Based in Hem, in the north of France near Lille and the Belgian border, Kiabi has set itself a goal of making fashion accessible to all, offering its own range of low-priced brands—including Winch, Decade, Tim Pouce, and P'tit Caïd—as well as a number of name brands, including Complices, Waikiki, Providence, and Fido Dido. One of France's pioneers of the ''category killer'' store, Kiabi's stores are typically located in commercial shopping areas outside France's mid- and large-size cities. Stores offer an average selling space of 1,500 to 2,000 square meters and feature some 50,000 clothing, accessory, and footwear items. The largest Kiabi store provides 4,600 square meters of floor space, while the smallest store stands at a nonetheless respectable 800 square meters. Kiabi stores features a full selection of women's, men's, and children's clothing, with each department further segmented into a number of ''stories,'' grouping similar colors, materials, and styles. Since 2000, Kiabi has been carrying out an extensive store remodeling program and plans to convert all of its store to the new interior and exterior design by mid-decade. The company has successfully developed its own fidelity card system, with more than 1.5 million cardholders. Kiabi also provides other services, such as free and paid in-store alterations and staggered payment plans. The company provides logistics support to its operations with three warehouse and distribution centers and operates through four primary divisions: Kiabi France, Kiabi Spain, Kiabi Italy, and Kiabi Logistique. Founded by CEO Patrick Mulliez, Kiabi remains under the control of the powerful Mulliez retailing empire, which includes Auchan hypermarkets, Leroy Merlin do-it-yourself (DIY) stores, Boulanger home appliance stores, Decathlon sporting goods, the Flunch restaurant chain, among many other formats.

Discount Fashion in the 1980s

The Mulliez family had already established itself as one of the leading lights of France's retail sector by the time the first Kiabi store opened in 1978. The Mulliez's started out as manufacturers, founding Phildar, a textile company, in 1903. By 1946, however, the family had begun a shift to the retail sector, opening its first stores and producing a new range of Phildar-branded knitting and sewing supplies as well. The Phildar chain took off in 1956 when it began franchising the Phildar format.

The company's rise to retail giant status began with Gerard Mulliez, a high-school dropout who started his career in the Phildar manufacturing plant. In 1961, Mulliez decided to launch his own retail business, setting up a grocery store in Roubaix called Auchan.

Mulliez's initial venture failed. Yet, with family support, he tried again, this time adopting the self-service discount supermarket format just then being introduced into France. Opened in 1967, the new Auchan supermarket clicked with the shopping public, and Mulliez began opening new stores in northern France. By the mid-1970s, aided by the difficult economic climate brought on by the Arab oil embargo, Auchan had already established itself as one of northern France's major supermarket chains. At the end of that decade, Mulliez prepared to take on the rest of the country, beginning a national expansion that positioned Auchan and the Mulliez family in the top ranks of French retailers.

Gerard Mulliez's success inspired other family members to enter the retail world as well. By the early 1980s, Mulliez

Company Perspectives:

Kiabi. Fashions for low prices. A name, a brand, a slogan, a symbol recognized by many. To the point that one might easily believe that Kiabi has always existed. And yet, Kiabi is just 25 years old. Twenty-five years of success, of a relationship with its public. But also a maturity that has led the company, in the context of the current market, to wish reinforce its position with its clients in all areas. Areas such as its product, with its collections developed across a larger universe in order to dress the whole family. Market using new methods of presenting collections. Retailing with a new store concepts. Without neglecting the will—unchanged since its beginnings—to respect what has made the company popular with shoppers: knowing how to provide ''fashions for low prices.''

family members had founded many of the country's leading retail brands, adopting a ''category killer'' approach pioneered in the United States. The family's empire grew to include such dominant retailers as the Decathlon sporting goods chain and electrical appliance specialist Boulanger. The Mulliez family was also behind the launch of Flunch, a popular family-oriented, cafeteria-style restaurant chain and in the early 1980s acquired control of the Leroy Merlin DIY store chain.

In the late 1970s, another Mulliez family member, Patrick Mulliez, decided to build on the family's background in the textile industry to open a new style of clothing store. Called Kiabi, the new format became one of the first in France to offer a large-scale selling space devoted exclusively to clothing. Featuring its own clothing designs and labels, and later incorporating other branded items as well, Kiabi was launched as a low-priced fashion concept with the motto: ''La mode à petits prix'' (''fashions for low prices''). Backed by his family's know-how in the textile manufacturing sector, Mulliez was able to ensure a quality product.

Mulliez opened the first Kiabi in the town of Roncq, outside of Lille, in 1978. This store already displayed the company's preference for scale, with a selling space of 1,000 square meters. Accompanying the launch of the store were the company's first two in-house brands, Winch, representing the Kiabi's sportswear fashions, and Decade, featuring more classic, ''city'' styles.

The first Kiabi was an immediate success, and Mulliez quickly began adding new stores. By 1979, the company had three stores and 150 employees. Less than a year later, there were already seven Kiabi stores and 450 employees. From there, the company's growth accelerated, and by its 10th anniversary, Kiabi had already opened 35 stores, as well as two logistics and distribution centers. By then, the company had sold more than ten million pieces of clothing.

International Expansion in the 1990s

Kiabi initially targeted the men's and women's clothing segments. The growing retail clout of the children's clothing market at the end of the 1980s and into the 1990s encouraged the company to expand its line of styles to include the segment ranging from infants to teenagers. As part of this effort, Kiabi launched a new brand insignia and in 1990 included the Tim Pouce and P'tit Caid labels. The company continued to add to its range of items, offering accessories, maternity wear, and footwear. By the end of the 1990s, the typical Kiabi store had grown to 2,000 square meters—with the largest store at 4,600 square meters—and featured more than 50,000 different clothing, accessory, and footwear items.

Kiabi continued to conquer France in the 1990s, jumping from 50 stores at the beginning of the decade to 100 stores by 2000 and 110 stores by the end of 2004. By the mid-1990s, Kiabi had already established itself as one of the major clothing retailers in France, claiming the number four spot for all retail textile sales and the number one spot among specialized large-scale clothing shops. Kiabi's sales at mid-decade were estimated at FFr 4.4 billion ($800 million).

A large part of the group's success was due to its dual commitment to low prices and quality. As part of the latter effort, Kiabi launched a new clothing range called Kiabi 4 Etoiles, which included a two-year guarantee, in 1995. Also in that year, Kiabi introduced its fidelity program, and less than a decade later the company had built up a base of some 1.5 million cardholders.

In the meantime, Kiabi had set its sights on new horizons. In 1993, the company opened its first international store, in Valence, Spain. That marked the beginning of Kiabi's expansion into the Spanish market, bringing it head to head with the likes of Spanish retail clothing powerhouse Zara. Nonetheless, the first Kiabi met with success, and the company began constructing a Spanish retail network as well. In 1996, the company opened a second Spanish store, in Saragosse, followed by a store in Barcelona in 1998 and one in Madrid in 1999. By 2003, the company had opened a second store in Madrid, as well as stores in Pampeluna, El Ferrol, and Oviedo. In 2004, the company began construction on four new stores, bringing its total in Spain to 12.

Spain was not Kiabi's only international target. In 1996, the company turned to the Italian market, where it faced such rivals as Benetton and Diesel on their home turf. The first Italian Kiabi store was opened in Milan in 1996 and was joined by a store in Ferrara in 1999 and another in Bari in 2000. Deeper penetration into the Italian market appeared difficult for the company, however, especially given the difficult economic climate at the beginning of the decade. After putting its Italian expansion temporarily on hold in the early 2000s, Kiabi began developing a new expansion strategy, with new stores planned in the 2004 to 2007 period.

New Look for the New Century

Back in France, Kiabi began testing a new store format in 2000, converting its first three stores to the new look in August of that year. The positive reaction to the design led the company to plan a full-scale rollout of the new store format, with the conversion of all of the company's stores expected to be completed by mid-decade. As part of the change in format, the company redeveloped its in-store presentations as well, developing its clothing collections as a series of ''stories'' that each

Key Dates:

1978: Patrick Mulliez opens his first Kiabi clothing store in Roncq and launches in-house brands Winch and Decade.
1988: Celebrating its first decade, Kiabi opens its 35th store.
1990: Children's clothing labels Tim Pouce and P'tit Caid are launched.
1993: Kiabi enters Spain with a store in Valencia.
1996: Kiabi enters Italy with a store in Milan.
2000: The company begins converting all of its stores to a new design format and changes its name to Kiabi Europe.
2003: ''Coté Miss'' clothing collection is launched for girls 8 to 14 years old.
2004: Kiabi opens its 110th store in France, bringing its total number of stores to 125.

revolved around similar colors, fabrics, and styles. Kiabi also launched a new clothing collection, ''Coté Miss,'' in 2003. The new line was specifically targeted at the fast-growing clothing segment for girls 8 to 14 years old, who had a penchant for adult-like fashions.

In the early 2000s, Kiabi also redesigned its corporate structure, changing its name to Kiabi Europe and regrouping its operations under four primary divisions: Kiabi France, Kiabi Spain, Kiabi Italy, and Kiabi Logistique. The new structure gave the company an effective oversight for its future expansion plans, with new stores planned in each of its geographic markets. The success of the Kiabi concept appeared certain to appeal to a broader European market in the new century.

Principal Divisions

Kiabi France; Kiabi Spain; Kiabi Italy; Kiabi Logistique.

Principal Competitors

Redcats; Vivarte; La Redoute; La Halle; Somfy International S.A.; Damartex S.A.; Zara France S.A.R.L.

Further Reading

Cristofari, Jean-François, ''Kiabi,'' *Marketing Magazine*, January 1, 1998.
''Dossier de presentation,'' Kiabi SA, January 2004.
''Kiabi, 22 ans de succès,'' *Voix du Nord*, November 11, 2000.
''La PME-école de kiabi,'' *Nouvel Observateur*, September 23, 1999.

—M.L. Cohen

Kirby Corporation

55 Waugh Drive, Suite 1000
Houston, Texas 77007
U.S.A.
Telephone: (713) 435-1000
Fax: (713) 435-1010
Web site: http://www.kmtc.com

Public Company
Incorporated: 1969 as Kirby Jamaica, Inc.
Employees: 2,425
Sales: $613.5million (2003)
Stock Exchanges: New York
Ticker Symbol: KEX
NAIC: 483113 Coastal and Great Lakes Freight Transportation; 483221 Inland Water Freight Transportation

As the largest inland barge operator in the United States, Kirby Corporation and subsidiary Kirby Inland Marine LP oversee a fleet of approximately 900 active tank barges. The company transports petrochemicals and pressurized products, along with refined petroleum, black oil, and agricultural chemicals throughout the Mississippi River System and the Gulf Intercoastal Waterway. Kirby's liquid cargo capacity stands at nearly 16.2 million barrels and the company has 230 active inland tugboats. Subsidiary Kirby Engine Systems provides overhaul and other related services and also sells diesel engine parts. Kirby began focusing aggressively on its inland tank barge and diesel engine services businesses in 1997. It sold off its offshore tank barges and ships, harbor tugs, and its stake in Universal Insurance Company the following year.

A Petroleum Spinoff of the 1970s

Kirby started out as a subsidiary of Kirby Industries, Inc.; incorporated as Kirby Jamaica in 1969, the company was formed as part of an oil and gas concession in Jamaica. In the early 1970s, the company's name was changed to Kirby Petroleum Co. However, in 1974, despite earnings of $6.5 million on revenues of $85 million, Kirby Industries liquidated its activities because, as then president Peterkin told *Newsweek,* "the market did not value [Kirby's] assets at the proper price." As part of the liquidation, Kirby Petroleum was spun off as a public company, renamed Kirby Exploration Company. The new company brought with it two former Kirby Industries subsidiaries, Dixie Carriers, acquired in 1968, and Universal Insurance, started in 1972. Revenues for the new company were $51 million in 1976.

The company's sales reached $58 million by 1978, and $73 million by 1980, driven largely by a boom in the marine transportation market. The company's oil and gas business was sagging, however, and in 1980 the company agreed to merge with a company to be formed by the New York investment firm Kohlberg, Kravis, Roberts & Company. That merger was called off in 1981 after the parties could not reach agreement on the distribution of shares in the company to be formed. As the economy slid into the recession of the early 1980s, Kirby's oil and gas business began dragging down the company's profits, producing an operating loss of $118,000 in 1981. In 1982, the oil and gas units operating loss jumped to $29 million, sinking Kirby into the red by $15 million on $102 million in revenues. In 1983, the company acquired General Energy Corporation in a stock-swap merger, and the following year formed a new subsidiary, Kirby Exploration Company of Texas.

Kirby also made attempts to diversify its operations, moving into data processing, through an interest in Davenport Data Processors, Inc., and into semiconductor services, through a 97.7 percent ownership position in Materials Technology Corporation. The Davenport interest was sold to Bank of America in 1984. The company sold off the semiconductor business the following year. More successful was the 1982 acquisition of Marine Systems, bringing the company into diesel repair. Meanwhile, Kirby's oil and gas segment continued to falter. When the oil industry collapsed in the second half of the 1980s, Kirby discontinued its oil and gas operations. That portion of the business was sold to American Exploration Company for $62 million in cash in 1988. About half of that went to retiring debt and covering costs of the sale. With the rest, the company began weighing its options for the future, including investing in other industries or returning to the oil and gas industry. Instead, Kirby turned to its marine transportation unit.

Company Perspectives:

Our goal is to be the best. By listening to our customers and embracing the concept of continuous improvement, we will provide our customers the highest value for their dollar and create long-term value for our shareholders.

Sailing into the 1990s

Peterkin's involvement in the barge business reached back to 1948, when his father and uncle, who also controlled Kirby, invested in Dixie Carriers. Peterkin, who had graduated from the University of Texas, joined the company that year. Dixie by then operated a 20-barge fleet. Five years later, Peterkin became president of the family-owned company. In 1968, Dixie was acquired as a subsidiary to Kirby Industries. When Kirby Petroleum was spun off after the Kirby Industries liquidation, Dixie was included as a subsidiary to the new public company.

The marine transportation unit already formed a major part of Kirby's operations. By 1981, over half the company's revenues came from its barge business, which also produced nearly two-thirds of the company's operating income. That business, too, was under pressure throughout the 1980s. Several factors combined to turn the once-solid marine transportation industry into a financial minefield. Chief among these was rampant overbuilding of barges during an industry-wide boom in the 1970s. With demand rising and hauling rates high, companies rapidly began expanding their fleets. By 1981 there were some 28,000 barges, including a historic high of 4,900 tank barges, working the country's waterways. Investment interest from Wall Street helped fuel the expansion of fleets, as investors sought out barges as attractive tax shelters.

In 1980, however, President Carter declared a grain embargo against the Soviet Union—until then the country's biggest grain buyer. At the same time, new federal regulations imposed waterway user fees for the first time in the industry's 200-year history. (Waterways had been decreed free in the Northwest Ordinance of 1787.) The user fee was meant ultimately to recover 100 percent of the cost of waterway improvement and maintenance, which cost taxpayers some $300 million in the early 1980s. It started at six cents per gallon of fuel, then rose to ten cents per gallon. With fuel consumption reaching some 11,000 gallons or more for a single barge's return trip, coupled with a flattening of the market, the marine transportation industry underwent a shakeout, with many smaller—and larger—companies failing. By 1983, 20 percent of the country's barge fleet were idled. Moreover, new environmental regulations, imposed in the wake of such major oil disasters as the Exxon Valdez spill, demanded that companies carrying petroleum and other chemical products convert their fleets from single-skin hulls to more disaster-resistant double-skin hulls. The cost of converting a barge, as well as building new double-skin barges, finally proved too much for many of the companies that had survived the shakeout of the early 1980s.

Kirby's barge subsidiary struggled along with the rest of the industry, with revenues falling in the first half of the 1980s. Fortunately, Kirby had resisted the urge to expand its fleet during the 1970s boom, building new barges only when they were under contract. At the same time, the company focused on winning primarily long-term, fixed-rate contracts, which served the company well as the bottom dropped out of the spot contract market and rates plunged. By the end of the 1980s, Kirby emerged as one of only a handful of surviving independent barge lines.

Kirby, by then exiting the oil and gas business, recognized an opportunity to expand its marine transportation unit. With many of its competitors floundering, Kirby began adding to its fleet by acquiring other companies, starting with the $25 million cash acquisition of Brent Towing Co. in 1989. That acquisition was followed less than two weeks later by the acquisition of Alamo Inland Marine Co. for another $27 million in cash. The two acquisitions doubled Kirby's fleet to 164 tank barges and 64 towboats. The expanded operations helped raise Kirby's revenues from $98 million in 1988 to $141 million in 1989. The company also added to its diesel repair operations, opening a fourth service facility, located in St. Louis, Missouri. The following year, the company added nine new double-skin tank barges to its fleet, purchased four used double-skin tank barges and five towboats, and placed an order for the construction of six new double-skin tank barges. Then, in a stock and cash deal worth $145 million, Kirby acquired Western Pioneer, Inc. and its Delta Western subsidiary, bringing Kirby into the Pacific Northwest and Alaskan markets. The company also acquired the assets of International Barges, Inc., which included three cryogenic tank barges serving the anhydrous ammonia market, for $2.6 million.

Kirby changed its name to Kirby Corporation in 1990 to reflect the company's new direction. In 1992, Kirby was back on the acquisition path, purchasing in that year Sabine Towing & Transportation Co., a subsidiary of Sequa Corporation, for $36.9 million in cash; the assets of Ole Man River Towing, including that company's tank barges, towboats, and property holdings, for $25.6 million; and Scott Chotin, Inc., based in Louisiana, and that company's 29 inland tank barges and ten dry cargo barges for stock and cash worth $34.9 million. In its diesel repair arm, Kirby opened a fifth service facility, located in Louisiana. The company then made the first step toward exiting the insurance market, merging its Universal insurance arm with Eastern America Insurance Company, with Universal as the surviving entity. Terms of that deal called for Eastern/Universal to redeem Kirby's stock in the company—75 percent after the merger—over the next 12 years.

Kirby's expansion drive continued. In 1993, the company's fleet grew to 468 barges and towboats, adding 16 offshore vessels with the $24 million purchase of 72 inland tank barges from Ashland Oil Co. subsidiary TPT Transportation and the $25.5 million acquisition of AFRAM Lines Company, a worldwide shipper of dry bulk and container cargo, primarily for the U.S. government. The company completed the year with the $15 million purchase of 53 inland tank barges from Midland Enterprises, Inc. Revenues for 1993 reached $378 million, providing a net income of $22.8 million.

While not all of Kirby's endeavors were equally successful. In January 1994, the company attempted to open a new shipping line running from Memphis to Mexico and South America; the company aborted that line in August 1994 in the face of stiff competition. In 1996, Kirby was forced to idle its AFRAM fleet

Key Dates:

1968: Kirby Industries buys Dixie Carriers Inc.
1969: Kirby Jamaica is incorporated.
1974: The company activities are liquidated; Kirby Petroleum is spun off as a public company and renamed Kirby Exploration Co.
1982: Marine Systems is acquired.
1983: Kirby purchases General Energy Co.
1988: American Exploration Co. buys Kirby's oil and gas operations.
1990: The company changes its name to Kirby Corporation.
1998: Kirby sells its offshore tank barges and ships, harbor tugs, and its stake in Universal Insurance Co.
1999: Hollywood Marine is acquired.
2003: Kirby adds the SeaRiver Maritime fleet to its arsenal.

and began to look into exiting the government/military transport market. Nevertheless, Kirby continued to post impressive gains into the mid-1990s as demand for barge transportation underwent a new surge. The company added to its fleet with the purchase of 65 inland tank barges and leases on an addition 31 inland tank barges from Dow Chemical Company for $24 million in cash. At the beginning of 1995, the company placed an order for construction of 12 new double-skin inland take barges—double hulls were now required by federal environmental laws. The company's 1995 revenues surged to $440 million, including $45 million from the company's insurance operations. Kirby de-consolidated Universal from its revenue statement for 1996. In that year, the company faced a weaker market for its marine transportation. However, its diesel repair arm posted strong growth, boosting the company's profits to $27 million on revenues of $386 million for the year.

Late 1990s and Beyond

Costs related to restructuring and floods on the Mississippi River in 1997 weakened company sales. Late that year, however, Kirby revamped its business strategy and launched a plan to focus on its core inland tank barge and diesel engine services businesses. As part of that initiative, Kirby sold its offshore tank barges and ships, harbor tugs, and its remaining stake in Universal Insurance.

The company significantly expanded its holdings in 1999 with the $322.2 million acquisition of Hollywood Marine Inc., the third-largest inland barge operator in the United States. Hollywood's fleet included 256 inland tank barges and 104 towboats. C. Berdon Lawrence, Hollywood's president and owner, was named Kirby chairman after the deal.

Kirby's growth continued into the early years of the 21st century. In 2001, the company signed a long-term lease agreement with Dow Chemical for 94 inland tank barges that it had acquired as a result of its merger with Union Carbide. In March 2002, the company added Cargill's Cargo Carriers fleet to its arsenal. In October of that year Kirby purchased ten double hull black oil tank barges and 13 towboats from Coastal Towing. Ninety-four double hull tank barges were acquired from Union Carbide Finance Corporation in December.

The company made another move to strengthen its leading industry position in January 2003 when it purchased the SeaRiver Maritime fleet—Exxon Mobil's U.S. marine transportation affiliate. The deal included 48 double hull tank barges, seven towboats, and a lease of 16 double hull tank barges. Kirby bought a one-third interest in Osprey Line LLC in 2004.

While Kirby enjoyed success during this time period, the company faced distinct challenges brought on by a slowdown in the refining and chemicals industries as well as an aging locks system and river infrastructure that was in need of upgrades. CEO Joseph H. Pyne commented on the situation in a November 2003 *Journal of Commerce* article, claiming, "If Congress doesn't fund it, ports will have to close down. You close one port, and it would affect all the others." He went on to add, "It's always a fight to get full and adequate funding, but I can't imagine Congress doing something adverse to a system that's so fundamentally important to the U.S. economy."

Despite facing several industry obstacles, Kirby held an enviable position in the industry. It transported a considerable portion of the nation's chemicals on its barges. In fact, just after the terrorist attacks of September 11, 2001, the Coast Guard contacted Kirby to find out exactly where dangerous chemicals could be found on U.S. waterways. As the largest inland barge operator in the United States, and with a long-standing history of prosperity behind it, Kirby appeared to be on track for smooth sailing ahead.

Principal Subsidiaries

Kirby Corporate Services, LLC; KIM Holdings, Inc.; Kirby Terminals, Inc.; Sabine Transportation Company; AFRAM Carriers, Inc.; Kirby Engine Systems, Inc.; Kirby Tankships, Inc.; Dixie Offshore Transportation Company; Mariner Reinsurance Company Ltd.; Oceanic Insurance Ltd..

Principal Competitors

American Commercial Lines LLC; Crowley Maritime Corporation; Ingram Industries Inc.

Further Reading

Hensel, Bill, Jr. "The Water's Bounty," *Houston Chronicle*, November 24, 2002.

Jones, John A., "Kirby Adds to Its Barge Fleet as Need for Carriers Grows," *Investor's Business Daily*, September 2, 1993, p. 34.

——, "Kirby Expands Tank Barge Fleet while Demand Is Strong," *Investor's Daily*, July 30, 1991, p. 32.

"Kirby Closes Hollywood Deal," *Oil Daily*, October 14, 1999.

"Kirby Divests Interest in Insurance Firm, Sells Offshore Barge/Tug Unit," *Petroleum Finance Week*, October 26, 1999.

"Kirby Sells Off," *Business Week*, June 9, 1975, p. 30.

Leach, Peter T., "Barge Wars," *Journal of Commerce*, November 10, 2003.

Moreno, Jenalia, "Houston-Based Barge Company Bolsters Position as Industry's Largest," *Houston Chronicle*, July 30, 1999.

O'Donnell, Thomas, "Waiting for Ivan," *Forbes*, November 22, 1982, p. 50.

Palmeri, Christopher, "Barging Ahead," *Forbes*, August 30, 1993, p. 80.

—M.L. Cohen
—update: Christina M. Stansell

La Senza Corporation

1604 St. Regis Boulevard
Dorval, Quebec H9P 1H6
Canada
Telephone: (514) 684-7700
Toll Free: (877) 644-0551
Fax: (514) 684-0258
Web site: http://www.lasenza.com

Public Company
Incorporated: 1982 as Suzy Shier Inc.
Employees: 6,063
Sales: $189.1 million (2003)
Stock Exchanges: Toronto
Ticker Symbol: LSZ
NAIC: 448120 Women's Clothing Stores

La Senza Corporation is a major Canadian retailer of women's lingerie and apparel, avoiding the sexy niche carved out by Victoria's Secret and Fredericks of Hollywood in favor of focusing on high quality merchandise sold at affordable prices. Based near Montreal, the company owns and operates more than 200 La Senza Lingerie stores in Canada, and another 140 stores located in 18 countries, which includes licensed operations in the United Kingdom, the Middle East, and elsewhere. In addition, the company owns and operates more than 80 La Senza Girl stores, which target girls between 8 and 14 years of age. Through subsidiary Wet Seal, the company has operated in the United States since 1984, but only since 2003 has it attempt to crack the U.S. market with La Senza Lingerie. Although a public company, La Senza is 90 percent owned by chairman and CEO Irving Teitelbaum.

Suzy Shier: Mid-1960s to Mid-1980s

Teitelbaum, La Senza's cofounder, was born to Polish immigrants who came to Canada after World War I. He went to college at McGill University, then transferred to Sir George Williams College, where in June 1960 he graduated with a bachelor of commerce degree. Shortly thereafter he married and began his retail career, going to work for his father-in-law, Irwin Shier, who owned a junior department store in the Quebec area. Over the next several years he gained a practical education in the importance of catering to customers. He told *Canadian Business* in 2002 that working for a small town department store was an excellent training ground because "You're not making new customers every day, so you have to treat each person who comes into your store like a king or queen." In 1966, Shier was looking to open another department store when he came upon a mall in a desirable location, Sherbrooke, Quebec, but it only had a woman's wear shop available to lease. Aware that junior fashion was becoming very popular, he decided to lease the space and open a store, which would be named Suzy Shier, and offer trendy, yet moderately priced, apparel to the junior market. By this time, he had another son-in-law, Stephen Gross, who teamed with Teitelbaum to open the first Suzy Shier store in 1966. After Shier died in 1968, Teitelbaum and Gross began to aggressively expand the Suzy Shier concept.

Over the course of the next decade Suzy Shier grew into a 22-store chain with units spread across Canada, generating sales of $7 million Canadian in 1975. At this point, the brothers-in-law needed more capital for expansion and in September 1975 they sold a 50.1 percent interest in Suzy Shier to Dylex Ltd., a Toronto-based holding company with a number of retail chains in its portfolio. Teitelbaum and Gross remained in charge of Suzy Shier, with Teitelbaum assuming the lead management role. Over the next ten years, with Dylex's backing, the chain was able to add another 50 units, with shops located in every major Canadian city as well as other smaller locales, such as Timmins, Sudbury, Sault Saint Marie, and Thunder Bay.

Wet Seal Acquired in 1984

During this period, Teitelbaum and Gross became interested in the U.S. market and took notice of a 16-store, Irvine, California-based chain, The Wet Seal Inc., which sold contemporary fashion apparel and accessories to juniors. Convinced that Wet Seal, despite losing money, was a good complement to Suzy Shier, they acquired an 80 percent interest in 1984 (half of which was owned by Dylex), made it profitable, and steadily expanded the chain in the United States. A key executive

Company Perspectives:

La Senza offers women and men a unique shopping experience with outstanding lingerie presentation in a beautiful and intimate environment, featuring everything from bras & panties, to sleepwear, loungewear, bodycare, accessories, and men's underwear.

credited with the growth of Wet Seal was Kathy Bronstein, who in 1985 joined the subsidiary as the head of the merchandise group. She brought with her a good deal of experience in the junior market place. After earning an advertising degree from the University of Florida, she became an assistant buyer for a Philadelphia, Pennsylvania, chain called Deb Shops, then became the buyer for junior sportswear at Jordan Marsh. She relocated to southern California in 1979 to become a buyer for Fashion Conspiracy, followed by a stint with the Wild West chain before coming to Wet Seal. By 1992, she became the company's chief executive officer. In the meantime, in 1990, Wet Seal was spun off as a public company, raising $41 million. Of that amount, $20 million was used to repay loans from Dylex, which now needed the money because of recent losses as well as a heavy debt load. The remaining $21 million would be used by Wet Seal to fuel further expansion. Over the next dozen years, Wet Seal grew to include some 600 stores divided among three chains. While Wet Seal continued to serve the youth market, Arden B stores catered to women and Zutopia targeted ''tweens,'' girls between the ages of 8 and 14.

In the early 1980s, Teitelbaum and Gross launched another chain of apparel shops to cater to the junior market called L.A. Express, but by the end of the decade they sensed that both Suzy Shier and L.A. Express had peaked in Canada, and they looked for a new growth vehicle. At the time, lingerie retailer Victoria's Secret was making a splash in the United States, and the partners decided to try something similar in Canada, while avoiding the overtly sexual nature of Victoria's Secret. Suzy Shier was already carrying a modest line of undergarments and sleepwear, but because shelf space was limited and fearing that the traditional Suzy Shier customer might be confused by the sudden influx of lingerie, Teitelbaum and Gross elected to form a separate chain of lingerie shops under a new subsidiary. After toying with the Suzy's Secret as a name for the business, Teiltelbaum drew on the Italian word for ''without,'' *Senza.* He added the article ''la'' to feminize the name, creating ''La Senza,'' which he felt ''had a nice, luxurious ring to it.'' The basic business plan was to sell private-label lingerie—designed by the company with manufacturing outsourced—in a boutique format. The first La Senza shop opened in 1990 in Ottawa's Place D'Orleans Shopping Centre.

Placed in charge of the brand as president was British-born Laurence Lewin, who did not start out in the apparel industry. Rather he was an accountant by training who was working for Honeywell Information systems when he was sent to Montreal in the early 1970s to work on a project for Air Canada. In the mid-1970s, he accepted a chance to run a clothing chain, found that he loved the industry, and elected to make a career in apparel. Teitelbaum recruited him in 1987, initially hiring Lewin to serve as vice-president in charge of merchandising at Suzy Shier, but with the intention of eventually offering greater responsibility. With Lewin as president, La Senza grew quickly, so that by the end of 1992 the chain had grown to about 35 units.

As had been the case with Wet Seal, Suszy Shier's La Senza division needed more financial backing to support its growth than its corporate parent could provide. Because it was still strapped for cash, Dylex once again opted to make a public offering, spinning off Suzy Shier, which was one of its few consistent successes. In 1993, Dylex sold its entire 50.1 percent stake to underwriters, realizing approximately CAD $60 million, while Suzy Shier also made shares available, raising about CAD $18 million, which was used to double the size of the La Senza chain by the end of the year.

Over the next few years, Suzy Shier attempted to grow on a number of fronts. Looking to becoming international, the company targeted England, a large and fragmented market. It formed a company, La Senza plc, and in the final weeks of 1994 opened six La Senza stores in the United Kingdom. By early 1996, another 16 shops had opened and La Senza plc floated an offering on the Alternative Investment Market, garnering a great deal of attention by bringing pictures of lingerie-clad models to London's financial newspapers. In the United States, Wet Seal posted back-to-back unprofitable years, but because of aggressive cost-cutting measures, the unit was much better positioned than rivals who were not as quick to react to a downturn in the economy and lapsed into bankruptcy. In April 1995, Wet Seal was able to acquire the 237-store Contempo Casuals chain from Neiman Marcus, nearly tripling the size of Wet Seal, which operated 130 stores. A few weeks later, Suzy Shier, which had remained profitable despite difficult economic conditions, paid $12 million to acquire a controlling interest in Wet Seal from Dylex, which had just emerged from bankruptcy. A year later, in October 1996, Suzy Shier paid nearly CAD $5.2 million to acquire the 42-store Silk & Satin lingerie chain from Woolworth Canada Inc. By this stage, Suzy Shier was operating 257 stores under the Suzy Shier and L.A. Express names and 145 La Senza stores.

Even while La Senza was making plans to open stores in additional countries, such as Saudi Arabia, the U.K. venture was beset with mounting losses, primarily because it attempted to grow too quickly and property rentals spiraled out of control. In September 1997, the company announced that the projections used in its listing prospectus ''should be disregarded.'' By early 1998, however, the subsidiary was on the ropes and with no help forthcoming from the parent company, bankers were reluctant to step in to help out. As a result, the U.K. operation was sold for a token pound to a company owned by businessman Theo Paphitis, who owned Contessa Ladieswear among other assets. Going forward, Suzy Shier's La Senza shops in the U.K. would be run on a licensing basis.

Suzy Shier Adopts La Senza Name in 2001

Another venture that did not succeed for Suzy Shier was an attempt to open stores to serve women five-feet, four-inches and under in height. In general, it was the La Senza brand that was generating growth for the company. A new concept, La Senza Girl, aimed at 7- to 14-year-old girls, was quick to succeed

Key Dates:

1968: Suzy Shier Inc. is launched.
1975: Dylex Ltd. acquires a controlling share of Suzy Shier.
1984: Wet Seal is acquired.
1990: La Senza lingerie division is formed, and the company's first stores opens.
1993: Suzy Shier is spun off as a public company.
2001: Suzy Shier changes its name to La Senza Corporation.
2003: La Senza opens its first U.S. store.

and establish itself. The parent company, as a result, began to convert a significant number of L.A. Express and Suzy Shier stores to La Senza Girl outlets. In July 2001, Suzy Shier Limited became La Senza Corporation, a name which management believed was more in keeping with the direction the company was taking.

Not only was the Suzy Shier chain not doing as well as it had in the past, Wet Seal also endured a difficult stretch in 2002, which led to the dismissal of Bronstein as CEO. Teitelbaum replaced her on an interim basis. Effective June 30, 2003, a permanent CEO was hired, Peter D. Whitford, the former worldwide president of Disney Stores. In the meantime, the 178-unit Suzy Shier chain was put on the block. A buyer was found in YM Inc., which operated similar junior clothing stores, such as Stitches, Sirens, and Urban Planet. Hindering the transaction, however, was a probe launched by Canada's federal competition bureau, which charged that Suzy Shier had used misleading ''regular'' prices in order to convince consumers they were getting a better bargain. La Senza's management agreed to a CAD $1 million fine but did not admit guilt. Teitelbaum told the *Toronto Star* that the company felt the matter was holding up the sale of the chain, adding, ''It was obvious there was no way YM or anyone else was going to buy a Canadian retailer that had an ongoing investigation with the bureau hanging over its head.'' Just hours after the settlement was announced, the sale to YM was finalized. The terms of the agreement were not made public, but press accounts estimate the purchase price at CAD $8 million.

In the same month that Suzy Shier was sold, La Senza opened its first outlet in the United States in a Rockaway, New Jersey, shopping center. Establishing a presence was imperative in achieving the goal of building La Senza into a true international brand. Within the year, a store opened in Garden City, New York, as well as three more units in Massachusetts. Management was confident that it would achieve success in the United States. It had some 20 years of operational experience in the country through Wet Seal, an advantage not enjoyed by many Canadian retailers who failed to crack the market. La Senza was also debt free and held cash investments. With 2,400 regional malls in the United States, half of which management considered suitable for housing a La Senza outlets, the lingerie chain appeared well positioned to realize a goal of one day operating 500 stores in the U.S. market.

Principal Competitors

Frederick's of Hollywood, Inc.; Movie Star, Inc.; Victoria's Secret Stores, Inc.

Further Reading

Aarsteinsen, Barbara, ''Suzy Shier Expanding with New Lingerie Claim,'' *Toronto Star*, December 11, 1990, p. F1.
Bitti, Mary Teresa, ''Speaking of Unmentionables: Man of La Senza,'' *Financial Post*, February 1, 1994, p. 28.
Cohen, Elaine, ''La Senza a Leader in Canada's Lingerie Market,'' *Canadian Jewish News*, January 15, 1998.
Heinzl, John, ''Dylex to Take Women's Wear, Lingerie Unit Public,'' *Globe and Mail*, April 15, 1993.
Olijnyk, Zena, ''Va va va Boom,'' *Canadian Business*, May 13, 2002, p. 48.

—Ed Dinger

Life Time Fitness, Inc.

6442 City West Parkway
Eden Prairie, Minnesota 55344
U.S.A.
Telephone: (952) 947-000
Fax: (952) 947-9137
Web site: http://www.lifetimefitness.com

Public Company:
Incorporated: 1990 as FCA, Ltd.
Employees: 7,700
Sales: $256.9 million (2003)
Stock Exchanges: New York
Ticker Symbol: LTM
NAIC: 713940 Fitness and Recreational Sports Centers

Life Time Fitness, Inc., operates more than 35 large-format sports, athletic, fitness, and family recreation centers. The publicly traded company is based in Eden Prairie, Minnesota, a state that is home to 14 Life Time centers. Illinois, with seven centers, is the next largest area of operation for the chain, followed by Michigan with five, Arizona, Texas, and Virginia with two, and single locations in Indiana and Ohio. Life Time takes a big box approach to health clubs, using a model center that exceeds 100,000 square feet in size and has a target capacity of 11,500 memberships. About one-third of the units conform to this model, and another dozen are also large-format centers. Because of their size, the resort-style centers are able to offer a wide variety of sports, fitness, and family recreation programs and services at rates below the industry average. Life Time offers swimming pools with water slides, racquet ball courts, basketball courts, climbing walls, and large numbers of weight training stations and cardiovascular equipment. The centers also provide free child care and children's activities, including small gyms, playground equipment, televisions, and even computer labs offering both entertainment and educational games. Moreover, Life Time offers dining and full-service spas. Life Time is also attempting to leverage its brand name, publishing a magazine, *Experience Life,* and developing a line of apparel, nutritional, and other products.

Founder Emigrates to America in 1978

Life Time's founder, Bahram Akradi, grew up in Tehran, Iran. In 1978, when he was 17 years old—and a year before Iranian militants stormed the U.S. embassy, took 54 hostages, and severed ties between the two countries—Akradi emigrated to the United States, joining his brother who had settled in Colorado Springs, Colorado. He began studying electrical engineering at the University of Colorado, working in restaurants to pay his bills. As a college senior, he found work at a unit of a local health club chain, Nautilus Swim & Fitness, starting out cleaning the pool and club but soon taking on increasing responsibilities. He began selling memberships two days a week, but because he was so goal-oriented, setting daily targets that he insisted upon meeting, by the time he graduated from college he was the chain's top salesman. He decided to continue working for Nautilus Swim rather than pursue a career in engineering and in 1983 was sent to Minneapolis-St. Paul to launch the chain's first facility outside of Colorado. It was an immediate success and within a month, Akradi became a partner in the company. He directed site selection, development, and sales and operation as the company added three locations in 1984. Under his direction, the chain became the first to become a 24-hour-a-day operation, provide free child care, offer almost-hourly aerobics classes, and hire larger teams of trainers to assist customers. In 1984, the year the chain changed its name to U.S. Swim and Fitness Clubs, its success—eight clubs generating $33 million in annual sales—attracted the attention of Bally's, the largest chain of health clubs in the United States, and in 1986 Bally's bought the company. Akradi elected to stay on with Bally's, signing a five-year contract.

After three years with Bally's, Akradi quit to start his own health club business. In addition to providing the kind of customer service he introduced at U.S. Swim & Fitness, his idea was to build clubs large enough to accommodate the variety of choices that would appeal to an entire family. "I had worked in clubs," he told the Minneapolis *Star Tribune* in a 2003 profile, "They were dingy, smelly places. They were like torture chambers. And they forced you into contracts. It wasn't built from a customer perspective." Unable to open a health club in the Minneapolis market because of a non-compete clause in the

Company Perspectives:

Our cornerstones are exercise, nutrition and education so you can achieve a balanced and fulfilled life.

contract he signed with Bally's, Akradi attempted to open a large club in San Francisco. According to his research, Minneapolis had a health club for every 70,000 residents while San Francisco had one for every 470,000 residents, making the community a logical place to open a facility. However, he was unable to raise the necessary financing, and finally he moved back to Minnesota when the non-compete provision expired.

First Center Opens in 1992

In October 1990, Akradi formed FCA Ltd. In addition to liquidating all of his personal assets, he lined up a group of shareholders, the largest of which were Minneapolis businessman Wheelock Whitney and Sunfish Lake businessman John Driscoll. Akradi retained a 35 percent interest. In July 1992, he opened the first Life Time Fitness center, roughly 30,000 square feet in size, in Brooklyn, Minnesota, on a site that had not been kind to health clubs: three earlier attempts to establish a club at this location had failed. Akradi established a goal of selling 2,700 memberships in the first year, and as had been the case when he sold memberships during college, he was determined to meet the challenge. At the end of the year, the Brooklyn club sold 2,702 members, was well established, and would go on to become one of the most profitable units in the Life Time chain.

Late in 1994, Life Time, focusing on the suburbs of Minneapolis-St. Paul, opened its second club, located in Egan, Minnesota, which contributed partially to the $4 million in revenues the company posted for the year. The third club, in Woodbury, Minnesota, opened in the fall of 1995, and the chain made plans to establish another four units in Roseville, Minnetonka, Eden Prairie, and Coon Rapids. Some parties were interested in investing in the chain, but at this point, according to Akradi, Life Time did not have use for the money until its could line up more deals for club openings.

In the summer of 1996, Life Time completed an initial round of venture capital financing, receiving $6.5 million from Minneapolis-based Norwest Equity Partners. The chain began building its first "big box" centers, 94,000 square feet in size, roughly the size of two football fields, to realize Akradi's dream of offering recreational centers for the entire family at a value price point. To further this concept, Life Time also began turning to municipalities to create public-private partnerships in building new centers. In 1996, Life Time forged such a relationship, the first of its kind in the United States, with the city of Plymouth, Minnesota, in conjunction with the local school district. With a contribution of land from the city which the company leased, Life Time built a 110,000-square-foot pool and fitness center, including an eight-lane competition pool, diving pool, indoor and outdoor leisure pools, two basketball courts, two gyms, an aerobics room, racquetball courts, and 160 pieces of cardiovascular equipment and 120 resistance-training machines. The facility was owned and operated by Life Time, but area residents were given a discount on memberships and the ability to use facilities on a daily-pass basis; the club also paid local property taxes. This public-private model would be used to open other Life Time clubs in Champlin and Savage, Minnesota, and Akradi hoped to put the idea to good effect elsewhere in the country. Aside from the money saved on real estate, these partnerships forged stronger ties with a community, resulting in increased membership rates.

In 1998, FCA Ltd. changed its name to Life Time Fitness, Inc. to help build the brand. It also completed its second round of venture capital financing, receiving $20 million. Norwest provided $18 million and Piper Jaffray Investors and a group of investors contributed the other $2 million. By the end of 1998, Life Time consisted of nine centers and with an infusion of cash from investors planned to open another six units in the next year. A major reason for investor enthusiasm over Life Time involved positive demographics. In 1990, the number of health club members in America totaled ten million, and over the course of the next decade that figure would triple to 30.5 million people. During the same period, however, only 1,200 health clubs were added, totaling 15,125 in 1999. In addition to growing demand, Life Time was staking out valuable territory, appealing to families and people who were not fitness buffs but just looking to improve their health. In the past, health clubs appealed to customers who were in shape, a situation that intimidated a large number of potential customers. The Life Time concept was more inviting and convenient, especially for parents with children.

One area that needed addressing at Life Time was its Member Management System (MMS), the information technology systems that was used to register, authorize, and track the usage of the facilities by Life Time members. Because the system was often down, many members simply bypassed it. The result was nonpayment of dues and a number of lapsed accounts that were recorded as paid. Moreover, Life Time had to foot the bill for consultants to step in to fix even the smallest glitch. To rectify the situation, a chief information officer was hired, Brent Zempel, who lacked technical expertise but knew the health and fitness industry and was a strong manager. He assembled an IT team and after dismissing available off-the-shelf MMS systems, developed a customized system based on Java. The architecture went live in August 2000, and because the Life Time clubs were all linked, members were now able to use any Life Time facility. The company continued to work out bugs as MMS was refined and became a major part of the company's expansion plans.

Chicago Entry in 2000

In 2000, Life Time began using its current model center, 105,000 square feet in size. Also during this year, the company conducted its largest round of equity financing, taking in $45 million, the financing managed by U.S. Bancorp Piper Jaffray and once again led by Norwest Equity Partners. New York-based Patricof & Co. Ventures Inc. also participated. At this stage, Norwest owned about 35 percent of Life Time, Arkadi and other employees around 20 percent, and Patricof 15 percent. Another major step taken in 2000 was Life Time's entry into the Chicago market. By the end of the year, the chain was operating 21 clubs and revenues totaled $92.9 million.

More than just expanding its geographic reach, Life Time began looking beyond the operation of health clubs to becoming

Key Dates:

1990: The company is formed as FCA Ltd.
1992: The first club opens.
1998: The company changes its name to Life Time Fitness, Inc.
2000: Life Time enters the Chicago market.
2002: The company enters the Southwest market.
2004: Life Time goes public.

a true health-and-fitness brand. The chain began adding amenities found in spas, as well as moving into such areas as apparel, food lines, and nutritional supplements. Life Time created a new position of chief operating officer and hired Bruce Fabel to fill the post. Fabel had worked in retail development for Calvin Klein, Nike, and Warner Brothers Studio Stores and was well experienced in branding strategies. A major factor in attaining the company's brand extensions involved Life Time's MMS, which could be used to inform members about the company's new programs, products, and services to help squeeze greater revenue out of the existing membership base. In addition, Life Time began thinking about spinning off its MMS unit as a consulting firm that would customize MMS for other companies. In this way, Life Time's IT unit would actually generate revenue rather than exist as a mere expense on the balance sheet. In 2002, about 5 percent of Life Time's revenues came from the sale of ancillary products, but that number would begin to increase significantly. Life Time also took steps to transform its in-house magazine, *Experience Life,* into a nationally distributed, bi-monthly glossy publication. In 2003, *Experience Life* became available at most Barnes and Noble, Borders, and B. Dalton locations around the country. Subscriptions to the magazine were also available. Contrary to the approach of some magazines that catered to the ''perfect body'' idea or peddled get-fit-quick fixes, *Experience Life* took a broader approach, appealing to the kind of audience its fitness centers targeted: people with a number of commitments, including family, career, and personal development.

In 2002, Life Time moved into the Southwest for the first time, opening a club in Tempe, Arizona. The Southwest was an appealing market for the company, which planned to open more centers in Phoenix and several in the Houston and Dallas areas. Revenues for the year increased to $192.4 million. That amount would grow to $256.9 million in 2003, and the company would record net income of $13.6 million. Life Time's efforts to grow its other income streams were also bearing fruit. Restaurants, nutritional supplements, personal training fees, and other sources of income generated $25.1 million in 2001, $38.2 million in 2002, and $54.2 million in 2003. The ability to show that the company had multiple ways to generate sales was also important to the company's next step: going public.

With Credit Suisse First Boston and Merrill Lynch serving as co-managers and Piper Jaffray acting as an underwriter, Life Time completed its initial public offering of stock in June 2004, raising $183 million. According to the company, the main reason for going public was to establish a market for its stock, which would allow equity partners like Norwest to realize a profit on their investment. Some of the money was also earmarked for opening new centers. The chain was 35 units strong by July 2004, with four centers in Texas scheduled to open in winter 2004 and others in the development stage. The prospects for Life Time were clearly trending upward, and there was no apparent end in sight to the company's ability to sustain its pattern of strong and steady growth.

Principal Competitors

24 Hour Fitness Worldwide Inc.; Bally Total Fitness Holding Corporation; Gold's Gym International, Inc.

Further Reading

Fiedler, Terry, ''Bulking Up,'' *Star Tribune*, November 16, 2003, p. 1D.

Tellijohn, Andrew, ''Life Time Fitness Bulking up, Shifting Focus,'' *CityBusiness*, August 3, 2001,p. 5.

Waters, Jennifer, ''Life Time Fitness Pumped for Expansion,'' *CityBusiness*, April 28, 1995, p. 4.

Youngblood, Dick, ''Entrepreneur Gets Healthy Return on His Investment,'' *Star Tribune*, November 5, 2000, p. 1D.

—Ed Dinger

Lonmin plc

4 Grosvenor Place
London SW1X 7YL
United Kingdom
Telephone: (+20) 7201-6000
Fax: (+20) 7201-6100
Web site: http://www.lomnin.com

Public Company
Incorporated: 1909 as London & Rhodesia Mining & Land Company
Employees: 20,668
Sales: $1.29 billion (2003)
Stock Exchanges: London
Ticker Symbol: LMI
NAIC: 212221 Gold Ore Mining; 212299 All Other Metal Ore Mining

Lonmin plc—formerly known as Lonrho plc—is the third-largest platinum producer in the world. The company's Lonplats arm mines platinum group metals, or PGMs, which include platinum, palladium, rhodium, and iridium through two South African subsidiaries. In 2002, the company sold its gold mining business in Zimbabwe as a result of political conditions in the region. At its peak, Lonmin controlled 900 subsidiary companies operating in Africa, Europe, Asia, and North America, generated revenues in excess of $7 billion, and employed more than one-quarter million workers. Anemic market prices and cumbersome debt forced the company to shed many of its businesses during the 1990s, as a hasty retreat from many industries took place. By the late 1990s, the company was focused mainly on its mining activities in Africa, where the Lonmin enterprise was born and built into an empire by one of the century's most notable businessmen, R.W. Rowland.

Origins of an Empire Builder

During Lonrho's first century of business, no individual figured more prominently than Roland Walter "Tiny" Rowland. No one even came close. His influence on the company's development was immense, enough to transform a moribund mining and ranching company named London & Rhodesia Mining & Land Company into a sprawling conglomerate that straddled much of the world, with operations blanketing all of Africa. Annual sales during the three decades of Rowland's stewardship increased 787-fold. Profits rose 1,365 times. A company with struggling operations in Rhodesia was shaped into a pan-African empire that, once established, threw its massive corporate weight into Europe, Asia, and North America with resounding success. There was one individual responsible for the meteoric ascension of Lonrho, and that person was the six-foot, two-inch "Tiny" Rowland, the enigmatic corporate baron whose critics numbered as many as his supporters. Combative, secretive, and more successful than any outsider in the tempestuous political waters of Africa, R.W. Rowland was a flamboyant, buccaneering entrepreneur, a corporate maverick who turned Lonrho into one of the world's largest conglomerates.

More inclined to let intrigue reign than to divulge facts, Rowland kept purposefully silent about his life before joining Lonrho. Despite his love for secrecy, Rowland did not escape entirely the scrutiny of his many investigators. He was born Roland Walter Fuhrhop in 1918, the son of a German father and British mother. Reports differ as to whether he was born in India or in Germany, but the young Roland did spend his youth in Hamburg, where his parents were regarded as respected merchants. By the time Hitler assumed control over Germany, Roland Fuhrhop was a teenager, and, like many of his peers, Roland joined the Hitler Youth, briefly becoming a part of the swelling nationalist movement sweeping across Germany. The young Fuhrhop managed to escape any personal stigma associated with being pro-Nazi, however, and in 1939, for unknown reasons, abandoned his surname, becoming, during the inaugural year World War II, Roland Walter Rowland.

During the war, Rowland's parents were deported to the Isle of Man as illegal aliens, interned there while their two sons joined the war effort. Rowland's brother joined the Wehrmacht as an officer and Rowland joined the Royal Army Medical Corps, serving a three-year tenure as a private before he was discharged from the service, supposedly for creating trouble because his mother was dying in internment. Subsequently,

Company Perspectives:

Our purpose is to be a cost-effective, innovative and profitable resources company that is accountable to all our stakeholders in an honest, open and proactive manner. We align ourselves with internationally recognized sustainable practices that ensure a safe and healthy working environment and a long-term responsibility towards the welfare of our communities and the environment within we operate.

Rowland was detained and interned himself, confined to a camp on the Isle of Man that was inhabited by members of the British fascist party founded by Sir Oswald Ernald Mosley.

Conditions for Rowland improved following the war, when for the first time the young entrepreneur began to demonstrate his prowess in the business world. During the immediate postwar years, Rowland engaged in a diverse range of business activities, as would be his predilection in his later career. He produced refrigerators, car radios, and washing machines, and started his own air cargo business before making his life-defining move overseas. In 1948, at age 30, Rowland moved to southern Rhodesia (later Zimbabwe), where he began to develop what he later referred to as his ''deep and abiding love for Africa.'' Africa presented Rowland with a number of different opportunities, and over the course of the next decade he unleashed his energies in several different directions, cementing his reputation as a savvy entrepreneur. Rowland entered into the farming business, he jumped into mining, he distributed Mercedes automobiles, and he landed a well-paid job as finance and commercial director of Rio-Tinto Zinc, a company making its way toward becoming one of the world's largest mining concerns. By the end of the 1950s, Rowland had accumulated a small fortune from his variegated business activities and the time had come for his path to cross with Lonrho's.

Rowland Joins Lonrho in 1961

Despite his less-than-conventional background and his troubles with the British establishment, Rowland, the discharged private and smoldering iconoclast, soon found himself mixing with British royalty and presiding as a managing director of a British-controlled firm. His introduction to royalty and to Lonrho came from the same person, the Honorable Angus Ogilvy, husband to Queen Elizabeth's cousin, Princess Alexandra, and the director of Lonrho. Ogilvy recruited Rowland, convinced that the 44-year-old mining consultant could cure Lonrho's ills. Rowland was ready for the challenge, and he exchanged some of his African assets for a 48 percent stake in Lonrho, joining the company in 1961 when it was more commonly known as the London & Rhodesia Mining & Land Company. At the time, Lonrho was a modestly sized ranching and mining company that was not doing very well. Founded in 1909, the company's sales volume hovered around a mere $10 million, and its payroll comprised fewer than 200 employees, including six in London. Once Rowland joined the company, however, torpid growth became a thing of the past. In a few short years, his actions would outstrip what had taken a half-century to achieve.

Once named a managing director of Lonrho, Rowland moved quickly to expand the company's interests, using his own portfolio of African holdings as a map for Lonrho's expansion and diversification. The company's involvement in mining and ranching was deepened, and forays into automobile and oil distribution were made. Concurrently, the geographic scope of the company was widened considerably until it embraced nearly all of the African continent. Expansion took Lonrho out of Rhodesia, north of the Limpopo River, and into neighboring Malawi, Zambia, Kenya, Zaire, and Tanzania, transforming the company into an African conglomerate without rival.

It was during his crusade to broaden Lonrho's geographic base that Rowland displayed a talent no one could match, an ability that gave Lonrho a decisive advantage over other companies competing in Africa and made its flamboyant leader a legend. While shuttling throughout Africa in search of business opportunities, Rowland struck lasting personal and political friendships with the men who became leaders of their respective nations. Rowland's ability to win over Africa's disparate political personages was astounding, the stuff of the greatest diplomats, effective no matter what the ideological leanings of others involved. Rowland was befriended by rightist authoritarians and leftist revolutionaries alike, confidant to Malawi's Kamuzu Hastings Banda, Zambia's Kenneth Kaunda, Kenya's Daniel arap Moi, and Zaire's Mobutu Sese Seko. With these powerful allies generally amenable to his business plans, Rowland was able to secure vast and diverse holdings for Lonrho, creating a tangle of operating companies that numbered in the hundreds. Annual sales increased exponentially as a result, and soon Rowland reigned over Lonrho's operations with resolute and absolute control, his rule autocratic.

As Rowland shaped Lonrho into a corporate archipelago and his power grew, the aggressive, confrontational managing director gained his detractors, perhaps the inevitable outcome of his singular influence over the fortunes of Lonrho and the way in which he exerted such influence. Feuds with both those within the company and outside its ranks were rampant during Rowland's stewardship of Lonrho, the most notable of which stemmed from a deal Rowland engineered during his first year with the company. In 1961, Rowland obtained the lucrative Beira oil pipeline connecting landlocked Rhodesia to what was then the Portuguese colony of Mozambique. The control of the pipeline was regarded as a coup of sorts, but when Rhodesia's Ian Smith announced his Unilateral Declaration of Independence in 1965, British sanctions forced Rowland to shut down the pipeline. Rowland evidently did so, but when a faction of Lonrho insiders were trying to oust him during the early 1970s, the question of whether or not Rowland had complied with British sanctions touched off a highly publicized investigation by the British government, the timing of which did not strike Rowland as a coincidence. The British government launched an investigation into charges that, among other violations, Lonrho had not honored the Rhodesian sanctions, and against this backdrop a power struggle waged by pro-Rowland and anti-Rowland factions ensued.

In 1973, the British government gave its answer, issuing a 600-page report that essentially cleared Rowland of the sanctions-busting charges. Prime Minister Edward Heath took the opportunity to utter his much-quoted feelings on the matter,

Key Dates:

1909: The London & Rhodesia Mining & Land Company is established.
1961: Roland "Tiny" Rowland joins the company.
1981: Rowland purchases the *Observer* newspaper.
1985: Mohammed Al-Fayed acquires House of Fraser plc; Rowland publicly opposes the deal and launches a near-decade long fight against Al-Fayed.
1993: Al-Fayed and Rowland settle their dispute; Dieter Bock becomes Lonrho's largest shareholder and shares the CEO position with Rowland.
1994: Rowland is ousted from his chief executive position.
1998: Lonrho spins off its Lonrho Africa Plc trading arm and repurchases 21 percent of its issued share capital.
1999: The company changes its name to Lonmin plc.
2000: Duiker Mining Ltd. is sold.
2002: Lonmin sells its Independence Gold assets.
2003: Incwala Resources Pty Ltd. is created.

however, declaring that Lonrho was "the unpleasant and unacceptable face of capitalism," a characterization that in the years to follow was used to describe Rowland. One African leader offered his own riposte, referring to Rowland as "capitalism with a human face," but Rowland did not let others do his fighting and launched his own attack on Britain in 1976, charging that Britain, through its half-ownership of British Petroleum, was violating Rhodesian sanctions itself. Further acrimony followed, leading to an inclusive end, but the power struggle within Lonrho ended with a decisive victory. From the early 1970s forward, Rowland was in charge as he had never been before.

Expansion and Controversy in the 1980s

With a firm grip on the reins of command, Rowland guided Lonrho along the path of expansion and diversification, increasing the breadth and scale of the company's operations. Between 1979 and 1981, Rowland paid $200 million for the Princess Hotel Group. In 1981, he purchased one of Britain's largest Sunday newspapers, the *Observer,* which he would use as a bully pulpit to articulate his stance on controversial issues stemming from Lonrho's activities. In 1986, Rowland paid $173 million for oil and gas properties, including 600 producing fields. Myriad deals were made during the 1970s and 1980s, each strengthening Lonrho's position in a wide spectrum of businesses that included mining, farming, ranching, automobile distribution, sugar production, communications, financial services, and nearly anything Rowland could get his hands on. Annual sales by the mid-1980s neared $5 billion, a volume, minus the $10 million Lonrho was generating before his arrival, entirely developed by Rowland.

The continuing sprawl of Lonrho carried the company from its base in Africa into North America, Europe, and Asia, creating a genuine multinational conglomerate crowded with a labyrinthine assortment of subsidiary companies. Lonrho, as one industry pundit observed, was like Rowland, "perplexingly diverse and hardly seeming to make a comprehensible whole." Rowland, with his forceful personality, managed to embody the eclectic, confusing mash of businesses over which he presided. Despite Lonrho's stature, Rowland's personality and his propensity never to stray too far from controversy made the development of Lonrho, even as it was growing by a billion dollars in sales a year, a subsidiary story next to the highly publicized life of its creator. This was true during the 1970s, when the acrimony over the Beira pipeline erupted, and it was true during the 1980s, when Rowland's pursuit of a prestigious British retail business stole the headlines.

The trouble began in the mid-1980s when Rowland was attempting to add another plume to Lonrho's hat. For years, Rowland had wanted to acquire House of Fraser plc, the parent company of, among many other retail properties, London's Harrods department store. On several occasions, his efforts to acquire the prestigious retail business had been parried by the British government on technical grounds, and by the mid-1980s, when he held 29.9 percent of House of Fraser, he was contemplating his next move. Rowland wanted to launch another bid for the company, but he was afraid his bid would be rebuffed again by the government, which, he thought, would reduce the value of his stock once the denial was made public. Consequently, Rowland sold his stock in House of Fraser to an Egyptian businessman and former sidewalk Coca-Cola vendor named Mohammed Al-Fayed, whose rise in the business world was a mystery to many. Al-Fayed, Rowland figured, lacked the resources to acquire House of Fraser on his own, and, furthermore, would have great difficulty in gaining the nod of approval from the British government. Rowland was incorrect on both presumptions. In March 1985, in an unusually speedy decision, the British government granted Al-Fayed permission to acquire House of Fraser, and by the time Al-Fayed had received approval he had acquired the cash to complete the deal quickly, reportedly receiving $900 million from Muda Hassanal Bulkiah Muizzadin Waddaulah, otherwise known as the sultan of Brunei.

Rowland, vigilantly on the prowl for suspected conspiracies and seemingly in pursuit of fostering corporate intrigue, was furious. In essence, he had attempted to use Al-Fayed to launch his own attack on House of Fraser, but before he knew what was happening Al-Fayed had tucked House of Fraser into his pocket. Never one to turn the cheek, Rowland bitterly opposed the deal, touching off a feud with Al-Fayed that lasted nearly a decade. Five publicly funded official investigations were undertaken into the acquisition of House of Fraser before Al-Fayed and Rowland settled their dispute behind closed doors in 1993, by which time Rowland was involved in the fight of his life.

Power Struggle and Divestiture in the 1990s

As the dispute between Al-Fayed and Rowland occupied the interests of industry observers, Lonrho held sway in a variety of industries. The company was a more than $6 billion enterprise during the late 1980s, generating the bulk of its revenue from Africa but realizing significant income from its worldwide operations. There were 900 subsidiary companies composing Lonrho by this point, and more than 125,000 Lonrho employees were scattered throughout the globe. The company was one of the world's largest automobile distributors, selling Rolls-

Royces, Volkswagens, Audis, Mercedes, and French, Japanese, and American vehicles in Britain, Europe, and Africa. It was the third-largest producer of platinum in the world through its ownership of Western Platinum mines in South Africa, which turned out more than one-quarter million ounces annually, and a major gold producer from mines in Ghana and in Zimbabwe, which yielded nearly 500,000 ounces a year. Lonrho also ranked as the largest single producer of food in Africa, owner of 1.5 million acres of land and 125,000 cattle spread across ten countries. Rowland's acquisition of the *Observer* had been supplemented with the addition of 23 provincial newspapers in the United Kingdom, adding to the might of the company. There were scores of other businesses within the company's fold; together, they created a hard-to-follow tangle of companies all contributing to the coffers of Lonrho.

The massive armada of Lonrho companies exited the 1980s at their peak. The early 1990s witnessed the beginning of serious difficulties for the company, but its problems did not stem from the loose amalgamation of businesses that stretched across the globe—they were born from the company's core business, the mining operations that predated Rowland's arrival. Prices for precious metals began to slide as the decade began, such as the precipitous drop registered by rhodium, a platinum-group metal used in catalytic converters and mined by Lonrho. Between 1990 and 1991, the price of rhodium was cut in half, plunging from $4,200 an ounce to $2,100 an ounce. For a company as diverse as Lonrho, depressive market prices in one of its many sectors should have had no adverse effect on the company's balance sheet. The wide range of the company's business activities presumably would mitigate the effect of slumping business in one area, but this was not the case. Although mining accounted for only a marginal 7 percent of Lonrho's total revenue volume, the proceeds derived from mining contributed a significant 36 percent toward the company's total profit. Moreover, Rowland's seemingly endless feud with Al-Fayed was still raging on, and investor confidence began to wane as considerable effort, cash, and attention were devoted to the resolution of Rowland's contentious struggle. Profits began to slip, and then they plummeted. Between 1990 and 1992, income dropped from £273 million to £79 million, and debt neared £1 billion. Changes were needed, and many considered that Rowland would be unable to take the actions necessary to restore Lonrho's financial health. Though few questioned Rowland's power as a merchant-statesman, his conduct was perceived as part of the problem contributing to Lonrho's woes. The stage was set, and the drama that followed disappointed no one.

Enter Dieter Bock, a German financier who made his reputation by dealing in property in Germany. Well known only to a tight circle of German financiers, Bock was described as cautious and self-effacing, a mild-mannered businessman without the vociferous aplomb characteristic of Rowland. Bock, as he later related, discovered Lonrho "by coincidence" while doing research into large companies during the 1980s. Though he lacked any appreciable experience in international business on the scale and breadth of Lonrho, he was nevertheless interested in the company. Bock met Rowland in the fall of 1992 for the first time, and from there the two began to negotiate; what they would agree upon would surprise nearly all those who watched from the wings.

Bock, it was announced in late 1992, would become Lonrho's largest shareholder by January 1993. Perhaps more surprising, he would also share the chief executive's position with Rowland from that month forward. When those familiar with Lonrho heard the news, they were shocked by this turn of events. Not only had Rowland allowed someone else to eclipse his commanding position as the largest shareholder, but he had evidently conferred upon Bock—a little-known businessman young enough to be his son, with negligible international business experience—the title of heir apparent to the Lonrho empire. It was odd, but soon normalcy—the Rowland breed of normalcy—returned to reassure those who were distressed by the mysterious upheavals within the company.

Bock immediately took the initiative. "You can really use your business fantasy to create wonderful situations," he confided to *African Business* shortly after gaining power. "That is the most interesting thing about Lonrho." Bock was not about to play the role of protege to Rowland's mentor, and he quickly set about turning his fantasy into reality. Bock wanted to change Lonrho's management structure, a plan met by stiff resistance from Rowland. Bock cited Rowland's never-ending feud with Al-Fayed as a deleterious drain on company resources, but Rowland's unexpected appeasement with Al-Fayed in 1993 ended the effectiveness of Bock's rallying point before it could gain momentum. Next, Bock claimed that several directors of the company were beyond retirement age and drawing substantial pensions on top of already substantial salaries. A compromise between Bock and Rowland was reached to add new, younger blood to Lonrho's board of directors. Soon after the agreement to admit two new non-executives to Lonrho's board, Bock charged that Rowland's salary and expenses were too rich for Lonrho. Bock also wanted Rowland stripped of his executive duties.

Battle after battle took center stage among the upper echelon of Lonrho executives, with Rowland eventually losing the war. Four of his staunch supporters, Chairman Rene Leclezio and board members Sir Peter Youens, Paul Spicer, and Robert Dunlop resigned in January 1994, signaling the end. In November 1994, Rowland, who had once negotiated a cease fire in Mozambique and later that same day mediated for an end to civil war in Sudan, was ousted from his chief executive position, effective on the last day of 1994. Part of the agreement reached on November 3, 1994 called for Rowland to resign his seat on Lonrho's board of directors in March 1995. When that month arrived, however, Rowland was his quintessential self. Promising to sue Lonrho for breach of contract, Rowland leveled his words directly at Bock, vowing to pursue him "until the end of my days."

On that somewhat ominous note, Bock set about unraveling the tangled web of subsidiary companies built up by Rowland during his 34-year tenure. The objective, as Bock saw it, was to shed the superfluous layers of Lonrho to expose its core: the businesses involved in mining, trade, agriculture, and hotels. Slated for the auction block were sundry Lonrho businesses involved in automaking, textiles, communications, and financial services, the divestiture of which would reduce the company's staggering debt and lead to a leaner, more profitable enterprise. As Bock spearheaded the dismantling of the Lonrho empire and business and after business was removed from the company's portfolio, the scope of the divestiture program was widened. By mid-1996, the decision had been made to sell the company's hotel holdings, principally its Princess Metropole hotel business, as well as its African and United Kingdom trading operations and its African sugar business.

The sales spree of the 1990s stripped Lonrho of more than half its revenue volume by the time it entered the late 1990s and faced its future as a company almost wholly devoted to mining. Princess Metropole, the trading operations, and the sugar business were expected to be sold in 1997, the same year the company gained a new controlling shareholder. In January 1997, Anglo American Corporation of South Africa Ltd., South Africa's largest company, acquired a controlling stake in Lonrho, purchasing a 26 percent interest in the company. From this juncture, Lonrho prepared for the future, its focus on the production of platinum, gold, and coal in Africa.

Changes in the Late 1990s and Beyond

Lonrho made several additional restructuring moves in the years leading up to 2000. There were multiple changes in management—Bock left in 1997—and the company narrowed its focus even further as the sell-off of non-core assets continued. In 1998, Lonrho spun off its Lonrho Africa plc trading arm and repurchased 21 percent of its issued share capital. In early 1999, Lonrho adopted the Lonmin plc moniker to symbolize the return to its mining roots. The name change and the death of Tiny Rowland months earlier marked the end of a very colorful era in the company's history.

In its first year of business as Lonmin, the company continued to make strides towards its goal of becoming a leading platinum producer. During 2000, the company exited the South African coal mining industry by selling Duiker Mining Ltd. and Tweefontein Collieres Ltd. to Glencore International AG. Nick Morell stepped down as CEO that year and mining executive Edward Haslam was tapped as his replacement. Haslam, together with chairman Sir John Craven, worked to solidify the company's metamorphosis into a premier platinum group metals concern. In 2001, the company partnered with Anglo Platinum to create the Pandora joint venture, which strengthened its platinum group metals production capacity. It also continued to invest in Platinum Australia Ltd., a company working to launch the first platinum/palladium mine in Australia. Political unrest in Zimbabwe led Lonmin to sell Independence Gold in 2002. The sale marked the end of Lonmin's gold mining involvement in the region and was in line with its strategy to focus on platinum group metals.

During 2003, Lonmin began to lay the groundwork for a complex deal that would meet the requirements of the Mining Charter set forth by the South African Minister of Minerals and Energy. As part of the charter, mining companies were required to transfer 15 percent ownership of their South African mining assets to historically disadvantaged South Africans (HDSAs) within five years, and then 26 percent over the next ten years. The company set plans in motion to enact a black economic empowerment transaction in 2003 when it created Incwala Resources Pty Ltd. Lonmin hoped to find suitable HDSAs to buy into Incwala, which would control 18 percent of the company's Lonplats mining operations.

Lonmin turned to former BHP Billiton executive Bradford Mills to take over as CEO upon Haslam's retirement in 2004. By now, rumors began to surface that the company would once again resume an aggressive acquisition strategy or quite possibly merge with another mining concern. A February 2004 *Financial Times* article speculated about the company's future. "Lonmin is going through an identity crisis," the article claimed. "Does it carry on as it is, riding the high platinum price and trying to please investors with hefty dividend payments but risk falling from favour when and if precious metals prices fall? Or does it move into other businesses, in an attempt to become a larger diversified mining group that can weather the commodities cycle?" Indeed, Lonmin's options for the future were plentiful. It had transformed itself over the past decade and looked to be on the brink of making significant changes in the future. Only time would tell how the next chapter in Lonmin's notable history would play out.

Principal Subsidiaries

Eastern Platinum Ltd. (73%); Western Platinum Ltd. (73%).

Principal Competitors

Anglo American plc; AngloGold Ashanti Ltd.; Inco Ltd.

Further Reading

Barnes, John, "Tit for Tat on London's High Street: A Tiff over the Crown Jewel of British Retailing," *U.S. News & World Report*, January 30, 1989, p. 63.

Bream, Rebecca, "Mills Joins Lonmin as Chief Executive," *Financial Times*, February 6, 2004, p. 24.

Buckingham, Lisa, "Sudden End for Britain's Last Tycoon," *Guardian*, November 4, 1994, p. 26.

Edgecliffe-Johnson, Andrew, "Lonrho Plans to Take Full Control of Platinum Arm," *Financial Times*, January 26, 1999, p. 21.

"Glencore Completes Acquisition of Lonmin's Stake in Coal Companies," *African Mining Monitor*, May 29, 2000.

Gupte, Pranay B., "Inside Lonrho Today," *Forbes*, March 21, 1988, p. 100.

——, "The Swami with the Golden Touch," *Forbes*, March 7, 1988, p. 34.

Hall, Richard, "As a Friend, I am Good . . . As an Enemy, I Am Excellent," *African Business*, November 1994, p. 12.

"Impala-Lonmin Deal Could Advance Black Empowerment," *Platt's Metals Week*, September 29, 2003, p. 12.

King, Ralph, Jr., " 'If Anything Happens to Tiny,' " *Forbes*, January 12, 1987, p. 291.

LaRue, Gloria T., "Rowland Agrees to Quit Lonrho at End of Year," *American Metal Market*, November 8, 1994, p. 2.

Moore, John, "Tiny versus Bock: Another Epic Battle Begins," *African Business*, November 1994, p. 8.

"More Changes on the Way, Says Lonrho," *Yorkshire Post*, January 26, 1999, p. 12.

Munford, Christopher, "Bock Wrests Lonrho from Rowland," *American Metal Market*, January 27, 1994, p. 2.

——, "It's a Lonrho to Hoe as 4 May Quit," *American Metal Market*, December 22, 1993, p. 6.

O'Connor, Brian, "Action is Brewing So Make Mine Lonmin," *Daily Mail*, March 13, 2004.

"A Riddle within an Enigma: Lonrho," *Economist*, December 19, 1992, p. 66.

"Sale Brings Lonrho Closer to Demerger," *American Metal Market*, February 24, 1997, p. 16.

Simpkins, Edward, ''A New Oligarchy Rises in South Africa Since the End of Apartheid,'' *Sunday Telegraph*, February 1, 2004, p. 6.

Tieman, Ross, ''When Breaking up Is Hard to Do,'' *Financial Times*, July 26, 1996, p. 17.

''Tiny Feat,'' *Economist*, December 14, 1991, p. 72.

''Tiny in Africa: Private Diplomats,'' *Economist*, September 26, 1992, p. 43.

—Jeffrey L. Covell
—update: Christina M. Stansell

McAlister's Corporation

731 South Pear Orchard Road, Suite 51
Ridgeland, Mississippi 39157
U.S.A.
Telephone: (601) 952-1100
Fax: (601) 957- 0964
Web site: http://www.mcalistersdeli.com

Private Company
Incorporated: 1989
Sales: $126 million (2003 est.)
NAIC: 722211 Limited-Service Restaurants

McAlister's Corporation, based in Ridgeland, Mississippi, operates fast-casual restaurants under the McAlister's Deli, McAlister's Gourmet Deli, and McAlister's Select names. There are more than 100 units in the chain, one-quarter of which are company owned. They are located in 16 Southern and Southwestern states and Ohio, primarily in college towns. McAlister's menu offers approximately 100 items, concentrating on sandwiches, salads, baked potatoes, desserts, and the chain's signature sweet ice tea. The company pays higher wages than most restaurants, allowing it to implement a no-tipping policy. Any tips that may be left by customers are donated to charity. The family-oriented chain also maintains a no-smoking policy and does not sell alcohol.

Origins

McAlister's was founded by Oxford, Mississippi, dentist Don Newcomb. He grew up in Ripley, Mississippi, where as a teenager in the 1950s he gained his first experience in the restaurant business while working at the only soda fountain in the county. Newcomb earned a degree in dentistry from the University of Mississippi, followed by a stint in the military that included time aboard a navy aircraft carrier and work in a veterans hospital. Upon his discharge he decided to return to Mississippi to set up a dental practice and settled on the thriving college town of Oxford, home to the University of Mississippi. There, his business interests expanded beyond dentistry. He developed rental properties, catering to the student population, and in the early 1980s he once again became involved in restaurants, launching franchise operations for the Sonic's and Danver's chain.

Ever since his days as a soda jerk, Newcomb had wanted to start his own restaurant, something more upscale than his fast food franchise ventures. In 1987, he recognized a opportunity to realize that dream when a movie, *The Heart of Dixie,* was filmed in Oxford and an old gas station, located about a mile from the university, was turned into a 1950s diner and hangout. After the production company was finished with the site, Newcomb bought the property, turned the movie set into a real restaurant, and along with his dentist office manager, Debra Bryson, and two sons, Chris and Neil, opened a sandwich shop called ''Chequers'' in 1989. To avoid confusion with the Checkers chain of restaurants, the name was soon changed to McAlister's Gourmet Deli. McAlister was the last name of his wife's parents.

The McAlister's format was simple yet engaging. The menu was presented on large boards that hung above the cashier station and meals were served in baskets with plastic utensils. In the beginning, the restaurant's line of sandwiches and salads were assembled from precooked ingredients and heated in Lincoln steamers, the bread was toasted in rotary toasters, and potatoes were baked in convection ovens. The restaurant's distinctive decor, for which Bryson was responsible, featured exposed ceilings, a garage door, and many local artifacts.

Branching Out in the Early 1990s

The McAlister's format proved especially popular with college students, and, building on the success of the Oxford restaurant, Newcomb and his team opened a second location in 1992 in another college town, Hattiesburg, Mississippi. Newcomb was so convinced that McAlister's was a winning concept that he also closed his dental practice in 1992 to concentrate on his restaurant business. A year later, he opened another McAlister's Gourmet Deli in Tupelo, Mississippi, where the University of Mississippi maintained a branch campus. In 1994, McAlister's expanded to another college town, Jackson, Mississippi. At this point, management decided to build McAlister's into a chain by way of franchising. The company turned for help in navigating the legal and business process issues to Chicago-based Francorp, a franchise consulting firm. Newcomb told the *Mis-*

Company Perspectives:

People today crave fresh tastes, quick service and a welcoming friendly atmosphere where they can relax for hours or eat and run. And that's precisely what McAlister's Deli delivers, with a special touch that's uniquely our own.

sissippi Business Journal in 1995, "We quickly saw that this was totally different from opening and operating a sandwich shop or two locally. . . . In franchising, our job as the management team [was] to teach potential franchise owners everything we know about how to operate the business successfully while maintaining McAlister's standards for quality." He said his top priority became maintaining quality control, making sure that "franchise owners receive all the training and support they're going to need to implement our system in their own locations."

Many of McAlister's early franchisees were strong believers in the concept because they were first satisfied customers of the restaurant and then became interested in the franchising opportunity because of their positive dining experience. As McAlister's evolved into a franchise operation, the management team took on clearly defined roles. As Newcomb explained to the *Mississippi Business Journal,* Bryson was an excellent organizer, his son Chris was a strong operations person, and Neil proved to be an effective communicator with franchisees, "making sure they [did] things right." Neil was also in charge of new store development. As for Newcomb, according to Bryson, he was the visionary of the group. He was responsible for applying lessons learned about teamwork in his dental practice to the restaurant business. "With each dental case," he explained to the *Mississippi Business Journal,* "you foster teamwork by sitting every member of your staff down and discussing each case in minute detail. With sandwich shops, customers want to get in there, get quick service with a smile, and get out on time with exactly what they ordered. That takes a lot of time and effort in training our employees and taking good care of them, because they really are our most important asset." To support that conviction, McAlister's paid higher-than-average restaurant wages, and for employees working 35 hours a week, medical coverage was included, a rarity in the industry.

McAlister's enjoyed such strong growth that during the mid-1990s it made *Inc.* magazine's list of the 500 fastest-growing companies in back-to-back years. In the fall of 1997, McAlister's added some outside executive talent, hiring attorney Patrick Walls from Francorp to serve as general counsel. He had worked with McAlister's for the previous three years as the company launched its franchising efforts. At this point, the McAlister's chain numbered 27 restaurants in nine states, with 13 located in Mississippi, and another 50 under development. To spur internal growth, McAlister's now began to offer catering services. In addition to hiring Walls, the company also hired a marketing team to help build name recognition and to develop new menus and promotions. It was also interested in adding further to the management team to facilitate faster growth.

More than just supplementing McAlister's management team, Newcomb was interested in finding someone with enough experience to take the chain to the next level—moving from a successful entrepreneurial company to a professionally managed organization. Newcomb interviewed a number of CEO candidates, and in early 1998, at a technology conference, Newcomb found his man in Michael J. Stack, a 35-year-veteran in the restaurant business. Over the years, Stack had held important management positions at Host International/Marriott Corporation, Pizza Hut, and Western Sizzlin', as well as spending time as a Chi-Chi's franchisee. Since the mid-1980's, Stack had run his own LaJolla, California-based consulting firm. Initially, Newcomb approached Stack to ask for some advice about buying a point-of-sale system. Stack admitted that he took Newcomb for a "small timer," but when he heard the volumes McAlister's was enjoying, in excess of $1 million per restaurant, his interest was piqued. He went to work for the chain on a consulting basis for six months and became convinced that the McAlister's concept was "a rare find." Newcomb then interviewed Stack for the CEO position, and like the other candidates Stack wanted a piece of the business. Unlike the others, however, Stack wanted to lead a management buyout, an idea to which Newcomb was receptive.

New Ownership in the Late 1990s

In October 1998, Stack accepted the CEO position and moved along with his wife from Los Angeles to Mississippi, a relocation that was actually not that drastic for him. His wife came from Mississippi, and they had paid regular visits to the state for 30 years. He also coaxed an ex-partner, Phil Friedman, to join him as president and chief operating officer. Friedman, who held an MBA from the Wharton School of Business, was strong in financials and was an experienced restaurant man. Together they formed a holding company, Mississippi Holdings Inc., and raised $8.3 million, much of its coming from local insurance companies, to buy a 70 percent stake in McAlister's. Newcomb stayed on as a director of the company and held the exclusive franchise rights to Kentucky. Stack took on the additional post of chairman, while Friedman became president and chief financial officer. Chris and Neil Newcomb retained their management positions.

Stack and Friedman initiated a number of changes following the buyout. Foremost, they recognized that the chain did not have the necessary infrastructure in place to support rapid growth in franchising. As a result, they opted to step back, regroup, and bolster the chain's training program. They also became more restrictive about whom they accepted as franchisees. Previously, McAlister's franchisees may have had business experience but little prior involvement with restaurants. Now the chain was interested in attracting larger players, people who were interested in a second concept as a way to grow market share. The new owners also hired an experienced restaurant designer, Scottsdale, Arizona-based Kathy Diamond, to bring some continuity to the look of the McAlister's locations. Architect David Cromley was also hired to shrink the chain's prototype, which was too large and costly. The one area that Stack and Friedman were reluctant to change was McAlister's culture, which had been a major part of the chain's success.

By the end of 1999, McAlisters generated sales of $46.3 million from 42 units, 11 of which were company owned. A year later, revenues improved to about $65 million. In 2001, McAlister's reached a major milestone when it opened its first

Key Dates:

1989: The first McAlister's Deli opens in Oxford, Mississippi.
1992: A second unit opens in Hattiesburg, Mississippi.
1994: The company begins franchising.
1999: Michael Stack and Philip Friedman acquire a chain of stores.
2002: Stack resigns as CEO.

nontraditional store. While the chain had enjoyed a great deal of success over the years in college towns, it now opened its first restaurant on campus, located in the student center of the Appalachian State University in Boone, North Carolina. As had been the case with many of the early franchised operations, this restaurant resulted from a customer's firsthand experience with McAlister's. The school director of foodservice was introduced to McAlister's while visiting his daughter at the University of North Carolina in Chapel Hill. They ate a meal at a McAlister's and he was impressed with the large number of students, the upscale decor, and the quality of the food. Appalachian State became a franchisee and operated the unit with university employees.

In early 2002, McAlister's began a process of restructuring and, in a surprise move, Stack decided to step down as CEO, turning over the reins to Friedman. Just a month later, Chris Newcomb also quit the company, although he maintained that his decision had nothing to do with Stack's departure. He, along with his father and Debra Bryson, decided to become involved in a different restaurant venture, this time as franchisees for a new fast-casual restaurant concept, Moe's Southwest Grille, which featured Mexican food and a fun atmosphere. Two years later, the three partners would once again try their hands at launching a restaurant concept, opening Newk's Express Café in Oxford, serving sandwiches, gourmet pizzas, and salads.

Friedman, along with Walls, who became chief administrative officer, carried on growing the McAlister's chain. There was some talk of taking the company public, but those plans failed to materialize. In 2002, sales topped the $100 million mark as the chain continued to add new locations, expanding concentrically from Mississippi into surrounding states. For the first time, in 2002, McAlister's opened a food court prototype, McAlister's Select, which debuted in the Northpark Mall in Ridgeland. The hope was that the smaller design would open up more possibilities in colleges where food courts were located and the McAlister's concept was strong.

The McAlister's chain continued to grow in 2004 and appeared poised to expand well beyond its southern roots. One of the chain's major franchisees, the Bistro Group, announced it would significantly increase the number of McAlister's Delis it planned to open in the Cincinnati area. Bistro was also interested in moving into other Ohio cities, as well as Pennsylvania.

Principal Competitors

Applebee's International, Inc.; The Quizno's Master LLC; Doctor's Associates Inc. (Subway).

Further Reading

Farkas, David, ''New Deli,'' *Chainleader*, December 1999.
——, ''Product Placement,'' Chainleader, March 2004, p. 1.
Gillette, Becky, ''McAlister's, Despite Tried-and-True Success, Trying New Things,'' *Mississippi Business Journal*, January 20, 2003, p. 33.
LaHue, Polly, ''McAlister Deli—Something to Cheer About,'' *Restaurant Hospitality*, November 2000, p. 120.
McAlister's Makes 'Inc. 500,' '' *Mississippi Business Journal*, November 6, 1995, p. 1.
McCann, Nita Chilton, ''With 1500% Sales Growth in 6 Years, Monteith, Libby, ''McAlister's Focusing on New Horizons,'' *Daily Mississippi*, July 7, 1998.

—Ed Dinger

McPherson's Ltd.

5 Dunlop Road
Mulgrave 3170
Australia
Telephone: 03395663300
Fax: 0395749075
Web site: http://www.mcphersons.com.au

Public Company
Incorporated: 1913
Employees: 935
Sales: AUD 333.32 million ($242.65 million) (2004)
Stock Exchanges: Australian
Ticker Symbol: MCP
NAIC: 332211 Cutlery and Flatware (Except Precious) Manufacturing; 339912 Silverware and Plated Ware Manufacturing

McPherson's Ltd. is a holding company encompassing three strategic activities: housewares, printing, and, since 2003, health and beauty care products. Housewares represents the company's closest link to its origins as an 1880s Melbourne-based pig iron trader, with the company's extensive range of silverware and kitchenware brands. McPherson's markets and distributes cutlery, kitchen tools, glassware, bakeware, dinnerware, cookware, knives, and other kitchen and tableware, as well as household goods including scissors, scales, barbecue accessories, door mats, garden tools, bathroom accessories, and the like. The company's range of brand names includes Crown, Strachan, Wiltshire, Grosvenor, Staysharp, and Eterna, among its own brands, as well as distribution agreements for international brands such as Oxo, Chef'n, and Selfix in the United States, Salter in the United Kingdom, Kinox/Kin Hip in Hong Kong, and Trudeau in Canada. Although formerly itself a diversified manufacturer, McPherson's now sources its housewares products from manufacturers through its Hong Kong office. McPherson's holds leading positions in many of its markets, such as the hospitality market, where it supplies some 80 percent of all beer mugs in Australia. Printing is the company's largest division, under McPherson's Printing Group, and is Australia's largest commercial printer, leading both the book printing and catalogue and commercial printing segments, with two book printing plants and a third dedicated commercial printing facility. McPherson's also controls a major segment of the country's telephone directory business, with long-term contracts with Telstra to print its white and yellow pages directories. That division, formerly known as William Brooks & Co., was renamed under the McPherson's name in 2003. In that year, McPherson's acquired Cork Asia Pacific for AUD 101 million in order to add a third division, Health and Beauty products, under such brands as Lady Jane and Manicare. Listed on the Australian Stock Exchange, McPherson's Ltd. posted sales of AUD 333 million (US $254 million) in 2004.

Pig Iron Origins in the 19th Century

Thomas McPherson was born in 1822 in Kingussie, in Inverness, Scotland. Like many Scotsmen of the period, McPherson decided to emigrate to Australia to try his luck in the newly established colony. McPherson arrived in Melbourne in 1852. McPherson launched his own business on Collins Street West, acting as a supplier for pig iron to the local foundry industry. The pig iron stock was brought in by trading ships coming to Australia to bring back wool and wheat to the United Kingdom.

McPherson's dealings with foundries led him to develop other trade streams, such as supplying equipment and machinery and parts for workshops, machine tools, steam engines, and the like. By 1860, McPherson's business had evolved into a general hardware wholesaler and retailer. In that year, McPherson renamed his business as Thomas McPherson & Sons.

McPherson continued building the business into the latter half of the century, while becoming a prominent citizen in his own right—becoming an alderman in the 1860s, and even serving a brief stint as mayor in 1870 before going on to become a member of the Australian parliament. The company grew in stature as well, and in 1881, son Hunter McPherson opened the company's first branch in Sydney.

Thomas McPherson died in 1888 and the business was taken over by Hunter McPherson and his brothers. The company

Company Perspectives:

Vision: To be a superior performing and internationally competitive company. Mission: To achieve long-term superior growth in the value of each share and its attendant dividends.

continued to operate as a wholesale and retail merchant to the hardware, building, and industrial trade. But the company also began a transition into becoming an industrial company in its own right. Indeed, McPherson's willingness to reinvent itself remained a company hallmark into the 21st century. The company marked this change by reincorporating in 1913 as a proprietary company, McPherson's Pty. Ltd. The company remained based in the state of Victoria, but increasingly began to focus on sales throughout Australia.

By the early years of the 20th century, McPherson's had emerged as leading manufacturer and supplier of metal fasteners, fittings, and components. As such, the company participated in a number of landmark public works projects, including the building of the Transcontinental Railway—the company produced all of the dog spikes needed for the 1,200-mile railroad, completed in 1917, which connected the country's coasts and made possible the formation of the Australian Commonwealth. McPherson's also manufactured the five million rivets needed to build the Sydney Harbor Bridge, a project launched in 1926 and completed in 1932.

McPherson's also became an important contributor to the Australian war effort in World War II, converting much of its production to the manufacture of machine tools. In 1944, the company went public and, with the end of the war, began seeking new directions.

Printing and Housewares in the 1980s

Although McPherson's developed a variety of activities over the next two decades—the company became, for example, the largest manufacturer and distributor of nuts, bolts, and screws in Australia—its interests narrowed more specifically to two fields, printing and tableware, in the 1980s.

McPherson's involvement in printing started back in the 1940s, when it acquired a stake in Maryborough, Victoria-based Hedges & Bell. In 1956, McPherson's acquired full control of Hedges & Bell, which remained the focus of its printing division through the 1970s. In the early 1980s, however, the company began building its print division, buying Dominion Press in 1981. That company, based in Blackburn, also in Victoria, was then merged with Hedges & Bell in 1983. The larger company continued operating under the name Dominion Press Hedges & Bell until 1986, when it changed its name to The Book Printer.

McPherson's continued adding printing business as its focus narrowed. In 1988, the company bought Mulgrave, Victoria's Owen King Printers Pty. Ltd., which then moved to a new printing plant the following year. At the beginning of the next decade, McPherson's boosted its book printing operation again, acquiring Globe Press in 1991. Following that purchase, McPherson's restructured its book and commercial printing division, merging Globe, Owen King, and The Book Printer into a single subsidiary, McPherson's Printing Pty. Ltd. in 1992.

At the same time, McPherson's also had begun to explore other printing areas. In 1982, the company acquired William Brooks & Co. Founded in 1887 as a printer of invitations and similar items, William Brooks began printing telephone directories in the early part of the 19th century.

By 1917, the company had been awarded a significant contract with the Postmaster General's Office to print some of the company's earliest telephone directories. William Brooks maintained that relationship over the course of the century, even as the Postmaster General's telecommunications wing evolved as Telstra. In 1992, William Brooks began a major investment program, building a new state-of-the-art printing plant. Completed in 1994, the new plant was capable of producing the entire run of Telstra directories in just three months. This investment enabled William Brooks to retain its position as Telstra's largest supplier into the 2000s, with a long-term contract to supply 50 percent of Telstra's directories.

New Horizons for a New Century

McPherson's had meanwhile been building another division, more closely related to its longstanding manufacturing wing. In 1980, McPherson's made its first step into developing itself as one of Australia's leading supplier of housewares, tableware, and kitchenware when it purchased the Wiltshire File Company. That company specialized in kitchen knives and cutlery, as well as other cookware, emerging as a leader in there categories in Australia. Two years later, McPherson's added a significant silverware brand, Strachan Silverware.

By the early 1990s, McPherson's began seeking to extend its tableware offerings, and in 1991 the company acquired the Grosvenor and Rodd brands from Mytton Rodd. Other brands in the McPherson's stable by the end of the 1990s included Staysharp, Deco, Ai-de-Chef, Kitchen Class, Richardson, and Gripi, among others. Hit hard by the recession of the early 1990s, and by what some observers considered a lack of direction, McPherson's began a new transformation at mid-decade. Led by new managing director David Allman, the company shed its manufacturing operations and instead fixed its focus on its Printing and Housewares division.

Housewares took on greater focus for McPherson's into the new century. In 1999, the division took a significant step forward with the acquisition of CPS Housewares Pty. Ltd., which boosted McPherson's range of kitchen utensils, as well as kitchen equipment and household cleaning products.

McPherson's Housewares division expanded again the following year, now through the acquisition of Crown Glassware. Among other products, Crown was a major supplier to the Australian and New Zealand hospitality markets, including an 80 percent of the commercial beer glass segment. Crown itself had been established in 1926 by a group of Sydney glassmakers, who originally produced crystal and flint glass. Crown Crystal later merged with Corning in 1961, then split off from Crown Corning and became part of ACI Packaging, becoming known as ACI Crown in 1988.

Key Dates:

1852: Thomas McPherson, a native of Scotland, emigrates to Australia and sets up business as a merchant for pig iron in Melbourne.
1860: McPherson incorporates the company as McPherson & Sons.
1882: McPherson's son Hunter opens a branch in Sydney.
1913: The company incorporates as McPherson's Pty. Ltd.
1944: McPherson's goes public and acquires a stake in Bell & Hedges printing company.
1956: The company acquires full control of Bell & Hedges.
1980: The company acquires Wiltshire File Company as part of its entry into the housewares sector.
1981: The company acquires Dominion Press.
1982: The company acquires William Brooks & Co., telephone directory printer; the Strachan tableware brand is acquired.
1983: Dominion Press and Bell & Hedges are merged.
1986: Dominion Press Bell & Hedges changes its name to The Bell Printer.
1988: The company acquires Owen King Printers Pty. Ltd.
1991: The company acquires Globe Press, based in Brunswick; the Grosvenor and Rodd tableware brands are acquired from Mytton Rodd.
1992: Globe, Owen King, and Dominion are merged to form McPherson's Printing Pty. Ltd.
1999: The company acquires CPS Housewares Pty. Ltd.
2000: Crown Glassware is acquired.
2003: William Brooks is merged into McPherson's Printing Group; the company acquires NBL Business and Cork Asia Pacific.

McPherson's continued to add to its housewares division into the 2000s, notably with the purchase of NBL Business, based in Sydney, in 2003. That company enabled McPherson's to come full circle, as it were, adding a range of hardware products such as the Primeline brand of lawn mower blades and trimmer accessories; Mastertool, a maker of soldering irons and glue guns; and Unibilt, which sold hinges and brackets.

Yet McPherson's also began seeking out new growth opportunities. The company launched a new direction in June 2003 when it purchased Cork Asia Pacific for AUD 101 million. That purchase brought McPherson's into the health and beauty care market for the first time, forming the basis for a new division. The purchase also gave the company a strong logistics and distribution operation, as an added benefit. With nearly 150 years of corporate evolution behind it, McPherson's remained a mainstay in Australia's business community.

Principal Subsidiaries

Domenica Pty. Ltd.; Owen King Holdings Pty. Ltd.; McPherson's Printing Pty. Ltd.; Yevad Products Pty. Ltd.; Wiltshire (NZ) Ltd. (New Zealand); 947413 Ltd.; 718932 Pty. Ltd.; Regent-Sheffield (Canada) Ltd.; McPherson's Housewares Pty. Limited; McPherson's America, Inc.; McPherson's Publishing, Inc. (U.S.); Regent-Sheffield Ltd. (U.S.); McPherson's (Hong Kong) Ltd.; McPherson's CPG Limited (Hong Kong); McPherson's (U.K.) Ltd.; Richardson Sheffield Ltd. (U.K.); V. Sabatier Ltd. (U.K.); Revlect Pty. Ltd.; McPherson's Enterprises Pty. Ltd.

Principal Competitors

Gillette Co.; Wella AG; Kenwood Silver Company Inc.; Union Industries Inc.; BIC S.A.; Fiskars Oy Ab; IMBEL; Lord Precision Industries; Tefal S.A.S.

Further Reading

''Cost Cutting Helps Lift McPhersons,'' *Advertiser,* March 13, 1996, p. 41.
''McPherson's Adds Cork to Make-Up Mix,'' *Age,* June 28, 2003.
''McPhersons Hit by US Operation,'' *Australian,* May 19, 1997, p. 31.
''McPherson's to Acquire ACI's Crown Glassware Businesses,'' *AsiaPulse News,* January 13, 2000.
Porter, Ian, ''McPherson's Lands Cash, Growth, Value,'' *Age,* November 8, 2003.

—M.L. Cohen

Milliman USA

1301 5th Avenue, Suite 3800
Seattle, Washington 98101
U.S.A.
Telephone: (206) 624-7940
Fax: (206) 340-1380
Web site: http://www.milliman.com

Private Company
Incorporated: 1947
Employees: 1,850
Sales: $323 million (2002)
NAIC: 541611 Administrative Management and General Management Consulting Services; 511210 Software Publishers

Milliman USA is one of the largest independent consulting and actuarial firms in the United States. The company works with corporations, government entities, union organizations, and financial institutions in the areas of healthcare; property and casualty insurance; pension, employee benefits, and compensation; and life insurance and financial services. Owned by more than 200 principals, Milliman has offices in more than 29 locations in the United States, Bermuda, Brazil, Hong Kong, Japan, Korea, Mexico, and the United Kingdom. Milliman is a founding member of Milliman Global.

1947–70s: New Company Gains Ground in a New Industry

In 1947, Wendell Milliman, a specialist in life and health insurance, returned home from New York and rented a two-room office in Seattle. The actuarial profession was just beginning to develop broadly in the United States at the time, and Milliman had in mind creating a national actuarial firm—a company whose business it was to evaluate risk for its clients, primarily insurance companies and pension plans. As an actuarial company, Milliman's business would use statistical evidence to answer questions about the future, such as: How long is someone likely to live after retirement? How much money would a start-up company need today to create a pension fund for its employees in 20 years? What is a woman's average stay in the hospital after childbirth? What are executives in the Northwest paid and how much more might they expect to earn the following year?

Three years later, Milliman hired Stuart Robertson, a young actuary from Northwestern Life Insurance Company of Seattle. Robertson chose to join Milliman—turning down a second offer to become chief actuary at a mid-sized New York-based life insurer—even though, as he explained in a 1998 *Puget Sound Business Journal* article, ''The job in the East carried a salary exactly double that which Milliman could afford.'' Nonetheless, he and Milliman shared a vision, and together the two formed Milliman & Robertson.

Although Milliman and Robertson began small (they at first shared a single office, desk, and telephone), the two men's vision was larger than their workspace. Unlike other firms, theirs was organized from the bottom up around four principal consulting practices—health, life insurance, property and casualty insurance, and pensions and employee benefits—each of which enjoyed a great deal of autonomy. Priding themselves on ''quality work, good client relationships and a solid reputation,'' according to Robert Collett, who was president and chief executive of the company from 1990 to 2002, they set about steadily to grow. Throughout the 1950s, M & R, as the company came to be called, expanded down the West Coast, and in the 1960s, it spread coast to coast.

1970s–80s: Becoming a National Presence

Beginning in the mid-1970s, when the government mandated that pension plans meet stringent regulations, and when insurance companies began to spin off their actuarial services to outside companies, M & R's client list grew rapidly. By 1983, when James A. Curtis replaced Robertson as president and chief executive of the company, M & R had become the nation's sixth largest actuarial firm and specialized in the field of employee benefits. Curtis, who had studied actuarial science at Drake University, had joined the company at age 19, when he turned down a job playing the bass with the Tommy Dorsey Band. As Curtis later explained in a 1983 article in the *New York Times,*

Company Perspectives:

A consulting firm is defined, in large part, by the quality, experience and skills of its professionals. Over time, Milliman has earned a solid reputation for its independence, excellent work product, practical advice, and dedicated client focus. Our structure, which is entrepreneurial, attracts independent men and women who seek out challenges and are willing to take risks. Clients recognize that dealing with business owners translates directly into hands-on, client-driven service and lends itself to forming long-lasting relationships characterized by strong client communications and a ''business advisor'' approach to problems and opportunities.

as head of M & R, he saw his biggest challenge as seeing to it that the company continued to grow, yet maintained ''that small company feeling.''

Curtis served as president only until 1990, when Robert L. Collett replaced him. That same year, the company headed up the creation of Woodrow Milliman, an affiliation of 11 actuarial and consulting firms operating in North America, Europe, and the Pacific Rim. Two years later, Collett also assumed the role of chief executive of M & R. By this time, the company was organized officially as a sort of franchise operation with ''equity principals'' who worked in separate, functionally independent offices that specialized in different parts of the company's overall practice. The individual offices paid a fee to the centralized structure, but functioned as independent profit centers.

The 1990s: Growth and Expansion into Healthcare

Throughout the 1990s, M & R also continued its involvement in the area of employee benefits. In 1991, it purchased Fleet/Norstar Employee Benefit Services Inc. In the late 1990s, the Pennsylvania Insurance Department hired M & R to estimate the potential financial savings from the state's new workers' compensation law. And in 1997, in a move that the California State Employees Association opposed, M & R performed a feasibility study to determine whether the state of California ought to privatize the State Compensation Insurance Fund, and, if so, how.

By the late 1990s, insurance companies had become increasingly dependent upon actuarial outsourcing firms, which, as a result, were growing at double-digit rates. M & R expanded from its traditional line of business, the design and administration of employee benefits, to help companies develop managed healthcare plans.

Healthcare financing had undergone a fundamental shift in the mid-1980s as the federal government started paying hospitals flat rates for different treatments through Medicare programs. Healthcare executives, as a result, sought ways to make their practice more consistent. M & R's consultants, who had already been helping HMOs and hospitals measure their performance against that of the industry, began to formalize the company's ''notebooks'' filled with recommended ''best practices'' (for different conditions that achieved the desired results most consistently) into official guidelines.

In 1990, the healthcare segment of M & R began to sell its guidelines. Based on data the company collected from medical articles, hospital records, and doctors, the guidelines served as a means of advising medical institutions on appropriate lengths of hospital stays and assisting insurance companies to determine whether to pay for treatments. Throughout the 1990s, M & R published nine updated versions of the guidelines, which it sold for an average of $500-$900 per book.

In 1993, as healthcare reform moved to the top of the nation's agenda, M & R also introduced a service for consumers, offering them access to healthcare cost data. Any individual could consult M & R's database of more than 150 million claims for the cost of a 900 telephone call.

M & R was by now one of the most influential firms with insurers and HMOs and one of the key players in the national move to curb medical practices and to slow the growth of medical costs. Annual sales of its guidelines topped 6,000 copies—not including electronic copies—up from about 600 in 1990. As the 1990s wore on, M & R's sway became ever more significant, and it became embroiled in the healthcare debates sweeping the nation.

Although the chief author of the guidelines insisted that ''quality of care and efficiency of care'' were convergent, in a 1995 *New York Times* article, the A.M.A. fought the use of the guidelines on the grounds that they were being used to help insurance companies cut medical costs at the risk of endangering patients. Doctors insisted that they needed to place more emphasis on saving patients' lives than on saving money. M & R responded that the guidelines should never be used to deny treatment, but only as reference points for discussion. Its recommendations were for uncomplicated cases only and, in these cases, represented the ''best practice'' in medicine. By 1995, the company had issued four volumes of guidelines—for hospital admission and stays, doctor's office treatments, home healthcare, and recovery times before returning to work.

By 2000, the guidelines covered everything from major surgeries to prescription drugs and were a lucrative part of M & R's business. M & R then served more than 50 million people in the United States; by 2001, that number was at 100 million. Then, in 2000, the disagreements between the medical profession and M & R concerning appropriate pediatric medical practice exploded. Drs. Thomas Cleary and William Riley brought suit against M & R for listing them as contributing authors on its pediatric guidelines. (Two unrelated class action suits filed against insurers in New York and Florida also blamed those insurers for relying two heavily upon the guidelines.) The doctors contended that the guidelines had no basis in sound medical practice—implying that M & R had bought scientific legitimacy by paying the pediatrics department at University of Texas-Houston for the school's stamp of approval—and asserting that in following the guidelines, a doctor might jeopardize a patient's health. M & R insisted that the guidelines were evidence-based, but, doctors insisted, only 15 percent of M & R's guidelines came from articles describing organized studies, which much of the medical profession considered the best evidence. M & R insisted that studies tended to be out of date by the time M & R published its volumes.

Key Dates:

1947: Wendell Milliman founds Milliman & Robertson.
1983: James A. Curtis replaces Stuart Robertson as president and chief executive officer of M & R.
1990: M & R introduces its first healthcare guidelines; Robert Collett becomes president of M & R; the company heads up the founding of Woodrow Milliman.
1991: M & R purchases Fleet/Norstar Employee Benefit Services Inc.
1992: Collett becomes chief executive of M & R.
2001: The company changes its name to Milliman USA and buys Dorn, Helliesen & Cottle; Milliman UK opens; Milliman Global forms.
2002: Patrick J. Grannan becomes president and chief executive officer of Milliman; the company purchases Evaluation Associates, Am-Re Consultants, and Morgan Consulting.
2003: Milliman USA purchases Insurance Actuarial Software and Focus Solutions.

M & R sent letters to those who purchased the guidelines saying that Riley, Cleary, and two other University of Texas doctors wanted their names removed from the list of contributors and stressing that neither the university nor the remaining contributing authors ''stood by the book.'' It issued a CD-ROM version of the guidelines with changes.

2000 and On: Restructuring and Going International

While the debate raged over its healthcare guidelines, M & R took on the broader role of advisor on mergers and acquisitions, demutualizations, new product development and asset management, and financial analysis in the late 1990s. In 1997, for example, it performed an analysis of the financial stability of Lloyd's of London and helped its client restructure its organization. On the property/casualty side, M & R helped develop homebuilder warranties, auto warranties, and credit card warranties. By 1998, the company, which had grown throughout the 1990s at double digit rates, employed 1,200 people in 28 offices in the United States, Bermuda, and Japan and had revenues of $230 million.

Woodrow Milliman, by the late 1990s, had grown to represent 31 companies in more than 100 cities. By 2000, it brought in revenues of $390 million. Believing the time was right to strengthen its position in China, the management of Woodrow Milliman established new employee benefit consulting practices in Hong Kong and Shanghai owned jointly by its member firms. M & R began engaging in work overseas, too, assisting several countries in central and eastern Europe to assess the demographic, economic, and financial implications of welfare reform. It formed a Denver-based practice to focus on international as well as local clients with insurance and financial interests in Latin America.

M & R also undertook major restructuring moves in 2001. Having become increasingly involved in international and cross-border mergers, M & R renamed itself Milliman USA and opened Milliman UK Ltd., Milliman Asia, Milliman Japan, and Milliman Australia to focus on financial services. At the same time, Woodrow Milliman metamorphosed into Milliman Global, an international group of 22 actuarial and consulting firms focused on serving the international insurance, employee benefits, and healthcare industries.

The company also engaged in a series of acquisitions between the years 2001 and 2003 as a means of planning for its long-term growth. In 2001, it bought Dorn, Helliesen & Cottle, an investment consulting firm specializing in advising institutional sponsors of investment funds. In 2003, it signed a long-term co-marketing and technology sharing agreement with SS&C Technologies Inc., provider of investment and financial management software, to distribute, develop, and service software. It also purchased the Insurance Actuarial Software practice from IBM Business Consulting Services, whose products were marketed under the Triton Systems name, and Focus Solutions, an insurance software technology company. IAS brought with it a suite of valuation software products, now known as MG-Triton, and ReservePro and Affinity, leading loss reserving software for property and casualty industry. The merger of Focus Solutions and Milliman's FAST life administration system led to STEP Solutions, which provided for the automation of all insurance business processes.

After Patrick Grannan took over as president and chief executive officer in 2002, Milliman also acquired the consulting business of Evaluation Associates, into which it folded the company's existing consulting practice in 2003. It added Am-Re Consultants that same year and strengthened its presence in Europe—especially Italy and Spain—with the acquisition of Morgan Consulting, a prominent actuarial and management consulting firm.

In 2003, Milliman's consultants collaborated with the member firms of Milliman Global on international projects—such as cross-border mergers, the restructuring of Lloyd's of London, the reshaping of the Japanese life insurance market, and the first insurance actuarial assignment in China. In 2004, Milliman USA introduced BenPulse, a web-based employee benefit evaluation tool that allowed client companies to compare their benefit programs with that of other companies in their region and industry. Its Employee Benefits Research Group, consisting of a team of actuaries, lawyers, and research and communications experts, monitored legislative and regulatory activities taking place in Washington, D.C. In other arenas, the company took final steps toward the release of MG-Hedge, trademarked software allowing clients to evaluate hedging strategies. It developed a single suite of life products to cover the entire spectrum of client needs.

In 2003, Milliman USA released its guidelines in handheld/PDA format. In 2004, the guidelines were in use by more than 100 insurers in the United States and by several insurers in Chile. The company—which now called itself just Milliman—issued a new, expanded *General Recovery Guidelines* that covered hospital admissions with a web-based transaction version that allowed for interactive access. Milliman also completed guidelines for use in the United Kingdom and in Latin American and Asian countries.

Principal Subsidiaries

Evaluation Associates, LLC, a Milliman Company.

Principal Competitors

Hewitt Associates; Marsh & McLennan; Towers Perrin; Mercer Human Resource Consulting; Watson Wyatt Worldwide.

Further Reading

Barker, Kim, ''Seattle Firm Has Sway Over Hospital Stays: Cost-Saving Role in Managed Care Brings Lawsuit by Doctors,'' *Seattle Times,* March 14, 2000, p. A1.

Beason, Tyrone, ''Decisions, Decisions,'' *Seattle Times,* August 13, 2000, p. F1.

Frishberg, Manny, ''Milliman USA Grows into Worldwide Actuarial Company,'' *Puget Sound Business Journal,* June 15, 2001, p. 81.

Long, Steven, ''Helping Put the Lid on Health Care; Hot Line Has Median Costs for Procedures,'' *Houston Chronicle,* October 14, 1993, p. 1.

Neurath, Peter, ''M & R Insures Success of Others: M & R's Rapid Rate of Growth Has Been Characterized As 'Quiet,' '' *Puget Sound Business Journal,* June 29, 1998.

Nissimov, Ron, ''Cost-Cutting Guide Used by HMOs Called 'Dangerous'; Doctor on UT-Houston Medical School Staff Sues Publisher,'' *Houston Chronicle,* March 5, 2000, p. 1.

Panko, Ron, ''Actuarially Speaking—It's a Growth Business,'' *Best's Review Property/Casualty Edition,* April 1998, p. 65.

—Carrie Rothburd

Modern Woodmen of America

1701 First Avenue
P.O. Box 2005
Rock Island, Illinois 61204-2005
U.S.A.
Telephone: (309) 786-6481
Toll Free: (800) 447-9811
Fax: (309) 786-1701
Web site: http://www.modern-woodmen.org

Nonprofit Company
Incorporated: 1884
Employees: 1,600
Sales: $1.15 billion (2003)
NAIC: 524113 Direct Life Insurance Carriers; 524210 Insurance Agencies and Brokerages; 522130 Credit Unions

Modern Woodmen of America (MWA) is a leading fraternal life insurance society in the United States, with more than 750,000 members and assets of more than $6 billion. In addition to providing insurance and financial services, Modern Woodmen maintains nearly 2,200 local chapters, or ''camps,'' and 700 youth service clubs. The group provides an array of free community benefits, such as youth educational programs on topics such as bicycle safety, scholarship programs, and a national student speech contest. MWA is strongest in the Midwest and the South.

Fraternal benefit societies are organized along ethnic, religious, or vocational lines. As nonprofits, they do not have to pay federal income tax. MWA is not connected to the Woodmen of the World fraternal benefit society, although the two groups were started by the same person.

Fraternal Roots

Modern Woodmen was formed in Lyons, Iowa on January 5, 1883 by Joseph Cullen Root. Born December 3, 1844 in Chester, Massachusetts, Root moved to Illinois and Iowa at a young age. He attended Iowa's Cornell College, Northern Illinois College, and graduated from Eastman Business College in Poughkeepsie, New York. He then operated a number of businesses.

Root became involved with a number of fraternal societies over the years, most notably the Freemasons, which he entered around 1877, as well as the Knights of Pythias, the Odd Fellows, and the Ancient Order of United Workmen. He also led Vera Amicitia Sempiterna, a fraternal benefit society exclusive to the state of Iowa. He founded Modern Woodmen in 1883, organizing the new society around the lodge system.

Fraternal benefit societies were typically formed by groups of immigrants or religious orders. But Root envisioned one that would ''bind in one association the Jew and the Gentile, the Catholic and the Protestant, the agnostic and the atheist.'' Membership was at first limited, however, to rural residents of midwestern states (Illinois, Minnesota, Iowa, Nebraska, Wisconsin, Michigan, Kansas, North Dakota, South Dakota, Missouri, Indiana, and Ohio).

The health and moral requirements were vigorous. Members had to be white and between the ages of 18 and 45. A whole slew of dangerous jobs also was grounds for disqualification, writes one historian in a Rochester, New York newsletter.

The organization's mission was to help families survive after the loss of a breadwinner. MWA also arranged for community-building events through its local chapters, called ''camps.'' These included meetings, parades, and baseball games.

The name Modern Woodmen alluded to the foresters who cleared the land to build their communities, an image Root culled from a sermon by a local preacher. There was also an element of connection with Root's own name, notes one historian in the *Scottish Rite Journal.* A patriotic reference was added later, and the group became Modern Woodmen of America (MWA).

Modern Woodmen relocated to Illinois after being incorporated in that state on May 5, 1884. First located in Fulton, the head office moved to Rock Island in 1897.

By 1889, noted the *New York Times,* the Woodmen had 40,000 members in Iowa and neighboring states. The group also

Company Perspectives:

Members of Modern Woodmen share an active commitment to three things: Financial Security. Modern Woodmen members believe in keeping families together, financially secure and independent; Positive Family Life. Members believe that the developmental, emotional and social needs of individuals are important for the future of families and communities; Community Service. Members believe each family, each individual, can make a positive contribution through service to others and to community.

Key Dates:

1883: Modern Woodmen of America is founded in Lyons, Iowa.
1884: MWA moves to Fulton, Illinois.
1897: MWA relocates to Rock Island, Illinois.
1909: A tuberculosis sanatorium opens in Colorado Springs.
1947: The sanatorium is closed.
2001: Renovation of Rock Island headquarters begins.
2002: A financial services subsidiary is formed.
2003: MWABank goes online.

spawned other organizations. A ladies' auxiliary, the Royal Neighbors of America, had been formed in 1888.

After a heated dispute with MWA Head Physician P.L. McKinnie, Root left MWA and launched another fraternal benefit organization, the Woodmen of the World Life Insurance Society, formed in Omaha in 1890.

The group's most visible ambassadors were the Modern Woodmen Foresters, a precision drill team that performed at numerous parades and competitions around the country between 1890 and the early 1930s. According to MWA, more than 160,000 men drilled in 10,000 units over the years.

At the turn of the century, MWA was among the largest of the 188 fraternal insurance companies doing business in the United States, reported the *New York Times.* These groups had several million members overall.

MWA raised $6 million to pay war claims during World War I. As the *New York Times* reported, however, influenza and pneumonia deaths nearly caused the group's general fund to drop precariously from $10 million to $640,000 between October 1918 and March 1919.

1909–50: "Chasing the Cure"

The group also had been touched by another epidemic, tuberculosis (TB). In the 19th century, the highly infectious disease had been the leading cause of death in the United States. In 38 years, the Modern Woodmen Tuberculosis Sanatorium treated more than 12,000 members (all of them male) at no cost.

Monument Park, its site nine miles northwest of Colorado Springs, was later renamed Woodmen Valley. According to the *Gazette* of Colorado Springs, there were 16 other TB sanatoriums in the Pikes Peak region. MWA's facility, which opened on January 1, 1909, was not the first, but it was one of the largest. The region's altitude, dry climate, and clean air were the basis of the therapy. A hearty diet including six raw eggs and up to ten glasses of milk per day was prescribed.

The isolation of the area was another factor in managing the highly contagious disease. According to the *Gazette,* the sanatorium's tree-lined campus had space for up to 200 patients, housed in individual, octagonal tents (a local doctor had designed them after teepees). The complex had its own dairy and cows.

The sanatorium claimed a 60 percent cure rate. It closed on May 1, 1947 after new drugs became the preferred treatment for TB. The site was sold in 1950 and eventually came into the hands of the Sisters of St. Francis Seraph, who operated it as a health retreat until about 1980. Some of the historic structures, including the dairy barn, were razed in a 1994 fire. MWA kept up its high moral standards in the 20th century. Bootleggers were banned from membership during Prohibition.

A.R. Talbot had become president of Modern Woodmen in 1903. A native of Warren County, Illinois, he had been president of the Nebraska legislature as well as a law partner of William Jennings Bryan. Talbot remained in office for more than three decades and was succeeded in November 1938 by MWA's treasurer, Oscar E. Aleshire of Chicago.

From shortly after MWA's founding to about 1950, members wore a variety of different types of jewelry. These included rings, cuff links, necklaces, and other articles that have become collectors' items. Symbols representing the society and its values included the axe (industry), the wedge (power), and beetle (progress).

There were about 200 fraternal benefit societies in the United States in the early 1990s, reported the *New York Times,* with a combined customer base of about ten million people. In 1993 A.M. Best Company rated 42 fraternals and found Modern Woodmen to be one of the top six. Assets were then more than $2 billion. While some of the largest fraternal benefit societies were open only to members of certain faiths (particularly Lutherans and Catholics), membership in Modern Woodmen was open to anyone except residents of Alaska, Hawaii, and Nevada. Total revenue reached $609 million in 1995, when assets were more than $3 billion.

New Ventures, New HQ After 2001

Modern Woodmen began a three-year, $25 million renovation of its Rock Island, Illinois headquarters in 2001. Two subsidiaries were soon added: MWA Financial Services, Inc. for investments and MWABank for banking products.

MWABank was an Internet thrift with only one physical branch office in Rock Island, Illinois. It contracted with several ATM networks so its customers across the country could access cash and make deposits. MWABank went online in the spring of 2003.

Assets exceeded $6 billion in 2003. Total income rose $50 million to $1.15 billion. According to *American Banker,* there were 80 comparable fraternal benefit societies in the United States at the time.

More than 750,000 people were members. MWA's community events continued to be well attended. Nearly 100,000 students from 1,200 schools competed in the 2003 School Speech Contest.

Principal Subsidiaries

MWABank; MWA Financial Services, Inc.

Principal Competitors

Independent Order of Foresters; Woodmen of the World Life Insurance Society.

Further Reading

Amidon, Carol, ''The Woodmen Societies and Their Presence in Mount Hope Cemetery,'' *Epitaph: The Friends of Mount Hope Newsletter* (Rochester, N.Y.), Fall 1998.

''A. R. Talbot Is Dead; Nebraska Lawyer, 84; Ex-Partner of W.J. Bryan, Long Head of Modern Woodmen,'' *New York Times*, January 30, 1944, p. 38.

Ascent Capture in Action; Insurance: Fraternal Society Speeds & Secures Life Insurance Policy Processing, Irvine, Calif.: Kofax Image Products, 2001.

Blanchard, Steve, ''Florida Fraternal Life Insurance Company Offers More Than Insurance,'' *Sun* (Port Charlotte, Fla.), April 27, 2002.

Davant, Jeanne, '' 'Chasing the Cure' Led to Pikes Peak Region,'' *Gazette* (Colorado Springs), Life Sec., July 3, 2001, p. 1.

Gjertsen, Lee Ann, ''750,000-Strong Modern Woodmen Starts Web Thrift,'' *American Banker*, January 29, 2003, p. 12.

Glissmann, Bob, ''Sandwich Speech Scores National Win for Student,'' *Omaha World-Herald*, September 30, 2003.

''Insurance Tax in the West,'' *New York Times*, August 22, 1900, p. 2.

Koco, Linda, ''New EIAs Built with Insurer 'Partners,' '' *National Underwriter Life & Health-Financial Services Edition*, June 15, 1998, p. 21.

Loretz, Carol, ''Private, Public Vitality Evident in Rock Island,'' *Quad-Cities Quest*, Rock Island, Ill.: Moline Dispatch Publishing Co., 2002.

''Modern Woodmen Fight; Bloody Battle at Fulton (Ill.) Over Removal of Headquarters to Rock Island,'' *New York Times*, August 14, 1897, p. 3.

''Modern Woodmen in Battle; Hose, Special Trains, Brass Knuckles, and Injunctions as Weapons,'' *New York Times*, February 17, 1987, p. 7.

''Modern Woodmen of America,'' *Oregionality, The Best of Eastern Iowa & Western Illinois*, 2003.

''New Head of Modern Woodmen,'' *New York Times*, November 28, 1937, p. 47.

Scherreik, Susan, ''Off the Beaten Path in the Insurance Field,'' *New York Times*, December 25, 1993, p. 45.

Thompson, Dennis R., ''Growth and Success,'' *Managers Magazine*, August 1994, pp. 13f.

Uzzel, Robert L., ''Ill. Joseph Cullen Root, 33','' *Scottish Rite Journal*, September 1998.

Vogrin, Bill, ''Old Barn Sits in Crossfire; Neighborhood Can't Decide If It's an Eyesore or Landmark,'' *Gazette* (Colorado Springs), August 29, 2002.

''Woodmen at Odds; Trouble in the Camp of a Western Beneficiary Society,'' *New York Times*, December 18, 1889, p. 10.

''Woodmen Bar Bootleggers from Membership in Order,'' *New York Times*, June 25, 1925, p. 1.

''Woodmen Expand Scholarship Program,'' *Knoxville News/Sentinel*, Sec. A., September 13, 2000.

''Woodmen in Financial Straits,'' *New York Times*, March 26, 1919, p. 10.

—Frederick C. Ingram

Naspers Ltd.

PO Box 2271
Cape Town
8000
South Africa
Telephone: (+27) 21 406 2121
Fax: (+27) 21 406 2913
Web site: http://www.naspers.com

Public Company
Incorporated: 1915 as Nasionale Pers
Sales: ZAR 12.8 billion ($2.09 billion) (2004)
Stock Exchanges: Johannesburg NASDAQ
Ticker Symbol: NPN NPSN
NAIC: 511110 Newspaper Publishers; 323110 Commercial Lithographic Printing; 323111 Commercial Gravure Printing; 511130 Book Publishers; 515210 Cable and Other Subscription Programming; 518111 Internet Service Providers; 551112 Offices of Other Holding Companies

Naspers Ltd. is one of South Africa's leading and most diversified media companies. South Africa remains the company's single most important market, at 64 percent of its 2004 sales of ZAR 12.8 billion ($2.1 billion). Naspers is also one of the leading media groups in sub-Saharan Africa, with operations in some 40 countries, including the continent's islands states. Naspers has also begun building a presence in Europe, notably with operations in Greece, Cyprus, and the Netherlands, as well as in Asia, especially in Thailand and China. Naspers operates in five core areas. The company's television component includes its control of MIH, MultiChoice South Africa, MultiChoice Africa, and M-Net; the NetMed pay-tv service in Greece and Cyprus; and a 31.1 percent stake in United Broadcasting Corporation in Thailand. The company is also targeting an entry into the future Chinese satellite television market. Internet services is another major part of the group's operations, and includes M-Web in South Africa and Thailand; majority control of SportsCn, a leading Internet portal in China; control of Hong Kong-listed Tencent Ltd., which provides the QQ instant messaging service in China, Taiwan, Thailand, and elsewhere in Southeast Asia and in South Africa; and the Media24 Digital brand of e-media Web sites. Print media represents Naspers origins and includes its 60 newspaper titles, such as *Die Burger, Beeld, Volksblad, Rapport, City Press,* and 30 magazine titles, including *Drum, Family, Huisgenoot, You, Finansies & Tegniek,* and *Finance Week,* as well as licensed and localized editions of *Cosmopolitan, Runner's World, Sports Illustrated,* and others. The Book Publishing and Private Education division encompasses Naspers' Via Afika unit, the leading African book publisher operating under a number of imprints, and its Educor private education component, South Africa's leading private provider of onsite and correspondence courses for adults, as well as corporate training programs. Naspers is listed on the Johannesburg, NASDAQ, and Euronext Amsterdam Stock Exchanges.

Afrikaner Voice after the Boer War

Naspers origins lay in the rise of the National Party following the Afrikaner defeat in the Boer War at the turn of the 20th century. The development of the Afrikaner population as a political force in South Africa at the approach of World War I brought a need for the creation of a pro-Afrikaner media that could escape the domination of the country's English-speaking population. In 1915, sympathizers of the National Party launched the first Afrikaans-language paper, *Die Burger,* in Cape Town. A new company was created as a holding company for the paper. The company was called Nasionale Pers (or National Press), underscoring its relationship with the National Party. Naspers, as the company came to be called, remained a dedicated supporter of the National Party throughout its later dominance of the South Africa government. Nonetheless, Naspers remained financially and editorially independent from the National Party and later became somewhat critical of at least some of the National Party's apartheid policies.

The success of *Die Burger* led Naspers to add its first magazine title in 1916, a monthly called *De Huisgenoot.* The company also began extending into book publishing, with its first Afrikaans-language books appearing in 1918 and its first English-language book in 1919. The company also began publishing in Xhosa in the 1922. By then, Naspers had emerged as a

Company Perspectives:

Our mission statement. To build shareholder value by operating subscriber management platforms that provide content, services and means of communication to paying users; to licence related technologies and to be useful to the communities we serve.

prominent South African book publisher, producing many of the country's most prominent authors. During that decade, Naspers also developed a strong textbook publishing business, particularly for the Afrikaans-language market.

Naspers also expanded its newspaper business beyond Cape Town, launching a newspaper, *Die Volksblad,* in Bloemfontein. *Die Volksblad* became a prominent daily in 1925, and, like *Die Burger,* maintained a editorial policy in support of the National Party. In the years following World War II, as the Afrikaner population took control of the South African government, both *Die Burger* and *Die Volksblad* emerged as important South African newspapers.

Entering the Media Market in the 1980s

Naspers transferred its textbook publishing business to a separate company, Nasionale Boekhandel, in 1950. The new company grew quickly, and by the late 1950s began to extend into the general publishing business as well with the acquisition of Tafelberg Uitgewers in 1959. Naspers, which created a new educational publishing operation, Nasou, in 1963, took back control of Nasionale Boekhandel in 1973, then acquired another prominent South African publisher, Human & Rousseau, in 1977. Naspers continued to develop its book publishing business during the 1980s, forming the Afrikaans-language book club Leserskring in 1979, followed by Leisure Hour, an English-language book club. In 1986, Naspers acquired publisher JL van Schaik.

In the meantime, Naspers had continued to develop its newspaper and magazine operations. During the 1960s, the company extended its magazine publishing to include its first English-language titles, signaling the group's intention to develop itself as a South African—and not merely Afrikaner—media group. The company's first English-language title was *Fairlady,* launched in 1965.

In 1970, the company took two of its Sunday newspapers, *Beeld* and *Dagbreek,* and merged them together to create a new national Sunday paper, *Rapport.* This move was followed by the relaunch of *Beeld* as a daily newspaper for the Johannesburg market in 1974. The following year, the company created a national distribution structure, Nasionale Nuusdistrubeerders.

Naspers took a new step forward in the 1980s when it acquired Drum Publications, a company that specifically targeted the black African reading market. The 1984 purchase gave Naspers a number of leading magazine titles, including the weekly *Drum* and *True Love & Family,* as well as the Sunday newspaper *City Press.* The acquisition was also instrumental in positioning the company for the post-apartheid era.

The 1980s also marked Naspers transformation into a multimedia group. In 1984, Koos Bekker had finished his graduate studies in the United States and was returning to South Africa. Bekker had written a thesis on the emergence of pay-television, especially HBO, while a student at Columbia University, and had recognized that the HBO model provided a model for developing a South African pay-television service. Bekker brought his idea to Ton Vosloo, Naspers' new CEO, in 1984. Together, Vosloo and Bekker formed a new company, M-Net, with Naspers and several other South African publishing groups, including Argus, Times Media, and Perskor, becoming major shareholders. The company then applied for permission to begin broadcasting, which was promptly refused by the government-controlled television monopoly, South African Broadcasting Corporation (SABC). In exchange for permission, however, Naspers had to agree to broadcast only non-news entertainment programming.

M-Net hit the air in 1986 to an enthusiastic reception. Less than three years after its launch, the new company was already posting profits. Bekker, who served as M-Net's CEO, then took the company public, launching its listing on the Johannesburg Stock Exchange in 1990. The listing enabled the company to begin plans to extend its coverage to the entire sub-Saharan African region, and in 1991 M-Net began building its own satellite network. Satellite broadcasting began the following year. In 1992, M-Net entered Europe with a 40 percent stake in pay-television group FilmNet. Then, in 1993, M-Net was split up into two publicly listed companies, the M-Net television channel and MultiChoice International Holdings (MIH), which took over subscriber management and the group's international broadcasting operations. The successful public offering encouraged Naspers to go public as well, with a listing on the Johannesburg exchange in 1994.

A Simplified Structure for the 21st Century

While Naspers' share of M-Net and MIH provided its major growth momentum into the new century, its publishing operations remained a steadily growing and stable cash generator. The company debuted its financial magazine, *Finansies & Tegniek,* in 1985. In the 1987, the company launched the successful English-language family magazine *You.* That year, Naspers relaunched its Nasionale Boekhandel stores under the Van Schaik name. In 1988, the company extended its academic publishing business into a new area—that of correspondence education—with the acquisition of two correspondence course providers, Lyceum and Success.

The company acquired Jonathan Ball Publishers, an English-language publishing house, in 1991. Naspers then acquired the South African branch of HarperCollins in 1994. By 1997, Naspers had decided to unite its various book publishing interests under a single structure, merging Nasou into a newly created entity, Via Afrika, in 1997.

Beyond publishing, the company became a major player in the South African Internet market with the launch of M-Web in 1997. The company's media operations were also growing strongly, backed by the launch of NetMed pay-television service in Greece and Cyprus in 1995 and the beginning of digital satellite broadcasting operations in Europe and Asia as well as

Key Dates:

1915: Publication begins of *Die Burger,* a newspaper for Afrikaner readers.
1916: Nasionale Pers is created as a holding company for *Die Burger* and other publishing interests.
1918: The company begins book publishing operations.
1925: *Die Volksblad* is launched as a daily newspaper.
1950: Nasionale Boekhandel is organized as a separate publishing business.
1959: Nasionale Boekhandel acquires Tafelberg Uitgewers.
1965: The company starts publishing its first English-language magazine, *Fairlady.*
1970: *Rapport,* a national Sunday newspaper, is founded.
1973: Nasionale Boekhandel becomes a Naspers subsidiary.
1974: A daily newspaper, *Beeld,* begins publication for the Johannesburg market.
1977: Human & Rousseau book publishers is acquired.
1986: M-Net pay television service is launched.
1988: Correspondence education services begin with the acquisitions of Success and Lyceum.
1990: M-Net is listed on the Johannesburg Stock Exchange.
1993: M-Net is split into MIH Holdings and MultiChoice (later MIHL).
1994: Naspers is listed on the Johannesburg Stock Exchange.
2000: Naspers simplifies its structure under five primary subsidiaries.
2002: Naspers acquires full control of MIH Holdings; the company gains a secondary listing on the NASDAQ.
2004: Tencent is listed on the Hong Kong Stock Exchange.

in Africa. The company bought a 50 percent stake in Touchline Media in 1996, increasing its content component, then gained nearly one-third of leading Thai pay-television broadcaster United Broadcasting Corporation (UBC) in 1997. In that year, MIH also became a major shareholder in interactive television services provider OpenTV, a position stepped up to 80 percent in 1999. By then, Koos Bekker had taken over as CEO of Naspers, while Ton Vosloo became the group's chairman.

In recognition of its expansion beyond its original publishing business, the company officially adopted the Naspers name in 1998. In that year, the company also debuted its Media24 brand of Web content, starting with the sites pages24.com, news24.com, fin24.com, as well as online bookseller Kalahari .net. On the publishing side, Naspers acquired a 50 percent stake in religious publisher Lux Verbi in 1999.

Naspers moved to simplify its corporate structure in 2000, regrouping its operations under five primary subsidiaries: MIH Holdings, M-Web, Media24, Nasboek, and Educor. That year also marked the company's entry into the China market with the launch of the sports-oriented web portal SportCN. The following year, Naspers increased its position in China by acquiring a 46.5 percent share of Tencent, which owned the popular QQ instant messaging service.

Naspers continued simplifying its structure in 2002, when it took full control of both MIH Holdings and MIHL (formerly MultiChoice). Naspers then listed its stock on the NASDAQ. The company also sold off its stake in OpenTV that year.

As it turned into the 21st century, Naspers continued seeking new growth avenues. The company targeted further international expansion, launching a Hungarian version of its *Women's Value* magazine title in 2003. Closer to home, the company debuted the monthly *Kick Off* in Nigeria that year and also began publishing the weekly newspaper tabloid *Kaapse Sun* for the Western Cape market. In 2004, another of the company's holdings went public, as Nasper listed its shares in Tencent on the Hong Kong Stock Exchange. The public offering marked Naspers commitment to positioning itself for the Chinese market, particularly with a view to gaining a share at the start up of the country's satellite television industry, which was expected to take off with China's admission to the World Trade Organization in 2005. With the largest part of its revenues generated by its pay-television holdings, Naspers had transformed itself into one of the world's major media groups.

Principal Subsidiaries

Educor; Media24; MIH Holdings; ViaAfrika.

Principal Competitors

New Africa Investments Ltd.; Central Group of Cos.; News Corporation Ltd.; Reed Elsevier PLC; Independent Newspaper Holdings Ltd.; VNU N.V.

Further Reading

Bloom, Kevin, and O'Toole, Sean, "Continental Heavies," *Mail & Guardian: The Media Online*, March 17, 2004.

"Foreign Pay-TV Ventures Put Naspers in the Picture," *Africa News Service*, November 26, 2003.

Mathews, Charlotte, "Naspers to Simplify Its Corporate Structure," *Business Day*, September 27, 2002.

"Naspers Debuts on NASDAQ," *Moneyweb*, December 24, 2002.

"Naspers Looks to China as Earnings Reach R2.4bn," *Business Day*, June 30, 2004.

"Naspers Offer Signals Wider Partnership," *Africa News Service*, December 29, 2003.

Paul, Donald, "Naspers: Bigger Brother," *Mail & Guardian*, February 24, 2003.

"Pushing Limits Ever Further, M-Net Pioneer Talks Himself out of His Job," *Business Times*, June 29, 1997.

"The Worst Is Over: Naspers," *Moneyweb*, December 5, 2002.

—M.L. Cohen

National Oil Corporation

Bashir Sadawi Street
Tripoli
Libya
Telephone: (218) 21 444-6181
Fax: (218) 21 333-1930
Web site: http://www.noclibya.com

State-Owned Company
Incorporated: 1970
NAIC: 211111 Crude Petroleum and Natural Gas Extraction; 213111 Drilling Oil and Gas Wells; 213112 Support Activities for Oil and Gas Operations

The National Oil Corporation of Libya (NOC) is a state-owned company that controls Libya's oil and gas production. The company is the biggest oil producer in Africa. Linoco's main export market is Italy, followed by Germany, Spain, and France. The company is rich in reserves and also controls unexplored land presumed to be rich in oil. The Libyan National Oil Corporation (Linoco) was created under Law No. 24 of March 5, 1970. It replaced the older Libyan General Petroleum Corporation (Lipetco) with a new national oil company. Its mandate, similar to Lipetco's, was "to endeavor to promote the Libyan economy by undertaking development, management and exploitation of oil resources . . . as well as by participating . . . in planning and executing the general oil policy of the state." The fortunes of NOC, therefore, cannot be separated from those of Libya, since the corporation acts as a government instrument of control, supervision, and participation in the oil industry and particularly in its relations with other oil companies. The company suffered from a lack of foreign investment through most of the 1990s because of United States and United Nations sanctions against Libya, which was accused of backing terrorists and shielding men accused of blowing up Pan Am Flight 103 over Locherbie, Scotland, in 1988. As the Locherbie case wound down in 2003, Libya expected a new round of foreign investment in its oil fields in the mid-2000s.

Lipetco in the 1960s

The role earmarked for NOC was largely a product of the political and economic events of the 1960s and 1970s in Libya. During the 1950s, Libya was an impoverished agrarian economy practicing a near-subsistence level of agriculture. The discovery of oil and the application of the much-needed oil revenues to other sectors of the economy reversed this trend, and the economy attained growth rates as high as 20 percent a year in the 1960s. There was considerable readjustment in the structure of the Libyan economy, as the oil sector gained prominence and became the vehicle of growth for the economy as a whole. With oil revenues going straight to the government, the latter took the responsibility for planning expenditure derived from these revenues. The outcome was the creation, by royal decree, of the Libyan General Petroleum Corporation (Lipetco) in 1968.

The creation of a state-owned oil company allowed Libya to follow in the footsteps of other oil-producing economies, where control of such a revenue-generating resource lay with the government. Lipetco's first chairman and director general was Mohammed Jeroushi. The company was based in Tripoli but was physically distinct from the Ministry of Petroleum Affairs. NOC would be similar to its predecessor in that it, too, would function under the supervision and control of the Minister of Petroleum. There was very little difference between Lipetco and NOC in terms of responsibilities. It is quite probable that NOC was formed in 1970 to highlight the political change from a monarchy to a republican government.

In 1969, the monarchy in Libya was overthrown by a group of young army officers led by Colonel Moammar Khadafi. In the years immediately following the coup d'état, the government continued to follow the economic policies of the past. However, the new regime's espousal of the creed of self-reliance and socialism indicated that in the future the government would play a major role in economic policy. Planning, in other words, was to be more widespread, encompassing national issues rather than those of the oil industry alone. This became immediately apparent with a more aggressive policy on oil pricing and the structure of ownership in the oil sector. In May 1970, a series of cuts in

Company Perspectives:

NOC is carrying out exploration and production operations through its own affiliated companies, or in participation with other companies under service contracts or any other kind of petroleum investment agreements. This is in addition to marketing operations of oil and gas, locally and abroad. For this purpose, NOC has its own fully owned companies which carry out exploration, development and production operations, in addition to local and international marketing companies. NOC also has participation agreements with specialized international companies. Such agreements have developed into exploration and production sharing agreements, in accordance with the development of the international oil and gas industry, and international petroleum marketing.

OPEC-determined production levels was introduced to force up prices. This policy gained Libya influence in OPEC (Organization of Petroleum Exporting Countries), where its radical stance met with considerable support.

Simultaneously, agreements on ownership were initiated with foreign oil companies, mainly in the form of joint ventures. The first joint venture was signed between Lipetco and the French state companies, ERAP (later Elf) and SNPA (Aquitaine) in 1968. Subsequently, in June 1969, joint ventures were introduced with Royal Dutch/Shell, ENI's Agip subsidiary, and Ashland Oil & Refining.

Joint Ventures in the 1970s

Lipetco was reestablished as the Libyan National Oil Corporation (NOC) in 1970. Linoco's first chairman and director general was Salem Mohammed Amesh, who was subsequently replaced by his deputy, Omar Muntasir. The latter remained in charge until 1980. The law under which NOC had been established restricted new joint ventures with foreign firms to those in which the latter took on all the risks of the pre-commercial exploration period. Only contract-type agreements were authorized and NOC's share was fixed at a given percentage from the start of operations. Contract-type agreements referred to production-sharing agreements as opposed to those simply allowing exploration to proceed. Furthermore, in July 1970, a new law was passed which made NOC responsible for the marketing of all oil products in Libya. The Brega Petroleum Marketing Company, a subsidiary of NOC, was set up to carry out the marketing activities of NOC, and the marketing assets of all the foreign oil companies were nationalized.

NOC played a major part in the Libyan government's new strategy of higher oil prices and production-sharing. The strategy was to lead to confrontation with the foreign oil companies. Foreign oil companies that did not voluntarily surrender concessions as part of the new policy were forced by economic and political pressure to relinquish these in full to the government. These were then taken over by NOC.

Soon after its establishment, NOC signed a joint venture agreement with the U.S. Occidental Petroleum involving production-sharing. In 1971, NOC arranged a processing deal with Sincat of Italy for refining oil products for domestic consumption, thereby providing a cheap supply of oil for internal Libyan consumption. A joint drilling company was formed with Saipem, a subsidiary of the Italian ENI, in early 1972. NOC took over the production operations of the Sarir oil field after the nationalization of British Petroleum's Libyan concession in 1971 and the U.S. company Hunt Oil in 1973. Similarly, Phillips' Umm Farud field was taken over in 1970. Other fields taken over by NOC included Amoseas's Beida oil field in 1974 and Amoco's Sahabir oil field in 1976.

By April 1974, production-sharing agreements had been reached with Exxon, Mobil, Compagnie Française des Pétroles, Elf Aquitaine, and Agip. All these agreements provided for production-sharing on a 85–15 basis onshore and 81–19 basis offshore. Each agreement had commitments in terms of expenditure on exploration by the foreign company. Development costs incurred by NOC were reimbursable by the partner. By using the surplus funds and technical expertise of the foreign oil companies, the problem of stimulating investment in exploration was resolved.

By the mid-1970s, NOC was faced with complications as a result of legal actions brought against it by British Petroleum (BP) over claims of ownership. Fears of an oil price rise in 1973 had led to a demand for Libyan crude oil. However, BP's legal position had made buyers wary of purchasing oil over which NOC may not have had legal title. NOC compensated for this position by arranging barter deals with both France and Argentina. Eventually all the foreign oil companies in Libya, except BP, agreed to the conditions imposed by Libya of partial nationalization, and as a result NOC had a substantial surplus of oil to sell. This was because Libya received share entitlements from the foreign companies, giving it rights on production by the foreign companies. It was part of the policy of production-sharing introduced by the government of Libya. However, by 1974–75, declining oil prices and oil consumption led NOC to sell back its shares of production to companies which had agreed to the partial nationalizations. This amounted to about 425,000 barrels per day (b/d) from its entitlement. Overall, NOC produced about 281,000 b/d in 1975 and 408,000 b/d in 1976. It exported 908,000 b/d in 1975 and 1.2 million b/d in 1976. The topical status of NOC's dispute with BP gradually faded away, and BP, Libya, was nationalized in 1974, as were the American companies Amoseas, Hunt, and Atlantic Richfield. Complementing its upstream activities and acquisitions, NOC itself had built two refineries at Azzawia between 1974 and 1976, with a capacity of 120,000 b/d.

The 1970s were a decade of great corporate activity. It saw the further consolidation of NOC's power. Nationalizations, the seizing of company assets, and buying out company shares were among NOC's activities. Esso Libya agreed to sell its share to NOC in April 1974. It subsequently withdrew from its Libyan operations in November 1981 and reached a compensation agreement with NOC in January 1982. Esso Sirte companies, Esso's Libyan subsidiaries, also relinquished 51 percent of their shares to NOC. In November 1982, Exxon's share in Esso Sirte was purchased by NOC and formed into a subsidiary company, Sirte Oil Company. The largest oil company in Libya at the time of the nationalizations was OASIS. Shell's original share of

Key Dates:

1968: Libyan General Petroleum Corporation (Lipetco) is founded by royal decree.
1969: The Libyan monarchy is overthrown in a coup led by Colonel Moammar Khadafi.
1970: The company is reestablished as Libyan National Oil Corporation (NOC).
1980: Libyan Arabian Gulf Oil Company (Agoco) subsidiary is established.
1986: U.S. sanctions against Libya begin.
1999: United Nations suspends its sanctions against Libya.
2003: United Nations sanctions are lifted, and NOC enters licensing agreements with European companies.
2004: U.S. sanctions are lifted.

16.7 percent was seized by the government in 1974, giving the government of Libya 59.2 percent ownership of OASIS in the early 1980s. Occidental Libya had agreed to a 51 percent nationalization in August 1973. This gave NOC a 51 percent share in Occidental, Libya. Mobil-Gelsenberg was owned 51 percent by NOC, 31.85 percent by Mobil, and 17.15 percent by Gelsenberg, the West German refining and marketing company. Mobil, however, left in 1982. In this period, NOC held 81 percent of Elf Aquitaine.

Political Conflicts in the 1980s

The 1980s was a decade of emphasis on joint venture projects. However, it was also characterized by a conflict of interests between Libya and the United States. The latter had instituted sanctions against Libya, based on assertions that Libya was supporting international terrorism, which had seriously affected the operations of U.S. oil companies in Libya. The Libyan government responded by freezing the royalties of the U.S. companies, restricting the repatriation of profits, and threatening to take over the entitlement rights to production of these U.S. companies.

During the 1980s, Libya's oil interests became less insular and more outward-looking. Libya relaxed its confrontational attitude, and NOC entered into new production-sharing agreements with a number of companies to ensure partial control. These included Rompetrol (Romania) and the Bulgarian Oil Company in 1984–85. Other agreements were signed in 1988–89 with Royal Dutch/Shell, Montedison of Italy, the International Petroleum Corporation of Canada, INA-Naftaplin of Yugoslavia, and a consortium of companies comprised of ÖMV in Austria, Braspetro in Brazil, and Husky Oil of Canada. These new agreements included guarantees ensuring rapid payment by Libya to these companies for the development costs incurred. These guarantees represented an important change from earlier Libyan regulations on joint ventures. The change was designed to offset the U.S. sanctions by offering incentives in joint venture terms to other foreign companies.

In 1980, the Libyan Arabian Gulf Oil Company (Agoco) was established by NOC through the amalgamation of the Arabian Gulf Exploration Company, Umm-al-Jawabi Oil Company, and direct NOC exploration and production interests. By 1989, Agoco's production was 400,000 b/d, making it was the largest individual oil producer in the country. Agoco was wholly Libyan-owned and fit into the overall oil policy of the government, which was to initiate and invest in new projects while maintaining control. NOC was also instrumental in the policy of downstream expansion. It was one of the shareholders, together with the Libyan Arab Foreign Bank and the Libyan Arab Foreign Investment Company, in Olinvest, a Libyan holding company established in 1988 for investment purposes and intended to permit a high degree of integration all the way to end consumers. Furthermore, Olinvest was responsible for ensuring that the downstream activities continued and so invested in Italian and German refineries. By 1990–91, the company was handling some 400,000 to 450,000 barrels per day.

The Reagan administration had introduced economic sanctions against Libya in January 1986. The sanctions were in reaction to the bombing of a Berlin disco and banned all trade, import and export activity, and travel between the United States and Libya. The sanctions were renewed in December of 1988 following a review of U.S. government policy by Congress after two years. The immediate impact of the sanctions was on the production and financial operations of five U.S. oil companies: Marathon, Conoco, Amerada Hess, Occidental, and W.R. Grace. In June 1986, these five companies had a total production entitlement of 263,000 b/d. As a result of the U.S. sanctions, the holdings and entitlements of the U.S. companies were kept in suspension and their operations were handled by NOC. Much of the latter part of the 1980s was spent in negotiations between the U.S. companies and NOC over the treatment of their equity holdings. The U.S. companies had offered to return to Libya to meet their commitments with regard to capital expenditure but continued U.S. sanctions did not allow them to bring in new technology, equipment, and spare parts. Even an easing of the ban by the Reagan administration in early 1989 only allowed the companies to transfer their equities to a third party and did not change the core issue of a transfer of technology. Due to the lack of overall progress, some of the companies were willing to extend their suspended status until a more viable political solution could be found.

Under Abdallah al-Badri, the chairman of the NOC management committee until November 1990, a new policy was introduced for the 1990s. This focused on reducing the number of new projects and upgrading the existing facilities of the national oil producers. NOC continued to make production-sharing agreements. New joint ventures were initiated between NOC and Veba, Petrofina, North African Petroleum Limited, and a consortium led by Lasmo and the Petroleum Development Corporation of the Republic of Korea. However, an additional emphasis was also placed on encouraging foreign companies to produce exclusively for export and on confining the sale of crude oil to a select number of national oil companies that already owned equity in Libyan production. This limited the crude being offered in the spot market through third-party traders and increased the input into Libya's downstream system. As a result, the national oil marketing company, Brega, ceased operating in 1990, and marketing became a responsibility of the National Oil Corporation itself.

Doing Business with Europe in the 1990s

Political relations between Libya and the United States worsened in the 1990s. In December 1988, Pan Am Flight 103 from London to New York blew up over Locherbie, Scotland. In 1991, the United States and Great Britain claimed that two Libyan men had carried out the bombing, and in 1992 the United Nations imposed new sanctions on Libya to pressure the government to extradite the suspects. The U.S. Congress then passed the Iran-Libya Sanctions Act in 1996, which extended the Libyan sanctions to firms doing more than $20 million of business annually in either Libya or Iran. The slow unwinding of the Locherbie case thus significantly impeded NOC's ability to do business around the world. Though the U.N. sanctions were less comprehensive than the U.S. sanctions, and NOC continued to work with several European companies, they apparently prevented NOC from obtaining needed technology. A reporter for the *Washington Report on Middle East Affairs* (November 2003) claimed that on a visit to Libya in 2000 "the whole country looked tired and run-down. No new computers could be acquired because every computer has at least one American component. The oil industry is limping along."

Yet NOC continued to maintain close relationships with some European companies. The largest foreign operator in Libya in the 1990s was the Italian firm Azienda Generali Italiana Petroli S.p.A., known as AGIP. In the mid-1990s, AGIP and NOC undertook the joint development of NOC's Bouri Field gas field, building a gas treatment and separation facility and starting work on a 1,040 kilometer undersea gas pipeline to Italy. NOC also continued to do business with other European oil companies, including Elf Aquitaine and Total of France, Spain's Repsol, the Austrian firm OeMV, and the German companies Veba AG and Wintershall AG. A consortium of other European companies also began development of NOC's Murzak Field in 1994 and began exporting oil from that field in 1996.

Improved Libyan Relations in the 2000s

United Nations sanctions against Libya were suspended in 1999, when the country agreed to extradite two men accused of planning the Locherbie bombing. Libya began revising its key petroleum regulations that year, and it held 137 blocks of acreage open to foreign oil companies for exploration. However, it took several years to iron out the new regulations. In 2001, NOC executives claimed to be negotiating foreign contracts on a case-by-case basis in the absence of the promised new petroleum legislation.

Then, in 2003, the Locherbie case seemed to come to a close when the Libyan government accepted responsibility for the bombing and set up a fund to compensate victims. The United Nations lifted its sanctions (as opposed to the earlier suspension) in 2003, though the United States sanctions remained in place until April 2004. Some doubt remained over the Locherbie case, and some parties close to the proceedings believed that Libya had accepted responsibility for the bombing merely as an expedient to get the sanctions lifted. Libya's foreign minister revealed in 2003 that the country's goal was to increase oil production from 1.2 million to three million barrels a day over the next 15 years. To do this, it was essential to broaden NOC's contacts with foreign oil companies. Toward that end, in 2003, NOC signed agreements with Austrian energy company OMV and Repsol of Spain, allowing those companies to explore for oil and gas in Libya both onshore and off.

In the spring of 2004, Libya seemed to come in from the cold when it made amends with Britain and the United States, promising to cease the pursuit of weapons of mass destruction. British Prime Minister Tony Blair met with Libya's Khadafi in March 2004, and a few weeks later NOC officials traveled to Houston, Texas, to meet with U.S. oil company executives. At that time President George W. Bush lifted the sanctions against Libya that had been in place for some 22 years. Libya was then able to sell oil to the United States, and U.S. oil companies were then able to invest in Libyan operations. The company opened leasing to U.S. corporations in the summer of 2004. NOC revealed that it had run short of drilling rigs in 2003 and was more than eager to attract new foreign investment. In 2004, NOC's estimated crude oil output was 1.23 million barrels per day. The company hoped to raise its production to two million barrels per day by 2007. It had more than 250 blocks of land to be leased for exploration. In 2004, NOC seemed to have turned a crucial corner in its history. The company was again able to look outward and to embrace many new corporate partners.

Principal Subsidiaries

Arabian Gulf Oil Company; Waha Oil Company; Sirte Oil Company; Oilinvest; Zawia Oil Refining Company; Hamada Pipeline Company; Jowfe Oil Technology Company; Brega Petroleum Marketing Company; Zuetina Oil Company.

Principal Competitors

Nigerian National Petroleum Corporation; Cathargo Oil Company Tunisia.

Further Reading

Antosh, Nelson, "Offshore Technology Conference: Emissary Says Bring Business to Libya," *Houston Chronicle*, May 5, 2004, p. B1.

Barker, Paul, and Keith McLachlan, "Development of the Libyan Oil Industry," *Libya Since Independence: Ecomomic and Political Development*, edited by J.A. Allan, London: Croom Helm/St. Martin's, 1982, 187 p.

Bearman, Jonathan, "U.S. Oil Companies Could Lose out in Libya as Western Firms Return to Develop Fields," *Oil Daily*, April 21, 1999.

Dinesh, Manimoli, "White House Lifts Sanctions Against Libya," *Oil Daily*, April 26, 2004.

"Energy: OMV Ups Links with Libya," *Utility Week*, June 6, 2003, p. 13.

"Extra Oil," *Weekly Petroleum Argus*, September 18, 2000, p. 1.

Ghanem, Shukri, "The Oil Industry and the Libyan Economy: The Past, The Present and the Likely Future" in *The Economic Development of Libya*, edited by B. Khader, London: Routledge, 1987.

Jones, Sally, "Companies Face Big Obstacles in Libya," *Wall Street Journal*, August 5, 2004, p. A6.

Killgore, Andrew I., "Pan Am 103 Case Winding Down, Despite Continued Doubts about Libya's Guilt," *Washington Report on Middle East Affairs*, November 2003, p. 18.

"Libya: Oil Law Suffers Continuing Delays," *Petroleum Economist*, August 2001, p. 38.

McLachlan, Keith, ''AlKhalij, the Libyan Oil Province: A Review of Oil and Development'' in *Libya: State and Region, a Study of Regional Evolution*, edited by M.M. Buro, London: School of African and Oriental Studies, Centre for Near and Middle Eastern Studies, 1989.

Mortishead, Carl, ''Al Fayed Shops for Oil in Libya,'' *Times* (London), April 19, 2000, p. 27.

O'Connell, Dominic, ''The Brits Who Beat Blair to Gadaffi's Tent,'' *Sunday Times* (London), March 28, 2004, p. 16.

The Oil Industry in the Great Jamahirya: Achievements Despite Challenges, Tripoli: Libyan National Oil Corporation, 1990.

Robbins, Carla Anne, and Susan Warren, ''U.S. Opens Door for Oil Concerns' Return to Libya,'' *Wall Street Journal*, February 27, 2004, p. A7.

Waddams, Frank C., *The Libyan Oil Industry*, London: Croom Helm, 1980.

Wright, John, *Libya: A Modern History*, London: Croom Helm, 1983.

—Sarah Ahmad Khan
—update: A. Woodward

National Railroad Passenger Corporation (Amtrak)

80 Massachusetts Avenue N.E.
Washington, D.C. 20002
U.S.A.
Telephone: (202) 906-3860
Toll Free: (800) USA-RAIL
Fax: (202) 906-3864
Web site: http://www.amtrak.com

Private Company
Founded: 1971
Employees: 22,000
Sales: $2.07 billion (2003)
NAIC: 482110 Rail Transportation

The National Railroad Passenger Corporation, better known as Amtrak, is the United States' national rail passenger service, providing train transportation between major cities as well as commuter service and delivery of mail and express freight. A private corporation, Amtrak is almost wholly owned by the U.S. Department of Transportation.

The Creation

On May 1, 1971, the first passenger trains operated by the National Railroad Passenger Corporation pulled out of stations around the country, beginning what was depicted as a two-year federal undertaking to revive (and save) long-distance, intercity rail passenger service in the United States.

Congress had created the company the previous year with the passage of the Railroad Passenger Service Act. The Act established a private company, incorporated in the District of Columbia. Most of the new company's stock was owned by the Department of Transportation, and it was governed by a board of directors made up of the Secretary of Transportation, the head of the corporation, and 11 other members, the majority appointed by the president. During its first year of existence, the corporation was known as Railpax. After it began operations, the nickname was changed to Amtrak, a contraction of the words America and track.

Amtrak was charged with accomplishing three goals, described in the Amtrak Source Book as: "To operate rail passenger service on a for-profit basis; to use innovative operating and marketing concepts to fully develop the potential of modern railway passenger service to meet intercity transportation needs; and to provide a modern, efficient intercity rail passenger service." Congress authorized grants of $40 million for operations and loan guarantees of $100 million for new equipment. Direct funding was to last only two years, by which time the corporation was to be completely self-supporting.

Background

By the time Congress created Amtrak, intercity rail passenger service in the United States had been in a 20-year decline. Until the 1950s, railroads were the only way to travel long distances. But during that decade, the federal government began financing the interstate highway system, a $41 billion, 16-year project, and, as jet airplanes were introduced, significantly increased its support for the construction and improvement of airports.

Airplanes, personal automobiles, and buses began competing with the country's railroads for long-distance travel. The railroads responded to the competition with new equipment on their prestige long-distance routes, replacing steam locomotives with diesel engines, and introducing lightweight stainless steel passenger cars with air-conditioning and double glazed windows. But as the number of passengers continued to drop, the rail companies had little incentive to make major capital investments to upgrade their tracks, signaling, stations, and maintenance facilities. Why, they thought, should their profitable freight business subsidize a means of intercity transportation that was competing with systems receiving federal and state tax dollars? By 1958, rail service accounted for just 4 percent of intercity travel.

The decline in rail passenger service and the deterioration of passenger facilities continued during the 1960s. By the end of the decade, the number of passenger trains had dropped to 500, down from more than 20,000 some 40 years earlier, and only 12,000 passenger cars remained in service. Losses from passenger service operations in 1970 came to more than $1.8 billion

Company Perspectives:

We are America's passenger railroad. Our mission is to consistently deliver a high-quality, safe, on-time rail passenger service that exceeds customer expectations.

dollars in 1997 dollars. Most of the loss was on long-distance, intercity travel. Commuter and suburban lines obviously were less affected by airlines and, at least during the 1960s, lost little ridership to buses and private cars. Many of the railroad companies filed applications to get out of the intercity service on most or all of their routes. Among the most critical was the proposal by Penn Central (the merged Pennsylvania Railroad and New York Central Railroad) to eliminate all its passenger service in the Northeast and Midwest.

Federal Action

The Railroad Passenger Service Act allowed the railroad companies to transfer their money-losing passenger operations to Amtrak in exchange for either a tax write-off or Amtrak stock. Only three lines, the Denver & Rio Grande Western, the Rock Island, and the Southern, did not join Amtrak, opting to continue their own passenger service.

The basic network of routes for the new corporation was developed by the Transportation Department with assistance from the Interstate Commerce Commission, the railroad unions, 15 railroad companies, 43 states, some 3,000 members of the public, and numerous U.S. Senators and Representatives. Factors considered in selecting the routes included existing routes, cost, ridership potential, size of the terminal cities (had to have a population of at least one million), and the condition of the tracks and facilities (no funds were allocated for improving these).

Between January and May 1971, as the new corporation got itself organized, a major argument developed regarding the company's objective: was it to reintroduce the traditional, and well-known, long-distance routes of the past, such as the "Empire Builder," "San Francisco Zephyr," and "Super Chief," or should it concentrate on introducing high speed (150 mph) rail corridors? Those two visions of passenger service in the United States would haunt Amtrak for decades.

The 1970s: Amtrak's First Decade

Although it operated in 43 states over 24,000 miles of track, the enterprise Amtrak began managing on May 1, 1971 was hardly a national transportation system. Essentially, Amtrak was a travel broker. It operated 119 passenger trains, a multicolored assortment of some 1,200 cars—coaches, diners, sleepers, and observation cars—with an average age of 20 years. The individual railroads donated some cars to Amtrak but continued to own the stations, terminals, yards, locomotives, and maintenance facilities, and employed all the people who worked on the passenger trains and in the stations and yards. In its first year, Amtrak leased the crews and equipment, along with the seat reservation, booking, communication, and dispatching systems from the various freight lines. In 1972, Amtrak began buying the diesel locomotives from the railroads and initiated a program of rebuilding and refurbishing the engines to improve on-time performance.

The tracks Amtrak's "rainbow" trains ran on also were owned by the freight companies. For access to the rights of way, which was guaranteed by the legislation, Amtrak paid the freight companies a rental charge. That charge was determined by a formula established in the federal statute. The legislation also gave Amtrak trains priority dispatching over freight trains, but did not address the issue of liability in cases of injuries. Despite the logistical problems and uncomfortable rolling stock, Amtrak was able to keep the passengers it inherited in 1971, and during its first two years even increased ridership.

The creation of Amtrak seemed to generate three conclusions. Some people believed the new entity was really expected to revive intercity rail traffic. The more skeptical seemed to think that this was a last gasp effort and that once the equipment finally gave out, that would be the end of it. Others within the industry and among the passengers saw it as a ruse to eliminate routes in sparsely populated areas while keeping rail service along corridors between major cities in the Northeast and on the West Coast.

None of these occurred after Amtrak's first two years because OPEC, the cartel of oil-producing countries, cut back the production of oil. The resulting energy crunch in 1973 and 1974 caused the price of gasoline (and airline tickets) to increase and lines at gas stations to grow long. Many Americans (and politicians) increased their support of alternative means of transportation, including rail passenger service. Congress approved funding for fiscal years 1972 and 1973 totaling $179.1 million in grants and $100 million in guaranteed loans. In 1973, Amtrak began ordering new equipment.

The new silver trains with the red and blue Amtrak logo attracted more riders and marketing became easier. A centralized and computerized reservations system also helped improve service. During the decade, the company purchased 600 Amfleet and Amfleet II cars and 284 Superliners, including locomotives, coaches, lounges, sleepers, and dining facilities.

Amtrak also began to take control of yard and station facilities, reservation offices, and all personnel except for train and engine crews. In 1972, Amtrak employed about 1,500 administrative and clerical workers. Within two years, as the company assumed responsibility for more of the passenger service operations, employment climbed to 8,500.

The Northeast Corridor (NEC)

As Amtrak was placing its equipment orders, the major freight lines in the Northeast were going bankrupt. As creditors, shareholders, railroad unions, and other railroads (who shipped to and from the East) cried for some action, the federal government took a step that would have a huge impact on Amtrak. The Regional Rail Reorganization Act of 1973 created Conrail (Consolidated Rail Corporation), a federally supported freight company made up of seven bankrupt railroads operating in the Northeast. The legislation also supported funding for preliminary engineering work to improve the Northeast Corridor to cut passenger travel times between Boston, New York, and Washington, D.C.

Key Dates:

1971: The National Railroad Passenger Corporation is created by an Act of Congress to supervise the country's rail passenger train service.
1981: Congress petitions Amtrak to cut back on federal support dollars.
1983: Amtrak shifts from a supervisory to an ownership role of the rail services, employing crews and centralizing reservations.
1994: Given the company's impressive revenues, Congress demands that Amtrak become a self-sufficient corporation.
1997: On the verge of bankruptcy, Amtrak continues to rely on federal subsidies.
2000: Amtrak debuts the Acela Regional passenger service linking Boston, New York, and Washington, D.C.
2004: Amtrak avoids insolvency, being approved for $2 billion a year in assistance for six years.

Three years later, following the passage of the Railroad Revitalization and Regulatory Reform Act in 1976, Amtrak acquired 621 miles of right-of way from Conrail. Most of the routes, about 450 miles, were in the Northeast Corridor, from Washington, D.C. to Boston. The acquisition also included lines from Philadelphia to Harrisburg, Pennsylvania; from New Haven, Connecticut, to Springfield, Massachusetts; and from Porter, Indiana, to Kalamazoo, Michigan. For a switch, now freight trains would have to pay Amtrak to use these rails. As part of the legislation, Congress authorized $1.9 billion over five years to rebuild and improve the tracks and facilities in the NEC.

Along with the tracks, Amtrak also came into possession of rail yards, maintenance facilities, and all the stations along their new routes. The real estate included Pennsylvania Station in New York City and 30th Street Station in Philadelphia, along with some 100 smaller station properties, and half interests in Chicago's Union Station and in Washington, D.C.'s Union Station. With these acquisitions, Amtrak employment nearly doubled, to 16,500, as the company assumed new operations and maintenance responsibilities.

The capital investments made to reduce travel time in the Northeast Corridor by rebuilding tracks and introducing new equipment received most of the attention during the late 1970s. But development was begun on another high-speed corridor, between Los Angeles and San Diego, and other corridors were being studied for high-speed potential.

During the last half of the 1970s, Congress changed the way it financed Amtrak's capital improvements. Instead of loan guarantees, which had mounted to $900 million between 1971 and 1975, or a designated source of income as was provided for highways and airports, Amtrak began receiving direct capital grants, which had to be requested and approved annually, making it difficult to plan and finance capital investments. Amtrak continued to receive separate annual operating grants.

The company's annual revenue during the decade averaged $252 million, and represented less than 40 percent of its operating expenditures. The growing deficits led the Carter Administration to push for more efficient operations and cuts in costs. Proposals to eliminate routes as a means of reducing costs generally went nowhere as Senators and Representatives fought to keep trains running in their states, whether the routes were profitable or not. In fact, by 1977, the number of miles in the Amtrak system had grown to 27,000. Finally, under restructuring in 1979, several routes were dropped as the basic network was cut to 24,000 miles.

1980s: Amtrak's Second Decade

During the 1980s, Amtrak continued to move from supervising to operating the nation's passenger rail system. Early in the decade, Amtrak installed its new Arrow reservation system, with faster computers, and acquired the last non-Amtrak intercity passenger train, the Rio Grande Zephyr, from the Denver and Rio Grande Western.

In 1983, Amtrak, for the first time, directly employed engineers, conductors, and their assistants, beginning on Northeast Corridor trains. The takeover of the operating crews continued for the next several years, until, by 1987, Amtrak employed most of the crews operating passenger trains around the country. After 1982, under Amtrak's bargaining agreements, crews were paid based on a 40-hour work week, not on mileage and other factors as had been the case with the freight lines.

The company also expanded its position in the commuter train business, taking over the commuter trains in the northeast previously operated by Conrail. The company set up a wholly-owned subsidiary, Amtrak Commuter Services Corporation, to oversee its commuter operations.

Amtrak's partnerships with various states improved passenger service in their jurisdictions. Under Section 403(b) of the legislation that established it, Amtrak could operate intercity trains or routes funded by states. California, for example, paid for more trains between Los Angeles and San Diego, in the San Joaquin Valley, and, eventually, between San Jose and Sacramento. New York was one of the first to take advantage of Section 403(b), improving passenger service for the New York-Albany-Buffalo corridor.

But the core route and services faced financial cuts as the Reagan Administration convinced Congress to significantly reduce both the operating and capital grants each year. As President Reagan told an audience, ''On the New York to Chicago train, it would cost the taxpayer less for the government to pass out free plane tickets.''

Most historians agree that things would have been even worse for Amtrak except for Graham Claytor, a lawyer and railroad executive and the new president and CEO of Amtrak. According to Stephen Goddard, ''The grandfatherly attorney left his comfortable office . . . to give Amtrak what it needed—credibility before Congress, in whose hands the troubled railroad would rise or fall.'' Yet even as the cuts were being made, when Reagan fired the striking federal air traffic controllers, people turned to intercity trains.

In 1981, Congress told Amtrak to make better use of all its resources to minimize federal support. In addition to revenues from the commuter and 403(b) trains, by 1981, Amtrak's real estate revenues were generating about $9 million a year. In 1984 the company acquired the remaining one-half interest in Chicago Union Station.

To help increase its assets, the company established a corporate development department. One of its ventures was to lease the NEC right-of-way to telecommunication companies for installing fiber optics communications systems. MCI Communications was the first company to enter into such a lease, with MCI providing Amtrak with specific fibers and communication circuits as well as with cash. Amtrak used those high capacity circuits for their own network and marketed and leased them to large telecommunication users. Amtrak also turned to mail and express freight service for additional income.

In 1985, Amtrak's supporters argued that shutting down Amtrak completely would result in costly drops in productivity due to traffic jams and crowded airports in the major corridors, especially in the northeast. The prospect of more cars and planes (and the resulting pollution) effectively dampened enthusiasm for eliminating all support for Amtrak, at least for a while.

In 1986, Amtrak became the dominant carrier between New York and Washington, with 38 percent of the total air-rail market. In 1989, the company began another period of capital investment, as Amtrak purchased 104 short-distance passenger cars to alleviate crowding on routes in the Midwest and in California's San Joaquin Valley.

By the end of the decade, Amtrak operations were bringing in more than $1.2 billion in revenues. But with operating expenses in fiscal 1989 of nearly $2 billion, it continued to have an operating loss larger than the $554 million operating grant it received from the federal government. The general capital grant fell from $221 million in fiscal year 1981 to $2 million in fiscal 1986 then averaged $34 million for the rest of the decade.

1990s: Moving Toward Self-Sufficiency

In 1994, Congress and the Clinton Administration demanded that Amtrak operations become self-sufficient by 2002. To accomplish this, the company, under new CEO Thomas Downs, adopted a strategic and business plan for the period 1995 to 2000. As part of the plan, Amtrak decentralized itself into three business units to increase accountability and responsiveness: Northeast Corridor, covering services from Virginia to New England; Amtrak West, which operated state-supported corridor trains and the long-distance Coast Starlight on the West Coast; and Amtrak Intercity, responsible for most of the long-distance routes as well as corridor trains in the Midwest. The company also began raising fares, cutting routes and service, and implementing cost reduction programs for its operations.

However, Amtrak needed new rolling stock to replace old equipment, to achieve better travel times, and to meet the requests from states for new intrastate rail services. Through 1990, Amtrak had spent $1.6 billion for cars and locomotives and the capital investment continued during the decade with the delivery of new diesel locomotives, 195 bi-level Superliners, and, in 1996, 50 Viewliners, the first single-level sleeping cars made in the United States in 40 years. In California, 14 new dual-level dining cars were introduced on the state-supported routes, and in Washington, three pendular "tilt" Talgo trains were ordered by Amtrak and the Washington Department of Transportation for delivery in 1998. Trains able to travel 150 miles an hour were added to service the Northeast Corridor beginning in 1999.

Although revenues increased to $1.6 billion in fiscal year 1996, debt and capital lease obligations were almost $1 billion. By 1997, Amtrak was in danger of going bankrupt (in December of that year Downs resigned as CEO and a search was underway for his successor). Congress debated the company's request to designate one-half cent of the Interstate Highway Trust for capital expenditures, but instead passed a tax rebate package of $2.3 billion for Amtrak capital spending over two years and adopted a package of reforms changing various labor requirements, allowing Amtrak to alter the basic system of routes inherited in 1971, setting a cap on liability costs, and establishing a new Reform Board. Funding for the Department of Transportation for fiscal year 1998 included $344 million for Amtrak operations and $250 million for Northeast Corridor capital. It also included $23 billion for highways, $9 billion for aviation, and $4 billion for transit.

Growing Budgets and High Speed Service in the 2000s

Despite the shakeup at the top and numerous skeptics, Amtrak survived. The company continued its efforts to improve service, spending $26.6 million to overhaul 212 passenger cars. Buttressed by the Taxpayer Relief Act of 1997 Amtrak launched a $360 million capital improvement program. They spent $100 million for eight new five-car train sets for San Diego service, purchased eight locomotives, 64 carriers, 43 coaches, several improved refrigerator cars, and numerous expensive equipment updates. New lines and improved travel times resulted in several cities. In December 1998 Amtrak agreed to purchase 44 RoadRailer Mailvans. Acting President and CEO George D. Warrington cited increasing rail revenues—which had been rising 10 percent each year—as reason for the investment, which he stated could only bolster their bottom line.

In January 1999 the Department of Transportation released a report accusing Amtrak of underreporting its losses, stating specifically that the 1998 year's loss was not the reported $95 million, but $854 million. A brief flap followed, but some in Congress pointed out that it was difficult for Amtrak to succeed when expectations for them constantly changed. Warrington continued to assemble a new management team, envisioning an Amtrak that featured high speed rail corridors across the country and high-quality service. Statistics backed up Warrington's assertions that Amtrak continued to improve—between 1998 and 1999 the percent of riders was the highest it had been in a decade, on-time arrival was the highest it had been in 13 years, and passenger revenues had topped $1 billion for the first time.

In March 2000 Amtrak introduced the Acela Regional passenger service, creating the long-awaited electrification of the Northeast Corridor linking Boston, New York, and Washington, D.C. The result was a reduction in travel time from Boston and New York by up to 90 minutes. Further improvements were unveiled in November 2000, after months of delay. The Acela

Express, the nation's first high-speed rail system began travelling the Northwest Corridor's tracks at up to 150 miles per hour, reducing a Boston to New York trip to 3 hours and 15 minutes, a New York to Washington, D.C. trip to 2 hours and 28 minutes. The Acela beat its projected profits by 12 percent in the first quarter of 2001 and launched Amtrak into its most profitable year yet. The success prompted Congress to reconsider a controversial bill to allow Amtrak to issue bonds to raise $12 million dollars for the high-speed rail system.

Rail use rose significantly due to security concerns in the wake of the terrorist attacks of September 11, 2001, and Congress allocated over a billion dollars to improve Amtrak's security. Yet Congress had legislated a time bomb for Amtrak in 1997 that was set to go off by December 2002. Amtrak was to attain self-sufficiency by that December or prepare for liquidation. By December 2001, CEO Warrington was told by the federally appointed Amtrak Reform Council that he would have to prepare a liquidation plan. Amtrak was absolved of the responsibility to prepare its own liquidation plan by a defense act signed into law by President Bush in early 2002, but was told they still needed to attain self-sufficiency. Numerous ideas were floated by congressional agencies, including breaking Amtrak up into separate privatized industries.

In July 2003 two competing funding plans warred for prominence. The Bush administration announced that it would allocate $90 million, while a house committee approved a bill that would fund the company for $6 billion over the next three years. Congressional debate continued, with Senator John McCain and the Bush administration arguing for breaking Amtrak up and selling it. They faced stiff opposition from both Democrats and other Republican congressional leaders. By February 2004 the Amtrak supporters had won, and Amtrak was approved for $2 billion a year for six years.

Amtrak had won at least a reprieve. By the fall of 2004 it looked as though the company would remain intact, though it still faced significant hurdles. Throughout its history it was funded at a rate tens of times lower than the rate at which Congress has funded highways and aviation, and continued to own little of its own track. Still, with the new high-speed trains, rising passenger rates, and improved funding, the future looked, if not rosy, then far more promising than it had in many years.

Principal Competitors

Greyhound Lines Inc.

Further Reading

Bradley, Rodger, *Amtrak: The U.S. National Railroad Passenger Corporation,* Dorset, England: Blandford Press, 1985.

DePalma, Anthony, ''Amtrak Tries to Learn How to Run a Railroad,'' *International Herald Tribune,* February 4, 2002, p. 2.

Goddard, Stephen B., *Getting There: The Epic Struggle Between Road and Rail in the American Century,* New York: Basic Books, 1994.

Hosansky, David, ''Struggling Amtrak Seeks Share of Federal Highway Money,'' *Congressional Quarterly Weekly Report,* March 29, 1997, p. 737.

Johnson, Bob, ''States Show Amtrak the Way,'' *Trains Magazine,* July 1997, p. 36.

Miller, William H, ''Amtrak's Unforgiving Timetable,'' *Chief Executive (U.S.),* December 2001 p. 29.

''Perspective—Derailing Amtrak,'' *Investors Business Daily,* November 6, 1997.

Vantuono, William C., ''Blue-Ribbon Panel Spells the Blues for Passenger Rail,'' *Railway Age,* August 1997, p. 161.

Wilner, Frank N., ''Amtrak at 25: The Railroad That Just Won't Quit,'' *Railway Age,* May 1996, p. 39.

—Ellen D. Wernick
—update: Howard A. Jones

Nexity S.A.

8 rue du General Foy
Paris F-75008
France
Telephone: +33 1 44 70 23 00
Fax: +33 1 44 70 28 06
Web site: http://www.nexity.fr

Subsidiary of Veolia Environment and EdF
Incorporated: 1996 as CGIS
Employees: 1,300
Sales: EUR 1.3 billion ($1.45 billion) (2003)
NAIC: 237210 Land Subdivision; 236115 New Single-Family Housing Construction (Except Operative Builders); 236116 New Multi-Family Housing Construction (Except Operative Builders)

Nexity S.A. is France's leading real estate developer, operating in both residential and commercial markets. Spun off from Vivendi in a management buyout in 2000, Nexity operates through four primary divisions. Residential Real Estate is handled by the group's Nexity Georges V and Nexity Foncier Conseil subsidiaries. Real Estate Development, which serves especially investors and third-party promoters, includes Nexity Sari and Nexity Geprim. Nexity Services provides a full range of real estate services including design, acquisition, day-to-day management, and others, for an institutional investor client base. Last, Nexity's fastest growing division is Nexity International, including Nexity Spain, Nexity Portugal, and, since 2003, Nexity Belgium. That division accounted for 36 percent of Nexity's revenues of EUR 1.3 billion (US $1.45 billion) in 2003. More than 68 percent of Nexity's revenues are generated by its residential real estate activities; institutional developments accounted for just 25 percent of the group's total revenues. Although Services represented just 6 percent of the company's revenues, it remains a fast-growing segment, and is helping to spearhead typically Paris-focused Nexity's drive to achieve greater penetration into the French regional market. Led by Stéphane Bernard and Alain Dinin, Nexity is said to be eyeing a public offering in the mid-2000s.

Grouping Real Estate Holdings in the 1990s

Nexity's origins were linked to the origins of former parent company Vivendi, which itself was known as Compagnie Générale des Eaux (CGE) for most of its existence. CGE was established in the mid-19th century in order to provide water supply services to France's rapidly industrializing cities. By the turn of the 20th century, CGE was already one of France's largest private companies.

Through the first half of the century, CGE remained focused on its core water utilities operations. In the 1960s, however, CGE launched a new diversification strategy that led it into a variety of new markets over the next two decades, including the construction and real estate sales and development sectors. By the late 1970s, CGE not only supplied water to French homes, it had begun to build them as well. In 1979, the company stepped up this activity with the acquisition of Maison Phenix.

Founded in 1946, Maison Phenix had played a prominent role in the rebuilding and modernization of France's housing stock. Maison Phenix was one of the first companies in France to offer American-style development homes, using standardized floor plans and prefabricated parts. In 1949, however, the company expanded its housing offerings with the launch of Maison Familiales, which provided more individual and artisan homebuilding services.

By the time of its acquisition by CGE, Maison Phenix was already a leader in the French home building market. CGE continued to extend its range of home brands over the next decade, adding such companies and their home brands as Maison Catherine Mamet, Maison FIL, Castor, Promidi, Florilège, Cévenol, and Sprint. A major boost to CGE's real estate operations came with its acquisition of Société Générale d'Entreprise in 1988. The purchase of the future Vinci placed CGE at the top of France's construction and real estate development industries. Other CGE acquisitions included Seeri, and Sari, which enabled the company to participate in such high-profile developments as the La Défense business district in Paris.

CGE began restructuring its real estate holdings during the housing crunch of the early 1990s. That process led the com-

Company Perspectives:

As the leading French residential and commercial real estate developer, Nexity is present throughout France. Nexity combines all areas of expertise. To address the concerns of its many clients—local communities, businesses, investors and individuals. Today, Nexity continues to grow in the area of real estate development, strengthening its presence in France and throughout Europe, while developing its commercial real estate services. Pursuing a targeted strategy of international development, Nexity aims to become a major player in European real estate.

pany to place its various residential and single family home businesses (also known as ''Maisons Individuelles'' division) under a single subsidiary, MI S.A., in 1993. MI S.A. then became the clear leader in the French residential real estate and development market.

Just two years later, CGE's real estate division took on an entirely new scale. In 1995, CGE bought up the George V real estate division from Groupe Arnault, of LVMH fame. Bernard Arnault, who became one of France's most visible business leaders, started his career at his family's construction firm, Ferret-Savinel, in 1971. Originally specialized in public works projects and industrial construction, Ferret-Savinel began developing its real estate and development operations under the younger Arnault. In 1975, Arnault convinced his father, then head of the company, to sell off its public works and industrial construction operations to Quillery, later a founding member of leading French construction group Eiffage.

Following that sale, Ferret-Savinel changed its name, becoming Ferinel, and, focused on the real estate market, began developing its portfolio. By the early 1980s, Ferinel had emerged as an important player in that market, particularly in the Parisian housing sector. Ferinel also was to provide the launch pad to Arnault's later success—particularly after it gained control of Groupe Boussac in 1984.

Boussac had been founded by Marcel Boussac in 1911 as textile firm Comptoir de l'Industrie Contonnière (CIC). That company grew into France's dominant textile concern by the 1950s. Boussac began to diversify his holdings, acquiring, among many others, fashion house Dior in 1947, then branching out into perfumes, with Parfums Dior. By the 1960s, Boussac also controlled his own real estate empire, governing some 30 different companies, which in turn held and managed Boussac's various real estate interests.

Boussac sold his business to Agache-Willot's Saint Frères in 1978, then died two year later. The two companies were then merged, creating Boussac-Saint-Frères. Yet by 1981, the new business had collapsed, and both Boussac-Saint-Frères and Agache-Willot declared bankruptcy. The takeover by Arnault met with some controversy, a controversy that only grew as Arnault refocused Boussac around Dior, selling off most of the group's industrial operations, before engineering the takeover of LVMH that created Groupe Arnault as one of the world's leading luxury goods groups.

Restructured and Independent in the 2000s

CGE's acquisition of Ferinel, which included its Georges V real estate arm and its Savinel home building brand, among others, proved to be a turning point in CGE's history. By then, CGE had swollen to an internationally operating giant with more than 2,200 subsidiaries and operations spanning such disparate sectors as construction, telecommunications, pay television, facilities management, the operation of amusement parks, and others. Yet for the first time in its history, CGE slumped into losses in the mid-1990s, and these losses were attributed in large part to the company's unwieldy construction and real estate components.

While the construction wing was restructured and ultimately spun off as Vinci, the company also took steps to reorganize its real estate division. In 1996, CGE grouped all of its real estate-related activities under a single subsidiary, Compagnie Générale d'Immobilier et de Services, or CGIS. Placed in charge of restructuring the new subsidiary and in restoring it to profitability were the three-man team of Stéphane Bernard, Alain Dinin, and Jean-Louis Charon.

CGIS started out as a highly diversified business, involved in all aspects of the real estate market. As such, the company operated a string of vacation resorts, under the Maeva name, some 85 hotels, a chain of exercise clubs, Groupe Gymnase, as well as a vast portfolio of industrial holdings, including a number of Marseilles-based docks. The company also operated engineering services under its Coteba subsidiary.

CGIS's new management team set to work restoring the subsidiary's profits. The lack of synergy among its disparate operations led it to launch a sell-off of its assets. By 1998, CGIS had raised more than EUR 1.75 billion for CGE—including the 1997 sales of two company flagships, including CGE's former headquarters near the Elysée Palace and its future headquarters, as Vivendi, on Avenue Friedland, near the Arc de Triomphe. The following year, CGE changed its name to Vivendi, and let it be known that it intended to refocus itself as a media and communications group.

CGIS's sell-off continued into 1999, as the company sold off its hotels to Accor for nearly EUR 1.4 billion, then spun off MI S.A. in a management buyout that same year. The company also sold a swath of Parisian commercial real estate properties, including a number of La Defense sites, to Unibail for EUR 900 million. CGIS went looking for a buyer for its Maeva resorts chain, reaching an agreement with Pierre et Vacances, which paid EUR 90 million in 2001. Also in that year, the company sold its Gymnase Club to Club Med for EUR 41 million, then shed its Marseilles docks and its suburban Paris office portfolio, among others, netting some EUR 692 million.

By then, CGIS itself had been sold off, in a management buyout backed by CDC Ixis Capital, LBO France, and Lehman Brothers in 2000 in a deal worth some EUR 700 million. CGIS then changed its name to Nexity. Already France's leading real estate group, Nexity now turned its attention to building an international presence. The company had been operating in Spain since the early 1990s, primarily for French investors seeking properties in that country. In 2002, the company stepped up its Spanish presence, as well as began development plans in Portugal, where it created subsidiary Nexity Portugal.

Key Dates:

1979: CGE acquires Maison Phenix, creating a residential home-building division.
1992: CGE enters the Spanish real estate market.
1993: CGE regroups its home-building operations under MI S.A.
1995: CGE acquires Georges V (formerly Ferinel) from Groupe Arnault.
1996: Property, real estate development, and related operations are restructured under the new subsidiary CGIS, which begins selling off assets.
2000: Vivendi (formerly CGE) spins off CGIS in a management buyout, and its name changes to Nexity.
2001: Nexity sells Maeva resorts, Gymnase Club, and a portfolio of properties.
2002: Nexity acquires 75 properties from Vivendi.
2003: Nexity Belgium is formed; the engineering services arm Coteba is spun off in a management buyout.
2004: Nexity acquires Saggel, property services group, and announces a possible public offering.

In 2003, Nexity's international interests turned to Belgium, where it founded Nexity Belgium and began developing projects, including the Radisson Hotel in Brussels, as well as the City Gardens project in that city. In the meantime, Nexity continued its restructuring. In 2002, Nexity acquired a portfolio of 75 properties from former parent Vivendi for EUR 130 million. By the end of 2003, Nexity's refocusing effort drew to a close with the spin-off of its engineering services wing, Cotebo, in a management buyout.

Nexity was now a focused property development and property services group. In January 2004, the company boosted its small services division with the purchase of Saggel, founded in 1999. Nexity also acknowledged its interest in going public, perhaps by as early as the end of 2004.

Principal Subsidiaries

Nexity Belgium; Nexity Espagne; Nexity Foncier Conseil; Nexity Georges V; Nexity International; Nexity Portugal; Nexity Sari.

Principal Competitors

Fortis N.V.; Société Centrale Immobilière de la Caisse des Depots; Gensec Property Services; Casino Guichard-Perrachon S.A.; ABN AMRO Bouwfonds Nederlandse Gemeenten N.V.; Granaria Holdings B.V.; George Wimpey PLC; Unibail S.A.; Lixxbail S.A.

Further Reading

''Immobilier Nexity: 'Je croyair en l'equipe, j'ai plongé sans hésitation,' '' *Challenges,* October 3, 2002.

Iskander, Samer, ''Move to Extend the Company's Liquid Assets,'' *Financial Times,* February 22, 2000, p. 2.

''Nexity cherche des relais de croissance,'' *Le Figaro,* December 10, 2002.

''Nexity envisage une entrée en bourse,'' *BatiActu,* July 15, 2004.

''Nexity organise son pôle logement,'' *BatiActu,* July 2, 2004.

''Nexity se renforce dans les services,'' *BatiActu,* September 1, 2004.

Rivlin, Richard, ''Vivendi in Talks on Properties,'' *Financial Times,* January 7, 2000, p. 22.

''Vivendi Universal se débarrasse d'une partie de son immobilier,'' *BatiActu,* May 30, 2002.

—M.L. Cohen

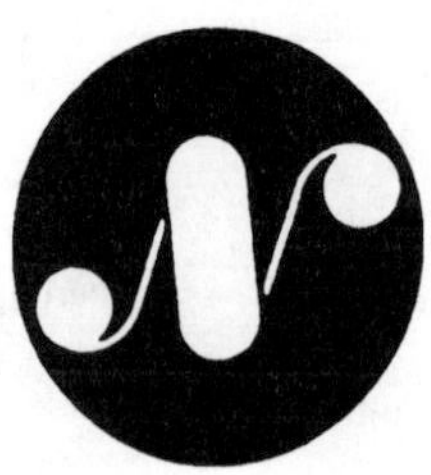

Nisshin Seifun Group Inc.

25 Kanda-Nishiki-cho
1-chrome, Chiyoda-ku
Tokyo 101-8441
Japan
Telephone: (+03) 5282-6650
Fax: (+03) 5282-6185
Web site: http://www.nisshin.com

Public Company
Incorporated: 1908
Employees: 5,185
Sales: $4.1 billion (2004)
Stock Exchanges: Tokyo
Ticker Symbol: 2002
NAIC: 311211 Flour Milling

Nisshin Seifun Group Inc., formerly Nisshin Flour Milling Company, operates as a holding company with subsidiaries involved in flour milling, processed foods, health foods, pharmaceuticals, pet food, engineering, yeast manufacturing, mesh products, and livestock feed. The company's processed foods division accounts for nearly 50 percent of sales. Flour milling—the company's original core operation—is responsible for approximately 35 percent of Nisshin Seifun's sales.

Origins

Founded in 1900 by Teiichiro Shoda as the Tatebayashi Four Milling Company, Nisshin's initial business operations focused on wheat-flour production. The company continued to be one of Japan's leading flour producers into the year 2000. When Tatebayashi merged in 1908 with the new Yokohama-based Nisshin Flour Milling Company, the company incorporated under the Nisshin Flour Milling Company name and moved its head office to Tokyo. A research center was established in 1916 to develop new products, including the world's first synthetic vitamin B6. With construction of the company's largest mill at Tsurumi in 1926. Nisshin's flour milling division expanded its production capacity for Japan's growing export market.

Postwar Growth

Nisshin's milling plants, damaged during World War II, were rebuilt and expanded between 1945 and 1949 to meet postwar demands for wheat flour. Further modernization occurred in 1957 with the installation of state-of-the-art pneumatic conveying equipment from West Germany and Switzerland.

In the early 1960s, Nisshin diversified into areas related to its flour-milling technology and expertise. For example, the feed division was formed in 1961 to take advantage of Japan's increasing meat consumption and the corresponding growth of the livestock industry. The division currently ranks third in Japanese livestock-feed production and has since grown to include the Nisshin Stockfarming Center Company for the commercial breeding and selling of hogs.

In the 1960s, Nisshin moved into the commercial processed-food market. Nisshin Foods Company was established in 1962 to manufacture cake mixes and other flour-based products for the consumer market. Nisshin-DCA Foods was created in 1966, through a joint venture with DCA Food Industries of the United States, to produce doughnut mixes. In 1967, the company purchased Ma. Ma-Macaroni Company, a pasta manufacturer. Nisshin Foods Company was the first food company to improve product quality in response to consumer demand by using imported 100 percent durum semolina flour, which was better for processing, instead of domestic wheat flour. New products included convenience foods like frozen noodles, frozen dough, and flour mixes for fried food.

In the early 1970s, Nisshin expanded its product line by forming or purchasing subsidiaries to market pet food, ham, and sausages, create stock-breeding operations, and develop restaurant and catering services. The fine chemicals division, part of Nisshin Pharmaceutical Company, marketed vitamins and other pharmaceutical products manufactured by another division, the Nisshin Chemicals Company. The company also established several international divisions. Nisshin Seifun do Brasil was

Company Perspectives:

Nisshin Seifun Group Inc. has been positioned as the holding company of the Nisshin Seifun Group of the 21st century. Its function is to establish business objectives in alignment with the company's guiding principles of "trust," being "in tune with the changing climate" and "contributing to a healthy and fruitful life for all" to maximize group value.

formed in 1977 to develop business in Brazil, and Nisshin Badische Company produced and sold feed additives through a joint venture with BASF of West Germany.

In anticipation of its 90th anniversary, Nisshin initiated a company-wide strategy known as "NI-90" to encourage innovation and commitment to continued growth. Led by president Osamu Shoda, Nisshin faced the challenges of international trade, changing consumer tastes, increased foreign competition, and a fluctuating yen in the early 1990s. As a member of the powerful Fuyo Group, a leading Japanese industrial group with close ties to Fuji Bank, Nisshin had a solid financial backing for future undertakings.

Changes in the 1990s and Beyond

As Nisshin headed towards the 21st century, it began to position itself to better compete in a challenging business environment. In 1994, the company took full ownership of Nisshin DCA Foods, a U.S.-based joint venture. Two years later, it established Medallion Foods Inc. in Tacoma, Washington, in order to produce and market pasta in the United States. The facility in Tacoma manufactured 72 tons of pasta each day.

The company also worked to strengthen its pharmaceutical holdings. It partnered with Kyorin Pharmaceutical Company Ltd. to establish Nisshin Kyorin Pharmaceutical Company Ltd. in 1996. One year later, Nisshin Flour restructured its frozen food operations in an attempt to increase sales. Wholly owned subsidiary Nisshin Foods Company Ltd. was created as a result.

Nisshin celebrated its 100th anniversary in 2000. Over the past ten years, the company and its peers in the industry had witnessed changes in business laws, deregulation, wavering domestic and international economies, and heightened competition brought on by globalization. That year, the company decided to launch a major reorganization. As part of its strategy for the new century, Nisshin adopted a holding company structure and changed its name to the Nisshin Seifun Group Inc.

Osamu Shoda—Nisshin's president at the time—explained the decision in the firm's 2002 annual report. "Like most companies," Shoda claimed, "Nisshin Seifun has a hand in an array of businesses. While there is some overlap, each of the businesses face different market condition, services a different customer base, and provides a different line-up of products. For a business to be competitive it must structure itself so that it is ideally suited to respond to the unique environment in which it operates." Shoda also added, "The aim of the reorganization is to put our businesses in a better position to respond quickly and closely to changing markets by providing them a greater degree of autonomy while allowing them to more freely form collaborative alliances inside and outside the Group."

Key Dates:

1900: Teiichiro Shoda establishes the Tatebayashi Flour Milling Company.
1908: Tatebayashi Flour Milling merges with Nisshin Flour Milling and incorporates under the Nisshin Flour name.
1916: A research center is established.
1926: The company opens its largest mill at Tsurumi.
1957: State-of-the-art pneumatic conveying equipment is installed at company plants.
1961: Nisshin Flour forms a feed division.
1962: Nisshin Foods Company is established.
1967: Ma. Ma-Macaroni Company is acquired.
1987: Nisshin Foods and Nisshin Chemicals are purchased.
1996: Medallion Foods Inc. begins producing and marketing pasta in the U.S.
2001: Nisshin Flour adopts a holding company structure and reorganizes as the Nisshin Seifun Group Inc.

Under the new structure, Nisshin Seifun was focused on five core areas—flour milling, processed food, pet food, animal feed, and pharmaceuticals. The company eyed new product development as crucial for future growth. In 2003, for example, Nisshin Flour developed three allergen detecting systems, which were designed as a result of stricter food labeling directives set forth by the government. The company also began expanding its health food offerings and planned to launch CoQ-10 enriched food and drink products, according to a June 2003 *Japan Food Service Journal.* CoQ10 is a coenzyme found in mitochondrion, a substance that converts food to energy in cells and also controls the cell aging process. In March 2004, Initio Foods Inc. was created as a subsidiary to market freshly prepared foods.

During fiscal 2004, Nisshin Seifun secured record sales and income. The company's restructuring appeared to have paid off and chairman Shoda and president Hiroshi Hasegawa were confident the company would continue down a successful path. With over 100 years of experience under its belt, Nisshin Seifun was well positioned to handle future challenges.

Principal Subsidiaries

Nisshin Flour Milling Inc.; Nisshin Foods Inc.; Nisshin Petfood Inc.; Nisshin Engineering Inc.; Marubeni Nisshin Feed Company Ltd.; Oriental Yeast Company Ltd.; NBC Inc.; Nisshin Pharma Inc.

Principal Divisions

Flouring Milling; Processed Foods; Pet and Animal Food; Pharmaceuticals.

Principal Competitors

Ajinomoto Company Inc.; Nestlé S.A.; Nippon Flour Mills Company Ltd.

Further Reading

"Japanese Companies in the United States: Food and Agricultural Products," *Japan-U.S. Business Report*, July 30, 1998.

"Nisshin Flour Group to Reorganize under Holding Company," *Dow Jones International News*, April 2, 2001.

"Nisshin Flour Milling Allergen Detector for Wheat, Buckwheat and Peanuts," *Japan Food Service Journal*, July 5, 2003.

"Nisshin Flour Milling to Form Holding Company by Summer 2001," *Japan Weekly Monitor*, July 31, 2000.

"Nisshin Flour Mills Strengthens Health Food Range," *Japan Food Service Journal*, June 11, 2003.

"Nisshin Flour to Buy out Nisshin-DCA Foods," *Jiji Press English News Service*, November 9, 1994.

"Nisshin Flour to Spin Off Frozen Food Division as Subsidiary," *Nikkei English News*, May 14, 1997.

"Nisshin Kyorin Pharmaceutical to Be Started in April," *Pharma Japan*, February 5, 1996.

—update: Christina M. Stansell

Paul-Son Gaming Corporation

1700 South Industrial Road
Las Vegas, Nevada 89102
U.S.A.
Telephone: (702) 384-2425
Toll Free: (800) 728-5766
Fax: (702) 384-1965
Web site: http://www.paulsongaming.com

Public Company
Incorporated: 1993
Employees: 540
Sales: $36.2 million (2003)
Stock Exchanges: NASDAQ
Ticker Symbol: PSON
NAIC: 339932 Game, Toy, and Children's Vehicle Manufacturing

Paul-Son Gaming Corporation is a Las Vegas-based company that manufactures a wide variety of casino table game equipment. Although the company is best known for its playing cards, chips, and dice, it also makes table game layouts, gaming furniture, and table accessories such as dealing shoes, chip trays, and drop boxes. To a lesser degree Paul-Son offers scaled-down accessories and gaming furniture for the home market. The company's main manufacturing facilities are located in San Luis, Mexico, and sales offices are maintained in Reno, Nevada; Atlantic City, New Jersey; Gulfport, Mississippi; Portland, Oregon; and Ontario, Canada.

1960s Origins

Paul-Son was founded by Paul S. Endy, Jr., in 1963. He was born in Monterey Park, California in 1928 and learned the gaming business from his father. After college, Endy worked as an electrician for Bethlehem Steel, then took a job with T.R. King & Company, a gaming supply distributorship and dice manufacturing operation owned by his father and a partner. During the 1940s and 1950s, the company was the leading supplier of cards and chips to California's legal card rooms. Endy emerged as his father's top salesman, but when his father retired in 1963, Endy, who did not get along with the partner, decided not to succeed his father at T.R King. Rather, he planned on moving his family to Utah where he would work on a ranch. Traveling ahead of his wife, he stopped at Las Vegas, where by chance he noticed in a local newspaper an ad for a bankruptcy sale of a dice manufacturer. He quickly changed his plans, borrowed $40,000 from his father, and bought the dice company. Endy sent his family back to California while he launched his new business, which he called Paul-Son Dice and Card Company. ''Paul-Son'' was a reference to his standing as Paul Endy's son.

The new business struggled during the early years, with Endy living in a 16-foot trailer behind the manufacturing facility and showering with a garden hose. Years later, Endy told *Forbes,* ''If we got an order for 500 dice, we'd say, 'Wow, what a week.' '' He took on a partner, Curley Ashworth, who handled operations while Endy packed up a van with merchandise and drove to California ten days a months selling to his father's old customers and eventually stealing them away from T.R. King. In 1974, Paul-Son opened an office in Reno, Nevada, to serve the casinos in that city and received a major boost later during that decade when New Jersey legalized casino gambling in Atlantic City. Paul-Son opened an office in Atlantic City in 1978. According to *Forbes,* Paul-Son held a major advantage entering this market: ''a known record in a business where huge amounts of cash change hands and tamper-proof equipment is imperative. Says Endy: 'In this business they [casino operators] want to know who they're doing business with.' ''

Growth in the 1980s

In 1983, Endy's son, Eric P. Endy, who held a master's degree in audiology, joined the company. As the casino business grew, so did Paul-Son, which expanded beyond cards and dice to offer chips and furniture. Each new casino required layouts and tables and an initial supply of chips, playing cards, and dice, but the real volumes came in replacement sales. Cards and dice had to be replaced every few hours, felt was worn down after just two months, and even chips lasted only about five years. In 1982, much of the manufacturing was moved to San Luis, Mexico, close to the Arizona border, as a way to cut

Company Perspectives:

Paul-Son Gaming Corporation manufactures and supplies casino table game equipment such as casino chips, table layouts, playing cards, dice and gaming furniture.

costs. The elder Endy, seeing that major manufacturers, such as automakers, were setting up plants in Mexico, decided to follow suit, transferring dice, chip, and furniture making operations to the new site. Only playing cards and felt table layouts continued to be produced in Las Vegas. As a result, Paul-Son was able to lower prices and gain a competitive edge.

Aside from price, the company also produced a quality products, which were becoming increasing more sophisticated. Paul-Son was the first to embed a small piece of encoded microfilm in chips to help prevent counterfeiting. In the early 1990s, the company developed a proprietary molding system that made it possible to produce full-color graphics on a chip. While previous chips featured an inlay of the casino's logo less than an inch in diameter, the Paul-Son molded chip had an inlay that measured 1⅜ inches, almost the entire surface of the 1.54-inch chip. This allowed for more detailed graphics, which Paul-Son was able to do in-house with computers. While many of the new chips simply featured a larger version of the casino's logo, the new technology led to the idea of special-event chips, including those that commemorated the Super Bowl, championship boxing events, and even the wedding of Donald Trump to Marla Maples. The chips cost some 60 cents each to casinos, but many customers opted to keep the $5 or $25 chips as a souvenir rather than cash them in. Any chip not cashed in meant more profit to the casinos, which quickly embraced the idea of special-event chips.

In 1988, Congress passed The Indian Gaming Regulatory Act, granting Native American tribes ''the exclusive right to regulate gaming on Indian lands if the gaming activity is not specifically prohibited by federal law and is conducted within a State which does not, as a matter of criminal law and public policy, prohibit such gaming activity.'' As a result, new casinos began opening across the country on tribal lands, resulting in increased business for Paul-Son. The idea behind tribal gaming was to encourage economic development and promote tribal self-sufficiency, and soon states turned to gaming as a way to fund their own programs, establishing legalized casinos, in particular on riverboats in such places as Gulfport and Greenville, Mississippi. Although Paul-Son did some international business, selling to casinos in Monte Carlo, the Caribbean, England, and South Africa, 90 percent of its sales came from the domestic market. During the first five years of the 1990s, the number of table games at U.S. casinos grew from 6,200 to 10,000. As a result, the company's revenues grew from $7.4 million at the start of the decade to $22.8 million in 1994, and net income improved from break-even to $1.4 million.

To take advantage in the explosion in casino gaming, Paul-Son began taking steps to become a public company. In December 1993, Paul-Son Gaming Corporation was formed to house all of the Paul-Son subsidiaries, and in March 1994 the company made an initial public offering of stock, underwritten by an investment banking group headed by Rodman & Renshaw, Inc. Paul-Son sold 44 percent of the company, netting $11 million, which was earmarked to pay down debt and for expansion.

Paul-Son produced mixed results after going public. In 1994, it forged a joint venture with JP Retail Enterprises of Louisiana, its distributor in the state, and opened a retail store, ''Jacks or Bettor,'' to sell dice, chips, and playing cards as well as clothing, jewelry, and memorabilia with gaming motifs to the general public. Early in 1995, Paul-Son opened a new 45,000-square-foot manufacturing facility in San Luis to help meet the increasing demand for replacement products. The company also installed a new state-of-the-art playing card cartoning machine capable of packaging 2,000 decks of playing cards per hour, a 50 percent increase over the speed of previous equipment. The system could also wrap bridge size and blackjack size cards simultaneously and possessed optics able to detect a deck's color and automatically assemble the appropriate box. However, the company also suffered setbacks. Craps was rapidly losing popularity because it was deemed too complicated by younger gamblers, thus cutting into the sale of dice. During fiscal 1995, two riverboat operations in New Orleans and a dockside casino in Mississippi folded, leaving Paul-Son and other creditors unpaid. To prevent a future occurrence, Paul-Son adopted stricter credit policies for riverboat casinos.

Challenges in the Late 1990s and Beyond

In 1997, Paul-Son acquired a 66,400-square-foot playing card plant located adjacent to its San Luis facility, allowing the company to consolidate its playing card operations in Mexico, a move that it hoped would make its playing cards more competitive in the marketplace. Also in 1997, Paul-Son entered into a joint venture with DeBartolo Entertainment to form Brand One Marketing to market collectible and commemorative chips and playing cards, as well as to pursue marketing opportunities outside the gaming industry. Paul-Son bought out DeBartolo's share in Brand One a year later. Despite these steps, Paul-Son failed to realize its growth potential in the eyes of investors, especially in light of the consolidation that was taking place in the gaming supply industry. In October 1997, the company hired Ladenburg Thalmann & Company as a financial advisor to review strategic alternatives, including the sale of the company. *Mergers & Restructuring* quoted one analyst as saying, ''I don't know why someone would buy them.'' He added that the company should have transformed itself into a fully integrated gaming manufacturer instead of devoting so much of its resources to manufacturing dice, which was labor intensive, and playing cards, which anyone could make. Most of a casino's revenues now came from slot machines and video poker. In 1998, Paul-Son attempted to grow the business by forming a new Games Division to develop and lease new casino gaming products. The first offering was ''Paul-Son's Draw Poker,'' a five-person game played on a blackjack-size table. Players did not play against the dealer or others players. Instead, they chose among Draw Poker, Jokers Wild, and Dueces Wild and were permitted to draw up to five new cards. Hands are then compared to a pay table to determine winnings.

In October 1998, Paul Endy was on a fishing trip in Mexico when he suffered a severe stroke. He was transported to south-

Key Dates:

1963: Paul Endy founds company.
1974: The company opens an office in Reno, Nevada.
1978: Another office opens in Atlantic City, New Jersey.
1994: The company is taken public.
1999: Paul Endy dies.
2002: The company combines with Bourgogne et Grasset.

ern California to be hospitalized. Eric Endy stepped in as chief executive officer on an interim basis while his father recovered, but that post became permanent in April 1999 when his father died. The company was now majority owned by the Paul S. Endy, Jr., who carried on his father's legacy. Paul-Son continued to offer the same traditional products, although in 1999 it turned to the Internet, establishing a Web site on which its products could be purchased.

Three years after announcing it might consider selling the business, Paul-Son began posting a string of quarterly losses. Then, in January 2001, the company announced it had signed a letter of intent to combine with the French company Establissements Bourgogne et Grasset SA and its subsidiary The Bud Jones Company, Inc. Bourgogne et Grasset had been founded in 1923 and primarily served casinos in Europe and the Far East, providing plaques, jetons, chips, roulette wheels, layouts, tables, and accessories and equipment. In October 2000, it acquired Bud Jones, a Las Vegas-based company founded in 1965 that manufactured and distributed casino gaming equipment and accessories. By merging operations, the companies hoped to become the leader in the global casino table game market.

The merger fell through, however, and in April 2001 Paul-Son placed a demand on Bourgogne et Grasset for a $1 million termination fee, which was part of the letter of intent. More than a year would pass before the two sides could iron out the terms of a new deal, but in April 2002 they finally reached an agreement, which in September Paul-Son stockholders approved. Although Bourgogne et Grasset and Bud Jones became subsidiaries of Paul-Son, the transaction was really a reverse merger. Bourgogne et Grasset received a controlling interested in the company, and Bourgogne et Grasset's controlling stockholder, Francois Carrette, took over as chairman of the board while its CEO, Gerard Charlier, became Paul-Son's president and CEO. Eric Endy stayed on as executive president, but the company his father had founded 40 years earlier was now set to embark on a new chapter in its history.

Principal Subsidiaries

Establissements Bourgogne et Grasset; Paul-Son Gaming Supplies, Inc.; Paul-Son Mexicana, S.A. de C.V.

Principal Competitors

Midwest Game Supply.

Further Reading

Cohen, Judy Radler, "A Deal in Paul-Son Gaming's Cards," *Mergers & Restructuring*, October 13, 1997.
"Founder of Casino Supply Company Dies," *Las Vegas Review-Journal*, April 15, 1999.
Hawk, Joe, "Gaming-Supply Company Cashing in on . . . Chips Cards, and Dice," *Las Vegas Review-Journal*, August 9, 1993, p. 1e.
Randall, Lane, " 'Let the Big Guy Come,' " *Forbes*, December 5, 1994, p. 72.

—Ed Dinger

Penaflor S.A.

Cuyo 3066
Martinez, Buenos Aires 1640
Argentina
Telephone: (+54) (11) 4717-8000
Fax: (+54) (11) 4717-8030
Web site: http://www.penaflor.com.ar

Private Company
Incorporated: 1941 as Bodegas y Vinedos Hnos. S.A.
Employees: 1,250
Sales: 208 million pesos ($70.51 million) (2003)
NAIC: 312111 Soft Drink Manufacturing; 312112 Bottled Water Manufacturing; 312130 Wineries

Penaflor S.A., together with its sister company, Bodegas Trapiche S.A.I.C.A., is Latin America's largest wine producer and the world's fifth-largest producer of wine. Based in a high-yielding area of Argentina, the company serves one of the world's largest wine-drinking populations, and its products are increasingly found abroad as well. Penaflor is at the heart of a larger grouping of Argentine wineries that account for one-sixth of the nation's consumption. The company's wines are marketed abroad under the Trapiche label.

Bodegas Trapiche: 1883–1970

A Spaniard living in what is now Chile brought vines of the *criolla,* or mission, grape, to what is now Argentina in 1556. Soon after, Spanish monks planted the first vines in or about Mendoza, a city founded a few years later. The industry was very small-scale but gradually increased to supply Buenos Aires, which grew to be the principal area of consumption. Tiburcio Benegas, a native of Rosario, came to Mendoza in 1864 to oversee a family business. There he met and later married the daughter of Eusebio Blanco, who transmitted to Benegas his knowledge of and enthusiasm for winemaking. Benegas, considered one of the three founders of the wine industry in the Americas, bought a property with a small vineyard in Godoy Cruz—now located within or just south of the city limits of Mendoza—in 1883. The coming of the railroad in 1885 made possible a flourishing business worked by immigrant labor. Benegas's property, El Trapiche, grew to 6,653 hectares (16,433 acres).

Some 700 miles west of Buenos Aires, the province of Mendoza produces most of Argentina's wine. The sun shines an average of more than 300 days a year, the summer temperature rarely varies from year to year, and irrigation channels pure water from the melting snows of the nearby Andes Mountains to provide necessary moisture, enabling the area to produce more grapes per area than California's Napa Valley. These conditions enabled Argentina to become the third- or fourth-largest wine producer in the world.

When Tiburcio Benegas died in 1908, his business was incorporated as Benegas e Hijos S.A., with creditors converting their loans into company shares. Of his three sons, Pedro was the winemaker, having studied in Paris and become partial to the vintages of the Bordeaux region. He created wines such as Fond de Cave and Broquel in an effort to meet European standards of quality. Alberto ran the business end from Buenos Aires. Although Argentine wine was still mediocre at best in this period, vintners could count on a large clientele, since the population consisted largely of immigrants from Spain and Italy, both countries where wine was the alcoholic beverage of choice. As late as 1970, Argentines drank more wine per capita than any nationality except for Italians and French.

Trapiche introduced Monitor, a sparkling wine, in 1925, and Crillon, a white wine, in 1935. The former was a blend of chardonnay, chenin, and ugni blanc and the latter of chenin and chardonnay. Fond de Cave was a blend of cabernet sauvignon, merlot, and petit verdot, while Broquel blended cabernet sauvignon and cabernet franc. The company's other wines were Puento Viejo (syrah and ugni blanc), Feudo Viejo (sangiovese and malbec), Trapiche Viejo (malbec and merlot), and Vezely (chardonnay).

After Pedro Benegas died in 1943, his sons assumed the winemaking business. Alberto retired in 1949 and was succeeded in Buenos Aires by his brother Eduardo and later by his sons and those of Eduardo. After World War II, the company became Benegas Hermanos y Cia. S.A.I.C. and shifted toward marketing

Key Dates:

1883: Tiborio Benegas purchases the Trapiche vineyard in Mendoza province.
1914: Antonio Augusto Pulenta buys a vineyard in San Juan province.
1941: The Pulenta enterprise takes the name of Penaflor.
1971: Penaflor purchases the Trapiche properties.
1995: Grupo Penaflor's eight firms are producing mineral water and soft drinks as well as wine.
1998: Luis Alfredo Pulenta buys out all but one of his relatives.
2000: Penaflor buys two more wineries: Lavaque and Santa Ana.
2002: Pulenta sells his majority stake to DLJ Merchant Banking Partners L.P.

its better-quality wine, selling the ordinary vintages to third parties for resale in bulk wines. Direction of the company passed to Alberto's son, Federico Benegas Lynch, in 1957. In 1965, the company owned six vineyards yielding ten million liters annually and had deposit branches in seven cities. Like other Argentine vintners, it was subject to government-imposed quality safeguards: the use of all-fresh grapes and restrictions on the use of chemicals and alcoholic strength. Only after a protracted struggle with the bureaucracy were the big wineries allowed to import European and American presses and oak casks.

Quality grapes were harvested by hand and collected with great care in stone jugs weighing about 150 pounds each for use in the Fond de Cave, Broquel, and Puente Viejo labels. Trapiche also produced vinegar and had fruit orchards yielding cherries, plums, and bitter oranges. Surrounding the company's offices were 15 acres of lawn and English gardens planted with roses developed by Pedro Benegas, as well as a great variety of trees, including enormous lindens, chestnuts imported from India, gingkos, and so-called bald cypresses that turned red in fall before the needles fell.

Penaflor and Penaflor/Trapiche: 1902–98

This idyllic state of affairs came to an end in 1971, when Benegas Hermanos was sold to the Pulenta family, except for its brands of sparkling wine, which were sold to Seagram Argentina. Angelo Antonio Pulenta, a penniless Italian immigrant, arrived in Argentina in 1902 and in 1914 purchased a property with vineyards in San Juan province, where warmer temperatures resulted in heavier wines than in Mendoza, including sweet white wines, fortified wines, vermouth, and brandy. Pulenta's eldest son Quinto took over leadership of the enterprise in 1924. Incorporated as Bodegas y Vinedos Pulenta Hnos. S.A. in 1941, it was later renamed Bodegas y Vinedos Penaflor S.A. and then simply Penaflor S.A.

Penaflor, originally devoted to ordinary table wine, opened its first Mendoza vineyard, for better-quality wines, in 1951. Quinto Pulenta and his three brothers decided in 1968 to diversify and, in the following year, began producing a line of fruit juices labelled Cepita. The company began bottling its own brand of mineral water, Villa del Sur, in 1972 in association with the French group Danone. Exports of Penaflor wines began in 1970, and the company was the national leader from the first. During the early 1980s, the Argentina wine most widely sold in the United States was Andean, made by Penaflor in a joint venture with Byron Tosi, a New Yorker. Within Argentina, Penaflor created the Perle, Bordolino, and Termidor table-wine brands. The company became the largest user of Swedish-made Tetrabrik laminated cardboard-and-foil cartons to package Termidor, a cheap bulk wine.

The Pulentas thought big and built big. A Frenchman who visited their main property about this time marveled at their underground storage tank of wine, with a diameter of over 100 meters and a holding capacity of more than five million liters. Penaflor continued the Trapiche wines, although modifying their characteristics to market requirements, and it renovated the vines and modernized the installations, adding, for example, casks of French oak to age the wines and experiment with fermentation.

By the early 1980s, Trapiche, with an eye to export sales, was concentrating on developing its white wines, with new fermentation processes based on lower temperature levels to maintain the aroma and fruitiness present in the grape. Fresh, light, and transparent, these new white wines contrasted with the heavier, yellow-tinted white wines typical of local Argentine production. Trapiche's red wines were also being modified to meet the international trend toward softer flavor and coloring lighter than the traditional Argentine ruby. Broquel's cabernet sauvignon, for example, was now being blended with merlot and malbec grapes, and Puente Viejo and Trapiche were being made now with chenin and malbec. The less-regarded Vieja Abadia was now available in cardboard cartons as well as bottles. Export markets, for bulk wine and grape-juice concentrate, included Japan, the leading client, as well as 18 U.S. states. The company also had installed an operation, jointly with a Spanish company, in Puerto Rico to produce wine from imported grape concentrate, principally under the Castillo Real name. It also bottled and distributed a line of imported fruit juices under the name Richy.

To celebrate its centennial, Trapiche, in 1983, introduced a Medalla wine in red and white. These wines changed in composition each year. The company also introduced a pinot noir and a rose composed of cabernet sauvignon. In 1995, it introduced Trapiche Milenium, a blend of cabernet sauvignon and malbec.

The need to improve Argentine wine quality and raise exports became critical by 1990. Argentine wine consumption had fallen precipitously, partly because of competition from beer and soft drinks and partly because even cheap wine had become a luxury in a time of economic crisis. As Carlos Pulenta, president of Bodegas Trapiche told *New York Times* wine columnist Frank Prial, "We must export or we will die." Prial reported that Pulenta had opened an importing company in New York and had invested heavily in improving the quality of Trapiche's wines, converting thousands of acres of *criolla* and Pedro Ximenes grapes to cabernet sauvignon, chardonnay, and malbec, which Prial called "as good as and often better than cabernet sauvignon." Penaflor was selling large quantities of bulk wine to government monopolies in the Nordic countries and even in France and Spain. Japan was importing grape-juice concentrate for conversion into wine. However, to hedge its bets, Grupo Penaflor—the family holding company that included Penaflor and Trapiche—diversified further by securing, in 1992, the Cadbury Schweppes PLC license to produce the Canada Dry, Schweppes, Crush, and Gini soft drinks in Argentina, and by purchasing a brewery, Bieckert, in 1994. In 1995, Grupo Penaflor consisted of eight firms with sales of $340.3 million, and table wine was accounting for only half of this revenue.

The opening of the Argentine economy to liberalized trade and commerce in the early 1990s brought in foreign investors who spent more than $250 million over five years to open new wineries, modernize old ones, and form joint ventures with operators short of capital. They brought in new grapevines, computerized irrigation equipment, and introduced French and American oak barrels and stainless-steel (in place of concrete) vats. The growing emphasis on developing fine wines (defined in 1996 as a modest $7 or more per bottle) was aimed not only at foreign markets but to the growing number of Argentines no longer satisfied with ordinary table wine. The Pulentas hired two leading oenologists, an Australian and a Frenchman, to ensure that the right grape varieties were planted in the right areas of the company's vineyards. Even so, foreign gastronomists maintained that Argentine wines were overly oxidized and allowed to remain in oak barrels for too long.

Under New Management: 1998–2004

The Pulentas were presiding over an empire of 1,800 hectares (nearly 4,500 acres) of vineyards by 1997 when Luis Alfredo Pulenta, a United States resident with Wall Street contacts, returned to Argentina. Armed with $40 million from the investment firm of Donaldson Lufkin & Jenrette Inc. (DLJ), which took a 20 percent share of the enterprise (later raised to 33 percent by converting notes issued), he bought out all his relatives—more than 20 brothers and sisters, uncles and aunts, and cousins—for about $80 million. The only holdout was Lilia Pulenta de Munoz, who retained 7.5 percent of the shares.

Under Luis Pulenta, Penaflor invested $25 million to found a new vineyard, Finca Las Moras, on 750 hectares (about 1,750 acres) in San Juan province. In 2000, he purchased Bodegas Lavaque S.A., a smaller Mendoza-based winery that also, in 1993, had acquired Michel Torino, a winery with high-altitude vineyards farther north, in Catamarca and Salta provinces. Bodegas Lavaque was renamed Bodegas y Vinedos Andinos (BVA), and, still later, Vinas de Altura S.A. Penaflor also purchased Bodegas y Vinedos Santa Ana S.A., a winery with four production facilities in Mendoza and San Juan provinces and a significant presence abroad under its own label. This winery was added to BVA. During the 1990s, Santa Ana introduced Rincon del Sol, a "soft wine" with reduced alcoholic content by means of a process called "reverse osmosis."

DLJ was acquired by Credit Suisse Group in 2000 and became Credit Suisse First Boston, Inc. Its DLJ Merchant Banking Partners L.P. fund acquired Luis Pulenta's 60 percent stake of Penaflor and Trapiche, plus all of BVA, in 2002, shortly after the devaluation of the Argentine peso had in effect virtually tripled Grupo Penaflor's debt of $150 million to various enterprises, including a group of banks, that financed the operation. The group's 2002 revenues of 399 million pesos came to only about $135 million as devaluation ended the Argentine peso's parity with the dollar, and 2003's total of 208 million pesos for Penaflor and 83 million pesos for BVA constituted a further reduction. Nevertheless, the group produced nearly 87 million liters of wine under 33 labels in 2003, and Trapiche was exporting to 40 countries.

Penaflor was reported, in 2003, to have recently acquired, in part or whole, the labels Crespi, Facundo, Algarves, and Casa de Troya. In the field of nonalcoholic beverages, it shared with Danone ownership of the Villa del Sur, San Francisco, and Waikiki brands of mineral water and the license from Cadbury-Schweppes to produce, bottle, and distribute the Crush, Gini, and Schweppes soft-drink lines in Argentina. Penaflor was reported to be on the verge of selling the Carioca, Cepita, Cipolletti, and Montefiore brands of fruit juices to Coca-Cola de Argentina.

Principal Competitors

Bodegas Chandon S.A.; Bodega y Vinedos Edmundo J.P. Norton S.A.; Bodegas y Vinedos Lopez S.A.I.C; Grupo Catena.

Further Reading

"Bodegas Trapiche cumple 120 anos," *Nacion*, August 10, 2003.

Moyano, Julio, ed., *The Argentine Economy*, Buenos Aires: Julio Moyano Comunicaciones, pp. 493, 496, 504.

Penning-Rowsell, Edmund, "Argentina: Where Wine Flows Like Beer," *Financial Times*, April 6, 1971, p. 12.

Prial, Frank J., "Uphill Struggle to Adapt Wine to the World's Taste," *New York Times*, June 6, 1990, pp. C1, C6.

"Productividad de sector de vinos finos es de 59.722 litros por empleado en 2003," *Nacion*, May 2, 2004.

Ruiz-Velasco, Laura M., "Salud, che!," *America economia*, June 1996, p. 30.

Sanguinetti, Andres, "DLJ Merchant Banking se queda con 93% del capital de Penaflor y Trapiche." Available from www.lavaque.com.

Schumacher, Edward, "Wine Industry Flourishes in Argentina," *New York Times*, February 15, 1984, p. C8.

Villa Buzzi, Fernando, *Mendoza: Los terranos del sol*, Mendoza: Editorial Foix Freres, 1994, pp. 196–201.

——, *Vino y pasion: La familia Benegas y el vino argentino*, Buenos Aires: Editorial El Ateneo, 2002.

—Robert Halasz

Pittsburgh Steelers Sports, Inc.

3400 South Water Street
Pittsburgh, Pennsylvania 15203-2349
U.S.A.
Telephone: (412) 432-7800
Fax: (412) 432-7878
Web site: http://www.pittsburghsteelers.com

Private Company
Founded: 1933
Sales: $159 million (2004)
NAIC: 711211 Sports Teams and Clubs

Pittsburgh Steelers Sports, Inc., is the operating company for the National Football League's Pittsburgh Steelers, four-time winners of the Super Bowl. The company is privately owned by a second generation of the Rooney family. With the opening of a new football stadium, Heinz Field, the Steelers are now involved in developing the real estate that surrounds the facility. The team, founded in 1933, is only one of five NFL franchises still in existence from that period.

1930s Origins

The Steelers were founded in 1933 by Arthur Joseph Rooney, better known as Art. He was born in Coultersville, Pennsylvania, in 1901, one of nine children. Two years later his family moved to Pittsburgh's North Side, then known as Old Allegheny, where they lived over their father's saloon. Close by was Exposition Field where the Pittsburgh Pirates baseball team played its home games. Baseball was actually Rooney's first love, but he grew to love most sports, and despite his slight frame, standing just five-feet-seven, he proved to be a versatile athlete. He was a good enough boxer to win Amateur Athletic Union titles in the welter-weight and middleweight classes and to earn a berth on the U.S. Olympic boxing team in 1920, although he would not participate in the games. He was also a good enough football player that legendary coach Knute Rockne recruited him to play at Notre Dame. Rooney, however, elected to stay home in Pittsburgh to play football at Duquesne University and college baseball at Georgetown University and Indiana State Normal School of Pennsylvania. Rooney attempted to make a career out of base-ball, playing minor league ball in Wheeling, West Virginia, from 1921 to 1925, but an arm injury ended his pitching career and he was unable to entertain offers to play major league ball with the Boston Red Sox or Chicago Cubs.

Rooney now turned his attention to football. He played semi-professionally for the Canton Bulldogs, then from 1926 to 1932 organized his own Pittsburgh clubs under several names: the P.J. Rooneys, the North Side Majestics, and the Hope Harveys. He also staged boxing events and became active in horse racing. He began breeding racehorses in 1930 and became an adept handicapper. According to family lore, one day at Empire City Raceway in 1936 (or perhaps 1937) Rooney placed a $10 bet (or perhaps $500) on a long shot and went on to win over $100,000 that afternoon. The next day he took his bankroll to Saratoga Raceway where he increased his winnings to $300,000 (or perhaps $380,000). It had been another good day at the track that supposedly allowed Rooney to buy a franchise in the fledgling National Football League in 1933. For $2,500 he was awarded the NFL's fifth franchise.

Rooney named his new football team the Pittsburgh Pirates after the local baseball club. (Other early NFL teams also latched onto the names of their hometown baseball teams, such as the New York Giants, New York Yankees, and Brooklyn Dodgers.) The Pirates became a member of the Eastern Division in the ten-team league and played most of their games at the University of Pittsburgh's Forbes Field, home to the baseball Pirates. In the early days of its history, however, the team was at the end of the pecking order of area sports teams. The Univer-sity of Pittsburgh football team was a winning program, so that when scheduling conflicts occurred with baseball or college football, the football Pirates were forced to play their home games elsewhere. Given the team's lack of success, winning just 22 games in its first seven seasons, it was little wonder that Rooney's club played "home" games as far away as Louisville and New Orleans—as well as in Johnstown and Latrobe, Penn-sylvania, and Youngstown, Ohio. One of the team's star players of this period was Byron "Whizzer" White, an All-American at the University of Colorado who would lead the league in rushing in 1938. He would also go on to become a Justice of the U.S. Supreme Court for 31 years.

Company Perspectives:

In 1933, Art Rooney purchased an NFL franchise for $2,500. Over the next eight decades the Pittsburgh Steelers have become a beloved part of the city, bringing so many great moments to the league and the Steel City.

To keep his losing team afloat Rooney often had to rely on his track winnings to meet the payroll and pay the bills. At this stage, the club was little more than a hobby for Rooney, who did not seem overly troubled that the franchise lost money during its first seven years. In 1940 the Pirates became the Steelers, following a contest in which a fan submitted the name in homage to the city's predominant industry. The fan won free tickets for a year; the switch in names, however, failed to change the team's losing ways. Rooney, discouraged, sold the team to Alexis Thompson and bought a half-interest in the Philadelphia Eagles, which were owned by his friend Bert Bell. Thompson tried to relocate the Steelers to Boston, but the NFL denied permission. Rooney had second thoughts about leaving his hometown, and soon a deal was worked out that satisfied all parties. Bell had not done well in Philadelphia and agreed to swap franchises with Thompson. Bell and Rooney would co-own the Steelers until 1946 when Rooney bought out Bell, who became the NFL Commissioner.

Wartime Reorganization

The Steelers enjoyed their first winning season in 1942, winning seven and losing four, but with the United States now involved in World War II, many football players were drawn into the military, and NFL clubs were forced to adjust to thinned-out rosters. Once again the Steelers and Eagles were linked together, this time merging their teams for the 1943 season. Officially known as the Phil-Pitt Combine, the resulting team would be popularly known as the "Steagles," dividing their home games between Pittsburgh and Philadelphia. In 1944 the Steelers merged with the Chicago Cardinals. The Card-Pitt Combine suffered through a winless season and earned the unenviable name of the "Carpets." In 1945, with the war having ended, the Steelers were able to be reformed. Still, other than the 1947 season, when the team won a share of the Eastern Division title but lost in a playoff game to the Philadelphia Eagles, the Steelers continued to be a perennial loser.

The Steelers were destined to endure another 25 years of futility. It was very much a rag-tag organization, the team offices located in a downtown hotel and financial records maintained in a black notebook. For years, Rooney, who had little love for lawyers, entered only into handshake contracts with his players. During the 1950s the team managed just two winning seasons, while making a number of poor player decisions. The Steelers cut future quarterback John Unitis, traded Quarterback Len Dawson, and passed on drafting running back Jim Brown. All three would win championships and be elected to football's Hall of Fame. One highlight of this period came in 1962 when the Steelers posted its best record to date, nine wins and five losses. By virtue of finishing second in its division, the team played in what was dubbed the "Playoff Bowl," losing to Detroit 17–10. What was essentially an exhibition game between also-rans failed to captivate the interest of America's football fans and the format was soon dropped. The year 1962 was also noteworthy in the team history because it was the first season the Steelers adopted its Steelmark logo, which had been created by U.S. Steel Corporation and later turned over to the American Iron and Steel Institute (AISI) so that the design could represent the industry as a whole. While other NFL teams adopted logos during the 1950s, the Steelers simply added the players' numbers to the side of their gold helmets. It was at the suggestion of a Cleveland company, Republic Steel, that the team began to apply the Steelmark to its helmets. Unsure how well the logo would look against a gold background, the team elected to place the Steelmark on just one side. The word "Steel" inside the logo was changed to "Steelers" with the permission of AISI. When the team played in the 1962 Playoff Bowl, management, to mark the occasion, painted the Steelers helmets black, a change which served to better highlight the logo. The new combination was so well received that the team decided to make the look permanent. As a result, the Steelers became the only NFL team with its logo on just one side of the helmet.

With the advent of the American Football League in the 1960s and the heated rivalry with the NFL that ensued, football was becoming very popular. The leagues would merge, resulting in the playing of the Super Bowl and ever-escalating television contracts. Because professional football decided to evenly share television revenues, even losing clubs like the Steelers became profitable concerns. The fortunes of the Steelers on the field were also about to change. In 1969 Rooney hired a new head coach, 37-year-old Chuck Noll, a former defensive coach with the Baltimore Colts and San Diego Chargers. Although Noll would post three consecutive losing seasons, he began to put together the foundation of a team that would become a dynasty during the 1970s.

Other changes were also taking place. As part of the merger agreement between the NFL and AFL, the Steelers along with the Cleveland Browns and Baltimore Colts joined the AFL teams in the new American Football Conference in 1970. In that same year the team moved into a new home, Three Rivers Stadium, after nearly 40 years of either playing at Forbes Field or the University of Pittsburgh's Pitt Stadium. Even though Three Rivers was a multipurpose stadium shared with the Pirates, it was a dramatic improvement over the club's prior arrangements and added to the club's profitability.

Super Success in the 1970s

The Steelers made the playoffs in 1972 and the first playoff game ever held in Three Rivers would prove to be one of the most famous NFL games after played, almost entirely because of one play, the so-called Immaculate Reception. Trailing 7-6 in the final minute, quarterback Terry Bradshaw hurled a desperation, fourth-down pass that was deflected into the hands of running back Franco Harris, who ran the ball into the end zone for the winning score with five seconds left on the clock. Although the Steelers would lose the next week to the Miami Dolphins, they served notice that they were now contenders. With a defense known as the Steel Curtain and offensive stars such as Harris, Bradshaw, Lynn Swann, and John Stallworth, the team would win Super Bowls in 1975, 1976, 1979, and 1980.

Key Dates:

1933: Art Rooney acquires NFL franchise.
1940: Team changes name from Pirates to Steelers.
1962: Steelmark logo adopted.
1970: Three Rivers Stadium opens.
1975: Steelers win first Super Bowl title.
1988: Art Rooney dies.
2001: Heinz Field opens.

Well before he experienced the success of winning, Art Rooney in 1964 was inducted into the Pro Football Hall of Fame for his contributions to the game. He then began to turn over day-to-day responsibilities to his son, Daniel M. Rooney, who was in his mid-30s and had been involved with the club since childhood, attending his first training camp at the age of five and becoming a water boy when he was 14. He was only 18 when he began to negotiate player contracts. After graduating from Duquesne University with a degree in accounting in 1955 he joined his father with the Steelers and became involved in all aspects of running the business. In 1975 he was named president. Art Rooney, known affectionately as The Chief, remained involved in the running of the Steelers, as chairman, until his death. In August 1988 he suffered a stroke while walking to his office at Three Rivers and died several days later. Despite being a multimillionaire—he also owned three horse racing tracks and a breeding farm—he continued to live in a house across the street from where he was raised. He was beloved by his players and a revered figure in the city of Pittsburgh and within the football community.

The 1990s and Beyond

Although the Steelers failed to win additional Super Bowls in the final two decades of the century, they generally fielded winning teams. When the Steelers suffered through a losing season, the Rooney family, unlike many NFL owners, were patient and not quick to fire the head coach. Noll retired after the 1991 season, during which the Steelers won seven and lost nine. He was replaced by 35-year-old Bill Cowher, a former Browns and Chiefs assistant, who quickly turned around the team. In his first year, Cowher led the Steelers to their first Central Division title since 1984. Following the 1995 season, Cowher became the youngest head coach at the time to take a team to the Super Bowl. The team lost to the Dallas Cowboys, the only time the Steelers lost a Super Bowl game in franchise history. Even when the Steelers suffered back-to-back losing seasons in 1998 and 1999, and missed the playoffs in 2003, the Rooney family remained patient, electing to retain Cowher.

In the 1990s the economics of the NFL began to shift as some teams began to enjoy the benefits of new state-of-the-art stadiums, replete with an abundance of luxury suites that brought in extra income. The Steelers operated in a small market where ancillary income, such as radio rights, were modest. The Steelers, because of the league's policy of sharing television revenues and the imposition of a cap on player salaries, remained profitable, but not to the same extent as other NFL franchises. Moreover, the Steelers lacked amenities such as a modern training facility, a feature becoming very important in teams' ability to attract free agent talent. The Steelers, as well as the Pirates, began pleading for new stadiums, ones that would be devoted purely to their respective sports. The same situation prevailed on the other end of the state in Philadelphia, where the Phillies baseball team and the Eagles were making similar demands. The Steelers, immensely popular in Western Pennsylvania, talked about finding a new home outside of Pittsburgh, but still in the region, which added some pressure for the state officials to act. Similar threats also emerged from the other sports franchise in the two cities. Several years passed before the Commonwealth of Pennsylvania and the cities of Pittsburgh and Philadelphia were able to secure the necessary funding and negotiate the teams' contribution to the financing of four new stadiums in the state. In the end, the Steelers agreed to pay $76 million. Groundbreaking took place on June 18, 1999.

Before the new stadium opened, the team, in 2000, moved into a new training facility it would share with the University of Pittsburgh football program, The UPMC Sports Performance Complex. As for the new stadium, the Steelers wanted to name it after Art Rooney, but because the money received from naming rights was such an important economic factor the team tried to find a corporate sponsor that would share the name with the Steelers founder. That effort failed and the team ultimately sold the naming rights to H.J. Heinz Co. for $57 million over 20 years, an amount that was less than what the Steelers had hoped for. The 65,000-seat Heinz Field opened in August 2001. The new facility also brought with it real estate development possibilities, as the Steelers and the Pirates acquired the development rights to 25 acres of land that separated their new stadiums. Thirty years earlier there had been plans to develop the area around Three Rivers, including restaurants, stores, hotels, and office buildings, but in the end nothing significant resulted other than the paving of vast parking lots. Because the sports teams received parking revenue they were disinclined to invest in real estate projects. This time, the Pirates and Steelers were determined to maximize the value of the surrounding land. They hired Continental Real Estate Cos. to pursue a number of projects, including a new office building that would serve as the headquarters for Equitable Resources and a 5,600 seat amphitheater.

Principal Competitors

Baltimore Ravens L.P.; Cincinnati Bengals, Inc.; Cleveland Browns, LLC.

Further Reading

Bernstein, Andy, "Assessing the Deal: Steelers Couldn't Prolong Trend of Rising Rights Fees," *Pittsburgh Business Times,* June 29, 2001, p. 55.

Carroll, Bob, et. al., *Total Football.* New York: HarperCollins Publishers, 1997.

Elliott, Suzanne, "Steelers, Pirates Design Real Estate Game Plan," *Pittsburgh Business Times,* March 2, 2001, p. 1.

—Ed Dinger

Punch International N.V.

Duwijckstraat 17
Lier
B-2500
Belgium
Telephone: (+32) 3 443 19 11
Fax: (+32) 3 443 19 06
Web site: http://www.punchinternational.com

Public Company
Incorporated: 1982 as New Impriver
Sales: EUR 175.89 million ($191.24 million)(2003)
Stock Exchanges: Euronext Brussels
Ticker Symbol: PUN
NAIC: 333293 Printing Machinery and Equipment Manufacturing

Punch International N.V. is a diversified manufacturing company with historic roots in manufacturing services, specifically the manufacture of plastic and metal components and the production of component assemblies for third-parties, such as Philips and Sony. Manufacturing Services remains the Belgian company's primary activity, accounting for nearly 60 percent of its turnover. Since the early 2000s, Punch has made an effort to diversify its operations and especially to aim the company more toward the production of end products and complete systems. As such, Punch has made a number of strategic acquisitions, such as the purchases of graphics systems makers Xeikon and Strobbe Graphics in 2002 and of Advantra International in 2001 and Acunia in 2004. These acquisitions have enabled Punch to extend into two new divisions, Graphics Solutions and Wireless Applications. Graphic Solutions, based around Xeikon and Strobbe, add digital color presses for the commercial and industrial printing industry, as well as computer-to-plate machinery for pre-press systems. Under Wireless Applications, the company is preparing wireless telemetry and messaging applications through Advantra and fleet management systems through Acunia. Punch is an international business, with manufacturing capacity in Belgium, Slovakia, Mexico, Hong Kong, and mainland China, as well as sales and distribution operations in a number of markets, including Germany, France, the Netherlands, Ireland, the United Kingdom, and the United States. The company has been listed on the Euronext Brussels Stock Exchange since 1999. In 2003, Punch International posted revenues of nearly EUR 176 million ($191 million).

From Supplying Parts to Systems Solutions in the 1980s

Punch International started out as a small supplier of semifinished metal components to the local manufacturing community in Ghent, Belgium. Originally known as Impriver, the company was taken over by new management led by Freddy Gysel and Jean Braem in 1982 and renamed as New Impriver BV. Over the following years, the company began developing beyond its local market. By 1988, it became determined to relaunch itself as a components supplier for the international market. Helping to steer the company's new strategy was Guido Dumarey, who later became company CEO and chairman.

In 1988, the company began constructing a new factory for the manufacture of machined punch metals in Evergem, also in Belgium. Production at the new facility began in 1989 under the name of Punch Products NV. The name Punch quickly became adopted as the designation for the overall group, which expanded again in 1991 with the creation of a new research and development division, Punch Engineering, based in Haasrode. The new operation enabled the company to extend its presence in the growing consumer electronics field.

That market was then undergoing its own transformation. Manufacturers were increasingly turning to third-party suppliers of components and subsystems and even entire assemblies in an effort to achieve greater profitability. Punch became an early beneficiary of this trend, and by the early 1990s the company had already established a strong relationship with consumer electronics giant Philips. In 1991, the two companies strengthened their relationship when Punch agreed to establish Punch Electronique in Dreux, France, in order to produce PCB assemblies for Philips.

Soon after, Punch attracted another of the world's major consumer electronics groups. In 1993, the company founded a

Company Perspectives:

Our goal is to provide our customers with total solutions while meeting their requirements for quality, cost and service. This approach enables Punch to continuously increase the added value for all its stakeholders: including partners, shareholders, clients, suppliers, employees and society. Punch operates as a subcontractor with tailor-made services for Television, Consumer Electronics and Specialized Communication Technology industries. Punch also delivers complete systems and services to end-users in the Graphics Industry.

new subsidiary, Punch Precision in Brigdend in the United Kingdom. That facility was established in order to produce display components for Sony. The two companies deepened their relationship that same year as Punch began building a second production plant in order to produce monitors and cathode-ray tubes for Sony televisions.

Punch's work for Philips brought it into new territory in 1994. In that year, the company set up a new plant in Travna, the Slovak Republic, in order to produce metal components for Philips. Slovakia became the company's most important production site next to its base in Belgium.

By the second half of the 1990s, Punch had grown into a specialist provider of components and assemblies for the electronics industries. By 1996, the company's sales had topped the equivalent of EUR 40 million. The consumer electronics market accounted for more than half of that figure.

Diversifying for a New Century

Punch continued to respond to the needs of the electronics industry into the late 1990s. In 1998, for example, the company agreed to acquire United Electronics, based in Namestovo, Slovakia, a move that enabled the company to begin production components for a new customer, Panasonic. That year, also, Punch followed Philips into Hungary, launching a new production subsidiary, Punch Manufacturing KFT, in Székésfehervar.

As it turned toward the new century, Punch began to seek new areas of growth. The company at first stayed close to its core manufacturing services, adding injection molding capacity through its purchases of Stevens NV, an injection molding specialist, in April 1999. Soon after, the company began construction of a new plant in Evergem, combining its Punch Products and Stevens operations into a single unit. The company continued to build up its plastics operations, buying up Bruges-based Trelleborg NV in June of that year. Trelleborg was then renamed as Punch Plastics.

Fueling the company's new expansion drive was its public offering, in March 1999, and a listing on the Brussels Stock Exchange's main board as Punch International N.V. In addition to its own expansion moves, Punch also began looking for new partnerships. Among the first of these was formed in November 1999 when the company teamed up with Buro- und Datentechnik GmbH, based in Germany, to produce paper-handling products and systems. The partnership then launched construction of a new plant in Guadelajara, Mexico, in order to supply the American markets.

Before the end of that year, Punch had also added a partnership in Korea, forming the joint venture Punch Donghwa Corporation for the purchase and distribution of components in Korea and elsewhere in the Asian region. Then, in January 2000, the company reached an agreement with Philips Display Components in which Punch agreed to begin producing rimbands for Philips' North American display operations. The company opened its U.S. production plant in July of that year in Lima, Ohio.

By then, Punch had made a significant step in a new strategic direction, that of transforming itself from a components supplier to a producer of end products and systems. In January 2000, the company acquired Strobbe Graphics, which supplied computer-to-plate pre-press systems for Agfa-Gaveart. Strobbe had been founded in 1961 by Dirk Strobbe, who came from a family with a long history in the printing industry. Strobbe had concentrated on photomechanical film systems in the 1960s and became an early adopter of new digital technologies, releasing its first computer-based systems in 1975.

Punch moved Strobbe into new and larger production facilities in Ypres, Belgium, in December 2000. By then, the company had began integrating a new addition to its array of complete end products with the takeover of Dufour Automation, based in Roubaix, France, in a 50–50 joint venture with that company's management. The Dufour purchase enabled Punch to extend into the market for payment terminals and other machinery and equipment for the industrial automation market. That venture proved short-lived, however. Unable to achieve profitability, in part because of the difficulties in France's industrial and technological sectors in the early 2000s, Punch shut down its Dufour operations in 2002.

Punch found more promising prospects elsewhere. The company continued to build up its manufacturing base in Slovakia, launching development of its own 25,000-square-meter industrial campus in Namestovo at the end of 2000. In 2001, the company moved into mainland China, launching a joint-venture manufacturing operation in Jiin Hui.

Punch also took on a new products category in 2001 with the acquisition of Avantra International, which specialized in wireless two-way data communication devices. That company had previously been separately founded and operated by Guido Dumarey.

Punch celebrated the opening of its Namestovo campus at the beginning of 2002. In April of that year, the company extended its range of operations again with that acquisition of Xeikon NV. Belgium-based Xeikon had been a leading global maker of digital color production systems but had slumped into bankruptcy amid the general tech industry crash at the beginning of the 2000s. Punch's acquisition of Xeikon included the company's Belgian operations as well as its U.S. and Japanese sales and service subsidiaries. Punch immediately set out to revive Xeikon, relaunching its sales and service operations at new quarters in Lier.

Punch bought another company out of bankruptcy in May 2002, acquiring MCMS Belgium, based in Colfontaine. That

Key Dates:

1982: New Impriver is launched as a components supplier to local industry in Ghent, Belgium.
1989: The company shifts to operating in the electronics industry, beginning with opening of a new production plant, Punch Products, in Evergem, Belgium.
1999: The company goes public as Punch International.
2001: Avantra, a maker of wireless communication equipment, is acquired.
2003: Punch rolls out Xeikon direct sales and service network in Germany, France, the Netherlands, and the United Kingdom, among other countries.

company was then renamed as Punchtronics; soon after, the group's Avantra operations were moved to the Colfontaine site as well.

Punch's move into end products encouraged it to exit a number of its existing business. In 2002, the company sold off its 51 percent stake in Punch Mécanique in July 2002. In 2003, the company shut down its Bridgend plant in the United Kingdom as well. Following the transfer of Avantra to Colfontaine, Punch sold off Punchtronics to the Valorics group in 2003.

In the meantime, the company began building up its Xeikon business. The company focused specifically on boosting Xeikon's direct sales network. In 2003, Punch added new subsidiaries in France, Germany, and the United Kingdom. By the end of that year, the company had added new Xeikon subsidiaries in Italy, the Netherlands, and Finland, with the last-named subsidiary covering the entire Scandinavian market.

As it continued to shift toward end products, Punch shut down its Punch Plastic plant in Bruges in October 2003. Early in 2004, the company announced its intention of forming a joint venture with OVP that was to take over Punch's plastics manufacturing operations. Punch retained 75 percent of the joint venture, however. As the company phased out its European manufacturing operations, it also reorganized its North American manufacturing presence, shutting down the Ohio plant and transferring its production activity in the region to a new site in Mexico. In the meantime, Punch strengthened its presence in the mainland China market with the creation of a second joint venture in that market, in Shenzhen.

By the end of 2003, Punch's sales neared EUR 176 million ($191 million), and a rising share of its turnover came from its Graphics Solutions division. The company also moved to boost its small Wireless division, purchasing Acunia International NV in 2004, adding that Belgian company's wireless fleet management systems. While Manufacturing Services continued to represent nearly 60 percent of the company's sales, Punch clearly pinned its future on its manufacturing extension, particularly on its Xeikon division. In February 2004, Xeikon launched its latest digital color press, the Xeikon 5000, which was expected to become a strong seller for the company. Meanwhile, Punch continued to oversee the extension of Xeikon's global direct sales and service network, launching a new subsidiary to cover Eastern Europe in May 2004. In little more than two decades, Punch International had transformed itself from a local components supplier to an international manufacturing group.

Principal Subsidiaries

Advantra International NV; New Impriver NV; Page Plus NV; Punch Plastics NV; Punch Products NV; Punch Property International NV; Punchtronics S.P.R.L.; Strobbe Graphics NV; Xeikon International NV; Strobbe Graphics Patrimonium BVBA; Punch Electronique SA (France); Xeikon Deutschland GmBH (German); Punch Management Ltd (Ireland); Advantra Nederland BV (The Netherlands); Xeikon Japan Ltd (Japan); Punch de Mexico S. De RL de CV (Mexico); PI Products SRO (Slovakia); Punch Assemblies Namestovo (Slovakia); Punch Campus Slovakia SRO (Slovakia); Punch Products Trnava SRO (Slovakia); Punch Property Orava SRO (Slovakia); PP Property Investments Ltd (United Kingdom); Punch Precision Ltd (United Kingdom); Xeikon GB (United Kingdom); Punch Donghwa Ltd (Hong Kong); Punch Components Inc (United States); Xeikon America Inc. (United States); Jiin Hung Industry Ltd (Hong Kong); Jiin Hui Industry Ltd (China); Shenzhen Sunrise Precision Electronic Co. Ltd. (China).

Principal Competitors

Agfa-Gevaert Ltd.; Scitex Vision Ltd.; Maschinenfabrik Wifag; Oce UK Ltd.; Scangraphic PrePress Technology GmbH; A.B. Dick Co.; Helvar Merca Oy Ab; Kodak Versamark Inc.; Esko-Graphics A/S.

Further Reading

"Punch Eyes Esko Digital Arm," *Print Week*, July 10, 2003, p. 11.
"Punch Pulls Out," *Converting Today*, October 2003, p. 7.
"Punch Purchses Xeikon's Belgian, US Assets," *American Printer*, May 1, 2002.
Wallis, Lawrence, "Hoping a Saviour Will Be Found for Troubled Xeikon," *Print Week*, February 8, 2002, p. 27.
"Xeikon Gets UK Subsidiary," *Converting Today*, July-August 2003, p. 9.

—M.L. Cohen

Real Times, Inc.

2400 South Michigan Avenue
Chicago, Illinois 60616
United States
Telephone: (312) 225-2400
Fax: (312) 225-6954

Private Company
Incorporated: 2002
Employees: 110
Circulation: 175,000/week
NAIC: 511110 Newspaper Publishers; 511120 Periodical Publishers

Real Times Inc. is the owner and publisher of the *Chicago Defender*, the most respected and history-laden of all publications written for the African American population. Real Times publishes the *Defender* daily in Chicago and also operates three other regional weekly newspapers: the *Tri-City Defender* in Memphis, the *Michigan Chronicle* in Detroit, and the *New Pittsburgh Courier* in Pittsburgh. Real Times' papers have a combined circulation of approximately 175,000 every week.

Early 20th Century Origins

While Real Times was established in 2002, the company's holdings trace their histories to the beginning of the 20th century. Robert Sengstacke Abbott, the founder of the *Chicago Defender*, the newspaper that would one day be the hallmark of Real Times Inc., was born around 1870 at St. Simons Island, Georgia, to ex-slaves. Abbott's father Thomas, a grocer whose business catered to other freed slaves, died when Robert was still an infant. Shortly afterwards his mother married John Sengstacke, a minister with a formal education who provided early schooling to his stepson and then encouraged him to continue his education. Abbott would eventually attend college at the Hampton Institute, the alma mater of Booker T. Washington, a figure who inspired Abbott's later work on behalf of African Americans. While at college, Abbott sang with the renowned Hampton Quartet, and he visited Chicago for the first time in 1891 when the Quartet sang at the World's Fair Columbian Exposition.

Abbott eventually moved to Chicago. Even before he did, he had been learning the newspaper trade. In addition to learning printing at Hampton Institute, he apprenticed with the Savannah *Echo* and worked occasionally on the *Woodville Times,* a paper founded by his stepfather. Once in Chicago, he looked for work as a printer, but his applications were consistently rejected in favor of the white immigrant labor that was streaming into the city. Thinking to learn something more marketable, he attended Kent College of Law. However, rather than improving his prospects, he ran headfirst into the same prejudice: an attorney with such dark skin, he was told by another black lawyer, would *never* be able to make a go of it in Chicago. After nearly a decade of scraping by with odd printing jobs and whatever else he could find, in May 1905, Abbott decided to create his own career, and he launched the *Chicago Defender.*

Reportedly starting with only 25 cents, which he used to buy pencils and notebooks, Abbott was nonetheless able to obtain a $25 line of credit with Western Newspaper Union, a small printer of weekly newspapers. A friend got him another credit line with the *Chicago Tribune*, where engraving could be done. The first issue of the *Defender* was simply a four-page handbill, written entirely by Abbott and printed in a run of about 300. Thanks to his meager financial situation Abbott was soon forced to give up his small rented office. However, his landlady graciously allowed him to use her dining room to produce the paper, a favor he repaid later by purchasing her a large house. Abbott distributed the papers himself at first through Chicago's black community, gathering fresh news for future editions as he did so. Early editions were penned by Abbott, but gradually he found writers willing to produce articles for no charge.

Embraced almost immediately by the black community in Chicago, the paper grew rapidly. By 1910 the paper's weekly print-run was too large for Western Newspaper Union's facilities, and printing was taken over by *Daily Drover's Journal.* The *Defender*'s early success in Chicago was due in large measure to the first full-time employee hired by Abbott, managing editor J. Hockley Smiley. Smiley introduced the techniques of sensationalistic journalism upon which newspaper moguls William Randolph Hearst and Joseph Pulitzer had built empires. As important, however, was Abbott's crusading stance on is-

> **Company Perspectives:**
>
> *Real Times is dedicated to ending illiteracy, reducing crime and encouraging self-empowerment by re-establishing values in the family structure.*

sues of importance to African Americans. Abbott wrote the paper's platform, pledging to fight race segregation and prejudice in all its forms, to abolish lynching, to extend to black Americans equal economic, educational, and social opportunities, and to help enforce the right to vote.

While the political stance established the *Defender* was popular with its audience in Chicago, a novel system of distribution made the *Defender* into a paper of national scope. Chicago was a major hub of the nation's railroads, and every week bundles of the *Defender* were given to the touring black entertainers who rode the trains and the black Pullman porters who worked them. They, in turn, would leave copies at all of the towns along the train's route, particularly on the routes through the South where the largest percentage of African Americans lived at the time. When trains arrived in Chicago, the porters collected out-of-town newspapers and magazines left behind by passengers and gave them to the *Defender*, where the staff combed through them to find stories that could be used in upcoming editions.

Successes and Challenges in the 1920s–30s

By the onset of World War I, the *Defender* had established itself as the first black newspaper with a national circulation. Between 1915 and the 1920s Abbott would pursue perhaps the most famous crusade in the paper's history. ''The Great Northern Drive'' was an ongoing series of editorials and articles that urged southern blacks to leave that land of lynching and bitter segregation and move north where economic and social opportunities awaited them. The result was the onset of the so-called Great Migration, in which 1.5 million African Americans left the South and moved to northern cities such as Detroit, Pittsburgh, Cleveland, and Chicago, where they found work in factories deprived of German immigrant labor because of the war. Chicago's black population almost doubled between the years of 1916 and 1918 alone, to about 110,000.

Each issue of the paper was eagerly awaited in the South. Outside Chicago, the *Defender* had its biggest readership in Deep South states such as Georgia, Alabama, Mississippi, Kentucky, and Tennessee. By 1920, it boasted a weekly circulation of nearly 230,000 copies, although the company estimated that each paper sold was eventually passed on to another four readers. The paper was circulated and discussed, and even read aloud in churches. With its crusade for civil rights and its advocacy of the North, the *Defender* soon came to be viewed as a threat among white southerners. Reading or selling the paper in the South was even sometimes a dangerous act of rebellion, punishable by arrest or even lynching. *Defender* readers bought the paper for more than politics and civil rights news. It offered a health column, a full page of comics, regular news and gossip about entertainers and other public figures, and sensational tabloid crime and sex stories.

The Chicago race riot of 1919 was a turning point for the *Defender*. The paper was almost forced to shut down temporarily when white workers, for fear of reprisals, refused to print it. The edition came out, thanks to printing presses in nearby Gary, Indiana, but the incident showed Abbott how vulnerable the *Defender* was to the whims of white businesses. So the Robert S. Abbott Publishing Company, which had been established in 1918, purchased a large building on Chicago's South Side and installed its own printing plant. By ceasing to subcontract the work, the *Defender* cut its weekly costs by $1,000. Abbott's work force was comprised of both black and white laborers, and the company permitted the Chicago Typographical Union to unionize the facility. Thus, the *Defender* was the first black newspaper with an integrated work force and the first to unionize.

With circulation surpassing the 200,000 mark the *Defender* was an unquestioned success, and Abbott was a millionaire. The *Defender* relied on circulation rather than advertising for the bulk of its revenues. Copies sold for ten cents apiece in the 1920s, from which the paper garnered one cent in profit.

In 1929 Abbott launched a new publication, *Abbott's Monthly*. The magazine presented a broad range of feature articles and eventually photographs more than 15 years before Johnson Publishing introduced *Ebony* in 1945. Unfortunately, despite press runs of 100,000 and regular tinkering with the format, the magazine never caught on with the public. It folded in 1934.

The onset of the Great Depression also threatened the *Defender* itself with insolvency. With hundreds of thousands suddenly unemployed, virtually all spending on nonessential goods—like newspapers and magazines—stopped. The *Defender*'s ten-cent cover price, more than twice that of its competitors, made the paper particularly unaffordable, and circulation fell dramatically. Nonetheless, the *Defender*, together with two new Abbott newspapers, the *Michigan Chronicle* and the *Louisville (Kentucky) Defender*, survived the hard times. A third contributor to the *Defender*'s woes in the 1930s was Robert Abbott's declining health. At the end of the decade, on February 29, 1940, he died.

New Leadership in the 1940s

Before his death Abbott had chosen a successor, his 28-year-old nephew John H.H. Sengstacke. Sengstacke's life mirrored his uncle's in many respects. He too had worked for the family newspaper in Woodville, Georgia; he too had attended Hampton Institute; and he too had moved to Chicago after he graduated, going to work for the *Defender* and learning the operation one job at a time. At the same time he continued his education, taking classes at both Northwestern University and The Ohio State University. By the mid-1930s, Sengstacke was the *Defender*'s general manager as well as Abbott's personal assistant.

As the country was plunging into World War II Sengstacke took over Robert S. Abbott Publishing. One of his first major achievements was the establishment—in the face of suspicion and doubt from other black publications—of a trade association of the black press, the National Negro Publishers Association (NNPA). After America's entry into the war, the company supported the ''Double V'' campaign (initiated by the *De-*

Key Dates:

1905: Robert Sengstacke Abbot publishes the first issue of the *Chicago Defender.*
1918: Robert S. Abbott Publishing Company established.
1920: *Defender* puts its own printing facility into operation.
1940: Robert S. Abbott dies, and John Sengstacke takes over the reins of the company.
1940: Sengstacke forms the National Negro Publishers Association.
1952: The *Defender* purchases the *New York Age.*
1956: Daily edition of the *Chicago Defender* is introduced.
1975: John Sengstacke puts *Defender* papers in trust for his grandchildren.
1997: John Sengstacke dies at 84.
2002: Real Times, a group headed by John Sengstacke's nephew, acquires Sengstacke Enterprises, including the *Defender* newspaper.

fender's main rival, the *Pittsburgh Courier),* which advocated victory over fascism overseas and victory over discrimination at home. The *Defender*'s advertising revenues and circulation increased once again during the war, the latter reaching 100,000 throughout the nation by 1945. Two years later, although national circulation had climbed still further to 193,000, competition in the field had escalated, and the *Defender* was only the third largest African American newspaper in the country. The *Pittsburgh Courier* was the most-read with circulation of 277,000, followed by the *Afro-American* with 235,000.

By the late 1940s, a lengthy court battle with Abbott's widow over control of the *Defender* had been resolved in Sengstacke's favor. He set to work expanding the publishing empire. In addition to introducing new features and sections to the *Defender,* Sengstacke established new papers throughout the Midwest, including the *Columbus News, St. Louis News, Toledo Press,* and the *Cincinnati News.* In 1951 he launched the weekly *Tri-City Defender* in Memphis. The following year, the company acquired the venerable *New York Age.* During this time, home delivery of the *Defender* in Chicago was offered for the first time.

Sengstacke's boldest move came on February 6, 1956, when he relaunched the paper as the *Chicago Daily Defender.* From that point on the paper was published Monday through Thursday, along with a weekend edition that came out on Saturday. As circulation and revenues jumped, and new headquarters were established in downtown Chicago, the paper took on a greater scope with more in-depth reporting.

Industry Consolidation in the 1960s

The year 1965 saw the merger of the two giants of black journalism when Sengstacke purchased the *Defender*'s long-standing rival, the *Pittsburgh Courier.* The *Courier* had grown largely through the efforts of Robert Lee Vann, an attorney practicing in Pittsburgh. In 1909 Vann was engaged by a group from the local Methodist church to draw up incorporation papers for a small newspaper it had been publishing for a couple of years. The *Courier* was largely the vehicle for the writings of one of the churchmen, Edwin Nathaniel Harleston. Vann helped the venture incorporate, and it was agreed that he would be paid in *Courier* stock. Before long he was not only the paper's editor and publisher, but its sole owner as well.

The *Courier* was the only paper serving Pittsburgh's black population of 25,000, and it gained popularity over the years for many of the same reasons as had the *Defender.* Like Abbott, Vann tried his hand at other publications in the 1920s, including *The Competitor,* a magazine that was apparently remarkably similar to *Abbott's Monthly* in concept and also folded after only a few months. While the *Courier*'s revenues and circulation soared during the 1920s, the company plunged deep into debt just as the Great Depression was starting and flirted with bankruptcy but managed to survive and even thrive by the late 1930s. By 1938 circulation had passed 250,000 and *Courier* stockholders received a dividend for the first time since the early 1930s.

In October 1940, just nine months after the death of Robert Abbott, Robert Vann died. The paper continued to flourish under P.L. Prattis, a former *Chicago Defender* editor. During World War II the paper helped maintain readership with its Double V campaign, and by war's end, with circulation at an all-time high of 357,212 the *Courier* had become the most influential, widely read black newspaper in the United States. As it had for many of its rivals, however, the 1950s brought declining sales for the *Courier.* And by 1965, in the face of apparently irreversible losses, Chairman S. B Fuller advised the sale of the paper to the *Defender.* Under the new management, the paper was renamed *The New Pittsburgh Courier* and was completely revamped.

As the 1960s ended, the crusading days of the black press seemed to come to a close. The goals Robert Abbott had set in the *Defender*'s 1910 platform had largely been achieved through the civil rights movement. Moreover, the white press began hiring *Defender* and *Chronicle* journalists, in a halting and extremely fragmented attempt to cover black issues. Furthermore, television was largely replacing newspapers as the main source of daily news for most people. The *Defender* was hit especially hard. By 1966 its circulation had dropped to about 50,000 copies daily. Another Sengstacke paper, the *Michigan Chronicle,* was able to sell that many copies of its weekly in a much smaller Detroit market. Circulation would continue to drop through the 1970s.

Declining Fortunes in the 1980s–90s

By the beginning of the 1980s Sengstacke Enterprises, a holding company that had taken over ownership of Robert S. Abbott Publishing, had ten newspapers in Illinois, Michigan, Pennsylvania, Ohio, Tennessee, Georgia, and Florida and had annual revenues of $7 million. In 1980 it was 73rd on *Black Enterprise*'s list of the 100 largest African American businesses in the United States, but it was the last time the company would appear in the rankings. Two years later the *Daily Defender* had a circulation of a meager 18,000. By contrast the *Courier* in Pittsburgh was selling almost twice at many copies of its weekly, while the *Michigan Chronicle,* though smaller than other Sengstacke papers, was the most consistently profitable, probably because of its tight focus on local issues of interest to Detroiters.

By 1990 Sengstacke's newspaper holdings had shrunk by more half. The only papers he still owned were the *Chicago Defender*, the *Michigan Chronicle*, the *Tri-State Defender*, and the *New Pittsburgh Courier*. The flagship paper, the *Defender*, had fallen on particularly hard times. Its daily distribution in Chicago, a city of approximately 1.3 million African Americans, was estimated at 26,000—although no accurate figures had been collected in more than 25 years. Apparently, the once-great paper had failed to change with the times. First, changing demographics hit the paper hard. The *Defender* readership had moved from Chicago's Southside, the area of greatest distribution. Furthermore, the *Defender* and other papers had been supplanted by radio stations and dozens of black alternative weekly newspapers, many of which were distributed free of charge. Finally, after 50 years at the helm, John Sengstacke was resistant to change. One symbol of this resistance was the company's old headquarters on South Indiana in Chicago. Established by Robert Abbott in the 1920s, it was on the National Register of Historic Places, but had fallen into such a state of extreme disrepair that in the early 1990s it looked as if it would have to be demolished.

On May 29, 1997, change was forced on the *Chicago Defender*. After a long illness John H.H. Sengstacke died at age 84. Unlike his predecessor Robert S. Abbott, he had refused steadfastly to name a successor. As a result, upon his death his publishing companies were plunged into a half decade of chaos. The one thing Sengstacke definitely intended was that the *Defender* and its affiliated papers remain in the hands of his family. Before his death, he extracted a promise from his eldest grandchild, Myiti Sengstacke, that she would not allow the company to be sold. Some 23 years earlier, however, in 1975 he had arranged for most of his holdings to be put in trust with instructions that the trustee, Northern Trust Co., do whatever was necessary to provide for the future financial security of his grandchildren. Further complicating matters, Sengstacke also left a $4 million tax bill and no cash reserves with which to paid it.

Reorganization and the Birth of Real Times

In January 1998, the Northern Trust Co. announced that it was putting Sengstacke Enterprises, the owner of the *Defender* and its sister papers, up for sale. Most analysts believed that, even though the Sengstacke newspapers were performing poorly, they had great potential as money makers and might sell for up to $10 million. Chicagoans, however, reacted angrily at the thought that as sacred an institution as the *Defender* could fall into the hands of non-African American owners who might abandon it as an advocate of minorities and the poor. Efforts were put in motion to organize an African American group to purchase the company, which ultimately came to naught.

Board members of Sengstacke Enterprises, including Sengstacke's son, voted to approve the sale. However, Sengstacke's granddaughter Myiti, who had promised her grandfather not to let the company be sold, took advantage of a clause in the trust agreement to block it. She and two of her brothers began a search for a new trustee and an acceptable buyer. By December 1998 two contenders had emerged. PublicMediaWorks, an African-American investment group, offered $12.5 million in cash. Myiti Sengstacke, however, favored a $10 million recapitalization plan offered by Detroit businessman Don Barden that would give him a majority share in the firm, while placing the remaining holdings in the hands of the Sengstacke grandchildren, and pay off the tax debt.

Events moved at a snail's pace. In May 1999 the impasse seemed about to resolve itself when a Cook County Circuit Court authorized the new trustee that had in the meantime been found to accept Barden's offer. However, for reasons that were never made public, in the end Barden did not purchase the firm. A year later in summer 2000 another Circuit Court judge approved new $11 bid by PublicMediaWorks. That firm was unable to secure financing to close the purchase, however, and Sengstacke Enterprises remained on the market. Finally, in June 2002, a group headed by John Sengstacke's nephew, Thomas Sengstacke Picou, reached a deal to by the *Defender* for about $10 million—$3 million up front, another $3 million with interest over five years, and a final payment of $2.5. The new owner was to be called Real Times Inc.; it was a company founded specifically to purchase the newspapers. In the deal the new company acquired all of Sengstacke Enterprises' newspaper holdings which, included the *Defender*, the *Michigan Chronicle*, the *New Pittsburgh Courier*, and Memphis' *Tri-State Defender*.

Picou, who headed Real Times and became the publisher of the *Defender*, had a long history with his uncle, working as a reporter, editor, advertising manager, and eventually from 1981 to 1984, as president of the *Defender*. He had left the paper only when he disagreed with Sengstacke about how the paper should be managed. After the Real Times takeover, Sam Logan, one of the partners in Real Times Inc. returned to edit the *Michigan Chronicle*. He had left the paper after his own disagreements with Sengstacke and formed another weekly in Michigan, *Front Page*. The Real Times 2 LLC subsidiary was formed to purchase the new paper from Logan.

Real Times planned significant changes for the *Defender*. Sengstacke hoped to incorporate the best features of alternative weekly papers, which were one of the fastest growing segments of the newspaper market. In July 2004 media consultant Roland Martin was brought in to streamline and modernize the papers' operations and to get finances on solid footing. At the time, the paper had no full-time editor-in-chief and it was speculated that Martin would be offered the position after his 90-day contract expired. At the end of summer 2004, Real Times and the *Defender* prepared to give up the building that had been its headquarters since the 1950s. The company was looking at properties around downtown Chicago.

Principal Subsidiaries

Real Times 2 LLC; Sengstacke Enterprises.

Principal Competitors

Johnson Publications; Chicago Sun-Times; Detroit Free Press; New York Amsterdam News; Afro-American Newspapers.

Further Reading

Bey, Lee, "Defender Earned a Place in History," *Chicago Sun-Times*, November 15, 1997, p. 18.

Borden, Jeff, "Bidders Duel For Defender," *Crain's Chicago Business*, December 7, 1998, p. 1.

——, ''Defender Heirs Win Paper Chase,'' *Crain's Chicago Business,* May 24, 1999, p. 3.

——, ''Tax Deadline Looms For Defender Publisher,'' *Crain's Chicago Business,* December 21, 1998, p. 6.

——, ''Time Passing by Veteran Defender,'' *Crain's Chicago Business,* November 26, 1990, p. 3.

''Chicago Defender, Black-Owned Newspaper, Is Finally Sold,'' *Jet,* February 10, 2003, p. 32.

''Chicago Defender Stays in Family,'' *Editor & Publisher Magazine,* August 30, 1997, p. 35.

Christian, Nichole M., ''Heirs Try to Keep A Black Press Heritage Alive,'' *New York Times,* March 9, 1998, p. D1.

Doby, Hersh, ''End of the Road?,'' *Black Enterprise,* April 2000, p. 24.

Doreski, C.K., ''Kin in Some Way: The *Chicago Defender* Reads the Japanese Internment, 1942–1945,'' in *The Black Press: New Literary and Historical Essays*, edited by Todd Vogel, New Brunswick, N.J.: Rutgers, 2001, pp. 161–187.

Fitzgerald, Mark, ''Faded Black Daily Sees a Future in New 'Defender','' *Editor & Publisher,* January 27, 2003, p. 6.

——, ''New Aegis for the 'Defender','' *Editor and Publisher,* May 6, 2002, p. 4.

——, ''Protesters Invade Office of Famed Chicago Paper,'' *Editor & Publisher,* December 16, 2002, p. 8.

Golson, Jennifer, ''Carrying the Torch,'' *Black Enterprise,* April 1999, p. 19.

Harsch, Jonathan, ''America's Leading Black-Owned Newspaper Enters its 75th Year,'' *Christian Science Monitor,* May 14, 1980, p. 3.

Herman, Eric, ''Period of Change Continues at Chicago Defender,'' *Chicago Sun-Times,* July 29, 2004, p. 63.

Hughes, Alan, ''Sengstacke,'' *Black Enterprise,* April 2003, p. 30.

Jeter, Jon, ''Black Readership Fears for Future of Chicago Defender,'' *Washington Post,* January 18, 1998, p. A3.

Lallande, Ann,''Defending a Chicago Legacy,'' *Presstime,* September 2002, p. 8.

Lydersen, Kari, ''Purchase Keeps Newspaper in the Family,'' *Washington Post,* June 24, 2002, p. A3

Moore, Aaron, ''The Pro Bono Plagiarist,'' *Columbia Journalism Review,* July 1, 2003, p. 10.

Parker, Suzi, ''African-American Newspapers Fall on Tough Times,'' *Christian Science Monitor,* February 15, 2000, p. 2.

Staples, Brent, ''Citizen Sengstacke,'' *New York Times,* January 4, 1998, Sec. 6, p. 27.

Strahler, Steven R., ''Defender Saga Turns Yet Again,'' *Crain's Chicago Business,* April 30, 2001, p. 54.

Steinberg, Neil, ''Publisher Sengstacke Dies,'' *Chicago Sun-Times,* May 29, 1997, p. 3.

Walker, Juliet E.K., ''The Promised Land: The Chicago *Defender* and the Black Press in Illinois, 1862–1970,'' in *The Black Press in the Middle West, 1865–1985*, edited by Henry Lewis Suggs, Westport, Conn.: Greenwood Press, 1996, pp. 9–50.

—Gerald E. Brennan

Réseau Ferré de France

92 Ave. de France
Paris F-75648 Cedex 13
France
Telephone: +33 1 53 94 30 00
Fax: 33 1 53 94 38 00
Web site: http://www.rff.fr

Government-Owned Company
Incorporated: 1997
Employees: 521
Sales: $2.69 billion (2002)
NAIC: 482111 Line-Haul Railroads; 561110 Office Administrative Services

Réseau Ferré de France (RFF) owns France's railroad infrastructure. The government-owned company is responsible for building, upgrading, and maintaining the company's rail lines and related infrastructure, including stations, bridges, and viaducts, as well as planning and engineering new rail extensions. RFF is also responsible for managing the traffic on the country's rail system—charging fees to historic operator Société Nationale des Chemins de Fer Français (SNCF) for its use of the network. Since March 2004, the country's rail network has been opened to use by third-party and foreign rail freight operators, and RFF has become responsible for coordinating that traffic as well. RFF was formed in 1997 when the French government split the SNCF into its train operations and infrastructure management segments—then transferred most of SNCF's huge debt to RFF. As such, RFF is also responsible for paying down the massive debt accrued in constructing France's world-leading high-speed train system. At the end of 2004, that debt was expected to near EUR 27 billion. The SNCF remains RFF's main customer, contributing nearly all of the company's EUR 2.6 billion in annual revenues. Because the RFF contracts with the SNCF for its railroad building and maintenance operations, most of the company's revenues are ultimately returned to the SNCF. Altogether, RFF oversees more than 29,000 kilometers of railroad, including more than 14,000 kilometers of electrified rail, and more than 1,500 high-speed train lines. The company also oversees more than 1,300 tunnels, nearly 30,000 rail bridges, more than 7,000 kilometers of fiber-optic cable, and nearly 31,000 kilometers of subterranean cable. RFF continues an active program for developing the country's rail system. In 2001, the company completed the highly touted high-speed line, directly connecting Paris and Marseilles for the first time. In summer 2007, the company expects to have completed the new Paris-Strasbourg line; development also has begun on high-speed lines serving the southern Atlantic coast and connecting the Brittany and Loire regions.

Laying the Foundations of France's Rail System in the 1800s

Railway development in France was marked from the start by a high degree of government involvement. The country's relatively low level of industrialization in the early 19th century, in comparison with England, the United States, or Germany, left little possibility of private investment in the construction of railroads. At the same time, the country's economy remained highly focused on Paris, a factor that further discouraged the construction of provincial rail lines. Meanwhile, the country's powerful shipping interests, both along its coasts as well as along an intricate inland canal and waterway network, helped stall railroad construction in order to head off competition from the younger form of transportation. Popular sentiment, particularly in the rural provinces, also viewed the arrival of railroads with suspicion.

The first French railroad was constructed in order to transport coal between Saint Etienne and Andrézieux in 1827. That railroad still required the use of animals to pull its wagons. The country's first steam locomotives began operating on the Saint Etienne-Lyons line, for which construction was completed in 1830. Yet, a lack of consensus among the French parliament led to the government refusing permission to allow construction of any major railroads into the 1840s.

The passage of legislation in 1842 gave new hope to France's railroad system. Under that legislation, the government became responsible for awarding concessions to the private sector for building and operating the country's railroad system. Planning for the system was placed under the guidance of the department of Ponts et Chaussés, which had overseen the development of the

Company Perspectives:

As manager, project leader and owner of the national rail network, RFF has been given five main missions: Manage and maintain the network; Dispatch the capacities; Upgrade and develop the network; Managing railway property; Managing the debt.

country's highly regarded road, bridge, and canal network. An important feature of the new railroad concessions was that the government essentially leased the operation of the lines, rather than allow outright private ownership of the rail system. In exchange, the French government took responsibility for funding most of the rail system's infrastructure requirements, building the bridges, tunnels, track beds, and embankments.

The relative political stability under Napoleon III paved the way for the first major extension of France's railroad system. By 1870, the country had completed more than 17,000 kilometers of rail lines, connecting most of the country's larger cities to Paris. The railroad sector also had consolidated. If originally the country's railroads were built and operated by a large number of small companies, by the 1870s these had become grouped into six large regional companies—Chemin de Fer de l'Est; Chemin de Fer du Nord; Chemin de Fer Paris-Lyons-Mediteranée; Chemin de Fer Paris-Orleans; Chemin de Fer Ouest; and Chemin de Fer du Midi.

These companies, however, jealously guarded their territory, leading to a somewhat absurd situation: if all of the country's major cities were connected to Paris, none were connected to each other. The six regional operators refused to allow their railroad networks to be connected to the others. The situation had a number of side effects, such as reinforcing Paris's position as the country's single political and economic focal point. The lack of coordination of its rail system also became a major military problem during the Franco-Prussian War in 1870.

Nationalized Rail System in the 1930s

The passage of the Plan Freycinet, developed by then minister of public works Charles Freycinet in 1879, sparked the next development phase in the country's national railway system. The Freycinet plan called for the construction of some 9,000 kilometers of new railroad, in part in order to connect and coordinate the country's grid.

The effort met with success. By the outbreak of World War I, France had one of the world's densest railroad grids, with more than 60,000 kilometers of line in operation. The cost of building the railroad, coupled with periods of economic hardship, had caused a number of railroads to begin operating at a loss during this period. The French government bailed out the failed lines, taking over their operation, and became more and more responsible for managing the coordination of the railroad sector.

World War I came as a new blow to the country's private railroad sector, especially in those regions torn by battle during the war. Rebuilding the infrastructure and otherwise recovering from the loss of business during the war became too much for the private sector to bear, and by 1920, all of the country's railroad companies were operating at a loss.

The rise of automobile traffic during this period and the growing popularity of delivering freight by truck added to the sector's troubles. Approximately one-third of the country's railroads were narrow-gauge lines, which proved unable to compete with the more flexible and less expensive automobiles. The economic collapse in the Depression Era coupled with the rising competition from automotive track forced the closure of most of the narrow-gauge lines during the 1930s.

At the same time, the sector's difficulties led to the decision to nationalize the railroad system during the 1930s—a process made easier by the earlier policy of granting lease-based concessions, rather than outright ownership of the railroad system. In 1937, the government established the legislation for the creation of a new government-owned railroad body. The new organization, Société Nationale des Chemins de Fer Français (SNCF), came into being at the beginning of 1938.

Under the SNCF, the country's railroad network was brought together into a single system. Yet soon after its creation, the SNCF found itself under control of the collaborationist French government and placed into service supporting the Nazi and German occupational policies.

Following the war, the SNCF became responsible for rebuilding the country's railroad network, which had experienced heavy damage during Allied bombing raids. In the 1950s, the SNCF began redeveloping its network, eliminating nearly all of the remaining narrow-gauge lines as well as a number of minor lines. By the end of that decade the country's system had been reduced to just 40,000 kilometers. Yet at the same time the SNCF had implemented a program of technical upgrades, such as the introduction of electricity-driven locomotives, enabling its trains to roll faster than ever before.

By 1955, the SNCF had succeeded in establishing a world railroad speed record at 331 kilometers per hour. This victory, and the resulting prestige, encouraged the SNCF to begin developing a true high-speed train network. Another factor in this development was the conversion of the SNCF's status in 1971, in legislation that required the group to become responsible for generating the funds for its own budget needs. With the freight market all but taken over by the trucking industry, SNCF turned its attention toward developing its passenger business.

Work on the high-speed train—called the TGV, for "train de grand vitesse"—began in earnest in the early 1970s. The high cost of fuel brought on by the Arab Oil Embargo led to the adoption of electricity—backed by the country's nuclear energy program—as the power source for the new locomotives. The SNCF began construction of the Paris-Lyons line in 1974, adapting the exiting rail to the new TGV standards. That line was inaugurated in 1981 and enabled the SNCF to set a new world train speed record, at 380 kilometers per hour.

Dedicated Infrastructure Company for the 2000s

The SNCF extended the TGV network during the 1980s and into the 1990s. The next phase, the TGV Atlantique, began operations in 1989, with full completion in 1990. In 1993, the

Key Dates:

1842: Legislation codifying construction of the French national rail system by the private sector is passed.
1938: The French railroad system is nationalized under the newly created SNCF.
1955: SNCF sets a train speed record, encouraging the development of a high-speed train line.
1974: Construction begins on the first leg of a high-speed train (TGV) line between Paris and Lyons.
1981: The first TGV line is inaugurated.
1991: The European parliament drafts a directive for the separation of the railroad infrastructure from railroad operation in Europe.
1997: Réseau Ferré de France, which takes over ownership of France's railroad network, as well as most of the SNCF's debt, is created.
2001: The new TGV line linking Paris and Marseilles is opened.
2004: RFF opens the French rail network to competition.

SNCF completed the TGV Nord-Europe, then joined in its extension to complete the Eurostar line, connecting France to England beneath the English Channel, in 1994. Another brand of the TGV network was added in 1996, when the Thalys line connected Paris and Brussels.

By then, however, the SNCF had come under pressure from the European Parliament, which had passed a ruling in 1991 stating that, in order to stimulate competition among the Union's railroad systems and operators, countries were required to separate ownership of their railroad networks from their operation. The French government had dragged its heels on implementing the directive into the mid-1990s.

Yet the SNCF also had racked up a huge debt, as ridership levels were nowhere near enough to compensate for the some EUR 45 billion (US $50 billion) spent on developing the country's TGV network. By the middle of the 1990s, with just half of the proposed network completed, the SNCF faced long-term debt levels of nearly EUR 21 billion and total debt of nearly EUR 29 billion.

In order to improve the SNCF's books, therefore, in 1997 the French government decided to split the organization in two, creating a new government-controlled company, Réseau Ferré de France, or RFF. That company took over ownership of the country's railroad network, as well as most of the SNCF's debt. As owner of the rail network, the RFF was responsible for managing its traffic—receiving toll payments from the SNCF, which retained for the time being its monopoly of the network. RFF was also responsible for developing, upgrading, and maintaining the network, work that was subcontracted to the SNCF.

Another of RFF's responsibilities was to pay down its huge debt, while continuing to finance the construction of the high-speed network. If the latter progressed smoothly—culminating in 2001 with the opening of the highly anticipated Paris-Marseilles line and the setting of new speed records—the former proved far more difficult. By 2001, RFF's long-term debt levels had actually increased, to nearly EUR 23 billion. By 2003, the company still faced down close to EUR 27 billion in debt.

The improbability of ever seeing RFF balance its books led to calls for the French government to forgive the company's debt—which could be considered as the cost of constructing one of the world's most respected high-speed train networks. In the meantime, RFF continued pursuing the network's extension, with the next phase, the TGV Est, already under construction—the company expected to have completed the new Paris-Strasbourg line by 2007. RFF also entered the planning and development phases for the high-speed lines serving the southern Atlantic coast and connecting the Brittany and Loire regions.

RFF meanwhile added a new facet to its range of operations in March 2004, when the French rail system was officially opened for competition. RFF now became responsible for coordinating the entry of foreign and private rail operators onto the French network. RFF promised to continued France's history as a technological leader in the world's railroad industry.

Further Reading

''French National Railways (SNCF),'' *Railway Age,* August 1996, p. 68.

Godault, Thierry, ''Les 4 scléroses de la SNCF,'' *L'Expansion,* March 2003.

Jacquin, Jean-Baptiste, ''Claude Martinaud, dialecticien des Ponts,'' *L'Expansion,* March 6, 1997.

Slessor, Catherine, ''French Lessons: Backed by Political Will and Financial Muscle, France's High-Speed Rail System with Its Sleek New Stations and Infrastructure, Is Reshaping the Country's Geography,'' *Architectural Review,* April 2003.

''TGV Sud-Europe-Atlantique: Réseau Ferré de France veut coller au terrain,'' *Charente Libre,* November 11, 2001.

''Tres Grand Void; French Railways,'' *Economist (U.S.),* June 2, 2001, p. 6.

—M.L. Cohen

RestaurantAssociates

Restaurant Associates Corporation

36 W. 44th Street, Fifth Floor
New York, New York 10036
U.S.A.
Telephone: (212) 789-7911
Fax: (212) 302-8032
Web site: http://www.restaurantassociates.com

Wholly Owned Subsidiary of Compass Group USA Inc.
Founded: 1919
Employees: 10,000 (est.)
Sales: $250 million (2003)
NAIC: 722110 Full-Service Restaurants

Based in New York City, Restaurant Associates Corporation (RA) is a subsidiary of Compass Group USA, a unit of the United Kingdom's Compass Group plc, the world's largest foodservice company. Acclaimed for developing the concept of theme restaurants and other accomplishments in the 1950s and 1960s, RA operates a dozen restaurants in Manhattan, including Brasserie, Rock Center Café, and Tropica. It also operates restaurants and concessions at major museums and performing arts centers, such as the Metropolitan Opera House, Avery Fisher Hall, the American Museum of Natural History, The Guggenheim Museum, and the Metropolitan Museum of Art. Outside of New York, RA handles dining at Boston's Museum of Fine Arts; the National Gallery of Art; the National Museum of American History; Smithsonian National Museum of Natural History; John F. Kennedy Center for the Performing Arts in Washington, D.C.; the Philadelphia Museum of Art; The Music Center of Los Angeles County; and San Francisco's War Memorial Performing Arts Center. RA has been the longtime provider of foodservice at the U.S. Open Tennis Championships in New York, and also handles foodservice for the PGA Championship and Ryder Cup. In addition it controls the franchise rights for Krispy Kreme in the New York area and the franchise rights for Au Bon Pain across North America.

Growing Out of a 1950s Coffee Shop Chain

The two men most responsible for the growth of RA were Jerome Brody and Joseph H. Baum. Brody was born in Manhattan in 1922, the son of a well-to-do family. While attending Dartmouth College, shortly before joining the Army Air Force during World War II, he married Grace Wechsler, the daughter of coffee importer Abraham F. Wechsler. After his stint in the military Brody attended Columbia Law School, but his education was interrupted by his father-in-law, who insisted he join him in his coffee business, which was struggling after three top executives died in succession. Wechsler, who had no background in restaurants, had picked up the Riker's chain of underperforming coffee shops as payment for a debt and put Brody in charge. The company was called Riker's Restaurant Associates, founded in 1919, the name of which would later be shortened to Restaurant Associates. Not having much money to work with, Brody took incremental steps in turning around the Riker's chain. To bring in much needed revenue he bid on concessions to run. His first contract was with the Mitchell Air Force Base on Long Island, followed by the employees' cafeteria at the Ohrbach's department store in Manhattan. Next, he won the food concession at Newark Airport, a turning point for RA, which now moved into the fine dining market. To launch the airport restaurant, which would become known as the Newarker, Brody recruited Joseph Baum, who had a strong background in hotels.

Baum was born in 1920 in Saratoga Springs, New York, where his parents operated a seasonal hotel. After graduating from high school he worked two years in New Jersey and Florida hotels as a busboy, waiter, and cook to earn enough money to attend Cornell University. In 1943 he graduated with a degree in hotel administration. After serving two years in the Navy, he went to work for the Manhattan accounting firm of Harris, Kerr, Foster & Company, and in 1947 became manager of one of its New York accounts, the Monte Carlo Hotel. Two years later he became director of restaurants in Florida for the Schine hotel chain, a position he held until Brody came calling in 1953, asking him to take on the dubious task of introducing luxury dining to an airport terminal.

Company Perspectives:

Restaurant Associates: a name that has been synonymous with exciting restaurant concepts and high quality foodservice for well over half a century.

The Newarker a Major Success in the Early 1950s

Baum hired a classically trained Swiss chef, Albert Stockli, to develop the menu, then invested in fine china and furnishings. The Newarker would become famous for its large portions: the oysters were so large they had to be eaten with a knife and fork, and Baum would add a seventh on a separate plate for orders of a half-dozen. He also added a third claw to lobster orders. In addition, Baum displayed the flair that would one time earn him the moniker, ''the Cecille B. DeMille of restaurateurs.'' He was the first to place a sparkler in a birthday cake, and had a penchant for setting dishes on fire. As he once explained, ''The customers like to see things on fire, or accompanied by fiery props, and it doesn't hurt the food that much.'' Although the restaurant would lose $25,000 in its first year, Baum and Stockli continued to make improvements to the menu, so that after three years it was turning a profit and grossing $3 million in annual sales. About 90 percent of the 1,000 meals served by the Newarker each day were to nontravelers. Moreover, the restaurant was earning half as much as the entire Riker's chain.

Brody enjoyed further success in the concession business, winning contracts on the New York State Thruway from Syracuse to Buffalo. But building on the success of the Newarker, RA would now embark on developing the theme restaurants that would make the company famous. In 1955 Baum was named to head RA's specialty restaurant division. He and Brody soon found their next project, taking over the money-losing Hawaiian Room in Manhattan's Hotel Lexington, a club that had once been a city hot spot. They completely transformed the Hawaiian Room, returning it to popularity. In 1957 RA opened what was regarded as the first theme restaurant on the ground floor of the United States Rubber Company Building in Rockefeller Center. It was called the Forum of the Twelve Caesars. The upscale Forum invoked ancient Egypt, with servers wearing togas and wine served in gladiator helmets. Equally exotic dishes could be found on the menu and so many of them were flambéed that the air conditioning system had to be upgraded.

Other RA restaurants in Manhattan would follow in the late 1950s, aided by James Beard and Julia Child, hired by Baum to consult on the menus. There was the La Fonda del Sol, a Latin theme restaurant located on the ground floor of the Time and Life Building. There was Tavern on the Green, occupying a precious slice of Central Park, featuring panoramic windows to allow diners to enjoy a theatrical view of trees strung with thousands of white lights. There was the Brasserie, employing a Paris bistro theme and becoming the best known 24-hour restaurant in the world, attracting an impressive array of athletes, movie stars, and royalty. RA also acquired a theatre district restaurant, Mamma Leone's, and turned it into a perennial cash cow. But the crowning achievement of RA in this period came with the 1959 opening of the Four Seasons, a three-level restaurant in the Seagram's Building. According to most accounts Baum named the restaurant after a haiku collection he had read. His inspiration was to create a restaurant that would change with the seasons, so that every three months the menu, color scheme, and foliage would be replaced. A minority opinion held that Brody did not receive as much credit as he deserved for the development of the Four Seasons and RA's other famous eateries. He was in many ways an ideal manager for the flamboyant and creative Baum, keeping him on ''a very long leash,'' according to some intimates. Whatever the truth of the matter, there was little debate about the influence of the Four Seasons in the restaurant industry. The restaurant's Grill Room epitomized New York's ''power lunch.''

RA became a public company and entered the 1960s at the peak of its reputation. In 1963 Brody was divorced and Wechsler subsequently forced out his former son-in-law. Baum took over as president and the company continued to prosper. It took over the dining at the Metropolitan Museum of Art, opened two restaurants at the 1964 New York World's Fair, and launched the Zum Zum chain of sausage shops. By 1965 RA was operating 130 restaurants and foodservice operations around the world. The price of RA stock during this period topped out at $47. But RA had overexpanded and Baum's disregard for costs led to thin margins. By 1970 RA stock dipped below $2 per share and it was merged with Waldorf Systems, a company that ran a chain of lunch rooms and a poor fit for Baum, who quit to start his own company. Nevertheless, Baum left a lasting legacy with RA, credited for many innovations in his field, some of which are taken for granted today. It was his idea for servers to replace a full ash tray by cupping it with an empty one, to refold a napkin when a guest left to use the rest room, and to introduce themselves to diners. Baum was responsible in large part for making American cuisine respectable, at a time when a restaurant had to be French to be considered elegant. He also commissioned Americans to design the dinnerware and serving pieces.

With Baum gone RA lost much of it cachet, although it remained a major force in the foodservice industry, continuing to operate many of the restaurants created by Brody and Baum. In 1974 RA acquired the New Jersey steakhouse chain, Charlie Brown's. It became the caterer for the U.S. Open Tennis Championships in 1976, a contract it would hold for the next 20 years and for many people would become the company's best known venture. In 1984 RA acquired the California-based Acapulco Mexican Restaurants chain.

Management Buyout in 1988

In 1988 RA's senior management, headed my Max Pine, who had been the company's chief executive officer since 1976, engineered a leveraged buyout to take RA private, paying $150 million for a 54 percent stake. The price proved too heavy, however, and RA was hard pressed to meet 13 percent interest payments. Expansion plans had to be shelved and RA sold off 152 Eastern Lobby newsstands for $25 million. RA independence lasted just two years. In 1990 Tokyo-based foodservice conglomerate, Kyotaru Co., became the first of many Japanese firms to take over an American company involved in retailing, entertainment, real estate, and technology. It paid approximately $120 million for RA and assumed $80 million in debt. RA expected an infusion of cash from its new corporate parent

Key Dates:

1953: The Newarker opens in Newark Airport.
1959: Four Seasons opens.
1963: Joseph Baum replaces Jerome Brody as president.
1970: The company merges with Waldorf Systems; Baum quits.
1988: The company is taken private in a management LBO.
1990: A Japanese company acquires RA.
1996: Management buys back the company.
1998: Compass Group USA acquires RA.
1999: The company acquires the Los Angeles-based Patina Group.
2003: Nick Valenti announces plans to step down as president, to be replaced by Richard Stockinger.

in order to resume growth plans, which called for RA to double in size in five years. Kyotaru was supportive at first, but after a year, as the Japanese economy began to falter, RA found itself sending its money to Japan to support Kyotaru.

In January 1994 Max Pine quit and was replaced as CEO by Nick Valenti, a longtime RA executive. According to the company, Pine left as part of a succession plan that had been put in place when Kyotaru bought RA. Valenti joined the company out of college in 1968, starting out as a management trainee. He took over at a time when not only was RA's corporate parent struggling but so was the New York economy. Revenues continued to rise, but RA could not reinvest in its own operations because of Kyotaru. In 1995 Brasserie closed, a restaurant that was in much need of a makeover. In 1995 RA suffered another blow when it lost the U.S. Open contract.

Starting in 1995 Valenti began lobbying Kyotaru to sell RA back to management, afraid that a third party might step in and attempt to buy the company. In July 1996 the two sides reached a deal, the terms of which were not disclosed. Management was backed by two Manhattan-based venture capital firms—Bruckman, Rosser & Sherill Co. L.P. and Furman Selz LLC. Valenti claimed that RA had not taken on excessive debt, as had been the case in the 1988 buyout, and he maintained that the company would have the capital necessary to grow the business. But almost immediately Valenti began searching for a new corporate backer. In 1997 it sold the Charlie Brown's chain and The Office Beer Bar & Grill chain to pay down debt.

In June 1998 RA agreed to be sold to Compass Group USA, the $2.3 billion North American division of Compass Group PLC, the world's largest contract caterer. The price was $87.5 million for RA and another $50 million for the Acapulco chain. Compass Group resulted from the 1987 spin-off of the contract services division of Grand Metropolitan, a London-based food and spirits company. After going public in 1988, Compass Group expanded rapidly. In 1994 it acquired Canteen Corporation, the third largest vending and foodservice company in the United States, forming the basis for the North American Division. A major step for the unit was winning a $250 million contract to serve 100,000 IBM employees located at sites in 29 states. In the months before acquiring RA, Compass Group won contracts for the Smithsonian National Museum of Natural History, National Museum of American History, and the American Art & Portrait Gallery—all of which would be administered by RA. By acquiring RA, Compass Group wanted to establish a strong presence in the premium concessions business. RA, for its part, would receive the financial backing it needed for expansion, while retaining a high degree of independence. Compass Group recognized the value of the RA name and its heritage—and would likely not have made the deal if management staying on were not part of the deal.

Under Compass Group ownership, RA advanced on a number of fronts in the late 1990s. It won back the U.S. Open contract in 1998, and in 1999 added the Intrepid Sea, Air & Space Museum, housed in a World War II-era aircraft carrier docked in Manhattan, as well as the cafeteria operations for Swiss Re, a financial firm relocating from Manhattan to Armonk, New York. Also in 1999 RA gained a strong West Coast presence with the acquisition of Los Angeles-based Patina Group, which operated a number of upscale restaurants and also served institutional contracts. In 2000 RA opened a wide range of operations, including three public restaurants in Rockefeller Center; steakhouses in Madison Square Garden and the MCI Center in Washington, D.C.; four foodservice operations in Macy's flagship department store in Manhattan's Herald Square; a food court in the Natural History Museum; an upscale cafeteria in the new Conde Nast Building in Manhattan; and two restaurants in Cleveland's Severance Hall. Of even greater importance, at least from a symbolic point of view, was the reopening of the completely remodeled Brasserie.

Over the next few years, RA opened a number of other notable eateries, including Macy's Cellar Bar & Grill in the basement of the Herald Square store, and a new cafeteria and restaurant at the Metropolitan Museum of Art. RA was growing at a 10 percent clip and expanding in a number of directions across the country, from operating fine restaurants and handling the catering for cultural and sporting venues, to controlling the franchise rights to Krispy Kreme and Au Bon Pain. In late 2003 Valenti announced that he planned to step down as president, but there was another seasoned RA executive waiting in the wings, Richard Stockinger, the chief financial officer and a 19-year veteran of the company. There was every reason to believe that he would be able to sustain RA's resurgence, as it continued in its efforts to expand on existing restaurants, acquire new ones, and grow its contract business.

Principal Subsidiaries

Patina Group.

Principal Competitors

Ark Restaurants Corporation; Levy Restaurants, Inc.; The Riese Organization.

Further Reading

Carlino, Bill, "75 Years: The Odyssey of Eating Out," *Nation's Restaurant News,* January 1994, p. 11.

Collins, Glenn, "Top Restaurant Will Buy Stock Back from Japanese," *New York Times,* July 26, 1996, p. B3.

Fabricant, Florence, "Love Theme Restaurants? Here's the Man to Thank," *New York Times,* September 13, 1995, p. C8.

Klara, Robert, "Atomic Baum," *Restaurant Business,* September 1, 1996, p. 40.

——, "Back in Control," *Restaurant Business,* November 1, 1996, p. 65.

Frumkin, Paul, "Restaurant Associates: Ready for Prime Time," *Nation's Restaurant News,* August 13, 2001, p. 66.

Grimes, William, "Joseph Baum, American Dining's High Stylist, Dies at 78," *New York Times,* October 6, 1998, p. B10.

Martin, Douglas, "Jerome Brody, 78, Is Dead; Guided Elegant Restaurants," *New York Times,* May 18, 2001, p. C15.

—Ed Dinger

Ryan Beck & Co., Inc.

220 South Orange Avenue
Livingston, New Jersey 07039
U.S.A.
Telephone: (973) 549-4000
Toll Free: (800) 342-2325
Fax: (973) 597-6414
Web site: http://www.ryanbeck.com

Wholly Owned Subsidiary of BankAtlantic Bancorp, Inc.
Incorporated: 1965 as John J. Ryan & Co., Inc.
Employees: 1,255
Sales: $221.41 million (2003)
NAIC: 523110 Investment Banking and Securities Dealing; 523930 Investment Advice; 523120 Securities Brokerage

Ryan Beck & Co., Inc. is an investment banking and brokerage firm. Ryan Beck offers services to individuals, institutions, and corporate clients, operating 36 offices in 13 states. The company provides services to individual investors, offering its clients advice on investments and retirement plans. For institutional clients, Ryan Beck underwrites municipal bonds. The company provides consulting and merger and acquisition advisory services to corporate clients. Ryan Beck operated primarily in New Jersey and New York until its 2002 acquisition of Gruntal & Co. increased its physical and geographic presence considerably, turning a nine-branch, five-state operation into a firm with more than 30 offices in 13 states. The company is owned by BankAtlantic Bancorp., Inc., a bank holding company based in Florida.

Origins

Ryan Beck's founder, John J. Ryan, launched his entrepreneurial enterprise shortly after the end of World War II. During the war years, Ryan was employed by Lehman Brothers, where he worked as a bond buyer. In 1946, he started his own investment banking firm. During its formative years, the company was devoted to underwriting and distributing tax-exempt municipal bonds, bidding on city, county, and state bonds that were used to finance public projects in New Jersey. The company earned distinction as an underwriter of municipal bonds but recognition came later for John J. Ryan & Co., as the company recorded only modest growth during its first years in business. By the time the company celebrated its fifth anniversary, it employed only a half-dozen people, holding slightly more than $40,000 in capital. The company's anniversary year marked the arrival of Roy G. Beck, who, while working as a bond salesman, met Ryan in 1951. Ryan and Beck were both bidding on a bond issue for a project in Monmouth County, New Jersey. Both failed to enter winning the bids, but their introduction led Ryan to offer the younger Beck a job at his small firm. Beck accepted the offer, becoming John J. Ryan & Co.'s lead bond salesman.

John J. Ryan's company did not begin to distinguish itself until the 1960s, when it diversified into the areas that later defined its expertise. The majority of the company's customers were New Jersey-based banks, which naturally led it into covering bank stocks. In 1963, a dozen years after joining the firm, Beck formed a bank-stock trading and research subsidiary, an action that the company's historians later hailed as one of the most important events in Ryan Beck's development. The company's bank stock business, which represented a second source of revenue, grew during the decade, as did the company's municipal bond business. In 1966, John J. Ryan & Co. was named co-manager of the $179-million bond issue for the New Jersey Turnpike. Although John J. Ryan & Co. had been guaranteeing the issue of municipal bonds for 20 years by 1966, the scale of the New Jersey Turnpike project did much to cement the company's reputation as one of the elite underwriters in the state.

Before the end of the 1960s, Ryan Beck added a third source of revenue, rounding out its portfolio of financial services. New Jersey's banking laws were slated for significant changes at the end of the decade, changes that enabled the company to diversify into corporate finance. In 1969, the company established a department equipped to oversee mergers and acquisitions, which quickly led to its first assignment, the merger of the Bank of Sussex County into the National Community Bank. Although the company would continue to diversify into other financial services, by the end of the 1960s Ryan Beck had established its

Company Perspectives:

Our focus is clear—whether we create strategic alliances, build proprietary products or commit to new technology, our goal is to provide our clients with outstanding opportunities. Helping our clients invest for their long-term goals is the premise upon which Ryan Beck & Co. was founded, and this premise will continue to be our inspiration. We look forward to continued expansion and profitability in the coming years. We could not have achieved our past goals—nor our vision for the future—without our dedicated employees and clients. We truly appreciate the opportunity to continue to provide you with innovative solutions to your financial needs.

involvement in its three principal business areas. In the years ahead, the company increased its stature by underwriting municipal bonds, by facilitating mergers and acquisitions, and by providing research and analysis of stocks, primarily bank stocks.

Development into a Regional Firm Begins in the 1980s

Ryan Beck recorded steady growth during the 1970s, gradually developing into a firm that attracted national attention. Toward the end of the decade, the company promoted and oversaw the first competitive bid for the sale of a bank branch, pioneering a concept that later would become commonplace in the industry. The company performed well during the 1980s as well, prospering during turbulent market conditions. In 1982, after changing its name to Ryan, Beck & Co. the previous year, the company opened a branch office in Philadelphia. The Philadelphia office was established to assist in the company's corporate finance business, serving as a satellite operation in support of the company's corporate finance efforts at its headquarters in West Orange, New Jersey. The mid-1980s were years of diversification, growth, and change. In 1984, Ryan Beck converted its first savings bank, Central Jersey Savings and Loan. In 1985, the company was selected as co-manager of a $2 billion New Jersey Turnpike issue, the largest public issue in the history of municipal financing. The following year, the company's 40th anniversary was celebrated with its conversion to public ownership after two million shares were sold in an initial public offering of stock.

The 1990s brought significant change to Ryan Beck, as the company completed its first half-century of business. The company opened a branch office in West Palm Beach in 1995, the same year Ryan, Beck Planning & Insurance Agency was formed, which served as the company's entry into business related to insurance, estate planning, and annuities. In 1997, when the company moved its headquarters from West Orange to Livingston, Ben A. Plotkin was appointed president and chief executive officer. Plotkin had joined Ryan Beck ten years earlier as an investment banker at the company's branch in Philadelphia. Eventually, he was promoted to steward the company's entire investment banking department, recording sufficient success to warrant his appointment as Ryan Beck's principal strategist.

Not long after Plotkin's tenure began, Ryan Beck embarked on a new era. In February 1998, the company acquired Cumberland Advisors, Inc., a leading fixed income money management firm, but the most significant event of the year occurred several months later. In June, Ryan Beck was acquired by BankAtlantic Bancorp, Inc., the largest bank based in Florida. BankAtlantic, whose primary subsidiary was a savings bank with 68 branches, acquired Ryan Beck for $39.4 million in stock, marking only the third time a thrift and securities firm had merged during the previous ten years. For Plotkin and his executive team, the affiliation with BankAtlantic gave them the chance to focus on larger deals. At the time the merger was announced, Ryan Beck held $56.5 million in assets, produced $35 million in annual revenues, and operated five branch offices. Historically, the company had limited itself to smaller bank deals because of its size, but with the access to capital provided by BankAtlantic, Ryan Beck could begin to focus on larger deals. The merger also allowed the company to keep its own identity, positioning Ryan Beck as an autonomous subsidiary of BankAtlantic: No offices were slated for closure, no employees were to be laid off, and the company was allowed to remain in Livingston with its existing management team.

Ryan Beck exited the 1990s buoyed by the financial resources of its new parent company. BankAtlantic, for its part, entered the lucrative business of underwriting, market making, and merger advisory work. The years immediately following the merger proved to be positive for Ryan Beck, as the company expanded, most notably through acquisitions. For much of its history, Ryan Beck had confined its activities to New Jersey, gradually building its reputation over the course of decades. Expansion outside New Jersey, begun in 1982 with the opening of the branch office in Philadelphia, started the firm down the road to becoming a regional concern. After opening branches in Chicago and Florida, the company began to broaden its geographic scope beyond that of a regional enterprise. In the wake of the merger with BankAtlantic, the company strengthened its position as an eastern U.S. financial services firm. In 1999, Ryan Beck acquired a Boca Raton, Florida-based company named Southeast Research Partners, paying $1.9 million in cash and stock for the firm. Founded in 1990, Southeast Research comprised a dozen stock analysts who covered industries such as energy, homebuilding, and health care, as well as a team of brokers who sold stocks and other investments to institutional clients.

Acquisition of Gruntal in 2002

Ryan Beck embarked a new era in the 21st century, concluding a deal that exponentially increased the company's stature. In the spring of 2002, the company announced it was acquiring the retail brokerage operations of one of the oldest investment firms in the country, New York-based Gruntal & Co. The transaction was by far the largest deal Ryan Beck had been involved in, adding 34 offices in 13 states and more than 600 account executives to its fold. The acquisition, completed in June 2002, quadrupled the size of Ryan Beck's brokerage business, giving the company nearly $19 billion in assets.

In the wake of the Gruntal acquisition, Ryan Beck emerged as a far more comprehensive investment bank. The company's focus on investment banking for regional commercial banks and thrifts and underwriting tax-free municipal issues remained, but the addition of Gruntal enabled Ryan Beck to offer a number of new services to its clients. The company added trust services,

Key Dates:

1946: John J. Ryan founds an investment banking firm.
1951: Roy G. Beck joins the company.
1963: The company begins covering bank stocks.
1969: Ryan Beck establishes its corporate finance department.
1982: A branch office in Philadelphia is opened.
1986: Ryan Beck completes its initial public offering of stock.
1997: Ben A. Plotkin is named president and chief executive officer.
1998: Ryan Beck is acquired by BankAtlantic Bancorp.
2002: Ryan Beck acquires the retail brokerage operations of Gruntal & Co., quadrupling its size.

residential mortgages, mutual fund programs, and several other products as it ''morphed into a full service retail firm,'' according to Ryan Beck's head of marketing in the July 1, 2003 issue of *On Wall Street.* As the company prepared for the future, the integration of Gruntal continued, as did Ryan Beck's efforts to expand its product offerings.

Ryan Beck's achievements in 2004 promised to put its greater geographical and operational scope to the company's advantage. During the spring of that year, the company expanded its stock coverage to include the business and consumer services sectors, hoping to distinguish itself from other brokerage firms. ''There aren't many middle market firms that have a focus on the consumer and finance sectors,'' the company's director of research explained in a May 31, 2004 interview with *Wall Street Letter.* ''If you look down the road, we're going to be one of the very few or maybe the only one that has a focus on the services economy versus the manufacturing economy,'' he added. In the summer of 2004, Ryan Beck launched a new advertising campaign designed around the slogan ''Let's Get Down to Work.'' The campaign focused on the company's direct, no-nonsense approach to investing, a message—after the acquisition of Gruntal—that was delivered to many more markets than previous marketing programs had addressed. Ryan Beck's senior vice-president, Eric Siber, explained the thinking behind the advertising campaign in a July 6, 2004 interview with *PR Newswire.* ''With nearly 500 financial consultants operating out of 36 offices in 13 states,'' he stated, ''we needed to move away from our market positioning as one of the best-kept secrets in financial services.'' Siber continued, hinting at a more aggressive Ryan Beck in the future: ''In the past, we've relied solely on clients to spread the word about Ryan Beck. Now it's time to blow our own horn.''

Principal Subsidiaries

Ryan Beck Financial Corporation.

Principal Competitors

Banc of America Securities LLC; Friedman, Billings, Ramsey Group, Inc.; Morgan Stanley.

Further Reading

Chapelle, Tony, ''Ryan Beck Digest Gruntal and Expands,'' *On Wall Street*, July 1, 2003.

Elstein, Aaron, ''BankAtlantic Has $38M Deal to Buy Ryan Beck,'' *American Banker*, February 11, 1998, p. 26.

''Florida-Based BankAtlantic Bancorp. to Buy New Jersey-Based Ryan, Beck & Co.,'' *Knight Ridder/Tribune Business News*, February 11, 1998.

Freer, Jim, ''BankAtlantic Subsidiary Acquires Boca Research Firm,'' *South Florida Business Journal*, July 2, 1999, p. 4A.

''Livingston, N.J.-Based Bank Plans Purchase of New York-Based Brokerage Firm,'' *Knight Ridder/Tribune Business News*, April 23, 2002.

''Looking for a Financial Advisor to Toast Your Daughter at Her Wedding?,'' *PR Newswire*, July 6, 2004, p. 34.

Martin, Robert Scott, ''Gruntal Switches Dance Partners,'' *Research*, June 2002, p. 24.

''Ryan Beck Plans Research Augmentation,'' *Wall Street Letter*, May 31, 2004, p. 4.

—Jeffrey L. Covell

Scheid Vineyards Inc.

305 Hilltown Road
Salinas, California 93908
U.S.A.
Telephone: (831) 455-9990
Fax: (831) 455-9998
Web site: http://www.scheidvineyards.com

Public Company
Incorporated: 1972 as Monterey Farming Corporation
Employees: 75
Sales: $26.4 million (2003)
Stock Exchanges: NASDAQ
Ticker Symbol: SVIN
NAIC: 111332 Grape Vineyards; 312130 Wineries

Scheid Vineyards Inc. is a leading independent vineyard, controlling 5,600 acres of vineyards along California's central coast. The company, the first vineyard not owned by a winery to be publicly traded in the United States, produces 17 varieties of premium wine grapes, supplying more than 30 wineries. Scheid Vineyards' most important grape varieties are Chardonnay, Cabernet Sauvignon, Merlot, Pinot Noir, Sauvignon Blanc, and Syrah. The company produces a small amount of wine under its own label, approximately 5,000 cases a year, to showcase the quality of its wines. Scheid Vineyards contracts with wineries, usually under long-term agreements, to grow wine grapes according to the wineries' specifications. The company is managed and majority-owned by the Scheid family.

Origins

Alfred Scheid's entry into wine grape farming had nothing to do with an interest in viticulture. Scheid's interest was in finance. A graduate of Harvard Business School, Scheid spent most of his early professional career working for the well-known brokerage firm E.F. Hutton & Company. He spent a decade at E.F. Hutton working as an investment banker, enjoying his work enough to start his own investment banking firm at the beginning of the 1970s. One of the first clients of Scheid's fledgling entrepreneurial career was his former employer, E.F. Hutton, who wanted Scheid to explore the idea of establishing what would become the rage in the 1970s: agricultural tax shelters. E.F. Hutton wanted to establish a tax shelter for its senior executives, and the company asked Scheid to look at vineyards as a potential business opportunity. In 1971, Scheid began exploring possibilities, eventually focusing his investigation in Monterey County, situated between San Francisco and Santa Barbara. His findings were promising, prompting E.F. Hutton to move ahead with the project.

In 1972, Scheid, working at E.F. Hutton's behest, formed an enterprise that would become his life's work. He acquired 2,100 acres that stretched for 15 miles between Greenfield and King City. Unlike most agricultural tax shelters, which preferred to use contract farm management, Scheid formed a genuine company to provide the labor and the management of the proposed vineyard, creating Scheid Vineyard's predecessor, Monterey Farming Corporation. A second important decision was made at the start: Scheid opted against planting on speculation, preferring instead to sign long-term contracts for the grapes grown by the vineyard, a practice observed by Scheid Vineyards into the 21st century. Scheid signed a contract with Almaden and planted on the 2,100 acres under Monterey Farming Corporation's control. With the company and crops in place, there was only the question of leadership to be answered, a post Scheid accepted without relish. "I became president of the company, Monterey Farming Corporation, because nobody else wanted the position," Scheid reflected in the winter 1999 issue of *Adventures in Dining*. "I didn't particularly want it either," he added, "because this was really just a sideline operation."

After establishing Monterey Farming Corporation, Scheid continued with his entrepreneurial endeavors. His efforts to build his own investment banking firm took him into the field of biotechnology, a foray that again drew its impetus from his former employer. In 1982, E.F. Hutton approached Scheid about starting a biotechnology company in Palo Alto, California. Scheid started the company with $120,000 and within three years created a company with a market value of nearly $400 million. His success in Palo Alto led to the creation of another biotechnology company in Texas, but Scheid's attention was soon drawn back to the vineyards in Monterey Country.

Company Perspectives:

Scheid Vineyards has been farming wine grapes in Monterey County since 1972. We service an array of winery clients up and down the coast of California with 13 distinct vineyard properties from Soledad down to Hames Valley. One principle has remained constant throughout our company's 30 years in business . . . our commitment to delivering what our clients want. This commitment brings our vineyard team and winery client together to realize the common goal of producing outstanding wines.

Changes in the tax laws had substantially reduced the worth of agricultural enterprises as tax shelters, which prompted some growers to abandon their vineyards. By the end of the 1980s, Monterey Farming Corporation had lost its worth as a tax shelter, and E.F. Hutton's senior executives wanted to divest their investment in the company. Scheid, who had initially assumed his duties at the vineyard with a measure of reluctance, felt differently about farming by the late 1980s. Scheid offered to buy out his partners and devote himself wholly to wine grape growing. ''I wanted to get out of the biotech business anyway,'' he explained in his interview with *Adventures in Dining*. ''The farming company had been a moneymaker from the first day,'' he added. ''But more than anything, it was a labor of love.''

Alfred Scheid Buys out His Partners in 1988

Scheid become sole owner of the vineyard operation in 1988, renaming the company Scheid Vineyards and Management Co. As Scheid set out, he was joined by his son Scott Scheid, who had left his job as an options trader for E.F. Hutton in 1986 to serve as vice-president for Monterey Farming Corporation. The two Scheids were joined by a third family member, Heidi Scheid, Alfred Scheid's daughter, who left her job as a senior valuation analyst at Ernst & Young LLP in 1992 to serve as the vineyard's director of planning.

By the time Scheid was joined by his son and daughter, the business of growing wine grapes had changed considerably since the formation of Monterey Farming Corporation. When the company was formed, low-quality jug wine was the predominate output of California wineries. Wineries bought in bulk, paying little attention to the quality of grapes they contracted vineyards to grow. ''It used to be you'd get a call from a winemaker who'd ask you to send them 100 tons of whatever you've got,'' Scott Scheid remarked in an April 21, 2001 interview with *Monterey County-The Herald*. In the years separating the formation of Monterey Farming Corporation and Scheid's purchase of the company, consumers' tastes had changed, as premium varietal table wines enjoyed increasing popularity. Between 1980 and the late 1990s, sales of these California wines increased from 6.6 million nine-liter cases to 70 million nine-liter cases, which fueled revenue growth of premium wines at an 18 percent compounded annual rate. As a result of the growing trend, winemakers became more discerning about the quality and type of grapes they purchased and the art and science of growing wine grapes became increasingly sophisticated. The Scheids positioned their vineyard as a producer of high-quality premium grapes, reaping the rewards of the trend favoring premium varietal wines.

Scheid Vineyards was regarded as custom farmer, a role and reputation the company strengthened during the 1990s, as it honed its viticultural skills and held sway as a vineyard particularly attuned to its customers' needs. Typically, a winery client contracted for a specified area of vineyard acreage, referred to as a vineyard ''block.'' Scheid Vineyards then farmed the block according to the specific winemaking goal of the client. The company produced more than a dozen varieties of wine grapes but devoted the majority of its acreage to Chardonnay and Cabernet Sauvignon. Nearly all of the company business was focused on wine grape production, but at the beginning of the 1990s, Alfred Scheid decided to make his own ultra-premium wine. The wine, made commercially available in 1996 to a limited audience, was produced primarily to showcase the vineyard's grapes in the company's tasting room.

Scheid Vineyards celebrated its 25th anniversary in 1997, the year the company made U.S. business history. After spending more than $11 million in capital improvements during the previous four years, the company converted to public ownership, completing its initial public offering (IPO) of stock in July 1997. Scheid Vineyards became the first independent (not owned by a winery) vineyard in the United States to trade on the public market. The company sold 2.3 million shares, raising $18.5 in proceeds from the offering.

Scheid Vineyards' IPO offered industry observers a closer look at the company's operations. The company operated 5,150 acres of vineyards at the time of its IPO, 3,470 acres of which the company operated for its own purposes. The remaining acreage was operated under management contracts with other concerns. Scheid Vineyards produced 14 varieties of premium wine grapes, including Chardonnay, Merlot, Cabernet Sauvignon, Chenin Blanc, Gewurztraminer, and Sauvignon Blanc. The company's two largest winery customers were Canandaigua Brands, Inc. and International Distillers and Vintners North America (IDV). IDV accounted for more than 80 percent of Scheid Vineyards' revenues, which totaled $19.8 million.

The company's 25th anniversary also marked a year of expansion. In June 1997, Scheid Vineyards acquired the Riverview Vineyard in Monterey County for $5.5 million. The purchase included 370 acres planted with several grape varieties, including 120 acres of Chardonnay and 100 acres of Pinot Noir. Also in 1997, the company acquired a lease option for a 655-acre property in Hames Valley in Monterey County. The year's harvest was record setting in terms of both revenue and tonnage, as Scheid Vineyard collected 15,600 tons of grapes and generated $18.6 million in revenues.

Struggles and Prosperity: Late 1990s–Early 2000s

The late 1990s were difficult years for the vineyard, as weather conditions negatively affected grape production. In 1998, unseasonably cool and cloudy weather between May and July delayed and reduced the vineyard's harvest, resulting in production falling to 10,900 tons. Revenues fell as well, dropping to $17.8 million. Late in the year, the company expanded again, providing one moment of celebration in an otherwise depressing

Key Dates:

1972: The Monterey Farming Corporation is founded with 2,100 acres of undeveloped land.
1988: Alfred Scheid acquires his partners' interests in Monterey Farming Corporation and renames the company Scheid Vineyards and Management Co.
1997: After a four-year capital improvement program, Scheid Vineyards completes its initial public offering of stock.
2001: Scheid Vineyards offers its proprietary VitWatch program to clients.

year. In December, Scheid Vineyards signed a long-term lease for 750 acres of undeveloped land in Greenfield, two miles away from the company's headquarters. The first harvest of the vineyard, renamed Mesa del Rio Vineyard, was expected in 2001. In 1999, adverse weather conditions again stunted the company's harvest. Warm weather, which promoted wine grape growth during the summer months, never materialized to any sustained extent, delaying the harvest by three to four weeks. Tonnage for the year fell to 7,700 tons, less than half the total harvested in 1997, and revenues declined 27 percent, dropping to $12.8 million.

Although Scheid Vineyards, like all farming enterprises, was at the mercy of the weather, the company did everything in its power to ensure it secured the greatest yields and produced grapes of the highest quality. The business of growing wine grapes at the turn of the 21st century was becoming an increasingly high-technology endeavor, and Scheid Vineyards stood at the vanguard of viticultural sophistication. The company mapped all of its vineyards using global positioning system (GPS) technology, which, when used with information about soils, topography, and slopes, gave it enhanced capabilities to manage erosion. At the vine, Scheid Vineyards growers used neutron probe technology to monitor soil moisture and pressure bomb technology to monitor the amount of water in plants. The technology used by the company not only helped it to improve its farming methods, but it also provided a wealth of information to its clients, the wineries who were in a perpetual state of anxiety about their grapes. Scheid Vineyards had five weather stations on its vineyards that recorded information every 15 seconds. The information gleaned from the company's weather stations was used to compile reports, which were updated every 15 minutes and accessible via telephone.

After two years of lackluster results in tonnage harvested and revenues collected, Scheid Vineyards began the 21st century positively. In 2000, the company harvested 10,700 tons of grapes, a 39 percent increase, and generated $17.4 million in revenues, a 35 percent increase. In 2001, Scheid Vineyards recorded a 25 percent increase in sales, posting revenues of $21.7 million, but the company's most notable achievement occurred on the technological front. During the harvest, winery clients were offered the company's proprietary VitWatch program, giving the wineries, most of which were located in the Sonoma and Napa regions, an opportunity to obtain information that their distance from Monterey County precluded. By logging onto the password-protected VitWatch Web site, a Scheid Vineyard client could obtain a wealth of information related to the client's specific blocks and vines. Data concerning weather, soil moisture, and sugar percentage in ripening vines was made available. Users were provided with satellite and radar weather images, information about historical weather trends, soil moisture level, vine water stress, and irrigation profiles. Winery clients, who typically inundated Scheid Vineyards with a plethora of faxes, pages, and cell phone calls beginning in mid-August, were desperate for information about their grapes as the decision on when to pick the grapes neared. VitWatch helped calm this growing anxiety, giving wineries a wealth of data relevant to their crops, a service that was highlighted by VitCam, a stationary Web camera that users controlled to scan and zoom in on their vines. In 2002, VitCam was made mobile, allowing users travel down stretches of vineyards to examine the state, pruning, and harvesting of their grapes. "We're trying to reach unprecedented levels of service," Scott Scheid remarked in a July 1, 2002 interview with *The Californian*, referring to the company's VitWatch program.

Scheid Vineyards' 30th anniversary provided encouragement for future success. The company, by 2003, was under day-to-day control of Alfred Scheid's children. Alfred Scheid, who served as the vineyard's chairman, appointed his son Scott chief executive officer in 2002. His daughter Heidi, having been promoted to chief financial officer in 1997, served as senior vice-president during the company's 30th anniversary. This management team enjoyed a banner 2003, as the vineyard's harvest increased 18 percent to 20,700 tons of wine grapes, fueling revenue growth to $26.4 million. As the company prepared for the future, its attention to customer service, coupled with its sophisticated knowledge of viticulture, promised to make Scheid Vineyards one of the leading vineyards in the United States.

Principal Subsidiaries

Scheid Vineyards California Inc.

Principal Competitors

The Robert Mondavi Corporation; E. & J. Gallo Winery; Golden State Vintners, Inc.

Further Reading

Franson, Paul, "Scheid Vineyards," *Wine Business Monthly*, December 2001, p. 27.
Fulmer, Melinda, "Grape Growing Going High-Tech," *Los Angeles Times*, September 1, 2002, p. C4.
Gaylord, Brian, "Click, There's Your Grapes," *Californian*, July 1, 2002, p. 17.
Livernois, Joe, "Scheid Moves to Where the Grapes Are," *Monterey County-The Herald*, April 2001, p. 34.
"Meeting the Challenges of Tomorrow," *Patterson's California Beverage Journal*, July 1999, p. 32.
Oliveira, Theresa, "Planning for the Future," *American Vineyard*, July 1999, p. 45.
Patterson, Tim, "Wired for Winegrowing," *Central Coast Adventure*, September 2002, p. 9.
Weir, Christopher, "Scheid Vineyards," *Adventures in Dining*, Winter 1999, p. 63.

—Jeffrey L. Covell

Scottish and Southern Energy plc

Inveralmond House
200 Dunkeld Road
Perth PH1 3AQ
United Kingdom
Telephone: (1738) 456000
Fax: (1738) 457005
Web site: http://www.scottish-southern.co.uk

Public Company
Incorporated: 1989
Employees: 9,474
Sales: $6.39 billion (2003)
Stock Exchanges: London
Ticker Symbol: SSE
NAIC: 221111 Hydroelectric Power Generation; 221112 Fossil Fuel Electric Power Generation; 221119 Other Electric Power Generation; 221121 Electric Bulk Power Transmission and Control; 221122 Electric Power Distribution

Scottish and Southern Energy plc (SSE) operates as one of the largest energy concerns in the United Kingdom. The company generates, transmits, and distributes electricity to more than three million electricity customers and 1.5 million gas customers in the United Kingdom through subsidiaries Scottish Hydro-Electric, Southern Electric, SWALEC, and Atlantic Electric and Gas. SSE is also involved in energy trading, gas marketing, electrical and utility contracting, and telecommunications. The company is heavily committed to protecting the environment—it stands as the United Kingdom's largest generator of renewable energy. SSE was born out of the 1998 merger of Scottish Hydro-Electric plc and Southern Electric plc.

The History of Scottish Hydro-Electric

The smaller of the two Scottish electric companies, Scottish Hydro-Electric was involved in generation, transmission, and supply of electricity to the Scottish Highlands and Islands. Hydro-Electric's position in the U.K. electricity industry was unique, serving a region comprising some 25 percent of Britain's total land area—and encompassing some of the United Kingdom's loveliest yet least hospitable terrain—but containing only 3 percent of its population. Although it got a late start relative to electricity suppliers in England and Wales, Scottish Hydro-Electric brought electricity to the north of Scotland virtually singlehandedly, first as a public sector utility and later as a privatized company. The generation and provision of electricity in the Highlands remained the company's core business, but in the 1990s it significantly broadened its market to include areas south of the border.

The harnessing of electricity for public use developed more slowly in Scotland than in England and Wales, where nearly 500 separate electricity suppliers had arisen within just 40 years following the introduction of street lighting in 1881. In Scotland the first electricity was supplied in 1890 via a water turbine at Fort Augustus. The first commercial use of water power in Britain came in 1896, when the British Aluminum Company set up a factory at Foyers on Loch Ness, utilizing the water coursing down the slopes of the Great Glen to power its aluminum smelting. But subsequent development, particularly in the remote and sparsely populated Highlands, was slow. There were few schemes until 1930, when the Grampian Electricity Supply Company began operating projects at Rannoch and Tummel Bridge, Perthshire, and at Luichart, Ross-shire.

These projects were by no means far-reaching, however; as late as 1943, five out of six farms and 99 out of 100 crofts in the Highlands had no link to publicly supplied electricity. In that year the North of Scotland Hydro-Electric Board was established by an act of Parliament. When, five years later, the electricity industry was nationalized, the projects of Grampian Electricity and other independent suppliers came under the jurisdiction of the new board.

The formidable work of harnessing water power in the Highlands now began in earnest. Within Britain, only in the Scottish Highlands could hydro power be utilized so extensively for electricity generation. The Highlands boast some of Britain's highest mountains, large expanses of uninterrupted high ground, vast tracts of moors, and numerous large and deep lochs. All these features provide ideal conditions for the use of

Company Perspectives:

At the heart of Scottish and Southern Energy's strategy is the belief that the highest priority should always be attached to managing existing businesses well through seeking operational excellence. The effective management of all operations throughout S.S.E. is the best means of achieving a financial performance which allows the delivery of long-term and sustainable real growth in the dividend.

hydro power. At the same time, those very features of the landscape often proved a barrier to development. Coupled with the scattered and isolated nature of Highland settlements, they made transmission of power a difficult task indeed. Nonetheless, work progressed with a labor force averaging between 4,000 and 5,000, and at one time reaching as high as 12,000. By 1965 about half of the area's estimated potential had been realized. This equated to 54 main power stations with a generating capacity of more than 1,000 megawatts, 56 primary dams, 300 kilometers of excavated rock tunnels, 300 kilometers of aqueducts and pipelines, 32,000 kilometers of overhead cables, and 110 kilometers of submarine cables.

Despite its history and even its name, only a proportion of Scottish Hydro-Electric's power was generated by water. In 1994, the breakdown of the company's power generation sources was as follows: 16 percent hydro; 51 percent oil and gas; 11 percent coal; 19 percent nuclear; and 3 percent other. The use of hydro power, however, fluctuated year by year, sometimes considerably, depending on rainfall; in 1993 the hydro figure had been 26 percent. The high percentage of oil and gas use was accounted for primarily by one station: Peterhead.

In the early 1970s the North Sea oil boom brought rapid development to the northeast of Scotland, and with it a heavily increased demand for electricity. Hydro-powered electricity had served the region previously, but this was inadequate for the surge in requirements for geographical reasons. Scotland's northeast, which mainly consists of a low plateau, is unusual in the Highlands in that it has no proximity to a major river system. Thus plans were laid for Hydro-Electric's major thermal power station.

Begun in 1973 and based at Boddam, near Peterhead, the plant was fully operational by 1982. Originally oil had been the favored fossil fuel, but by the time the project was completed natural gas had become a more popular option for the electricity industry (although the Peterhead plant retained its oil capability). In 1988 Hydro-Electric arranged to buy the entire natural gas yield of the Miller Field in the North Sea, thus securing itself a continuing supply from 1992, when the gas came on stream, until well into the next century.

In the late 1980s Britain's Conservative government laid plans to privatize the electricity industry, and Scottish Hydro-Electric was accordingly incorporated as a private company in 1989. The company's shares were sold on the stock market in 1991. The privatized electricity industry in Scotland was structured differently from that in England and Wales. In Scotland, Hydro-Electric and its southern counterpart ScottishPower were fully integrated: that is, they generated, distributed, and supplied electricity. In England and Wales, however, the system was more fragmented. The electricity generators, principally National Power and PowerGen, produced electricity, which was then distributed via the National Grid to the Regional Electricity Companies (RECs), who in turn supplied electricity to consumers.

The Scottish electricity boards were originally slated to be privatized first, but eventually the government decided to proceed with the English RECs first, at the end of 1990. Hydro-Electric and ScottishPower were offered for sale in the summer of the following year. Some investors argued that in the interim the government changed the rules so that the munificent premiums enjoyed by investors in the RECs were not available to those who invested in Hydro-Electric and ScottishPower. For reasons that have never been entirely clear, shareholders in the English and Welsh companies made five times more in capital gains than their Scottish counterparts. This history of inequity played a part in the controversy that arose in 1994 between Hydro-Electric and the Office of Electricity Regulation (Offer).

Although privatized, Hydro-Electric remained a monopoly supplier of a public utility, and as such was subject to government regulatory control. It was Offer's task to balance the interests of Britain's electricity consumers against those of the industry's shareholders. The job proved to be a particularly sensitive one in 1994, when Offer assessed the position of the electricity industry for the first time since privatization with a view to setting a new round of pricing controls. The English and Welsh RECs were reviewed first, and the consensus among financial analysts was that the RECs had been treated very leniently. Happy shareholders agreed, and the companies' share prices rocketed to record levels. Some politicians and consumer groups were less pleased, however, and Offer was widely criticized.

Suspiciously minded observers speculated that Offer was mindful of that criticism the following month, when the Scottish companies were assessed with quite a different result. (Bowing to pressure, Offer subsequently announced its intention to re-review the English and Welsh companies, but a decision date was not revealed.) The main point of contention was Offer's proposed price formula for electricity distribution, which allowed the RECs a rate of return of 6.5 to 7 percent, ScottishPower 6 percent—and Hydro-Electric 2 percent. Hydro-Electric's share price dropped dramatically after the regulator's announcement.

ScottishPower accepted Offer's decision, but Hydro-Electric protested vigorously. The company claimed that the stringent pricing controls would render it unable to undertake necessary improvements to its distribution network, on which it spent some £50 million a year. Hydro-Electric warned that power cuts would inevitably be suffered in its rural areas. When outraged critics labeled this nothing short of blackmail, Hydro-Electric chief executive Roger Young replied bleakly: "It isn't blackmail, it's a statement of fact." After a month of deliberations, Hydro-Electric refused to accept Offer's price caps, forcing the regulator to refer the matter to the Monopolies and Mergers Commission (MMC) for arbitration.

After privatization, Hydro-Electric looked to expand its market, in terms of both geography and product. Toward that end, the company began aggressively seeking opportunities

Key Dates:

1881: Street lighting is introduced in the United Kingdom.
1921: By now, more than 480 authorized electricity suppliers operate in England and Wales.
1926: The passing of the Electricity (Supply) Act creates a central authority to encourage and facilitate a national transmission system.
1947: The Electricity Act of 1947 consolidates control of utilities into one government-controlled authority.
1957: A new Electricity Act creates the Central Electricity Generating Board (CEGB).
1989: Scottish Hydro-Electric PLC and Southern Electric PLC are privatized.
1990: Southern Electric goes public.
1991: Hydro-Electric's shares are sold on the stock market.
1998: Scottish Hydro-Electric and Southern Electric merge to form Scottish and Southern Energy PLC.
1999: The U.K. retail power market deregulates.
2000: The company acquires SWALEC.
2004: The company announces a deal with National Grid Transco PLC that, upon completion, will position it as the second largest energy distribution company in the United Kingdom.

south of the border. In 1994–95, Hydro-Electric opened three new power stations in England, each as a 50-50 joint venture with another firm. The biggest project was at Keadby, South Humberside, where Hydro-Electric, in conjunction with Norweb, finished a 680-megawatt combined cycle gas turbine plant, operated through the subsidiary Hydro-Electric Production Services. The other two projects were combined heat and power (CHP) schemes: a 157-megawatt plant built at Sellafield in cooperation with British Nuclear Fuels, and a Dover-based nine-megawatt plant built to deliver steam and electricity to the project's partner, the papermakers Arjo Wiggins Appleton. These three projects together accounted for 15 percent of Hydro-Electric's total generating capacity; add to this electricity generated in Scotland but supplied to England, and Hydro-Electric's production south of the border rose to 30 percent, or about 2 percent of the entire English market.

In 1993 Hydro-Electric launched an important project as a joint venture with the U.S. oil and gas company Marathon: Vector Gas Ltd. With the gas industry well on the road to deregulation, Hydro-Electric was eager to penetrate a wider energy market. Vector sold gas to commercial and industrial customers throughout the United Kingdom under its ''HE Energy'' brand. One of the company's highest-profile clients (among the more than 1,000 it served) was beer and leisure industry giant Scottish & Newcastle.

Gaining experience in the retail gas market was an important move for Hydro-Electric, because its core electricity business was in a region where 40 percent—an unusually high percentage—of water and space heating was provided via electricity. Competition from gas was sure to arise in the future, and Hydro-Electric hoped to be able to persuade its electricity customers to become its gas customers, too, rather than switching to other suppliers.

Clearly Hydro-Electric viewed its future as stretching beyond the boundaries of its traditional role as electricity supplier to the Highlands. While the company stressed that its commitment to its home base of the north of Scotland remained its first priority, it also became apparent from the firm's initiatives and pronouncements that Hydro-Electric intended to continue to expand beyond its borders and beyond its core business to play a significant role in the production and supply of energy in the United Kingdom. Indeed, its merger with Southern Electric plc in 1998 positioned it as one of the United Kingdom's leading energy companies.

The History of Southern Electric

Before its merger with Hydro-Electric, Southern Electric was the second largest regional electricity company in England and Wales, serving 2.5 million domestic, commercial, and industrial customers. Its 16,900-square-kilometer region extended from London in the east to Somerset in the west, and from Oxfordshire in the north to the Isle of Wight in the south. Originating in the public sector as the Southern Electricity Board, Southern Electric was privatized, along with the whole of Britain's electricity industry, in 1989. After that time, the company became involved in separate but related business opportunities. By 1995, Southern Electric's subsidiary interests included utility contracting, investments in power generation projects, environmental engineering, electrical retailing, and supplies of natural gas. In addition, as the electricity industry became increasingly deregulated, Southern Electric began competing directly with other distributors to capture a wider customer base. Southern Electric's principal activity remained, however, its core business of marketing and distributing electricity to central southern England.

Electricity was first harnessed for practical use in the United Kingdom in the late 19th century, with the introduction of street lighting in 1881. By 1921 more than 480 authorized but independent electricity suppliers had arisen throughout England and Wales, resulting in a rather haphazard system operating at different voltages and frequencies. In recognition of the need for a more coherent, interlocking system, the Electricity (Supply) Act of 1926 created a central authority to encourage and facilitate a national transmission system. This objective of a national grid was achieved by the mid-1930s.

The state consolidated its control of the utility with the Electricity Act of 1947, which collapsed the distribution and supply activities of 505 separate bodies into 12 regional area boards, at the same time assigning generating assets and liabilities to one government-controlled authority. A further Electricity Act, in 1957, created a statutory body, the Central Electricity Generating Board (CEGB), which dominated the whole of the electricity system in England and Wales. As generator of virtually all the electricity in the two countries as well as owner and operator of the transmission grid, CEGB supplied electricity to the area boards, which they in turn distributed and sold within their regions.

Such was the situation for 30 years, until the government raised the idea of privatizing the electricity industry in 1987.

The proposal was enshrined in the Electricity Act of 1989, and a new organizational scheme was unveiled. The CEGB was splintered into four divisions, destined to become successor companies: National Power, PowerGen, Nuclear Electric, and the National Grid Company (NGC). The generators National Power and PowerGen were to share between them England and Wales's fossil-fueled power stations; Nuclear Electric was to take over nuclear power stations; and the NGC was to be awarded control of the national electricity distribution system. The 12 area boards, Southern Electric among them, were converted virtually unchanged into 12 regional electricity companies (RECs), and these were given joint ownership of the NGC. Southern Electric was incorporated as a private company in 1989, and its shares, along with those of the other RECs, were the first to be sold to the public, at the end of 1990.

The provision of electricity consisted of four components: generation, transmission, distribution, and supply. In England and Wales, generation was the province of National Power, PowerGen, and Nuclear Electric. Transmission was the transfer of electricity via the national grid, through overhead lines, underground cables, and NGC substations. Distribution was the delivery of electricity from the national grid to local distribution systems operated by the RECs. Supply, a term distinct from distribution in the industry, referred to the transaction whereby electricity was purchased from the generators and transmitted to customers. Under the terms of their licenses, the generators could supply electricity directly to consumers, but that right was comparatively little exercised; their usual customers were the RECs, who in turn sold the electricity to the end users.

A new trading market was devised with the privatization scheme for bulk sales of electricity from generators to distributors—the pool. A rather complicated pricing procedure existed in the pool, according to which each generating station offered a quote for each half-hour of the day, based on an elaborate set of criteria including the operating costs of that particular plant, the time of day, the expected demand for electricity, and the available capacity of the station. The NGC arranged these quotes in a merit order and made the decisions regarding which plant to call into operation when. The pool system was not relied upon exclusively, however, as the generators and distributors frequently made contractual arrangements for a specified period of time as a means of mutual protection against fluctuations in the pool price. Southern Electric's contracts with the generators were arranged for periods of anywhere from 1 to 15 years.

The privatized Southern Electric took as its core business that of the former Southern Electricity Board, in which fully 60 percent of its staff was employed—supplying electricity from the National Grid to its 2.5 million customers via 71,000 kilometers of cables, both above and below ground, and about 51,000 substations. All in all, the company dealt with more than 5,000 megawatts of electricity per year. This immense and complex network cost the company about £100 million each year in development and maintenance costs. About 40 percent of Southern Electric's customers were private homes, 35 percent offices and shops, and 25 percent factories and farms.

The deregulation of the electricity industry changed the face of the business. Under the state-controlled system, customers and suppliers were matched on a purely geographical basis. Beginning in 1991, however, consumers with larger electricity requirements of more than one megawatt, including hospitals, industrial sites, and ports, were free to choose their own suppliers. From 1994, customers demanding more than 100 kilowatts, such as superstores and office buildings, had a similar freedom of choice, and come 1998 a completely free market would be in operation. In this new environment Southern Electric had to compete not only with the other RECs but also with suppliers of other forms of energy, such as British Gas.

In the light of the new competitive era, Southern Electric targeted three key areas in its marketing strategies—industrial, commercial, and domestic—offering free specialist advice to each sector to attract customers. Industrial applications of electricity were myriad and could be refined to suit individual needs with an eye to energy efficiency and cost savings. Southern Electric's clients in this sector included such varied corporations as Parrs Quality Confectionery Ltd., Westinghouse Brakes Ltd., and BICC-Vero Electronics Ltd.

In its bid for commercial clients, Southern Electric offered a range of specialist advisory services, including its Building Energy Appraisal Service (BEAS) and Energy Efficient Design (EED). The company also advised on such applications of electricity as space heating, water heating, ventilation and air conditioning, catering, and lighting. Southern Electric won clients in commercial fields as diverse as education, retailing, leisure, and healthcare. In the domestic sphere, Southern Electric concentrated on providing information and advice to woo customers to electricity in preference to other energy sources where choice was possible, as in cooking, heating, and water heating.

Privatization and increased competition also allowed Southern Electric to move beyond its core business and expand into other, related ventures. Southern Electric Contracting Ltd., which began as a branch of Southern Electric, moved to subsidiary status in 1992. Its business ran the gamut of electrical design and installation work, encompassing everything from domestic needs—such as insulation, fitted kitchens, replacement doors and windows, and rewiring—to complex and often dangerous work for the petrochemical industry. The subsidiary also boasted a public lighting division that was the largest contractor of its kind for local authorities' street lighting, a security systems area, and a datacom division. Operating not only in Southern Electric's traditional region but in Edinburgh, Leeds, Birmingham, and Middlesbrough as well, the subsidiary's clients included public utilities, government departments, universities, and health authorities.

M.P. Burke plc was a post-privatization acquisition. The company was established in 1983 in Yorkshire as a general civil engineering firm, but over the years it became a specialist in utility contracting for the water, gas, electricity, telecommunications, and cable TV industries. Southern Electric Power Generation Ltd., formed in 1992, was Southern Electric's entry into the field of energy generation. During its short existence the subsidiary has invested, as full or part owner, in four combined cycle gas turbine (CCGT) or combined heat and power (CHP) projects. Thermal Transfer Ltd., which was established in 1972 and was later added to Southern Electric's stable, was an environmental engineering company serving the heating, ventilation, and air conditioning markets. The company also served the pharmaceutical, biotechnology, microelectronics, and food industries with design and installation of sterile facilities and mechanical and electrical services. It counted among its clients Bass Brewers, British Aerospace, and Motorola.

In a 1992 joint venture with Phillips Petroleum Company United Kingdom Ltd., Southern Electric formed Southern and Phillips Gas Ltd. Phillips, with its history of oil and gas exploration and production in North Sea fields, provided the gas, while Southern Electric controlled the service, sales, and marketing end of the business. The alliance enabled Southern Electric to offer its customers a choice of energy supply. Clients included Oxford University, Toys 'R' Us, bookseller W.H. Smith, and local government authorities.

Southern Electric also owned, in conjunction with fellow RECs Eastern Electricity and Midlands Electricity, the appliance retailing operation Powerhouse. Formed as a partnership between Southern and Eastern in 1992 and originally known as E & S Retail Ltd., the company had more than 300 outlets in the South, the Midlands, and East Anglia. Powerhouse was the third largest electrical retail group in the United Kingdom, but nonetheless was the most disappointing performer in Southern Electric's portfolio, consistently making losses.

On the whole, however, Southern Electric had fared well since privatization: in 1994 its profits were the highest of all the RECs. This success was due in part to the company's own efforts. Like virtually all privatized companies in Britain, Southern Electric instituted a rigorous program of cost-cutting and efficiency improvement after leaving the public sector. Procedures were streamlined, management structures pared, and fully one quarter of its staff was cut—with more jobs likely to be eliminated in the future.

Another cause of Southern Electric's consistently rising profits was the straightforward expedient of higher prices charged to customers—a sensitive issue for all connected with the industry. Because electricity is an essential utility in the modern world, the privatized industry remains subject to governmental control through the Office of Electricity Regulation (Offer). Offer's task was to ensure that the electricity companies provided a fair deal to customers while at the same time not unduly depressing profits to the detriment of shareholders. Offer's role in maintaining this balance was a highly controversial subject. For example, many observers maintained that the RECs enjoyed a very easy ride after privatization. Some 80 to 95 percent of the RECs' profits derived from the distribution side of their core business. After privatization, the companies were permitted to raise their distribution prices by an average of 1.1 percent over inflation every year. This situation, commented the Independent, "has proved a virtual license to print money."

Offer's first post-privatization review of the industry came in August 1994. The stock market was wary, and the RECs' share prices fluctuated, but in the end Offer was extremely lenient with the RECs, allowing them a significantly higher price cap than had been anticipated. Indeed, many consumer groups and some politicians were outraged by the decision, believing that Offer had weighted the balance too far in favor of the profit motive. Offer was apparently not impervious to this criticism, because some months later, in the spring of 1995, the regulator unexpectedly announced that it would re-review the electricity companies with the intention of tightening price controls. A decision date was not announced. The prolonged suspense returned the stock market to a state of uncertainty.

In one possible scenario, much favored by consumer groups, Offer would limit pricing to 4 percent below inflation as well as insist that the RECs provide cash rebates to customers, although at least one REC publicly questioned the legality of this proposal. If Offer and the RECs found themselves unable to reach an agreement, the Monopolies and Mergers Commission would step in to arbitrate—resulting in a long, drawn-out process to no one's advantage. The uncertainty delayed indefinitely the proposed privatization of the National Grid, jointly owned by the 12 RECs.

Joining Forces in 1998

As Southern Electric, Scottish Hydro-Electric, and their REC peers dealt with changes in pricing structure, they began to experience a wave of merger activity brought on by competition and continued deregulation in the energy sector. By 1999, Britain's retail market would be deregulated, which would allow approximately 23 million customers to choose their energy supplier and end the monopolistic position held by the 12 RECs in England, Wales, and Scotland.

As such, the RECs began looking for deals designed to increase their customer base and generating capacity. The industry began consolidating at breakneck speed. Southern Electric and Scottish Hydro-Electric eventually opted to join forces in a $4.54 billion deal. Completed in 1998, the merger created a well-rounded entity involved in the supply, distribution, and generation of electricity—and one of the largest energy concerns in the United Kingdom. The merged company adopted the Scottish & Southern Energy plc (SSE) name and set plans in motion to expand power generation assets.

Indeed, SSE made several key moves in the early years of the new millennium that strengthened its position in the United Kingdom. In 2000, the company added SWALEC, an energy and gas supplier in Wales, to its arsenal. The success of the deal left SSE looking to make additional purchases. It set its sights on Midlands Electricity, a company owned by U.S.-based Aquila Inc. and First Energy Corp. The deal, worth nearly $1.8 billion, would add 2.3 million customers to SSE's base and increase its hold over the U.K. market. SSE and Midlands' parents failed to agree on a price and the merger was called off in 2003.

Undeterred, SSE forged ahead with its growth strategy. The company acquired Medway Power Station in 2003 and Fife Power in early 2004. Later that year, it purchased the coal-fired Ferrybridge and Fiddler's Ferry Power plant from U.S.-based American Electric Power for $454 million. With both sales and net income on the rise, SSE set its sights on making the largest purchase in its six-year history. In September 2004 it announced a deal with National Grid Transco plc that would position it as the second largest energy distribution company in the United Kingdom. The £3.16 billion purchase would include two gas distribution networks and was expected to be completed in April 2005.

SSE enjoyed success in the years after the 1999 deregulation. It stood as the largest renewable power generator in the United Kingdom and its nonutility businesses—gas storage and telecommunications—were growing rapidly. The company also stood to benefit from the 2005 introduction of the British Electricity Trading and Transmission Arrangements (BETTA). According to the company, the BETTA would create a single, unified electricity market across the United Kingdom and would extend electricity trading agreements currently operating in England and Wales to Scotland.

In the coming years, SSE planned to focus on maintaining and investing its networks, strengthening and adding to its generation holdings, growing its energy supply business, and fostering new growth in the areas of contracting, new connections, and gas storage. With the National Grid deal in the works, the company appeared to be on track for success in the U.K. energy market for years to come.

Principal Operating Units

Southern Electric plc; SWALEC; Scottish Hydro-Electric plc; Generation; Power Distribution; SSE Network Solutions; Gas Storage; SSE Telecom; SSE Contracting Group; hienergyshop; Simple2; Neos.

Principal Competitors

Centrica plc; E.ON UK plc; RWE Innogy.

Further Reading

Baur, Chris, "The Words and Pictures of the Noble Adventure," *Hydro-Electric Business,* Spring/Summer 1993, pp. 20–21.

" 'Blackmail' Claim Over Electricity Pricing," *Herald,* December 10, 1994.

Buckley, Christine, "Corporate Profile-SSE," *Times,* October 18, 1999.

Calder, Colin, "Vector Puts New Gas into Brewing," *Hydro-Electric Business,* Spring/Summer, 1994, pp. 30–32.

"Electricity Price Controls Thrown into Confusion," *Scotsman,* November 16, 1994.

"Fifty Years of Hydro-Electric," *Hydro-Electric Business,* Spring/Summer 1993, pp. 18–19.

Frank, Robert, "Southern Electric, Scottish Hydro to Join," *Wall Street Journal Europe,* September 2, 1998.

Fraser, Ian, "SSE Defends (pounds) 3bn Transco Asset Deal," *Sunday Herald,* September 5, 2004.

Holberton, Simon, "Rewiring Britain's Electricity Industry," *Financial Post,* December 7, 1996.

"Hydro Drive South Starts to Pay Off," *Scotsman,* December 9, 1994.

"Hydro in Highland Power Cuts Warning," *Times,* December 9, 1994.

"Hydro Is Looking South to Offset Highland Limitations," *Herald,* December 9, 1994.

"Merged Power Generators Set for Speedy Expansion," *Engineer,* September 4, 1998, p. 1.

"Plugging into the Power Profits," *Scotsman,* September 30, 1994.

"Power Firms Spurn Concern Over Bills by Pegging Prices," *Guardian,* March 4, 1994.

Power from the Glens, Perth: Scottish Hydro-Electric PLC, n.d.

"Power Struggle," *Herald,* December 10, 1994.

Reguly, Eric, "Southern Electric Plans to Eliminate 1,200 More Jobs," *Times,* December 14, 1994.

"Scots Electric Shares Slide As Price Curbs Put in Place," *Guardian,* September 30, 1994.

"Scots Power Runs into Littlechild," *Daily Telegraph,* September 30, 1990.

"Scots Power Shares Plunge on Price Review," *Herald,* September 30, 1994.

"Scottish Power Groups Hit by Tougher Price Controls," *Daily Telegraph,* September 30, 1994.

"Southern Chief Warns Regulator Over Service Standards," *Guardian,* June 24, 1994.

"Southern Electric Powers On to Lift Payout and Profit," *Times,* June 24, 1994.

"Southern Electric Surges to £222 Million," *Independent,* June 24, 1994.

"Southern Electric's Buyback Triggers a Buzz," *Independent,* May 4, 1994.

"Southern Seeks Efficiency Reward," *Daily Telegraph,* June 24, 1994.

This Is Southern Electric, Maidenhead: Southern Electric PLC, 1993.

"UK Company News: Scottish Hydro-Electric Declines 23 Percent to Pounds 35 Million," *Financial Times,* December 9, 1994.

"UK Company News: Southern Electric Up at £222 Million," *Financial Times,* June 24, 1994.

"VAT Adds Cold Comfort to Order to Cut Power Bills," *Herald,* September 30, 1994.

Waller, Martin, "Eastern Doubts Legality of Electricity Bill Rebates," *Times,* April 10, 1995.

——, "Work Resumes on Flotation of Grid," *Times,* April 3, 1995.

Wilkinson, Paul, "Building on Experience at Keadby," *Hydro-Electric Business,* Spring/Summer 1994, pp. 14–17.

Wilson, Andrew, "Scottish & Southern Energy Generates Heat," *Herald,* November 16, 2000.

Yilmaz, Eral, "Scottish & Southern Buy AEP Power Plants," *WMRC Daily Analysis,* August 2, 2004.

—Robin DuBlanc
—update: Christina M. Stansell

SENNHEISER

Sennheiser Electronic GmbH & Co. KG

Am Labor 1
D-30900 Wedemark
Germany
Telephone: (+49) (5130) 600-0
Fax: (+49) (5130) 600-300
Web site: http://www.sennheiser.com

Private Company
Incorporated: 1945 as Laboratorium Wennebostel (Labor W)
Employees: 1,579
Sales: EUR 237.2 million ($297.8 million) (2003)
NAIC: 33431 Audio and Video Equipment Manufacturing; 33422 Radio and Television Broadcasting and Wireless Communications Equipment Manufacturing

Based near Hannover, Germany, Sennheiser Electronic GmbH & Co. KG is one of the world's leading manufacturers of audio equipment. The company's Berlin-based subsidiary Neumann GmbH is the world market leader for top quality studio recording microphones. An established supplier to the global music and entertainment industry and to the broadcasting media, most of Sennheiser's revenues come from high-end microphones and headsets for professional and personal use, including special noise-canceling headsets for pilots and headsets for call centers and multimedia applications. Sennheiser also makes hearing aids and wireless broadcasting systems and equips conference centers, museums, and trade shows with audio-communication systems. While roughly 60 percent of the company's output is manufactured in Germany, Sennheiser exports four-fifths of its total output, with the United States the company's largest geographical market. Foreign production facilities are located in Tullamore, Ireland, and in Albuquerque, New Mexico, in the United States. Sennheiser products, which received numerous industry awards, are distributed by authorized dealers all around the world. The family enterprise is owned and directed by the founder's son.

From Scientist to Entrepreneur after World War II

Company founder Fritz Sennheiser was a realist by nature, and it was this quality that put him on track to entrepreneurial success. In the early 1930s, when confronted with the decision of what professional path he should pursue, the young man abandoned his dream of becoming an landscape gardener. At a time of economic depression, he had concluded, the demand for such services would be very limited. Therefore, Sennheiser decided to pursue his second career choice and became an electrical engineer. He studied wave technology at the Technical University's Heinrich-Hertz-Institute—at the time Germany's center for radio technology—in his home town of Berlin. In 1938, Sennheiser followed his professor to Hannover's Technical University, where he helped him establish a new research institute for radio frequency technology and electro-acoustics. The institute worked on encoded language transmission and developed radio devices for the German army. Sennheiser received his Ph.D. and later became the institute's deputy head. During World War II, the institute's building was destroyed by heavy bombing and its staff of roughly 50 moved into an old farm house in Wennebostel, a small town north of Hannover. After Germany's defeat in the spring of 1945, the Hannover region was occupied by the British Allied Forces. The British military administration made all research in the area of radio frequency and encoding a capital crime but offered Sennheiser the opportunity to continue his work at Cambridge, England.

Sennheiser did not want to leave his country and declined. However, with Germany's academic landscape in ruins, there was no other place where he could make his living as a scientist doing research in his field. With the former institute's remaining staff of seven, Sennheiser decided to make a new start and to found a private enterprise. In 1945, with his personal savings as his start-up capital, Sennheiser established a radio mechanics workshop and research laboratory on the former institute's premises, which he called Laboratorium Wennebostel, in short, "Labor W." Equipped with some of the old institute's machinery the British had forgotten to dismantle, Sennheiser and his seven employees went to work.

Labor W's first products were made out of seven measuring devices the British had left behind on the institute's premises.

Company Perspectives:

Our commitment to the world of audio is simple: we offer products that provide the finest combination of performance and value available anywhere, and back them up with superlative service. Success is a result of good planning combined with good luck. Yet today, one might be the very best planner, and enjoy incredible luck, yet still be limited in pursuit of success unless he or she recognizes an additional ingredient in the success formula. PEOPLE . . . because no matter how great the product or service offered; no matter how attractive the price/performance ratio; no matter how grand and innovative the marketing efforts; the bottom line is that today's knowledgeable and demanding consumers require the service and support that is only possible through high quality people. Delight our Stakeholders; our associates, customers and suppliers. Demand Excellence; in our products; services and people. Deliver Results; to do what we say we will do. *Our team understands fully that consumers have many choices today. The consumer's commitment to a company and/or product is predicated on a number of things including products, performance, price, services, and among other things; their loyalty, however, is primarily due to people. The Sennheiser team is dedicated to a singular goal; your Total Satisfaction.*

Sennheiser and his staff converted the devices into valve voltmeters, and Sennheiser made his first successful sale at the Hannover branch of German electric appliances manufacturer Siemens. Siemens bought all seven instruments. Some time later, Sennheiser heard back from them again. The company asked if Labor W could take over the production of a special microphone for radio stations. Sennheiser's team agreed to rebuild the ''MD1'' microphone from the model they were given by Siemens, since the former supplier's factory had been destroyed in the war. During the postwar years, Labor W developed valuable know-how in microphone technology that laid the foundation for a successful private enterprise.

Commercial Success with Innovative Microphones in the 1950s

Two years after Sennheiser's team of researchers had begun to build the ''MD 1'' for Siemens, they came up with their own, improved model, the ''MD 2.'' Beginning in 1949, the company decided to market the patented model under the ''Labor W'' label and to establish the necessary distribution network. However, most of the company's business was still done with Siemens, which in turn helped ''Labor W'' to become a respected manufacturer in the field of electro-acoustics. Dedicated to pushing the limits in the chosen field, Sennheiser's research team began to put out a constant stream of innovative microphone designs that often set industry standards for many decades.

In 1950, Labor W introduced the ''MD 3'' ''invisible microphone''—an extremely slim design with a tiny head did not obstruct an audiences's view of a performer's face as conventional models did. In 1951, the company launched the ''MD 4'' noise-canceling microphone that suppressed feedback and ambient noise—a novelty in the market. A major success was the introduction of the ''MD 21'' reporter's microphone in 1954. It's rugged and sturdy design and extreme reliability made it a long-term bestseller among the world's radio and TV-broadcasters. In 1958, the company launched the wireless transmission system ''Mikroport.'' Consisting of a small microphone and a pocket radio transmitter, it allowed TV-show hosts to move more freely in the studio. Besides microphones for the broadcasting and entertainment industry, Labor W developed magnetic acoustic transducers for use in dictating machines and hearing aids. For many years, the company became the sole supplier of these miniaturized microphones, which were roughly the size of a dime, to German manufacturers of dictating machines and hearing aids. The company also developed amplifiers and microphones for telephone receivers.

Due to the quickly rising demand—driven by the growing number of TV and radio stations and the introduction of dictation devices—Labor W grew rapidly. Sennheiser, whose goal initially was merely to create a source of income for himself and his former co-workers, was repeatedly overwhelmed by his own success. He had never intended to employ more than 100 employees. However, that number was soon surpassed. Even the next limit he set himself of 300 employees did not last long. Labor W was riding the wave of rapid expansion, fueled by the German ''economic miracle'' following World War II. Between 1950 and 1960, the company's sales exploded, from roughly half a million deutsche marks in 1950 to almost ten million a decade later. During the same time period, the company's payroll grew from 67 to 695 employees. Labor W had become a major supplier to the German electronics industry, selling its products to brand name manufacturers such as Telefunken and Grundig. However, with the number of competitors on the rise, the original equipment manufacturer (OEM) business became less profitable. To lower the company's dependence on its industrial clients, Labor W focused its marketing efforts on its own brand name. In 1958, the company was renamed Sennheiser Electronic, which also became the company's new brand name.

Sennheiser Brand Takes off in the 1960s

Slowly but steadily, Sennheiser established a network of authorized dealers and expanded the company's production facilities. Determined to preserve the company's independence from outside investors, the pace of this expansion was dictated by the cash flow available for investment. Sennheiser's own brand name business took off during the 1960s. Sales from products with the Sennheiser label rose to roughly two-fifths of total sales by 1966 and reached 50 percent by the end of the decade. At the same time, the company's export business began to thrive, reaching about one-third of total sales by 1969.

Much of this success was due to two new Sennheiser products that became instant bestsellers. One of them, the MD 421 dynamic studio microphone, was introduced in 1960. Its flexibility of use, excellent sound reproduction, and long durability made the MD 421 a long-term bestseller. Another commercial success of the 1960s in the professional microphone market were Sennheiser's condenser gun microphones, which featured a highly directional pickup pattern that was able to capture the sound in TV and film studios within the viewing angle of the

Key Dates:

1945: Fritz Sennheiser establishes Laboratorium Wennebostel.
1949: Labor W begins to market its products independently.
1954: The ''MD 21'' reporter's microphone is introduced.
1958: The company is renamed Sennheiser Electronic.
1960: The ''MD 421'' studio microphone is successfully launched.
1968: The ''open'' hi-fi headphone set ''HD 414'' becomes an instant bestseller.
1976: Sennheiser is transformed into a limited partnership.
1977: A production subsidiary in Burgdorf near Hannover begins operations.
1982: Jörg Sennheiser takes over management of the family business.
1988: The ''NoiseGuard'' headset for pilots is launched.
1991: Headset production is moved to Ireland.
1991: Sennheiser Electronic Corporation is established in the United States.
1992: The company acquires Berlin-based microphone manufacturer Neumann GmbH.
2000: Sennheiser introduces the ''AudioBeam'' technology.
2003: The joint venture Sennheiser Communications A/S is founded.

camera while remaining free of ambient noise outside this range. The ''gun mics'' became a mainstay in Hollywood's dream factories and elsewhere in the world.

In 1968, Sennheiser entered the headset market with the HD414, the first dynamic stereo headphones with an ''open'' design. Patented in 1967, the HD414 was the result of experiments at Sennheiser that led to a completely new headset design. Until then, headsets had a closed capsule to insulate the listener's ear from outside noise. The experiments showed that an open design that allowed that kind of noise created a more natural sound impression. However, with portable audio devices such as Walkman cassette players merely in the research pipeline of the world's consumer electronics giants, the market for such headsets seemed very limited. A conservative market prognosis predicted a world market of under 1,000 such headsets. Sennheiser was optimistic and produced 5,000. Yet the market success of the HD414 was so overwhelming that the company struggled to catch up with demand for many years.

Sennheiser's success in continually developing innovative products was made possible by the company founders' conviction that his engineers needed a lot of freedom to experiment. In the company's 50th anniversary chronicle, this attitude was described in Fritz Sennheiser's own words: ''I am convinced that you cannot be an innovator in product design and development if your engineers are not allowed to tinker around and come up with new ideas. After all, business isn't only about selling products. Above all, it's about selling ideas.'' A scientific researcher and technological innovator by heart, Sennheiser protected this ''freedom to play'' of his engineers against the constant attacks from his bottom-line oriented sales manager, who pressed him to focus the company's development efforts solely on marketable products. Lavishly funded with 11 percent of the company's total sales, Sennheiser's research and development department was easily able to compete with that of a large consumer electronics manufacturer.

Naturally, not all of the ideas Sennheiser's engineers came up with were accepted by the customers they had in mind. One example was ''Philharmonic,'' the first hi-fi system with active speakers and a remote control. The expensive system sold poorly and its production was phased out a few years after it was introduced. However, Sennheiser's continuous innovation efforts provided the basis for the company's success in the following decades.

Expansion and Leadership Change: 1970s–80s

By the beginning of the 1970s, Sennheiser was an established brand name for high-quality professional audio equipment such as microphones and headsets. At a time when Japanese consumer electronics manufacturers flooded the world market with new audio equipment at low prices, Sennheiser decided to stick with the company's policy of developing innovative new products of high quality in its established niche markets that allowed higher profit margins. However, in order to secure future growth, the company began to expand its network of authorized dealers and sales subsidiaries in Europe and all over the world. By the end of the 1970s, there were 57 authorized dealers and sales offices for Sennheiser products: 23 in Europe, 25 in Asia, and nine in North America. Even the speeches of Soviet political leaders in the Kremlin were captured by Sennheiser microphones. These efforts to expand the company's markets yielded impressive results. Sennheiser's sales increased from DEM 18 million in 1970 to DEM 63 million in 1980. By the late 1970s, the company's production capacity reached its limits. However, Fritz Sennheiser was able to solve this problem almost immediately. When the premises and buildings of a bankrupt company only 15 miles from Wennebostel were auctioned off, he walked in with a suitcase of cash and bought the new site on the spot. The new production subsidiary opened in 1977.

The year 1982 marked an important milestone in Sennheiser's history. Company founder Fritz Sennheiser decided to hand over the reins to his son Jörg. Jörg Sennheiser had practically grown up with the company. He began to play with spare parts from the factory as a young boy and later started building his own devices—often with the help of Sennheiser's engineers. Not surprisingly, the junior Sennheiser became an acoustic-electric engineer himself. After receiving his Ph.D., Sennheiser began to work for the company's very first customer—Siemens. It was there that he decided to take over the family enterprise. In 1976, the company was transformed into Sennheiser KG, a limited partnership, and the founder's son became the limited partner. After taking over as CEO in 1982, Jörg Sennheiser initiated some changes in management. The company's marketing efforts were geared at two different segments—professionals and consumers—and each segment was managed by a designated product manager. In 1984, Sennheiser launched a product development plan for the next decade and focused its efforts on putting out tailor-made products for these different market segments.

During the 1980s, Sennheiser's engineers pioneered wireless transmission and noise reduction technologies and refined its existing product lines. In 1980, the company introduced its first wireless vocal microphone, followed one year later by a pocket-sized radio transmitter and an accompanying receiver. Partly funded by Germany's second public TV station, ZDF, the new wireless technology made possible complete freedom on stage with flawless sound reproduction of live stage shows such as musicals. In 1983, Sennheiser launched a new kind of hearing aid based on infrared technology. Sennheiser's efforts in refining the company's line of professional studio microphones were intensified to match the new technical standards of the upcoming digital recording technologies. The company founder's life work culminated in 1987, when Fritz Sennheiser received the ''Scientific and Engineering Award,'' the ''technical Oscar'' awarded by the American Academy of Motion Picture Arts and Sciences, for the MKH 816 interference tube microphone.

Becoming a Global Player: 1990s–2000s

In the late 1980s, competition among manufacturers of audio equipment—and consequently cost pressures—began to intensify. Sennheiser reacted by entering new markets with a number of innovative products and technologies, by expanding the company's network of foreign subsidiaries, by intensifying the company's marketing communication, by moving production to countries where labor was cheaper, and by taking over one of its competitors. Following an inquiry from the German airline Lufthansa, Sennheiser introduced the ''NoiseGuard'' headset for pilots in 1988. The NoiseGuard technology cut the ambient noise pilots are exposed to in the cockpit in half and was subsequently adopted by many of the world's airlines. The technology was later developed further for use in Sennheiser's hearing aids. Throughout the 1990s, Sennheiser continued to refine radio frequency- and infrared-based wireless technologies for microphones, headphones, and transmission systems as well as for high-end hi-fi consumers. Another invention, the ''AudioBeam'' technology, was presented by Sennheiser in 2000. AudioBeam made it possible to focus sound waves similar to beams of light. The result was that sound could be projected upon a limited area very precisely. Museums and trade shows were among the first applications of the AudioBeam technology, where the sound of multimedia exhibits could be directed from above at the visitor in front of it, while it was not audible farther away from the exhibit.

Beginning in 1988, Sennheiser founded a number of foreign subsidiaries to strengthen the company's presence in major markets, such as France, the United Kingdom, Belgium, the Netherlands, Singapore, the United States, Canada, and Mexico. To complement Sennheiser's product range, these subsidiaries also took on the distribution of speakers and amplifiers from other brand name manufacturers. The company's subsidiary in the United States, Sennheiser Electronic Corporation, was established in 1991 and soon gained a considerable market share. In 1999, a production plant was built in Albuquerque, New Mexico, to satisfy the growing demand for Sennheiser products in North and South America. By 2001, the United States had become the company's single most important geographical market.

In 1991, Sennheiser moved its headset production to Ireland to cut cost. One year later, the company acquired German microphone manufacturer Georg Neumann GmbH. Founded in 1928, the Berlin-based company had achieved a reputation for making the best studio microphones in the world. After the takeover, production of ''Neumann'' microphones was moved to Wennebostel, while product development, distribution, and customer service remained in Germany's capital. The production of high-tech components for microphones was outsourced to suppliers in Asia in the late 1990s but later moved back to Germany for quality reasons. However, Sennheiser outsourced the production of cables and components made from plastic.

After a short dip in sales accompanied by higher cost caused by the reorganization after the Neumann-takeover in the early 1990s, Sennheiser got back on the growth track in a generally stagnating market. In 2003, the company launched a joint venture, Sennheiser Communications A/S, together with Danish William Demant Holding A/S. Headquartered in Kopenhagen, Denmark, the new subsidiary entered the expanding market of telecommunications and multimedia with the introduction of five headsets designed for use in call centers and for facilities with computer-based multimedia applications.

In 1996, Jörg Sennheiser handed over the day-to-day management of the business to an external management team. Sennheiser became the president of the newly established advisory board of Sennheiser Electronic GmbH & Co. KG and focused mainly on public relations and the future direction the company might take. In the near future, he saw NoiseGuard and AudioBeam applications for passenger cars. Convinced that the area of electro-acoustics would be able to sustain the company into the 21st century, he foresaw appliances that automatically adapted to the users' personal preferences and mood and that improved communication between people. Standing on a sound financial basis, Sennheiser still financed its expanding research and development programs from the company's cash flow. Since the founding family's goal remained to keep the company vital in the long run, there were no plans to go public. Jörg Sennheiser's three children—all in their twenties or thirties—may or may not become actively involved in the family enterprise. ''They can apply for a job, if they want to work for Sennheiser,'' the founder's son told *Süddeutsche Zeitung* in 2000 and added: ''There is no family privilege.''

Principal Subsidiaries

Sennheiser Electronic Corporation (United States); Sennheiser Electronic ASIA Pte. Ltd (Singapore); Sennheiser France SARL; Sennheiser U.K. Ltd.; Sennheiser Belux BVBA; Sennheiser Canada Inc.; Sennheiser Nederland B.V. (Netherlands); Sennheiser Mexico S.A.

Principal Competitors

AKG Acoustics GmbH; BEHRINGER Spezielle Studiotechnik GmbH; Shure Incorporated; Harman International Industries, Incorporated; Telex Communications, Inc.; Nady Systems Inc.; CAD Professional Microphones; RODE Microphones; JVC Company of America; Pioneer Corporation; Audio-Technica Corporation.

Further Reading

''Brakhan, Former President of Sennheiser, Dies,'' *Pro Sound News*, March 1, 2004, p. 14.

Fifty Years Sennheiser, Wedemark, Germany: Sennheiser Electronic KG, 1995, 102 p.

''Fritz Sennheiser 90 Jahre,'' *Frankfurter Allgemeine Zeitung*, May 7, 2002, p. 23.

''Neue Rechtsform für Sennheiser,'' *Frankfurter Allgemeine Zeitung*, March 28, 1996, p. 22.

''Sennheiser and Marc Look to Web Lounge to Reach Young Men,'' *Brandweek*, June 14, 2004, p. 32.

—Evelyn Hauser

Shoppers Food Warehouse Corporation

4600 Forbes Boulevard
Lanham, Maryland 20706
U.S.A.
Telephone: (301) 306-8600
Fax: (301) 306-8855
Web site:http://www.shoppersfood.com

Wholly Owned Subsidiary of Supervalu Inc.
Incorporated: 1956 as Jumbo Food Stores
Employees: 5,000
Sales: $971.7 million (2002)
NAIC: 445110 Supermarkets and Other Grocery (Except Convenience Stores)

A subsidiary of Supervalu Inc., Shoppers Food Warehouse Corporation operates a chain of 57 warehouse-style supermarkets, serving Delaware, Maryland, Virginia, and the Washington, D.C., markets. The company's headquarters is located in Lanham, Maryland. Although its takes a no-frills approach—items are presented for sale in their own packing cartons and customers bag their own food—Shoppers offers a wider range of products and services than other warehouse chains, including baked goods, cookware, produce, salad bars, and prepared food.

Founder Opens First Grocery Store in 1929

The founders of Shoppers were two brothers, Irving and Kenneth Herman. Their parents were Russian immigrants who opened a small delicatessen in northwest Washington, D.C., in 1919. The boys worked in the store, sweeping floors and stocking shelves, while the family lived in the back. Irving did not intend to devote his life to the grocery business and was instead interested in becoming a lawyer. While attending George Washington University Law School, however, he opened a grocery store in Washington, financed by a $300 wedding present and a loan of some $500, and ran it with his wife Toby. After finishing law school the next year, he was prepared to get out of the business and start practicing law, but with the country lapsing into the Great Depression of the 1930s, his prospects for a legal career were dim. His bank loan officer, who had been keeping tabs on Herman's grocery store, weighed in with his opinion, "I've seen many unemployed lawyers. Stay in business." Herman took his advice. Several years later, he was joined by his brother, and in the late 1930s they launched the first Jumbo Food Stores—Shoppers' predecessor.

With the population boom during the post-World War II years and the rise of the supermarket concept, the Herman brothers successfully added several Jumbo stores in the area surrounding Washington, D.C. Irving's son, Michael, also became involved in running the business. By the mid-1970s, however, the company grew stagnant and was in trouble financially. In order to stay afloat, it had to seek concessions from an employee union. Desperate for a way to turnaround the company, the Hermans decided to try the warehouse approach and opened their first Shoppers Food Warehouse in 1978. A key factor in the move was the computer technology that by this time had become instrumental in the supermarket industry. By scanning items at the cash register, the Hermans realized, a store could maintain much better control of both inventory and prices. The concept was to eliminate private-label goods and sell only name brand products, but at prices 20 to 30 percent lower than conventional supermarkets. Shoppers would be able to maintain a pricing edge by keeping employment and services to a minimum. Hence, items were simply stacked in their packing boxes and customers bagged their own groceries.

The Shoppers formula worked, and the company began to convert all of its Jumbo stores to the new warehouse format. In 1986, the company dropped the Jumbo name in favor of Shoppers. The Hermans were not the only grocers to try the warehouse format, but they were more successful at its implementation than others, a key factor in the highly competitive Washington market. The area was dominated by Giant and Safeway, and a number of major chains—Acme, Grand Union, Memco, and Pantry Pride—had all attempted to break into the market and failed. Shoppers was able to take advantage of the situation, buying some of the shuttered stores and opening warehouse units in their place. As a result, Shoppers, with 11 stores, rose to third place in the market, albeit a distant third, controlling just 5.7 percent, or $211 million of a $3.6 billion market.

Company Perspectives:

Your one-stop shop for groceries, prescriptions, and all your banking needs.

Ownership Changes in the Late 1980s–Early 1990s

Shoppers reached a turning point in 1988. Irving Herman was ready to retire, and his son Michael wanted to exit the business to pursue other interests. As a result, the family was open to selling part of the company and found an ideal suitor in Dart Group Corp., which operated the Trak Auto discount auto parts chain and the Crown Books chain. Dart's chairman was Herbert Haft, who was also the son of Russian immigrants and had attended high school and George Washington University with Kenneth Herman. Haft had made his fortune in the drugstore business. His father had owned a Baltimore drugstore, where Haft worked as a child, and after becoming a pharmacist he opened his first Dart drugstore in downtown Washington in 1954. He eventually built his business into a 73-store discount chain and became a major player in real estate. Haft's son Robert, who held a Harvard MBA, joined Dart in 1977 and launched Crown. Two years later, Dart established the Trak Auto. In 1984, Dart sold off the original drug store chain and the Hafts became involved in takeover bids as a way to enter the supermarket business. They failed in their attempts to land Safeway Stores Inc., Supermarkets General Corp., and Stop & Shop Co. However, they made money selling their shares at a premium, which led to the perception that they were not truly interested in food retailing, just stock speculation. The hope was that by becoming involved with Shoppers, the Hafts would gain some credibility as food retailers, and when making future bids in the industry they would not simply be dismissed as hostile raiders.

Upon the completion of the sale of a 50 percent interest in Shoppers to Dart, for approximately $17 million, Irving Herman retired as chairman and son Michael resigned as executive vice-president. Shoppers' board would now be co-chaired by Kenneth Herman and Herbert Haft. Although Dart now held a controlling interest in Shoppers, Herman retained an option to reacquire one share and regain control of the company. The Hermans continued to run the chain on a day-to-day basis, while Dart was expected to help the chain grow internally by using its knowledge and connections in drugs and cosmetics to bolster sales in those areas, help in improving the look of the stores, and use its real estate expertise in the selection of new locations.

Over the new few years, Shoppers enjoyed steady growth. Its market share in Washington increased to 7.7 percent in 1989, 8.5 percent in 1990, and 10.3 percent in 1991. The total number of stores also grew to 27. The chain's success was due in part to a recession that made the chain's price-conscious approach more appealing to many consumers, as well as an aggressive advertising campaign. The Shoppers logo was prominently displayed on the scoreboard at Washington Redskins football games at RFK Stadium, and newspaper ads featured comparisons of cash register tapes from Shoppers, Giant, and Safeway. Shoppers' television advertisements were also prevalent. Although Giant and Safeway remained the undisputed market leaders, Shoppers' inroads forced the larger chains to take countermeasures, such as doubling coupons. Shoppers positioned itself for further growth by continuing to open new stores and acquiring existing stores from smaller competitors, such as Basics. In 1992, the chain opened seven new stores, and its market share improved to 11 percent. Nevertheless, all was not well with the company. Much of its recent success was due to the large number of new store openings. Same-stores sales, however, were either flat or negative. Some of the problem stemmed from the real estate choices made by Dart, which sometimes located stores too close to one another, more concerned with what was good business for the real estate unit rather than what made sense from a food retailing point of view.

Shoppers' relationship with Dart was also complicated by a Haft family feud that broke out in 1993 and soon turned into a virtual soap opera. Herbert Haft, 72 years old, had made plans to retire as Dart's CEO and turn over the reins to his 40-year-old son Robert. However, he changed his mind, which according to some sources was prompted by a *Wall Street Journal* article that called Robert the "de facto chief executive for the last two years." At a contentious board meeting, Herbert's wife Gloria took the side of their son, and Herbert responded by having both of them ousted from the board. She then divorced him after 50 years of marriage, ultimately winning a $14 million settlement, and the son sued over being fired, winning $40 million. Herbert Haft promoted younger son Ronald to the presidency of Dart, but this faction in the family squabble—which pitted them against Gloria, Robert, and a sister named Linda—proved short-lived. They would fall out when Ronald accused his father of borrowing $18 million from Dart without board approval and insisted he return the money. The two then began hurling accusations at each other in stormy board meetings, which in recent years had become a forum for family squabbles. In an attempt to shelter control of Dart from his wife, Herbert had sold his voting shares to Ronald, who now took advantage of the situation to sell those shares back to the company, thus diluting his father's controlling interest to less than 50 percent. In this way, he was able to have his father removed as chairman.

Another person with whom Herbert Haft had a falling out during this period was his old friend Kenneth Herman. In June 1994, Herman elected to exercise the option to reacquire one share of Shoppers and wrested back control of the chain. In this way, Shoppers would no longer be pushed into unsuitable locations and Herman's son, Robert, would be in line to succeed him as chairman. According to press reports, Herbert Haft opposed the nomination of Robert Herman to the top post, preferring instead to have the chain brought under his management control.

Over the next four years, Shoppers operated with Dart and the Herman family each owning 50 percent of the company. Despite internal friction during this time, the chain managed to add stores and market share. In 1996, Shoppers totaled 34 units, generating $830 million in sales with a 13.5 percent market share. Shoppers also introduced a new, larger format, some 75,000 square feet in size, called Shoppers Club. These four units combined elements of price clubs and warehouse supermarkets. In addition, Shoppers began introducing cafes in its 30 other warehouse stores. Both the Hermans and Dart were by now interested in severing their ties and dissolving the uncomfortable board arrangement of Kenneth Herman, Robert Her-

Key Dates:

1929: Irving Herman opens a Washington, D.C., grocery store.
1956: Jumbo Food Stores is incorporated.
1978: The first warehouse format store opens.
1986: Jumbo Foods changes its name to Shoppers Food Warehouse.
1999: Supervalu Inc. acquires Shoppers chain.
2002: Irving Herman dies at age 95.

man, Herbert Haft, and Ronald Haft. However, any sale would be subject to the terms of a complicated buy-sell agreement, which stipulated that if one side wanted to sell, it had to set a price. The other side then had 120 days to either buy half the business at that price or sell its half. Thus, there was a great deal of pressure on the initiating partner to set the right price: too low and the other side bought the business on the cheap, while too high a price would likely saddle the initiating partner with a heavy debt load. As a result, neither side wanted to make the first move. To speed the process along, Shoppers hired New York-based investment firm Lazard Freres to help in determining the market price of the chain, but Dart was clearly in a position where it needed to take action. In December 1996, Dart triggered the buy-sell provision, setting a $210 million price for a 50 percent interest in Shoppers. The Herman family agreed to sell its stake, and the transaction was completed in February 1997. Two months later, Dart settled its differences with Herbert Haft, who agreed to a $41 million settlement to relinquish control of the company and step down as CEO and chairman.

Late 1990s and Beyond

Shoppers was only fully owned by Dart for little more than a year. In April 1998, Richfood Holdings Inc., a regional wholesale distributor, agreed to acquire Dart's outstanding stock in order to acquire Shoppers. Dart's other assets—Trak Auto, Crown Books, and Total Beverage—were either sold or spun off. The addition of Shoppers, along with the acquisition of the 45-store Farm Fresh supermarket chain a month earlier and 17 Metro stores already owned, made Richfood into a regional powerhouse in the area with nearly 100 stores. Acquiring Shoppers was also a necessity for Richfood because its supply contract with the chain was set to expire, and the distributor could not afford to lose the business—although Richfood's CEO, John E. Stokely, maintained that Richfood did not "do things for defensive reasons."

With the supermarket industry undergoing a period of intense consolidation, Richfood was dealt a severe blow in 1999 when major wholesale customer Giant Food Stores elected not to renew its contract to buy dry goods through Richfood after 1999. The decision came in anticipation of Giant's corporate parent acquiring Pathmark Stores and establishing its own internal distribution operation for its extensive supermarket holdings. Less than two months later, Richfood was sold to Minneapolis-based SuperValu Inc. for $882 million, a move that both parties had to make given the consolidation going on in the industry.

Despite a number of changes in ownership during a short period of time, Shoppers continued to grow in the Washington market. With Supervalu's backing, the chain acquired four former Superfresh stores in Maryland and Virginia. In 2003 and 2004, Supervalu demonstrated its commitment to the Shoppers format by converting all of the 15 Metro supermarkets acquired from Richfood to Shoppers. When the conversion was completed, the Shoppers chain had 58 stores in the Washington, D.C., area. In the meantime, in September 2002, Shoppers co-founder, Irving Herman, the law school graduate who decided to sell groceries rather than practice law, died at the age of 95.

Principal Competitors

Giant Food LLC; Safeway Inc.; Wal-Mart Stores, Inc.

Further Reading

Lundegaard, Karen M., "One Share Makes All the Difference with Shoppers Food," *Baltimore Business Journal*, August 26, 1994, p. 40.

Mayer, Caroline E., "Jumbo Hungry for Larger Share of Grocery Pie," *Washington Post*, p. F01.

Orgel, David, "Theory of Evolution," *Supermarket News*, October 28, 1996, p. 1.

Sun, Lena H., "Survival in the Land of Giants—and Safeways," *Washington Post*, June 5, 1989, p. F01.

Swisher, Kara, "Shoppers Takes on the Titans," *Washington Post*, September 16, 1991, p. F01.

—Ed Dinger

Siderar S.A.I.C.

Avenida Leandro N. Alem 1067
Buenos Aires, C.F. C1001AAF
Argentina
Telephone: (54) (11) 4018-2100
Fax: (54) (11) 4318-2460; 4318-6417
Web site: http://www.siderar.com

Public Company
Incorporated: 1962
Employees: 4,724
Sales: ARS 2.73 billion ($925.42 million) (2003)
Stock Exchanges: Buenos Aires
Ticker Symbols: ERAR
NAIC: 331111 Iron and Steel Mills

Siderar S.A.I.C. is the leading Argentine integrated steel-making facility, converting iron ore, coke, and pig iron to raw steel in order to produce hot- and cold-rolled coils and plates of steel and other steel products. These goods are destined primarily for tube and pipe manufacturing and for the automotive, home-appliance, construction, and agricultural sectors. The company is majority owned by Organizacion Techint, Argentina's largest holding company, which also has majority control of Tenaris S.A., the world's largest producer of seamless steel pipes and tubes.

State-Run Steelmaking Enterprise: 1947–92

Only one recently established steel manufacturer was operating in Argentina in 1947, when the government founded Sociedad Mixta Siderurgia Argentina (Somisa). Its first director, Manuel Savio, was a military engineer who had previously organized a government agency charged during World War II with securing arms and munitions in case Argentina entered the war or was subject to naval blockade. Promoted to the rank of general, Savio headed Altos Hornos Zapla, an enterprise owned by the nation's ministry of defense that, in the late 1940s, began making steel in the province of Jujuy, but on a very small scale.

A decade later, Somisa established a steel plant in the district of Ramallo, Buenos Aires, on a site extending about two miles along the bank of the Parana River, 232 kilometers (144 miles) north of the capital near the town of San Nicolas. Officially inaugurated in 1960 to produce a wide range of hot- and cold-rolled steel coils, sheets, and plates and also tin plate, it turned out its first ribbon of molten steel the following year. As a military-run company under a military regime, Somisa had little to fear from competition. Acindar Industria Argentina de Aceros S.A., closest to it in size, received 70 percent of its raw steel from Somisa and generally confined its output to rods and special steels. The government rejected, until 1975, Acindar's proposal to build a new blast furnace and produce an additional 800,000 tons of steel a year. But after Acindar opened fully integrated facilities in 1978 and acquired several smaller steelmakers in 1981, it became a serious competitor to Somisa.

Somisa added a second blast furnace to its facilities in 1974 and now had the capacity to raise its raw-steel production to 2.5 million metric tons a year, 55 percent in the form of rods, rails, and structural steel, and 45 percent as hot- and cold-rolled coils, sheets, and plates. The enterprise even had a plan to double its steel production to five million tons a year. Economic conditions, however, were restricting actual production to about 1.5 million metric tons annually. Somisa was Argentina's fifth largest enterprise in 1975, with sales of ARS 8.08 billion (about $230 million). By 1980, however, it had fallen to 13th, and by 1985, when it lost 40.86 million australes (about $49 million), it had dropped to 16th, behind Siderca S.A.I.C., Organizacion Techint's corporation for making seamless steel tubes, used chiefly for oil and gas projects.

Anticipating a growing domestic market and seeking greater volume in order to improve productivity, Somisa both expanded its manufacturing capacity and its range of products. It led Argentina in production of raw steel, cold-rolled products, steel profiles, and rods, and it was the only Argentine producer of hot-rolled products and tin plate. Unfortunately, domestic demand did not increase, and so the company was forced to seek new customers in the highly competitive export market, where capacity also far outstripped demand. In 1990 Somisa was

Key Dates:

1947: Sociedad Mixta Siderurgia Argentina (Somisa), a military-run enterprise, is founded.
1960: Somisa establishes a steel plant near San Nicolas, Buenos Aires.
1974: The Somisa plant has capacity to produce 2.5 million metric tons of steel a year.
1975: Somisa ranks fifth in revenue among Argentine enterprises.
1985: Somisa drops to 16th place among Argentine companies.
1991: Seeking to cut its losses, Somisa reduces employment by one-half.
1992: The company is sold to private sector investors for $163.6 million.
1993: The company merges with a smaller steel producer to form Siderar.
1996: Restored to profitability, Siderar sells shares to Argentine and foreign investors.
1998: Siderar takes a stake in Sidor, Venezuela's steelmaking giant.
2003: Siderar remains profitable after peso devaluation but restructures its debt.

exporting more than half of the output from the 2.3 million metric tons of steel it was producing. As a result, the company was losing $20 million each month in operating costs. Moreover, its debt was rising, and there were no funds available for necessary maintenance and modernization of the plant.

Carlos Menem, who was elected president of Argentina in 1989, adopted a program of free trade that involved selling heavily protected major state-owned enterprises, among them Somisa. The company's plant included two blast furnaces, two continuous casters, four coke-furnace batteries, a hot-strip mill, and other finishing facilities. Its value to a private investor, however, had very little to do with its claimed book value of $2 billion, since the older pieces of equipment were becoming obsolete and the enterprise was also one of Argentina's largest employers—a liability. Its 12,094 workers at the end of 1990 were far in excess of those employed by Somisa's foreign competitors, in terms of manpower per ton of steel output. In 1991, on the eve of privatization, nearly 6,000 employees were dismissed. The company's sales came to $624.2 million that year.

A total of 80 percent of Somisa—which had been renamed Aceros Parana S.A.—was sold in 1992 for $163.6 million to a consortium that also assumed $250 million of the company's estimated debt of $900 million. The main share was taken by Propulsora Siderurgica S.A.I.C., a cold-rolled steel unit of the privately owned Organizacion Techint holding company, which included Siderca, the Argentina-based multinational manufacturer of the seamless steel pipes used in oil and gas projects. Other members of the consortium were Brazilian and Chilean mining and metals enterprises. Twenty percent of the shares were set aside for offer to the mill's workers. Aceros Parana was merged with Propulsora Siderurgica S.A. and Aceros Revestidos S.A., a manufacturer of coated steel products, in 1993 to form Siderar S.A.I.C.

Siderar in the 1990s

Siderar was now in the hands of Organizacion Techint's owners, the Rocca family. Agostino Rocca had become vice-president of the Dalmine S.p.A steel plant, largest in Italy, in 1931. He continued in this capacity when the plant was nationalized by Benito Mussolini's government during World War II and came to Argentina in 1946, establishing an industrial empire that included Dalmine Siderca (later Siderca), founded in 1954, and Propulsera Siderurgica (1961). The latter was originally intended to be a fully integrated steelmaking facility like Somisa, but the military junta ruling Argentina at the time did not want it competing with a state company and approved it only as a plant for making cold-rolled steel products. To sweeten its decision, the military, according to muckraking journalist Luis Majul, allowed Propulsora Siderurgica to buy hot-rolled steel from Somisa at a price so low that Somisa lost $80 million to $100 million a year on the contract for 20 years. By the 1990s Propulsora Siderurgica was turning out 600,000 metric tons of cold-rolled steel a year and had annual revenue of some $200 million to $250 million.

Siderar's management embarked on a five-year, $438 million investment program, with priority given to retiring the older blast furnace, renovating the newer one, and installing a new electrogalvanizing line. The program also called for upgrading the coke batteries and increasing the hot-strip mill output. Siderar also closed facilities that were turning out products seen as continuing to be unprofitable in the near future. In addition, the company contracted out operation of the central thermoelectric plant—its supply of electric energy—production of industrial gases, and management of the river port where the enterprise received its raw materials. Siderar also reorganized operations, creating separate business units to serve its various clients: the automotive, container, commercial products, and home-appliance industries, and construction, agriculture, roadbuilding, and international customers. In general, these customers tended to be, as before, small and medium-sized companies. A heavy emphasis was placed on personnel training, both in Argentina and abroad, in keeping with longstanding tradition within Organizacion Techint as a whole. At the same time, the company outsourced to third parties areas in which it did not specialize in order to concentrate on its core business, rolled-steel products. Between 1992 and 1996 Siderar raised its share of domestic consumption of flat-steel products from about 56 percent to about 79 percent.

By 1996 Siderar was considered attractive enough to investors to go public, selling $78 million worth of shares (12 percent of its capital) on the Bolsa de Comercio de Buenos Aires and through private placement of American depositary shares to U.S. and European institutional investors. The company's sales rose from $669.2 million in 1993 to $1.01 billion in 1997, when its net profit reached $90.9 million. Productivity almost tripled during this period, costs per ton fell by 28 percent, and operating profit margin more than doubled.

Siderar turned out some two million tons of steel products in 1997, with 80 percent destined for the then-booming domestic market, which basically consisted of small and medium-sized businesses. There were seven programs oriented toward these clients, including one that audited the industrial engineering of these enterprises and offered plans to correct detected flaws in these operations. Another program, available over the Internet, included market analysis and software for managers. In addition, in that year, Siderar paid $60 million for Comesi San Luis S.A.I.C., a company that galvanized and painted metal sheets. A Siderar executive said that in less than six months Comesi's production rose 43 percent although staffing was cut by one-third.

Siderar, through its Prosid Investments S.C.A. subsidiary, took, in 1998, a 17.5 percent stake in Consorcio Siderurgica Amazonia Ltd., which had acquired 70 percent of Siderurgica del Orinoco C.A. (Sidor) from the Venezuelan government. Sidor was Venezuela's biggest steel producer. By the end of 2003, Siderar had raised its share of Sidor to 21.1 percent. Handicapped by political and economic turmoil in Venezuela, Sidor registered a $131 million loss for Siderar in 2002 but contributed $46 million in profits in 2003.

Siderar in the New Century

As the Argentine economy fell into recession, Siderar compensated for reduced domestic demand by increasing its exports from 340,000 metric tons in 1998 to one million in 1999. By late 2000 it had delayed for two years a planned three-year investment program of $1 billion. When the economy collapsed under the weight of heavy debt toward the end of 2001, Siderar continued to operate at 90 percent of its installed capacity of 2.3 million metric tons of raw steel per year, but exports now came to 60 percent of production. As the domestic economy recovered, exports fell to 45 percent of the total in 2003. The company lost money in 1999 and 2001 but then regained profitability.

Siderar's furnaces produced 2.41 million metric tons of raw steel in 2003. Its continuous casters turned out 2.54 million tons of molten steel. Hot-rolled steel production came to 2.47 million tons, cold-rolled steel, 1.54 million tons, and coated steel, 739,000 tons. The latter included electrogalvanized and electrozinced steel, and electrolytic tinplate. The company's net sales came to ARS 2.73 billion ($925.42 million) and its net profit to ARS 422.22 million ($143.13 million). During 2003 Siderar restructured $473.6 million in debts, which had grown increasingly burdensome after the value of the peso fell 70 percent against the dollar at the end of 2001. Siderar's total debt at the end of 2003 was $781.9 million.

Siderar was the dominant supplier for the high-quality and high-performance products used in the auto industry and of tin-plated steel for canning by the food industry and of coated steel products to meet the demands of the construction and electric home-appliance industries. All seven of its plants were in the province of Buenos Aires. The main Ramallo plant produced pig iron in its blast furnace from iron ore, coal, limestone, and coke. The pig iron was then purified into raw steel in basic oxygen furnaces. Casting produced slabs that were reheated into hot-rolled coils, which were sometimes cut into sheet steel. Alternatively, hot coils were sent to a cold-rolling mill. There was a second plant in the Ramallo complex for chromium coating.

The former Propulsora plant, in Ensenada, produced cold-rolled coils and plates and electrogalvanized hot-dipped galvanized and coated sheets. At Florencia Varela, two former Aceros Revestidos plants electrogalvanized sheets and coils and color-coated the sheets. Haedo was a specialized galvanizing plant for coated sheets. At the acquired Comesi canning plant at Estaban Echeverria, cold-rolled sheets and coils coated with tin underwent electrolytic cleaning and other steps to produce tin plate.

Agostino Rocca had died in 1978 and had been succeeded as president of Organizacion Techint by his son Roberto, who retired in 1993 and was succeeded by his son Agostino. He died in an aviation accident in 2001 and was succeeded at the head of Techint and as president of Siderar by his brother Paolo.

Organizacion Techint's Sidertubes S.A. unit owned 50.7 percent of Siderar's common stock in 2003. Inversora Siderurgica held 10.76 percent, Brazil's Usinas Siderurgicas de Minas Gerais S.A., 5.32 percent, and Iterbira, 4.85 percent. Employees held 10 percent of the enterprise, and company shares also traded on the Bolsa de Comercio de Buenos Aires.

Principal Subsidiaries

Comesi San Luis S.A.I.C.; Prosid Investments S.C.A.

Principal Competitors

Acindar Industria Argentina de Aceros S.A.

Further Reading

"Argentina Sells Somisa to Multinational Group," *American Metal Market,* October 30, 1992, pp. 1, 8.

"Experiencia y racionalizacion," *Mercado,* January 1998, pp. 46–47.

Friedland, Jonathan, "Siderar's Share Sale Caps Success Story," *Wall Street Journal,* May 1, 1996, p. A10.

Kepp, Michael, "Argentina's Siderar More Competitive," *American Metal Market,* June 21, 1994, p. 4.

——, "President, Board Quit at Argentina's Somisa," *American Metal Market,* April 19, 1990, pp. 1, 12.

Majul, Luis, *Los duenos de la Argentina,* Buenos Aires: Editorial Sudamerica, 5th ed., 1995, pp. 191–252.

Mooney, Reynold W., and Scott Griffith, "Privatizing a Distressed State-Owned Enterprise," *Columbia Journal of World Business,* Spring 1993, pp. 18–24.

Moyano, Julio, ed., *The Argentine Economy,* Buenos Aires: Julio Moyano Comunicaciones, 1997, p. 544.

"Siderar Mulling $1-Billion Investment to Boost Output," *American Metal Market,* November 21, 2000, p. 6.

Silveti, Edgardo A., "Un tercero alto horno para SOMISA," *Mercado,* July 28, 1977, pp. 20–21.

"SOMISA: Un nuevo desafio," *Mercado,* Nocember 29, 1984, p. 42.

—Robert Halasz

ULTRA
Slim·Fast®

Slim-Fast Foods Company

777 South Flagler Drive
West Tower, Suite 1400
West Palm Beach, Florida 33401
U.S.A.
Telephone: (407) 833-9920
Fax: (407) 822-2876
Web site: http://www.slim-fast.com

Wholly Owned Subsidiary of Unilever Group
Incorporated: 1945 as Thompson Medical Company
Employees: 110
Sales: $28 million (1999)
NAIC: 311514 Dry, Condensed, and Evaporated Dairy Product Manufacturing; 311999 All Other Miscellaneous Food Manufacturing

Slim-Fast Foods Company sells its popular meal replacement shakes, drink powders, snack bars, and meals throughout the United States, Europe, Asia, and Latin America. Created in 1977 by S. Daniel Abraham, Slim-Fast grew rapidly in the 1980s due in part to successful advertising featuring celebrities like Los Angeles Dodgers manager Tommy Lasorda. The company was spun off from Thompson Medical Co. in 1990, and consumer products giant Unilever acquired it in 2000. Following the high protein, low-carbohydrate diet craze that swept the United States in 2003, the Slim-Fast has been forced to rethink its product strategy.

The Early Years

What would become Slim-Fast Foods Company began with S. Daniel Abraham's ability to sell itch relief cream. Abraham exited the U.S. Army in 1945 at age 21 and went to work at his uncle's small drug company in New York. While working there, he read an advertisement in a trade journal for an itch-relief cream and decided to purchase the product and its maker for $5,000. Abraham left his uncle's company and began traveling throughout neighboring states to offer doctors and pharmacists samples of his product while distributing his advertisement posters. Abraham's fledgling enterprise soon became known as the Thompson Medical Company.

Abraham used his profits to hire chemists and pharmacologists to modify other manufacturers' existing products. In addition, he purchased the rights to other pharmaceutical companies' smaller and less-successful product lines, which he then revamped and marketed as Thompson Medical products. In 1956, Abraham unveiled his first diet product, called Slim-Mint gum, which contained a hunger suppressant called benzocaine. By 1960, his company had also added a line of diet pills called Figure-Aid.

It was not until 1976, with the introduction of Dexatrim, that Abraham's experimentation in the diet-control market began to pay off big. Dexatrim was a diet pill containing the appetite suppressant phenylpropanolamine (PPA). Although the use of PPA was somewhat controversial at the time, Dexatrim soon became the best-selling diet pill on the market and helped Thompson Medical's sales surpass $50 million by the end of the decade.

Slim-Fast Is Born: 1970s–1980s

Thompson Medical introduced Slim-Fast in 1977. When mixed with low-fat milk, the powdered formula took on the taste and texture of a milkshake. Marketed as a 1,200-calorie-per-day meal-replacement product, Slim-Fast was engineered to be used at both breakfast and lunch, and then supplemented with a sensible and healthy dinner. Unfortunately, during its first year on the market, Slim-Fast was pulled from circulation along with all other fluid meal-replacement products after almost sixty dieters died while using 300-calorie-per-day liquid diets made by other manufacturers. To counter the loss of earnings that had been generated by the Slim-Fast product, Abraham engineered a public offering in 1979 of approximately four million shares of Thompson Medical stock. The offering brought in $8.4 million in earnings, most of which was spent on advertising and promotion of the company's products.

Luckily, Abraham was able to reintroduce his Slim-Fast product in the early 1980s, at the same time that Dexatrim sales began to decline due to the Food & Drug Administration's growing concerns regarding the use of PPA in consumer products. The readmittance of Slim-Fast to the diet control market helped Thompson Medical achieve sales of approximately $197 million in 1984 and laid the foundation for the product's future success.

Company Perspectives:

For more than 25 years, we have been committed to the development of wholesome and balanced nutritional products to aid in weight management and improved health.

Throughout the mid-1980s, Thompson Medical's sales fluctuated as more manufacturers entered the diet-control market and competed for market share. In late 1987, just after the October stock market crash, Abraham decided to make the company private once again and began repurchasing shares of Thompson's stock. A year later, he had acquired 33 percent of the company's stock, a controlling interest that he maintained into the mid-2000s. At this time, he also stumbled upon what would become the most successful advertising tool used by Slim-Fast in the coming years: televised celebrity endorsements.

In 1988, Los Angeles Dodgers manager Tommy Lasorda needed to lose 20 pounds, and Slim-Fast was in need of a celebrity to promote its product in the same way that Oprah Winfrey was promoting competitor Opti-Fast. The company signed Lasorda as its spokesman and offered to contribute $20,000 to his favorite charity if he would stick to the diet plan. Within months, Lasorda had lost almost 30 pounds, and a Nashville-based group of nuns received a new convent in his name. Research showed Lasorda to be an especially effective spokesman with female consumers, who found him to be credible because he was a man admitting to a weight problem on national television, and he was seeing successful results due to his use of the Slim-Fast product.

On Its Own in the 1990s

Throughout the 1980s, Thompson Medical had diversified its product offerings and had begun to market such over-the-counter remedies as Aspercreme, Sportscreme, and Cortizone-5. By 1990, in response to Slim-Fast's rapid growth in the diet and nutritional foods segment, Abraham spun off the division to become its own company, although he retained his position as chairman and majority stockholder.

Just after the split, Slim-Fast began to experience a decrease in sales, due in part to Oprah Winfrey's highly publicized weight gain after discontinuing use of a fluid meal-replacement product. Without Thompson Medical's diverse portfolio to back it, Slim-Fast had to find a way to support itself through this time period. Thus, the company began planning the introduction of a variety of new products under the Slim-Fast brand name, and Slim-Fast Nutritional Foods International, Inc. was born.

The new Slim-Fast offerings were accompanied by a broadening of the company's focus to combine weight loss with an emphasis on the importance of a healthy lifestyle and the nutritional benefits of Slim-Fast products. A new slogan was introduced, advertising the company's products as a part of the ''Slim-Fast way of life.'' New product offerings stressed convenience and included pre-mixed Slim-Fast in cans and refrigerated cartons, hot chocolate mix, frozen entrees and desserts, and snacks such as cheese curls and popcorn. ConAgra, a leading force in the health and diet business with its Healthy Choice product line, manufactured and distributed the frozen foods. The pre-mixed Slim-Fast was manufactured by Farmland Dairies, and the snack items were made in partnership with Borden.

In another effort to move the company beyond its typical weight-loss products, Slim-Fast produced new television advertisements featuring celebrity testimonials to the health benefits derived from the ''Slim-Fast way of life.'' While many people questioned Slim-Fast's ability to compete in the health-food arena against giants such as Weight Watchers and Lean Cuisine, Slim-Fast hoped its advertising campaign would generate increased sales. A new spot featuring Lasorda was aired, as were other spots containing media personalities Frank and Kathie Lee Gifford, actor Peter DeLuise (Dom's son), ex-New York Mayor Ed Koch, and singer Mel Torme.

In 1992, about a year after Slim-Fast separated from Thompson Medical, Ron Stern was promoted to the position of president of Slim-Fast. Stern had previously been with the company as a vice-president and was instrumental in the signing of Lasorda as spokesman three years earlier. Although Slim-Fast held a 70 percent share of the meal-replacement market at that time, Stern noted that a rapidly increasing amount of competition threatened the company's market share. Slim-Fast decided to lower the wholesale price of its products by an average of 55 cents, thereby making its competitors' products more expensive to stock.

The following year, Slim-Fast began airing a talk-show style infomercial in an attempt to counter the growing segment of companies that were offering mail-order diet products. Interestingly, Slim-Fast did not actually sell its products through the infomercial. Instead, the television spot tried to persuade consumers to go to retail stores for weight control products, rather than purchase such items through the mail. Using this method, Slim-Fast made efforts to retain its market share without having to enter the mail-order arena to compete effectively.

Slim-Fast Nutritional Foods International entered the mid-1990s in a position of dominance in the weight management and health-food industry. With a controlling share of the market, Slim-Fast was beginning to receive accolades for its performance. ''No single brand has demonstrated the vitality, marketing savvy and well-timed ability to tie into Americans' desire for weight management and proper nutrition as has Slim-Fast,'' according to *Supermarket Business.* As one of the few brands that followed the Surgeon General's recommendations on diet and health and as a recipient of the Good Housekeeping Seal of Approval, Slim-Fast appeared to be equipped to handle the pressures of an increasingly cautious consumer society. An expanding array of product offerings and a growing base of customers interested in better health left Slim-Fast well positioned to face future challenges.

Late 1990s and Beyond

In order to maintain its market share, Slim-Fast introduced new products and spent heavily on advertising in the late 1990s. Over $46 million was earmarked for advertising in 1996. The company launched a $10 million campaign in May 1997 for its new quick diet product, Jump Start, which claimed consumers could lose five pounds in five days. ''Give us a week, we'll take

Key Dates:

1945: S. Daniel Abraham incorporates the Thompson Medical Company.
1956: Abraham unveils his first diet product, Slim-Mint gum.
1976: The Dexatrim diet pill is launched.
1977: Thompson Medical introduces Slim-Fast.
1979: The company goes public.
1987: Abraham decides to take the firm private.
1988: Tommy Lasorda becomes a Slim-Fast spokesman.
1990: Slim-Fast is spun off; Abraham remains a majority stockholder.
2000: Unilever acquires Slim-Fast.

off the weight'' was a popular tagline during this time. Slim-Fast also added a new line of Slim-Fast Meal On-The-Go bars to its arsenal, introducing consumers to the products via a $60 million advertising campaign in 1999.

Slim-Fast now held a 46 percent share of the diet liquid/powder segment of the weight loss market, selling over $611 million of its products in 1999. With the diet/weight loss market slated to grow by at least 10 percent per year, Slim-Fast entered the 2000s on solid ground. Its annual sales were growing at a rate of 20 percent per year, and the company soon caught the eye of consumer products conglomerate Unilever. In April 2000, Unilever announced that it would buy Slim-Fast in a $2.3 billion deal. Unilever also bought ice cream maker Ben & Jerry's at the same time, thereby tapping into two groups of consumers—those that craved sweets and those searching for weight loss products. An April 14, 2000 *Wall Street Journal* article wrote about the benefits of the deal, reporting that ''only six percent of its [Slim-Fast] sales are outside North America, offering Unilever an opportunity to push the brand through its world-wide distribution and sales network.''

Indeed, under Unilever's ownership Slim-Fast began an aggressive expansion plan. The company—now called Slim-Fast Foods Co.—opened a new manufacturing plant in Tucson, Arizona. It also expanded into twelve global markets in Europe, Asia, and Latin America.

By 2003, intense competition forced the company to launch a line of convenient-meals, including pastas, soups, and a new frozen novelties line that included a low-calorie fudge bar. The company and its peers in the diet industry faced a major challenge at this time as the low-carbohydrate/high protein diet craze swept the United States. Weight loss programs like Atkins and South Beach, which focused on low sugar and low carb diets, began to cut severely into Slim-Fast revenues. In 2003, the company's sales fell by 21 percent. In an attempt to attract low-carb conscious consumers, Slim-Fast launched a line of high protein and low carbohydrate products in late 2003 and early 2004.

While the recent shift in consumer preference was indeed a setback, Slim-Fast was confident it would remain the leading weight management brand in the United States. The company claimed that nearly one billion people across the globe were overweight or obese and that for the first time there were more over-nourished people in the world than under-nourished. With a consumer products giant as a parent, Slim-Fast appeared to be well positioned to face the challenges brought on by changing customer demands.

Principal Competitors

GNC Corporation; Jenny Craig; Weider Nutrition International Inc.

Further Reading

Berman, Phyllis, and Amy Feldman, ''An Extraordinary Peddler,'' *Forbes*, December 9, 1991, p. 136.
Branch, Shelly, and Ernest Beck, ''For Unilever, It's Sweetness and Light,'' *Wall Street Journal*, April 13, 2000.
Cotton, C. Richard, ''Slim-Fast to Plump up When Facility Expands,'' *Commercial Appeal*, December 28, 1998.
Dagnoli, Judann, ''Heavying up on Diet Ads,'' *Advertising Age*, December 23, 1991, p. 3.
——, ''Slim-Fast Beefs up Menu of Food Items,'' *Advertising Age*, May 27, 1991, p. 33.
''Dieters Ready for More Ready-to-Eat/Drink Formulas,'' *Drug Store News*, February 1, 1999.
Doherty, Katherine, ''Farmland Carton-Packages Slim-Fast,'' *U.S. Distribution Journal*, May 15, 1991, p. 40.
Freeman, Laurie, ''Ultra Slim-Fast: Ron Stern,'' *Advertising Age*, July 6, 1992, p. S8.
Levin, Gary, ''Infomercials Take a Different Spin,'' *Advertising Age*, September 20, 1993, p. 8.
Liesse, Julie, ''Frozen Novelties Look for Hot Summer,'' *Advertising Age*, May 13, 1991, p. 6.
Lucas, Sloane, ''Slim-Fast Intros Meal Bars in $60m Push,'' *Brandweek*, January 11, 1999.
''Meal Replacements,'' *Supermarket Business*, April 1991, p. G22.
Pollack, Judann, ''Slim Fast Touts Its Quick Fix,'' *Advertising Age*, May 19, 1997.
Reed, Stanley, ''Niall Fitzgerald: Sweet Dreams Are Made of This,'' *Business Week*, April 24, 2000.
Rigg, Cynthia, ''After Binge, Slim-Fast Is Thinning,'' *Crain's New York Business*, March 18, 1991, p. 3.
''Unilever Expands Slim-Fast to Create a Diet Megabrand,'' *Advertising Age*, June 23, 2003.
Winters, Patricia, ''Slim-Fast Dishes up New Foods,'' *Advertising Age*, January 7, 1991, p. 38.

—Laura E. Whiteley
—update: Christina M. Stansell

Sovran Self Storage, Inc.

6467 Main Street
Buffalo, New York 14221
U.S.A.
Telephone: (716) 633-1850
Fax: (716) 633-8397
Web site: http://www.sovranss.com

Public Company
Incorporated: 1995
Employees: 824
Sales: $113.6 million (2003)
Stock Exchanges: New York
Ticker Symbol: SSS
NAIC: 525930 Real Estate Investment Trusts

Based in Buffalo, New York, Sovran Self Storage, Inc. is a real estate investment trust (REIT) trading on the New York Stock Exchange and involved in the self-storage industry under the Uncle Bob's Self Storage banner. As of March 2004, the company owned or managed 265 properties in 21 states, mostly in the eastern part of the United States but also in Arizona and Texas. With 15.5 million net rentable square feet, Sovran is the fourth largest self-storage company in the country. It is also one of the most innovative in the industry. Sovran offers free truck rentals to customers, flexible storage spaces that allow a customer to rent the minimum amount of needed space, and a humidity control system.

Early 1980s Origins

The predecessor to Sovran, Sovran Group, was founded in 1982 and incorporated in New York state in 1983. It was primarily involved in the syndication of limited partnerships, which bought and managed a variety of real estate interests. In 1985, Sovran first became involved in the self storage industry, which was in its infancy at the time. Self-storage facilities, mostly mom-and-pop operations, had sprouted up to meet the needs of a changing America. Because people were now more likely to change jobs, and sometimes careers, on a more regular basis, many people found themselves in need of storage facilities for many of their belongings, either on a temporary basis or as a way to supplement limited storage available in their apartments or condominiums. Aside from demand, self storage facilities presented an attractive investment opportunity because they could be constructed at less than half the price of an apartment building, cost much less to maintain than apartments, yet still achieve the same rent quota.

For the next decade, Sovran Group built up its self storage business while remaining involved in other areas of real estate. In 1987, one of Sovran's four partners, Ronald Mariellos, sued the other three—Charles Lannon, Kenneth Myszka, and Robert Attea—contending that they ousted him as a director and officer of the company in order to prevent him from collecting a bonus associated with the purchase of Florida Storage Properties. His partners offered $125,000 to buy out his share of the business, but he refused and took his grievances to court. At the time, Sovran Group was comprised of six subsidiaries: Sovran Capital Inc., Sovran Blend Inc., Sovran Management Inc., Sovran Ltd., Sovran Securities, and McKenzie Construction Corp. Mariello eventually settled with his partners, leaving Lannon, Myszka, and Attea to carry on Sovran's transformation into a pure play self-storage company. Another key player would be David L. Rogers, who joined Sovran as controller and due diligence officer in 1984 and in 1988 became chief financial officer.

REIT Formed in 1996

Late in 1994, Sovran Group initiated a number of moves that would separate out the company's self-storage facilities, which would be packaged into a REIT called Sovran Self Storage, Inc., incorporated on April 19, 1995 under Maryland law. In recent years, REITs had become an attractive investment vehicle for many sectors of the real estate industry, such as apartments and commercial properties, so that forming a REIT to roll up assets in the highly fragmented self storage industry held an obvious appeal.

REITs had been created by Congress in 1960 as a way for small investors to become involved in real estate in much the same way a mutual fund permitted them to pool resources in order to buy stock. REITs could be taken public and their shares traded like any other stocks; likewise, REITs were also regulated

Company Perspectives:

Sovran operates its stores under the trade name Uncle Bob's Self Storage, and serves over 125,000 customers in 21 states.

and monitored by the Securities and Exchange Commission. Unlike stocks, however, REITs were required by law to pay out at least 95 percent of their taxable income to shareholders each year, thus severely limiting the ability of REITs to raise funds internally. During the first 30 years of existence, REITs were hindered in their growth because they were only allowed to own properties. Third parties had to be engaged to operate or manage them. Moreover, the tax code made direct real estate investments an attractive tax shelter for many individuals, thereby absorbing funds that might have been invested in REITs. The situation changed with the Tax Reform Act of 1986, which greatly reduced interest and depreciation deductions and prevented taxpayers from generating paper losses in order to lower their taxes. The Act also permitted REITs to provide customary services for property, in effect allowing the trusts to operate and manage the properties they owned. Despite these changes, REITs were still not embraced as an investment options. In the late 1980s, banks, insurance companies, pension funds, and foreign investors (in particular, the Japanese) provided the lion's share of real estate investment funds. That period also witnessed overbuilding and a glutted marketplace. Commercial property values fell dramatically in the early 1990s, and lending institutions, following the savings and loan debacle, were forced by regulators to be more circumspect about their investments. Capital essentially dried up and REITs finally became an attractive way for many private real estate companies to raise funds. They also gave many limited partnerships a way to provide liquidity for investors, leading to many REITs that rolled up assets and became giant real estate companies.

At the time Sovran made its public offering in June 1995, the REIT owned 74 Uncle Bob's self-storage facilities, with 3.8 million square feet of rentable space in locations that reached from Connecticut to Pensacola, Florida. Of those facilities, 62 had been owned by Sovran's limited partnerships and another 12 were purchased in connection with the offering. Sovran netted about $136 million from the offering, of which $70 million was earmarked to pay down debt. The balance made up a war chest to pursue further acquisitions. Sovran was only one of five REITs involved in the self-storage area, and given that combined they controlled only 10 percent of the market, there was ample opportunity for growth. A few weeks later, the offering's underwriting group, led by PaineWebber Inc., exercised an over-allotment option, which raised an additional $16 million for the REIT.

In the last half of 1995, Sovran acquired eight more self storage properties; the next year, it bought another 29. For its first full year in operation, Sovran generated $33.6 million in revenues and net income of $15.7 million, establishing a pattern of steady growth that would continue through the rest of the 1990s. The company issued another 1.5 million shares of common stock in 1997 to help fuel expansion. During the course of the year, Sovran acquired 28 storage facilities to strengthen its position in such cities as Cleveland, Fort Lauderdale, and Dallas/Fort Worth. It also opened units in new markets: Houston, northern Michigan, central Virginia, and Baton Rouge. To better manage its portfolio of self storage assets, management in 1997 established four geographical regions, each headed by a regional vice-president. Sovran also took steps to refine its Uncle Bob's brand and improve marketing efforts. A new logo and signage were developed and a new color scheme adopted. In addition, the company took steps to improve its shareholder distribution, launching a Web site and taking other steps to make investors aware of Sovran's potential. Because the company was mostly owned by institutional investors, there was no need at this point to hold a local annual meeting. Instead, a meeting with a handful of institutional investors in New York City sufficed. After posting $49.4 million in revenues in 1997 and net income of $23.1 million, Sovran in 1998 acquired 50 self storage facilities to boost its total number of stores beyond the 200 mark. As a result, rental income improved by 40 percent over the previous year to $69.4 million, although net income was relatively flat compared to 1997, totaling $23.4 million.

"Flex-a-Space" Introduced in 1999

The self-storage business was now mature, occupancy rates were tailing off, competition was keen, and overhead costs had already been trimmed. To attract new business and grow profits, self storage operators became eager to find a competitive edge through innovation. The industry leader, Public Storage Inc., made an unsuccessful attempt to offer a delivery service of sorts, with storage containers dropped off at customers' houses and retrieved later. Some competitors formed alliances with moving companies as a way for both parties to take advantage of each other's customer lists. In 1999, Sovran introduced an idea that it hoped would differentiate it from the field: "Flex-a-Space" movable walls. It used a track-and-wheel system that allowed a wall to be brought in to accommodate the actual amount of space a customer needed. According to one example, a customer renting a ten-by-ten-foot space for $85 a month but who only needed a space measuring eight-by-ten could have the flexible walls adjusted accordingly and reduce his monthly rent to $75. Not only would the customer save money, the Uncle Bob's facility would benefit as well, improving its revenue by 9 percent on the cost per square foot. What also made "Flex-a-Space" so appealing was that competitors were not able to quickly emulate the idea. Aside from installing the track-and-wheel system, on which Sovran filed a patent, competitors also faced a problem with their management software, which was not set up to help site managers deal with the variables of track space rentals. Sovran rolled out "Flex-a-Space" to 62 locations in six major markets—Atlanta, Cleveland, Phoenix, Tampa, Dallas/Forth Worth, and Norfolk/Virginia Beach—in 1999 and launched a $10 million program to convert all of its locations by the end of 2001. Another enhancement introduced during the year was a Corporate Alliance Program, which offered companies discount rates as well as a uniform leasing and invoicing system when using Uncle Bob's facilities across 50 different markets. In 1999, Sovran acquired 18 more facilities and moved into three new markets, as well as upgrading 31 other stores. Revenues for the year improved to $84.3 million and net income grew modestly to $25.6 million, suppressed somewhat

Key Dates:

1982: Predecessor real estate company, Sovran Group, is founded.
1985: Sovran becomes involved in the self storage industry.
1995: Sovran is reorganized as REIT and taken public.
1999: Flex-a-Space system is introduced.
2000: Dri-guard humidity control system is introduced.

by the investment in the ''Flex-a-Space'' program and the cost of acquisitions.

In 2000, Sovran moved into a new $6 million headquarters in Buffalo, eschewing offers from southern communities to relocate. This was also the first year that the company held an annual shareholder meeting in Buffalo, attracting 65 people, a surprising turnout that prompted management to make the local session a yearly event. Sovran continued to bring innovations to the Uncle Bob's chain, introducing to 11 facilities in 2000 its exclusive Dri-guard dehumidifying storage system, the same type of humidity control system used by the U.S. military, which proved helpful in protecting metal, papers, fabric, furniture, and electronics. Sovran acquired only five stores in 2000, primarily due to a scarcity of attractive targets and high interest rates. However, the company was able to boost sales internally with the opening of a new central call center at its Buffalo headquarters, which picked up overflow calls to the company's more than 200 stores. As a result, business was picked up that in the past would have gone to a competitor. For the year 2000, Sovran grew revenues to $90.2 million and net income to $25.7 million.

Growth Continues in the 2000s

In 2001, Sovran began taking steps to have all Uncle Bob's stores connected to the central call center, and ultimately all sales inquiries would be handled from company headquarters. The company also ramped up its Internet sales. Another improvement to the Uncle Bob's chain was the launch of a fleet of rental trucks, some of which were available for free use by storage customers. The trucks were geared toward the amateur mover and offered all the blankets, ramps, and dollies needed for a move. An added benefit was that the trucks also served as rolling billboards promoting Uncle Bob's Self Storage. Conditions were not conducive to strong growth in 2001. The company acquired just eight stores and sales were flat, totaling $91 million, while net income fell to $24.2 million. Nevertheless, the company was able to extend a practice of increasing the dividend it paid to shareholders each year.

In 2002, Sovran continued to bring its Flex-a-Space, Driguard humidity control, and truck rental business to all of its locations. It also returned to an aggressive pursuit of external growth, over the course of the year spending $82 million to acquire 23 stores, of which 19 were in existing markets in Texas and New York and another four in a new market, the Hamptons, Long Island. In addition, the company added 130,000 square feet of new space to existing properties, which helped Sovran bring new growth to their balance sheet. For the year, the company posted sales of $102.1 million and net income of $26.3 million.

Sovran shied away from acquisitions in 2003, buying just two properties because management considered prices too high, as a number of investors now recognized the reliability of self-storage cash flows and were looking to become involved in the sector. This situation led to overbuilding of facilities and ultimately to lower pricing. Despite these factors and the effects of a poor economy, Sovran was able to grow internally. At the same time, management prepared to return to a more aggressive approach to acquisitions by refinancing its long-term debt and increasing its borrowing capacity by $100 million. For the year, revenues improved to $113.6 million and net income to $28.4 million. Once again the company increased its dividend, which had grown from $2.05 in 1996 to $2.41 per share in 2003.

Early in 2004, Sovran took advantage of high prices for self storage facilities by selling four units located in non-core markets—Akron and Elyria, Ohio; Allentown, Pennsylvania; and Nashville, Tennessee—for $10.2 million. At the same time, the company was lining up a number of properties to acquire in its high-growth markets, earmarking $40 million for acquisitions in 2004. The industry in general was enjoying good conditions, reducing the need for discounts, and setting up Sovran for a banner year. With the industry still composed of many mom-and-pop operations and the need for self storage continuing to rise, there was every reason to expect that Sovran would enjoy steady growth for the foreseeable future.

Principal Subsidiaries

Sovran Holdings, Inc.

Principal Competitors

AMERCO; Public Storage, Inc.; Shurgard Storage Centers, Inc.; Storage USA, Inc.

Further Reading

Connelly, Katherine, ''Sovran Group Partners Feuding,'' *Business First—Buffalo*, August 3, 1987, p. 1.

Glynn, Matt, ''Williamsville, N.Y.-Based Real Estate Investment Trust Ready for Buying Binge,'' *Buffalo News*, May 14, 2004.

Linstedt, Sharon, ''New Headquarters Bolsters Sovran's Ties to Region,'' *Buffalo News*, June 1, 200, p. E1.

Robinson, David, ''Sovran's Stock Sale Raises $136 Million,'' *Buffalo News*, June 22, 1995, p. C1.

Williams, Fred O., ''Williamsville, N.Y.-Based Storage Firm Introduces Movable Walls,'' *Buffalo News*, September 23, 1999.

—Ed Dinger

Spartan Stores Inc.

850 76th Street Southwest
Grand Rapids, Michigan 49518
U.S.A.
Telephone: (616) 878-2000
Fax: (616) 878-8802
Web site: http://www.spartanstores.com

Public Company
Incorporated: 1918
Employees: 6,900
Sales: $2.05 billion (2004)
Stock Exchanges: NASDAQ
Ticker Symbol: SPTN
NAIC: 422410 General Line Grocery Wholesalers; 445110 Supermarkets and Other Grocery (Except Convenience) Stores

Once a wholesale grocery cooperative, Spartan Stores Inc. now operates as the eighth-largest grocery distributor in the United States. The company supplies over 40,000 name brand and private label products to 330 independent grocery stores in Michigan, Ohio, and Indiana and operates warehouse facilities in Grand Rapids and Plymouth, Michigan. Spartan is also involved in retailing—the company owns and operates 54 supermarkets and 21 discount food and drug stores in Michigan and Ohio.

Early History as a Cooperative

Seeking to lower grocery prices by providing greater economies of scale, a group of nearly 100 independent store owners met at the Livingston Hotel in Grand Rapids, Michigan, on December 27, 1917. The meeting had been prompted by a recent increase in competition from emerging national grocery store chains, such as A&P, which were able to provide customers with one-stop shopping and lower prices. By the end of the day, 43 of the grocers decided to form a cooperative whose purchasing power they hoped would help their business. Signing Articles of Incorporation, the grocers formed the Grand Rapids Wholesale Grocery Company. Only 27 bought stock in the corporation.

Stock in the company was privately held. Stores becoming members of the cooperative were required to maintain a stock investment, which could be sold back should a store decide to leave the cooperative. In 1957, the wholesale company changed its name to Spartan Stores Inc., a name management believed would achieve wide recognition in the area due to the popular association in Michigan between the name Spartan and the state university. The Spartan logo, featuring a warrior of ancient Sparta holding sword and shield, colored in a bright green, was reproduced on labels, grocery bags, and on the sides of the company's trucks. Although the retailers for whom Spartan acted as distributor did business under different names, the stores were united under this logo, which was displayed on the doors of all Spartan stores and also featured on the neon-lit signs of many.

Changes in the 1970s Lead to Success in the 1980s

In 1973, Spartan's status changed from that of a cooperative to a Michigan business corporation. During this time, the grocery business changed considerably, as the rate at which new products became available and the competition among grocery chains increased. Product volume at the Spartan warehouses also increased dramatically, and a new computerized vending system, known as Big Blue, was installed at the Grand Rapids complex, helping to distribute around 174 million pounds of fresh produce, 115 million pounds of meat, and four million cases of frozen foods in 1984. As both sales and the company's stock, available to businesses and individuals who operated grocery retail outfits, steadily climbed, the wholesaler expanded its membership to 475 stores.

Over the next ten years, Spartan also became involved in several humanitarian projects, including sponsorship of several area food bank and youth programs and a golf tournament to benefit the American Cancer Society. The company's most notable community project, however, has been its exclusive sponsorship of the Michigan Special Olympics Summer Games, which it took on in 1984. Spartan's role as sponsor is highly publicized every year through television, radio, and newspapers. Furthermore, Spartan designates around 200 products that are carried by its retailers as Special Olympics items; the products are advertised and five cents from each sale of these items

Company Perspectives:

The company's mission is to consistently satisfy customers with quality food and related retail and distribution products and services. Spartan's new strategic focus is based on the customer and they are working to become a total consumer driven organization and to accumulating the best total knowledge of consumers and independent retail operators in their market.

goes to the support and promotion of this annual event. In addition to paying the way for athletes to travel to and participate in the games, Spartan provides printed programs and entertainment, as well as food for the hundreds of volunteers who supervise and officiate the games.

The 1980s were a very productive and successful period for Spartan Stores. Annual sales rose by nearly 10 percent through 1989. In 1985, sales reached $1.3 billion, up from $1.2 billion the year before. By 1986, Spartan controlled 20 percent of the Michigan grocery market, and its sales had risen to $1.4 billion. That year, the company was ranked as Michigan's largest grocery wholesaler, and the 12th largest in the country. Sales steadily increased to $1.7 billion in 1988.

Although financially successful during this time, Spartan began to receive complaints from some of its member stores, who charged that Spartan seemed more interested in maintaining the status quo than fostering communication and cooperation between retailer and distributor. Agreeing that management lacked a vision for the company's continued growth and improvement, the board decided to elect a new president. When Patrick Quinn, formerly a vice-president at the 14-store chain of D&W Food Stores, became Spartan's president and CEO in 1985, he was the third person to fill the post in four years. Quinn was charged with reestablishing positive relationships and developing a specific and detailed long-term plan for the company.

When questioned about his lack of background in retailing, Quinn told Supermarket News that "it puts me in a naive position, so I can ask questions that may not have been asked in a long time, such as why something is done a certain way. It causes people to think, reexamine why things are done as they are." Quinn proceeded to reexamine nearly every aspect of the company and determined that distribution centers needed expanding and that both Spartan's data processing system and its policy of owning corporate stores needed further consideration.

Considering himself a "visible" manager who would strive to be available and responsive, Quinn pledged to visit stores and warehouses in an effort to establish good relations with employees and become better educated about retailers needs. Quinn's vision for the company was characterized as "getting back to basics," a practice realized through several of his early decisions as Spartan's president. He eliminated the computerized vending system in Spartan's Grand Rapids distribution center when he found numerous bugs in the system and noted the increasing expense of its maintenance. He also brought back the conventional wooden pallet, used to move boxes in and out of the company's truck trailers, when he observed that newer high-tech metal mechanisms were more cumbersome and less reliable. Quinn also stressed the importance of keeping Spartan retailers happy. Toward that end, he created the position of a customer service director who, by reporting directly to Quinn, could help improve communication and solve problems in all areas of the business.

In September 1985, hoping to gain more warehouse and office space, Spartan entered negotiations to purchase Eberhard Foods, a Grand Rapids chain of 22 stores. The following month, negotiations were indefinitely postponed, however, when Eberhard was faced with a lawsuit filed by union members and employees charging the company with mishandling their stock option plan. Plans to acquire Viking Food Stores Inc. of Muskegon, Michigan, fell through two years later when an agreement could not be reached regarding the purchase price and several other terms.

Focusing on Wholesale Operations in the Late 1980s

In 1987, Spartan disclosed plans to sell some of its corporate retail stores. Not only did the company wish to refocus its business as that of wholesale and not retail, but it was also concerned that the role it had assumed in both supplying stores and operating competing stores represented a conflict of interest. Thus, Spartan decided to auction off 80 percent, or 22 of its 25, retail stores. The stores were first offered to Spartan's retail members, and in October 1987 D&W Food Stores, Inc., announced its intention to purchase six of the stores. Other stores were bid on by smaller local chains.

At this time, Spartan's operations were generally divided into four segments: distribution, insurance sales and underwriting, real estate and finance, and retail stores. As a distributor of groceries and grocery related items, Spartan carried over 46,000 items, including general merchandise and health and beauty care products, which it received from suppliers. Spartan made available to its retailers both nationally advertised brands and Spartan's own private label items. Products reached individual stores via Spartan's fleet of over 300 trucks, one of the largest private fleets in Michigan. Insurance was offered to retailers through Spartan's subsidiaries, which made group health plan programs available for store employees and provided Spartan stores with fire, casualty, liability, and several other types of insurance. Those in the Spartan network who wished to either expand or remodel their stores could petition to borrow funds from Spartan's real estate and financing division.

The retail store segment, having been scaled back under Quinn's leadership, consisted of one corporate store in 1993, which was maintained through the company's Valueland subsidiary. In addition to its four main business segments, Spartan offered numerous support services to its retailers including market research, training programs, advertising design and printing, and accounting services. The company strengthened its wholesale convenience holdings in 1993 with the purchase of J.F. Walker Co. It began its foray into the wholesale convenience market with the 1987 purchase of L&L Jiroch.

In the early 1990s, the Spartan board voted to allow individual employees of Spartan Stores, its subsidiaries, and its retailers, as well as certain "approved shareholders," to purchase

Key Dates:

1917: A group of 43 grocers decide to form the Grand Rapids Wholesale Grocery Company.
1957: The company changes its name to Spartan Stores Inc.
1973: Spartan's status changes from a cooperative to a Michigan business corporation.
1986: Spartan controls 20 percent of the Michigan grocery market and is ranked the largest grocery wholesaler in the state.
1987: The company begins to sell of some of its corporate retail stores.
1993: J.F. Walker Co. is acquired.
1999: The company re-enters retailing by acquiring eight Ashcraft's Markets, 13 Family Fare stores, and 23 Glen's locations.
2000: Spartan goes public after its purchase of Seaway Food Town Inc.
2003: The company sells off non-core assets in order to focus on retail and distribution.

Spartan stock. In 1992, the company expected to generate more than $27 million from the sale of 175,000 shares of its Class A stock, which would be used for working capital. Quinn was characterized by *Progressive Grocer* magazine as cautiously optimistic in his projections for the company's success in 1993. While planning to expand Spartan's network to include more stores in the Midwest, the company faced tough competition from the larger chain supermarkets as well as the challenge of recovering from a national economic recession. Nevertheless, by continuing to reevaluate and improve its procedures and products, while maintaining the image of its stores as unique, local alternatives to the giant supermarket chains, the company expected to see continued growth in sales and earnings.

Mid-1990s and Beyond

After Quinn retired, Jim Meyer was appointed president and CEO in 1997. The company had just experienced the one of the worst financial losses in its history—$21.7 million—due to restructuring costs. A July 1997 *Supermarket News* article quoted the new leader, who proclaimed, "Growth is not an option for the 80-year old company, it is imperative for our long-term survival." Meyer firmly believed that the company needed to expand back into retailing in order to remain competitive. According to a November 2000 *Grand Rapids Press* article, his decision was based on several industry and demographic changes: consumers were spending over half of their food dollars outside of the home; a slowdown in the U.S. population, and therefore new customers, resulted in a need for a growth through acquisition policy; aggressive competition by large companies like Wal-Mart was wreaking havoc on the market share of smaller grocers; and industry consolidation made it nearly impossible for small chains to secure efficiencies of scale.

In view of these factors, Spartan acquired a handful of neighboring chains in 1999. It added eight central Michigan-based Ashcraft Markets, 23 Glen's Markets, Family Fare Supermarkets, and Great Day to its arsenal. The company marked its entrance into the new century with the acquisition of Ohio-based Seaway Food Town Inc., an operator of 39 supermarkets and 21 discount drug stores. Upon completion of the merger, Spartan Stores made its debut on the NASDAQ, going public at $11 per share. In 2001, it purchased Prevo's Family Markets, a ten-store chain in western Michigan.

The company's aggressive return to retailing proved to be problematic on several fronts. As a result of its recent acquisition spree, Spartan found itself in direct competition with many of its customers. Its largest client, D&W Food Centers, took issue with Spartan's strategy and opted to use a different distributor in 2000. At the same time, a faltering economy and intense competition coupled with major operational changes began to put a strain on the company's financials. Sales were stagnant in 2002, and net income began a downward spiral. In 2003, the company posted a net loss of $122.4 million. As a result, Spartan announced that it would shutter its Food Town stores in an attempt to shore up profits and reduce debt. It also sold convenience wholesalers L&L Jiroch and J.F. Walker. The sale of United Wholesale Grocery Co. in early 2004 signaled the company's exit from convenience operations.

Meyer retired in 2003, leaving Craig C. Sturken, a grocery business veteran, at the helm. He immediately set plans in motion to restore Spartan's profits. The company's retail stores were consolidated under the Family Fare Supermarkets and Glen's Markets names. Sturken hoped to revitalize the brand with a new logo, replacing the Spartan soldier with a green and white banner-style logo. Spartan also planned to add more pharmacies to its stores and convert to a 24-hour format. While Spartan's fortunes appeared to be changing, only time would tell if its new leader could orchestrate a successful long-term turnaround.

Principal Subsidiaries

Spartan Stores Distribution, LLC; JFW Distributing Company; LLJ Distributing Company; United Wholesale Grocery Company; Market Development Corporation; Spartan Stores Holding, Inc.; Spartan Stores Fuel, LLC; Family Fare, LLC; Prevo's Family Markets, Inc.; Spartan Stores Associates, LLC; MSFC, LLC; MDP, L.L.C.; Seaway Food Town, Inc.; The Pharm of Michigan, Inc.; Buckeye Real Estate Management Co.; Valley Farm Distribution Co.; Port Clinton Realty Company; Gruber's Food Town, Inc.; Gruber's Real Estate, LLC; Custer Pharmacy, Inc.; SI Insurance Agency, Inc.; Spartan Insurance Company Ltd. (Bermuda).

Principal Competitors

D&W Food Centers Inc.; IGA Inc.; Meijer Inc.

Further Reading

Bennett, Stephen, "Spartan Shows Sporting Spirit," *Progressive Grocer*, December 1991, pp. 34–35.

Crawley, Nancy, "Spartan Pays Painful Price," *Grand Rapids Press*, November 5, 2000, p. B1.

De Santa, Richard, "Renewing the Spartan Philosophy," *Progressive Grocer*, January 1988, pp. 28–36.

Hogan, John, ''Spartan Finds a Buyer for United Wholesale,'' *Grand Rapids Press*, January 28, 2004, p. A10.

Natschke, Patricia, ''Quinn Leads a Spartan Life,'' *Supermarket News*, September 2, 1985, p. 1A.

Radigan, Mary, ''Meyer's Decision to Leave Spartan Not a Performance Issue,'' *Grand Rapids Press*, October 30, 2002, p. A13.

——, ''Repackaging Spartan,'' *Grand Rapids Press*, August 8, 2004, p. E1.

——, ''Spartan Stores Ends Rough First Year as Public Company,'' *Grand Rapids Press*, May 9, 2002, p. C1.

Shellenbarger, Pat, ''Big-Volume Spartan Just Clicks Along,'' *Grand Rapids Press*, April 21, 1985.

''Spartan Becomes a Public Company,'' *Supermarket News*, August 7, 2000, p. 4.

''Spartan CEO Says Growth Is 'Imperative',,'' *Supermarket News*, July 21, 1997, p. 6.

Veen, Jeffrey, ''Technology Boosts Spartan Inc. Efforts,'' *Grand Rapids Business Journal*, May 18, 1992, p. 5.

Weinstein, Steve, ''It Won't Be Easy,'' *Progressive Grocer*, January 1993, pp. 36–40.

—Tina Grant
—update: Christina M. Stansell

Spear, Leeds & Kellogg

30 Hudson Street
Jersey City, New Jersey 07302
U.S.A.
Telephone: (212) 433-7000
Fax: (212) 433-7310
Web site: http://www.slk.com

Wholly Owned Subsidiary of The Goldman Sachs Group, Inc.
Founded: 1931 as Spear, Leeds & Co.
Employees: 2,500
Operating Revenues: $1.3 billion (2000)
NAIC: 523120 Securities Brokerage

A subsidiary of The Goldman Sachs Group, Inc., Spear, Leeds & Kellogg (SLK) is a Jersey City-based company that offers execution and clearing services to the investment community. SLK has long been known as a leading specialist on the New York Stock Exchange. Such firms have been at the heart of the system since 1792 when the open auction approach for each stock trade was introduced. Specialists manage the sale of stocks on the floor of the exchange, in effect ''making a market'' by matching up sellers and buyers at a fixed price, a service for which they receive a commission. Specialists also step in to buy stock when there is an imbalance between sellers and buyers, and make most of their money through buying and selling from their own account, a practice known as ''principal'' trading. Because of their unique position in the stock market, possessing inside knowledge about the demands to buy and sell specific stocks, specialists hold a highly profitable advantage, one open to abuse. In 2004 SLK and four other specialist firms paid $240 million to settle with the Securities and Exchange Commission (SEC), which accused them of ''front-running,'' artificially inflating the price of shares they held as a way to skim additional profits. In recent years, SLK has expanded beyond its traditional function as a market maker to offer other services, such as clearing, trading, and reporting tools. SLK also offers financing to customers and loans out stocks, especially hard-to-borrow securities. In addition SLK provides custody reporting services—helping customers to keep track of their daily trading activity, combined with profit and loss information—and a Web-based portfolio accounting system.

Origins Dating to the Early 1930s

SLK was founded as a partnership in 1931 by Harold Spear and Lawrence Leeds. Spear bought his seat on the floor of the New York Stock Exchange in 1927, and Leeds bought his the following year. In 1941 they took on a third partner, 26-year-old James Crane Kellogg III, who would be highly influential in the growth of the firm. ''Jimmy'' Kellogg was born in New York City in 1915. His family ran a detergent bluing company that struggled with the advent of the Great Depression, and with the death of his father, Kellogg was forced at the age of 16 to leave Williams College to find work to help support his family. He became an odd lot broker with Carlisle, Mellick & Co. In 1936 he was able to raise $125,000 to buy a seat on the New York Stock Exchange and at the age of 21 became the youngest seatholder. Although his mother's connections helped Kellogg establish himself on the Exchange, Kellogg also proved to be highly talented. According to the recollections of SLK partner Al Rubin, ''Jimmy Kellogg was one of the finest professional short players I've seen in my life.'' It was no wonder that Spear and Leeds, in search of new blood, would eagerly bring in the young man. Not only was he a good clubman, able to use his natural geniality to his advantage in doing business, he also possessed strong organizational skills.

In 1951 Kellogg became a managing partner in the firm, which in 1954 became known as Spear, Leeds & Kellogg, L.P. In 1955 he became the managing partner when Spear and Leeds retired and became limited partners. Under his leadership the company was quick to buy out the books of stock owned by other specialists, and Kellogg helped drum up new business by playing the old boy's network, always ready to help out fellow Exchange members. As a result, when specialists retired, SLK often picked up their business. In many ways Kellogg laid the foundation for today's firm, responsible for its diversification beyond market making, into such areas as clearing. In the early

Company Perspectives:

With over 70 years of dominance in the U.S. equities markets, Spear, Leeds & Kellogg (SLK) provides one of the industry's most comprehensive suites of prime brokerage solutions.

1950s he became a New York Stock Exchange governor and in 1956 was elected chairman of the Exchange. Also in 1955 Kellogg became a commissioner of the Port Authority of New York and New Jersey. He played a crucial role in the building of the World Trade Center, serving as an unpaid chief executive from 1968 to 1974.

Kellogg's son, Peter Rittenhouse Kellogg, although not the eldest of four sons, would be the one to carry on the Kellogg tradition on Wall Street and build upon what his father started. Unlike his father, however, Peter Kellogg preferred to operate in the background and shunned the press. Nevertheless he would become, in the words of the *Investment Dealer's Digest,* "the most powerful and feared man on Wall Street. . . . Kellogg's detractors call him 'Peter the Predator.' " He grew up in Elizabeth, New Jersey, attended the exclusive Berkshire School, a 100-year-old prep school that primarily served the monied classes and where his father served as a trustee. Kellogg studied at the Babson Institute of Business Administration but dropped out after only four semesters. Because his father had instituted a rule at SLK that forbade the hiring of kin, Kellogg found a job on Wall Street in the early 1960s with Stern, Frank Meyer & Fox, initially working as a clerk on the New York Stock Exchange floor. It was here that he gained a practical education from the people who worked for his employer's agent, Dominick & Dominick. Like his father, he proved to be an adept trader, so much so that the partners at SLK petitioned the elder Kellogg to bend his rules and bring Peter into the firm. Thus, in 1967, Peter Kellogg became a partner at SLK at the age of 25.

Becoming Computer-Oriented in the 1960s

Some of SLK's attempts at diversification in the 1960s did not prove as successful as the firm envisioned. For a time it sold a mutual fund and launched a retail branch network, but neither made much money and were discontinued. "The real master stroke," according to the *Investment Dealer's Digest,* "proved to be clearing—settling trades for other firms for a fee. Clearing forced Spear Leeds to pay strict attention to costs, unhindered by optimism of a retail sales department. Transaction processing forced the firm to apply computer technology, long before the iron discipline of economics made it a necessity. Finally back office work prepared the firm for the large trading volumes that became routine as the decades progressed." Unlike other securities firms that used operations as support for the sales office, SLK ran "from the back office outward." By focusing on cost control, SLK made sure that revenues generated by the front of the operation ended up as profits on the balance sheet.

SLK started the 1970s with just 50 employees, but over the course of the next decade it swallowed up a number of longtime Wall Street specialist firms, such as Pears Duffy & Stern; Frost Stamler & Klee; Schaefer, Collins & Tuttle; Murray & Co.; Wisner Declairville & Hoffman; and R.S. Dodge. Jimmy Kellogg retired in 1978, replaced as SLK's managing partner by his son. Jimmy Kellogg died from a stroke in December 1980, and although his death was unexpected, he had recently established trusts that allowed the firm to continue acquiring specialty firms, so that by the early 1980s SLK employed more than 700 people.

Many of the acquisitions were a response to changing conditions that diminished the role of market making. According to the *Investment Dealers' Digest,* "Most of Spear Leeds' acquisitions in the late 1970s and beyond stem from an attempt to capture the flow of orders leaving the specialists' order books. The deregulation of commission rates contributed—as did institutional trading in blocks of stocks far too large for the specialist to handle—to what is euphemistically called upstairs trading by major firms. Spear Leeds pursued the business off the exchange, because the specialist saw less and less of the order flow." One of SLK's most successful upstairs traders was John Mulheren, who made a great deal of money for the firm with a takeover bid on Conoco. He left to start his own firm and in 1985 offered $350 million to acquire SLK. The bid was rejected, but the firm then floated the idea of making an initial public offering (IPO). Brokerage firms like Bear, Stearns & Co. and Morgan Stanley & Co. had recently completed highly successful offerings, making the idea of taking advantage of investor interest in Wall Street firms an attractive one. SLK went as far as to retain the investment banking firm Drexel Burnham Lambert Inc. to study options, including an IPO, a leveraged buyout, or selling to a larger corporation. Another area SLK entered as a way to pick up some of the business moving away from the exchange floor was over-the-counter dealers. In 1977 SLK acquired dealer Troster Singer, making it a subsidiary, and later forged a less direct relationship with another dealer, Sherwood Securities.

The partners ultimately dismissed the idea of an IPO, opting instead to raise money in 1986 by selling a valuable asset, First Options, the largest clearing operation in the stock option business. Continental Illinois Bank of Chicago paid $125 million for First Options plus $35 million in subordinated debt. To outside observers the deal appeared too expensive and too risky for Continental. When the stock market crashed in October 1987, Continental was severely crippled. Five years later, SLK was able to reacquire First Options for a song, paying just $15 million and a small percentage of future earnings. SLK was then able to successfully rebuild the business.

In the 1980s SLK started to get caught up in controversies in which its conduct was called into question. In 1988 the firm's arbitrage operation came under the scrutiny of the SEC, an outgrowth of the Ivan F. Boesky case concerning illegal stock parking. This practice conceals the ownership of securities by having one investor buy stock for a party, which might want to quietly accumulate large positions in the stocks of takeover targets. But such arrangements run afoul of disclosure regulations. In 1989 SLK paid $2.5 million to settle a class action lawsuit by investors who claimed that the firm profited from deceptive practices involving shares of J.P. Morgan & Co. in October 1987. SLK was accused of setting the opening price artificially high, well aware that it would fall, and knowing it could buy back the shares at a lower price. On the day of the

Key Dates:

1931: Harry Spear and Larry Leeds start a specialist brokerage.
1941: Jimmy Kellogg joins the firm.
1951: Kellogg becomes a named partner.
1957: Kellogg becomes managing partner.
1967: Kellogg's son, Peter, joins the firm.
1978: Kellogg retires, replaced by Peter Kellogg.
2000: Goldman Sachs acquires the firm.

market crash in 1987 the price of Morgan stock increased 69 percent between the final trade of the day and the opening price for the next day, which was set at $47. Within hours, the price plunged to $29. According to the suit, SLK sold about half of the 500,000 shares traded at the opening from its own account. A fair opening price, according to plaintiffs, would have been around $34, the stock's closing price for the day. In settling the suit, SLK admitted to no wrongdoing. Later SLK and one of its specialists would be fined by the New York Stock Exchange for a number of violations during the mini-crash of the stock market in 1989. The firm also would be fined by the New York Stock Exchange for violations of exchange rules and federal securities laws for a large account transfer done by its futures division in 1990.

Peter Kellogg began cutting back his role at SLK during the 1990s. According to the firm he relinquished his role as senior partner in mid-1990. Whatever his title at SLK, he retained control of the firm and remained a powerful force on Wall Street. In 1994 SLK acquired Foster, Marks, Natoli & Safir, a medium-sized specialist firm, the addition of which gave SLK control over some 11 percent of the Exchange's 2,343 listings. Only recently had the New York Stock Exchange increased its longtime rule of limiting specialist firms to no more than 10 percent of the listings. The next largest specialist controlled a 7 percent share of the listings, prompting many on the Street to view SLK "as a subtle threat to the NYSE's ability to regulate the auction system." In the words of the *Investment Dealers' Digest:* "Unlike the NYSE, Spear Leeds Kellogg refuses all public comment and is under the control of one man." SLK also had ties to more listings through Sherwood, which owned a controlling interest in another specialist with 40 New York Stock Exchange stocks. Other than market making, there was concern about SLK's other activities: "Spear Leeds has diversified into all forms of trading, from over-the-counter markets which handle NASDAQ listed shares and bonds, to options and block trading. These holdings give Spear Leeds an equally vested interest in the dealer markets." Moreover, SLK could influence the market in more subtle ways by acting as the clearing broker for several specialists, thereby gaining "an insider's advantage when it comes to acquiring firms."

New Century, New Ownership

SLK continued to diversify in the 1990s, especially in the area of electronic communication networks (ECN). It developed RediBook, a system that connected customers to various exchanges and integrated order routing. To supplement the business, in 1999 SLK acquired TLW Securities LLC, a big program trading operation, and Pantechnia LLA, a technology firm that designs trader work stations. It was the breadth of the firm's capabilities that led to Goldman Sachs buying SLK for $6.3 billion in September 2000. Because there was uncertainty about the future structure of the market, Goldman Sachs was in effect hedging its bet in picking up SLK. Whether trades would one day go completely electronic or not, there would still remain the need for the match-making intervention of market makers like SLK.

With Peter Kellogg now out of the picture, SLK was headed by Todd J. Christie, who had joined the firm in 1987 when he was in his early 20s and used his talent as a trader to quickly rise through the ranks. SLK was initially allowed to operate as an autonomous unit, but the marriage between SLK and Goldman Sachs soon proved rocky in a number of ways. It became apparent, although Goldman Sachs officials were reluctant to admit it, that SLK was bought at the top of the stock market. Business fell off sharply, leading to the March 2003 resignation of Christie without explanation, and the retirement of Joe Della Rosa, the head of the institutional trading business. Senior Goldman stock managers John Lauto and Duncan Neiderauer were installed as co-CEOs to oversee the business.

SLK also was implicated in more regulatory problems. In 2001 SLK agreed to pay $1 million to the American Stock Exchange for failing to supervise an executive accused of making fraudulent trades. In 2003 the firm and four former employees paid $435,000 to the American Stock Exchange for violations such as quoting erroneous prices and putting their own interests ahead of their customers. Later in 2003 SLK agreed to pay $450,000 to settle accusations from the SEC that in 1999 its employees helped Baron Capital to inflate the share price of the Southern Union Company, which was more than 10 percent owned by Baron affiliates. Southern Union was then able to use more of its stock in its acquisition of Pennsylvania Enterprises, thus saving a significant amount of cash. Also in 2003 SLK and four other specialist firms came under investigation by the New York Stock Exchange for questionable trading practices, such as using inside information about pending orders to engage in "front-running"—buying stock low and reselling at a high amount after the orders start driving up the price. The matter would be settled in March 2004 when the five firms agreed to return a combined $154.1 million and pay $87.7 million in civil penalties. In exchange, they neither admitted nor denied guilt. The New York Stock Exchange also had been caught up in scandal, which led to the resignation of its chairman, Richard Grasso. The Exchange cleaned house, hiring a new CEO and approving major governance changes. How these changes would affect the business of SLK remained to be seen.

Principal Operating Units

Clearing Services; Prime Brokerage; SLK Fixed Income; Electronic Transaction Services; SLK Specialists LLC.

Principal Competitors

Bear/Hunter Specialists; Knight Trading Group, Inc.; LaBranche & Co. Ince.

Further Reading

Kelly, Kate, and Susanne Craig, ''Ouster at Goldman HITS NYSE,'' *Wall Street Journal,* March 27, 2003, p. C1.

Santini, Laura, ''A Big Stake in Market Making,'' *Investment Dealers' Digest,* January 8, 2001, p. 1.

Sorkin, Andrew Ross, ''Goldman Bought Questions Along with Spear, Leeds,'' *New York Times,* April 22, 2003, p. C1.

Willoughby, Jack, ''A Modern-Day Rockefeller,'' *Investment Dealers' Digest,* December 12, 1994, p. 12.

——, ''Spear Leeds Kellogg Buys Specialist Foster Marks,'' *Investment Dealers' Digest,* February 21, 1994, p. 4.

Wipperfurth, Heike, ''Spear Leeds Adds Program Trading to Growing Empire,'' *Investment Dealers' Digest,* December 6, 1999, p. 1.

—Ed Dinger

Stanley Leisure plc

151 Dale Street
Liverpool
L2 2JW
United Kingdom
Telephone: (+44) 151-237-6000
Fax: (+44) 151-237-6100
Web site: http://www.stanleyleisure.com

Public Company
Incorporated: 1958
Employees: 6,631
Sales: $1.6 billion (2003)
Stock Exchanges: London
Ticker Symbol: SLY
NAIC: 713990 All Other Amusement and Recreation Industries

Based in Liverpool, Stanley Leisure plc is the United Kingdom's largest casino operator and fourth-largest operator of betting shops. In addition, the publicly traded company is involved in online betting and has interests in betting ventures in Italy and Bermuda. Stanley divides its business between two operating divisions: gaming and betting. The gaming division is responsible for running Stanley's 41 casinos, of which 37 are located in the provinces and four in London. The best-known casino is Crockfords, one of London's oldest and most exclusive gambling clubs. Stanley also owns the largest casino in the United Kingdom, Star City in Birmingham. The gaming division runs two online gaming businesses: www.crockfords casinos.com, taking advantage of the Crockfords name, and www.acropoliscasinos.com, which represents the combined businesses of two acquired online casinos, "Acropolis" and "Avalon." Stanley's betting division operates 600 shops under the Stanleybet banner in Britain, the Isle of Man, Jersey, Northern Ireland, and the Republic of Ireland. The shops concentrate on small wagers placed on horse racing and soccer games. The division also runs its own online sports betting site, www.stanleybet.com., which is dedicated to sports wagering as well as occasional specialty bets, such as the eventual winner of the *Big Brother* reality television series. Stanley's executive chairman is its founder, Leonard Steinberg.

Company's Founder Dabbles in Bookmaking with 1954 Derby

Leonard Steinberg's grandparents were Jews who escaped the pogroms in Poland and Russia during the early 20th century, settling in Manchester, England, and then Northern Ireland. Steinberg grew up in Belfast, the son of Stanley Steinberg, who owned and operated an optical manufacturing business and a milk bar in addition to running an illegal betting shop as a hobby. As a teenager, Leonard Steinberg placed an occasional bet, and when he was 18 years old he first tried his hand at bookmaking. Some school friends asked him to stake their bets on the 1954 Derby, but realizing that the bets covered only nine of the 20 horses in the field, Steinberg and a friend decided that the odds favored them taking on the risk themselves instead of placing the bets with bookies. Because only one of the horses placed and required a payout, Steinberg and his partner each walked away with more than one pound.

After this modest foray into bookmaking, Steinberg decided to pursue a career as an accountant and had begun a trainee program with a Belfast firm when his father died in 1954. As the oldest child in the family, he stepped in to take over his father's businesses to support his mother, two brothers, and a sister. He hired someone to operate the milk bar and attempted to keep the optical manufacturing business running as well. However, his employees absconded with £3,000, and optics proved too technical for the young man, forcing him to shut down that business. All that remained was his father's illegal betting shop. It was here that he found success. After Northern Ireland legalized betting shops in 1957, he was able to expand the business. With the ownership of two Belfast betting shops, Steinberg founded Stanley Leisure in 1958, naming the company after his late father.

Relocating to England in the 1970s

Stanley concentrated on the lower-end of the betting market and over the next decade added some ten shops across Ulster. He also began taking bets from customers in England before

Company Perspectives:

The Company has pursued a focused policy of expanding its betting and gaming divisions through organic growth and a steady acquisition programme.

betting shops were legalized there. It was in England that his future lay, especially in light of the increased level of violence that afflicted Northern Ireland. ''At that time,'' he told the press in a 1997 interview, ''there was no great difference between the IRA and the extremists on the Protestant side. They were all at the protection racket. We refused to pay.'' Some of his shops were set ablaze and his workers threatened. By the early 1970s, Steinberg, who as an Ulster Unionist was a target of the IRA, decided to relocate his business across the Irish Sea. He started out by operating two betting shops on the Isle of Man, which were followed by four in Yorkshire. During the middle years of the decade, he acquired more than 100 betting shops spread across northwest England. They were in poor condition and hardly attractive to the big three in the industry: William Hills, Ladbrokes, and Coral. In general, Steinberg did business in the places his larger rivals disdained, and he was willing to invest the time and money needed to grow them into healthy ventures. To achieve some diversification, he bought a provincial casino in Stockport. In 1979, he established his headquarters in Liverpool to manage his slate of betting operations.

Steinberg took the betting shop division, Stanley Racing, public in June 1986. At this stage, Stanley Racing was the sixth largest betting shop chain, but Steinberg clearly had more ambitious goals in mind. Not only did he want to add to his chain of betting shops, now numbering 117, he was interested in building up his gaming business, which consisted of three casinos. For the time being, however, he elected to stay away from London, where the rewards were greater than in the provinces but so were the risks. In September 1989, Stanley became involved in the Republic of Ireland market by acquiring the 58-shop Mecca chain. Also in 1989, the company grew the gaming side of the business by acquiring five casinos in England from Brent Walker. A year later, Stanley added eight more casinos from Leading Leisure.

Stanley's growth was held back in the early years of the 1990s due to a recession, but by mid-1993 profits began to show improvement, especially in the casino trade. On the horizon was a national lottery, which was a cause of concern to many, but Steinberg maintained that while his betting shops, which now numbered 355, might be adversely impacted in the beginning, the lottery would in the end carve out its own clientele of bettors and simply serve to grow the gaming market. Moreover, the lottery was not expected to have any impact on Stanley's string of 18 casinos.

In 1994, Stanley raised an additional 21 million pounds in the equity market for further expansion. Over the course of the year, the company added another provincial casino and 70 more betting shops. However, in the fall of that year Steinberg also underwent heart by-pass surgery and had to take about three months to convalesce. He used this time to plan a strategy for Stanley's ongoing growth, looking to move into southern England and ultimately London. Steinberg also remained committed to serving the middle market and was loath to overpay on acquisitions. A major factor in the expansion of the company, as well as the growth of British gaming in general, was the move towards deregulation, an issue on which Steinberg had emerged as one of the industry's chief champions. An area of particular contention was the addition of slot machines, so-called fruit machines, to casino operations. The new regulations permitted three machines per gaming table, a change that Steinberg expected to significantly alter the casino business and lead to greater profitability. Betting shops would also be allowed to install two slot machines. In addition, at the end of the 1990s the government opened up 20 new markets to casinos in England, but several of the proposed sites—such as the seaside towns of Morecambe, Weymouth, and Hastings—were not considered large enough to support a casino. Steinberg was also eager to offer gaming machines with payoffs in the £100,000 range, but the government was reluctant to move too quickly on that front. As part of his effort to improve gambling's image and influence the government, Steinberg established in 1997 a Centre for Gambling and Commercial Gaming at the University of Salford.

The next major event in Stanley's history came in 1999. After failing to buy the Coral betting shop chain, Steinberg was successful in acquiring troubled Capital Corporation plc for £86 million, a deal that brought Stanley into the London market with the addition of three city casinos: the Colony Club, Cromwell Mint, and Crockfords, Britain's top venue and London's oldest private gaming club. While Crockfords added luster to Stanley's portfolio, and fulfilled a goal of becoming a major presence in London, Steinberg was not interested in relocating his headquarters to the city. Rather, he preferred to stay in Liverpool, in keeping with his belief that the provincial casinos, although far less glamorous than the London clubs, remained the backbone of his gaming division's success. Even as he was staking out the London market, Steinberg had to contend with competition on another front—the Internet, which threatened to revolutionize the gaming industry.

Internet Gambling Sites Acquired in 2000

Internet gaming was illegal in the United Kingdom in 1999, but the lure was so great that U.K.-based companies began looking for a way to become involved in the business by going offshore. Ladbrokes, the country's largest chain of betting shops, was already gearing up to offer Internet bookmaking and casino games, and Coral, the third-largest bookmaker, bought a Gibraltar-based Internet betting service called Eurobet. Steinberg expressed his displeasure with these moves by U.K. bookmakers, but because he risked being left behind he began shopping for an Internet gaming company to acquire for Stanley. Finding the right candidate, however, proved difficult, as so few of the Internet gambling sites were profitable. In March 2000, Stanley acquired two offshore gaming sites, Acropoliscasinos.com and Avaloncasinos.com, then announced he was taking the associated infrastructure and wedding it to the Crockfords name, one of the most prestigious in the gaming world. As a result of taking Crockfords online, which debuted in 2002, Stanley would become the first company to combine a virtual casino with a real one. Players with an interest in archi-

Key Dates:

1958: The company is formed in Northern Ireland.
1979: Headquarters are relocated to Liverpool.
1986: The company is taken public.
1999: Crockfords casino is acquired.
2003: Star Casino opens.

tecture would also be able to take a virtual tour of Crockfords' 18th century premises. In addition to virtual casinos, Stanley launched a sports betting site, Stanleybet.com, in 2000.

The advent of online gaming also provided Steinberg and U.K. gambling interests with leverage in their lobbying efforts with the government. Steinberg maintained that the gambling industry was taxed far more than any other leisure industry and that it actually paid more in betting and gaming taxation and duty than it made in profits. He also claimed that if taxes on betting shops and casinos were reduced, the treasury would not lose money because gaming revenues would increase and generate the same amount in taxes. In February 2001, the country's five largest bookmakers, all with offshore gaming operations offering tax-free bets, gave the government an ultimatum: Either eliminate the 9 percent tax on bettors in exchange for a 15 percent tax on the gross profits of the bookmaker or risk the destruction of the domestic gambling industry. The government gave in to the demand and most of the British bookmakers closed down their tax-free offshore operations.

In the early years of the 21st century, Stanley increased its holdings in land casinos. In 2001, it added casinos in Plymouth and Torquay. A year later, it bought casinos in Brighton and Luton and picked up another five from Tower Casino Group, adding two locations in Birmingham and ones in Reading, Blackpool, and Derby. In May 2002, Stanley opened a new casino in Manchester called The Circus that featured four of the new games the government now permitted as part of its deregulation effort. These games were Sic Bo, a dice game popular in the Pacific Rim; the Wheel of Fortune, a vertical spinning wheel game; three card poker; and progressive casino study poker, which featured a linked jackpot.

Stanley continued to expand in 2003. Although it failed in its bid to acquire London Clubs International, it was able to buy one of the London Clubs' casinos it coveted, the Palm Beach Club in Mayfair. This addition further solidified Stanley's presence in the London market. In November 2003, Stanley opened Star City Casino, the largest to date in the United Kingdom at 70,000 square feet. The facility featured 40 gaming tables, 200 slot machines, and 80 automated games. Star City also offered entertainment, restaurants, and bars—more in keeping with Las Vegas-style casinos than the staid English gaming clubs in the mold of Crockfords. Other changes were also underway in 2003. The company took steps to refine its branding and elected to rename Stanley Racing as Stanleybet, a name which was also applied to the company's telebetting operation, now known as Freephone Stanleybet, while online gambling operations became Stanleybet.com.

However, Stanley also faced uncertainties, as the 66-year-old Steinberg, who held 20 percent in the company he founded, announced his intention to relinquish his executive post. Speculation arose that Stanley's chief executive, Bob Wiper, was about to lead a management buyout effort to take the company private, or that possibly a U.S. casino operator, keen on entering the U.K. market before even more deregulation took place, might make a bid. Such talk continued in 2004, leading to volatility in the price of the company's stock. Stanley's stock would tumble in 2004 when the government announced stricter controls, adversely impacting the smaller casinos, which would now be blocked from offering Las Vegas-style slot machines offering unlimited prize money. These slots would be available only in the largest casinos, and the provincial casinos would continue to be limited in the number of slot machines they could offer per table. Although Stanley operated several large casinos, its portfolio included many of the smaller casinos facing a limited future. Moreover, U.S. interests were clearly poised to enter the U.K. market, making Stanley's prospects very much uncertain.

Principal Competitors

Camelot Group plc; Coral Eurobet plc; Ladbrokes.

Further Reading

Bowers, Simon, ''Interview: Leonard Steinberg, Chairman, Stanley Leisure,'' *Guardian*, February 17, 2001, p. 30.
Terry, Fiona, ''Teenage Bookie Beats the Odds,'' *Sunday Times*, October 7, 2001.
Walsh, Dominic, ''Stanley Can't Rest on Its Laurels,'' *Leisure Report*, February 2004, p. 18.
''Winner: As Leonard Steinberg Ponders His Next Move in Stanley Leisure's Bid to Gain Control of Casinos . . . ,'' *Manchester Evening News*, December 11, 2002.
Woolf, Marie, ''Mammon—One Man Who Knows How to Call the Odds,'' *Observer,* January 19, 1997, p. 9.

—Ed Dinger

STARCRAFT

Starcraft Corporation

P.O. Box 1903
1123 South Indiana Avenue
Goshen, Indiana 46527-1903
U.S.A.
Telephone: (574) 534-7827
Fax: (574) 534-1238
Web site: http://www.starcraftcorp.com

Public Company
Incorporated: 1903 as Star Tank Company
Employees: 419
Sales: $192.1 million (2003)
Stock Exchanges: NASDAQ
Ticker Symbol: STCR
NAIC: 811121 Automotive Body, Paint, & Interior Repair & Maintenance

Starcraft Corporation, through its joint-venture ownership interest in Tecstar Inc., is a leading supplier to the original equipment manufacturer (OEM) automotive supply market. As a ''second-stage manufacturer,'' Starcraft's Tecstar receives new trucks and sports utility vehicles (SUVs) from General Motors and then outfits them with high-end groupings of bumpers, mirrors, wheels, grills, rocker panels, and other items, before returning the vehicles to GM for sale to the public. Starcraft also supplies after-market parts and accessories to wholesale and retail customers throughout North America. Once known for its fishing boats and then for its van conversions, Starcraft has again regrouped and shed those businesses to focus on the OEM market.

Early History

The forerunner to Starcraft Corporation, the Star Tank Company, was founded in 1903 in Goshen, Indiana, a tiny town near the Michigan border. Its founder, Arthur Schrock, first began the business to manufacture metal feeding and watering tanks for livestock. In the 1920s, however, Schrock broadened his manufacturing operation to include aluminum boats, and the company was renamed Star Tank and Boat. In the mid-1960s, the company diversified yet again, entering the recreational vehicle industry with a line of fold-out campers that were sold under the trade name Starcraft. The Schrock family sold the business to a conglomerate in 1969.

In 1977, the company entered a new and rapidly growing market, when it began customizing vans through a newly formed subsidiary, Starcraft Van Conversions Corporation. To convert a vehicle, the company took incomplete van chassis, obtained directly from major automotive manufacturers, and added a variety of customer-chosen features, which might include anything from curtains, to specially built seating, to coordinating upholstery and interior decor.

The vehicle conversion industry had started in the early 1970s and had gathered steam steadily through the middle of the decade. When Starcraft joined the fray in 1977, young recreational users comprised the main market for the vehicles. Starcraft bucked that trend, however. The company targeted an older market, offering an upscale luxury product for middle and upper income buyers.

The company's sales of conversions increased steadily through the 1980s, driven by the growing demand for custom luxury vans. Moreover, the Starcraft name became well-known for high quality in design and implementation. In 1987, Star Tank and Boat's management team acquired the company in an expensive leveraged buyout that left it heavily in debt. The following year, the new management sold off the company's boat-building business, Starcraft Power Boats, to Brunswick Corporation, one of the nation's largest boat and marine engine producers. The financial picture did not improve, however, and in November 1990, Starcraft filed for Chapter 11 bankruptcy protection. The company was auctioned by the bankruptcy court and purchased by Kelly Rose, an entrepreneur from northern Indiana, and his partner Stephen Kash.

Coming up Roses in the Early 1990s

Rose was a resident of Elkhart, Indiana, a city just northwest of Goshen. In 1977, he had cofounded an electronics supply business in Elkhart that catered to the van conversion industry. By 1990, however, he had sold his interest in the electronics

Company Perspectives:

Our commitment, with utmost integrity, is to continually improve quality, innovation, safety, service and value. Our focus is to exceed the expectations of our customers, associates, community and shareholders. We will remain the worldwide manufacturer of choice in custom, automotive-related products.

company and was ripe for a new challenge. As soon as Starcraft filed for bankruptcy, Rose knew he wanted it. ''I wanted to buy Starcraft badly,'' he said in a September 1994 interview with *Indiana Business Magazine.* ''There's no other company that enjoys as much of an elite reputation,'' he explained. Rose enlisted Kash, who worked in the conversion business in Elkhart, as a partner and made the purchase. Simultaneously, he sold Starcraft's recreational vehicle business to a third-party RV company, Jayco.

Rose made major changes at Starcraft, hiring new upper-level management and restructuring its production process. Sinking more than $2.5 million into capital improvements, he converted the company's manufacturing floor into team-centered production lines. A firm believer in employee empowerment, Rose also implemented a more bottom-up style of management. Striving to give his employees the tools they needed to be successful, he instituted ''Starcraft U''—a series of classes on business skills, which were held in onsite classrooms.

Under Rose, Starcraft's fortunes quickly reversed. For the 49 weeks ending December 29, 1991, the company posted a $1.3 million profit on sales of $43.5 million. The numbers for 1992 were even more encouraging: a $2.9 million profit on $57.4 million in sales. In 1993, Rose took the company public in an offering that generated approximately $13 million.

Mid-1990s Diversification and Innovation

Since it had begun converting vehicles in the late 1970s, Starcraft had established a reputation for its high-end custom vans. The market for these luxury vans was particularly strong through the boom years of the 1980s, when discretionary income was high and consumer spending grew steadily. By the early 1990s, however, consumer confidence in the economy was growing shaky, and the spending spree was drawing to an end. As consumers grew more cautious in their buying habits and more sensitive to price, the market for more affordable vehicles outstripped the luxury market. To respond to the market shift, in 1994 Starcraft purchased Imperial Industries, Inc., a maker of lower-priced conversions. With the inclusion of the Imperial line, Starcraft was positioned to offer a full line of vehicles that fit a wide range of budgets. In 1995, the company built a state-of-the-art, 110,000-square foot factory in Goshen for its newly purchased subsidiary.

Starcraft caught national media attention in the mid-1990s with the introduction of the Integrated Seat Belt, a new safety feature for its custom vans. The IBS was a new belt designed to prevent seat-back failure during rear-impact collisions. In addition to the conventional lap belt and shoulder harness, the IBS incorporated a second belt that ran through the seat back. In lab and crash tests, the system held the seat back in an upright position during impact, preventing crash-test dummies from slamming backward. IBS was named one of the 100 most technologically significant new products of 1994 by R&D Magazine and was featured in 1995 on a nationally televised segment of Inside Edition.

Starcraft had sales of $81.6 million in 1994, and profits of $3.8 million, an increase of 13 percent over 1993. Unfortunately, it would be the last increase in profits for several years to come, as a trend was beginning that would prove seriously detrimental to the van-conversion industry. Sport utility vehicles were taking over the automotive market.

Market Downturns and New Opportunities in the 1990s

The movement toward sports utility vehicles (SUV) and pickup trucks had been gathering momentum for several years. Since Ford first introduced its Explorer in 1990, SUV sales had skyrocketed, growing 130 percent by 1996. By the middle of the 1990s, consumer obsession with the boxy SUVs had drawn buyers away from full-sized vans, which were the bread and butter of the conversion industry.

Not surprisingly, as sales of van conversions were faltering, sales of SUV and pickup conversions were climbing. Starcraft addressed this trend by opening a new manufacturing operation—Starcraft Southwest—to specialize in conversion pickups and sport utility vehicles. Based in McGregor, Texas, Starcraft Southwest marketed its products under the trade name Lonestar. In 1995, it began developing special conversion packages for the Ford Explorer and Ford Windstar minivan. The following year, the company was asked to develop luxury conversions for the Jeep Grand Cherokee and the Plymouth Voyager, marking the first time it had ever worked with Jeep and Plymouth. Starcraft also worked with GMC to develop a new conversion package for the Jimmy sport utility vehicle.

Already reeling from the effects of the SUV craze, the conversion industry was further hurt by a shortage of key chassis. GM's production of full-size vans decreased by 22 percent in 1995, significantly curtailing the number of van chassis available for conversion. The following year, all three major automakers cut back their production of light trucks, limiting the number of chassis available to fill orders for minivans, SUVs, and pickup trucks. This chassis shortage was worsened by an extended General Motors strike in the spring of 1996.

In October 1996, faced with declining sales and the need to trim costs, Starcraft announced its plan to consolidate its Imperial and Starcraft manufacturing operations. Imperial was moved into Starcraft's 650,000-square-foot facility in Goshen, thereby reducing overhead and allowing for integration of engineering and production.

Such cost-containment strategies could not counterbalance the effect of the market slump. Net earnings declined by 27 percent in 1995, then plummeted 96 percent in 1996. Still, Starcraft fared much better than its competitors, remaining profitable and debt-free while most conversion companies slid deep into red ink. By the end of 1996, there were approximately

Key Dates:

1903: Star Tank is founded as a farm equipment manufacturer.
1920: Company begins manufacturing fishing boats.
1956: Starcraft is incorporated.
1964: Starcraft introduces a pop-up camper.
1977: Company begins doing van conversions.
1988: Company sells its boat division.
1990: Starcraft files Chapter 11.
1993: Starcraft reemerges as a public company specializing in van conversions.
1998: Tecstar, a joint venture with an engineering firm, is formed.
2001: Starcraft divests its van conversion business to focus on Tecstar's operations.

100 van upfitters in the United States; just ten years earlier, there had been more than 2,000.

In early 1997, Starcraft began looking for new income sources to offset the shrinking sales of its van-conversion business. Its first such effort was the acquisition of National Mobility Corp., an Elkhart, Indiana-based manufacturer of modified vans for the disabled. Founded in 1992, National Mobility specialized in making minivans wheelchair accessible by lowering the rear floor and installing fold-out ramps. Most of the company's sales were made to taxi fleets, government agencies, and private transit companies that served healthcare organizations. Once the National Mobility acquisition was complete, Starcraft established a new retail division to handle the subsidiary's products and began selling them through a dealer network.

The market for van conversions continued to decline in 1997. In addition, the demand for SUV and pickup truck conversions had also fallen off. As a result, Starcraft decided to close its Texas operation, and the company's Goshen plant took over manufacture of the vehicles previously sold under the Lonestar name. Starcraft closed out 1997 with total sales of $99 million, a decrease of 12.5 percent over 1996. The company posted a net loss of $11.3 million for the year.

Starcraft expanded its product line again in 1998, when it began producing shuttle buses. The buses, which were marketed under the Starcraft name, ranged in length from 20 to 35 feet and contained seating for 12 to 25 passengers. Starcraft offered a range of features on the vehicles, including interior and exterior storage compartments, wheelchair lifts, and various seat types and arrangements. The primary markets served by the company's new enterprise were nursing homes, churches, and hotel resorts.

A second 1998 initiative took Starcraft into the taxicab market. In the early part of the year, the company partnered with GM's Chevrolet division to convert Venture minivans into taxis. To convert the vans, Starcraft replaced their sliding side doors with hinged ones, added temperature controls in the passenger area, and installed a plexiglass shield behind the driver's seat. The first converted Venture taxis were shipped to New York City in February for a trial period, and another batch went to Chicago for a similar trial. The endeavor proved successful, and in April of that year both the New York and Chicago Taxi Commissions approved the Starcraft Taxicab Minivan, opening the door for Starcraft to further penetrate the cab market in those two cities.

Starcraft formed a second partnership in 1998 with Troy, Michigan-based engineering firm Wheel to Wheel, Inc., which specialized in building show cars and engineering prototypes for General Motors. The joint venture, named Tecstar, Inc., was formed to win a three-year contract with Chevrolet to upfit its 1999 S10 Xtreme pickup. Under the contract, Tecstar would add ground effects, wheels, and badging to the standard S10 trucks, and Chevrolet would then market them as factory vehicles. The arrangement marked a change in the way Starcraft had historically marketed and sold its products. ''This is a significant event for Starcraft, enabling us to participate directly in the OEM market for the first time and benefit from the marketing expertise and national advertising strength of Chevrolet,'' Rose said in a February 17, 1998 press release. ''The Xtreme program,'' he added, ''has brought Starcraft into the Tier 1 automotive business.'' Tecstar leased a manufacturing facility in Shreveport, Louisiana, near the GM plant that produced the S10. In the fall of 1998, Tecstar won another General Motors contract, this one to outfit two new versions of the Chevrolet Tahoe. The company leased 100,000 square feet of production space in Grand Prairie, Texas, near the Arlington, Texas GM plant that produced the Tahoe.

Starcraft's total sales for 1998 were $53.1 million, down 26.5 percent from 1997. For the second year in a row, the company posted a loss, albeit a smaller one than in 1997. The loss was primarily attributable to the continuing slowdown in the vehicle conversion market; during 1998, the company's conversion sales declined 27 percent. Conversely, Starcraft's National Mobility sales grew 39 percent.

2000 and Beyond

Recognizing the need to continue developing and nurturing new businesses and products as the conversion industry dried up, Starcraft entered the 2000s focused on cost-containment and diversification. As the demand for SUVs continued to increase in the United States, Starcraft expanded its facility in Grand Prairie, Texas, to 192,000 square feet, where Tecstar produced up-fit appearance packages for the GM Suburban and the GM Tahoe. The demand for up-fit, or customization, packages showed no sign of abating, and had even grown to become a $3.2 billion industry in which Starcraft was gaining significant ground.

Thus, Starcraft sold its conversion assets and turned its attention to conversion vehicle parts sales and building vehicle appearance packages for OEM. In October 2003, Starcraft and its partner in Tecstar, Wheel to Wheel Inc., merged, with Tecstar becoming a wholly owned subsidiary of Starcraft. CEO Kelly Rose remarked that Tecstar provided ''substantially all of the revenues and net income of Starcraft Corporation. This move enables us to become a single-focus company with improved financial flexibility.'' Rose expected the merger to strength shareholder value. At the end of fiscal year 2003, Starcraft annual revenues rose to $192 million, an increase of 84 percent from the previous year. The company's financial picture had improved dramatically. More importantly, after posting a loss of $3 million in 2001, the company was able to report a profit in 2003 of $3 million. Industry analysts took note of the remarkable turnaround.

Having exited the van conversion business, Starcraft nevertheless formed Conversion Warranty, Inc., in 2002, to provide all van conversion customers one central source to serve their service and parts replacement needs. Starcraft and IPMCO Technologies, Inc., of California, jointly formed Powertrain Integration LLS, in July 2004. With this partnership, Starcraft planned to better meet the emissions needs of low-volume, on-highway vehicle applications, including delivery vehicles, motorhomes, buses, military, and other light and medium duty vehicle applications. IMPCO Technologies supplied advance alternative fuel systems and designed systems for clean burning gaseous fuels.

In 2004 Starcraft hit a bump in the road when third quarter profits dropped dramatically. Like all automotive parts suppliers, Starcraft was experiencing the effects of the decline in the U.S. auto industry. Moreover, Starcraft's Canadian operations, which produced equipment for the Chevrolet Silverado, saw dramatically reduced sales during this time. Management expressed disappointment with the financial performance but remained optimistic that its business would realize long-term growth.

Principal Subsidiaries

Tecstar Inc.; Starcraft Automotive Group Inc.

Principal Competitors

ASC Inc.

Further Reading

Couretas, John, ''Van Plans Vary As Upfitters Cope with Slumping Market,'' *Automotive News*, September 14, 1998, p. 20.

Erickson, Arden, ''Believing in the Team Make Starcraft Work,'' *Elkhart Truth*, March 16, 1993.

Kaeble, Steve, ''The Conversion,'' *Indiana Business Magazine*, November 2003, p. 10.

Kerfoot, Kevin, ''Starcraft Corp. Expanding in Goshen,'' *Indiana Manufacturer,* June 1, 1995, p. 1.

Kurowski, Jeff, ''Starcraft's Set to Survive,'' *South Bend Tribune,* February 27, 1997, p. B7.

''Starcraft Corporation—DaimlerChrysler and Starcraft Corporation Form New Partnership,'' *Market News Publishing,* January 1, 2002.

Swift, Shelley, ''Starcraft Corp. Put Profit Pedal to the Medal in 2003,'' *Indianapolis Business Journal,* May 24, 2004, p. B6.

''Van Converters Diversify Due to Shrinking Market,'' *RV Business,* May 1, 1998, p. 12.

—Shawna Brynildssen
—update: Catherine Holm

Steel Authority of India Ltd.

Ispat Bhavan
Lodi Road
New Delhi 110 003
India
Telephone: (91) 24367481
Fax: (91) 24367015
Web site: http://www.sail.co.in

Public Company
Incorporated: 1973
Employees: 137,496
Sales: $3.73 billion (2003)
Stock Exchanges: Mumbai
Ticker Symbol: SAIL
NAIC: 331221 Rolled Steel Shape Manufacturing; 331111 Iron and Steel Mills

The Steel Authority of India Ltd. (SAIL) is the largest steel manufacturer in India. The company's four integrated steel plants and three specialized facilities produce a variety of steels used in the construction, engineering, utilities, railway, automotive, and defense industries. SAIL's product line includes hot- and cold-rolled sheets and coils, galvanized sheets, electrical sheets, structurals, railway products, plates, bars and rods, stainless steel, and alloy steels. While India's government owns approximately 85 percent of the company, SAIL operates under a ''navratna'' status, that is, it enjoys substantial operational and financial autonomy.

Early History

The history of the iron and steel industry in modern India is closely bound up with political and economic developments since the country achieved independence from Britain in 1947. Most of the productive units run by SAIL were built as state ventures with aid and assistance from industrially developed countries, and operated by SAIL's predecessor, Hindustan Steel Ltd. SAIL's main subsidiary, the Indian Iron & Steel Company Ltd., India's largest single iron and steel company, developed separately as a private company before nationalization, but it depended on state subsidies from 1951 onward and had to function within the terms of the government's planning system.

The industry, however, did not spring from nowhere in 1947. Iron had been produced in India for centuries, while Indian steel was superior in quality to British steel as late as 1810. With the consolidation of the British raj the indigenous industry declined and the commercial production of steel did not begin in earnest till 1913, when the Tata Iron and Steel Company began production at Sakchi, on foundations laid by Jamsetji Tata, whose sons had raised the enormous sum of INR 23 million to set up the company, partly from family funds but mostly from Bombay merchants, several maharajahs, and other wealthy Indians who supported the movement for Indian self-sufficiency (Swadeshi) but did not want to appear openly anti-British. Tata was to dominate the Indian steel industry until the 1950s. The Indian Iron & Steel Company was set up in West Bengal in 1918 by the British firm Burn & Co., with plans to become a rival steelmaker. Steel prices declined in the early 1920s, however, and the company produced only pig iron until 1937. The acute depression suffered by the iron and steel industry after World War I was alleviated by the government's protective measures. The industry continued to make steady progress.

From the late 1920s, when the British authorities introduced a system of tariffs that protected British and Indian steel but raised barriers against imports from other countries, the Indian market was divided in the ratio of 70 to 30 between British producers on the one hand and the Tata company on the other—thus effectively excluding indigenous newcomers. By 1939 the Tata works were producing 75 percent of the steel consumed in what was then the Indian Empire, consisting of the present-day India, Sri Lanka, Pakistan, Bangladesh, and Burma.

In the late 1930s, as European rearmament pushed iron and steel prices upward, the export of Indian pig iron increased and two small firms began to compete directly with the Tata company in steel production. The first was the Mysore State Iron Works, which had been set up by the maharajah of Mysore in 1923 to produce pig iron at Benkipur, now Bhadravati. The second was the Steel Corporation of Bengal, a subsidiary established by the Indian Iron & Steel Company in 1937, the year after it had bought up the assets of the bankrupted Bengal Iron

Company Perspectives:

SAIL strives to be a respected world class corporation and the leader in Indian steel business quality, productivity, profitability, and customer satisfaction. We build lasting relationships with customers based on trust and mutual benefit. We uphold the highest ethical standards in conduct of our business. We create and nurture a culture that supports flexibility, learning, and is proactive to change. We chart a challenging career for employees with opportunities for advancement and reward. We value the opportunity and responsibility to make a meaningful difference in people's lives.

and Steel Company. The Steel Corporation of Bengal was reabsorbed into its parent company in 1953. All three companies profited from the British connection during World War II. Annual output rose from one million tons in 1939 to an average of 1.4 million tons between 1940 and 1945.

In 1947, when India became independent as the biggest, but not the only, successor state to the British raj, the three major iron and steel companies had a total capacity of only 2.5 million tons. A great deal of their plant was already more than three decades old, and badly in need of repair and replacement, while demand for iron and steel was growing.

Industry Changes in the Late 1940s–50s

Like other Third World states that achieved political independence but found their economic prospects determined by their subordinate position in the world economy, the new republic's policymakers decided to seek economic growth through a combination of protection for domestic industries, heavy public investment in them, encouragement of savings to finance that investment, and state direction of production and pricing. The Mahalanobis model of the Indian economy, based on the assumptions that exports could not be rapidly increased and that present consumption should be curbed for the sake of long-term growth through import substitution by the capital goods sector, provided the theoretical justification for this set of policies, which closely resembled what was done in the Soviet Union in the 1930s, in China in the 1950s, and in Africa and Asia in the 1960s, though with much less loss of life than in most of these cases.

Under the terms of the new government's Industrial Policy Statement of 1948, confirmed in the Industries Development and Regulation Act three years later, new ventures in the iron and steel industry were to be undertaken only by the federal government, but existing ventures would be allowed to stay in the private sector for the first ten years. Thus the First Five Year Plan, from 1951 to 1956, involved the use of government funds to help Tata Iron and Steel and Indian Iron & Steel to expand and modernize while remaining in the private sector. As for new projects, in 1953 the government signed an agreement with the German steelmakers Krupp and Demag on creating a publicly owned integrated steel plant, which was sited at Rourkela, in the state of Orissa, to make use of iron ore mined at Barsua and Kalta. Krupp and Demag were chosen after the failure of Indian requests for aid from Britain and the United States, but were excluded from the project by 1959, when the Estimates Committee of the Lok Sabha, the lower house of the Indian Parliament, concluded that getting investment funds from them was equivalent to borrowing at an interest rate of 12 percent.

In order to carry out its side of the agreement the government set up Hindustan Steel Ltd. in 1954, as a wholly state-owned company responsible for the operation of the Rourkela plant. By 1959, when the plant was commissioned, Hindustan Steel had become responsible for two more plants, at Bhilai in Madhya Pradesh and at Durgapur in West Bengal, under the Second Five Year Plan, which started in 1956. The Bhilai plant, located between Bombay and Calcutta, was designed and equipped by Soviet technicians, under an agreement signed in 1955, and by 1961 it included six open-hearth furnaces with a total capacity of one million tons, supplied from iron ore mines at Rajhara and Dalli. The Durgapur plant, meanwhile, was built with assistance and advice from Britain and sited near the Bolani iron ore mine. Hindustan Steel took over the operation of all the iron ore mines supplying its plants, all three of which had been located to take advantage of existing supplies. This policy of locating steel production near raw materials sources reflected the relatively small and dispersed nature of the domestic market for steel at that time, and contrasted with the market-related location policies of companies in more advanced steel-producing countries, such as the United States.

Hindustan Steel's other major venture was its Alloy Steels Project, also based at Durgapur, which was inaugurated in 1964. Hindustan Steel's tasks included not only steel production but also the procurement of raw materials, and its subsidiaries included, in addition to the iron ore mines already mentioned, limestone and dolomite mines and coal washeries. It also operated a fertilizer plant at Rourkela.

The modernization of the two private sector leaders and the program of public sector investment together raised Indian steel output from about one million tons a year in the 1940s to three million tons in 1960, then to six million tons only four years later. Pig iron output rose by an even greater margin, from 1.6 million tons in 1950 to nearly five million tons in 1961. Both wings of the iron and steel industry contributed to the expansion of the engineering and machinery industries envisaged in the Mahalanobis model, and in turn were stimulated by the increased demand to raise production volume and quality. In 1965 Hindustan Steel's latest project, for an iron and steel plant with an associated township at Dhanbad in the state of Bihar, was transferred to a new company created one year earlier, Bokaro Steel Limited. Contact continued between the two companies, however, mainly through an arrangement whereby the chairman of each company was made a part-time director of the other. Like the Bhilai plant the Bokaro project was initiated with aid and advice from the Soviet Union, including blueprints, specialist equipment, technical training, and a loan at 2.5 percent interest. After the establishment of SAIL the Bokaro company was changed back into a division of the public sector steel company.

Throughout its first five years of production, 1958 to 1963, Hindustan Steel's losses rose steadily from INR 7.51 million to INR 260 million. It made a small profit in 1965 and 1966, only to slip back into the red and stay there until 1974, the last year of the company's existence under that name. Among the reasons

Key Dates:

1913: Production of steel begins in India.
1918: The Indian Iron & Steel Co. is set up to compete with Tata Iron and Steel Co.
1948: A new Industrial Policy Statement states that new ventures in the iron and steel industry are to be undertaken only by the federal government.
1954: Hindustan Steel Ltd. is created to oversee the Rourkela plant.
1959: By now, Hindustan is responsible for two more plants in Bhilai and Durgapur.
1964: Bokaro Steel Ltd. is created.
1973: The Steel Authority of India Ltd. (SAIL) is created as a holding company to oversee most of India's iron and steel production.
1993: India sets plans in motion to partially privatize SAIL.
1999: The company posts losses as a result of an industry downturn.
2003: SAIL's output surpasses ten million tons of saleable steel.

the company gave for these disappointing results were the losses incurred at the Rourkela fertilizer plant, the Steel Alloys Project, and the Durgapur steel plant; an increased rate of interest on government loans; an increase in provision for depreciation; and the high costs of imported plant and equipment.

Problems Leading to the Creation of SAIL in 1973

The rate of growth of the iron and steel industry, and of the engineering and machinery producing sectors with which its fate was so closely linked, declined significantly once the phase of import substitution was complete and the droughts of the mid-1960s had forced a diversion of resources from industry. Pig iron output, which had risen so spectacularly in the 1950s, rose from seven million tons in 1965 to ten million tons in 1985, while production of steel rose from 6 million tons to 12 million tons in the same period. The industry suffered due to state intervention to keep its domestic prices low as an indirect subsidy to steel users, and—though the technical problems were different—from a heritage of outdated and inefficient plants and equipment.

Indian government policy since 1965 has been to use its iron ore less as a contribution to domestic growth than as an export, earning foreign exchange and helping to reduce the country's chronic deficit on its balance of trade. Production of ore increased, from 18 million tons in 1965 to 43 million tons in 1985, in order to supply a growing number of overseas markets.

With the expansion and diversification of Hindustan Steel, the separate establishment of Bokaro and the beginning of planning for new plants at Salem, Vishakhapatnam, and Vijaynagar, it became increasingly clear that public sector iron and steel production would need some new form of coordination to avoid duplication and to channel resources more effectively. The Steel Authority of India Ltd. was established in January 1973 for this purpose, to function as a holding company along the lines of similar but older bodies in Italy and Sweden. The new organization was placed on a secure footing when the Indian Iron & Steel Company was nationalized, giving SAIL control of all iron and steel production apart from the venerable Tata Iron and Steel Company and a number of small-scale electric-arc furnace units. At the time of nationalization the Indian Iron & Steel Company included a steel plant at Burnpur in West Bengal; iron ore mines at Gua and Manoharpur; coal mines at Ramnagore, Jitpur, and Chasnalla; and a specialist subsidiary, the IISCO-Ujjain Pipe and Foundry Co. Ltd., based at Kulti.

Both SAIL and its predecessor sought to expand capacity to meet predicted rises in demand for steel. In 1971 Hindustan Steel had unveiled plans for India's first coastal steel plant, at Vishakhapatnam. The project, which in 1991 was in the process of being opened, with one blast furnace already in operation, was expected to allow productivity of 230 tons per man year compared with less than 50 in SAIL's existing plants. The Authority also invested heavily in modernizing its oldest plants, at Rourkela and Durgapur.

Challenges in the 1980s

The 1980s were not a happy decade for SAIL. It suffered losses between 1982 and 1984 but went back into the black in the following two years. Meanwhile Tata Iron and Steel was consistently profitable. By 1986, when the Indian steel industry's total capacity was 15.5 million tons, only 12.8 million were actually produced, of which SAIL produced 7.1 million. Thus imports of 1.5 million tons were needed to meet total demand, after years of exporting Indian steel. By 1988 all the main steel plants in India except Vishakhapatnam were burdened with obsolescent plants and equipment, and Indian steel prices were the highest in the world. The government proposed a ten-year plan to modernize the plants, based on aid from West Germany, Japan, and the Soviet Union just at a time when the worldwide economic recession was deepening and the World Bank was recommending the privatization of SAIL and the liberalization of steel imports.

In 1989 SAIL acquired Vivesvata Iron and Steel Ltd. In its first year under SAIL's wing this new subsidiary's production and turnover showed an improvement over its last year in the private sector. This progress contrasted with results for SAIL as a whole in 1989–90, since production declined, and once again planned targets were not met. Various factors contributed to this disappointing outcome, including unrest at the Rourkela plant as a result of the management's decision not to negotiate with a new union, Rourkela Sramik Sangha, which had challenged the established union, Rourkela Mazdoor Sabha, and had even won all the seats on the plant's elected works committee. Another problem, continuing over several years, arose from defects in power supply; the impact of power cuts on steel output in 1989–90 was estimated as 170,000 tons lost, and the supply of coal was unreliable.

During this time period, SAIL remained in the public sector as a central instrument of state plans for industrial development. The country's reserves of iron ore and other raw materials for iron and steel made the industry central to the economy. At the beginning of the 1980s India had recoverable reserves of iron ore amounting to 10.6 billion tons, a natural endowment that it would take 650 years to deplete at then current rates of production. The high-grade ore within this total—that is, ore with an iron content of at least 65 percent—was, however, thought likely to reach depletion in only 42 years; yet it still represented about one-tenth of the world total. SAIL struggled to maintain production, let alone expand it, in large part because of circumstances outside its control. Since the purchase of raw materials typically accounted for 30 percent of the Indian steel industry's production costs, any rise in the prices of coal, ferro-manganese, limestone, or iron ore cut into the industry's profitability. In the first half of the 1980s, for example, prices for these materials rose by between 95 and 150 percent, at the same time as electricity charges rose by 150 percent. Most of these increases were imposed by other state enterprises.

Nor did it help SAIL that the high sulfur content of Indian coal required heavy investment in desulfurization at its steel plants. Indeed, the industry had chronic problems in trying to operate blast furnaces designed to take low-sulfur coking coal. The more suitable process of making sponge iron with non-coking coal, then converting it to steel in electric arc furnaces, was introduced in the private sector later, though by 1989 only 300,000 tons were being produced in this way. India's basic output costs of INR 6,420 per ton in 1986 compared well with the averages for West Germany (INR 6,438), for Japan (INR 7,898), and for the United States (INR 6,786). What finally kept Indian steel from being competitive was the imposition of levies that raised its price per ton by about 30 percent, and which included excise duties, a freight capitalization surcharge, and a Steel Development Fund charge.

In spite of such problems, and in response to them, SAIL announced in December 1990 an ambitious plan to increase its annual output of steel from 11 million to 19 million tons, thus transforming itself from the world's thirteenth largest steel producer to its third largest, within ten years. SAIL's use of its steel production capacity, running at about 77 percent in 1990, would be raised to 95 percent by 1996, thus permitting output of crude steel to rise by two-fifths over its current level. Output for 1990 had actually been only six million tons, however, compared with 6.9 million tons in 1988, and eight million tons in 1989. SAIL was no more able than large steel companies in other countries to achieve the optimum balance between demand and supply, between increasing the quantity of output and improving its quality by modernizing, and thus escaping from its heritage of outdated plant and equipment. Neither Hindustan Steel nor SAIL was ever in a position to defy the circumstances of the Indian economy or of the world steel industry on their own, but they achieved, in large part, the more modest goal of contributing to India's postwar economic growth.

The 1990s and Beyond

As part of an economic reform policy, India set plans in motion to partially privatize its nationalized industries in 1993. As such, 10 percent of SAIL was offered to private investors over the next several years. In 1994, the company announced its plans to offer an additional 10 percent to international investors in order to raise funds for plant modernization and expansion.

While SAIL worked to reach the goals set forth in the early 1990s, the company faced severe challenges in the latter half of the decade. Falling international steel prices, high costs related to its modernization program, increased inventory levels brought on by private sector growth, the Asian economic crisis, and falling export sales took their toll on SAIL's bottom line. In fact, during the 1998–99 fiscal year, the company posted one of the largest net losses in its history—$360 million.

Overall, the global steel industry struggled during the late 1990s and into the new millennium. By 2002, a turnaround appeared to be on the horizon and demand in India had increased by 5.7 percent. V.S. Jain was named chairman that year and was tapped to reverse SAIL's fortunes. Under his leadership, the company planned to raise its production capacity to 20 million tons by 2011. SAIL's output surpassed ten million tons of saleable steel in 2003 while exports grew by 53 percent over the previous year. By 2004, the company was producing 12.5 million tons.

Although SAIL appeared to have weathered the industry downturn, it continued to face problems related to coking coal supplies. Jain explained the issue in a June 2004 *Hindustan Times* article. ''Coking coal has been a global problem,'' he claimed. ''Since China restricted exports to bolster its domestic industry, global prices have gone through the roof. Our current coking coal requirements are 13 million tons, of which 9 million tons is imported. Due to constraints, we had to cut production last year and make exorbitant spot purchases.'' Jain added, ''We are exploring the option of buying equity stakes in coking coalmines in Australia and New Zealand. We are also looking at substitutes like coal tar and other petroleum derivatives.''

Along with the challenges brought on by the coking coal concerns, SAIL was forced to deal with rising steel prices. Over the past several years, the company had worked to overcome industry problems by diversifying into new business areas in an attempt to bolster profits. In 2001, the company formed a joint venture with the National Thermal Power Corp. to create NTPC SAIL Power Company Ltd., a company designed to manage the Captive Power Plants. Other newly formed joint ventures included the Bokaro Power Supply Co. Ltd. and the Bhilai Electric Supply Co. Ltd.

Believing that it had a solid strategy in place, SAIL's management team remained optimistic about the company's future. India's economy was growing, leading SAIL to assume that the country's steel consumption would nearly double the 2004 levels, reaching 55 to 60 million tons by 2012. Although the company's bottom line stood to benefit from this estimate, the cyclical and turbulent nature of the steel industry left SAIL's future hanging in the balance.

Principal Subsidiaries

Indian Iron & Steel Company Ltd.; Bhilai Oxygen Ltd.; Maharashtra Electrosmelt Ltd.

Principal Competitors

Arcelor S.A.; JFE Holdings Inc.; United States Steel Corporation.

Further Reading

Agrawal, G.C., *Public Sector Steel Industry in India,* Allahabad: Chaitanya Publishing House, 1976.

Behara, Meenakshi, and C.P. Chandrasekhar, *India in an Era of Liberalisation,* London: Euromoney Publications, 1988.

Choudhury, Santanu, and Bhupesh Bhandari, ''Global Factors Will Govern Steel Prices,'' *Business Standard,* May 7, 2004.

''India Steel Consumption Expected to Double by 2001,'' *Dow Jones International News,* September 9, 2004.

''India's Steel Authority Taps Merrill Lynch to Lead Equity Sale,'' *Wall Street Journal,* December 2, 1994.

Karkada, J.S., ''Steeling Itself for Change,'' *TQM Magazine,* June 1993, p. 43.

Pingle, Vibha, ''Managing State-Owned Enterprises: Lessons from India,'' *International Journal of Sociology and Social Policy,* 1997.

Rothermund, Dietmar, *An Economic History of India,* London: Croom Helm, 1988.

''SAIL Remains on Sick Bed,'' *Iron Age New Steel,* October 1999, p. 12.

Sharma, Kuber, ''SAIL Expanding But Not Going Global,'' *Hindustan Times,* June 21, 2004.

Sharma, Rahul, ''India to Raise More from Sell-Off of State Firms,'' *Reuters News,* March 1,1994.

—Patrick Heenan
—update: Christina M. Stansell

Tembec Inc.

800 Rene-Levesque Boulevard, Suite 1050
Montreal, Quebec H3B 1X9
Canada
Telephone: (514) 871-0137
Toll Free: (514) 397-0896
Web site: http://www.tembec.ca

Public Company
Incorporated: 1972 as Tembec Forest Products Inc.
Employees: 9,290
Sales: $2.12 billion (2003)
Stock Exchanges: Toronto
Ticker Symbol: TBC
NAIC: 321113 Sawmills

With headquarters in Montreal, Quebec, Tembec Inc. is a publicly-owned integrated Canadian forest products company involved in four product groups. Tembec's forest products group offers a range of commodity and value-added forest products, including softwood and hardwood lumber, pine lumber, oriented strand board, hardwood flooring, and engineered wood products. The group maintains more than 30 manufacturing facilities located in Canada, the United States, South America, and Europe. The pulp group produces kraft pulp, used for printing and writing, tissue and toweling, and the making of paperboard; high yield pulp, suitable for the manufacture of coated papers, cards, construction paper, as well as tissue, toweling, and boards; and specialty cellulose pulp, used in textiles, pharmaceuticals, food additives, industrial chemicals, nursing pads, sanitary napkins, non-woven products, diapers, and other absorbent products. The Tembec Paperboard Group produces fully bleached coated paperboard used in commercial printing, packaging, high-impact graphic corrugated boxes, litho-laminated packaging, and point-of-purchase displays. The paper group manufactures newsprint, specialty printing paper used in book publishing, light-weight coated papers used in magazines and catalogs, and converted specialty paper used to make such items as cups, coffee filters, file folders, and crepe paper suitable for medical and industrial applications. All told, Tembec operates more than 50 manufacturing plants and generates annual sales in excess of C$4 billion.

1970s Origins from the Shutdown of a Pulp Mill

Tembec was founded in the small town of Temiscaming, Quebec, a single industry town wholly dependent for the previous 50 years on a pulp mill owned by a multinational corporation, Canadian International Paper Company. Late on a Friday in 1972, the company issued a press release announcing that the mill would be closing. Within three months 500 people were out of work, and the town itself was on the verge of collapse. Heated demonstrations resulted, but some of the employees took a different approach. Believing that the company had made a mistake and that the mill remained a viable business, they launched an effort to buy the operation and operate it on an employee-run basis. Spearheading this small group of determined men was the plant's 33-year-old general superintendent, Frank Dottori. Born in Timmins, Ontario, he earned a chemical engineering degree from the University of Toronto and had gone to work for Canadian International Paper in 1963. Three years later he took a position with Texas Gulf Sulphur, then returned to his former employer, assigned to the Temiscaming facility as a control engineer. The mill manager, Jim Chantler, became a major influence, convincing Dottori and other young engineers that they needed to understand business as well as science. After the plant was closed, Dottori joined forces with other ex-employees, Jack Stevens and George Petty, to find a way to buy the business as an employee-owned enterprise, a rarity at the time. They later recruited Chantler as Tembec's fourth founder.

In July 1972 Tembec was incorporated as Tembec Forest Products Inc., to acquire the pulp mill. However, its owners were more interested in demolishing the plant than selling it. The matter received national publicity as the demonstrations continued and the Quebec government became involved, supporting the employee takeover, as did the Canadian Paperworkers Union. The law was also changed to allow union members to serve on a company's board of directors. After more than a year of effort, the former employees were finally successful, buying the pulp mill for C$2.5 million.

Company Perspectives:

Tembec's corporate mission is to be a low-cost, profitable integrated forest products company converting forest resources into innovative and competitive quality products for customers while protecting the environment and creating positive long-term social, cultural and economic benefits for the region and its people, employees and shareholders.

The sting of being fired by press release, and being treated like numbers instead of people, led the new management team to take a groundbreaking approach in building the company. Because Tembec was employee owned, the workers developed a greater sense of pride and were motivated to be more innovative. They also shared in the profits, which allowed the company to be more competitive. Employees earned less in salary, so that during difficult business conditions everyone made less, but when the company was doing well, they would share in the profits and earn more. Tembec also pursued a participatory management approach. A dozen committees were established and all employees were able to participate. The committee had equal representation from management and the union, and majority decisions were binding on the company. An open door policy was also established, and all financial information was made available to employees on a regular basis. As a result of this management model, Tembec was free of labor strife. Labor agreements that might take several months to hammer out at other companies were finalized in a matter of days at Tembec.

Tembec Goes Public in 1979

Tembec's successful launch was helped by a growing pulp market. Dottori started as the mill's production manager and a year later became mill manager. He then became vice-president of operations in 1977 before being named president and chief of operations in 1979, the same year that Jack Stevens became the first of the founders to retire. Also that year the company changed its name to Tembec Inc. and was taken public. Employees still retained a 50 percent ownership stake, however. Also of note in the 1970s was the 1977 incorporation of Temfibre Inc., a research subsidiary that looked to develop marketable products from mill effulent and waste streams.

Tembec marketed its products around the world, to Japan, Taiwan, Indonesia, Iraq, Italy, France, Germany, Cuba, England, as well as to Communist Bloc countries. The company first attempted to grow by external means in 1981 when it acquired Temfor of Ville-Marie, a plywood operation. Dottori became chief executive officer in 1982, a year when the pulp and paper industry began enduring one of its worst recessions in history. The company lost C$4 million in 1983 before business began to improve the following year. Despite these challenges, Tembec was able to survive without resorting to layoffs, a testament to the flexibility of the company's business model. Tembec returned to profitability in 1984 and prospects appeared bright, enough to warrant the investment of C$102 million to build a new state-of-the-art mill to produce a new product, bleached chemi-thermo-mechanical pulp (BCTMP), used to make file folders, printing papers, and disposable diapers.

After recovering from the recession, Tembec was faced with an increasingly competitive market for pulp and paper products. To meet the challenge, the company began to grow several fronts, the result of acquisitions as well as startup operations. In 1984 the company established Temcell to run its new BCTMP mill, the first in North America to sell its output on the open market. Sciere Bearn Inc. was acquired in 1986, and a year later Tembec added sawmills in Taschereau and Delebo. The company also acquired Equipement Boreal Hydraulique in 1987 and half-ownership of the TKL Sawmill a year later (the remaining 50 percent interest would be acquired in 1990). In 1988 Tembec established Temboard and Co. LP to take advantage of Temcell and other Tembec pulps.

Construction was started on a new mill, which became operational in December 1989. It produced a new three-ply paperboard, the top layer consisting og bleached chemical pulp, the middle ply from Temcell, and the bottom layer from bleached chemical pulp. Temcell provided stiffness and the chemical pulp enhanced the boards printing capabilities. Temboard was found useful in the folding carton business—appropriate for packaging cosmetics, frozen foods, health foods, pharmaceuticals, and tobacco—and the graphic arts market, for such uses as brochures, greeting cards, and post cards. To close out the 1980s, Tembec took steps to become a vertically integrated company with the acquisition of saw mills acquired from the G.W. Martin company, picking up facilities in Mattawa, Alban, and Huntsville.

Tembec continued its growth program in the 1990s. It acquired Howard Bienvenu Inc., picking up a sawmill in La Sarre, in 1990. The following year the company started up a second Temcell plant and opened a distillery to turn wood waste into ethanol, which could either be used as a fuel or a gasoline additive. Also in 1991 Tembec established EnviroTem, a subsidiary that was devoted to the development of new technologies to minimize the environmental impact of Tembec activities.

In 1991 Tembec became involved in a deal very much reminiscent of its own founding some 20 years earlier. Spruce Falls Power & Paper Ltd., which operated a newsprint milling operation in Kapuskaning, Ontario, was slated by its co-owners, Kimberley-Clark and the New York Times Company, for a significant downsizing. They were, however, willing to sell the plant to employees, ala Tembec, in exchange for the government giving it clear sale to Spruce Falls' other major asset, Ontario Hydro of the Smoky Fall hydroelectric station. Should the sale be held up because of a drawn-out environmental review, however, the owners threatened to close three out of four newsprint mills, putting 1,200 out of 1,450 employees out of work and threatening the very existence of Kapuskaning. Buyout talks were initiated, the employees put together a C$12.5 million bid backed by area residents, but after several months the deal fell through. A new buyout team stepped in, Tembec agreed to invest in the deal, and Quebec's premier took part in the negotiations. After twice extending their deadline, the U.S. co-owners agreed to a deal in October 1991. They sold the hydroelectric generating station to the Ontario government for C$140 million. The mill employees gained a 60 percent stake in the mill operation, and Tembec paid C$25 million for a 40 percent interest and promised to invest another C$15 million over the next three years in upgrades. Tembec would serve as

Key Dates:

1972: Employees of a shuttered pulp mill form a company to buy the mill.
1973: The mill acquisition is completed.
1979: Tembec goes public.
1986: The Temcell subsidiary is launched.
1995: Malette Inc. is acquired.
1997: Company acquires 100 percent of Spruce Falls.

managing partner. The mill enjoyed immediate success, as production increased by 40 percent over the next year, and the operation posted a C$4.5 million profit. In 1993 profits improved to C$15.7 million and C$50.9 million in 1995. In addition a C$36 million modernization program was launched. In 1997 Tembec acquired 100 percent of the Spruce Falls business.

In 1994 Tembec merged it Temfibre and Temeco operations to form its Chemical Products Group. Also in that year it forged a 50–50 joint venture with another Canadian company, Cascades Paperboard International Inc., to buy a sulfite fluff pulp mill in Landes, France, which was on the verge of closing. The price was a single franc. Tembec provided marketing and technical expertise, while Cascades took over management services.

Fully Integrated for the Future

Tembec fulfilled its effort to become an integrated forest products company when in 1995 it paid approximately C$350 million to acquire Malette Inc., a Timmins, Ontario-based, family-owned company. Unlike other acquisitions Tembec made throughout its history, Malette was a healthy company. Tembec picked up a number of attractive assets, including a lumber mill capable of producing 250 million board feet each year and a bleached kraft pulp mill. Malette also owned a 41 percent interest in a machine finish coated paper mill. As a result of this acquisition, Tembec rounded out its product profile. To help sell the expanded product line in Europe, the company established a new trade office in Switzerland. To bump revenues even further, Tembec invested C$65 million to build an oriented strand board line. The addition of Malette contributed to strong growth in the company's balance sheet, which benefited from higher pulp prices and a weak Canadian dollar. In fiscal 1995 sales totaled C$873.2 million, a 75 percent increase over the C$489.8 million posted the previous year. Net earnings improved from C$72.7 million to C$118.6 million.

In the second half of the 1990s, Tembec completed a number of acquisitions. In 1998 it acquired the Pine Falls Paper Company newsprint mill located in Pine Falls, Manitoba, which was no longer able to compete effectively in an industry that was undergoing consolidation. Tembec paid C$70.4 million in cash and stock and assumed more than C$200 million in debt to buy Crestbrook Forest Industries Ltd., a financially troubled British Columbia pulp and lumber company. The addition of Crestbrook facilities made Tembec Canada's largest market pulp producer and fourth-largest in lumber production. Also in 1999, Tembec acquired a BCTMP mill in Matane, Quebec.

Tembec's expansion program continued in the early years of the new century. It acquired Marks Lumber Inc, an Ontario lumber remanufacturing operation. It bought two French pulp mills; A.R.C. Resins International Corporation, producer of formaldehyde and adhesives for use in fiberglass insulation, binders, and laminates; Duratex Hardwood Flooring Inc., Davidson Industries Inc., supplier of specialty woods; and a St. Francisville, Louisiana, paper mill. In 2002 Tembec acquired a high yield pulp mill in Chetwynd, British Columbia, and a year later added sawmills in La Sarre and Senneterre, Quebec, and Chapleau, Ontario.

In 2001 Tembec added other Canadian forest products companies facing challenging conditions. It was already a soft year for lumber sales when the terrorist attacks that struck the United States had an adverse impact on the world economy. Moreover, the U.S. Commerce Department decided to impose antidumping duties on Canadian products, based on Canada charging forest companies low fees to cut timber on government-owned land. As a result, Tembec and other Canadian companies saw their sales drop significantly. The matter would linger into 2004. Tembec encountered other obstacles as well. Overall there were too many sawmills and not enough available lumber in North America, a situation that prompted the company to look to make more value-added products. Aside from the rising cost of raw materials, energy prices were also rising. In addition, Tembec faced the emergence of lower-priced competition from such countries as Brazil, China, and Russia, all of which possessed large forest resources and low monetary values. Nevertheless, Tembec had proven over the course of three decades that its employee-empowered business approach was flexible enough to meet any challenge.

Principal Subsidiaries

Pine Falls Paper Company Ltd.; Crestbrook Forest Industries Ltd., Spruce Falls, Inc.; Malette Quebec Inc.; Davidson Industries Inc.

Principal Competitors

Abitibi-Consolidated Inc.; Canfor Corporation; Cascades Inc.

Further Reading

Curry, Don, "Tembec: A Model Turnaround," *Northern Ontario Business,* March 1985, p. 65.
"Case of Deja Vu for Tembec," *Financial Post,* December 28, 1991, p. 16.
"Frank Dottori: PINA's Man of the Year," *PIMA Magazine,* August 1990, p. 32.
"Tembec's Grab for Malette Propels Company into Big Leagues," *Canadian Papermaker,* July 1995, p. 5.
Wareing, Andrew, "Limited Wood Supply Demands Innovative Thinking, CEO Says," *Northern Ontario Business,* May 2004, p. 5.

—Ed Dinger

Tom's Foods Inc.

900 8th Street
Columbus, Georgia 31902
U.S.A.
Telephone: (706) 323-2721
Fax: (706) 323-8231
Web site: http://www.tomsfoods.com

Wholly Owned Subsidiary of Heico Acquisitions
Incorporated: 1925 as Tom Huston Peanut Company
Employees: 1,583
Sales: $195.7 million
NAIC: 311919 Other Snack Food Manufacturing

Tom's Foods Inc. is a privately owned, Columbus, Georgia-based company that distributes more than 300 snack food products, 250 of which it manufactures. Tom's specializes in single-serve and vending machine sales. Its business is divided among five food categories: nuts, sandwich crackers, chips, baked good, and candy. In the 1920s, the company was built on its toasted peanuts, but Tom's now offers a variety of flavored peanuts, cashews, pistachios, and sunflower seeds. Peanut butter filled sandwich crackers was another early success and the sandwich category is now supplemented by cheese filled crackers and cream filled cookies. Tom's chips products include potato, tortilla, and corn chips, as well as popcorn, pretzels, and extruded products like cheese puffs. Tom's baked goods include cookies, cakes, and pastries. In the candy category, Tom's sells candy coated nuts, candy bars, hard and rolled candies, and novelty candies. Tom's maintains manufacturing facilities in Columbus, Georgia; Knoxville, Tennessee; Perry, Florida; Corsicana, Texas; and Fresno, California. Although Tom's products are best known in the South, they are distributed in 43 states through company-owned and independent distributors.

1925 Origins

Tom's was founded in 1925 by Tom Huston, who was born in Alabama, raised in Texas, and relocated to Columbus, Georgia. With a penchant for invention, a fondness for peanuts, and a dislike for shelling them, Huston as a young man invented a shelling machine. Peanuts (technically a legume and not a true nut) were originally cultivated in Peru and came to America from Africa by Spanish slave traders who fed them to their captives. Farmers in Virginia were the first to plant peanuts in the United States, but they did not become a popular crop in the Deep South until the 20th century. After decades of cotton cultivation, southern soil was exhausted and rapidly eroding. Ironically, it was a man born into slavery, George Washington Carver, through his research at the Tuskegee Normal and Industrial Institute, who would convince Southern farmers to plant peanuts and soybeans, which—because they were legumes—would restore nitrogen to the soil. In addition, the crops would also provide much needed protein to the diets of Southerners. Carver also developed hundreds of products that could be derived from peanuts, which would become one of the largest cash crops in the South. When Huston invented his shelling machine, however, the peanut was far from an established crop and most farmers could not afford to buy his $5,000 machine, at least not in cash. Instead they paid him in peanuts.

Forever creative, Huston decided to sell roasted peanuts. He was not the first to hit upon this idea. In 1906, an Italian immigrant named Amedeo Obici who was selling peanuts at his Wilkes-Barre, Pennsylvania, fruit stand began jobbing two-ounce bags of peanuts. His business would take on the name of Planters Peanuts. Huston developed his own roasting process, fashioned a toasted peanut log, and invented a narrow cellophane sleeve as packaging. With three employees, he hit the streets of Columbus in April 1925 to sell ''Tom's Roasted Peanuts'' at a nickel a package. Huston turned to Carver for advice on improving peanut crops, making a number of trips to Tuskegee. Tom Huston Peanut Company was the only one of its kind to seek Carver's expertise. As a result, Huston was able to improve the peanuts crops he relied on, which led to increased growth and new products. Within two years of the company's founding, Tom's peanuts were being sold around the country, generating more than $4 million in sales, and the company was relocated to its present day site. Also during the 1920s Tom's added a line of peanut butter, Red Robin Peanut Butter, and began producing peanut butter sandwich crackers under the Red Robin label. The crackers were made by outside bakeries and prepared in the factory by hand feeding into machines for sandwiching.

Company Perspectives:

Quality snacks for every taste.

Huston continued to grow the business into the 1930s, but his inventiveness got the best of him. His attempt to launch a business in frozen peaches failed, the bank holding his notes foreclosed, and Huston lost his peanut company. Far from ruined, however, Huston would move to Miami, Florida, where he launched a pet equipment manufacturing company called House of Huston.

In 1932, the bank hired Walter Richards as president of Huston Peanut. He then formed an investment group to buy the business from the bank and eventually took the company public. Tom Huston Peanut, as well as the entire snack food industry, enjoyed tremendous success during the post-World War II era. In 1950, the company posted sales of $8.9 million, but five years later that number would grow to $16.4 million. Earnings also showed strong growth, jumping from $2.45 a share in 1953 to $4.34 in 1955. To take better advantage of its close proximity to an excellent peanut crop, the company built 14 silos to replace warehouses for storing peanuts, in this way providing more efficient storage and handling while freeing up more space for manufacturing. Not only was production done in Columbus but also through a dozen affiliates located around the country. For distribution, Tom Huston Peanut steadily added to a fleet of trucks that grew to number more than 1,200. Potato chips and popcorn, made by outside companies under the Tom's label, would also be added for distribution. By the 1960s, Tom Huston products could be found in 44 states, sold through 250,000 retailers. A key to the company's success was its network of independent distributors. Unable to match the marketing budgets of larger rivals, Tom's kept its distributors happy by frequently bringing out new products and offering strong point-of-sale support. Many of Tom's distributors would stay on generation after generation. To keep pace with the rising demand for snack foods, Tom Huston Peanut upgraded its manufacturing facilities, installing new production and wrapping machinery, and opened a state-of-the-art plant in Corsicana, Texas. By 1964, the company was approaching $20 million in annual sales and posting a string of record-breaking profits. It was especially strong in the vending segment.

New Ownership in the 1960s

In 1966, ownership of Tom Huston Peanut passed out of the control of local ownership. It was acquired by General Mills, Inc. for $75 million in stock. The name of the company was now changed to Tom's Foods. While a subsidiary of General Mills, Tom's ran afoul of the United States Justice Department, which charged that the company conspired to restrain trade by entering into agreements with competitors, requiring them to gain Tom's approval before selling their products to independent distributors. Starting in the late 1970s, Tom's attempted to move beyond independent distribution and enter the national supermarket channel. General Mills brought in people with marketing experience in this area, and the Great American Chip product line was developed. However, it never took off, failing to achieve national penetration.

Tom's changed ownership again in 1983, this time to an overseas owner, Rowntree-Mackintosh, which paid $215 million in cash for a company that at this point was posting annual sales in the neighborhood of $225 million. Rowntree-Mackintosh was a British company with roots dating back to 1725, when a Quaker woman named Mary Tuke opened a grocer's shop in York, a city that would emerge as England's chocolate capital. In 1862, the company that Tuke founded sold its chocolate and cocoa business to Henry Isaac Rowntree. In the 1890s, J. Mackintosh Limited, which made soft toffees, was established. Later, the company began making chocolates and other candies, and in 1969 it merged with Rowntree's Cocoa Works. Over the next decade, Rowntree-Mackintosh grew to become an international marketer of confections and grocery products, with revenues in excess of $1 billion. Its best known brands were Kit Kat, Rolo, and After Eight, which in the United States were either licensed or marketed by Hershey Foods. In the early 1980s, Rowntree began looking to the United States, hoping to find an acquisition with a strong distribution network that it could use as a vehicle to handle its products into the U.S. market for itself. Rowntree eventually settled on Tom's to fill that role and later supplemented its U.S. holdings by acquiring Sunmark Inc., makers of Sweetarts, Willy Wonka, and Nerds.

Rowntree's ownership of Tom's would be short lived, however. During this time, the company launched a franchising program for its distributorships, and many of the independents converted to the franchise model. Nevertheless, after five years, Tom's saw its business improve only marginally, with 1987 sales estimated to be $247 million. Snack foods were falling out of favor with consumers, who were paying closer intention to nutritional considerations. The business was also becoming highly competitive as larger companies like Frito-Lay and Borden were able to dominate by spending more money. In January 1988, Rowntree announced that it intended to sell Tom's along with Rowntree Snack Foods in order to concentrate on its core confectionery business. Borden as well as Golden Enterprises of Birmingham Enterprises were reported suitors, but in April 1988 Tom's management team, leading a private group called T.F. Acquisition Corporation, emerged the winner, agreeing to pay $200 million. At the same time, Rowntree found itself the unwanted target of takeover attempts by Swiss chocolatiers Souchard and Nestlé. Several months after selling Tom's, Rowntree would be swallowed by Nestlé in a $4 billion takeover.

Tom's management was headed by president Mike Dillon. Funding was arranged through Citicorp bank. Tom's was back in the hands of local ownership after more than 20 years, and although the company was highly leveraged it was in relatively good shape. During the 1980s, Tom's had upgraded it production facilities, replacing all of its packaging equipment in the previous five years, overhauling the cracker-sandwich production line, and building a new state-of-the-art peanut shelling plan in Columbus as well as new potato chip plants in Perry, Georgia, and Knoxville, Tennessee. As the result, Tom's could put its money to use in growing the business and expanding its network of independent distributors.

Two years after buying the company, Tom's management announced an aggressive five-year plan to grow the business. According to *Food & Beverage Marketing,* Tom's was the third-largest snack food marketer in the United States, although it

Key Dates:

1925: The company is founded by inventor Tom Huston.
1932: The bank takes over the company from Huston.
1966: General Mills acquires the company.
1983: Rowntree-Mackintosh acquires the company.
1988: The company changes ownership after a management-led buyout.
1993: Tom's is sold to Heico Acquisitions.

trailed Frito-Lay and Borden by a considerable margin. Tom's strategy relied on the expansion of its franchisees to achieve greater coverage, which would translate into more calls to customers and better service. The company's system included more than 700 independent distributors, of which 320 were franchise operations. The goal was to grow that number to 1,200. In order to support that level the company would have to increase its sales by an estimated $400 million. Tom's was strong in the vending machine channel and with mom-and-pop retailers, which together accounted for about 40 percent of all sales. Convenience store sales were also strong, but Tom's was able to achieve only limited sales to supermarkets, where the snack food category was experiencing its best growth. The competition for supermarket shelf space was cut throat, with stores charging exorbitant slotting fees—from $200 to $1,000 per foot of shelf space for annual contracts—and manufacturers all too willing to pay. Even some independent retailers were now demanding slotting fees if they were a dominant force in their local markets. Given Tom's unsuccessful efforts a decade earlier, when it had the backing of General Mills, to make inroads into supermarket sales, the company's chances to achieve a better result under more difficult conditions appeared unlikely. The second part of Tom's strategy was adopting "unique price points," providing value to consumers and higher margins to retailers.

However, this idea, even when coupled with traditionally strong customer service, would not be enough to overcome disadvantages in the marketplace, and Tom's would fall far short of its goals.

Heico Acquires Tom's in 1993

In May 1993, Tom's was acquired by Heico Acquisitions, a Chicago-based investment company. Heico was founded by Michael Heisley in 1979 after buying conglomerate Conco, Inc. He sold all of Conco's assets except for Spartan Tool Company, maker of sewer cleaning equipment, and Field Controls Corporation, which made climate control components. Heisley then adopted the Heico name and during the 1980s began buying up distressed manufacturing companies in the Midwest, preferably business-to-business manufacturers, at a time when many Rust Belt factories could no longer compete against foreign companies. Heisley bought these companies on the cheap, then turned them around. After the region began to recover, Heisley looked elsewhere for opportunities. In the late 1980s, for example, he acquired Nutri/System, which was on the verge of bankruptcy. Buying Tom's Foods was out of character for Heisley, but he was a difficult man to pigeonhole. He would buy the Vancouver Grizzlies National Basketball Association team and at one point attempted to acquire New York's upscale department store Barney's, Inc.

Over the next decade, under Heico's ownership, Tom's upgraded its information technology and production facilities. It also moved away from the independent distributor model, instead launching a company-owned and operated direct store delivery/vending distribution network. As a result, Tom's gained better control over sales and improved earnings, but this did little to change the company's underlying limitations. Because it was too small to compete against the giants in the snack industry, sales fell below the $200 million level in fiscal 1995. A new management team was hired in January 1995, headed by Rolland G. Divin, the former CEO of Chun King, Inc. Soon a new program was instituted to increase profitability, update old products and introduce new ones, increase operating efficiencies, and expand the company's distribution network, but as Tom's entered a new century, these changes provided little help, and the company posted a string of losing years. Tom's carried too much debt and, according to Moody's, had a negative net worth. The Tom's brand remained strong in the Southeast and Southwest with its single-serve products sold in vending machines, convenience stores, and other small retailers, but it was not competitive in the supermarket and mass merchandise channels. Tom's had a rich heritage and strong brand recognition in some parts of the United States, but its future as an independent company was very in doubt.

Principal Competitors

Kraft Foods Inc.; Lance, Inc.; Wise Foods, Inc.

Further Reading

Chandler, Susie, "What Would Columbus, Georgia Be Like Without Tom's Foods, Inc.," *Columbus Times*, May 10, 1987, p. B3.
DuBois, Peter C., "Goobers to Cashews," *Barron's National Business and Financial Weekly*, June 19, 1961, p. 11.
Hallman, Tom, "Tom's Getting Back Its Hometown Flavor," *Atlanta Journal*, May 31, 1988, p. E1.
McDermott, Michael J., "Tom's Wants More," *Food & Beverage Marketing*, October 1990, p. 16.
Willatt, Norris, "Profits in Nibbling," *Barron's National Business and Financial Weekly*, June 4, 1956, p. 5.

—Ed Dinger

TTX Company

101 North Wacker Drive
Chicago, Illinois 60606
U.S.A.
Telephone: (312) 853-3223
Fax: (312) 984-3790
Web site: http://www.ttx.com

Private Company
Incorporated: 1955 as Trailer Train
Employees: 1,285
Sales: $918 million (2002)
NAIC: 532411 Commercial Air, Rail, and Water Transportation Equipment Rental and Leasing

TTX Company, which is privately owned by the six leading railroads in the United States and Canada, manages a fleet of over 127,000 railcars. The company's three types of railcars—intermodal, autorack, and general use—are utilized by the automobile, steel, lumber, agricultural, and construction industries. The U.S. military is also a TTX customer. TTX railcars are serviced by three maintenance divisions in Florida, California, and South Carolina. Thirty-one Field Maintenance Operations (FMOs) also provide inspection and repair services onsite.

Early History

While ''piggy-back'' transportation of horse-drawn wagons, and later highway trailers, on railroad flatcars was performed sporadically by individual railroads as early as the 1850s, the concept became popular with the shipping public only after the Korean War. However, the growth of piggyback, or intermodal, transport was limited by the absence of standards for flatcar design, particularly trailer tie-down devices, and the uncoordinated control of flatcars by the individual railroads, which resulted in low utilization.

TTX was formed to satisfy the increasing demand from railroads and their customers for a fleet of standardized intermodal flatcars under unified control at the lowest possible cost. Efficient utilization of intermodal flatcars was achieved through the pooling of these cars under TTX management. Unlike cars owned by the individual railroads, TTX cars did not have to be returned empty to the owning railroad after they were unloaded by another railroad. Instead, the cars could be reloaded and transported to any other destination where they could be reloaded again. If no loads were immediately available, TTX directed the movement of the empty cars to the closest location where loads are waiting. TTX's efficiencies and economies of operation were illustrated by the fact that, while TTX owned 8 percent of the U.S. railroad car fleet in the early 1990s, its cars accounted for 24 percent of all the car miles traveled in the United States. Since TTX cars were used more intensively and efficiently than railroad-owned cars, TTX could supply them at a lower cost per load.

The company was incorporated as Trailer Train Company in Delaware on November 9, 1955. Its initial railroad stockholders were the Pennsylvania Railroad and the Norfolk & Western Railway. TTX began operations on March 17, 1956 with a fleet of 500 75-foot flatcars. As the length of the standard highway trailer increased to 40 feet during the fifties, TTX introduced 85-foot and 87-foot flatcars capable of carrying two such trailers. TTX acquired its first 89-foot flatcars in 1961, and cars of this length became the industry standard for the next two decades. Some of these cars had low decks permitting piggyback operations over the older Eastern railroads, which were constrained by tighter clearances than their Western counterparts. By 1964, 41 railroads, including virtually every major line in the United States, had become a TTX stockholder. (By 2003, the number of major railroads in the United States and Canada had been reduced to six as a result of industry consolidation and merger activity.)

Railroads initially used chains, blocks, and jacks to attach trailers to flatcars, but this method was time-consuming and labor-intensive. A TTX employee introduced the concept of a collapsible hitch which could be raised and lowered quickly and efficiently by one worker using a power winch. This innovation, which both cut costs and improved ride quality, was subsequently produced by American Car and Foundry and quickly became the industry standard. An improved hitch, powered by the tractor used to load and unload the trailer, was introduced in 1966.

Company Perspectives:

Our goal is to supply well-maintained equipment wherever needed at the lowest cost possible, while permitting financing of equipment on reasonable terms. To accomplish this goal we must size our fleet in a prudent manner, balancing new equipment acquisitions with innovative modifications and upgrades to the existing fleet.

Postwar Growth

TTX began supplying 89-foot cars for motor vehicle movement in 1962. Prior to World War II, the railroad industry had dominated motor vehicle transportation, but as highways improved, the railroads' share of this market dropped to 10 percent by 1959. To regain this traffic, the railroads and their suppliers designed bi-level and tri-level racks carrying eight to twelve vehicles, each of which could be attached to the standard 85-foot and 89-foot flatcars operated by TTX. If traffic patterns changed, the racks could be detached and the cars returned to piggyback service. This innovation, which cut costs and improved the condition of the vehicles at their destination, proved popular with the manufacturers. By the 1980s, the railroad industry had recaptured nearly 60 percent of the vehicle transportation market, a position it maintained into the 1990s. In 1992 TTX continued to supply thousands of 89-foot flatcars for this service.

During the mid-1960s, TTX began to supply specialized flatcars designed for transportation of lumber, machinery, agricultural equipment, vehicle frames, and pipe to the railroad industry.

To provide reliable service at the lowest overall cost, TTX maintained its car fleet to high standards. In 1991 for example, TTX achieved 92 percent utilization of its intermodal fleet and 97 percent utilization of its flatcar fleet assigned to motor vehicle service. At first maintenance was performed by the individual railroads and independent car shops. However, as its fleet grew and aged, TTX determined that the most cost-effective approach would be to operate its own repair shops. TTX acquired its first shop on February 21, 1974, when it consummated its purchase of Hamburg Industries, operator of a repair facility at Hamburg, South Carolina. TTX subsequently constructed or acquired repair shops at Mira Loma, California, Jacksonville, Florida, and Drayton Plains, Michigan. In 1984, TTX established its first Field Maintenance Operation (FMO)—an FMO employs mobile repair vehicles to perform running maintenance on TTX cars when necessary, avoiding unproductive trips to repair shops. TTX operated 38 FMOs by the early 1990s.

On January 14, 1974, the American Rail Box Car Company, or Railbox, was incorporated as a subsidiary of TTX. At that time, high-quality boxcars were in short supply. The mission of Railbox was to establish a pool of standardized, high-quality 50-foot boxcars that, like TTX's flatcars, could be freely reloaded to any destination, thus optimizing utilization and efficiency. Railbox's car ownership peaked at 24,966 in 1981 and subsequently was reduced to 13,174 as of December 31, 1991, due to oversupply and declining demand for that type of equipment.

Another TTX subsidiary, Railgon Company, was incorporated on May 24, 1979. Railgon acquired a fleet of standardized, high-quality gondola cars which, like Railbox cars, were pooled and could be freely reloaded for optimal efficiency.

Changes in the dimensions of highway trailers and the introduction of intermodal containers led to changes in TTX's flatcar fleet. TTX acquired the first "all purpose" 89-foot flatcars equipped to carry either trailers or containers in 1966. By the early 1980s, highway operation of 45-foot trailers had become legal, and TTX modified thousands of its 89-foot flatcars to carry two trailers of this length. The introduction of 48-foot, and later 53-foot, highway trailers, however, necessitated the acquisition of new types of rail cars. Prominent among these was the five-unit articulated Spine car design, added to the TTX fleet in container-only configuration starting in 1986 and in all-purpose (trailer or container loading) configuration starting in 1989. These cars could carry trailers or containers up to 53 feet in length.

During the 1980s, ocean carriers began acquiring vessels too large to fit through the Panama Canal for their trans-Pacific trade. To reach markets on the East Coast and interior points, these carriers began moving large quantities of containers across the United States by rail on double-stacked, five-unit well cars. TTX acquired its first 320 double-stack cars in 1985. By 1991, double-stack cars made up over one-third of TTX's intermodal capacity, and 74 percent of the intermodal cars were equipped to carry containers. TTX's fleet at the time included single-unit and three-unit drawbar-connected cars with 125-ton trucks, capable of carrying two stacked 48-foot containers, as well as the five-unit design.

Updating the intermodal fleet to satisfy the demands of railroad customers required substantial investment. From 1987 through 1991 TTX acquired over $1 billion worth of new equipment. In 1991 TTX acquired 21 heavy-duty, depressed-center flatcars for transportation of heavy equipment, including transformers and pressure vessels.

During the early 1990s, TTX derived its revenues from its railroad owners in the form of charges for the use of its cars. These charges, which were set by TTX's Board of Directors, included two components: time and mileage. TTX charged no more for use of its cars than was absolutely necessary to recover the cost of owning the cars and maintaining them to high standards. In 1991, TTX's revenue was $621 million.

TTX's pooling operations were subject to the jurisdiction of the Interstate Commerce Commission (ICC) in the early 1990s but eventually fell under authority of the Department of Transportation's Surface Transportation Board. The TTX and Railbox pools were approved by the ICC in 1974, while the Railgon pool was approved by the ICC in 1980. The flatcar pooling agreement among TTX and its participating railroads that was approved by the ICC had a 15-year term. In 1989, the ICC re-authorized this pool for an additional five-year period.

Trailer Train Company changed its name to TTX Company on July 1, 1991, to better reflect the broadened scope of its activities. During that year, TTX also commenced a major quality improvement effort, which included vendor evaluations and internal review of maintenance facilities.

Key Dates:

1955: Trailer Train Company is incorporated.
1961: The company acquires its first 89-foot flatcars.
1964: By now, 41 railroads, including virtually every major line in the United States, has become a company stockholder.
1974: Hamburg Industries is acquired; American Rail Box Car Company is incorporated as a subsidiary.
1979: Railgon Company is formed.
1984: The first Field Maintenance Operation (FMO) is established.
1985: The company purchases its first 320 double-stack cars.
1991: Trailer Train Company officially changes it name to TTX Company.
2004: TTX accepts $600 million in flatcar deliveries—a company record.

Mid-1990s and Beyond

TTX entered the mid-to-late 1990s on solid ground due in part to an antitrust exemption it enjoyed in intermodal shipping. According to a 2003 *Crain's Chicago Business* article, the exemption was granted so that small rail lines could afford intermodal equipment. Industry consolidation during the 1990s, however, did away with smaller rail lines and left just six major companies in the United States and Canada. During this time period, intermodal shipping was the fastest-growing segment of the rail transport industry. From 1992 to 2002, intermodal shipping grew from 10 percent of all railroad revenues to 21 percent. With renewal of the exemption due in 2004, speculation regarding TTX's monopolistic position began to arise. The aforementioned *Crain's Chicago Business* article reported, ''leasing firms would like to get a crack at the intermodal business TTX controls. But leasing companies are worried about offending their railroad customers and thus haven't come out against renewal of the antitrust exemption—yet.''

Another trend that bode well for TTX was the continuing tendency for railroads to lease railcars instead of owning or buying them outright. In 1990, 37 percent of the 1.2 million cars in service were owned by leasing companies like TTX. By 2001, that number had grown to 52 percent.

Success followed TTX into the new millennium as railroad traffic reached record levels. The company's intermodal fleet continued to experience high demand, especially in late 2003 and early 2004. Higher fuel costs and insurance premiums plagued the motor carrier industry, and shippers turned to rail as a more affordable option.

In response to higher demand, TTX continued to focus on quality and maintenance, as well as ordering new equipment. In 2004, the company expected to receive $600 million in flatcar deliveries—a company record. TTX also began to revamp its fleet. According to a July 2004 company press release, the company was working to extend the length of the platform on five-unit spine cars from 48-feet to 53-feet. It also redesigned its tri-level autorack cars to accommodate a bi-level rack, which was used to transport sports utility vehicles. It also planned to modify its 89-foot cars, allowing them to carry new Class 8 highway tractors and recreational vehicles.

Favorable market conditions and its ability to adapt to changing industry demands left TTX in an enviable position among its competitors. By focusing on providing low-cost and well-maintained equipment to its customers, TTX appeared to be on track for success in the future.

Principal Competitors

GATX Corporation; The Greenbrier Companies Inc.; Pacer International Inc.

Further Reading

''Freight Car Market Takes an Upturn,'' *Railway Age*, December 1, 2002.
''How TTX Tracks Quality,'' *Railway Age*, April 1992.
''Ray Burton: Looking Back and Looking Ahead,'' *Railway Age*, January 1, 1993.
Tita, Bob, ''Fed Fuel Keeps TTX Chugging,'' *Crain's Chicago Business*, November 17, 2003, p. 4.
''TTX Fleet Changes to Meet Intermodal Demands,'' *Journal of Commerce*, July 26, 2004.
Welty, Gus, ''It's Time for Up-Sizing,'' *Railway Age*, December 1, 1993.
''Where Intermodal Is Headed: A TT View,'' *Railway Age*, March 1990.

—William F. Todd
—update: Christina M. Stansell

Turner Broadcasting System, Inc.

One CNN Center
100 International Boulevard
Atlanta, Georgia 30348
U.S.A.
Telephone: (404) 827-1700
Fax: (404) 827-2437
Web site: http://www.turner.com

Wholly Owned Subsidiary of Time Warner Inc.
Incorporated: 1965
Employees: 8,000
Sales: $8.4 billion (2003 Time Warner's Networks Group)
NAIC: 515210 Cable and Other Subscription Programming; 533110 Owners and Lessors of Other Non-Financial Assets; 711211 Sports Teams and Clubs; 713990 All Other Amusement and Recreation Industries

As a subsidiary of media giant Time Warner Inc., Turner Broadcasting System, Inc. (TBS) operates as the leading provider of programming for the basic cable industry. Its holdings include TBS Superstation, TNT, Cartoon Network, Turner Classic Movies, Turner South, CNN, CNN Headline News, CNNfn, CNNRadio, and CNN International. The company also owns the professional baseball team Atlanta Braves and oversees nascar.com and pga.com. Founder Ted Turner left Time Warner in 2003 to pursue philanthropic interests.

Beginnings

The history of TBS is closely tied to the personal history of its flamboyant founder, chairman, and president, Robert Edward ''Ted'' Turner III. Alternately seeking and shunning media attention, Ted Turner has accumulated colorful nicknames, including ''Captain Outrageous,'' ''the Mouth of the South,'' and ''Terrible Ted,'' and has earned a reputation for daredevil tactics. Turner's freewheeling entrepreneurial style was reflected in the strategic and financial risks the company took under his leadership.

Turner became president and chief operating officer of a $1 million billboard enterprise, Turner Advertising Company, upon his father's suicide in 1961, which occurred shortly after the elder Turner concluded an agreement to sell the firm's recently acquired Atlanta, Georgia, division. Turner offered the buyers $200,000 to rescind the deal and persuaded them to accept his offer by shifting employees and contracts to another division, threatening to destroy financial records.

In 1970, Turner's firm merged with Rice Broadcasting Company, Inc., a small Atlanta UHF television station. The transaction took the resulting company public, with Turner as majority stockholder, under the new name Turner Communications Corporation.

Turner Communications bought the right to broadcast the Atlanta Braves major league baseball games, then bought the team in 1976. The Braves were said to be losing money at the time and were on the verge of being transferred to another city; Turner's acquisition kept popular broadcasts on the air and provided diversification for his growing company. Turner increased his sports presence in 1977 by acquiring the National Basketball Association's Atlanta Hawks.

Expanding into Cable in the Late 1970s and Early 1980s

After reading that the cable television network Home Box Office (HBO) was transmitting programs nationwide via satellite, Turner saw an opportunity to expand his station's audience enormously and to make it more attractive to advertisers by beaming its signal to cable TV systems throughout the country. The resulting SuperStation WTBS, begun in December of 1976, became, in effect, another TV network. However, start-up costs were substantial, cable operators who signed up tended to have questionable credit records, and advertisers were reluctant to invest. Nevertheless, in the course of a few years the concept proved viable as WTBS-TV gradually became profitable.

Meanwhile, Robert J. Wussler, a 21-year veteran of CBS, joined TBS in April 1980 as executive vice-president, an office he would hold for several years. At CBS, Wussler had been instrumental in the expansion of satellite usage in news

Company Perspectives:

We thrive on innovation and originality—encouraging risk-taking and divergent voices. We value our customers—putting their needs and interests at the center of everything we do. We move quickly—embracing change and seizing new opportunities. We treat one another with respect—creating value by working together within and across our businesses.

coverage—which began as early as 1962—and in the development of the mini-cam for on-the-spot news coverage. His career included positions as president of the CBS television network and of the CBS sports division.

In its early years, Turner's SuperStation aired primarily reruns and sports. In June 1980, however, Turner created the Cable News Network (CNN) subsidiary to broadcast live news on a 24-hour basis. News bureaus were established in major cities throughout the United States and the world. The live, 24-hour format encouraged a more direct and unedited presentation of the news than the networks provided, as well as instant availability at viewers' convenience. The minimal editing and absence of star anchors sparked both positive and negative reactions: some thought the format lacked polish and professionalism, while others felt it brought viewers closer to the news items at hand. In January 1981, shortly after CNN began operation, another subsidiary, Turner Program Services, was created to serve as the syndication arm of TBS.

In January of the following year, Turner formed a second all-news television network. Officially named Headline News, the network aired a sequence of half-hour segments edited from the live material shown on CNN. If CNN was conceived as "a newspaper you can watch," in Turner's words, then Headline News permitted a quick scan of the top stories at any time. Just months later, in April of 1982, CNN Radio commenced operations, offering a 24-hour, all-news format on a network basis in the radio market.

By this time, the broadcast market was becoming increasingly competitive. TBS benefited as cable became available to an increasing portion of U.S. households. CNN's success pressured the three established networks to acknowledge the audience CNN had tapped and to provide late-night and early-morning news broadcasts for this group. In addition, Satellite News Channels (SNC)—a second 24-hour cable news headline service—opened direct competition, promising financial incentives to combat the loyalty of CNN's cable operators and viewers.

In January 1985, TBS spent $60 million for a 75 percent interest in an Atlanta real estate complex that contained approximately 470 hotel rooms and 775,000 square feet of office and retail space. By 1987, the company had acquired the remaining 25 percent of the facility, which was renamed CNN Center and housed the corporate offices as well as the Atlanta headquarters for CNN, Headline News, and CNN Radio.

In 1982, CBS had declined to comment on industry rumors that it wished to buy CNN but was not as quiet in April 1985, when TBC filed a preliminary exchange offer with the Securities and Exchange Commission (SEC) for CBS. CBS immediately bought back nearly six million shares of its common stock—amounting to almost $1 billion—forcing Turner to withdraw his offer in August. The aborted bid cost TBS approximately $20 million in underwriting, legal, and accounting fees, but Turner argued that the action, which forced CBS into significant borrowing to finance its repurchase and absorbed management time and attention, at least hindered CBS as a competitor.

In later years, Turner defended his bid for CBS as an attempt to protect his own company's vulnerability. In addition to the three major networks, there were by this time more than 25 independent ones, including Fox, Tribune, HBO, USA, Viacom, Time, and Showtime. Turner was worried that networks, as the distributors of television programming, could be held at the mercy of program producers, and he described his bid to gain control of CBS as an attempt to strengthen his bargaining position with them.

Turner also took a small step into the production business in the 1980s. He helped found the Better World Society in 1985, a nonprofit organization that produced documentaries on ecological and environmental issues. Turner's global consciousness was also behind his company's contribution to the Goodwill Games with the former Soviet Union. These games, patterned after the Olympics, were held in order to bring U.S. and Soviet athletes away from recent political boycotts of the Olympics and back into sporting competition. Conceived and organized in 1985, they were first held in Moscow in July 1986. TBS's production costs associated with the Goodwill Games amounted to more than $25 million, a sum not completely recovered through the increased revenues that resulted from the broadcast syndication of the games.

The MGM/UA Purchase in 1986

TBS's ventures into original programming were dwarfed, however, by its acquisition of the film company MGM/UA Entertainment in 1986. Turner contended with Kirk Kerkorian, the 50.1 percent owner of MGM/UA, which was losing money and valued on Wall Street at about $825 million in August 1985. Kerkorian was represented by Drexel Burnham Lambert, an investment-banking firm famed for dealing in high-risk junk bonds. In an unusual move, and with the consent of all parties, the bankers switched sides and represented Turner when it became apparent that he needed their expertise to finance the deal that was being discussed.

In the end, TBS bought MGM/UA Entertainment for $1.4 billion in March 1986, immediately sold the United Artists portion back to Kerkorian for $480 million, and assumed $700 million of MGM debt, resulting in a net purchase price of more than $1.6 billion. Because the purchase price was almost twice the street price, Drexel Burnham Lambert was at first unable to create securities acceptable to Turner and to potential investors. After Kerkorian was persuaded to accept approximately $475 million less in cash in return for a new issue of TBS preferred stock, financing for the remainder could be secured. When critics questioned the purchase price, Turner cited the enduring merit of the classic films in MGM's library, the programming

Key Dates:

1961: Ted Turner becomes president and COO of Turner Advertising Co.
1970: Turner's firm merges with Rice Broadcasting Co. Inc. and forms Turner Communications Corporation.
1976: SuperStation WTBS is launched.
1980: Turner creates Cable News Network (CNN).
1986: MGM/UA Entertainment is acquired.
1988: The company establishes Turner Network Television (TNT).
1992: Turner launches the Cartoon Network.
1996: Time Warner buys Turner.
2001: AOL and Time Warner merge.
2003: Turner resigns as vice-chairman of Time Warner; Philip Kent is named chairman and CEO of Turner Broadcasting System.

security he sought from this entertainment base, his fear of being outbid by another buyer, and, characteristically, his disinclination to haggle.

The new issue of preferred stock carried two provisions. The first was a necessary payment of $600 million of notes in September 1986. To meet this requirement, Turner was forced to sell all MGM assets except the film library; many were bought by Kerkorian himself just before the September deadline. The second provision involved dividend requirements that threatened corporate control, depending on market performance.

The entire MGM deal weighed heavily on the TBS's financial statements. As Turner conceded in his 1986 report to shareholders, ''The financial representation of 1986 is what it is—a net loss of approximately $187 million on revenue of more than $556 million.'' (In 1985, TBS had earned a net income of $1 million on $352 million in revenues.) Interest payments, together with amortization of the MGM purchase price, would lead to what Turner described as ''substantial accounting losses in the foreseeable future.''

In 1987, Turner called on the support of the cable industry to deal with the preferred stock problem created as a result of the MGM deal. A group of 31 cable operators—the companies that provide local cable service and choose what cable networks subscribers can get—headed by TeleCommunications Inc. (TCI), paid nearly $565 million for 37 percent of TBS. This capital secured Turner's control of voting stock and introduced new directors to Turner operations, including John Malone, president of TCI; Michael Fuchs, chairman of HBO; and Jim Gray, chairman of Warner Cable. While the backing of the cable industry virtually guaranteed the success of the Turner networks, the presence of major cable operators on Turner's board also posed certain problems. Since cable operators such as TCI purchase programming from TBS, Turner commented in the *New York Times,* the operators ''don't have much incentive to see us make healthy profits.'' Nevertheless, the rescue deal succeeded in keeping Turner afloat.

Although Turner's MGM purchase was criticized for putting TBS in nearly unmanageable debt, within two years the company's prospects were looking up. TBS's new Turner Network Television (TNT) channel, which was based on the MGM film library but also offered original programming, did exceptionally well. With eight of fifteen places on Turner's board in the hands of the cable consortium, TBS was moving more slowly and deliberately than in the past. Turner himself pointed to the completion of cable wiring in metropolitan areas as critical to his industry's growth, noting that major events would not receive adequate coverage while cable remained unavailable to large blocks of viewers.

In 1989, Turner Broadcasting made several important moves, including a $1.6 billion refinancing of its debt. The company also launched Turner Pictures, a filmmaking division, and Turner Publishing, a subsidiary that developed TBS properties for book publication.

With the onset of 1990s, Turner brought the Goodwill Games to Seattle, Washington. The games, intended to take place every four years, generated about $60 million in subscription and advertising revenues and created production costs of nearly $95 million. Naturally these figures skewed the company's overall performance statistics for the year: profit fell by about $65 million from 1989, and revenue increased significantly, reaching $1.39 billion. TBS instituted a one-dollar-per-viewer surcharge to cable operators for carrying the games, resulting in a blackout of TBS for nearly 17 percent of the 54 million households receiving the network. Ratings for the Goodwill Games were not as high as expected, and Turner felt obligated to compensate advertisers with costly ''make good'' time.

CNN's coverage of early 1990s events in the Persian Gulf resulted in spectacular ratings for the Turner networks, which beat out all other broadcast networks for the ten-week period from January 14 to March 24, 1991. CNN set new industry standards for war coverage during Operation Desert Storm, committing nearly 2,000 staff members, more than 4,000 hours of airtime, and $17.1 million to war-related telecasts. On the night of the invasion, 11 percent of U.S. households were tuned to CNN, compared with less than 1 percent on an ordinary day. The network's reputation soared when, at a press conference following the initial bombing runs, General Colin Powell and Defense Secretary Richard Cheney revealed that some of their information was coming from CNN.

Changes in the 1990s and 2000s

Turner continued to create specialized networks for particular markets in 1991, launching the Airport Channel and the Checkout Channel. The Airport Channel is broadcast in strategic places in airports, including gates and baggage claim areas. Its programming consists of a 30-minute loop of live news and features lifted from CNN as well as several advertising spots. Revenues for the Airport Channel approached $10 million for its first year, with broadcasts in Dallas-Fort Worth, Miami, Cincinnati, Denver, Minneapolis, and Washington, D.C.

Late in 1991, TBS purchased Hanna-Barbera Productions for $320 million. Turner and its joint-venture partner, Apollo Investment Fund, thus gained access to more than 3,000 half-hours of animated programming, including such classics as *Yogi Bear, The Flintstones, Scooby Doo,* and *The Jetsons,* as well as a total of 350 series and films. Prior to the purchase, TBS already owned approximately 800 animated half-hours, primarily from the MGM library. These included *Popeye, Tom and Jerry,* and a collection of Warner Bros. cartoons produced before 1948. With this impressive animation array in hand, Turner announced in early 1992 the creation of the Cartoon Network, a 24-hour animation channel for basic cable systems.

TBS strengthened its foothold in the film industry when it acquired Castle Rock Entertainment and New Line Cinema Corporation in 1993 and 1994, respectively. It also created Turner Classic Movies in 1994. Despite its growth over the past several years, Turner's appetite remained unsatisfied. By now, his competitors had gained substantial ground through merger activity. A February 1994 *Wall Street Journal* article claimed that Turner "wants a network more than ever. He says he is interested in new business alliances. And for the first time ever, the restless chairman, chief executive, and founder of Turner Broadcasting System Inc. says he is prepared to give up his 51% voting control of the company to accomplish those goals." In the same article, Turner revealed, "I don't like being the ninth—or 10th-largest—player in the game. Now Viacom, which was my size, is twice as big. Sony, which owns Columbia, is 10 times as big. . . . Murdoch is a lot bigger."

True to his word, Turner began to seek out a colossal deal of his own. He courted both NBC and CBS to no avail. Then, in 1995, he began talks with Time Warner Inc. After complex negotiations with Time Warner's Gerald Levin and TCI's John Malone, Time Warner finally agreed to acquire TBS for $7.6 billion. While it was met with resistance by certain shareholders and the Federal Trade Commission, the union was eventually cleared and completed in 1996. TBS and its subsidiaries fell under Time Warner's corporate umbrella, creating the largest telecommunications firm in the U.S. at the time with annual revenues reaching at $19 billion. Turner—named vice-chairman of Time Warner—and Levin immediately set plans in motion to reduce Time Warner's $17.5 billion debt load by cutting costs and eliminating certain cable holdings.

Under new ownership, TBS continued to look for ways to remain competitive in the cable industry. In 1999, it launched Turner South, its first foray into regional entertainment. The company debuted Boomerang, a classic cartoon network, the following year. Meanwhile, TBS's parent was once again on the prowl. Indeed, by 1999 Time Warner was looking for a deal that would ease its foray onto the Internet scene. As an old economy media company, its stock price was languishing compared with new Internet-based companies that were growing faster and faster each day. Levin, a well-known industry guru that had masterminded the deal between Time Inc. and Warner Communication Inc. in 1989 and launched HBO on cable networks across the nation, believed that moving onto the Internet was imperative for his company's future growth. Time Warner had tried on several occasions to launch Web sites related to music and videos but had yet to secure success in the online arena.

Despite his initial objections to the deal, Turner found himself in the middle of the one of the most contested mergers of the new century. The $112 billion union of online access provider America Online Inc. and Time Warner was the largest merger in U.S. history, creating a media powerhouse capable of touching consumers' lives over three billion times each month. Turner was named vice-chairman of AOL Time Warner but relinquished his role in early 2003. By that time, the merger had failed to produce successful results. Turner's stake in the company, once valued at $10.7 billion, had fallen to $1.4 billion. In October 2003, the company officially dropped AOL from its name, reverting back to Time Warner Inc.

TBS entered a new chapter in its history without its founder at the helm. Indeed, TBS dealt with several changes as a subsidiary of the new Time Warner. Over 400 jobs were cut at its CNN unit, and it sold its World Championship Wrestling unit. In March 2003, Philip Kent took over as chairman and CEO and launched a restructuring effort that organized TBS into three business segments—entertainment, news, and animation. While its parent company struggled, TBS remained one of its most profitable subsidiaries. TNT, TBS, and Cartoon Network continued to hold top spots in the industry, while Turner Classic Movies secured its 66 millionth subscriber in 2003, and CNN/U.S. achieved its highest audience levels in over a decade that year.

Principal Competitors

The NBC Television Network; Viacom Inc.; The Walt Disney Company.

Further Reading

Brown, Rich, "Turner Animated over New Channel," *Broadcasting*, February 24, 1992.

"A Contest Without a Cause," *Newsweek*, August 6, 1990.

"Crowd-Calmer," *Forbes*, February 17, 1992.

Harris, Kathryn, "Time Warner and Turner: Why Levin Is Willing to Risk Everything for a Deal," *Fortune*, October 2, 1995, p. 38.

Konrad, Walecia, "The Scoop on CNN's Bottom Line," *Business Week*, February 4, 1991.

Sellers, Patricia, "Ted Turner Is a Worried Man," *Fortune*, May 26, 2003.

Shapiro, Eben, "Ted's Way: Brash as Ever, Turner Is Giving Time Warner Dose of Culture Shock," *Wall Street Journal*, March 24, 1997, p. A1.

——, "Time Warner Completes Turner Deal," *Wall Street Journal*, October 11, 1996, p. B17.

Sharpe, Anita, "Two Dreamers, One Dream: To Be Media Kings," *Wall Street Journal*, February 4, 1994, p. B1.

Williams, Christian, *Lead, Follow, or Get out of the Way: The Story of Ted Turner*, New York: Times Books, 1981.

—updates: Robert R. Jacobson; Christina M. Stansell

Turner Construction Company

375 Hudson Street, 6th Floor
New York, New York 10014
U.S.A.
Telephone: (212) 229-6000
Fax: (212) 229-6390
Web site: http://www.turnerconstruction.com

Wholly Owned Subsidiary of The Turner Corporation
Incorporated: 1902
Employees: 5,000
Sales: $3.59 billion (2003)
NAIC: 236210 Industrial Building Construction; 236220 Commercial and Institutional Building Construction; 236116 New Multi-Family Housing Construction

Turner Construction Company is one of the most prodigious builders in the world, credited with building in part or in entirety many of the 20th century's most notable landmarks. Turner Construction contributed to the construction of the United Nations Secretariat building, Madison Square Garden, passenger terminals at JFK International Airport, LaGuardia Airport, and O'Hare International Airport, and numerous other commercial, industrial, and sports facilities. The company operates more than 40 offices throughout the United States and maintains a substantial international presence. Turner Construction has built or managed the construction of 19 of the 100 tallest buildings in the world. The company is the main operating subsidiary of The Turner Corporation, which is owned by a German construction firm named Hochtief AG.

Origins

Turner Construction's influential founder, Henry Chandlee Turner, was born in Maryland in 1871. Turner, as did a number of his descendants, attended Swarthmore College in Pennsylvania, where he studied civil engineering. Shortly after earning his degree at Swarthmore, Turner started working for Ernest Ransome, an engineer whose pioneering work in the nascent field of reinforced concrete provided the inspiration for Turner's career. Turner spent nearly a decade working with Ransome developing an enduring appreciation of the merits of reinforced concrete. Turner was convinced the material warranted greater use in construction, and in 1902 he set out to put his belief into practice, forming Turner Construction Company with $25,000 in start-up capital.

From the first day he opened his office in New York City on 11 Broadway, Turner aspired to make his company a major player in the construction industry. He did not begin his entrepreneurial career with modest ambitions; Turner wanted to construct large buildings for powerful clients. Turner Construction's first job, a $687 project to build a concrete vault for Thrift Bank in Brooklyn, fell well short of the stature Turner envisioned, but much larger projects soon came the company's way. In 1903, just a year after setting up shop, Turner secured two contracts that ensured his place among New York's construction elite. A Scottish industrialist named Robert Gair who made his fortune manufacturing paper products hired Turner Construction to build a new plant in Brooklyn. The facility, finished in 1904, measured 180,000 square feet, making it the largest reinforced concrete building in the United States. At the same time the company was developing plans for the Gair building, it began building staircases for the new subway system in New York. The stairs had been designed to be constructed with steel, but Turner thought concrete offered a less expensive alternative. After looking at public bidding records, Turner undercut competing offers and was awarded the chance to build several staircases in concrete. His alternative worked, leading to contracts for more than 50 staircases and platforms for the Interborough Rapid Transit. Aside from the gains to the company's bottom line and its stature within New York's construction community, the contracts to build subway staircases delivered one other important benefit to Turner Construction. The staircases were spread throughout the metropolitan area and needed to be built simultaneously, requiring Turner to hire a large number of foremen and engineers to complete the project. Because of the nature of the project, Turner Construction adopted the structure it would need in the coming years to successfully complete large-scale construction projects.

Once Turner Construction had established itself, the company's greatest challenge was expanding fast enough to keep

Company Perspectives:

We are proactive in finding solutions for our clients that best achieve their goals. Lasting relationships are the lifeblood of our business. We want the client to feel that our staff is even more committed to the effort than their own staff . . . that's what distinguishes us. Personal attention to our clients as individuals . . . caring about them as individuals. Our founder, Henry C. Turner, referred to our clients, appropriately, as our "respected friends."

pace with the volume of work it secured. Branch offices were established to help the company maintain its expanding geographic scope of operations, beginning with the opening of an office in Philadelphia in 1907. Additional offices followed, forming what would become a chain of offices that stretched nationwide by the end of the century. In 1908, a Turner Construction branch in Buffalo opened, followed by the addition of an office in Boston in 1916. When the United States entered World War I the following year, Turner Construction stood as one of the country's most successful builders. The first 15 years of the company's history saw it construct buildings for some the country's largest commercial concerns, including Western Electric, Standard Oil, Kodak, Colgate, and Squibb. In all, the company completed $35 million worth of work during its first 15 years, earning the esteem of clients who would turn to Turner's company in the years to come and provide the company with a sizable percentage of repeat business.

Turner Construction experienced its first setback at a time of supreme national crisis. From the beginning of World War I to the beginning of the Great Depression, the company's billings swelled from under $12 million to nearly $44 million. Like virtually every industry throughout the country, the construction business suffered severely during the economic collapse that began in 1929. The construction of new buildings came to a halt, causing Turner Construction's volume to plunge to $2.5 million by 1933. The company slowly began to recover as construction activity demonstrated a shade of its former vitality. Revenues increased to $12 million by 1937, but the company did not fully escape the ravages of the Great Depression until the rest of the country recovered, a moment marked by the United States' entry into World War II. The company's commercial construction largely was suspended during the war years, as it directed its efforts toward the construction of military camps, factories, and government buildings. The greatest change during the war years was not the shift toward military related construction, however. The same year the country entered the war, Henry Turner decided to end his nearly 40-year reign as president.

Henry Turner was 70 years old when he decided to cut back on his duties at Turner Construction. He relegated himself to serving as the company's chairman, making room for the ascension of his youngest brother, J.A. (Archie) Turner, to the post of president. Archie Turner, who also held a civil engineering degree from Swarthmore, guided the company through the war, but his failing health limited the length of his presidency. In October 1946, Henry Turner retired as chairman, handing the post to his ailing brother. For his replacement, Archie Turner selected the individual responsible for forming the Seabees, the construction battalions used during World War II. Admiral Ben Moreell was appointed president, but his stint in charge was fleeting. One month after his appointment as chairman, Archie Turner died of a heart attack. Four months later, Moreell resigned to take another executive position, leaving Turner Construction without a president or a chairman. To fill the leadership void, the company turned to Henry Turner's eldest son, Henry Chandlee (Chan) Turner, Jr., who had worked for the company since being graduated from Swarthmore in 1923. In Chan Turner, Jr., Turner Construction found a leader to give it the leadership stability it needed. Chan Turner presided over the company for the next quarter-century, overseeing a more than 1,000 percent increase in sales during his tenure.

Postwar Construction Projects

The substantial financial growth achieved during Chan Turner's leadership represented the rewards gleaned from numerous high-profile construction projects. After eclipsing the financial milestone of $100 million in revenues in 1951, Turner Construction built the United Nations Secretariat building in New York in 1952 and the New York headquarters of Chase Manhattan Bank in 1956. During the 1960s, Turner Construction's most notable projects included buildings for the Lincoln Center for the Performing Arts in the early 1960s and Madison Square Garden in 1967, the project most often referenced in the company's portfolio of accomplishments. The company also expanded physically in the decades following World War II. A branch office was opened in Cincinnati, Ohio, in 1954, followed by the establishment of offices in Los Angeles in 1964, Cleveland and Columbus, Ohio, in 1966, and San Francisco in 1968.

With operations spreading from coast to coast and an impressive list of projects to it name, Turner Construction held sway as one of the premier construction firms in the country. The investing public, well aware of the company's accomplishments during its nearly 70 years of existence, was given a chance to take part in Turner Construction's high-profile projects in 1969 when the firm issued over-the-counter stock. In 1972, Turner Construction' presence on Wall Street gained wider exposure when the company's stock began trading on the American Stock Exchange. The 1970s saw the company flesh out its network of branch offices, adding offices in Detroit, Michigan, and Denver, Colorado, in 1973; Pittsburgh, Pennsylvania, and Atlanta, Georgia, in 1976; Seattle, Washington, in 1977; and Miami, Florida, and Portland, Oregon, in 1979. Notable projects during the decade included the construction of Vanderbilt University Medical Center Hospital in 1974 and the John Fitzgerald Kennedy Library in 1977, the year Turner Construction eclipsed $1 billion in sales.

During the years leading up to the company's 75th anniversary, leadership changes at Turner Construction bridged the end Chan Turner's lengthy tenure of service and the beginning of the company's first era of non-Turner leadership. In 1965, eyeing his eventual retirement, Chan Turner appointed as president Howard Sinclair Turner, one of Archie Turner's three sons. A Swarthmore graduate, Howard Turner was appointed chairman in 1970 upon Chan Turner's retirement. Howard Turner, the last Turner to hold a senior management position at the company, served as chair-

Key Dates:

1902: Henry C. Turner forms Turner Construction Company.
1903: Turner Construction begins building staircases and platforms for New York City's subway system.
1919: Turner Construction builds the U.S. Navy and War Department Office Building.
1952: As part of a four-contractor team, Turner Construction builds the United Nations Secretariat building.
1967: Turner Construction completes construction of Madison Square Garden.
1977: Annual sales exceed $1 billion.
1996: Turner Construction completes construction of Ericsson Stadium, a 72,000-seat football stadium in Charlotte, North Carolina.
1999: Turner Construction's parent company, The Turner Corporation, is acquired by Hochtief AG.
2004: Turner Construction nears completion of the Taipei 101 Tower, slated to be the tallest building in the world.

man until 1978, when his successor, Walter B. Shaw, Turner Construction's president for the previous eight years, assumed the duties of chairman. Shaw, the first non-Turner to lead the company aside from Admiral Moreell's five-month stint following World War II, joined the company shortly before the war, served as one of Admiral Moreell's Seabee officers in the Pacific and returned to Turner Construction after the war. Shaw managed the company's Chicago office before rising through the executive ranks at Turner Construction's New York headquarters. In 1984, Shaw appointed Herbert Conant, a 34-year Turner Construction veteran, as president, one year before his retirement and Conant's appointment as chairman.

As Conant took the helm, Turner Construction was undergoing a structural change. In 1984, The Turner Corporation was formed as a holding company. Within the new structure, Turner Construction, as well as other facets of the company's business such as Turner International Industries and Turner Development Corporation, became subsidiaries of the holding company. Turner Construction served as the main operating subsidiary of Turner Corporation, representing the essence of the holding company. In this new guise, the company proceeded to add its to its physical presence. After opening an office in Connecticut in 1980 and three more California offices in 1983, Turner Construction opened an office in Orlando, Florida, in 1984 and offices in Phoenix, Arizona, and Nashville, Tennessee, in 1986. Another California office, located in San Jose, California, was opened in 1987, followed by the addition of a Dallas, Texas, office in 1988, and offices in Arlington Heights, Illinois, and Kansas City, Missouri, in 1989. Among the projects completed during the decade were the Texas Commerce Tower, a 75-story office building Houston, United Airlines Terminal One at O'Hare International Airport, and Los Angeles' First Interstate World Center, a 75-story office building.

Despite Turner Construction's aggressive physical expansion during the 1980s, the decade was remembered as a difficult period for the company. Conant and his successor, Al McNeill, who was named president in 1985 and chairman in 1988, were forced to contend with serious financial problems. Several foreign projects were partly to blame for the difficulties, but the weight of the blame fell on failed efforts undertaken by Turner Development Corporation, not by Turner Construction. The financial problems persisted, even as Turner Construction performed a record amount of profitable work. Although McNeill was credited with staving off more profound trouble, the holding company did not begin to recover until his successor, Ellis T. Gravette, took over after McNeill's resignation in 1996.

Turner Construction in the 1990s and 2000s

Against the backdrop of financial problems affecting the holding company, Turner Construction added to its already impressive portfolio of projects. The company's achievements in commercial and industrial construction were lengthy and legendary, but the 1990s saw the Turner Construction name behind the erection of several much-publicized sports stadiums. The field was not new to the company: Turner Construction's first major sports contract was completed in 1910, when the company constructed the promenade for the football stadium at Harvard Stadium. In 1925, the company played a much larger role by constructing a 62,000-seat football stadium for the University of Pittsburgh. The construction of Madison Square Garden in the late 1960s secured the company's lasting place in the realm of sports-facility construction, a standing that was enhanced by Turner Construction's efforts in the 1990s and early 21st century. In 1995, the company completed construction of the Rose Garden Arena, Portland, Oregon's 20,000-seat sports arena. The following year, Turner Construction built a 72,000-seat stadium in Charlotte, North Carolina, home of the National Football League's Carolina Panthers. In 2001, the company completed construction of INVESCO Field at Mile High, a 76,125-seat stadium designed for the National Football League's Denver Bronco's.

As Turner Construction cemented its reputation in sports-facility construction, a new corporate hierarchy within the Tuner organization took shape. In 1999, an Essen, Germany-based construction firm named Hochtief AG became Turner Construction's ultimate parent company. The German construction firm agreed in August to purchase Turner Corporation for $370 million in a bid to expand its worldwide presence in the construction business. ''It's not a hostile takeover in any way,'' Turner Construction's general manger for Detroit explained in an August 23, 1999 interview with *Crain's Detroit Business.* ''Hochtief is number five in the world, a 125-year-old construction company doing lots of jobs in Australia and the United Kingdom, where Turner isn't working.... Hochtief does heavy construction that Turner isn't into, such as dams, tunnels, and bridges.'' The corporate marriage wedded two companies not too far apart in either size or length of service. A 125-year-old, $6.7-billion company acquired a 97-year-old, $4.1 billion company. For Hochtief, the gain was a company with 41 offices in the United States and a presence in the Middle East and Asia, offering the opportunity for geographic expansion. Turner Corporation, and by extension Turner Construction, gained access to Australia and the United Kingdom and, perhaps more significantly, entry into the field of heavy construction.

Turner Construction celebrated it centennial in 2002. The company's historic achievements during its first century of business testified to its ability to manage and to build construction projects of the largest scale. As the company progressed in its second century of business, it continued to play a leading role in the global construction industry. The company planned complete construction in late 2004 of the Taipei 101 Tower in Taiwan, a 1,667-foot building that was expected to be the tallest building in the world. In the years ahead, Turner Construction's name figured to be behind some of the most high-profile projects of the future, as Henry Chandlee Turner's company fulfilled its founder's vision of a builder able to meet construction's greatest challenges.

Principal Subsidiaries

Turner Internationl Industries; Turner Universal; Service Products Buildings, Inc.

Principal Competitors

Bovis Lend Lease; Centex Corporation; Skanska USA Building Inc.

Further Reading

Ankeny, Robert, ''Turner Construction Expects Parent's Buyer Will Build Biz,'' *Crain's Detroit Business*, August 23, 1999, p. 31.

Edwards, Lynda, ''Recession-Proof, but Tricky,'' *Miami Daily Business Review*, February 14, 2002, p. AA2.

Elliott, Suzanne, ''Building Business at Turner,'' *Pittsburgh Business Times*, July 5, 2002, p. 7.

——, ''Turner Nails Down Cultural Trust Job,'' *Pittsburgh Business Times*, September 19, 1994, p. 1.

——, ''Turner, P.J., Dick Partnership Places Center Contract Before Competition,'' *Pittsburgh Business Times*, October 8, 1999, p. 36.

''First Century Leaders,'' *Turner News*, March 2002, p. 3.

Fredrickson, Tom, ''New Executive: Sidewalk Success Story,'' *Crain's New York Business*, March 10, 2003, p. 4.

Grone, Jack, ''Turner Lands Airport Plum,'' *St. Louis Business Journal*, March 9, 1992, p. 1.

''Growing Up Fast,'' *Turner News*, March 2002, p. 1.

''Known for Coors Field, Pepsi Center, Builder Has Varied Client List,'' *Rocky Mountain News*, September 1, 2001, p. 4C.

—Jeffrey L. Covell

U.S.Robotics®

U.S. Robotics Corporation

935 National Parkway
Schaumburg, Illinois 60173
U.S.A.
Telephone: (847) 874-2000
Toll Free: (877) 710-0884
Fax: (847) 874-2001
Web site: http://www.usr.com

Private Company
Incorporated: 1976
Employees: 114
Sales: $144 million (2003)
NAIC: 334418 Printed Circuit Assembly (Electronic Assembly) Manufacturing

U.S. Robotics Corporation supplies modems and wired and wireless networking devices designed for use in homes, home offices, and businesses throughout North America and Europe. The company was at the forefront of modem technology in the 1980s and 1990s and was among the leading suppliers of modems using the V.32, V.34, and eventually the V.90 56K standard. 3Com Corporation acquired U.S. Robotics in 1997. As part of a major restructuring, 3Com formed a joint venture with NatSteel Electronics Ltd. and Accton Technology Corporation in 2000. The venture, which included 3Com's analog modem business, adopted the U.S. Robotics name. The company began selling broadband modems—those used for digital subscriber line (DSL) and cable connections—in 2002. U.S. Robotics' management acquired a majority interest in the firm in 2004.

Early History: 1970s

U.S. Robotics was started principally by Casey Cowell, a native of Detroit who completed his degree in economics at the University of Chicago in 1975. He then pursued a doctorate in economics at the University of Rochester, where a friend informed him that after he graduated that he would be the only person in the unemployment line who knew exactly why he was there.

Cowell, at age 23, dropped out of the doctoral program, moved back to Chicago, and reestablished contact with former classmates Paul Collard and Steve Muka, who had an interest in computers. Eventually, the group grew to five men who pooled $200 and laid out plans to build a keyboard and acoustic coupler for communication over phone lines.

At the time, computers consisted of huge mainframes, and four-function calculators were expensive novelties. FCC regulations would not permit direct connection of any device not built by AT&T into the telephone network. While modems could translate digital signals into tones, these tones could be fed mechanically only into an AT&T handset.

In need of a name for the enterprise, one of Cowell's partners suggested a moniker from Isaac Asimov's 1950 science fiction novel *I, Robot,* which featured a company called U.S. Robot and Mechanical Men, Inc. Dropping the reference to mechanical men, the group settled simply on U.S. Robotics. Initially, the name was problematic, proving unfamiliar and therefore difficult for many people to spell. Furthermore, the name suggested that the company made robots.

Nevertheless, Cowell liked the name because it connoted advanced technology at a time when he and his partners were unsure what product the company would eventually produce. As it turned out, they perfected an acoustic coupler before the keyboard and, in need of cash, decided to begin marketing the device immediately.

Cowell later told the Chicago paper the *Reader* that, to his surprise, the city was replete with small factories that supplied plastic compounds, vacuum molding materials, electronic parts, and people willing to share their expertise with him. The first couplers were cast in mahogany molds, and the assembly line was located in Cowell's tiny Hyde Park apartment.

U.S. Robotics garnered sales initially through word of mouth. In time, customers started inquiring which terminal systems were recommended for use with the coupler. It soon occurred to Cowell that the company could generate additional revenue by distributing terminal connections made by other companies.

A range of equipment made by DEC, Teletype, General Electric, Applied Digital Data Televideo, and Perkin-Elmer was

Company Perspectives:

Leveraging its analog modem line's key strengths—brand equity and channel penetration—U.S. Robotics will continue to bring new products to its worldwide customer base quickly and competitively. Consumers can expect simplicity in setup and use, reliability and convenience, as well as the dependable service and support that U.S. Robotics' customers have enjoyed for decades.

added to the U.S. Robotics' product line. By the end of the first year, the company cleared $50,000 in sales, about half of which resulted from its distribution business.

Entering the Modem Market in 1979

The company launched its second product, a modem, in 1979 after FCC regulations were changed to allow non-AT&T equipment to be connected directly with the telephone network. The modem was operated by homemade circuit boards, created by silk screening paint over a copper-plated board, then immersing the board in an acid bath where all but the painted surfaces were dissolved. Cowell took out a classified ad in *Byte* magazine, and soon orders for the modems began rolling in. With its increased cash flow, Cowell rented manufacturing space west of Chicago's Loop.

In the early 1980s, Cowell approached the investment community for the first time in search of capital, most importantly for a new manufacturing facility. In addition to being small, the west Loop facility had no shipping door, forcing workers to hand boxes through doorways and pack palettes on a makeshift loading dock. The search for funding was successful, and in 1984 U.S. Robotics relocated to a large factory space, formerly a pharmaceutical building, in Skokie, a suburb north of Chicago. The modem became U.S. Robotics' only product. Through research and development, modems were by now eight times faster than they had been only a few years earlier. Rather than sending a page of text every minute, the devices could shuttle through nearly ten.

The company encountered a market dominated by three major competitors, Hayes Microcomputer Products and Motorola's Codex and UDS divisions. Nevertheless, U.S. Robotics held several advantages over these competitors. Most importantly, the company manufactured its own "data pump," the computer chip that controlled the modem's transmission features. As a result, U.S. Robotics' modems were built to its own specifications, not those of Rockwell and other chip manufacturers that supplied Hayes and Motorola. This allowed U.S. Robotics to develop faster modems and get them to market more quickly than its competitors.

While modems operating at a rate of 1,200 baud (signal variations per second) were once considered fast, by 1990 rates of 9,600 bits per second were becoming common. These systems multiplied the number of variations by using different forms of modulation on the signal. In 1990, the standard was known as V.32, or "V-dot 32." During this time, U.S. Robotics began development of a much faster modem system that could deliver 14.4 kilobits per second. Nevertheless, when the international standard, called "V.32bis," was adopted, U.S. Robotics also had a product meeting these specifications ready for manufacture.

The modem made it possible to send and receive information much more quickly, which was both a convenience for the computer user and, more importantly, a cost savings, involving less time that a user needed to keep expensive long distance telephone lines engaged. For many, the new modem represented a tremendous savings in operating expenses. While maintaining third place in the general modem market, with an 8.3 percent share, U.S. Robotics dominated the high-speed sector of the market, capturing a 43 percent share.

Expansion in the Early 1990s

The risky but successful coup in the high end of the market did much to further the legitimacy of the U.S. Robotics name. Companies previously unfamiliar with U.S. Robotics became customers and, in doing so, identified themselves for future marketing efforts.

U.S. Robotics also expanded into foreign markets; its first acquisition was Miracom Technology, Ltd. (later called U.S. Robotics Ltd. UK), with which the company established EEC sales and manufacturing capabilities in 1989. In 1991, U.S. Robotics' sales and marketing concern, U.S. Robotics, s.a., was established in Europe. Two years later, the company acquired P.N.B., s.a., a designer and manufacturer of data communications products for IBM-compatible personal computers and workstations. This overseas presence not only gave U.S. Robotics access to international market intelligence and standards but enabled the company to maintain the same level of local market support worldwide that it had in North America.

In 1993, U.S. Robotics changed the face of the personal communications market through aggressive pricing moves and an expanded retail presence with its Sportster line of modems. Capitalizing on the low-cost digital signal processor (DSP)-based architecture—developed for the company's line of Courier organizational modems—the company established its brand image as a technical leader, and its well-known quality allowed U.S. Robotics to become the dominant modem supplier to the personal communications market.

U.S. Robotics also served its worldwide corporate customers with three product lines at this time: Courier organizational desktop modems; Shard Access local area network (LAN) communications servers; and Total Control, analog and digital WAN Hubs.

Courier was the first modem on the market to include industry-standard V.32bis 14,000 bps data transmission. U.S. Robotics motherboard/daughterboard architecture enhanced the Courier's functionally and allowed the company to offer the first modem with a field upgrade to the upcoming V.34 28, 800 bps architecture.

U.S. Robotics' two WAN hubs served distinct markets. The Enterprise Network Hub served the corporate market, which required high-speed, error-free data transmission for applications such as file transfer and electronic mail. The Transaction Processing Hub provided the quick connections and multiple

Key Dates:

1976: Casey Cowell and his partners establish U.S. Robotics.
1979: U.S. Robotics launches its first modem.
1984: The company moves to a larger factory space in Skokie, Illinois.
1991: U.S. Robotics goes public.
1995: Megahertz, ISDN Systems, and Palm Computing are acquired.
1997: 3Com Corporation purchases U.S. Robotics.
2000: 3Com, Accton Technology, and NatSteel Electronics form an alliance to take over 3Com's analog-only modem business; the alliance adopts the U.S. Robotics name.
2001: Solectron Inc. acquires NatSteel Electronics and its majority stake in U.S. Robotics.
2004: Solectron sells its stake to U.S. Robotics' management.

protocols needed for applications such as credit card verification, point-of-sale terminals, and inquiry response.

Additional areas in which U.S. Robotics planned for future product introduction in 1994 included an even faster modem system run on the "V.Fast" protocol and a cellular modem system called HST Cellular (for "high speed technology"). This system would allow data transmissions over a cellular telephone network, again with adaptive speed leveling, even while traveling between cell sites at 60 miles per hour.

U.S. Robotics raised $28.3 million through an initial public offering in 1991 in which 2,380,000 million shares of common stock were offered by the company. U.S. Robotics worked to avoid excessive debt, keep a lean operation centered on customer needs, and maintain a generous research and development budget.

Changes in the Mid-1990s and Beyond

As surfing the Web became increasingly popular in the mid-1990s, U.S. Robotics was well positioned for success. As part of its growth strategy, the company added Megahertz, ISDN Systems, and Palm Computing to its arsenal in 1995. By 1996, it controlled over one-fourth of the North American modem market, and its earnings had increased by 158 percent over the previous year. In early 1997, it launched a 56K modem, called the x2, ahead of its competitors. The new modem allowed consumers to download information at 56,000 bits per second—a significant jump from the 28,800 bps that was standard at the time.

By 1997, U.S. Robotics had caught the eye of 3Com Corporation, a computer networking products manufacturer. 3Com was the second-largest networking company in the United States behind Cisco Systems Inc. In order to lessen the gap between itself and its main competitor, 3Com made a $6.6 billion play for U.S. Robotics. A February 1997 *Wall Street Journal* article described the deal as "a bold attempt by 3Com's chairman and chief executive, Eric Benhamou, to challenge Cisco by adding U.S. Robotics's modems to 3Com's growing product offerings."

The merger initially faced shareholder opposition. Nevertheless, 3Com completed its purchase of U.S. Robotics in July 1997. As one of the largest high-tech deals at the time, the union created a $5 billion networking giant that could provide customers with a wide variety of product offerings.

Additional changes were on the horizon for the company as it entered the 2000s. Just three years after purchasing U.S. Robotics, 3Com made the decision to focus on its lucrative networking business. As part of its restructuring, 3Com formed an analog modem joint venture with Taiwan-based Accton Technology Corporation and Singapore-based NatSteel Electronics Ltd. The venture, which took over 3Com's analog-only product lines and business, adopted the U.S. Robotics name and began official operation in September 2000.

During 2001, U.S. Robotics' focus on modems continued. It developed a modem based on the V.92 standard, which increased the speed of the 56K modems. It also set plans in motion to launch broadband modems—modems used for DSL and cable access—in 2002. Solectron Inc. acquired NatSteel Electronics in 2001 and, in turn, acquired a majority interest in U.S. Robotics. In early 2004, Solectron sold its interest to U.S. Robotics' management.

As a privately held company, U.S. Robotics remained a leading provider of analog modems and continued to develop cutting-edge new products related to wired and wireless networks and high speed Internet access. The company planned to focus heavily on the research and development of new technology and pledged to bring products to market that would simplify consumers' lives. With a history of success behind it, U.S. Robotics appeared to be well-positioned for future growth.

Principal Competitors

Creative Technology Ltd.; Multi-Tech Systems Inc.; Zoom Technologies Inc.

Further Reading

"The Disenchanted Professor," *Industry Week*, August 19, 1985, p. 49.
Gomes, Lee, and Evan Ramstad, "3Com Agrees to Acquire U.S. Robotics," *Wall Street Journal*, February 27, 1997, p. A3.
"How to Succeed in High Tech, Without Really Knowing What You're Doing," *Reader*, April 13, 1990, p. 1.
Lawrence, Aragon, "Robotics' Hat Trick," *PC Week*, December 2, 1996, p. A01.
"Making the Right Calls at U.S. Robotics," *Business Week*, December 21, 1992, p. R86.
Ramstad, Evan, "U.S. Robotics Defends Sale to 3Com Corp.," *Wall Street Journal*, March 6, 1997, p. B6.
Reinhardt, Andy, "One David Taking On Two Goliaths," *Business Week*, May, 19, 1997.
"U.S. Robotics Has High Aspirations for Lowly Modem," *Wall Street Journal*, July 27, 1993.
"U.S. Robotics Is Back," *Computer Dealer News*, August 3, 2001, p. 30.
"U.S. Robotics Not Shy about Plans," *Chicago Tribune*, March 17, 1991, Sec. 20, p. 5.

—John Simley
—update: Christina M. Stansell

U.S. Vision, Inc.

One Harmon Drive, Glen Oaks Industrial Park
Glendora, New Jersey 08029
U.S.A.
Telephone: (856) 228-1000
Fax: (856) 228-3339
Web site: http://www.usvision.com

Private Company
Incorporated: 1990 as Royal International Optical Inc.
Employees: 2,350
Sales: $134.8 million
NAIC: 446130 Optical Goods Stores

U.S. Vision, Inc., based in Glendora, New Jersey, operates some 600 company-owned retail optical departments in national and regional department stores in the United States and Canada, as well as a handful of freestanding locations. Approximately 400 of the units are located in JC Penney stores, about 65 in Sears locations, and another 85 in regional department stores. The company derives about one-third of its revenues from managed vision care programs. U.S. Vision outlets offer a full range of designer brand and private label prescription eyewear, contact lenses, sunglasses, and accessories. Independent doctors of optometry are available on the premises to provide eye examinations and write prescriptions for eyeglasses and contact lenses. Eschewing the trend of offering eyewear within an hour, U.S. Vision fills customers' orders at its optical laboratory, where lenses are prepared and fitted to frames, then shipped to the retail store within a few working days for customer pickup. If requested by the customer, an order can be completed overnight. The company is owned by a group of investors, including Chairman, President, and Chief Executive Officer William A. Schwartz, Jr.

Mid-1960s Origins

U.S. Vision dates its foundation to 1967 when William A. Schwartz and William A. Schwartz, Jr., bought Wall & Ochs Inc., a one-store Philadelphia optical company started in 1885. The elder Schwartz had been Wall & Ochs's president. With backing from area venture capital firms—Keystone Venture Capital Management Inc., the Philadelphia Industrial Development Corporation's Penn Venture Fund, and Fidelcor Capital Corporation—the company, renamed U.S. Vision, launched an expansion program, establishing operations in department stores under the Wall & Ochs and 20/20 Vision Center names. After 20 years, the company owned more than 200 stores in 24 states, all located east of the Mississippi River.

In the mid-1980s, the eyewear industry enjoyed tremendous growth, due in large part to the increasing optical needs of the aging Baby Boom generation and relaxed rules on advertising. Nevertheless, in order to keep U.S. Vision competitive, the younger Schwartz, who was now in charge, decided that the company had to become a national player. In 1990, the company found a way to achieve that goal by acquiring Dallas-based Royal International Optical Inc., whose main attraction was its connection to another Dallas company, JC Penney. Royalty was the department store chain's primary domestic optical licensee.

Royal Optical was one of the fastest growing retailers of eyeglasses and contact lenses. From 1982 to 1985, the company increased in size from 198 stores to nearly 400, and by the end of the decade Royal owned and operated 658 stores—400 free-standing and 258 in host department stores—making it the second-largest eyewear retailer in America, trailing only Pearle Vision. Royal's strong growth caught the attention of an investor group led by Edward Buchanan, which in 1988 and 1989 attempted to engineer a takeover and eventually accumulated 20 percent of the company's stock. Royal instituted some takeover defenses and finally settled with Buchanan by naming him to the board. Later in 1989, however, at a time when the effects of a recession were beginning to be felt and optical sales started to tail off, Buchanan and the board agreed to sell Royal to U.S. Vision, which offered $12 a share for 80 percent of the company, or $68 million. At the 11th hour, the bid was topped by Ipco Corp., a White Plains, New York company operating 240 Sterling Optical and Ipco Optical stores, offering $12.25 a share for all of the Royal stock, for a total of $87 million. On January 10, 1990, The Royal board rejected the Ipco offer, clearing the way for the sale to U.S. Vision. Westinghouse Credit Corp. provided the financing—$70 million in senior and subordinated debt.

Company Perspectives:

U.S. Vision, Inc. is a retailer of optical products and services through retail optical departments licensed to operate within national and regional department stores and through a limited number of freestanding retail locations.

A New Name in 1990

At the time of the acquisition, U.S. Vision had annual revenues in the $30 million range, while Royal's sales topped $100 million. The two now combined to create the largest publicly held optical retailer in the country. In addition to 658 retail outlets, U.S. Vision received Royal's main prescription laboratory, four regional laboratories, and subsidiary Styl-Rite, which manufactured and imported frames and sunglasses for sale in Royal stores as well as third-part retailers. Schwartz remained chairman and chief executive officer of the company, while a Royal executive vice-president, Donald Gross, was appointed president. Later in 1990, U.S. Vision reincorporated the business and for the next several years assumed the Royal International Optical Inc. name. Operations were split between New Jersey and Texas, but Dallas became the company's official headquarters. The company's strategy was to further develop the department store niche, in particular taking advantage of the JC Penney license.

Soon after the merger, the entire optical retail sector felt the full effects of the recession that arrived in the wake of the Persian Gulf War. Also saddled with large interest payments on the debt it took on, the company lost more than $2 million in both fiscal 1990 and fiscal 1991, forcing management to close 57 underperforming stores. Sales then dropped from $145.5 million in fiscal 1991 to $136.8 million in fiscal 1992, resulting in a $6.5 million net loss for the year. Another 148 freestanding stores were closed by the end of fiscal 1992. In his letter to shareholders in the 1992 annual report, Schwartz wrote that the previous two years had been a humbling experience: ''I for one have bought a smaller hat.'' Royal was now the fourth-largest optical retailer, lagging behind in annual sales to Lens-Crafters with $660 million, Pearle Vision with $634 million, and Cole Vision with $210 million. The damage to the company also extended beyond the balance sheet. In an August 1993 *Consumer Reports* survey, Royal was last among America's largest 18 optical chains in terms of customer satisfaction.

In August 1993, Westinghouse gained control of Royal as part of a financial reorganization that lowered the company's debt to $20 million. In return, Westinghouse took a 72 percent interest, while Schwartz retained a 10 percent stake. However, Westinghouse, with no expertise in the optical field, had no intention of holding onto the company. Its goal was simply to help Royal improve profitability in preparation for a sale. From fiscal 1993 through fiscal 1995, Royal took a number of steps to reposition itself. It shut down another 151 unprofitable freestanding stores, unloaded its Montgomery Wards licensed departments, severed its unprofitable relationship with Kmart, and closed five of its prescription laboratories, consolidating all operations into two facilities.

In December 1994, Grotech Capital Group, a Baltimore venture firm, bought the Westinghouse position, paying $20 million. Now that Royal was free of a heavy debt load, it was hoped that cash flow could now be directed towards expansion, especially in the department store sector. Also in December 1994, Schwartz was able to secure three low-interest loans totaling $4.7 million from the Delaware River Port Authority. The money was used to expand and renovate Royal's New Jersey eyewear factory and consolidate its administrative offices. As a result, in 1995 the company's headquarter was moved from Dallas to Glendora, New Jersey.

By the start of 1996, Royal had completed its repositioning plan and looked to future growth. The relationship with JC Penney was strengthened and its license agreement extended through 2003. Royal also extended its agreement with Vision One, an insurance plan for which it provided managed vision care on a national basis. The company began to place more emphasis on designer frames and made a conscious decision to avoid competing in the one-hour-service business. Schwartz told the *Star Ledger*, ''Only about 11 percent of customers want their glasses in one hour. So we got very humble and decided to chase the other 89 percent.'' In addition, Royal's manufacturing operations were consolidated into one facility, and a new computer infrastructure was incorporated into the chain of outlets and corporate headquarters. Royal's balance sheet was also cleaned up, as the company took write-downs on closed stores, laboratories, and the former Dallas headquarters. As a result of these efforts, by the end of fiscal 1997 (ending July 31, 1997) Royal operated 558 locations in 48 states, of which 368 were located in host JC Penney stores and only 63 were freestanding. The company had also enjoyed six straight quarters of growth in existing stores.

Going Public in the Late 1990s

In March 1997, the company was reincorporated in Delaware, and the name changed back to U.S. Vision in preparation for taking the company public once again. The subsequent initial public offering (IPO), managed by Salomon Smith Barney and Janney Montgomery Scott Inc., was completed in December 1997. The company hoped to sell 4 million shares at $11 to $13 a share, but because of limited interest, the number of shares was scaled back to 2.5 million and the share price fell to $9, resulting in a gross sale of $22.5 million. U.S. Vision used the proceeds to pay down debt of $19 million and provide some working capital.

U.S. Vision now entered a period of expansion, adding a number of stores through acquisition. In July 1997, it acquired 11 units from Ben Israel Optical located in Alabama, Arkansas, and Missouri, including nine Sears centers and two stores in medical office buildings. Then, in September 1998, U.S. Vision bought 16 optical departments from Dayton Hudson's department store division, six of the units located in Minnesota and the other ten in Michigan. U.S. Vision also pursued internal growth. In November 1998, it opened a unit in a Danbury, Connecticut, JC Penney store, which brought the total number of units to 600. Expansion continued into 1999, highlighted by the October 1999 acquisition of 24 optical departments from the Reading, Pennsylvania-based regional Boscov's department store chain. U.S. Vision also agreed to open new stores in two other

Key Dates:

1967: The company is founded by William A. Schwartz, Jr., and his father in Philadelphia, Pennsylvania.
1990: The company acquires Royal Optical International, assumes the Royal name, and move its headquarters to Dallas.
1997: The company is taken public as U.S. Vision.
2002: U.S. Vision is taken private.

Boscov's stores. Altogether, the company added more than 50 stores in 1998 and 1999, but expansion would quickly come to an end as U.S. Vision, whose stock languished at less than half its IPO price of $9, faced new challenges.

In August 2000, U.S. Vision received an unsolicited bid to buy the company for $4 a share, or $31 million. The suitor was Norcross Investment Group, which was led by George Norcross III, chairman of Commerce National Insurance Services and former South New Jersey Democratic party leader; Norcross's brother Phillip, an attorney; and New Jersey Democratic Assemblyman Joseph Roberts, who was also a nightclub owner. U.S. Vision rejected the offer, then promptly hired Philadelphia's Janney Montgomery Scott to explore its strategic options. Norcross continued its overtures through the fall of 2000 while buying up shares, so that by December it owned 24 percent of the outstanding shares. Norcross increased its offer to $4.50 a share and U.S. Vision accepted, but the deal was far from over and would prove a distraction for nearly two more years. U.S. Vision began to struggle, as did the economy in general, leading to the closing of some 100 unprofitable stores, the freezing of wages, and staff cuts. The Norcross offer was reduced to $4.25 and then fell through in November 2001. Almost another year would pass before the men involved in Norcross along with Schwartz arranged a leveraged buyout to take U.S. Vision private once more.

George Norcross put up 70 percent of the $33 million purchase price, and Assemblyman Roberts contributed 17 percent of the money. Both men maintained that a major reason for buying the company was to make sure in remained in South Jersey. But according to the *Asbury Park Press,* ''The new board of directors resembles a Democratic clubhouse,'' leaving U.S. Vision open to scrutiny on a number of issues. Roberts, for instance, sponsored state legislation that would allow optometrists to perform corrective laser surgery, which was limited by law to ophthalmologists. Because of his relationship to U.S. Vision, Roberts turned over sponsorship of the bill to another assemblyman. Schwartz ridiculed the insinuations that U.S. Vision stood to benefit from the proposed change, maintaining by way of e-mail that the company had no intention of becoming involved in laser surgery, adding, ''Who is going to get eye surgery in a department store?''

A far more serious matter associated with U.S. Vision emerged in the spring of 2003 when the U.S. Securities and Exchange Commission began to investigate the sale of U.S. vision to the Norcross group, which had been brokered by Commerce Bancorp Inc., on whose board both George Norcross and Schwartz sat. Moreover, it was revealed that U.S. Vision owed money to Commerce, some $8.5 million through a $20 million credit line extended in 1996 and that the law firm that helped a Commerce subsidiary to determine whether the offer was fair or not was headed by Phillip Norcross. Soon the New Jersey Attorney General's office became involved, launching an investigation to look into the circumstances of the 1994 Delaware River Port Authority development loans that brought the U.S. Vision headquarters back to New Jersey. Again, Schwartz was dismissive of the implication that the company was the unworthy beneficiary of political influence, asserting in a prepared statement, ''If not for the public and private support for U.S. Vision, the company's headquarters and 400 South Jersey jobs would be located in Dallas. This is exactly the way the public and private sector should work together to spur economic development and create jobs. If not for this successful cooperation, I would be in Texas wearing cowboy boots and a 10-gallon hat.''

In truth, U.S. Vision was a minor player in a larger controversy that surrounded the significant political influence of Commerce Bancorp's chairman, Vernon W. Hill II. According to the *Philadelphia Inquirer,* Schwartz and Hill had been partners since the late 1970s in a venture called Optical Equities, and both had been on the board from 1991 through 1994. The newspaper further revealed that $1 million of the 1994 development loans was used to buy property U.S. Vision was leasing from Optical Equities, Hill and Schwartz's partnership. They had purchased the property in 1977 for $305,000, then leased the property to U.S. Vision for more than 15 years at an average annual rent of $105,000. In addition, Hill earned about $280,000 in fees for providing financial advice to U.S. Vision in the early 1990s. The two men also leased other property and equipment to the company at an average annual rent of $236,000. According to the *Philadelphia Inquirer,* ''Schwartz also separately owned property with other U.S. Vision board members, including Harvey Johnson, a prominent member of the Black People's Unity Movement Impact Corp., a Camden-based nonprofit group with powerful political ties. That partnership rented office and retail space in Philadelphia to U.S. Vision for an annual average of about $110,000 between 1991 and 1993, records show. Together, Hill, Schwartz and Johnson also owned almost three-quarters of U.S. Vision's stock in early 1990.''

A year later, nothing had come of these investigations other than a good deal of unwelcome attention drawn to the way business and politics were sometimes conducted in South Jersey. The affairs of the now private U.S. Vision were difficult to judge as it endeavored to recover from a period of difficult economic conditions.

Principal Subsidiaries

Styl-Rite Optical Manufacturing Company.

Principal Competitors

Cole National Corporation; Luxottica Group S.p.A.; National Vision, Inc.

Further Reading

Armstrong, Michael W., ''U.S. Vision Setting Its Sights on Royal Stores,'' *Philadelphia Business Journal*, January 22, 1990, p. 3.

Bond, Helen, ''New Royal Optical to Be Based Here after Buyout by N.J. Firm,'' *Dallas Business Journal*, July 16, 1990, p. 13.

Cantu, Tony, ''Owner Eyes Sale of Royal Optical,'' *Dallas Business Journal*, August 6, 1993, p. 1.

Couloumbis, Angela, Wendy Ruderman, and Frank Kummer, ''N.J. Investigates Loans Made by Port Authority,'' *Philadelphia Inquirer*, May 1, 2003, p B1.

Olson, Thomas, ''Westinghouse Takes Control of Big Texas Optical Retailer,'' *Pittsburgh Business Times*, August 9, 1993, p. 1.

Patton, Carol, ''U.S. Vision See Its Future Clearly,'' *Philadelphia Business Journal*, December 22, 1997.

—Ed Dinger

United Defense

United Defense Industries, Inc.

1525 Wilson Boulevard, Suite 700
Arlington, Virginia 22209-2444
U.S.A.
Telephone: (703) 312-6100
Fax: (703) 312-6148
Web site: http://www.uniteddefense.com

Public Company
Incorporated: 1994 as United Defense L.P.
Employees: 7,900
Sales: $2.05 billion (2003)
Stock Exchanges: New York
Ticker Symbol: UDI
NAIC: 336992 Military Armored Vehicle, Tank, and Tank Component Manufacturing; 332995 Other Ordinance and Accessories Manufacturing; 334511 Search, Detection, Navigation, Guidance, Aeronautical, and Nautical System and Instrument Manufacturing; 336414 Guided Missile and Space Vehicle Manufacturing

United Defense Industries, Inc., designs, develops, and produces combat vehicles, artillery, naval guns, missile launchers, and precision munitions used by the U.S. Department and worldwide allies. United Defense is the sole-source prime contractor and systems integrator for many of its key U.S. Department of Defense Programs. The company's 5,300 employees conduct research and development efforts in key technologies, develop combat system operating software, and create efficient manufacturing processes. United Defense went public on the New York Stock Exchange in December 2001. The following year, the company acquired United States Marine Repair, the country's largest ship repair, modernization, and conversion service. With the additional acquisition of Bofors Weapon Systems, United Defense provides the U.S. armed services with a complete and diverse range of equipment.

Origins

One of the antecedents of United Defense L.P., Food Machinery Corporation (FMC), was a maker of agricultural equipment that began defense work in 1941, when it built the first amphibious landing craft for the U.S. Marines.

Over the years FMC produced some of the most enduring military equipment, such as the M113 Armored Personnel Carrier, used by the Army since the 1960s. The Navy became a client, purchasing the Mk45 naval gun system, which would be in use for another 40 years.

The M109 Self-Propelled Howitzer, the most widely used field artillery vehicle, was introduced in 1974. During the 1970s the company began developing the Bradley Fighting Vehicle, a troop carrier/fighting vehicle, which began production in 1981.

FMC's rival BMY Combat Systems, a unit of Harsco Corp., began upgrading the Army's Paladin howitzers in 1991. After the cost for each vehicle tripled, the Army awarded a new production contract to FMC Corporation.

Consolidation in the 1990s

A wave of consolidation swept through the defense industry in the 1990s. Between 1993 and 1997, there were 20 mergers among large defense contractors. The Pentagon encouraged this trend as a means of saving costs.

FMC's flagship product, the Bradley, was not well received overseas, which left the company vulnerable when the U.S. Department of Defense halved its annual orders to 200 vehicles per year, which it had been buying at a cost of $1 million each. FMC began planning its exit from the business. Defense sales accounted for a quarter of FMC's 1993 sales and 43 percent of income.

Harsco Corp., based in Camp Hill, Pennsylvania, also wanted to rely less on defense. It subsequently made a major metals acquisition. FMC and Harsco began discussing the possibility of merging their defense businesses in 1992. Their joint venture, United Defense, L.P., was formed in January 1994 out

Company Perspectives:

Our vision is to protect freedom worldwide by supporting U.S. and Allied security needs. To make this vision a reality, United Defense will provide soldiers, sailors, and marines with the finest combat capacity in the world. We will focus on serving eight major markets: Combat Vehicle Systems, Fire Support, Combat Support Vehicle Systems, Weapons Delivery Systems, Amphibious Assault Vehicles, Logistics and Training Support, Intelligent Munitions, and Marine Repair.

of FMC's Defense Systems Group and Harsco's BMY Combat Systems Division. FMC held a 60 percent stake in the new company; Harsco, 40 percent.

The deal reduced the number of combat vehicle makers to two: United Defense, maker of aluminum troop carriers, and General Dynamics, which specialized in tanks made of steel. Harsco brought lean and flexible manufacturing capabilities to FMC's technical expertise. Not included in the joint venture was a separate Harsco division which made trucks for the Army.

United Defense was based in Arlington, Virginia, and started with about 6,000 employees. It had annual sales of $1.6 billion in 1996, of which its armament systems division contributed $400 million a year. Parent FMC Corporation employed 17,000 people worldwide in its Performance Chemicals, Industrial Chemicals, and Machinery and Equipment divisions.

Besides pushing for consolidation, the Pentagon encouraged cooperation among competing firms. United Defense began producing missile launchers in cooperation with Lockheed Martin. United Defense provided the mechanical systems while Lockheed Martin created the electronics. In 1997, United was granted a $1 billion contract to develop the Crusader field artillery system in collaboration with General Dynamics. The project originally involved another two contractors.

Iraq's Russian and French artillery outperformed that of the U.S. Army during the Persian Gulf War, although the United States had more advanced missiles, tanks, and helicopters. The Crusader was designed to fire faster and farther than existing U.S. artillery pieces—ten rounds per minute to 25 miles. Crusader was fully automated, not dependent on the numerous manual tasks traditionally associated with firing artillery. Like the M109A6 Paladin, the Crusader used two vehicles—one carrying the gun plus an ammunition carrier.

Business was scarce for surviving defense firms. The Wall Street Journal reported that in the ten years since 1987, a quarter of the country's four million defense jobs were eliminated. United Defense employed 5,700 at ten sites in 1997. Its Minnesota plant employed 1,600 in 1997, half its mid-1980s level. Union manufacturing jobs were cut by 75 percent, to under 500. The Crusader program brought 250 mostly engineering jobs.

United Defense lost a multibillion-dollar contract to produce amphibious assault vehicles for the Marine Corps, a longtime client for whom FMC had developed the concept between the wars. The setback signaled to FMC executives it was time to leave the business entirely and concentrate on its core strengths of herbicides, insecticides, and food additives.

New Owners in 1997

FMC and Harsco began looking for bids in May 1997. By the summer of 1997, defense contractor General Dynamics and investors The Carlyle Group were vying to purchase United Defense from FMC and Harsco. General Dynamics offered $1 billion but raised antitrust flags since this deal would have left it the only armored vehicle manufacturer in the country. General Dynamics officials countered that the market was so small this was allowable, and the company could save taxpayers money by consolidating operations. In addition, despite its calls for cooperation and consolidation, the Pentagon preferred to have at least two sources for military equipment to ensure supplies in wartime.

FMC and Harsco ultimately accepted a lower offer from Carlyle, indicating their unease with the prospect of an antitrust fight from Republican Senator Arlen Specter, whose home state of Pennsylvania would have lost jobs in the event of a United Defense/General Dynamics merger. In October 1997, through its Iron Horse subsidiary, Carlyle acquired United Defense, L.P. from FMC and Harsco for $880 million, later adjusted to $863.9 million.

Carlyle intended to grow the business, then either sell it or hold a public offering, typical of its modus operandi. (Interestingly, it had already bought and sold the electronics division of rival bidder General Dynamics.) Carlyle was an investment trust formed in 1987. It owned a dozen other companies at the time of the acquisition, including several defense firms. (Holdings included waste recycler GTS Duratek Inc. and Baker & Taylor, a major book distributor.) Its properties had combined annual sales of $5 billion.

Carlyle's chairman, Frank C. Carlucci, had been Secretary of Defense under Ronald Reagan and was also a director at General Dynamics. The firm stated Carlucci had separated himself from involvement in the bidding process to avoid a conflict of interest. Carlyle specialized in undervalued companies affected by changes in government policy. According to the Washington Post, between 1990 and 1996, Carlyle averaged annual returns of more than 32 percent.

After the acquisition, sales and profits fell at United Defense due to fewer domestic and foreign shipments. Some aspects of United Defense's business, such as U.S. government contract work and the Crusader program, showed improvement. Gross profits were $59.2 million on sales of $1.22 billion in 1998. Exports accounted for $230.3 million of sales in 1998, up from $89.1 million in 1997.

The Future of Defense: 2000 and Beyond

After experiencing some quality problems in the late 1980s, United Defense set out to systematically improve its communications with suppliers. By the late 1990s, this resulted in more

Key Dates:

1994: United Defense L.P. is formed as a joint venture between Harsco Corporation and the defense division of Food Machinery Corporation (FMC).
1997: The Carlyle Group acquires United Defense.
2001: United Defense goes public on the New York Stock Exchange.

dependable and better quality deliveries and made the company's own receiving and inspection operations more efficient. On the design side, Electronic Product Definition software allowed United Defense to link its engineers around the world. Only the newest software could handle the complexity of the company's products, whose parts numbered in the tens of thousands.

Simulation-based acquisition took communications between Army purchasers and defense contractors to a new level. Simulation Modeling for Acquisition, Requirements and Training (SMART) was a joint Army/industry plan for reducing development costs. This concept integrated industry and government product development teams (IPTs). The new level of cooperation introduced soldiers into the development process and allowed trainers to be trained before systems were deployed. United Defense president and CEO Tom Rabaut pressed for more commonality among systems in various projects and more reuse and interoperability of components.

Rabaut warned of two obstacles to advancement in military technology. He complained the low burden of proof of the new Civil False Claims Act (a new law to encourage whistleblowers) scared technology entrepreneurs away from defense contracts, ultimately denying the Army the opportunity to benefit from the latest innovations. Rabaut also found it alarming that the U.S. Department of Defense seemed to be moving in a socialistic direction, while other industries across the world were becoming more privatized. He was referring to depots in particular, where the Defense Department maintained its own equipment. He argued this work should be in the private sector, since so little new equipment was being purchased.

The Bradley Fighting Vehicle was no longer in production at the end of the century, but BFV derivatives were, and United Defense was upgrading existing vehicles. The company was also busy developing the next generation Crusader Field Artillery System, designed to replace the M109A6 Paladin, and was hoping to land a $20 billion Crusader production contract in 2000. The company was also developing a Composite Armor Vehicle and a Grizzly minefield-breaching vehicle.

After the September 11, 2001, terrorist attacks on U.S. soil, President George Bush and his administration launched immense military initiatives in Afghanistan, Iraq, and other areas, and these initiatives greatly impacted the U.S. defense industry. In December of that year, United Defense went public on the New York Stock Exchange and was awarded many new contracts.

In July 2002, United Defense acquired United States Marine Repair, the country's largest non-nuclear ship repair, modernization, conversion, and overhaul company. United Defense's work with the U.S. Army was bolstered as well when, in 2003, the company was awarded a $2 billion contract by Boeing Co. to develop five types of manned ground vehicles (MGVs) for the Army.

In 2004, United Defense acquired Cercom Inc., which specialized in developing armor protection for soldiers as well as for defense vehicles. Also that year, in a strategic move to strengthen design and fabrication capabilities for navel and ground combat systems, United Defense purchased Kaiser Compositek, which provided custom designs for aircraft, missiles, engines, spacecraft, marine vehicles, and mass transportation. Through Kaiser, United Defense planned to incorporate technology to develop lighter-weight weapons systems to replace traditional metal components.

As the country's war efforts continued, United Defense's first quarter revenues in 2004 increased 17 percent, with sales from the Defense System division generating the bulk of the first quarter growth in 2004. These were attributed, in particular, to Bradley Fighting Vehicle upgrades, spare parts, and ramped-up development programs including the Army's Future Combat Systems and the Navy's new destroyer program, DD(X).

Principal Subsidiaries

United States Marine Repair; Cercom Inc.; FNSS Savunma Sistemleri A.S. (Turkey; 50%); Kaiser Compositek Inc.

Principal Divisions

Armament Systems; Ground Systems; Steel Products; Bofors; CTC; International; Homeland Security.

Principal Competitors

General Dynamics Company; Lockheed Martin Corporation.

Further Reading

Baumgardner, Neil, "United Defense Plans to Demonstrate NLOS Cannon Technologies Next Year," *Defense Daily International,* November 1, 2002.

Boatman, John, "United We Stand . . . ," *Jane's Defense Weekly,* May 20, 1995.

"Carlyle Beats Out Dynamics for United Defense," *Wall Street Journal,* August 27, 1997, p. A3.

"Crusader Completes Executive Level Review," *Defense Daily International,* July 20, 2001.

DeMeis, Rick, "Electronically-Linked Teams Design the Defense Systems of the Future," *Purchasing,* May 7, 1998.

Gilpin, Kenneth N., "Military Contractor Sold to Buyout Firm," *New York Times,* August 27, 1997, p. D2.

Litsikas, Mary, "United Defense Teams with Suppliers to Boost Quality," *Quality,* April 1997, pp. 74–76.

"Live-Fire Qualification Begins for United Defense Naval Gun and Ammo," *Defense Daily International,* January 16, 2004.

Machan, Dyan, "The Strategy Thing," *Forbes,* May 23, 1994.

Mintz, John, "Area Firms in Bidding War for Army Vehicle's Maker," *Washington Post,* August 14, 1997, p. E01.

Pasztor, Andy, "General Dynamics May Have to Rethink Game Plan—Failure to Acquire United Defense Makes Firm's Goal Appear Riskier," *Wall Street Journal,* August 28, 1997, p. B4.

Pearlstein, Steven, ''Carlyle Group to Buy Military Contractor; United Defense Makes Weapons, Transports,'' *Washington Post,* August 27, 1997.

Peters, Katherine McIntire, ''Unique Partnership Yields Results,'' *Government Executive*, April 1998, p. 69.

Peterson, Susan E., ''Bringing in the Big Guns: Crusader Artillery System Carries Hopes of United Defense,'' *Minneapolis Star Tribune,* May 26, 1997, p. 1D.

——, ''Carlyle to Acquire United Defense for $850 Million,'' *Minneapolis Star Tribune*, August 27, 1997, p. 1D.

''United Defense will Acquire Kaiser Compositek,'' *Performance Materials*, February 16, 2004, p. 3.

—Frederick C. Ingram
—update: Catherine Holm

Valeo

43, rue Bayen
75848 Paris
France
Telephone: (+33) 01 40 55 20 20
Fax: (+33) 01 40 55 21 71
Web site: http://www.valeo.com

Public Company
Incorporated: 1923 as Société Anonyme Francaise du Ferodo
Employees: 68,200
Sales: EUR 9.23 billion ($11.59 billion) (2003)
Stock Exchanges: Euronext Paris
Ticker Symbol: FR
NAIC: 336322 Other Motor Vehicle Electrical and Electronic Equipment Manufacturing; 336350 Motor Vehicle Transmissions and Power Train Manufacturing; 336399 All Other Motor Vehicle Parts Manufacturing

France's Valeo is the tenth-largest supplier of components and systems to the worldwide automobile and truck industry. Valeo operates approximately 129 manufacturing plants, 65 research and development centers, and nine distribution centers serving the European, North and South American, and Asian markets. The company is one of the largest automotive suppliers in Europe and has several times declared its intention of moving up to becoming one of the top five such companies in the world. Valeo is divided into ten industrial branches, making transmissions, climate control devices, engine cooling devices, lighting systems, electrical systems, wiper systems, motors and actuators, security systems, switches and detection systems, and electronics and connective systems. The company groups these industrial branches into four main areas: electrical and electronic systems, which account for more than 50 percent of total sales; thermal systems, which represent close to 25 percent of sales; aftermarket activity, at 17 percent of sales; and transmissions, which make up just 4 percent of sales.

Changing the Ferodo in 1980

When Valeo adopted its new name in 1980, it gave up what many manufacturers can only hope for: a name that had become synonymous with an entire product category. For more than 50 years, Société Anonyme Française du Ferodo had dominated the French brake linings market to the extent that the phrase "change your ferodo" all but meant "reline your brakes" in many of the country's service stations. Yet, by 1980, the founding company had grouped together many of France's most celebrated names in automotive equipment and systems, including Cibie, Marchal, Paris-Rhone, and SEV, representing some 30 product lines. Changing the company's name to Valeo (Latin for "I'm very well") created a consolidated and independent force in the global automotive supply market.

Ferodo's origins dated back to England of the 1890s. It was then that Herbert Frood witnessed a heavily loaded horse and carriage having difficulties braking and the driver thrusting his shoe between the brake and wheel to bring the carriage to a halt. Frood kept the event in his memory; 20 years later, as the newly emerging automobile industry was struggling with its own braking systems, Frood introduced the first brake lining, replacing the driver's shoe with a more durable sheet of asbestos. Frood dubbed the lining "Ferodo," and the product quickly became a mainstay in the British automotive industry's brake systems.

Frood's brake linings also caught the attention of the automobile industry on the Continent. In 1910, Frood agreed to give a French entrepreneur, Eugene Buisson, the right to import and distribute the Ferodo linings in France. Soon after, Buisson received the rights to begin manufacturing the Ferodo linings in France, and the Société Anonyme Française du Ferodo, founded in 1923, grew to become one of France's most prominent automotive equipment suppliers.

Although its initial success was based on brake linings, Ferodo soon diversified into other automotive equipment markets, adding first clutch linings and then complete clutch systems. The 1962 acquisition of Sofica added automotive heating systems, from which the company branched out into cooling systems by the mid-1960s. As with its other product lines, Ferodo soon came to dominate the French market for this

Company Perspectives:

Valeo ranks among the world's leaders in automotive suppliers. Valeo is an independent industrial company entirely dedicated to the design, manufacture and sale of components, integrated systems and modules for cars and trucks.

product category as well. Meanwhile, as automobile makers established international and then global markets for their cars and trucks, Ferodo also began its international development, opening subsidiaries and factories close to its customers. An early subsidiary, formed in Italy in 1964 to produce clutch systems, adopted the name Valeo for the first time. The Italian Valeo went on to capture the majority of the Italian clutch market. From Italy, Ferodo moved into Spain, then into the South American market through operations in Brazil and Argentina. North America and the crucial U.S. market followed soon afterwards; during the 1970s, the company turned east, entering the soon-to-boom Asian market. Meanwhile, Ferodo remained in the Buisson family, with André Buisson succeeding as CEO.

During the 1970s, the French automotive equipment market underwent a shift. Spurred by the 1973 oil crisis and the resulting economic chaos in the automobile industry on the one hand and, on the other, the French government's eagerness to consolidate—and later nationalize—much of French industry, Ferodo began to absorb a number of other prominent automotive equipment makers. By 1980, the company had been joined by SEV (Société Anonyme pour l'Equipement Electrique des Vehicules, founded in 1912), which had pioneered automotive electrical systems; Paris-Rhone (Compagnie Industrielle de Paris et du Rhone, founded in 1915), which retained a leading position supplying military aviation and radio-electric markets; Cibie, founded in 1919, France's pioneering and leading maker of lighting systems for automobiles and trucks; Marchal, founded in 1923, which specialized in headlamps and lighting systems; and a number of other similarly prominent automotive brands, including Soma, which added transmissions and hydraulic systems for the trucking industry, as well as IMCH, ISHA, PPB, SIME, UFAGA, and Flertex.

In 1980, Ferodo took the bold move of adopting a new name under which it grouped and later replaced its panoply of brand names. The new company boasted revenues of FFR 7 billion, a payroll of 27,000, and a product line of more than 30 products capable of providing most of the critical internal components of automobiles for some 26 automakers worldwide, supported by 100 factories and other facilities in 16 countries.

A Worldwide Leader for the 1990s

The 1980s would mark the company's strongest period of growth, with revenues reaching FFR 20 billion by 1990, establishing the company as the world's premier independent automobile components and systems supplier. Valeo's globalization strategy would also be put in place by the start of the 1990s, with the company's foreign sales topping its domestic sales for the first time. Yet not all of the company's strategies would be as successful. At its formation, Valeo determined to diversify its activities into the nonautomotive industrial and manufacturing market. A number of acquisitions made in the early 1980s brought the company into the construction industry, smelting and steelworks, industrial equipment, and other activities that would eventually stretch the company too thin and drag heavily on its profits.

Weathering the recession of the early 1980s, and its annual sales rising to FFR 11 billion by the middle of the decade, Valeo faced a new crisis in 1986. At a time when French industry was reemerging from the country's brief flirtation with nationalization, Valeo, which had steadfastly remained independent, found itself involved in a struggle for control. In a period that gave rise to a new breed of corporate raiders, Valeo became a target for one of the best known of these, Carlo De Benedetti of Italy. In February 1986, De Benedetti began buying up shares of Valeo, gathering 19 percent and effectively gaining majority control of the company. Valeo's CEO André Buisson turned to the French government in an attempt to head off this passage of the company into foreign control. Buisson was almost successful: Valeo succeeded in becoming classified as strategic to France's national defense. While the company was indeed manufacturing components for a model of a new French tank, this activity formed less than 1 percent of its revenues. Nonetheless, the action barred Valeo's takeover by a foreign concern.

De Benedetti was only temporarily thwarted, however. In June 1986, he purchased an inactive French holding company, Airflam. Renamed Cerus, the shell company received De Benedetti's 19 percent of Valeo, giving De Benedetti a controlling stake in the auto equipment maker after all. In fact, Valeo's years under Cerus proved a period of strong growth, if only because of the appointment of Noel Goutard to replace André Buisson as Valeo's CEO.

Goutard came to Valeo after a career that included stints with a number of the biggest companies in France as well as globally, including Warner Lambert and Pfizer, and leadership positions with Gevelot, Copmteurs Schlumberger, Pricel (later Chargeurs), and Thomson. Under Goutard, Valeo rapidly shed its nonautomotive activities, at the same time boosting its position in its core market with a new series of acquisitions, including Tibbe of Germany, Bongotti of Brazil, and Chausson Thermique and Neiman of France. By 1988, Valeo's revenues had climbed to FFR 16.5 billion and its profits soared, rising 127 percent in a single year to reach a net profit of FFR 817 million. Unsatisfied, Goutard would suggest that Valeo needed to attain a "critical mass" of FFR 25 billion in revenues—a milestone reached in 1995.

Goutard was also credited with foreseeing the economic crisis of the 1990s and proactively restructuring Valeo by shedding subsidiaries, and even entire product categories, while shutting 12 plants (representing 15 percent of the company's activity) to realign its manufacturing activities on an international scale. Cutting back its work force by some 2,000 helped the company boost its per-employee productivity from FFR 560,000 in 1988 to FFR 690,000 in 1990. The sale of a series of nonstrategic subsidiaries, which reduced Valeo's revenues by some FFR 1.2 billion, helped the company reduce its debt load, bringing its net debt/earnings ratio down from 0.70 in 1989 to 0.54 in 1990, and to 0.42 in 1991.

Key Dates:

1910: Inventor Frood sells the rights to his brake shoes to a French entrepreneur.
1923: Société Anonyme Française du Ferodo is founded.
1962: Sofica is acquired.
1980: The company changes its name to Valeo.
1986: Italian investor De Benedetti acquires 19 percent of the company.
1998: Valeo acquires the electrical business of ITT.
2001: The company's North American electrical unit declares bankruptcy.

The now leaner Valeo found itself in an enviable position as the recession of the early 1990s turned into a prolonged European economic crisis. Aided by Valeo's moves into the booming Asian market and its successful alignment with the major Japanese auto makers—along with its continued global implantation, including a policy of opening production facilities close to its clients' plants—Valeo would see a steady progression of its net profits through the first half of the 1990s despite the stagnant market. While its revenues stuck at around FFR 20 million through 1993 and would climb only slowly afterwards, reaching FFR 28 billion in 1996, the company attained net profits of FFR 1 billion by 1994.

In the mid-1990s, Valeo continued making key acquisitions, including Borg Instruments in 1995 and Brazil's Univel in 1997, while shedding other operations. Valeo had also embarked on the creation of a number of joint venture partnerships, among them a European project with Japan's Seiko-Seiki; the formation of and 50 percent participation in Nobel Plastiques Climatisation; partnerships with Siemens in automotive climate control systems; and 1997 joint venture agreements reached with France's Plastics Omnium, a world leader in plastics-based automotive components, and with Yuejin Motor Corporation of China, marking Valeo's fifth joint venture in that crucial market. In 1996, Valeo regained its ''independence'' when De Benedetti's Cerus sold off its stake in the company.

Valeo continued to invest heavily in research and development and, especially, capital expenditures. New Valeo plants started up operations in France, Spain, the United States, Canada, Mexico, China, Argentina, and Brazil. The company also moved into the former Soviet bloc, bringing production facilities to the Czech Republic and Poland. Valeo's global development strategy and its specialized focus would seem a model for a new industrial age. In addition, the company could begin eyeing its next milestone, that of becoming a FFR 40 billion company by the year 2000.

Stops and Starts in the Late 1990s–Early 2000s

In U.S. dollars, Valeo's sales stood at about $5.7 billion for 1997, and the company was one of only a handful of European firms in the automotive components industry to operate on a truly global level. At the close of 1997, Valeo revealed an expansion plan that would increase sales outside Europe. The company hoped to bring sales to about $8.6 billion in four years, with a larger percentage of sales coming from North America, South America, and Asia. Achieving this goal would make Valeo one of the top five in the automotive components industry. CEO Goutard wanted 50 percent of sales to come from outside Europe over the next few years, and he hinted that a North American acquisition would not be unwelcome. In 1998, Goutard engineered the biggest acquisition during his tenure at the company, paying some $1.7 billion for the automotive electrical business of U.S. conglomerate ITT. Shortly after the deal went through, Noel Goutard retired. He was succeeded by André Navarri.

The ITT deal made sense for Valeo, giving it a valuable slice of the North American market, where Valeo hoped to grow rapidly. Before the acquisition, North American revenue had stood at around $700 million, and the purchase of ITT's 11 plants were expected to boost that figure to $2.6 billion. A year after the acquisition, most business areas were doing well, and the ITT plants in Europe had been refitted. However, the former ITT plant in Rochester, New York, a facility that employed 3,500 workers to make electrical components, turned out to be a bugbear. The plant was outdated and in need of considerable new investment. Valeo contemplated shutting the Rochester complex, yet vehicle production in the U.S. was very high in the late 1990s, and the company was afraid it would miss out on new business opportunities if it closed the plant to move to Mexico or another lower-wage country. Relations with the labor union in Rochester were described as ''bitter,'' yet Valeo ultimately signed an eight-year agreement with the union, twice as long as the typical contract.

Then the auto market began to slow down in 2000, with the three largest auto makers cutting their production by 10 percent. By that time, missteps at the Rochester plant had taken a toll on Valeo. The company lost $159.5 million in the first quarter of 2001. Andre Navarri, in the job only ten months, was ousted as CEO and replaced by the former chief operating officer, Thierry Morin. Noel Goutard came out of retirement to act as head of the company's supervisory board, a position that made him responsible for long-range planning. Morin quickly sold or closed 26 of Valeo's 170 manufacturing plants. The company also cut the number of its suppliers from 4,600 to 3,900 by the end of 2001. Then two of Valeo's U.S. subsidiaries, Valeo Electrical Systems and Valeo Electrical Systems and Marketing LLC, filed for bankruptcy. These comprised most of the business bought from ITT in 1998, including the troublesome Rochester plant. Some industry analysts saw the bankruptcy filing as a ploy to pressure the Rochester union. In early 2002, Valeo announced more cost-cutting measures, axing 5,000 jobs worldwide on a pessimistic forecast of a further 10 percent fall in automotive output in both Europe and North America. A month later, the company announced its financial results for 2001, a net loss of $509 million (EUR $591 million). Sales had actually risen slightly over the year because of new acquisitions, but Valeo took a huge charge of EUR 526 million for its problematic Rochester facility.

Later in 2002, the company announced long-range plans that would turn the company around. Valeo planned to further reduce its number of suppliers and to work with its suppliers to improve quality and cut costs. The company also sold off non-core businesses and began to look more to low-cost countries in North Africa and Eastern Europe as well as to Mexico for new suppliers. The company also pinned its hopes again on growing sales in North America. CEO Morin announced in late 2002 that Valeo would double its sales in North America by 2007. The U.S. subsidiaries had just emerged from bankruptcy, and Morin predicted the Rochester plant would be consistently profitable by 2005. Valeo turned a profit in 2002, and by early 2003 its crisis seemed to be over. Noel Goutard announced that he was retiring again, leaving Thierry Morin with full responsibility for the direction of the company.

Morin felt that business conditions in the automotive industry would remain difficult for the next few years, and the company worked assiduously to prepare for the end of the decade. Valeo had had significant problems with quality control in the early 2000s, but it seemed to be on the way to solving them by 2004. In 2003, the company reported 200 problems per million parts, but by 2004 Valeo claimed it had only 53 problem parts per million. The company concentrated its technical expertise on what it called ''seeing and being seen'' systems, which it hoped would lead to greater North American sales. ''Seeing and being seen'' included advanced lighting devices, such as night vision systems, special ''bending'' lights for turning, and new sensors inside headlamps which offered obstacle detection. Initially, costs for these advanced features were high, but the company was confident it could bring prices down. This was to help Valeo double its North American sales by 2007. In a new strategic road map released in 2004, to take the company through 2010, Valeo also emphasized the increasing importance of Asia. By 2010, Valeo hoped to have 400 suppliers in China and to bring in 25 percent of its revenue from Asia, which accounted for only 10 percent of sales in 2004. In 2004, Valeo reiterated its hope to become one of the top five automotive suppliers in the world over the next few years. The company had first announced this vision in 1997 and had overcome several obstacles and significantly revamped its operations since then. Nevertheless, in 2004 the company remained in the number ten spot in the industry.

Principal Subsidiaries

Valeo Gmbh (Germany); ITT Automotive Inc. (U.S.); Valeo Electronique et Systèmes de Liaison; Valeo Espana S.A. (Spain); Valeo Thermique Habitacle; Valeo Sistemi S.p.A. (Italy); Valeo Thermique Moteur S.A.; Valeo Climate Control de Mexico, S.A.; Valeo Sécurité Habitacle; Valeo S.p.A. (Italy); Valeo Service; Valeo Termico Ltda. (Brazil); Valeo Termico S.A. (Spain); Valeo Vision Belgique (Belgium); Fiamm Technologies (U.S.); Valeo Group (China); Zexel Valeo Compressor USA Inc.

Principal Competitors

Delphi Corporation; Visteon Corporation; Robert Bosch GmbH.

Principal Divisions

Electrical & Electronic Systems; Transmissions; Thermal Systems Activity; Valeo Service.

Further Reading

Armstrong, Julie, ''Valeo Plans Major Shift to Low-Cost Countries,'' *Automotive News*, March 15, 2004, p. 16.

Armstrong, Julie Cantwell, ''Valeo Braces for Another Tough Year,'' *Automotive News*, May 26, 2003, p. 28.

De Saint-Seine, Sylviane, ''Navarri out as Valeo Restructures,'' *Automotive News*, March 26, 2001, p. 8.

——, ''Valeo's Goutard Retires (Again),'' *Automotive News*, February 24, 2003, p. 3.

Harnischfeger, Uta, ''French Group Victim of Sharp Edge of Car-Parts Production,'' *Financial Times*, April 10, 2001, p. 30.

Mallet, Victor, ''Loss Caps Grim Year for Valeo,'' *Financial Times*, February 4, 2002, p. 28.

Sherefkin, Robert, ''Valeo's Growth Hits a Pothole,'' *Automotive News*, October 2, 2000, p. 3.

Sherefkin, Robert, ''Valeo to Slash 5,000 Jobs in Sluggish Market,'' *Financial Times*, January 12, 2002, p. 8.

Simonian, Haig, ''Healthy Appetite Remains after a $1.7bn Purchase,'' *Financial Times*, March 1, 1999, p. 3.

Ulrich, Lawrence, ''Two U.S. Units of Paris Auto Supplier Valeo File for Bankruptcy,'' *Detroit News*, December 15, 2001.

''Valeo Aims to Be Top 5 Global Supplier,'' *Ward's Auto World*, May 1, 2004.

Whitbread, Colin, ''Valeo Trims Some Suppliers, Coddles Others,'' *Automotive News*, July 29, 2002, p. 22D.

Wilson, Amy, ''Valeo Wants to Double N.A. Business,'' *Automotive News*, October 28, 2002, p. 41.

—M.L. Cohen
—update: A. Woodward

Viewpoint International, Inc.

1071 Avenue of the Americas, 11th Floor
New York, New York 10018-3704
U.S.A.
Telephone: (212) 391-8688
Web site: http://www.tommybahama.com

Wholly Owned Subsidiary of Oxford Industries, Inc.
Incorporated: 1992
Employees: 2,500
Sales: $369.15 million (2004)
NAIC: 448110 Men's Clothing Stores; 448120 Women's Clothing Stores

Viewpoint International, Inc., a subsidiary of Oxford Industries, Inc., is best known for the Tommy Bahama brand. Tommy Bahama began as a line of elegant, casual men's clothing with a tropical flair. Later expanded to include womenswear, Tommy Bahama also pitches the island lifestyle through a broad range of licensed goods. The company has more than 40 of its own locations, including seven combination retail/restaurant compounds, and four outlets. Upscale department stores also carry the brand. In 2003, Viewpoint was acquired by Oxford, a large, publicly traded producer of private-label clothing.

Launching the Company in 1992

Viewpoint International, Inc. and the Tommy Bahama brand was created in 1992 by apparel industry veterans Tony Margolis, Bob Emfield, and Lucio Dalla Gasperina. The original product was upscale casual clothing for men. Margolis, a cofounder of Generra Sportswear Co. Inc., served as Viewpoint's president and chief executive officer. Emfield, a regional sales manager at Generra, became marketing director and former Seattle Pacific Industries (Union Bay Sport) vice-president Gasperina served as the new firm's design director. Margolis and Emfield had worked earlier as sales reps for the Britannia brand during the 1970s.

Start-up capital was $1.5 million, including $500,000 from Hong Kong manufacturer Whole Duty Inc., reported the *Puget Sound Business Journal.* Viewpoint began with three clothing brands, two of which would be eclipsed by Tommy Bahama: Gear for Urban Training, a line of skateboarder clothes, and Linguini & Bob, for ladies' men in the *Saturday Night Fever* tradition. According to *Inc.,* these were both distributed through Merry-Go-Round Enterprises Inc., a retail chain on the road to bankruptcy.

Margolis and Emfield reportedly first conceived the Tommy Bahama brand while at their vacation homes on Florida's Gulf Coast. It was designed to conjure an island attitude—''one long weekend.'' The name, by one account attributed to Emfield, referred to a fictional character living the good life in the tropics, decked out in classy but relaxed updates of ''Hawaiian'' shirts and khakis. Silk was a favored material since it was cheap to import, Margolis later told the *New York Times.* Other offerings included T-shirts and linen and canvas shorts. Businessmen longing for a bit of a holiday made up the target market.

The company motto was simply, ''Relax,'' and it was an appealing mantra. According to the *New York Times,* Tommy Bahama's first-year sales were $3.5 million. With department stores scaling back their offerings, the clothes were most successful with small men's shops at first.

Viewpoint was based in Seattle, where the clothes were designed under the direction of Gasperina. The other two partners worked in different cities—Margolis in New York, and Emfield in Minneapolis. Seattle was chosen for its port and its established apparel industry. Manufacturing was carried on in Asia; the garments were distributed through upscale department stores such as Nordstrom and Neiman Marcus. Resorts and country club pro shops also carried them.

The other two brands were dropped in late 1994, reports *Inc.* magazine. Feeling a cash pinch, the company resorted to producing private-label clothes.

In November 1995, the company's first retail shop opened near a Ritz-Carlton Hotel in Naples, Florida. Having a standalone store finally provided an opportunity to demonstrate how the tropical lifestyle should be merchandised. It was approached

Company Perspectives:

Life is one long weekend—who wouldn't find the thought intriguing? That relaxed casual state of mind is the philosophy behind TOMMY BAHAMA, the popular lifestyle brand that elevates the act of relaxation to a fine art. The inspiration behind the company is a fictional character whose celebration of island living encourages a slowed down, relaxed approach to the finer things in life.

as if they were constructing a house for the Tommy Bahama character. Old Chinese newspapers were used as wallpaper to suggest world travels, reports *Display & Design Ideas.* The environment was kept open, inviting, and exotic.

The founders later told *Inc.* that around the same time as the store was opening, they were wondering how to make the most of some money they had saved for advertising. Leery of high media prices, they wondered, ''What would Tommy do?''

They decided he would open a brewpub. Tommy Bahama's Tropical Café, a restaurant with a relaxed island flavor, was opened when space next to the store was offered at a steal. The cantina served Tommy Bahama beer to wash down the island dishes such as a grilled jerk chicken sandwich with roasted onions and shrimp BLTs. (Florida's Paradise Breweries produced the beer under license.) It was a hit with visitors, who loved being able to buy clothes at the Emporium while sipping tropical drinks.

Tommy Bahama's washable silk clothing got more exposure when Kevin Costner wore it in the movie *Tin Cup.* Tommy Bahama benefited from a trend toward more casual clothes throughout the decade. At the same time, its own fashions were becoming more sophisticated to appeal to a more upscale buyer. In the last half of the decade, reported the *New York Times,* the company started importing more muted floral prints from Europe.

The opening of the retail/restaurant compound proved to be the company's big break. Hugely successful in its own right, the location created a buzz that led to increased orders from department stores. A second store soon opened in Sarasota, Florida. Viewpoint's sales were about $100 million in 1998, reported the *Los Angeles Times.* During the year, the company opened two restaurant/retail compounds in California. A women's line was introduced in the late 1990s.

Tommy Bahama also expanded to sportswear and swimwear for men and women, as well as accessories like ties, forming a joint venture, Paradise Neckwear, to produce them. Footwear and belts were being made under license by Paradise Shoe Co. of Tempe, Arizona. Paradise Bags Co. of Millburn, New Jersey made the brand's handbags. Other offerings in line with the beach theme included hats and towels. According to *Brandweek,* licensees also included Wildwood Lamps, Geneva Watch, Shaw Rugs, L'Amy (eyewear), and Sferra Bros. (linens). The most successful was said to be North Carolina-based Lexington Home Brands, which reportedly sold $100 million of branded plantation furniture in the first year and a half.

All of the extensions kept within the tropical lifestyle. ''We don't really look at our brand as apparel,'' Gasperina told the *Seattle Times.* ''We look at it as a brand with a soul.''

New Brands After 2001

Sales exceeded $300 million in 2001. According to *Inc.,* royalty revenues from licensed goods brought in $16 million. Viewpoint had 2,500 employees, more than 300 of them at its Seattle headquarters and distribution center. The Tommy Bahama chain had 18 retail stores and six restaurant/retail compounds, as well as finer department stores in 34 states. None of the company-owned stores were in Seattle. Private-label manufacturing accounted for 10 percent of revenues, reported the *Puget Sound Business Journal.*

Viewpoint had another brand on the drawing board, a denim clothing chain called Indigo Palms. Viewpoint launched a line of men's jeans under this name in the fall of 2001. Jeanswear for women soon followed. The company also added sweaters and sweatshirts designed for winter walks on the beach to appeal to stores in the Northeast.

Model Andy Lucchesi had signed up to portray the Tommy Bahama character in the company's print advertising beginning in 1999. The company launched its first national advertising campaign in 2001, placing ads in fashion magazines such as *W* and *Town & Country.* The advertising budget was upped the next year to help restart the women's line with a focus on a younger audience. Another marketing activity was sponsorship of sporting events such as golf, auto racing, and speedboat racing.

A Stamford, Connecticut equity firm, Saunders, Karp & Megrue, acquired a minority holding in mid-2002. Viewpoint aimed to reach $1 billion in revenues by 2007, reported the *Puget Sound Business Journal.* According to the same publication, Saunders, Karp wanted to sell its stake within a couple of months of acquiring it, opening the way for the eventual acquisition of the company by Oxford International, Inc.

Former Seventh Avenue whiz kid Christian Francis Roth was brought in to restyle the women's line, which accounted for about one-third of sales. Hawaiian shirts for men then made up just 20 percent of total business.

Acquisition by Oxford in 2003

Venerable apparel group Oxford Industries, Inc. acquired Viewpoint International and its Tommy Bahama brand on June 13, 2003. The deal was worth $240 million in cash, $10 million in stock, and up to an additional $75 million if certain performance targets were met. Viewpoint, operated as Tommy Bahama Group, remained under the direction of its original founders.

Oxford produced licensed cotton clothing under a number of designer and department store brands, including Tommy Hilfiger, Oscar de la Renta, Geoffrey Beene, Lands' End, Nautica, and J.C. Penney's private label, Stafford. The Viewpoint purchase brought Oxford into a higher margin market heavy in silks. Oxford's stock, traded on the Big Board since the 1960s, nearly tripled in price after the company acquired Tommy Bahama, seen as much more glamorous and lucrative than Oxford's

Key Dates:

1992: Apparel industry vets launch the Tommy Bahama lifestyle brand.
1995: The first company store opens in Naples, Florida.
1996: The first café opens next to the first store.
2001: Indigo Palms jeans are launched.
2003: Oxford Industries buys Viewpoint; Island Soft casual clothing debuts.

private-label business. Oxford Chairman J. Hicks Lanier called it the "crown jewel" in the company's portfolio.

Viewpoint introduced a higher end brand of casualwear called Island Soft in the fall of 2003. Launched at Tommy Bahama stores, the line was not limited to a tropical theme. It also was sold at department stores and at Viewpoint's new Indigo Palms stores, the first of which opened in Newport Beach, California in November 2003.

In July 2004, Viewpoint announced that it was licensing Gemini Cosmetics to produce fragrances for men and women under the Tommy Bahama label. Other new brand extensions ran the gamut from ceiling fans (Emerson Fans) to sailing yachts (Beneteau U.S.A. Inc.).

The Tommy Bahama Group posted operating income of $50.6 million on net sales of $369 million in the 2004 fiscal year. The firm was celebrating its success by moving into a new headquarters building in Seattle. Oxford aimed to grow the chain to up to 80 stores by 2008, then cap the expansion to maintain the brand's exclusivity.

Principal Operating Units

Indigo Palms; Island Soft; Tommy Bahama.

Principal Competitors

Kahala of Hawaii; Nautica Enterprises, Inc.; Polo Ralph Lauren; Reyn Spooner Inc.; Tommy Hilfiger Corporation; Tori Richard.

Further Reading

Batsell, Jake, "Well-Stressed? Then Relax in These Clothes; Casual Outfitters Find Comfort Fits Country's Mood," *Seattle Times,* March 26, 2002, p. F1.

Bellafante, Ginia, "The Hawaiian Prints That Wouldn't Fade," *New York Times,* June 24, 2003, p. B7.

Bowers, Katherine, "Tommy's Bahama Mama," *Women's Wear Daily,* November 13, 2002, p. 10.

Clark, Julie, "Do You Like Piña Coladas?," *Display & Design Ideas,* November 2001, p. 25.

Cunningham, Tommy, "Tommy Bahama Hires Financo to Spearhead Growth Plans," *DNR,* April 23, 1999, p. 1A.

Dolbow, Sandra, "Brand Builders," *Brandweek,* March 4, 2002.

Hofman, Mike, "A Brand Is Born," *Inc.,* December 1, 2001.

"In Brief: Eyewear to Yachts," *Women's Wear Daily,* July 16, 2004, p. 2.

Jones, Jeanne Lang, "The Other Tommy," *Puget Sound Business Journal* (Seattle), August 23, 2002, p. 1.

Lloyd, Brenda, "Tommy Bahama Sends Oxford Soaring," *DNR,* October 13, 2003.

McCarrell, Pat, "Big Bucks for Bahama," *Puget Sound Business Journal,* May 2, 2003, p. 3.

McKanic, Patricia, "Tommy Guns for Exposure," *Sarasota Herald-Tribune,* March 18, 1998, p. 1D.

McKinney, Melonee, "Not Your Typical Tropical," *Daily News Record,* August 7, 1998, p. 2.

McNaughton, David, "Upscale by Design: Oxford Sizzles with Tommy Bahama Brand," *Atlanta Journal-Constitution,* September 30, 2003, p. D1.

Medina, Marcy, "Tommy Bahama Is Suiting Up," *WWD,* January 7, 2002, p. 3.

Moore, Booth, "Seeking Career Heat at Tropical Tommy Bahama," *Los Angeles Times,* January 31, 2003, p. E1.

Much, Marilyn, "Apparel Company Has a Brand New Strategy," *Investor's Business Daily,* August 15, 2003.

Newkirk, Margaret, "Oxford Buys a Piece of the Beach," *Atlanta Journal-Constitution,* April 29, 2003, p. D1.

O'Loughlin, Sandra, "Tommy Bahama Sails Out to Sea with Sights Set on Young Women," *Brandweek,* January 20, 2003, p. 14.

Quintanilla, Michael, "Bahama Papas," *Los Angeles Times,* April 30, 1999, p. E1.

Spector, Robert, "Seattle Sportswear Firms Rebound with New Names But Some Faces Are Familiar from the '70s, '80s," *DNR,* September 21, 1994, p. 4.

Stewart, Al, "Tommy Bahama Stretches Its Scions," *Daily News Record,* January 19, 2004, p. 4.

Tice, Carol, "Button-Down Meets Breezy at Tommy Bahama," *Puget Sound Business Journal,* March 5, 2004, p. A3.

Williams, Linda, "Generra Co-Founder Stitches Together New Apparel Firm," *Puget Sound Business Journal* (Seattle), September 11, 1992, p. 4.

Williams, Stan, "Tommy Bahama—They Call Him the Great Extender," *DNR,* February 5, 1996, p. 8.

—Frederick C. Ingram

Viking Range Corporation

111 Front Street
Greenwood, Mississippi 38930
U.S.A.
Telephone: (662) 455-1200
Fax: (662) 453-7939
Web site: http//:www.vikingrange.com

Private Company
Incorporated: 1984
Employees: 800 (est.)
Sales: $800 million (2003 est.)
NAIC: 335221 Household Cooking Appliance Manufacturing

Viking Range Corporation manufactures and markets a wide range of professional kitchen appliances for home use. The private company, based in Greenwood, Mississippi, is best known for it upscale ranges, but also offers ovens, refrigerators, freezers, dishwashers, disposals, and ventilation products. In addition, Viking offers professional-grade countertop appliances such as a blender and stand mixer, a line of cookware and cutlery, and a complete set of outdoor cooking products, including gas grills with hoods, warming drawers, gas woks, outdoor refrigerated beverage centers, stainless steel cabinets, as well as professional barbecue tool sets and gloves. Viking maintains three factories in Greenwood, and operates a dozen Viking Culinary Arts Centers across the country, where cooking lessons are given and the company's products are available for purchase. The company's products are also sold through high-end dealers, housing contractors, and kitchen specialists. Internationally, Viking products are retailed in more than 80 countries.

Early 1980s Origins

Viking was founded by Fred Carl, Jr., whose father and grandfather were building contractors in Greenwood, Mississippi, once the cotton capital of the world but a town that had fallen considerably in stature. Carl grew up wanting to be a designer or an architect. While he was in college at Delta State University studying architecture, his father lost his business, and because Carl had signed some loans for him, he had to go to work in construction and selling office furniture to pay off the bills. After a decade of toil he emerged as the leading contractor in the area, known for the industrial-style kitchens he incorporated into contemporary houses. He set up a showroom to display upscale kitchen products, such as cabinets by Rutt, ranges by Thermador, and Refrigerators from Sub-Zero and KitchenAid.

Around 1980, when he could finally afford to remodel his own kitchen, his wife, along with two clients, asked Carl to find a better stove than the residential models available through regular channels. His wife came from a family of cooks and had grown up using a massive, hand-built Chambers stove featuring six burners and two ovens, but these ranges were no longer available. Manufacturers had abandoned the upper-end market in favor of producing the least expensive models they could, choosing to compete on price rather than quality. Consumers who wanted something better, and could afford it, began installing commercial ranges, the kind found in restaurants, but they faced several problems. Commercial ranges were illegal in some communities for use in a residence, primarily because they weren't insulated and used large burners, posing a fire hazard when placed next to wooden cabinets in a typical home setting. They also required overhead venting, special gas lines, and sometimes overhead sprinkler systems in order to meet building codes. In addition, commercial ranges were energy hogs and did not come with a broiler, forcing consumers to buy a separate wall oven as well. Just as residential stove manufacturers were uninterested in this market, so too were the commercial food-service companies, who were afraid of liability risks. Carl recognized a niche opportunity and began to pursue a dream of building a professional-grade range for residential use.

After paying visits to restaurant-supply houses and meeting with salespeople, he began to work on a design, which he completed in 1981 after 18 months of work. In essence, he combined elements of the residential stove with ones used in commercial food service: keeping the look of a professional range along with the high performance, but adding automatic ignition and an oven broiler. He now took his "range project" to manufacturers, hoping to find a partner, but none were interested. Rather than quit, Carl decided to drum up interest in

Company Perspectives:

In spite of tremendous growth and success, Viking remains essentially the same entrepreneurial company it was at its inception. This small, close-knit company culture serves Viking and its customers well, and strongly contributes to the company's on-going growth and success.

his concept by contacting kitchen designers featured in trade magazines. He had his range design done in an airbrush version, printed a brochure, and mailed them to key designers. The ploy worked, as a buzz about upscale ranges began to circulate in certain circles, and he began to receive telephone calls from people around the country who urged him to press on. In 1983 Carl selected the Viking name and had a logo designed, a year later the company was incorporated, and in 1986 the first Viking prototype was approved and received AGA approval for meeting safety standards.

Carl arranged to have the Viking range manufactured by U.S. Range Corporation, based near Los Angeles. His first order came from New York City, from Patricia King who was a passionate cook and wanted a restaurant stove but had balked at the idea of giving up so much kitchen space for ductwork and insulation to comply with city ordinances. Her architect gave her one of Carl's brochures for the Viking stove, priced at $3,000, and she promptly sent a $100 deposit. At this stage Viking consisted of two unpaid employees, Carl and his assistant, Tawana Thompson. The contract manufacturer, which was undergoing a number of management changes and treated Viking like a poor country cousin, shipped King's range nine months later and six months late. The black enamel unit had a number of problems: electric pilots that didn't work, gas leaks, a wiring harness that melted, and oven doors that refused to stay open. Diligently, Carl and friends he recruited worked through the problems with King on the phone and even dispatched a local appliance repairman to help out and flew in engineers. According to King, her stove may have been rebuilt four times. It wasn't until early 1988 that it was finally working properly.

The initial Viking product line included ten models of gas ranges, ranging in price from $2,700 to $4,700. They featured oversize burners capable of handling large utensils and infra-red broiling. Because of the price, Carl had some difficulty lining up appliance dealers to handle Viking ranges and opted instead to set up his own network of dealers and regional distributors, creating an air of exclusivity. His timing proved fortuitous because a number of KitchenAid distributors had their franchises terminated in July 1986 when KitchenAid opted to go factory-direct. About half of Viking's initial 28 independent distributors were former KitchenAid distributors.

Because U.S Range proved unreliable, Carl tried a contract manufacturer in Tennessee in 1988 before deciding to make the ranges in-house. Carl and an employee, Ron Ussery, a former appliance repairman, took apart one of their own ranges to reverse engineer it, determining which parts could be bought and which ones they would need to have built. Carl took on ten partners—a group that included his doctor, several farmers, and an insurance agent—raising more than $125,000. He then rented a small abandoned factory in the area, hired a manufacturing chief and 30 workers, and in late 1989 the first Viking Range was assembled in Greenwood in a 35,000-square-foot facility. By 1990 all production was occurring at the Greenwood facility. Two years later the company opened a new 100,000-square-foot plant to handle production.

Because of the manufacturing problems the company endured in the beginning, it was fortunate that for about three years Viking had the market to itself and was able to stake out a strong position. The company added smaller ranges, hoods, and wall ovens. Because the Viking range had such a unique look compared to residential stoves, it did not match the other appliances in the home, offering the company an opening to apply the professional-grade idea to other appliances and create an integrated kitchen concept. In 1992 Viking added dishwashers to its lineup. A year later it began manufacturing its own line of commercial quality disposers for the home. The company also added trash compactors.

In 1992 some of Carl's investors grew impatient and threatened to take over the business, but Viking was able to obtain backing from Stephens Inc., the Little Rock, Arkansas, investment bank that took Wal-Mart public. Stephens bought the company with Carl and named him chief executive. He now had the resources to recruit seasoned executives and completely redesign Viking's range top product lines. The company was also able to launch a very successful print and television advertising campaign, created by Jackson, Mississippi-based Ramey Agency.

These investments would pay off in 1994, but the company almost became a victim of its own success. It hired more workers and went to three shifts, and was still unable to meet demand. It took customers 20 to 22 weeks to receive the Viking ranges they ordered, and the backlog was soon worth some $20 million in orders. The company was in danger of losing customers and dealers when it changed its manufacturing approach, adopting practices developed by Toyota, such as building each product from order and managing inventory at the assembly line. Eventually, the company was able to reduce the time between order and delivery to just nine days. Instead of 14 days, finished inventory would stay on the plant floor for little more than an hour.

Because Viking was so behind on orders there was no need to spend money on advertising, but as production got up to speed the company again began to advertise its products in 1996. The company was also able to take the next steps in creating an integrated kitchen. It created a new division, Viking Specialty Products, which received a $1 million empowerment grant from the Department of Agriculture's Rural Business Enterprise Grant Program. The division looked to develop stainless steel cabinets and outdoor grills. Later in 1996 Viking began shipping its first side-by-side commercial-style refrigerators, completing the basic integrated commercial-type kitchen. As had been the case with ranges, institutional refrigerators were robust but lacked certain features consumers had grown to expect from residential models, such as temperature controls, adjustable door shelves, ice makers, and separate meat and produce compartments. Maytag handled the manufacturing of the premium line of 84'' refrigerators, a contract that would be taken over by Amana in 1999. Viking acquired equipment from

Key Dates:

1981: The first drawing of a Viking range is completed.
1984: The company is incorporated.
1987: First Viking Range is sold.
1990: Production is moved to Greenwood, Mississippi.
1992: Stephens Inc. forms partnership with management to buy the company.
1996: The first Viking refrigerators are shipped.
2000: Refrigerator manufacturing operations are moved to Greenwood.

Amana a year later and moved it to Greenwood to take refrigerator production in-house.

New Products in the Late 1990s

Viking added outdoor gas grills and electric ranges and rangetops in 1997. A year later the company introduced electric thermal-convection ovens and gas woks. Viking also opened a new plant for ventilation products and began to produce its own hoods and warming drawers. In 1999 Carl came up with an idea to drum up more business and grow the Viking brand. Just as Land Rover had opened up driving schools where people could drive a SUV to see if they wanted to buy one, Carl decided to open what would be called Viking Culinary Arts Centers, where people could spend an evening or an entire weekend learning how to cook gourmet meals—using a Viking range, of course, which would then be available for sale along with professional caliber cooking utensils. The first centers were opened in 1999 in Memphis and Nashville. The program received a boost in 2000 when Viking acquired San Francisco-based HomeChef, Inc., picking up four HomeChef locations in California that were converted to Viking Culinary Arts Centers. Other centers would open in or near such cities as Atlanta, Cleveland, Dallas, New York, Philadelphia, San Francisco, San Jose, and St. Louis.

Viking continued to add new products in 2000. To complement its outdoor gas grills, the company brought out a set of high-end barbecue tools—spatula, tongs, fork, knife, and brush—priced at over $100, twice the price of the most expensive tool sets on the market. The tools were made out of stainless steel and used wooden handles impregnated with epoxy to make them weather resistant. The barbecue tools represented the next step in achieving the company's new goal: creating an integrated, virtual outdoor kitchen. Other products, such as an outdoor refrigerator, beverage dispenser, and warming drawer would also follow. Also in 2000 Viking introduced its Designer Series Line, which gave customers a look different from the commercial-style products, offering simple shapes, clean lines, and refined details that subtly accented a kitchen rather than making a statement.

In 2001 Viking established Viking Europe SAS, to distribute Viking products in the European market, In addition, the company grew by acquisition, picking up Rutt Custom Cabinetry of Goodville, Pennsylvania, and Heritage Custom Kitchens of New Holland, Pennsylvania, after their parent company, Classic Kitchen, filed for Chapter 11 bankruptcy protection.

Viking also ventured further afield, becoming involved in the hotel business in 2001 by acquiring Greenwood's historic Hotel Irving and adjoining downtown property, which was located within walking distance of Viking's corporate headquarters. The purpose was to provide comfortable housing for the company's many corporate visitors: Each year some 30 groups of 25 to 30 people traveled to Greenwood from around the world for three-day tours and training sessions. Hotel Irving would be remodeled to include 50 rooms and suites. Some of the nearby property was set to be converted into luxury condominiums. Revitalizing downtown Greenwood was also a long cherished dream of Carl, who now devoted considerable time to the endeavor.

Viking restructured its distribution network in 2002, creating three new distributorships in the eastern United States and another in western Canada. Later in the year the company broadened it international business by making Moscow-based Electromir the distributor of Viking products throughout Russia. In 2002 Viking also introduced smaller gas ranges, 24 inches wide, to accommodate urban apartment dwellers who had the money and the desire to buy a Viking range but lacked the space. Another unusual step the company took during the year was to become partners with its executive chef, Wally Joe, who earned acclaim as Chef de Cuisine of K.C.'s, a world-class restaurant in Cleveland. Joe's new establishment, located in Memphis, would serve as a laboratory of sorts for Viking, to help the company in its continued efforts to design equipment for the residential market.

Viking moved into the small appliance area with the introduction of a blender and stand mixer, and in 2004 opened a research and development center in Starkville, Mississippi, for advanced product development. On the retail side, the company launched a wedding and gift registry program at its Viking Culinary Arts Centers and Viking Home Chef stores. Although competitors had emerged in the high-end stove and kitchen appliance market, and took turns as the latest media darling, Viking had by now established a strong brand, and management continued to demonstrate an innovative spirit that was likely to keep the company growing and prosperous for some time to come.

Principal Divisions

Viking Specialty Products; Viking Capital Ventures.

Principal Competitors

Electrolux AB; Maytag Corporation; Sub-Zero Freezer Company, Inc.

Further Reading

DuPont, Ted, "Restaurant-Style Ranges From Viking," *HFD–The Weekly Home Furnishing Newspaper,* October 6, 1986, p. 150.

Harrington, Ann, "A Brand Built to Last," *FSB,* July/August 2001, p. 88.

Mikell, Ray, "Viking Range Corp. Thriving in Mississippi Delta," *Mississippi Business Journal,* August 1, 1994, p. 15.

O'Neill, Molly, "The Viking Invasion," *New Yorker,* July 29, 2002.

—Ed Dinger

Volunteers of America®

Volunteers of America, Inc.

1660 Duke Street
Alexandria, Virginia 22314-3427
U.S.A.
Telephone: (703) 341-5000
Toll Free: (800) 899-0089
Fax: (703) 341-7000
Web site: http://www.VolunteersofAmerica.org/

Nonprofit Organization
Founded: 1896
Employees: 14,000
Sales: $711 million (2003)
NAIC: 623220 Residential Mental Health and Substance Abuse Facilities; 623312 Homes for the Elderly; 62411 Child and Youth Services; 62421 Community Food Services; 62419 Other Individual and Family Services; 624221 Temporary Shelters; 62423 Emergency and Other Relief Services; 62431 Vocational Rehabilitation Services; 813319 Other Social Advocacy Organizations; 922140 Correctional Institutions

Volunteers of America, Inc., is a leading nonprofit human services organization in the United States. Volunteers of America considers itself a nondenominational Christian church with a ministry of service. Its programs serve nearly 1.8 million people a year. The organization prides itself on helping those with immediate, critical needs: the elderly, the disabled, the homeless, the incarcerated, abused children, and at-risk youth. The group underwent a sweeping reorganization in the early 1980s, doing away with military ranks and uniforms in favor of corporate-style titles and accountabilities. A number of business magazines have commended the group's efficiency.

1896 Origins

Volunteers of America was spawned by another well-known nonprofit group. Its founders, Ballington and Maud Booth, were son and daughter-in-law of Salvation Army founders William and Catherine Booth. They had arrived in America in 1887 to lead the U.S. branch of the Salvation Army, which had been founded in Britain in 1865. The Booths introduced programs such as social work in the New York slums and oversaw the construction of a new headquarters building.

Ballington and Maude left the Salvation Army in early 1896, complaining about the father's autocratic ways and the amount of money being sent back to England. On March 8, 1896, they told a throng of thousands at New York City's Cooper Union that they were forming a new organization with ''The Lord My Banner'' as its motto. This marked the birth of Volunteers of America, whose articles or incorporation were signed on November 4, 1896.

Ballington Booth was chosen as commander-in-chief, a rank soon changed to that of general, for a ten-year term. The group was well established by the end of the year, notes historian Herbert A. Wisby, Jr., with more than 140 posts in 20 states across America.

One of the group's early missions was serving prison inmates. Maud Booth was the first woman ever allowed into Sing Sing Prison. The Volunteer Prison League (VPL) was founded there in 1896 and involved 2,000 prisoners at eight institutions by the end of 1897. Within fifteen years, writes Wisby, VPL had 60,000 members. Maud Booth's work at Sing Sing led to the formation of the nation's first halfway houses, known as Hope Halls.

Volunteers of America took over existing meals programs in cities that included Chicago, where it fed 7,000 people on its first Christmas Day. Homeless shelters were also established there and in other locations. The group established its first home for unmarried mothers in Newark, New Jersey, in May 1899.

Innovations in the 20th Century

Volunteers of America had introduced a number of new programs in its first four years, and the innovations continued after 1900, when the group's first Sidewalk Santa rang his bell in Los Angeles. Ten years later, the Santas appeared in New York City. By the early 1900s, the organization was serving thousands of people each year. It had an annual budget of several hundred thousand dollars.

Company Perspectives:

In addition to being one of the nation's largest and most comprehensive human services organizations, Volunteers of America is an interdenominational church—a church with a distinctive ministry of service. For more than 100 years Volunteers of America has provided essential services to heal both body and soul. In fact, what sets Volunteers of America apart from most other human services organizations is that we are spiritually based. We provide services to people in need, and are motivated to service by our beliefs of compassion for people, forgiveness, and hope for mankind. Volunteers of America acknowledges service as an expression of faith. We believe that serving others is an important means of serving God. Building on that spiritual base, Volunteers of America provides human service programs and opportunities for individual and community involvement for people of all faiths. Volunteers of America offers people a very unique opportunity to put their faith into action. Working together with the help of our committed volunteer board members and volunteers we can achieve our collective mission and make the world a more compassionate place to live.

The new St. Gregory's Hospital, the only one in New York City offering free services for those unable to pay, was acquired in 1906. It was renamed Volunteer Hospital in December 1906. Another group took over St. Gregory's in 1922, and it later became part of the NYU Hospital system.

Volunteers of America's first headquarters was a few rooms at the Bible House on the corner of Fourth Avenue and 8th Street. After several moves, the group acquired a six-story headquarters building at 34 West 28th Street in April 1907.

The Volunteers found themselves weakened financially after World War I, and a huge challenge was a decade away. The Great Depression challenged the group with increased calls for assistance at a time when its financial backers were less able to help. Nevertheless, the group provided assistance to millions. From 1931 to 1936, reports Wisbey, Volunteers of America served nearly 25 million free meals, plus another four million paid for by money or work. The group help find employment for more than 416,000 people. More than 4.5 million in all were assisted with food or lodging, and another 7.5 million were afforded religious services.

Ballington Booth died in 1940, followed by his wife eight years later. Their son, Charles Brandon Booth, was commander-in-chief from 1949 to 1958, when he was succeeded by John McMahon.

Volunteers of America served a range of different populations, helping provide housing for low to middle-income families, the elderly, at-risk youth, and single mothers. There were group homes for the emotionally and physically disabled. Alcohol and drug addiction programs were another area of service. The organization also provided meals on wheels for senior citizens.

Other programs thrived in the 1950s. In the late 1950s, the Santas were raising money for about 50,000 meals per year in New York. Volunteers of America had 2,575 employees by that time, two-thirds of them trained social workers. The group began opening nursing homes in the early 1970s. Among the first was Maplewood Care Center near St. Paul, Minnesota.

Reorganization in Louisiana in 1980s

Raymond C. Tremont became the organization's general in 1980, succeeding John McMahon. The first reorganization in the group's history ensued over the next three years. The blue uniforms were dropped. The military ranks were replaced with titles from the corporate world, and the structure was made less authoritarian, with the addition of local boards that included more lay people. Tremont also moved the group's headquarters from New York City to Metairie, Louisiana.

Volunteers of America began operating prisons in 1984. The first was a 42-bed facility near St. Paul, Minnesota. Another new project was a literacy program operated in partnership with Literacy Volunteers of America and the American Association of Retired People (AARP).

The organization's revenues were $132 million in 1984. In the mid-1980s, the organization had a presence in 37 states. It ran the country's largest year-round shelter for homeless men, an 800-person unit in New York City. However, Tremont told the *Associated Press*, the group was known in some circle as "the invisible agency" since relatively few people were aware of it.

The Volunteers of America became identified with its thrift shops and bell-ringing Santas soliciting donations at Christmas. However, the latter appeared only in New York City, reported the Associated Press in 1985, and the stores accounted for only 5 percent of activity.

CEO Raymond Tremont retired in 1991 and was replaced by J. Clint Cheveallier, formerly a vice-president at the Baton Rouge office. Both were second-generation members of the group, reported the *Advocate* of Baton Rouge. The organization had a yearly budget of $230 million at the time; more than 85 percent of funding came from the government. It had 8,000 employees in 200 chapters, plus many thousands of volunteers. Cheveallier made raising the organization's profile a priority.

In 1990, Volunteers of America alcohol addiction specialists entered an exchange program with the Soviet Union, where treatment methods and facilities bore a greater resemblance to those of a gulag prison camp than a social service organization. The Soviet state was notorious for alcoholism. As part of the exchange, 16 Soviet "narcologists" visited Volunteers of America treatment centers in 12 U.S. cities. The group's drug and alcohol programs assisted 50,000 people a year.

Cheveallier retired as president and CEO in 1996 and was succeeded by Charles Gould. Gould, an attorney, had formerly led VOA Health Services, based in Eden Prairie, Minnesota, which operated nursing homes and retirement communities in five states. It had revenues of about $60 million a year.

A Web site, www.sidewalksanta.org, was launched in 1997 as part of the organization's holiday fundraising efforts. Visitors could also donate money and discover volunteer opportunities through the Volunteers' main site.

Key Dates:

1896: Volunteers of America is founded in New York City; halfway houses are opened.
1900: The group's first Sidewalk Santa appears in Los Angeles.
1907: A new headquarters building is acquired.
1936: Volunteers assists 4.5 million with food or lodging during the Great Depression.
1953: The group is serving two million people per year.
1981: Headquarters is relocated from New York to Louisiana.
1982: Military ranks are replaced with corporate job titles.
1984: The organization is restructured.
1989: An alcoholism treatment exchange program with Soviet specialists is conducted.
2000: The group's headquarters is moved to Alexandria, Virginia.

Volunteers of America's national headquarters were relocated to Alexandria, Virginia, in 2000. Its proximity to federal lawmakers and other nonprofits were a reason for the move. The head office had a staff of 35 people. The organization's programs were serving more than one million people a year. The annual budget exceeded $500 million in 2001. By fiscal 2004, that number had reached $711 million.

Principal Subsidiaries

Volunteers of America of Alaska, Inc.; Volunteers of America of Arkansas, Inc.; Volunteers of America Bay Area, Inc.; Volunteers of America Chesapeake, Inc.; Volunteers of America Colorado Branch; Volunteers of America of Florida, Inc.; Volunteers of America of Greater Baton Rouge; Volunteers of America of the Carolinas; Volunteers of America of Central Ohio, Inc.; Volunteers of America, Dakotas; Volunteers of America Delaware Valley, Inc.; Volunteers of America of Greater New Orleans, Inc.; Volunteers of America Greater New York; Volunteers of America Greater Sacramento & Northern Nevada, Inc.; Volunteers of America of Illinois; Volunteers of America of Indiana, Inc.; Volunteers of America of Kentucky and Tennessee, Inc.; Volunteers of America of Los Angeles; Volunteers of America of Massachusetts, Inc.; Volunteers of America of Michigan, Inc.; Volunteers of America of Minnesota; Volunteers of America North Alabama, Inc.; Volunteers of America of North Louisiana; Volunteers of America of Northeast & North Central Ohio, Inc.; Volunteers of America of Northern New England; Volunteers of America of Northwest Ohio, Inc.; Volunteers of America Southeast, Inc.; Volunteers of America Ohio River Valley, Inc.; Volunteers of America of Oklahoma, Inc.; Volunteers of America of Oregon, Inc.; Volunteers of America of Pennsylvania; Volunteers of America Southwest California; Volunteers of America of Spokane; Volunteers of America of Texas, Inc.; Volunteers of America of Utah, Inc.; Volunteers of America of Western Nebraska, Inc.; Volunteers of America of Western New York; Volunteers of America of Western Washington, Inc.; Volunteers of America of Wisconsin; Volunteers of America of Wyoming.

Principal Competitors

Salvation Army.

Further Reading

Bartlett, Kay, ''VOA Drops Military Look, Moves to Diversify Work,'' *Baton Rouge Sunday Advocate*, September 2, 1985, p. 5J.
——, ''Volunteers of America: Santa Claus and Thrift Shops?,'' *Associated Press*, August 23, 1985.
''Charles Brandon Booth Is Dead; Headed Volunteers of America,'' *New York Times*, April 17, 1975, p. 36.
''Gen. Booth of Volunteers of America Retiring to Life of Sailing and Writing,'' *New York Times*, September 5, 1957, p. 15.
Hattersley, Roy, *Blood and Fire: William and Catherine Booth and Their Salvation Army*, New York: Doubleday, 2000.
Heitman, Danny, ''America's Team; Volunteers of America Celebrating 100 Years of Service in American and 75 or So in Baton Rouge,'' *Baton Rouge Advocate*, April 15, 1996, p. 1C.
''La. Man to Lead National VOA,'' *Baton Rouge State Times*, May 24, 1990, p. 1B.
McKinley, Edward H., *Marching to Glory: The History of the Salvation Army in the United States of America, 1880–1980*, San Francisco: Harper & Row, 1980.
Martin, Karen, ''Last 'General' Views VOA Career; Ray Tremont Made Big Changes in Organization during His Service,'' *Baton Rouge Morning Advocate*, January 16, 1991, p. 1C.
——, ''New President Aims to Polish Image of VOA,'' *Baton Rouge Morning Advocate*, January 16, 1991, p. 1C.
Oliver, Daniel T., ''How Social-Service Contracting Has Transformed Charity,'' *World & I*, November 1, 1999, p. 323.
Renz, Christine, ''Built to Last: Ten Keys to a Long-Lived Organization,'' *Nonprofit World*, November 1, 1999, p. 33.
''Santas Are Back in Nylon Beards to Open 50th Appeal,'' *New York Times*, November 22, 1958, p. 8.
''VOA to Help Soviets with Alcoholism Treatment Plans,'' *Baton Rouge Sunday Advocate*, October 8, 1989, p. 9B.
''Volunteers of America to Move to Alexandria,'' *Washington Post*, August 30, 1996, p. D2.
Wisbey, Herbert A., Jr., *The Volunteers of America: 1896–1948: Era of the Founders*, Revised Edition, Metairie, Louisiana: 1994.
Youngblood, Dick, ''Having Your Corporate Heart in the Right Place Makes a Huge Difference,'' *Star Tribune* (Minneapolis), August 3, 1994, p. 2D.

—Frederick C. Ingram

Weber et Broutin France

rue de Brie, BP 84
Brie Comte Robert F-77253 Cedex
France
Telephone: +33 1 60 62 13 00
Fax: +33 1 64 05 47 50
Web site: http://www.weber-broutin.fr

Wholly Owned Subsidiary of Saint-Gobain S.A.
Incorporated: 1902 as G. Weber et Cie
Employees: 7,414
Sales: EUR 742 million (US $780 million) (2003)
NAIC: 327310 Cement Manufacturing; 325510 Paint and Coating Manufacturing

Weber et Broutin France is a subsidiary of Saint-Gobain S.A. and forms one of the pillars of the French giant's Building Materials division. Weber et Broutin focuses on the development and production of mortars and cements for facades, tile fixing, ground and foundation preparation, and other construction and engineering projects. The company produces full-scale fixing systems, including the mortars, tools, equipment, and accessories needed for their application. The company also produces decorative façade mortars and mortars for industrial use. Weber et Broutin has operations in 18 countries, primarily in western and eastern Europe, but with a growing presence in South America (Brazil and Argentina especially) and Asia (in China, Hong Kong, and Thailand). The company operates from more than 100 sites, including nearly 60 production facilities and 20 warehouses. This network helps Weber et Broutin claim the number one position in the world for tile fixing mortars, the top spot in Europe for decorative façade mortars, and the lead in both the European and Brazilian markets for industrial mortars. The company markets its products under a number of local brand names, as well as the primary brand name, Weber Building Solutions. The company employs more than 3,400 people, and generated sales of EUR 742 million (US $780 million) in 2003.

Early 20th Century Foundations

George Weber founded a business in 1902 producing gypsum- and lime-based mortars, used as a covering for building façades. Weber at first served his east Paris neighborhood, but soon began shipping a major part of his production to the United States. In this effort, Weber was joined by competitor, and neighbor, Jean-Baptiste Broutin, who opened his own factory just 500 meters from G. Weber & Cie. These companies were taken over by Edgar de Vigan in 1927, and two years later, Vigan merged them to form Weber et Broutin Réunis.

Exports remained a significant part of the united company's business until World War II. Following the war, Weber et Broutin turned much of its attention toward supplying the domestic market, adding reconstruction and renovation materials to its list. The company grew strongly during the reconstruction period and the surge in housing construction and renovation during the postwar economic boom.

The late 1960s and early 1970s saw a wave of consolidation and restructuring throughout the construction and building materials industries. This process was encouraged in large part by the French government, which sought the creation of a smaller number of large-scale companies capable of competing on a European and even global level. Weber et Broutin became part of this process when it was acquired by Groupe Poliet. That company, formerly known as Poliet & Chausson, was in the process of redefining itself as a specialist producer and distributor of building materials. Poliet sold off its cement production unit to Ciments Français in 1970, and instead added Weber et Broutin's more specialized mortars in 1971.

Under Poliet, Weber et Broutin extended its range of products to include tile adhesives and technical mortars. The company took advantage of Poliet's strong wholesale distribution network—regrouped as Point P in 1981—to extend its operations to a national level by the end of the 1970s.

With its domestic presence solidified in the early 1980s, Weber next turned to the international market. The company's first foreign move was the acquisition of Spain's Cemarska in

Company Perspectives:

Our mission is to maintain leadership by exceeding our customer's expectations in service excellence and product quality. We stand for: high quality materials and solutions, combining aesthetics, comfort and technical performances, improved through constant innovation; complementary services to satisfy all specific needs; respect of the environment, within our organization and externally. We measure our success through the success of our customers.

1982. The company next turned to Belgium, adding that country's Betraci in 1984. These acquisitions, and others, enabled the company to extend its reach into other European markets as well. By the 1990s, the company had established a presence in the United Kingdom, The Netherlands, Germany, and elsewhere.

During the 1990s, Weber et Broutin stepped up its foreign expansion. In 1990, Weber et Broutin formed a new subsidiary in Portugal in order to acquire that country's Fixicol, itself founded in 1978. The following year, the company acquired the Stickfit brand, and claimed the leadership in Portugal's tile adhesives market.

Solidifying Global Leadership in the 2000s

Weber et Broutin achieved a major milestone in 1993 when the company acquired the Terranova brand. That company had started out in Bavaria in 1893. By 1927, Terranova had entered Austria, then Italy, and later expanded throughout more of central and eastern Europe. The addition of Terranova not only gave Weber et Broutin one of Europe's leading building materials brands, it also brought the company footholds in new markets including the Czech Republic, Hungary, Poland, Slovakia, and Slovenia. In Italy, meanwhile, Weber and Broutin built on its local Terranova holding, merging that operation with a number of other Italian companies, including Into, Modenfix, Orsan, Pearl, and Pronit, among others.

Weber et Broutin also entered Switzerland in 1993, acquiring Stahel-Keller AG. Founded in 1906, Stahel-Keller had originally specialized in the production of soaps and detergents under the Favor brand name. In 1965, however, the company began an extension into technical products for building tiles, such as adhesives and cleaners, marketed under the Favo brand. The company grew into a Swiss market leader, and in 1987 expanded its production and storage capacity.

Groupe Poliet was acquired by French industrial giant Saint-Gobain in 1996. Saint-Gobain's origins dated back to 1665, and the founding of the Compagnie des Glaces, which gained a monopoly on glassmaking in France. After losing that monopoly following the French Revolution, Saint-Gobain began its first diversification effort at the turn of the 19th century, with the production of soda ash. By the middle of the century, Saint-Gobain had extended its range to include the production of chemicals. In the 1920s, Saint-Gobain began producing cellulose, then, after acquiring Italy's Balzaretti-Modigliana in 1935,

Key Dates:

1902: George Weber begins producing mortar in east Paris; Jean-Baptiste Broutin later sets up a similar business nearby.
1927: Edgar de Vigan acquires control of the two companies.
1929: A merger between Weber and Broutin creates Weber et Broutin Réunis.
1946: The company begins production for the reconstruction and renovation markets.
1970: The company is acquired by Poliet and begins expanding into tile adhesives and technical mortar sectors.
1982: The company acquires Cemarska, in Spain, in its first international expansion.
1984: The company acquires Betraci, in Belgium.
1990: Fixicol of Portugal is acquired.
1993: The company acquires Terranova in Germany and Stahel-Keller in Switzerland.
1996: Saint-Gobain acquires Poliet.
1997: The company acquires Quartzolit, in Brazil, in its first expansion into South America.
1998: The company acquires Montenovo in Germany and Wallmaster in the United Kingdom.
2002: The company acquires Batec in Romania and Metzger in The Netherlands.
2003: The company begins plans to open a production facility in Russia.

entered fiberglass production as well. These operations also led the company to develop a significant insulation division, particularly after 1945.

By the 1970s, however, Saint-Gobain's chemical sales had begun faltering. Already in 1965, much of this division had been sold off to Rhone Poulenc. After the company merged with steel and iron conglomerate Pont-a-Mousson in 1970, it continued hiving off its chemical operation, a process completed in large part by the end of the 1970s. By then, too, however, Saint-Gobain had shed most of the Pont-a-Mousson steel and iron operations, but remained nonetheless a highly diversified company, with operations ranging from packaging and pulp and paper, to computer technology, to its glass and growing building materials activities.

The latter division took on still greater importance within Saint-Gobain in 1990, when the company completed the takeover of the United States' Norton, the global leader in sandpaper and abrasives. At $1.9 billion, the acquisition was the largest-ever by a French company in the United States at the time.

When Saint-Gobain acquired Poliet, Weber et Broutin now found itself part of a globally operating industrial giant—one of the world's top 100 industrial companies with total revenues of more than $20 billion. Weber et Broutin quickly took advantage of Saint-Gobain's global reach. In 1998, the company extended beyond Europe for the first time, acquiring Quartzolit, the leading producer of industrial mortars in Brazil. That purchase was followed by another South American acquisition, of Concreto, giving Weber et Broutin access to the Argentinian markets. Closer to home, Weber et Broutin boosted its European leadership position with the purchase of Germany's Montenovo Werke. The company also boosted its position in the United Kingdom that year, acquiring that country's Wallmaster.

Into the 2000s, Weber et Broutin became one of the core units of Saint-Gobain's building materials division. The company now also became known as Saint-Gobain Weber, and enhanced its global position through the unified brand name, Weber Building Solutions.

Weber et Broutin made its first entry into the Asian markets in the 2000s, establishing subsidiaries in Thailand, Hong Kong, and on the Chinese mainland. The company also continued to seek out new growth in Europe, and in 2002 acquired The Netherlands' Metzger, a producer of powdered mortars, and Romania's Batec, which specialized in tile adhesives, giving Saint-Gobain Weber an entry into that country as well. Meanwhile, Saint-Gobain had begun extending its diversified operations in Russia, and by 2003, Weber had begun scouting out locations for a new Russian production site as well. With more than 100 years behind it, Weber et Broutin claimed global leadership for its tile adhesives operations, and European leadership for its industrial and decorative mortars into the new century.

Principal Subsidiaries

Saint-Gobain Weber Stahel-Keller AG (Switzerland); Royal Tile Fix Ltd. (Thailand); Saint-Gobain Quartzolit Ltda. (Brazil); Saint-Gobain Weber Argentina S.A.; Saint-Gobain Weber Cemarksa S.A. (Spain); Saint-Gobain Weber Cimenfix S.A. (Portugal); Saint-Gobain Weber Corporation (China); Saint-Gobain Weber Corporation (Hong Kong); Saint-Gobain Weber GmbH (Austria); Saint-Gobain Weber GmbH (Germany); Saint-Gobain Weber Ltd. (U.K.); Saint-Gobain Weber Markem A.S. (Turkey); Saint-Gobain Weber N.V./S.A. (Belgium); Saint-Gobain Weber S.p.A. (Italy); Saint-Gobain Weber Terranova d.o.o. (Slovenia); Saint-Gobain Weber Terranova S.R.O. (Czech Republic); Saint-Gobain Weber Terranova Sp. z.o.o. (Poland); Saint-Gobain Weber Terranova spol S.R.O. (Slovakia); Saint-Gobain Weber Terranova Kft (Hungary).

Principal Competitors

IFI; Lafarge S.A.; CRH PLC; HeidelbergCement AG; Italcementi S.p.A.; Rinker Group Ltd.; Société des Ciments Français S.A.

Further Reading

''La Russie attire les industriels de la construction,'' *BatiActu,* July 27, 2003.

''Mortier ultra rapide pour travaux de maçonnerie,'' *BatiActu,* June 16, 2004.

''Saint-Gobain achète la société allemande Montenovo,'' *Les Echos,* November 3, 1998.

''Saint-Gobain privilégie les acquisitions de proximité,'' *BatiActu,* March 21, 2003.

''Saint-Gobain rachète le premier producteur brésilien de mortiers industriels,'' *Les Echos,* December 3, 1997.

—M.L. Cohen

WGBH Educational Foundation

125 Western Avenue
Boston, Massachusetts 02134
U.S.A.
Telephone: (617) 300-2000
Fax: (617) 300-1026
Web site: http://www.wgbh.org

Nonprofit Company
Incorporated: 1951
Employees: 1,300
Sales: $187.43 million (2003)
NAIC: 515112 Radio Stations; 515120 Television Broadcasting

WGBH Educational Foundation is an umbrella organization overseeing a number of public broadcasting properties. WGBH's properties include three public television stations—WGBH 2 and WGBH 44 in Boston, Massachusetts, and WGBY in Springfield, Massachusetts—and three public radio stations, WGBH 89.7 in Boston and WCAI 90.1 and WNAN 91.1 serving Cape Cod, Martha's Vineyard, and Nantucket. WGBH also operates a Web site, www.wgbh.org. WGBH represents the flagship station of the Public Broadcasting Service (PBS), producing one-third of the programming broadcast during PBS's primetime schedule. WGBH also serves as a major source of public radio programs. The major sources of WGBH's funding are corporate donors (21 percent), other PBS stations (20 percent), and individual donors (14 percent).

Origins

From its earliest roots, WGBH's leading role in the development of public broadcasting sprang from the beneficence of John Lowell. Lowell's father, Francis Cabot Lowell, pioneered cotton manufacturing in the United States, amassing a fortune that enabled his son to pursue his intellectual desires with complete financial security. Lowell, a Boston native born in 1799, sat on the city council and in the state legislature, traveled widely, and read voraciously, acquiring a large personal library that reflected his passion for learning. Lowell lived only to the age of 36, but before his death he ensured that later generations would have access to the intellectual world he adored. Lowell bequeathed $250,000 for the establishment of the Lowell Institute, whose endowment was used to provide free lectures to the citizens of Boston. In the decades following Lowell's death, the prudent administration of the Lowell Institute created a renowned patron of learning, an organization whose liberal stipends attracted some of the world's leading scholars. Lowell, as a benefactor of learning, lived well beyond 36 years. His institute served as a font of information for the public, one that served Boston's residents in the 19th century and into the 20th century.

The lectures sponsored by the Lowell Institute became an institution unto themselves. Residents of Boston were offered access to the world's great minds, and, through the publication of the lectures, the Lowell Institute was able to deliver its mission to a much larger reading audience. It was through the institute's efforts to reach a bigger audience that WGBH came into being, years before the federal government became involved in public broadcasting. In 1946, the Lowell Institute formed a partnership with six Boston colleges to broadcast its lecture series on the radio. At first, the lectures aired on commercial radio, but the series eventually found a permanent home on WGBH, a station that would become the exemplar of non-commercial, or public, broadcasting. WGBH, from its base on Massachusetts Avenue in Boston, debuted on October 6, 1951, when the station broadcast a live radio concert by the Boston Symphony Orchestra.

It did not take WGBH long to make its mark in public broadcasting. The station's greatest achievements were made in television, an era that began in 1955 when Channel 2 debuted. WGBH began to distinguish itself in the 1960s, but the decade began sourly. The station's 10th anniversary was pocked by a fire that razed its facilities on Massachusetts Avenue, leaving WGBH homeless. The station relied on its community for space to house its operations until a new home could be found, using spare room offered by local broadcasters and universities to continue to broadcast and develop programs. WGBH operated without its own headquarters for three years, a chapter in the station's history that ended in 1964 when it moved to Boston's Allston neighborhood. Although the station's staff must have found their situation bothersome, they scored their first great success while WGBH searched for a permanent home. The

Company Perspectives:

WGBH enriches people's lives through programs and services that educate, inspire, and entertain, fostering citizenship and culture, the joy of learning, and the power of diverse perspectives.

station recorded its most notable achievements as a producer of programming for public broadcasting, and in 1962 WGBH unearthed what would become a fixture on television sets for decades to follow. One year after the fire dislocated the station, it produced three programs as part of its *French Chef* series, using a basement in a local gas company to feature the techniques of French cooking. Within a year, WGBH had educational television's first celebrity, a chef named Julia Child. For decades to follow, television viewers across the nation tuned in to watch Child prepare meals in her inimitable style.

A National Network Takes Shape in the 1960s

WGBH's commitment to the *French Chef* series produced what became the station's hallmark program, but it was a piece of legislation passed in the 1960s that enabled WGBH, as well as the other public broadcasting stations scattered throughout the country, not only to survive but to flourish. The one glaring difference between commercial and public broadcasters was the enormous advantage held by commercial stations to collect revenue from advertisers. Revenue from advertisers provided a wellspring of cash for commercial stations; public broadcasters, who were reliant exclusively on donations, struggled to stay afloat. Beyond the most obvious difference between the two breeds of broadcasters, non-commercial stations also suffered from a lack of support from among their own. Commercial stations operated as part of networks, giving them the same sort of advantages a chain of retail stores enjoyed over independent, mom-and-pop stores.

In the late 1960s, national leaders sought to ameliorate both disadvantages endured by public broadcasters: those of funding and those of structure. The federal government first funded public broadcasting in 1962 through the Education Television Facilities Act in 1962, but the U.S. Congress realized the necessity of greater action. In 1967, the Public Broadcasting Act was established, stipulating, according to the text of the legislation, that "a private corporation should be created to facilitate the development of public telecommunications and to afford maximum protection from extraneous interference and control." A nonprofit corporation, "which will not be an agency or establishment of the U.S. Government," was incorporated the following year, marking the formation of the Corporation for Public Broadcasting (CPB). (Once matured, the CPB would fund more than 1,000 public television and radio stations nationwide, using an annual appropriation from the U.S. Congress.) In 1969, a year after CPB was formed, the Public Broadcasting Service (PBS) was created, making public broadcasters such as WGBH into non-commercial versions of commercial networks.

With funding and structure provided by the Public Broadcasting Act of 1967, WGBH could play a much larger role on the airwaves, a medium not envisioned by John Lowell, Jr., but a means of fulfilling his mission, nevertheless. Through CPB and PBS, WGBH and other public affiliates could share programming of national interest and share in the benefits of a national distribution infrastructure. More than any other public broadcasting affiliate, WGBH seized the opportunity available to it in the wake of the Public Broadcasting Act, occupying a singular spot in the realm of public broadcasting. WGBH became the flagship station of PBS, the paradigm of a non-commercial broadcaster. Public broadcasting was generally not associated with producing programming of sweeping national interest—the "hit shows" more readily associated with commercial, network television—but WGBH produced a series of widely popular favorites, belying the stereotype of a public broadcaster.

WGBH came to the fore in the 1970s, a decade that saw the station fully exercise its skill as a producer of programming. WGBH's content, after the creation of CPB and PBS, could be shared nationwide with other public affiliates, but the station was also building its own collection of broadcasting properties, becoming a mini-network within a network. The year the Public Broadcasting Act was passed, Channel 44 debuted, first airing in September 1967. In 1971, WGBH licensee Channel 57, broadcasting from Springfield, Massachusetts, became part of the station's fold, the same year WGBH created its Caption Center, which introduced captioned television programs for deaf and hearing-impaired viewers. WGBH's three stations, as well as other PBS affiliates, were provided with several notable programs during the 1970s, all produced by WGBH. In 1971, *Masterpiece Theatre*, hosted by Alistair Cooke for the next 22 years, debuted. The following year, *Zoom* first aired, a television program created for children and performed by children that ran for nine years, winning three Emmys during its first incarnation. In 1974, WGBH unveiled *Nova*, a science-based program still viewed by PBS viewers 30 years later. One year after the debut of *Nova*, WGBH producers directed that a small section of the station's parking lot be removed to make room for a garden. *The Victory Garden* used the plot for its first show, beginning a run that would last for decades. In 1979, after a decade of spectacular success, WGBH added another arrow to its quiver of programming when the station's producers filmed the remodeling of a worn-down Victorian mansion, marking the debut of *This Old House*. The show became the most-watched half-hour series on television.

WGBH continued to demonstrate its creative skills as the station entered its fourth decade of existence. Among the most notable new shows that premiered during the 1980s was *Frontline*, a weekly program renowned for its style of investigative journalism that debuted in 1983. In 1988, WGBH produced *American Experience*, a weekly history series that became a mainstay of public broadcasting. Aside from the station's achievements as a producer of award-winning content, there were technological achievements to be celebrated during the decade. In 1985, the station's radio property aired the first transatlantic digital broadcast, broadcasting Bach's *St. Matthew Passion* live from East Germany's Leipzig Gewandhaus. Within two years, WGBH aired the first transpacific digital broadcast, enabling listeners to hear the New Japan Philharmonic play a live concert in Tokyo. WGBH's efforts to serve the deaf and hearing-impaired also made broadcasting history in

Key Dates:

1951: WGBH debuts on the airwaves, broadcasting a live radio concert by the Boston Symphony Orchestra.
1962: WGBH produces the *French Chef* series, starring Julia Child.
1967: The Public Broadcasting Act is passed, leading to the incorporation of the Corporation for Public Broadcasting the following year.
1969: The Public Broadcasting Service is formed.
1971: WGBH produces *Masterpiece Theatre*, the first of a series of popular shows produced during the decade, including *Nova*, *The Victory Garden*, and *This Old House*.
1985: WGBH broadcasts the first transatlantic digital radio broadcast.
1995: WGBH launches its Web site, www.wgbh.org.
2000: WGBH completes the largest fundraising campaign in its history, raising more than $43 million.
2004: WGBH adds WGBH World, WGBH Create, and WGBH Kids to the selection of channels available to New England-area viewers.

the 1980s. In 1986, WGBH and an affiliate of the ABC network, WCVB-TV, became the first stations to close-caption their newscasts on a regular basis on the local station level.

WGBH in the 1990s and 2000s

WGBH's influence as an innovative educator and entertainer increased during the 1990s, despite escalating pressure from politicians determined to reduce public broadcasting's funding. In 1990, WGBH's Descriptive Video Service (DVS) was introduced nationwide, giving blind and visually impaired viewers supplementary narration to television programs. In 1995, the station launched its Web site, www.wgbh.org, giving the station an online presence and the ability to distribute its content through another media format. The following year, WGBH Radio, Public Radio International, and the BBC World Service co-produced *The World*, a global news and public affairs program that aired daily coast-to-coast. In 1997, the station became the first broadcaster to win six George Foster Peabody Awards, which recognized outstanding achievement in radio and television. The station repeated its record two years later, the same year it produced a 25-hour international broadcast, *PBS Millennium 2000*, a series that was watched by an estimated one billion viewers.

As WGBH entered the 21st century and neared its 50th anniversary, the goal of securing the station's financial future grew paramount. Attracting capital had been a perennial obstacle since the station's founding, but after a decade of budget cutbacks and persistent efforts spearheaded by the Republican Party to further reduce funding to public broadcasting, WGBH executives looked toward fundraising with particular zeal. In 2000, the station began the most ambitious fundraising effort in its history, endeavoring to raise $33 million by the end of the year. ''Expanding the Vision,'' as the campaign was named, represented the station's efforts to gain the financial footing to fund the next generation of programs and services and to aid its further conversion to digital broadcasting. By the end of the year, WGBH exceeded the goal of the largest capital campaign in its history, raising more than $43 million from nearly 20,000 donors.

As WGBH prepared for its future as a noncommercial broadcaster, the station figured to remain the driving force behind public television in the United States. Although its sources of revenue declined during the first years of the 21st century, dropping from $207 million in 2000 to $187 million in 2003, WGBH stood on firm financial footing, buoyed somewhat by the sale of trademark rights and real estate in 2002 and 2003. The station balanced its operating budget for the 23rd consecutive year in 2003. In 2004, WGBH added several new channels to its roster, unveiling WGBH World, WGBH Create, and 'GBH Kids.

Principal Subsidiaries

WGBH 2; WGBH 44; WGBH World; WGBH Create; 'GBH Kids; WGBH On Demand; Boston Kids & Family TV; WGBY 57; WGBH 89.7; WCAI 90.1; WNAN 91.1.

Principal Competitors

ABC, Inc.; The NBC Television Network; The CBS Television Network.

Further Reading

Albiniak, Paige, ''Mission Most Mind-Boggling,'' *Broadcasting & Cable*, July 26, 1999, p. 41.
''Boston Stations to Closed-Caption,'' *Broadcasting*, January 6, 1986, p. 185.
Lambert, Peter D., ''FCC Gets Copy of WGBH-TV Mapplethorpe Broadcast,'' *Broadcasting*, August 20, 1990, p. 59.
Littleton, Cynthia, ''PBS Takes Proactive Approach to Sponsorship,'' *Broadcasting & Cable*, May 5, 1997, p. 39.
Whitney, Daisy, ''WGBH-TV Rolls out Digital Asset System,'' *TelevisionWeek*, November 24, 2003, p. 24.

—Jeffrey L. Covell

Wilbur Chocolate Company

20 North Broad Street
Lititz, Pennsylvania 17543
U.S.A.
Telephone: (800) 233-0139
Fax: (717) 626-3487
Web site: http://www.wilburchocolate.com

Wholly Owned Subsidiary of Cargill Inc.
Incorporated: 1909 as H.O. Wilbur & Sons
Employees 350
Sales: $10.76 million (2003)
NAIC: 311330 Confectionery Manufacturing from Purchased Chocolate; 311340 Non-Chocolate Confectionery Manufacturing

The second-oldest chocolatier in the United States, Wilbur Chocolate Company has been a leader in the manufacture of chocolate and cocoa products for over a century. Best known for its Wilbur Buds, a precursor to the Hershey Kiss, Wilbur supplies a wide range of chocolate items and chocolate coatings to candy makers, bakers, and dairies throughout North America. A wholly-owned subsidiary of Cargill, Inc., one of the largest privately held companies in the United States, Wilbur produces over 150 million pounds of chocolate products and other food ingredients a year. The majority of Wilbur's sales is made through its wholesale business, although it does offer some products through its one retail facility, the Candy Americana Factory Store in Lititz, Pennsylvania, as well as through catalog and phone sales. Wilbur also operates sales of Gerkens Cocoa, selling the Dutch company's cocoa powder, cocoa liquor, and cocoa butter to customers in the United States, Canada, and Mexico.

Sweet Beginnings: 1865–1900

Although Wilbur Chocolate is frequently overshadowed by the other Pennsylvania chocolate manufacturer, Hershey Foods Corporation, Wilbur has carved a solid niche in the chocolate and cocoa manufacturing market and has established its reputation on quality and consistency. Tracing its beginnings to 1865, Wilbur's is the second-oldest chocolate company in the United States, behind Massachusetts-based Baker's Chocolate, now a subsidiary of Kraft Foods, Inc., which got its start in 1765.

Henry Oscar Wilbur had a successful hardware and stove business when he seized an opportunity to enter the confectionery trade with Samuel Croft. They formed Croft & Wilbur in 1865 and set up their business in Philadelphia, Pennsylvania. Initially the two made molasses candies and hard candies that they sold to buyer from the railroad. In short time the business achieved great success as the candies were popular items bought by passengers from train boys.

After nearly two decades, during which the company outgrew its original plant location and expanded its second plant, Croft & Wilbur was split into two companies in 1884. Wilbur became head of H.O. Wilbur & Sons, which specialized in the manufacture of chocolate and cocoa products, and Croft headed Croft & Allen, which maintained production of all other nonchocolate candies. By 1887 continued growth necessitated H.O. Wilbur & Sons to make another move to larger quarters in Philadelphia. When H.O. Wilbur retired that year at 59, two of his sons, William Nelson Wilbur and Harry L. Wilbur, took over the family business. Bertram K. Wilbur, a third son who worked as a doctor in Alaska, joined the business after his brother Harry's death in 1900. Management also extended to French family members Steve and Mass Oriole, brothers of W.N. Wilbur, when they joined the company in the early 1890s, bringing their expertise in European chocolate-making techniques.

A Bud Is Born: 1893–1958

In 1893 Wilbur introduced its most enduring product—the Wilbur Bud—a bite-sized solid milk or dark chocolate molded into a flower bud. The big chocolate morsels and the innovative technique by which they were made came to represent a hallmark of the company. Although Hershey Kisses, introduced 14 years later in 1907, became the ubiquitous chocolate drop, many customers attested to the superior rich quality of the Wilbur Bud. Eric Asimov claimed in the *New York Times* in 2001, ''Kisses have the phantom flavor of insincere greetings, but Buds are as solid and substantial as a hearty handshake.''

The company continued to prosper, and in 1905 Lawrence H. Wilbur, a third generation Wilbur, joined the business. In 1909 the

Company Perspectives:

Our Vision: To be an innovator of unique functional ingredients for the food industry. Our Mission: Wilbur will be the preferred formulator of food ingredients by tailoring fats, flavorings and bulking agents. Our products will enable the food industry to meet the challenges of evolving consumer preferences.

company was incorporated as H.O. Wilbur & Sons. In 1913 the company built a new facility in Lititz, Pennsylvania, a small town eight miles north of Lancaster in the center of what became known as the chocolate capital of the United States. Also located in Lititz was the Ideal Cocoa and Chocolate Company.

In 1927 Wilbur entered into negotiations with the Swiss company Suchard Societe Anonyme, and the following year the two companies merged to form Wilbur-Suchard Chocolate Company, Inc. That same year Wilbur-Suchard merged with the neighboring Ideal Chocolate Company. In 1930 Wilbur began the process of relocating its manufacturing operations from Philadelphia to Lititz, and by 1933 production was carried out completely in Lititz. Over a period of time the company sold off Suchard production and sales, and the corporate name became Wilbur Chocolate Company on December 31, 1958.

Changes in Ownership through the Early 1990s

In 1968 Wilbur Chocolate was acquired by MacAndrews & Forbes Group Inc., a New York-based holding company that later sold off its interests in Wilbur in 1986 when sales of the chocolate company were over $100 million. Florida-based AmBrit Inc., the makers of Klondike ice cream bars, purchased Wilbur for $42 million. By 1989 AmBrit and the holding company Clabir Corporation, which had a 58 percent stake in AmBrit, experienced continued financial losses and the two holding companies merged as Empire of Carolina Inc. At that time AmBrit's board of directors strongly rebuffed an offer of $78 million cash and debt assumption by an investor.

In 1992 Empire of Carolina sold Wilbur Chocolate to Cargill Inc. for $42 million and the assumption of $9.1 million in debt. Cargill was the Minneapolis-based food conglomerate that ranked as one of the largest privately held companies in the United States. Among its many holdings Cargill had plants in Europe and Brazil that processed cocoa, as well as cocoa trading and sales operations. Wilbur president William J. Shaughnessy did not foresee the sale greatly affecting operations in the company's two plants in Lititz and Mount Joy, Pennsylvania, nor affecting its 326 employees. Shaughnessy was optimistic when he told *Lancaster New Era* reporter Doug Wenrich, "Wilbur has been sold many times before and we've now been purchased by a company of unquestionable financial strength and market reputation, with a very high level of integrity." He continued, "This is the first time since 1958, in fact, that Wilbur has been owned by a company with a time line that extends beyond the next interest payment." The year prior to Wilbur's sale to Cargill, revenues totaled $49.1 billion with earnings of $351 million.

Contract Disputes with New Parent in the Mid-1990s

Three years after the sale of Wilbur to Cargill, the union contract represented by the Bakery, Confectionery and Tobacco Workers expired, and workers at Wilbur entered into a protracted labor dispute with the company. In 1995 the main negotiator for Local 464 union, Earl E. Light, remarked that the primary issues concerned health care benefits, forced scheduling, management rights, and wages. He emphasized, however, in the *Intelligencer Journal* that the real issue was that the small Lititz union was attempting to gain respect from the giant Cargill. Light maintained, "This big company has come in and doesn't care. They want their way."

In September 1995, 11 months after working without a contract, union workers at Wilbur unanimously rejected (175 to 0) a contract put forth by the company. Light continued to assert that it was Cargill that stood as the major obstacle in achieving a contract agreement between workers and the company regarding health care and management issues. Finally in May 1997, nearly three years and over 20 meetings after talks had begun, Wilbur Chocolate and the union employees negotiated a three-year contract that reflected concessions by both workers and the company but that, according to a joint statement reported in the *Intelligencer Journal,* "gives employees a realistic competitive benefits package."

Smooth Operations in the New Millennium

After what had become a rocky start, operations under Cargill went smoothly at the start of the 21st century. Wilbur Chocolate was, in fact, in a position to acquire companies of its own. In June 2002 Wilbur bought the Canadian company Omnisweet, which manufactured a variety of products for the food ingredient industry, including specialty compound chips and low-melt ice cream flakes. Following the purchase, the Canadian operation was renamed Wilbur Ltd., and production of such value-added products as coatings, inclusions, and colored and flavored products remained in Burlington, Ontario. With this acquisition Wilbur expanded its product base, particularly adding new items to nutritionally-fortified products.

In October 2002, only months after the Omnisweet acquisition, Cargill announced that it had acquired Peter's Chocolate, the California-based unit of Nestlé, and that production of Peter's products would shift from its New York and Wisconsin plants to production at Wilbur's Lancaster County plants. With the addition of Peter's, Wilbur occupied the top-ranking spot as a supplier to confectioners and bakers in the United States. Peter's Chocolate, which gained its name from Daniel Peter, the inventor of milk chocolate, had long been an industry leader noted for its premium chocolates. In a press release, Shaughnessy conveyed his excitement about the merger, stating "This is the most noteworthy acquisition in our 118-year history. We are enthusiastic about bringing together two of the finest and oldest chocolate companies in the United States that share a heritage of loyal employees, customers, and unique products." At the time of the acquisition Wilbur employed approximately 320 employees and expected to increase its work force after production moved to Pennsylvania.

The chocolate industry as a whole received a big boost when the news media published findings about the possible health

Key Dates:

1865: Henry Oscar Wilbur and Samuel Croft begin partnership as Croft & Wilbur, a candy business in Philadelphia, Pennsylvania.
1884: Croft & Wilbur is separated into two businesses: H.O. Wilbur & Sons, manufacturer of cocoa and chocolate, and Croft & Allen, manufacturer of candy.
1887: H.O. Wilbur retires and his sons, William Nelson Wilbur and Harry L. Wilbur, head the company.
1893: Wilbur Bud Chocolates are introduced.
1900: Kendig Chocolate Company is established in Lititz, Pennsylvania.
1902: Kendig Company name is changed to Ideal Cocoa and Chocolate Company after purchase by new owners.
1909: Company is incorporated as H.O. Wilbur & Sons.
1928: H.O. Wilbur & Sons merges with Swiss company Suchard S.A. to form Wilbur-Suchard Chocolate Company, which in turn merges with Ideal Chocolate Company.
1930: Manufacturing operations move from Philadelphia to Lititz, Pennsylvania.
1958: Company ceases production and sales of Suchard products and name changes to Wilbur Chocolate Company.
1968: Company becomes wholly owned subsidiary of MacAndrews & Forbes Company.
1972: Penny Buzzard, wife of former president John Buzzard, opens the Candy Americana Museum in Lititz, Pennsylvania.
1992: Wilbur Chocolate is sold to Cargill, Inc.
2002: Wilbur acquires Canadian company Omnisweet and Peter's Chocolates from Nestlé USA.

benefits from moderate amounts of chocolate consumption derived from antioxidants present in chocolate. Already producing sugar-free and nutritionally fortified products, Wilbur was well-positioned to meet customers' demands for healthy chocolate choices. In 2003 Wilbur was the first chocolate-maker in the United States to launch a new line of chocolate coatings that used an innovative combination of artificial sweeteners—erythritol, inulin, and isomalt—to create sugar-free chocolate coatings containing high laxation tolerance, fewer calories, and lower glycemic indexes. Marketed under the brand New Frontiers, these new sugar-free chocolate coatings were fortified with fiber and calcium, were more easily digested than previous sugar-free products, and had the ''melt in your mouth'' sensation of regular premium chocolates, hitherto never achieved by sugar-free chocolates. Wilbur sold its new confection to the large candymaker Russell Stover, among other customers. As the second-oldest chocolatier in the United States Wilbur kept abreast with new technologies and marketing strategies to maintain its position as a premier supplier of chocolates in North America.

Principal Divisions

Wilbur Ltd.; Peter's Chocolate.

Principal Competitors

Hershey Food Corporation; Baker's Chocolate; Nestlé USA.

Further Reading

''AmBrit Agrees to Buy Wilbur Chocolate Co.,'' *Wall Street Journal,* January 14, 1986, p. 1.
Asimov, Eric, ''The Other Pennsylvania Chocolate,'' *New York Times,* December 12, 2001, p. F3.
Bomberger, Paul, ''NLRB Ruling Heightens Wilbur Chocolate Workers' Unrest,'' *Intelligencer Journal* (Lancaster, PA), September 6, 1995, p. B4.
——, ''Wilbur Chocolate, Union Contract Talks Get Sticky,'' *Intelligencer Journal* (Lancaster, Pa.), June 23, 1995.
——, ''Workers at Wilbur Reject Pact,'' *Intelligencer Journal* (Lancaster, Pa.), September 11, 1995, p. A1.
''Business Brief—Empire of Carolina Inc.: Chocolate Unit to be Sold to Cargill for $42 Million,'' *Wall Street Journal,* July 15, 1992.
''Cargill Inc. Acquires Peter's Chocolate Company Inc.,'' *Dairy Foods,* December 2002, p. 46.
Clark, Kim, ''Chocolate Pilgrims Find Paradise in Pennsylvania,'' *U.S. News & World Report,* April 24, 2000, p. 72.
''Empire of Carolina—Cargill Unit,'' *Wall Street Journal,* October 5, 1992.
Goldstein, Alan, ''AmBrit Declines Investors Offer,'' *St. Petersburg Times,* December 5, 1989, p. 1E.
Hopkinson, Natalie, ''The Dish on Candy,'' *Patriot Ledger* (Quincy, Mass.), April 25, 1998, p. F6.
''Ice-Cream Maker in Florida Buys Wilbur Chocolate,'' *Orlando Sentinel,* January 14, 1986, p. C3.
''Latest Buyout Makes Wayzata, Minn., Company Largest Chocolate Maker,'' *Saint Paul Pioneer Press,* October 15, 2002.
Mekeel, Tim, ''Wilbur Workers Reject Offer,'' *Lancaster New Era,* September 11, 1995, p. 1.
Meyer, Cheryl, ''Wilbur, Union Agree on Contract after Three-Year Struggle,'' *Intelligencer Journal* (Lancaster, Pa.), May 22, 1997, p. B4.
Pearce, Patty, ''A Nubbin of Pleasure,'' *Pittsburgh Post-Gazette,* June 6, 2004, p. G11.
Poist, Patricia A., ''Wilbur Chocolate Deal Will Deliver Jobs Here,'' *Lancaster New Era,* October 17, 2002, p. 1.
Powell, Joy, ''Cargill's New Foods Have a Purpose,'' *Star Tribune* (Minneapolis, Minn.), July 10, 2004, p. 1D.
''Quality is Wilbur Hallmark,'' *Candy Industry,* August 1997, p. 35.
Savage, Daina, ''Welcome to Candy Land,'' *Intelligencer Journal* (Lancaster, Pa.), April 5, 1996, p. 3.
''Sweet Revolution,'' *Lancaster New Era,* January 14, 2003, p. 1.
Wenrich, Doug, ''Biggest Private U.S. Firm Buys Wilbur Choc. For $51 Million,'' *Lancaster New Era,* October 10, 1992, p. 1.
''Wilbur Chocolate Buys Omnisweet,'' *Food Ingredient News,* July 2002.

—Elizabeth Henry

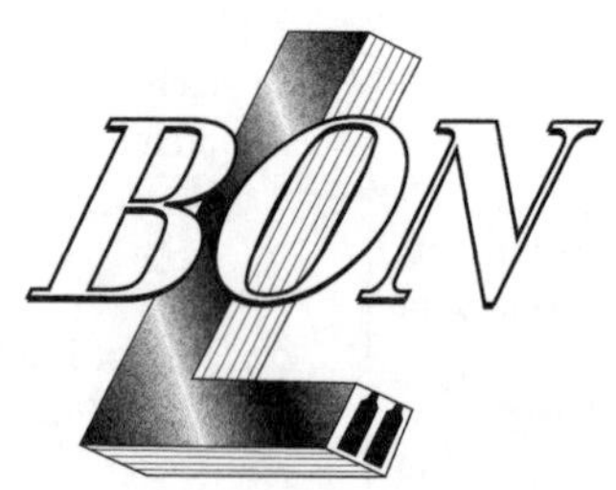

William L. Bonnell Company, Inc.

25 Bonnell Street
Newnan, Georgia 30263
U.S.A.
Telephone: (770) 253-2020
Fax: (770) 254-7711
Web site http://www.bonlalum.com

Wholly Owned Subsidiary of Tredegar Corporation
Incorporated: 1955
Employees: 1,200 (est.)
Sales: $360 million (2003 est.)
NAIC: 331316 Aluminum Extruded Product Manufacturing

Based in Newnan, Georgia, William L. Bonnell Company, Inc., is a subsidiary of Tredegar Corporation. Bonnell is a full service company involved in three product categories: aluminum extrusion, aluminum-cast billets, and ladders. Aluminum extrusion is the company's primary business, offering customers a variety of lengths and shapes, alloys, and finishes. Markets served include automotive, building and construction, electrical, consumer durable, and sporting goods. Bonnell operates 23 extrusion presses, three casting operations, four paint lines, and three anodizing lines in seven plants located across North America. Three of these plants also possess billet casting capabilities. In addition, Bonnell also manufactures and markets a wide range of aluminum, fiberglass, and wood climbing ladders, the result of an acquisition in the late 1990s. In the United States, plants are located in Newnan, Georgia; Carthage, Tennessee; and Kentland, Indiana. In Canada, Bonnell plants are located in Ste-Thersee, Quebec; Pickering, Ontario; Richmond Hill, Ontario; and Aurora, Ontario. Because of poor economic conditions and increased competition, the Aurora plant is scheduled to be closed by 2005 and its work moved to another plant as part of a cost-cutting initiative.

Origins

The company's namesake, William L. Bonnell, was born in 1903 on a Missouri ranch, where he learned how to trick ride, a talent that would provide his first employment. Later, he would go on to study metallurgy and find employment in Columbus, Ohio, with a flooring contractor, B&T Flooring. His expertise was important because the company offered decorative metal trims, which were highly popular at the time and led to B&T deciding to produce their own shapes suitable for a number of applications. Bill Bonnell became a partner in the business and responsible for B&T's growth in metals. The company started out with six basic shapes designed by Bonnell and extruded by Alcoa. In 1939, the company bought its own extrusion press to do the work in-house. Bill Bonnell was now able to take full advantage of his talent, developing more than 500 shapes in common use today. One of his most influential designs was a preformed sink frame. His expertise in the field of aluminum extrusion was so respected that during World War II scientists building the first atomic bomb turned to Bonnell for help in developing a way to extrude radioactive uranium samples.

Bonnell went to work for Youngstown, Ohio-based Trimedge Corp. in 1945, eventually becoming vice-president and general manager. Trimedge established an operation in Newnan, Georgia, in 1952 after acquiring a press from United Extruders, and construction on a new plant in the area began a year later. Bonnell and a partner owned Trimedge of Georgia, Inc., but in 1955 Bonnell decided to strike out on his own and bought out his partner. He also acquired the Trimedge patents and trademarks. The result was William L. Bonnell Company, Inc. Over the next five years, he added other popular products and finishes, tripled production capacity, and built a national sales force. In 1960, five years ahead of schedule, he made the final payment to his partner to gain full ownership of the company, but in December 1960 Bonnell died. Bonnell's wife Mae succeeded her husband as president of the company, a position she held until the company was sold in late 1965 to Ethyl Corporation.

Ethyl had been formed in 1924 as a joint venture between General Motors and Standard Oil to manufacture tetra ethyl, a gasoline lead additive that eliminated knocking in car engines. The company held a patent on the substance, providing it with a strong position in the gasoline additive market. As a result, even after the patent expired, Ethyl was able to maintain its leading

Company Perspectives:

The Bonnell family of companies is steeped in tradition, a tradition of trust and integrity which accompanies each order to completion. At Bonnell, our focus is on completing orders and making on time deliveries. We strive to understand our customer's needs and use an innovative team approach to solve problems and drive change. Bonnell believes in partnering with customers so value is added to the entire supplier/customer chain ensuring success for all.

position in the market. However, when General Motors and Standard put the company up for sale in 1962, large chemical companies like DuPont and Dow Chemical were prevented from bidding on the property due to antitrust laws. This allowed a small company named Albemarle Paper Manufacturing Company to buy Ethyl, leading to a famous *Wall Street Journal* headline, ''Jonah Swallows the Whale.''

Based in Richmond, Virginia, Albemarle had started out in the 1880s making blotter and kraft paper, but with the introduction of the ballpoint pen in 1945, the need for blotting paper used with fountain pens diminished greatly. Moreover, the demand for kraft paper dropped significantly when dry cleaners during the 1950s switched over to polyethylene garment bags. Albemarle, which put together a $200 million package in an early example of a leveraged buyout, acquired Ethyl as a way to begin manufacturing polyethylene bags. The company was restructured so the Albemarle became a subsidiary of Ethyl and was then sold off to help pay down the debt taken on to finance the deal.

Building Market Entry in 1973

Ethyl began to diversify in the 1960s. It acquired VisQueen, makers of polyethylene film used in food packaging, in 1963. Then, in 1966, it took control of Bonnell, installing E.M. Harvey as the new president. He continued to grow the business while the corporate parent continued its efforts in diversification, which took on even greater significance when lead gasoline was cited as a major cause of air pollution and leaded gasoline was banned and phased out. The aluminum business was augmented in 1969 with the opening of a new extrusion plant in Carthage, Tennessee. In 1973, the parent company acquired Capital Products, an aluminum window fabricator, in a deal which transformed Bonnell into a major supplier to the building and construction industry. Capital brought with it manufacturing plants located in Mechanicsburg, Pennsylvania, and Kentland, Indiana. In 1984, Ethyl added to its aluminum group with the acquisition of Fiberlux Inc., a major manufacturer of replacement windows and patio doors.

Harvey retired in 1989, the same year that Bonnell's parent company reached a turning point. As Ethyl withdrew from the tetra ethyl business, it became involved in specialty chemicals and pharmaceuticals. Late in 1988, Ethyl announced its intention to package its plastics, aluminum, and energy assets into a new subsidiary called Tredegar Industries Inc. The subsidiary was spun off to Ethyl shareholders as a publicly trade company in July 1989. The name of the company referred to Tredegar Iron Works, famous in Richmond for its Civil War role in providing cannon and other armaments to the South. The new Tredegar was faced with difficult economic conditions as it set to the task of weeding out weak assets and building the ones offering the most long-term potential.

Bonnell was hit especially hard by a downturn in housing starts, resulting in a drop in demand for aluminum extrusion products. At this stage the company operated four aluminum extrusion facilities: an eight-press plant in Newnan and a four-press plant in Carthage, both operating under the William L. Bonnell name, and a two-press plants in Kentland and Mechanicsburg operating as Capitol Products. To adapt to changing conditions, Bonnell began to restructure its operation. The Newnan plant, which had recently upgraded its anodizing capabilities and build a painting facility, would now focus on specialty products for markets requiring extruded products with high-finish properties. Some 400 workers, out of 1,100 employed at the plant, were terminated, as some of the plant's work was transferred to other facilities. A buyer was also sought for Capitol Products, but when that effort failed, the company in February 1991 closed down the Mechanicsburg plant.

Bonnell's restructuring effort began to pay off as the economy heated up in the 1990s. The company also benefited from reduced gas rates it negotiated from Atlanta Gas Light in 1995 when it threatened to get its gas directly from the Transcontinental Gas pipeline that ran close to the Newnan plant. Aluminum required a great deal of energy, and this concession allowed the Newnan plant to be more competitive in the industry, as well as with Bonnell's own Carthage plant, which bought federally subsidized power from the Tennessee Valley Authority that cost 35 percent less than power in Georgia. Tredegar, in the meantime, invested in a number of areas, including communications, life sciences, and information technology companies. It also exited the energy business. However, its old-line aluminum and plastics businesses prospered, prompting management to invest in these areas.

In May 1997, Bonnell, through a Tredegar acquisition, added a four-press aluminum extrusions and fabrication plant in El Campo, Texas, from Reynolds Metals Company, the world's third largest aluminum company, which was shifting its focus to basic aluminum and consumer products. Less than a year later, in February 1988, Tredegar and Reynolds agreed to another sale of assets. Now Bonnell, at the cost of $29 million, added its first facilities outside of the United States and became a major player in the North American extrusion market, picking up extrusion and fabrication plants located in Ste-Theres, Quebec, and Richmond Hill, Ontario. It was from Reynolds that Bonnell became involved in the ladder business, picking up Reynolds Ladder, a leader in the Canadian market. In June 1998, Bonnell added to its Canadian assets when Tredegar acquired Exal Aluminum Inc. and its two extrusion plants in Ontario. Exal added about $92 million in sales to the $267 million generated by Bonnell in 1997.

Demand Softens in 2000

As long as the U.S. economy soared during the late 1990s, Bonnell prospered, as sales for the unit approached $500 million. The situation would change in mid-2000, however, when Bonnell started to experience a decline in demand. Tredgar's

Key Dates:

1955: The company is formed by William L. Bonnell.
1960: Bonnell dies.
1965: Ethyl Corporation acquires the company.
1989: Bonnell is spun off as part of Tredegar Corporation.
1998: Canadian operations are acquired.
2001: Texas plant is closed.

film business also began to suffer. Sales of aluminum extrusions fell by 18 percent in the first six months of 2001. In September 2001, just days before the terrorist attacks that would further hurt the economy, Bonnell announced that it was closing the aluminum extrusion plant in El Campo. Other Tredgar groups were also suffered, in particular biotechnology. The company decided to exit this field and devote resources to the film and aluminum assets, which were more likely than the tech sector to rebound with an improving economy. In 2001, Bonnell's sales decreased 21 percent from the previous year, from $479.9 million to $380.4 million. Business remained sluggish in 2002, as sales fell another 5 percent, to $360.3 million. Aside from a drop in demand, Bonnell also faced pricing pressure from domestic rivals as well as foreign competitors, in particular the Chinese.

Bonnell completed an acquisition in 2003, buying Apolo Tool and Die Manufacturing Inc., a small Ontario, Canada-based aluminum fabricator with whom Bonnell had a long-standing relationship. Apolo possessed a variety of capabilities, including bending, CNC machining, drilling, mitering, punching, riveting, sawing, and welding of aluminum extrusions and other materials. It also had in-house tool and die design and manufacturing capability to support its fabrication services. Despite this versatility, the addition of Apolo offered no solution to Bonnell's immediate problem of declining business. In 2003, sales slipped further, decreasing 2 percent to $354.6 percent.

Bonnell made a number of changes in 2004. A new president, Albert A. Butler, was hired to head the unit. Butler was recruited from Minolta-QMS, a company involved in document printing solutions. He also brought with him 20 years of experience at General Electric Company, where he held a variety of management positions. Within a matter of weeks, Bonnell began taking steps to cut costs, reduce excess capacity, and become more competitive. In April 2004, the company announced it would close the Aurora plant by January 31, 2005, and transfer its work to the other Ontario locations. The largest press would be moved to the Pickering facility, which would be enlarged and upgraded. The company was also buoyed by improved market conditions in 2004. Through the first six months of 2004, sales were up 18 percent.

Principal Competitors

Alcan Inc.; Alcoa Inc.

Further Reading

Blackwell, John Reid, ''Subsidiary of Richmond, Va.-Based Specialty Metal Firm Buys Canadian Company,'' *Richmond Times-Dispatch*, November 22, 2003.
Hannon, Kerry, ''Life after Lead,'' *Forbes*, May 18, 1987, p. 65.
Lemons, Teresa, ''Tredegar's Quiet Growth, Dull Products, Exciting Profits,'' *Richmond Times-Dispatch*, January 26, 1997, p. F1.
Regan, Bob, ''Cutbacks under Way at Bonnell,'' *American Metal Market*, August 16, 1990, p. 1.

—Ed Dinger

Young & Rubicam, Inc.

285 Madison Avenue
New York, New York 10017
U.S.A.
Telephone: (212) 210-3000
Fax: (212) 370-3796
Web site: http://www.yr.com

Wholly Owned Subsidiary of WPP Group plc
Incorporated: 1923 as Young & Rubicam Advertising
Employees: 11,387
Gross Billings: $10.52 billion (2004)
NAIC: 541810 Advertising Agencies

A wholly owned subsidiary of WPP Group plc since 2000, and one of the largest advertising companies in the world, Young & Rubicam, Inc., specializes in advertising, public relations, direct marketing, corporate and product identity consulting, and health-care communications. Young & Rubicam operates more than 500 agency offices in 80 countries and counts Citibank, Cadbury Schweppes, Miller Brewing, Kraft Foods, Colgate-Palmolive, and AT&T among its largest clients.

Early History

The history of 20th-century advertising is populated by a handful of men. Stanley Resor, Claude Hopkins, Albert Lasker, Marion Harper, Bill Bernbach, Leo Burnett, and David Ogilvy are the names that come quickly to mind. Also included within this group would be Raymond Rubicam, the man cited by David Ogilvy as the single most important influence in his advertising career. Said Ogilvy, ''He taught me that advertising can sell without being dishonest.'' He was only the second living person ever elected to the American Advertising Federation Hall of Fame.

Born in Philadelphia in 1882 to a family that had prospered in the import-export business, Rubicam seemed destined to lead an easy and comfortable life. However, when young Raymond's grandfather died the estate fell to his wife's side of the family instead of to Rubicam's father, who was a writer for a trade journal. The situation worsened when Raymond's father died of tuberculosis. The young boy was then shuttled from relative to relative because his widowed mother could not care for him. Due in large part to his unconventional and lonely childhood, Rubicam was a poor and unruly student. He left school in his early teens to work as a grocery clerk in Denver and never attended school again. Later, he returned to his native Philadelphia hoping to become a short story writer, but he became an advertising man instead.

His first position was as a copywriter for the Armstrong Advertising Company in Philadelphia. The owner, F. Wallis Armstrong, was generally regarded as an autocratic tyrant who harassed his employees on a regular basis, and Rubicam more regularly than most. When offered a more lucrative position at the larger and more renowned N.W. Ayer Company, Rubicam accepted with gratitude. While at Ayer he wrote two advertisements which made him a reputation within the industry. The first was for Steinway pianos. Steinway had traditionally been averse to advertising. The owners of the company did not regard it as an estimable craft and consequently did as little of it as possible. To satisfy this particularly skeptical client Rubicam produced the famous ''Instrument of the Immortals'' ad. It not only caused a stir in the 1920s when it first appeared (Steinway sales rose by 70 percent), but has stood the test of time. It is still considered one of the most effective advertisements ever written. The other Rubicam creation of note was the ''Priceless Ingredient'' slogan developed for Squibb over-the-counter drugs.

Rubicam would have stayed indefinitely at the Ayer agency had the elder Ayer not died and left the business to his son-in-law. Rubicam was hoping to be made copy chief but was passed over in favor of an older man. Because of this unpromising situation, Rubicam decided to quit Ayer in 1923. Along with another dissatisfied Ayer employee, account executive John Orr Young, he started his own advertising agency in New York. The new Young & Rubicam firm had nothing but enthusiasm to offer prospective clients, but that proved enough to persuade General Foods to give it the struggling Postum beverage account. Postum was then followed by other General Foods accounts. Young & Rubicam did the advertising for products such as Grape-Nuts, Sanka Coffee, Jell-O, and Calumet baking powder.

The office atmosphere at the Young & Rubicam agency was different from that at any other ad firm. It was markedly loose,

Company Perspectives:

We make connections between our client partners and their customers. We are client-focused, insightful, pragmatic. We believe in ideas. Ideas based on rigorous analytic processes and human insights. Ideas that act as catalysts for building businesses. Big ideas that travel across borders and disciplines. Ideas that create real, measurable, positive change for client partners.

lively, and informal; it had the imprint of its founder Raymond Rubicam. Nearly all agency directors, both in the past and in the present, have emerged from the accounting rather than from the creative department. Rubicam was different. He was the creative man par excellence, and he ran his agency accordingly. What the office lacked in structure and standard operating procedure (no one made it to work before 9:30 in the morning) it more than made up for in talent and vitality. An example would be what were called ''gang ups'' at the agency. When work on a new campaign was initiated, all copywriters, artists, photographers, and copy chiefs involved in the project would lock themselves in a room to labor over the details. These ''gang ups'' usually lasted well into the night and were very exhausting. Only a rare breed of person could produce effectively in that kind of environment—but Rubicam always found such people. He hired his staff on the basis of their writing and artistic skill, and their willingness to work long and odd hours. He cared little about the typical qualifications of educational background and work experience. He wanted people with innovative ideas rather than impressive resumes.

The agency grew steadily throughout the 1920s and 1930s. Even the Depression did not hinder its ability to gain new clients and increase revenues. It may have been a loosely organized advertising company, but more often than not the ad campaigns were of exceptional quality. Billings went from $6 million in 1927 to $12 million in 1935, and then jumped to $22 million in 1937. During this period Young & Rubicam gained such lucrative accounts as Travelers Insurance, Bristol-Myers, Gulf Oil, and Packard automobiles. However, it also voluntarily resigned the extremely large Pall Mall account from the American Tobacco Company. The owner of American Tobacco, George Washington Hill, was notorious for badgering those who were unfortunate enough to do his advertising. The relationship between George Hill and Young & Rubicam grew so strained that Rubicam decided it would be in the best interest of the agency to forfeit the $3 million account. Rarely has the news of a large business loss met with such a sigh of relief at an advertising firm. The $3 million loss was well worth the boost in morale.

In 1934 John Orr Young retired. He had lost interest in the business and was allowing others to slowly take over his duties. Despite the great amount of money he was making, he wanted an early retirement. His position as head of new business was filled by Sigurd Larmon, who was to become an important influence at the agency for decades. Rubicam, who had been progressively exerting more and more influence at the firm, now had majority interest in the business. In the next 10 years Rubicam led an ascending firm through the advertising industry's first ''creative revolution.'' The agency was successful because Rubicam, while always encouraging his creative department to be original and take chances, was nonetheless careful with the gifted but fragile personalities who surrounded him. Although it is a cliche to say a business is its people, the maxim holds particularly true in advertising; an ad agency has no other form of inventory. The agency's staff was pushed but also nurtured, and resignations were rare. In the words of former copy supervisor George Gribbin, ''One of the great assets of this agency is that a man here feels he can express himself as a writer.''

Postwar Global Expansion

When Raymond Rubicam retired to Arizona in 1944, Young & Rubicam was the second largest advertising company in the world. Only the J. Walter Thompson agency did more business. The void left by a man such as Raymond Rubicam could have caused confusion at the agency and left it without direction, but that scenario did not happen. Rubicam had trained his successors well, especially George Gribben. Gribben had long been one of the most influential men at the firm and, upon Rubicam's retirement, was named creative director in charge of all advertising production. He was instrumental in bringing Young & Rubicam into the second advertising ''revolution'' which took place in the late 1950s and 1960s. In 1951 the agency reached the $100 million mark in total billings and by 1960 that figure had more than doubled to $212 million.

In the 1960s advertising grew as an industry. Firms such as Ogilvy and Mather, Doyle Dane Bernbach, and Leo Burnett initiated a period of innovation that broke all previous advertising rules and conventions. They helped re-establish advertising as an artistic craft. Though overshadowed by these smaller, more ''visible'' ad agencies, the larger companies like Young & Rubicam and J. Walter Thompson also benefited from the renaissance.

More money than ever was being spent by companies on advertising. The growth in business was paralleled by staff increases and subsidiary acquisitions within particular agencies. This internal growth, however, proved to be problematic. In 1971 the worldwide economic recession brought the rapid rise in advertising expenditures by manufacturers to a quick halt. Nearly all advertising companies suffered billings losses, and many of the smaller ''creative'' shops were forced out of business altogether. Young & Rubicam itself was in trouble. Its payroll and other expenses were too high, and the agency was not growing. A ''changing of the guard'' took place among the company's management. Ed Ney became chairman and chief executive officer, Alex Kroll became creative director, and Alexander Brody was placed in charge of international operations. These men were to lead the agency into a period of unprecedented growth.

Ney's first action was to reduce the staff at the New York office by one-third and relinquish some of the losing accounts that were draining the agency. One of those to go was the Bristol-Myers account; they had been a client for over 25 years. Then he set out to reorganize and increase the company's financial resources in order to renew its ability to purchase subsidiaries and broaden its range of services. Rather than sell shares to the public to raise capital, Ney instead manipulated retirement benefits and

Key Dates:

1923: The Young & Rubicam agency opens for business in New York.
1931: A Chicago branch office is opened.
1937: Gross billings reach $22 million for the year.
1951: Gross billings reach $100 million.
1973: A period of acquisitions begins with marketing company Wunderman, Ricotta & Kline and ad firm Sudler & Hennessey.
1998: Following a reorganization, Young & Rubicam goes public.
2000: Agency is acquired by WPP Group plc.

agency-held stock to generate the funds he needed. These maneuvers allowed him greater flexibility and privacy when it came time to decide when and where to use the money. For instance, in 1973 Ney supervised the acquisition of Sudler & Hennessey (a health care ad firm) and Wunderman, Ricotta & Kline (a direct marketing company). These two agencies added $62 million to the firm's balance sheet and pushed it past J. Walter Thompson to become number one in domestic billings. In a little over five years Ney had taken Young & Rubicam from third to first in the industry. Ney, however, was not yet satisfied. In addition to purchasing a number of small Midwestern and Southwestern ad shops, he also arranged in 1979 for Young & Rubicam to merge with the Marsteller agency, which had long been among the leaders in the public relations business. Not only did Marsteller's $306 million in billings help Young & Rubicam stay ahead of J. Walter Thompson, it also gave the agency the strong public relations department it needed.

While Ed Ney was building Young & Rubicam on the domestic fron' Alexander Brody was increasing the company's presence abro. '. The firm successfully broke through cultural and politic l b. riers by linking up with Hungary's leading advertising agenc 'Mahir), illustrating that the Eastern Bloc countries should no longer be considered "non-markets." More importantly, Brody was instrumental in orchestrating the agency's most important joint venture to date, the 1981 merger of Young & Rubicam's Tokyo office with Dentsu's Tokyo office. Never before had the number one and number two advertising companies in the world joined together on a business venture such as this one. The new subsidiary, called DYR, gave Dentsu a firmer foothold outside Japan and strengthened Young & Rubicam's position in Tokyo.

In 1985 Ed Ney announced that he was resigning as chairman and chief executive officer of Young & Rubicam. He named as his successor Alex Kroll, the former head of Young & Rubicam U.S.A. and the man responsible for resurrecting the agency from its creative doldrums. Under his leadership the firm reasserted itself as an "idea" shop. During a seven-month period in 1977 the agency procured $77 million in new business. Accounts included Pabst beer, Oil of Olay skin cream, and Kentucky Fried Chicken. When Young & Rubicam lost the Chrysler account in 1979, Kroll's persistence helped to win the very prestigious Lincoln-Mercury account, worth $65 million. Kroll was also the man who hired comedian and television personality Bill Cosby to do Jell-O Pudding commercials.

Following in the footsteps of Ney, one of the most effective administrators in the advertising industry, was no easy task. Kroll insisted he would try to emulate Ney's methods and patterns of success. Remaining the number one world agency required a commitment to growth and diversification. Kroll was prepared to take the necessary steps to secure Young & Rubicam's position at the top of the advertising industry, but not at the expense of the company's reputation for creativity.

Changes During the 1990s

As chairman and chief executive officer, Kroll enjoyed considerable success during his first half-decade at the helm of Young & Rubicam. The agency reigned as an industry power during the latter half of the 1980s, as it had during the first half of the decade. Young & Rubicam was praised by industry observers for its global might and the quality of its advertising, demonstrating a rare ability to be both creative and large, but by the end of the 1980s conditions in the U.S. advertising industry began to change swiftly. An industry-wide slump in 1990 called a quick end to the expansion years of the 1980s, when the prevailing trend among the larger advertising companies was to open agency after agency in a global race for domination. Further, an era of corporate cutbacks began, as a nationwide economic recession settled in during the early 1990s, which forced advertising companies not only to develop creative advertising ideas, but to convince cost-conscious clients that advertising spending should be spared from budget cuts.

At Young & Rubicam, the momentum built up during the 1980s was quickly lost. As economic conditions soured, the agency lost its edge, and those who once applauded the company's ability to meld creativity and worldwide clout were describing the early 1990s version of Young & Rubicam as "stodgy and musclebound." By 1993, the company's situation had become dire. Employee layoffs were imminent and several large clients such as Johnson & Johnson, Warner-Lambert, and AT&T took their business elsewhere, underscoring the need for dramatic changes.

Young & Rubicam's turning point occurred in late 1993, when a new generation of management took control and began to reshape the company. Kroll relinquished his command in December 1993 and passed the baton to Peter Georgescu, the Romanian-born son of an executive of Standard Oil of New Jersey. In describing Young & Rubicam's state before he took command, Georgescu said, "We were big, intellectual, conservative, and introspective," qualities that had led to uninspired advertising presentations and bred apathy among the company's employees. Georgescu was determined to change this. A strategy he conceived in 1990 was being implemented as he took charge in late 1993, one that was supposed to transform Young & Rubicam from a company with a geographical orientation to a company focused on client services. The years of establishing fiefdom after fiefdom throughout the world by opening new agency offices were over. As this was underway, Georgescu recruited a new team of senior executives who had made their mark in the advertising business at smaller, flexible, and innovative agencies. The addition of these new executives was intended to breathe new life into Young & Rubicam and spark a new era of advertising creativity.

New life was shown shortly after Georgescu began making wholesale changes, particularly in 1995 when Young & Rubicam picked up $500 million in new business in the United States alone. Young & Rubicam won Viacom's Showtime Networks account, prevailed in presentations for 7Up, Dimetapp, and Keycorp, and in early 1996 the company gained the $100 million Blockbuster Video account. Young & Rubicam increased its Sears business and reestablished its relationship with AT&T by developing a new corporate image campaign for the telecommunications giant. After several years of being described as stodgy and musclebound, "confused and staid," Young & Rubicam entered the mid-1990s with a refurbished corporate personality. Under Georgescu, the company's leadership was described as "warm," its creativity "passionate," and its presentations "fun." The turnaround had worked, and Young & Rubicam was once again recognized as a powerful, creative force in the advertising industry.

The Late 1990s and Beyond

By 1997, Georgescu's influence on Young & Rubicam's financial stature was readily discernible. Between 1994 and 1997, advertising billings nearly doubled, reaching $7.3 billion, making Young & Rubicam the fourth-largest advertising agency in the world. Early in 1997 Linda Srere replaced Steve Davis as Young & Rubicam's president and chief executive, the first female to hold the post in the company's long history. Her habitually casual dress (cowboy boots being a trademark) and plain speaking style helped promote the vision of a changed agency, one that was no longer a stuffy men's club, and billings rose quickly. Between 1997 and 1998 numerous lucrative contacts followed, including ones with the US Army, Sony, Kellogg, and AT&T.

A flurry of speculation and interest followed the 1998 announcement that Young & Rubicam planned to offer their stock to the general public. In June 1998 the stock opened three dollars higher than the initial price of $25 a share, likely due to the steady profits visible in the company's quarterly earnings statement. Not all was rosy in June, however. Reverend Al Sharpton led more than 100 protestors to the doorstop of the agency's New York offices, accusing the company (along with Macy's, Pepsico, and the Katz Radio Group) of depending upon minorities for sales while spending few dollars to advertise to them. Young & Rubicam responded to the rally by pointing out that it spent more than $150 million yearly in minority markets, and further noting that one-fifth of its employees were minorities; also that it was an annual contributor to the United Negro College Fund, the National Urban Coalition and the National Urban League. The protest seemed to have little effect on the agency's chain of successes; the company continued to accrue financial successes, notably multi-million dollar accounts for Schweppes beverages and mixers, and MGM's Grand Hotel & Casino in Las Vegas.

Other lucrative clients continued to be attracted by the company's success, and by 1999 Young & Rubicam was producing ads for Sony (a $60 million account). In May 1999 they acquired KnowledgeBase Marketing for $175 million, a company specializing in customer relationship marketing services, direct marketing, and marketing database programs. By June 1999 they had landed a $35 million contract to market a new line of Barbie toys, dubbed Generation Girl. By the third quarter of 1999 Young & Rubicam was able to report that profits were up 14 percent over the previous year.

As 2000 began Young & Rubicam made further strides into tackling new client types: technology-based companies like internet firms, herbal supplement maker Nature's Way, and Concert, the international venture between two telecommunications giants AT&T and British Telecom. Despite these developments, share prices for the company's stock fell from $72 to $41 between December and April, probably related to the U.S. Army and Citibank both deciding to reconsider their account status with Young & Rubicam. Rumors swiftly followed that British advertising firm WPP Group plc was poised to take over the company. By May the rumors proved true, and after protracted negotiations Young & Rubicam became an independent arm of the British firm in a friendly takeover.

Kentucky Fried Chicken, a major client since 1976, left Young & Rubicam in 2001, and job cuts at the agency soon followed. Over the next several years many major brands left the agency's fold, and by the middle of 2004 the company's earnings had dropped from a 1998 high of $3.4 billion to about $1 billion. Moreover, a succession of executive officers had come and gone, and morale was low. In May 2004 WPP executives decided that drastic measures were required, calling in a new CEO for Young & Rubicam. Ann Fudge was a former division head at Kraft Foods. Hopes were high that she could turn the ailing giant around, although some were skeptical, stating that she lacked both the industry expertise and the proper drive. Others praised her for her creativity and intelligence. Fudge herself saw that there would be resistance but looked forward to the challenges.

Further Reading

Brady, Diane, and Brian Grow, "Act II: Ann Fudge's Two-Year Break from Work Changed Her Life; Will Those Lessons Help her Fix Young & Rubicam?," *Business Week,* March 29, 2004, p. 72.

Cummings, Bart, "An Interview with Ed Ney," *Advertising Age,* January 3, 1983.

Daniels, Draper, *Giants, Pigmies, and Other Advertising People,* Chicago: Crain Communications, 1974.

Eleftheria, Parpis, "Young & Rubicam, New York," *ADWEEK Eastern Edition,* April 15, 1996, p. 38.

Farrell, Greg, "With a New Reel in Hand, Y&R's "Ted & Ed Show' Sends Ratings Soaring," *ADWEEK Eastern Edition,* November 13, 1995, p. 26.

Fox, Stephen, *The Mirror Makers,* New York: Morrow, 1984.

Hume, Scott, "JWT, Y&R Will Face Off for Kraft," *ADWEEK Eastern Edition,* July 7, 1997, p. 3.

Miles, Laureen, "Stalking the CEO: Campaign Spending, $1–$10 Million," *MEDIAWEEK,* May 20, 1996, p. 50.

Nokes, Roger, "Saved by the Bell," *ADWEEK Eastern Edition,* May 9, 1994, p. 26.

Richmond, Susannah, "How to Resolve Y&R's Troubles," *Campaign,* January 14, 1994, p. 20.

Rubicam, Raymond, "Memoirs," *Advertising Age,* February 9, 1970.

Taylor, Cathy, "Changing of the Guard at Y&R," *ADWEEK Eastern Edition,* December 20, 1993, p. 2.

Wascoe, Dan, Jr., "Young & Rubicam's 1,000-Mile Corridor," *Back Stage,* May 25, 1990, p. 24B.

—updates: Jeffrey L. Covell; Howard A. Jones

Ziebart International Corporation

1290 East Maple Road
P.O. Box 1290
Troy, Michigan 48007-1290
U.S.A.
Telephone: (248) 588-4100
Toll Free: (800) 877-1312
Fax: (248) 588-1444
Web site: http://www.ziebart.com

Private Company
Incorporated: 1959 as Ziebart Corporation
Employees: 90
Sales: $32.5 million (2004 corporate)
NAIC: 53311 Lessors of Nonfinancial Intangible Assets (Except Copyrighted Works); 811121 Automotive Body, Paint, & Interior Repair & Maintenance; 811122 Automotive Glass Replacement Shops; 811198 All Other Automotive Repair & Maintenance

Ziebart International Corporation, which offers a wide range of services and products for cars and trucks, is perhaps best known for its rustproofing and auto protection services, its primary line of business for its first 30 years. In the 1990s, the company began focusing on expanding its products and services. As a result, its franchised and company-owned retail locations offer a range of professional detailing services, appearance protection services, window tinting, glass replacement and repair, car accessories (such as sunroofs and alarm systems), and truck and van accessories (including trailer hitches and spray-on bedliners) in addition to rust protection. In 1998, Ziebart entered into a co-branding agreement with Speedy Auto Glass and began offering auto glass replacement in many of its locations. Ziebart has also partnered to co-brand with Rhino Linings USA, which offers polyurethane spray-on liners for truck beds.

Beginnings and Expansion through Franchising: 1950s–80s

In 1954, Kurt Ziebart, a master mechanic from Germany, living in Detroit, Michigan, developed a scientific process called rustproofing, the first successful method of protecting an automobile from corrosion. Using Ziebart's chemical method, car owners could protect the metallic body of their vehicles from rust caused by rain, snow, and ice. The first store, bearing the proprietary Ziebart name, was opened on Harper Avenue in Detroit in 1959 to rustproof automobiles. The system proved popular, particularly in the Great Lakes states, where the salt mixture sprayed on the roads during the winters caused rusting, as well as in coastal areas where the salt air encouraged rust. The company was soon establishing franchised locations, primarily in the Midwest, throughout the 1960s.

In 1969, Ziebart opened its first international operation in Windsor, Ontario, across the border from Detroit. The following year, Ziebart was bought by Swedish immigrant E. Jan Hartmann, who developed Ziebart's operations through its master franchise system into the Pacific Rim, the Middle East, Australia, Europe, and Mexico. Ziebart expanded overseas by finding a corporation within each country that had the ability to become a master franchisee for the country. The master franchisee would then be responsible for establishing locations through subfranchising.

The Mexican master franchise was given to Praxis Corporation in 1993, and average sales for the first location in Monterrey were twice the U.S. average. The first German location was also opened in 1993. By this time, Ziebart manufactured its own rust protection chemicals, paint sealants, fabric protectors, and various cleaners and polishes. It distributed most of its products worldwide from its warehouse in Detroit. The company also operated a separate Canadian warehouse for its Canadian locations.

Product Diversification in the 1990s

In 1990, Ziebart had more than 1,000 locations in 40 countries and more than $100 million in worldwide dealer sales. The company had also acquired Tidy Car in 1989, which included about 200 detailing locations in the United States, Canada, Sweden, and Denmark. Detailing was a type of deep cleaning that restored a vehicle to like-new condition. Ziebart eventually expanded the Tidy Car locations to include accessories and Ziebart protection services.

The year 1991 was good for growth at Ziebart Tidy Car, with revenues increasing by 12.5 percent. Tidy Car was the largest

Company Perspectives:

Ziebart has circled the globe with success for nearly four decades. We've launched and nourished hundreds of individual entrepreneurs and master franchise organizations. In more than 40 countries across six continents, people have recognized the Ziebart name for two generations. Vehicle owners know that Ziebart stores are the premier places on earth where, under one roof, they can find everything they need to help keep their cars and trucks beautiful, and exciting to drive.

franchise system of automotive detailing services in the United States. Ziebart began testing the possibility of combining the new Tidy Car franchises with the traditional Ziebart locations. It conducted market tests in six cities that combined detailing services with accessories and protection products. During the test, Ziebart and Tidy Car products were offered to owners of the separate franchises. The test proved successful, and toward the end of 1991 more than 400 franchises had the opportunity to convert to a joint Ziebart Tidy Car franchise. By October, nearly 60 percent had either made the change or were in the process of converting. Some 70 Canadian Ziebart-only franchises remained unchanged.

Ziebart recognized that consumers were spending more on their cars and trucks and keeping them longer. The company also noted that people were generally too busy to maintain their vehicles themselves, so they were willing to spend money on high-quality professional services such as those that Ziebart offered to protect their investment in their cars and trucks. In fact, new vehicle purchases in 1992 were down about 10 percent, and analysts observed that owners were keeping their vehicles for an average of more than seven years. With the trend of consumers driving older cars came the demand for services such as Ziebart's to keep cars looking like new.

In 1992, Ziebart introduced ChipFix, a detail service that restored paint surfaces that had been chipped or dinged, as part of its product diversification strategy. The ChipFix system could match more than 25,000 colors. ChipFix was priced at $89 and $100, making it much cheaper than a full paint job. Moreover, the process could be completed in a few hours. After being test marketed, the new service was launched in the late spring of 1992. At the time, Ziebart Tidy Car operated 700 locations in more than 40 countries.

By 1992, about two-thirds of Ziebart's revenues came from protection services, with detailing accounting for about 7 percent of sales. The company's marketing efforts stressed one-stop shopping for car care and the high quality and durability of its products and techniques that had been proven over the past 30 years.

When Mississippi River flooding paralyzed rail and truck traffic in 1993, Ziebart developed a special marketing campaign for its Tidy Car division in the Midwest. The program offered a 10 percent discount ($10 off the standard $100 price) to power-wash mud from car-engine compartments and remove mildew and odors from vehicle interiors.

In 1994, Ziebart's employees purchased the company through an employee stock ownership plan (ESOP). The franchise support system was expanded, and Ziebart's line of products and services broadened. The following year, Ziebart offered new Ziebart Tidy Car franchises that would focus on detailing and installing bolt-on accessories. The company planned to offer these franchises for less than the cost of the original rustproofing franchises. About 65 percent of the new franchises' business was projected to be detailing, cleaning, and protectants, with the remaining 35 percent being auto and truck accessories.

Sales of Ziebart's core service, rustproofing, fell by 25 percent during 1996 and 1997. During the 1980s, rustproofing had accounted for 80 percent of Ziebart's revenues, and by the mid-1990s it was accounting for less than 30 percent of the company's business, even though market research indicated that most customers associated Ziebart with rustproofing. The rise of auto leasing and better grades of metal being used in car production were among the factors contributing to a decline in the demand for rustproofing. Ziebart's business was also being affected by increased competition from the automotive aftermarket as well as from automakers themselves, who were starting to offer consumers such options as lighted running boards, an add-on that Ziebart had been offering as well. Franchise sales were flat for 1996–97, and the number of franchise locations was holding steady at around 600.

The company felt that detailing offered good prospects for growth. Detailing was estimated to be a $1 billion per year market and was highly fragmented. Ziebart estimated it was the largest detailing operation in the United States with about 2 percent of the market. In the auto accessories market, the challenge was to offer the newest, most popular accessories and to jettison them in favor of other accessories when the trends changed. In 1997, the hottest accessories were remote starters, which allowed drivers to warm up or cool off their vehicles before getting into them, and Ziebart promptly began offering these. Some franchisees supported Ziebart's diversification strategy, while others gave up their franchises because they felt that consumers associated Ziebart exclusively with rustproofing and that company efforts were going too far afield.

At the end of 1997, Ziebart introduced a new marketing slogan—"Survival Gear for Cars"—as part of an already-running ad campaign featuring Adam West, star of the 1960s television series *Batman.* A newly expanded line of products and services was marketed under the slogan, and Ziebart was offering such products and services as sunroofs, window tints, auxiliary lighting, sound barriers, keyless entry and electronic alarm systems, remote car starters, paint renewal, and fabric protection. "Survival Gear" also included a range of professional detailing services, appearance protection services, rust protection, accessories, and truck and van accessories such as trailer hitches and spray-on bedliners. Ziebart positioned itself to offer services and products for long-term car owners as well as individuals who kept their cars only for a couple of years. Services included cleaning, restoring, and renewing the paint finish; rust protection; installing underbody sound barriers to reduce noise levels; and spraying Ziebart's patented bed liners to protect truck beds and cargo areas. For a vehicle's interior, Ziebart locations could apply the company's own chemical

Key Dates

1954: Kurt Ziebart develops a process for rustproofing cars.
1959: Ziebart Corporation is formed and begins franchising operations.
1969: The company's expands internationally with a outlet in Windsor, Canada; Ziebart is purchased by E. Jan Hartmann and begins franchising operations world wide.
1989: Ziebart buys Tidy Car, a specialist in automotive detailing, and begins to move away from rustproofing and toward an expanded line of products and services, including the installation of sunroofs, sound barriers, electronic alarm systems, paint renewal, and fabric protection.
1998: Ziebart initiates a co-branding arrangement with Speedy Auto Glass and, later, with Rhino Linings, USA.
2004: The company has 400 locations across the world.

formulations to restore interior fabric and protect it from permanent spills, dirt, and stains.

While Ziebart's primary market was the individual car and truck owner, the company also serviced wholesale accounts, mainly car dealerships and fleet owners such as municipalities, utility companies, and even floral shops. Favorable market forces included higher car prices, which prompted owners to treat their vehicles as valuable investments that required care and protection.

Co-Branding and Franchise Standards in the Late 1990s

In 1998, Ziebart initiated a co-branding arrangement with Speedy Auto Glass, whereby Ziebart would offer the installation of Speedy Auto Glass at its stores, and Speedy would offer Ziebart products in its outlets. The co-branding plan between Ziebart and Speedy called for the opening of 150 new Ziebart stores within Speedy facilities and 225 new Speedy stores within Ziebart's franchise and company-owned operations. Speedy Auto Glass was a Canadian-based company that entered the U.S. market in 1984 and was the leading supplier of replacement auto glass in Canada as well as a leader in the western United States. Speedy had an established position with insurance companies and an established relationship with North American glass distributors. It had a strong franchise that was geographically compatible with Ziebart's and operated some 300 corporate stores and 200 franchise outlets in North America. The co-branding arrangement was part of Ziebart's strategy to add "need" products and services to its line of "want" products and services. Auto glass was considered a "need" product, because people needed to replace a cracked windshield or broken glass, while many of Ziebart's other products were used to upgrade vehicles and were classified as "want" products or services.

Once the auto insurance networks were notified that Ziebart stores would be offering glass replacement, business began coming in without any advertising or marketing efforts. "It's an insurance-driven business," noted one franchisee whose business increased 20 percent after taking on Speedy Auto Glass replacements. Ziebart dealers were given extensive training in glass replacement at Speedy's Seattle headquarters. By 2004, Speedy Auto Glass was offered at 86 Ziebart locations. However, Ziebart and Speedy Auto Glass terminated their co-branding agreement in January 2001 due to trade area overlap in Canada between Speedy (a Canadian company) and Ziebart franchises. Ziebart and Speedy Auto Glass considered redrafting a co-branding agreement. In the event of unsuccessful renegotiation of the co-branding agreement, Ziebart franchises offering Speedy Auto Glass services were eligible to remain Speedy dealers for the next ten years. Ziebart also initiated a co-branding partnership with Rhino Linings USA, to offer polyurethane spray-on bed liners for trucks, eventually offering Rhino Lining services at over 100 Ziebart locations.

Over the years, Ziebart developed an excellent reputation for its franchise operations and franchise support, earning recognition from such publications as *Entrepreneur, Success, Franchise Times,* and *Income Opportunities,* as well as numerous awards from the International Franchise Association for outstanding performance. These awards honored Ziebart for its long-term financial stability, growth rate, number of operating unites, affordability of start-up costs, relationships between the franchiser and franchisees, and long-term potential. In 2004, the company had 400 locations across the world.

Ziebart's franchise support included sophisticated marketing programs as well as sales and technical support. The company's worldwide training team conducted detailed, hands-on technical and business training for franchise operators. Moreover, the company produced an extensive plan that set franchise standards; potential franchisees were required to work in an existing Ziebart store before being given their own franchise. Once in business, franchisees had access to a well-staffed support hotline. Ziebart also provided information services support and equipped its stores with point-of-sale computer applications.

Ziebart also valued its advertising program, seeking to create high visibility television, radio, and print advertisements. In the late 1990s, the ads were designed to increase awareness in, and drive sales for, Ziebart's "Survival Gear for Cars" marketing campaign. Franchisees were supplied with merchandising materials for their stores, including signs, brochures, and other promotional materials.

Each year, Ziebart held an International Dealer Conference to encourage communication among its widespread franchisees and to provide information about new products, services, and marketing plans. Celebrating 40 years in business as it approached a new century, Ziebart expected to continue anticipating and meeting the wants and needs of car owners and to grow its franchise operations in the process. Ziebart also redesigned its image by strategically remodeling all of its stores inside and out. In the beginning of the 21st century, Ziebart targeted western Europe (France, Spain, and Germany) and locations in North America for further franchise expansion.

Ziebart was sued by 29 of its current and former franchises in 2001. The franchises claimed that Ziebart violated franchise agreements by overcharging for products. The franchises also questioned the safety of a particular rustproofing chemical that franchises were required, via Ziebart, to use. Franchise employees complained of headaches and nausea when using the new rustproofing sealant. The suing franchises represented about one-fourth of Ziebart's U.S. stores at the time. In December 2003, the court ruled in favor of the franchisees, awarding them $1.4 million and requiring Ziebart to make changes in its relationship with its franchises. In the same month, Ziebart's COO and treasurer, John Lynch, resigned to take a position with another company.

Ziebart rolled out an advertising campaign in 2002 which differed from recent marketing—the company emphasized its rustproofing heritage. Ziebart's vice-president of worldwide marketing justified the advertising strategy, claiming that ''we don't shy away from our heritage—we're proud of it.'' Opinion differed on the strategy. One competitor, David Hoot of Automotive Accessories Connection Inc., thought Ziebart should move away from its rustproofing image. Hoot also acknowledged the difficulty of breaking the association between Ziebart and rustproofing. However, a Ziebart franchisee, Bob Adams of Toledo, claimed that a significant portion of his sales continue to come from rustproofing and that Ziebart ''can't scrub rust from their name.''

Principal Competitors

FinishMaster Inc.; Earl Scheib Inc.

Further Reading

''Auto Finds Way to Add Space at Cobo,'' *Crain's Detroit Business*, December 15, 2003, p. 30.

Cunningham, Dwight, ''Flood's Impact Hitting Here, Even If You Can't See Water,'' *Crain's Detroit Business*, July 19, 1993, p. 3.

Geisler, Jennie, ''To Boldly Go Where No Other Specialty Retailer Has Gone Before,'' *Aftermarket Business*, October 1, 1993, p. 20.

Roush, Matt, ''Customers Picked Ziebart's New Slogan,'' *Crain's Detroit Business*, December 22, 1997, p. 13.

Snavely, Brent, ''In Rust They Trust,'' *Crain's Detroit Business*, March 25, 2002, p. 3.

——, ''Product Partners Come to Defense of Ziebart Programs,'' *Crain's Detroit Business*, September 3, 2001, p. 25.

——, ''Ziebart Franchisees Sue Company, Allege Overcharging,'' *Crain's Detroit Business*, August 13, 2001, p. 23.

''Ziebart and Speedy Tie a Ribbon on Bigger Cut of Auto Aftermarket,'' *Successful Franchising*, February 1999.

''Ziebart Debuts Detailing Franchises,'' *Aftermarket Business*, March 1, 1995, p. 31.

''Ziebart Franchises Marry Accessories, Detailing into One,'' *Aftermarket Business*, October 1, 1991, p. 5.

''Ziebart's Service Does Away with Dings,'' *Aftermarket Business*, May 1, 1992, p. 7.

—David P. Bianco
—update: Catherine Holm

INDEX TO COMPANIES

Index to Companies

Listings in this index are arranged in alphabetical order under the company name. Company names beginning with a letter or proper name such as Eli Lilly & Co. will be found under the first letter of the company name. Definite articles (The, Le, La) are ignored for alphabetical purposes as are forms of incorporation that precede the company name (AB, NV). Company names printed in bold type have full, historical essays on the page numbers appearing in bold. Updates to entries that appeared in earlier volumes are signified by the notation **(upd.)**. Company names in light type are references within an essay to that company, not full historical essays. This index is cumulative with volume numbers printed in bold type.

Xetra, **59** 151

INDEX TO INDUSTRIES

Index to Industries

ACCOUNTING

ADVERTISING & OTHER BUSINESS SERVICES

ADVERTISING & OTHER BUSINESS SERVICES *(continued)*

AEROSPACE

AIRLINES

AUTOMOTIVE

AUTOMOTIVE *(continued)*

BEVERAGES

BIOTECHNOLOGY

CHEMICALS

CONGLOMERATES

CONSTRUCTION

CONTAINERS

DRUGS/PHARMACEUTICALS

DRUGS/PHARMACEUTICALS *(continued)*

ELECTRICAL & ELECTRONICS

ELECTRICAL & ELECTRONICS *(continued)*

ENGINEERING & MANAGEMENT SERVICES

ENTERTAINMENT & LEISURE

ENTERTAINMENT & LEISURE *(continued)*

FINANCIAL SERVICES: BANKS

FINANCIAL SERVICES: NON-BANKS

FINANCIAL SERVICES: NON-BANKS *(continued)*

FOOD PRODUCTS

FOOD PRODUCTS *(continued)*

FOOD SERVICES & RETAILERS

FOOD SERVICES & RETAILERS *(continued)*

HEALTH & PERSONAL CARE PRODUCTS

HEALTH CARE SERVICES

HOTELS

INFORMATION TECHNOLOGY

INFORMATION TECHNOLOGY *(continued)*

INSURANCE

INSURANCE *(continued)*

LEGAL SERVICES

MANUFACTURING

MANUFACTURING *(continued)*

MANUFACTURING *(continued)*

MATERIALS

MATERIALS *(continued)*

MINING & METALS

PAPER & FORESTRY

PAPER & FORESTRY *(continued)*

PERSONAL SERVICES

PETROLEUM

PUBLISHING & PRINTING

PUBLISHING & PRINTING *(continued)*

REAL ESTATE

RETAIL & WHOLESALE

RETAIL & WHOLESALE *(continued)*

RETAIL & WHOLESALE *(continued)*

RUBBER & TIRE

TELECOMMUNICATIONS

TELECOMMUNICATIONS *(continued)*

TEXTILES & APPAREL

TOBACCO

TRANSPORT SERVICES

TRANSPORT SERVICES *(continued)*

UTILITIES

WASTE SERVICES

GEOGRAPHIC INDEX

Geographic Index

France *(continued)*

Germany

Ghana

Greece

Hong Kong

Hungary

Iceland

India

Indonesia

Iran

Ireland

Israel

Italy

Kuwait

Libya

Liechtenstein

Luxembourg

Malaysia

Mauritius

Mexico

United States *(continued)*

United States *(continued)*

United States *(continued)*

United States *(continued)*

United States *(continued)*

United States *(continued)*

United States *(continued)*

United States *(continued)*

United States *(continued)*

Venezuela

Vietnam

Virgin Islands

Wales

Zambia

NOTES ON CONTRIBUTORS

Notes on Contributors

BRENNAN, Gerald E. California-based writer.

CAPACE, Nancy K. Detroit-based writer, editor, researcher, specializing in history and biography.

COHEN, M. L. Novelist and business writer living in Paris.

COVELL, Jeffrey L. Seattle-based writer.

DINGER, Ed. Bronx-based writer and editor.

GREENLAND, Paul R. Illinois-based writer and researcher; author of two books and former senior editor of a national business magazine; contributor to *The Encyclopedia of Chicago History* and *Company Profiles for Students.*

HALASZ, Robert. Former editor in chief of World Progress and Funk & Wagnalls New Encyclopedia Yearbook; author, *The U.S. Marines* (Millbrook Press, 1993).

HAUSER, Evelyn. Researcher, writer and marketing specialist based in Arcata, California; expertise includes historical and trend research in such topics as globalization, emerging industries and lifestyles, future scenarios, biographies, and the history of organizations.

HENRY, Elizabeth. Maine-based researcher, writer, and editor.

HOLM, Catherine. Writer, editor, and Co-Active coach.

INGRAM, Frederick C. Utah-based business writer who has contributed to *GSA Business, Appalachian Trailway News,* the *Encyclopedia of Business,* the Encyclopedia of Global Industries, the *Encyclopedia of Consumer Brands,* and other regional and trade publications.

JONES, Howard A. Writer and editor.

LEMIEUX, Gloria A. Researcher and writer living in Nashua, New Hampshire.

ROTHBURD, Carrie. Writer and editor specializing in corporate profiles, academic texts, and academic journal articles.

STANSELL, Christina M. Writer and editor based in Farmington Hills, Michigan.

UHLE, Frank. Ann Arbor-based writer; movie projectionist, disc jockey, and staff member of *Psychotronic Video* magazine.